MyMarketingLab™: Improves Student Engagement Before, During, and After Class

- **Video exercises** – engaging videos that bring business concepts to life and explore business topics related to the theory students are learning in class. Quizzes then assess students' comprehension of the concepts covered in each video.
- **Learning Catalytics** – a "bring your own device" student engagement, assessment, and classroom intelligence system helps instructors analyze students' critical-thinking skills during lecture.
- **Dynamic Study Modules (DSMs)** – through adaptive learning, students get personalized guidance where and when they need it most, creating greater engagement, improving knowledge retention, and supporting subject-matter mastery. Also available on mobile devices.
- **Business Today** – bring current events alive in your classroom with videos, discussion questions, and author blogs. Be sure to check back often, this section changes daily.
- **Decision-making simulations** – place your students in the role of a key decision-maker. The simulation will change and branch based on the decisions students make, providing a variation of scenario paths. Upon completion of each simulation, students receive a grade, as well as a detailed report of the choices they made during the simulation and the associated consequences of those decisions.

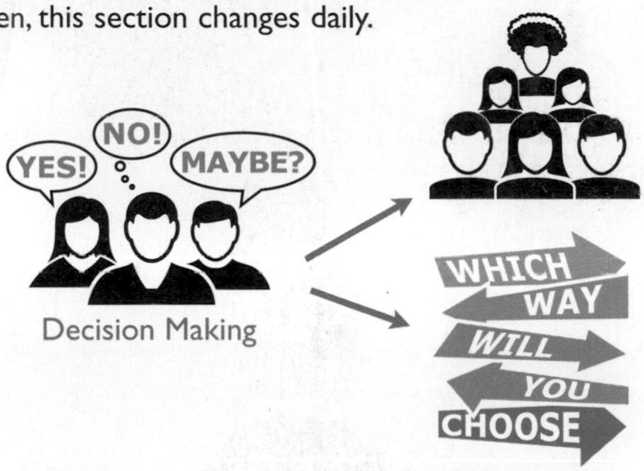

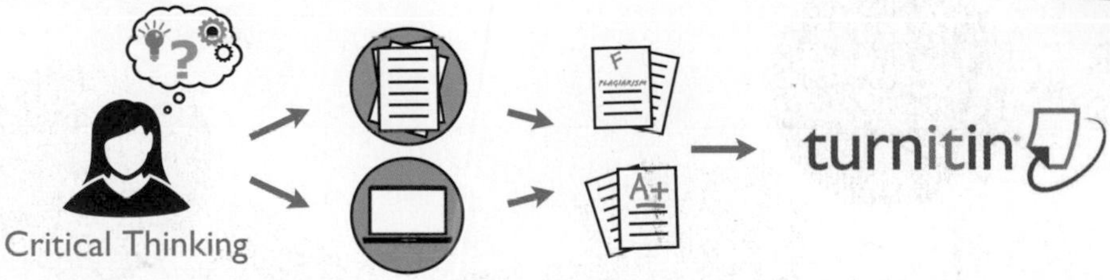

- **Writing Space** – better writers make great learners—who perform better in their courses. Providing a single location to develop and assess concept mastery and critical thinking, the Writing Space offers assisted graded and create your own writing assignments, allowing you to exchange personalized feedback with students quickly and easily.

  Writing Space can also check students' work for improper citation or plagiarism by comparing it against the world's most accurate text comparison database available from **Turnitin**.
- **Additional Features** – included with the MyLab are a powerful homework and test manager, robust gradebook tracking, comprehensive online course content, and easily scalable and shareable content.

Integrated Advertising, Promotion, and Marketing Communications

Integrated Advertising, Promotion, and Marketing Communications

Seventh Edition

Global Edition

Kenneth E. Clow
University of Louisiana at Monroe

Donald Baack
Pittsburg State University

PEARSON

Boston Columbus Indianapolis New York San Francisco Amsterdam
Cape Town Dubai London Madrid Milan Munich Paris Montréal Toronto Delhi
Mexico City São Paulo Sydney Hong Kong Seoul Singapore Taipei Tokyo

Vice President, Business Publishing: Donna Battista
Editor-in-Chief: Stephanie Wall
Acquisitions Editor: Mark Gaffney
Program Manager Team Lead: Ashley Santora
Program Manager: Jennifer M. Collins
Senior Acquisitions Editor, Global Edition: Steven Jackson
Senior Project Editor, Global Edition: Daniel Luiz
Media Producer, Global Edition: M. Vikram Kumar
Senior Manufacturing Controller, Production, Global Edition: Trudy Kimber
Editorial Assistant: Daniel Petrino
Vice President, Product Marketing: Maggie Moylan
Director of Marketing, Digital Services and Products: Jeanette Koskinas
Executive Product Marketing Manager: Anne Fahlgren
Field Marketing Manager: Lenny Ann Raper
Senior Strategic Marketing Manager: Erin Gardner
Project Manager Team Lead: Judy Leale
Senior Project Manager: Jacqueline A. Martin
Operations Specialist: Carol Melville
Interior and Cover Designer: Integra
Cover Image: © Ruth Black/Shutterstock
Vice President, Director of Digital Strategy & Assessment: Paul Gentile
Manager of Learning Applications: Paul Deluca
Digital Editor: Brian Surette
Digital Studio Manager: Diane Lombardo
Digital Studio Project Manager: Robin Lazrus
Digital Studio Project Manager: Alana Coles
Digital Studio Project Manager: Monique Lawrence
Digital Studio Project Manager: Regina DaSilva
Full-Service Project Management and Composition: Integra

Pearson Education Limited
Edinburgh Gate
Harlow
Essex CM20 2JE
England
and Associated Companies throughout the world

Visit us on the World Wide Web at:
www.pearsonglobaleditions.com

Authorized adaptation from the United States edition, entitled Integrated Advertising, Promotion, and Marketing Communication, 7th edition, ISBN 978-0-13-3866339, by Kenneth E. Clow and Donald Baack, published by Pearson Education © 2016.

ISBN 10: 1-292-09363-3
ISBN 13: 978-1-292-09363-5

British Library Cataloguing-in-Publication Data
A catalogue record for this book is available from the British Library.

14 13 12 11 10 9 8 7 6 5 4 3 2 1

Typeset in Times LT Std Roman by Integra.

Printed and bound by CTPS China in China.

To my sons Dallas, Wes, Tim, and Roy, who provided encouragement, and especially to my wife, Susan, whose sacrifice and love made this textbook possible.

Kenneth E. Clow

I would like to dedicate my efforts and contributions to this edition to my wife Pam.

Donald Baack

Brief Contents

Part One THE IMC FOUNDATION 22

Part Two IMC ADVERTISING TOOLS 140

Part Three DIGITAL AND ALTERNATIVE MARKETING 242

Part Four IMC PROMOTIONAL TOOLS 326

Part Five IMC ETHICS, REGULATION, AND EVALUATION 412

Contents

NOT FOCUSED
ON MY WORKERS' COMP
LUBA Workers' Comp
Which is precisely why we stay so sharp.
888.884.5822 • LUBAwc.com
Rated A- Excellent by A.M. Best

Part Three

DIGITAL AND ALTERNATIVE MARKETING 242

8 DIGITAL MARKETING 242

9 SOCIAL MEDIA 272

10 ALTERNATIVE MARKETING 298

Part Four

IMC PROMOTIONAL TOOLS 326

Lunches, made.
Backpacks, ready.
Hair, braided.
Shoes, tied.
Moment, to savor.
pheel
the joy
KRAFT
PHILADELPHIA
REGULAR
pheel the moment

Preface

Advertising, promotions, and communications constitute integral components of marketing. For marketing majors, understanding how companies effectively communicate and interact with customers and potential customers creates the foundation they need to develop effective marketing skills. This will help them succeed in their marketing careers.

If your students are not marketing majors, consider all of the marketing communications around them. Any company or organization they work for will be involved in marketing its products or services. Understanding how marketing communications are developed and why is valuable knowledge. It helps them comprehend the methods used by the people in the marketing departments where they will work and provides them with better information to function as a consumer.

We continue to refine *Integrated Advertising, Promotion, and Marketing Communications,* in part, to help students understand the importance of integrating all marketing communications (IMC) and how they are produced and transmitted. When the first edition was written, almost all marketing communication textbooks focused exclusively on advertising. As your students know from their everyday experiences and the courses they have taken in college, marketing communications incorporates much more than that. It includes promotions, such as coupons, price discounts, and contests. Marketing has expanded to extensive use of social media, blogs on the internet, customer reviews of products, messages delivered to mobile phones, and other programs, such as buzz marketing and stealth marketing. These venues are vital ingredients in effectively reaching consumers. These must also be carefully integrated into one clear message and voice for customers to hear.

We prepared this textbook and the additional materials in ways that will best help your students to understand integrated marketing communications. Students need opportunities to apply concepts to real-life situations. This helps them clearly understand and retain the ideas. As a result, we have composed a variety of end-of-chapter materials designed to help them practice using the concepts. These materials now include and ongoing blog, integrated campaigns in action, integrated learning exercises, discussion and critical-thinking exercises, creative exercises, blog exercises, and updated cases.

What's New in the Seventh Edition?

The seventh edition of *Integrated Advertising, Promotion, and Marketing Communications* offers several new features. The most exciting may be the addition of a blog devoted to supporting this textbook for both professors and students. The blog may be found at: blogclowbaack.net, but is also incorporated into the text in end-of-chapter exercises. These exercises have links to news articles, YouTube videos, social media networks and other websites presenting interesting and engaging marketing communications ideas and tactics.

- **Campaigns in Action.** Professors who adopt this text receive access to the MyLab resource that was developed to support classroom teaching. Each section contains an advertising and communications campaign, complete with power point slides, advertisements, collaterals, and other pieces of media that are designed to more fully explore the entire promotional process. Campaigns include Progressive Bank, The Snoring Center, Interstate Batteries and Wayport. Each of these *Integrated Campaigns in Action* is mentioned at the close of the chapter text to draw student attention to them. Additional Campaigns in Action are included through the authors' blog (blogclowbaack.net).
- **Increased emphasis on social media.** One of the most rapidly evolving aspects of advertising and promotion has been the demand for increased usage of social media. This edition presents an entire chapter devoted to these important changes. Coverage of social media has also been added throughout the text to illustrate how brands are integrating social media with other communication strategies.
- **Interviews with advertising professionals.** At various points throughout the text, interviews and quotes from advertising professionals have been integrated into the chapters. A full description of the development of the Motel 6 advertising program by Stan Richards, founder of The Richards Groups is provided. Marketing professionals from the mcgarrybowen agency, Zehnder Communications, Wholly Guacamole, The Richards Group, Spych Market Analytics, and Pink Jacket Creative add commentary and perspective on various marketing and promotions topics and will give your students an important perspective on real-world applications.
- **New opening vignettes and cases.** Many of the chapter opening vignettes and cases are new to this edition. These materials keep the book fresh and current.
- **New advertisements.** Throughout the text, a significant number of new advertisements have been added. Many of these resulted from interactions with advertising agencies. Philadelphia Cream Cheese, Wholly Guacamole, Scott Equipment, and other new advertisements are

included, all helping to keep the content as fresh and current as possible.

- **Updated examples.** New examples of marketing communications principles have been incorporated to provide up-to-date information about companies students can relate to. New discussion and critical-thinking exercises have been created to help students understand and apply the materials presented in each chapter.
- **Blog exercises.** End-of-chapter exercises have been added that incorporate the authors' blog. These exercises have students accessing YouTube videos, websites, social media sites, and other online resources. The blog then poses a series of questions that require students to utilize concepts in the chapter as they relate to the resources provided on the blog.
- **Active blog.** The authors have created and maintain a blog at blogclowbaack.net. The authors post weekly news articles, videos, and items of interest to individuals using this text. The goal of the blog is to provide information about current events that relate to the book. Textbook adopters can use these blog entries to enhance classroom presentations or as assignments for individual students or even small groups.

Integrated Learning Package

We have created several devices that are designed to help students learn the materials in this text. Advertising and marketing communications are interesting and enjoyable subjects, and these materials have been developed to make learning interactive and fun!

- **Integrated Campaigns in Action.** One unique new feature in this textbook is a series of presentations about actual marketing programs, as created and designed by professional agencies, provided in the MyLab resource center. These features are noted at the end of each section and in the instructor's PowerPoint materials. Additional Integrated Campaigns in Action can be found at the authors' blogclowbaack.net.
- **Lead-in vignettes.** Each chapter begins with a short vignette related to the topic to be presented. The majority of the vignettes revolve around success stories in companies and about products most students will recognize, such as Oreo cookies. In this edition, new vignettes have been introduced, including stories about Wholly Guacamole, Zehnder Communications, Hebrew Hot Dogs, and Huggies Pull-up. These accompany vignettes featured in the sixth edition regarding Miracle Whip, Applebee's, the mcgarrybowen agency, and Interstate Batteries. The vignettes introduce your students to the concepts presented throughout the chapter.
- **International marketing issues.** Some of you have traveled to other countries. Most of you interact with students from around the globe. This book features international concerns that match the presented materials. Also, a section called "International Implications" is found at the end of every chapter.
- **Critical-thinking exercises and discussion questions.** The end-of-chapter materials include a variety of exercises designed to help your students comprehend and apply the chapter concepts. These exercises are designed to challenge students' thinking and encourage them to dig deeper. The best way to know that your students have truly learned a concept or theory is when they can apply it to a different situation. These critical-thinking and discussion exercises require them to apply knowledge to a wide array of marketing situations.
- **Integrated learning exercises.** At the end of each chapter, a set of questions guides students to the internet to access information that ties into the subject matter covered. These exercises provide students an opportunity to look up various companies and organizations to see how they utilize the concepts presented in the chapter.
- **Blog exercises.** A new feature with this edition is a set of exercises from the authors' blog. These exercises can be fun for students to do and can be used for individual assignments or group assignments.
- **Creative Corner exercises.** Most students enjoy the opportunity to use their creative abilities. As a result, we feature a new exercise called the "Creative Corner," which asks students to design advertisements and other marketing-related materials. The exercises are designed to help students realize that they are more creative than they might think. Ken Clow has taught students who said they had zero creative ability. Yet these same students were able to produce ads that won ADDY awards in student competitions sponsored by the American Advertising Federation (AAF). If you are not familiar with the AAF student competition, go the organization's website at **www.aaf.org**. Entering the annual competition is exciting, and participating looks great on a student's resume.
- **Cases.** At the conclusion of each chapter, two cases are provided. These were written to help students learn by providing plausible scenarios that require thought and review of chapter materials. Many of the new cases relate to aspects of the food and restaurant industries, including Eight O'Clock Coffee, Pepsi Hispanic, the Japanese Steakhouse, Dannon Yogurt, and Taco Bell. The short cases should help students conceptually understand chapter components and the larger, more general marketing issues.

Instructor Resources

At the Instructor Resource Center, www.pearsonglobaleditions.com/Clow, instructors can easily register to gain access to a variety of instructor resources available with this text in downloadable format. If assistance is needed, our dedicated technical support team is ready to help with the media supplements that accompany this text. Visit http://247.pearsoned.com for answers to frequently asked questions and toll-free user support phone numbers.

The following supplements are available with this text:

- **Instructor's Resource Manual**
- **Test Bank**
- **TestGen® Computerized Test Bank**
- **PowerPoint Presentation**

Acknowledgments

We would like to thank the following individuals who assisted in the development of the previous editions through their careful and thoughtful reviews:

John Bennett, *Univeristy of Missouri–Columbia*
Donna Falgiatore, *St. Joseph's University*
Larry Goldstein, *Iona College*
Joni Jackson, *Robert Morris University*
Laurel Schirr, *VA Polytech Institute/State University*
Allen Smith, *Florida Atlantic University*
Debbie Campbell, *Temple University*
Rick Morris, *University of North Texas*
Steve Edwards, *Southern Methodist University*

We are grateful to these reviewers for the fifth edition:

Joni Jackson, *Robert Morris University*
Rick Morris, *University of North Texas*
Charles Larson, *Northern Illinois University*
Charlie Schwepker, *University of Central Missouri*
John Bennett, *University of Missouri*
Prema Nakra, *Marist College*
Linden Dalecki, *Pittsburg State University*
Kathleen Havey, *University of Maryland*
Bryan Johnson, *Pennsylvania State University*
Debbie Campbell, *Temple University*

We are grateful to these reviewers for portions of the fourth edition:

John Bennett, *University of Missouri–Columbia*
MaryEllen Campbell, *University of Montana, Missoula*
Donna Falgiatore, *St. Joseph's University*
Deanna Mulholland, *Iowa Western Community College*
Jim Munz, *Illinois State University*
Prema Nakra, *Marist College*
Allen Smith, *Florida Atlantic University*
Amanda Walton, *Indiana Business College*

We are grateful to these reviewers for the third edition:

Jeffrey C. Bauer, *University of Cincinnati–Clermont*
MaryEllen Campbell, *University of Montana, Missoula*
Sherry Cook, *Missouri State University*
Catherine Curran, *University of Massachusetts–Dartmouth*
Michael A. Dickerson, *George Mason University*
Donna Falgiatore, *St. Joseph's University*
Charles S. Gulas, *Wright State University*
Diana Haytko, *Missouri State University*
Al Mattison, *University of California–Berkeley*
Deanna Mulholland, *Iowa Western Community College*
Jim Munz, *Illinois State University*
Charlie Schwepker, *University of Central Missouri*
Eugene Secunda, *New York University*
Allen E. Smith, *Florida Atlantic University*
Bonni Stachowiak, *Vanguard University*
Rod Warnick, *University of Massachusetts–Amherst*
Patti Williams, *Wharton Business School*

We are grateful to these reviewers for the second edition:

Craig Andrews, *Marquette University*
Robert W. Armstrong, *University of North Alabama*
Ronald Bauerly, *Western Illinois University*
Mary Ellen Campbell, *University of Montana*
Les Carlson, *Clemson University*
Newell Chiesl, *Indiana State University*
Jerome Christa, *Coastal Carolina University*
John Cragin, *Oklahoma Baptist College*
J. Charlene Davis, *Trinity University*
Steven Edwards, *Michigan State University*
P. Everett Fergenson, *Iona College*
James Finch, *University of Wisconsin–La Crosse*
Stefanie Garcia, *University of Central Florida*
Robert J. Gulovsen, *Washington University–Saint Louis*
Thomas Jensen, *University of Arkansas*
Russell W. Jones, *University of Central Oklahoma*
Sreedhar Kavil, *St. John's University*
Franklin Krohn, *SUNY–Buffalo*
Dave Kurtz, *University of Arkansas*
Tom Laughon, *Florida State University*
Monle Lee, *Indiana University–South Bend*
Ron Lennon, *Barry University*
William C. Lesch, *University of North Dakota*
Charles L. Martin, *Wichita State University*
James M. Maskulka, *Lehigh University*
Robert D. Montgomery, *University of Evansville*
Darrel D. Muehling, *Washington State University*
S. Scott Nadler, *University of Alabama*

Ben Oumlil, *University of Dayton*
Esther S. Page-Wood, *Western Michigan University*
Melodie R. Phillips, *Middle Tennessee State University*
Don Roy, *Middle Tennessee State University*
Elise Sautter, *New Mexico State University*
Venkatesh Shankar, *University of Maryland*
Albert J. Taylor, *Austin Peay State University*
Janice E. Taylor, *Miami University*
Robert L. Underwood, *Bradley University*
Jerald Weaver, *SUNY—Brockport*
Robert Welch, *California State University–Long Beach*

We would also like to thank the following people for their contributions to MyMarketingLab:

Barbara S. Faries, Mission College, Santa Clara
Shirley Arlene Green, Indian River State College
Mahmood Kahn, Virginia Tech
Denise M. Lorenz, Wake Technical Community College
Jefrey R. Woodall, York College of Pennsylvania

Although there were many individuals who helped us with advertising programs, we want to thank a few who were especially helpful. We appreciate the owners and employees of advertising agencies Pink Jacket Creative, The Richards Group, mcgarrybowen, and Gremillion & Pou for providing us with a large number of advertisements. We want to thank Benny Black for his time explaining his highly successful company, Platinum Motorcars. Stan Richards, Mary Price, Dave Snell, Elena Petukhova, and Carrie Dyer (The Richards Group) were very generous with their time, as were Bill Breedlove and Elena Baca (Pink Jacket), Shama Kabini (Marketing Zen), Brian and Sarah Warren (Emogen Marketing Group), Charlie Brim (Interstate Batteries), Lee McGuire (Skyjacker), Paula Ramirez (1400 Words), Tim Clow and Jane Hilk (Oscar Mayer), Howard Friedman (Kraft), Tori Emery, Brittany Bowman, and Rick Thornhill (mcgarrybowen), Shauna McLean Tompkins (Boxcar Creative), Bo Bothe (Brand Extract) and Anne Gremillion (Gremillion & Pou). We also wish to thank W. Peter Cornish, former senior vice president for the J. Walter Thompson company and current professor at the University of South Carolina for his inputs and advice.

On a personal note, we would like to thank Leah Johnson, who signed us for the first edition of the book. Thank you to Mark Gaffney, Jennifer Collins, Ashley Santora, and Stephanie Wall for helping with this edition as it moved forward and to Jacqueline Martin and Valerie Iglar-Mobley (S4Carlisle) for guiding the production process. We would also like to thank the entire Pearson production group.

Kenneth Clow would like to thank the University of Louisiana at Monroe for providing a supportive environment to work on this text. He would like to thank students, Lindsey Atkins and Logan Dale, for all of their assistance in producing this text. He is thankful to his sons Dallas, Wes, Tim, and Roy, who always provided encouragement and support.

Donald Baack would like to thank Mimi Morrison and Paula Palmer for their continued assistance in all his work at Pittsburg State University.

We would like to especially thank our wives, Susan Clow and Pam Baack, for being patient and supportive during those times when we were swamped by the work involved in completing this edition. They have been enthusiastic and understanding throughout this entire journey.

Pearson wishes to thank the following people for their work on the content of the Global Edition:

Contributors
Diane Sutherland
Jon Sutherland

Reviewers
Dalia Abdelrahman Mohamed Zaki Farrag, Qatar University
Anne Morton, Swinburne University of Technology
Michael Tanas, Bethlehem University–Palestine
Lilian Yap, Wawasan Open University

Integrated Advertising, Promotion, and Marketing Communications

Part 1

THE IMC FOUNDATION

Chapter 1 Integrated Marketing Communications

Chapter Objectives

After reading this chapter, you should be able to answer the following questions:

1.1 How does communication take place?

1.2 What is an integrated marketing communications program?

1.3 What trends are affecting marketing communications?

1.4 What are the components of an integrated marketing communications program?

1.5 What does the term *GIMC* mean?

Overview

Advertising and promotion face a rapidly shifting landscape. A decline in traditional media viewing combined with the rise in internet usage and the use of social media have created a new order. The wide variety of available media means that an effective advertising and marketing campaign now requires more than just one well-made commercial. Current advertising and marketing methods range from simple stand-alone billboard advertisements to complex, multilingual global websites. As a result, the number of ways to reach potential customers continually increases while alternative methods expand and become increasingly popular.

In the face of these sophisticated and cluttered market conditions, firms seek to be heard. Marketing experts know that a company's communications should speak with a clear voice. Customers must understand the essence of a business along with the benefits of its goods and services. The new variety of advertising and promotional venues combined with a multitude of companies bombarding potential customers with messages makes the task challenging. In response, some advertisers and companies have moved to innovative new approaches that utilize the concepts presented in this chapter.

VIRGIN ATLANTIC AIRWAYS

MO_SES/Shutterstock

The airline industry is characterized by high levels of competition and increasingly price-sensitive travelers. Economic pressures can often result in reduced marketing communications and advertising budgets. An exception to this is Virgin Atlantic Airways. In the run up to their 25th anniversary in 2009, they launched their "Still Red Hot" advertising campaign, which featured an instantly recognizable sound track by *Frankie Goes to Hollywood*, together with glamorous and distinctive brand images, humor, and entertainment. The advert was broadcast on TV and online and was shared by viewers across social networking sites. The advert also featured in press and magazines, and was supported by direct marketing, resulting in a highly integrated marketing communications campaign. The advert was discussed widely by marketing commentators as an example of highly creative, emotion-based advertising. In 2010, Virgin Atlantic launched a new advert to build on the success of the previous campaign, entitled, "Your airline's either got it or it hasn't." The advert featured glamorous movie images that emphasized Virgin Atlantic Airways' key brand qualities of excellent customer service, distinctive brand character, and sense of humor. The continued investment in the use of TV advertising ensured continuing high levels of awareness of the brand and its services.

In addition to advertising, Virgin Atlantic Airways uses a wide range of marketing communications media and promotional tools to send messages about the brand and the services it offers. In the UK, in addition to TV and press, Virgin Atlantic Airways uses posters and transport media such as taxis. They also market to travel agents who sell tickets on behalf of the airline; promotions to this audience are carried by specialist travel trade press and magazines. Sales promotions such as special offers are also used together with a frequent flyer program that encourages brand loyalty. A direct marketing database is used to communicate personalized information, mail shots, and offers to customers. The Virgin Atlantic Airways press office prepares press releases, organizes press conferences, organizes photo opportunities for the press, and works with movie production companies to organize product placement opportunities. Celebrity endorsement is also used to promote the brand; in 2007 Virgin Atlantic Airways was chosen by the Spice Girls as the airline partner to provide the flights for their "Return of the Spice Girls" world tour and a Virgin Atlantic Boeing 747 was named "Spice One" to celebrate the tour. The Virgin Atlantic Airways website features a range of integrated features including the latest information on new products, routes, and latest news and information. There are links to Virgin Atlantic Airways' Twitter and Facebook pages, and links to enable customers to manage their travel arrangements. Customers can also register their details to join the loyalty program.

Virgin Atlantic Airways highlights many of the themes present in this chapter, including the planning and management of the right mix of media and promotional tools to ensure integrated campaigns that communicate clear and distinctive brand messages in a competitive market.[1]

The Nature of Communication

objective 1.1
How does communication take place?

Communication involves transmitting, receiving, and processing information. As a person, group, or organization attempts to transfer an idea or message, communication occurs when the receiver (another person or group) comprehends the information. The model of communication shown in Figure 1.1 displays the pathway a message takes from one person to another or others.[2]

Communication plays a key role in any advertising or marketing program. Consider a person planning to dine at a quick-serve chicken restaurant. In the communications model (Figure 1.1), the **senders** include the chains KFC, Chick-fil-A, Popeye's, Church's

▶ FIGURE 1.1
The Communication Process

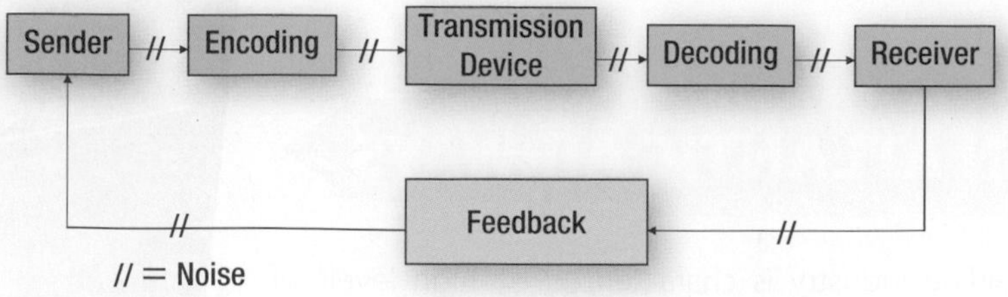

Chicken, Bojangles, and Raising Cain's Chicken Fingers. Each one tries to capture the customer's attention. Most of these firms hire advertising agencies, although some utilize in-house teams.

Encoding is forming verbal and nonverbal cues. In marketing, the person in charge of designing an advertisement takes an idea and transforms it into an attention-getting message. The commercial consists of cues being placed in various media, such as television, magazines, and billboards. The message may also be encoded on the firm's website, a social media page, or on a Twitter account.

Messages travel to audiences through various **transmission devices**. Marketing communications move through various channels or media. The channel may be a television station carrying an advertisement, a Sunday paper with a coupon placed in it, the internet, or a billboard placed along the interstate.

▼ Decoding occurs when a consumer sees this advertisement and understands JD Bank is a viable option for a home loan.

JD Bank

Decoding occurs when the message reaches one or more of the receiver's senses. Consumers both hear and see television ads. Other consumers handle (touch) and read (see) a coupon offer. It is even possible to "smell" a message. A well-placed perfume sample might entice a buyer to purchase both the magazine containing the sample and the perfume being advertised. Hungry people tend to pay closer attention to advertisements and other information about food.

Quality marketing communication takes place when customers (the **receivers**) decode or understand the message as it was intended by the sender. In the case of the JD Bank advertisement shown in this section, effective marketing communications depend on receivers encountering the right message and responding in the desired fashion, such as obtaining a home loan or refinancing a home's current mortgage.

Chick-fil-A's approach to social media provides an example of a successful communication strategy that integrates the web with both online and offline advertising to build a loyal customer base.[3] Before launching a social media site, Chick-fil-A's third-party digital agency discovered that more than 500 Facebook profiles mentioned Chick-fil-A and that one particular fan page had 25,000 "fans." Engaging consumers constituted the social media program's goal. John Keehler, director of interactive strategy at ClickHere, noted that, "One of the mistakes we'd seen is brands would gather a lot of friends but wouldn't get people to interact with them."

The Facebook page allows fans to network with Chick-fil-A. The company holds a "Cow Appreciation Day" each July that encourages

- Talking on the phone during a commercial on television
- Driving while listening to the radio
- Looking at a sexy model in a magazine ad and ignoring the message and brand
- Scanning a newspaper for articles to read
- Talking to a passenger as the car passes billboards
- Scrolling past internet ads without looking at them
- Becoming annoyed by ads appearing on a social media site
- Ignoring tweets on Twitter because they are not relevant
- Being offended by the message on a flyer for a local business

FIGURE 1.2
Examples of Communication Noise

customers to dress like cows and post their photos on Facebook. To build the base of members, coupons have been offered as part of a "Chicken Wave" during the kickoff of the college football season. Other promotions through Twitter and Facebook resulted in a Facebook community with more than 1 million members. Currently, the company announces any new Chick-fil-A store opening on Facebook first, and customers are invited to visit the restaurant and participate in grand-opening festivities.

Donald E. Baack
A Chick-fil-A contest winner.

A compatible offline program represents one key to the social media utilization. Successfully-integrated communications employ multiple channels providing a consistent message. Many Chick-fil-A commercials feature cows urging people to "Eat Mor Chikin." All advertising and promotional venues present the same tagline and theme, thereby increasing the chances that consumers will encounter and perceive the same message. A stronger brand presence has been the result.

In the communication process, **feedback** takes the form of the receiver's response to the sender. In marketing communications, feedback includes purchases, inquiries, complaints, questions, store visits, blogs, and website hits.

Noise consists of anything that distorts or disrupts a message, including marketing communications. It might occur at any stage in the communication process, as shown in Figure 1.1. **Clutter** remains the most common form of noise affecting marketing communications. Figure 1.2 provides examples of noise that can affect the advertising messages.

The marketing professionals involved in the communication process pay attention to each aspect of the communications model to ensure that all audiences encounter a consistent message. They try to make sure the message can cut through noise and clutter. In the case of quick-serve chicken restaurants, common objectives marketing teams seek to achieve include an increase in market share, sales, and brand loyalty.

Communicating with consumers and other businesses requires more than creating attractive advertisements. The upcoming section describes the nature of integrated marketing communications. An effective program integrates all marketing activities into a complete package.

Integrated Marketing Communications

objective 1.2
What is an integrated marketing communications program?

The communications model provides the foundation for an advertising and marketing program. **Integrated marketing communications (IMC)** is the coordination and integration of all marketing communication tools, avenues, and sources in a company into a seamless program designed to maximize the impact on customers and other stakeholders. The program covers all of a firm's business-to-business, market channel, customer-focused, and internally-directed communications.[4]

▶ **FIGURE 1.3**
Components of Promotion

Before further examining an IMC program, consider the traditional framework of marketing promotions. The **marketing mix**—price, product, distribution, and promotions—provides the starting point. For years, the view was that promotional activities included advertising, sales promotions, and personal selling activities. This approach has expanded to incorporate digital marketing, social media, and alternative methods of communication. It also includes activities such as database marketing, direct response marketing, personal selling tactics, sponsorships, and public relations programs (see Figure 1.3).

A complete IMC plan combines every element of the marketing mix: products, prices, distribution methods, and promotions. While this textbook primarily deals with the promotions component, note that, in order to present a unified message, the other elements of the marketing mix should be blended into the program.

An Integrated Marketing Communications Plan

A strategic marketing plan forms the basis for integrated marketing communications. The plan coordinates every component of the marketing mix in order to achieve harmony in the messages and promotions relayed to customers and others. Figure 1.4 lists the steps required to complete a marketing plan.

A *current situational analysis* process involves examination of the firm's ongoing market situation. Next, marketers conduct a *SWOT analysis* by studying the factors in the organization's internal and external environments. SWOT identifies internal company strengths and weaknesses along with the marketing opportunities and threats present in the external environment.

Defining primary *marketing objectives* establishes targets such as higher sales, an increase in market share, a new competitive position, or desired customer actions, such

- Current situational analysis
- SWOT analysis
- Marketing objectives
- Target market
- Marketing strategies
- Marketing tactics
- Implementation
- Evaluation of performance

▶ **FIGURE 1.4**
Steps of a Marketing Plan

◀ Matching marketing objectives with the key target market is an important step in developing the "Visit South Walton (Florida)" campaign.

as visiting the store and making purchases. Marketing objectives are paired with key target markets. A comprehensive understanding of these markets helps the marketing team prepare an effective integrated marketing communications program.

Based on the marketing objectives and target market, the team develops *marketing strategies*. These strategies apply to every ingredient in the marketing mix and include all positioning, differentiation, and branding strategies. Based on the strategies, *marketing tactics* guide the day-by-day activities necessary to support marketing strategies. The final two steps in the marketing plan consist of stating how to *implement* the plan and specifying methods to *evaluate performance*.

The steps of the strategic marketing plan help pull together all company activities into one consistent effort. The steps provide guidance to company leaders and marketing experts as they coordinate the firm's overall communications package.

Emerging Trends in Marketing Communications

objective 1.3
What trends are affecting marketing communications?

Many forces impact the field of marketing communications. Financial pressures have caused the company leaders who hire advertising agencies to conclude that they cannot pay out unlimited dollars for marketing programs. Competition, both domestically and globally, forces company leaders to examine their communications plans to ensure maximum effectiveness. The internet and emerging social trends impact marketing messages and means of communicating with consumers and businesses. Figure 1.5 highlights the current trends that have an impact on marketing communications.

- Emphasis on accountability and measurable results
- Explosion of the digital arena
- Integration of media platforms
- Shift in channel power
- Increase in global competition
- Increase in brand parity
- Emphasis on customer engagement

▲ **FIGURE 1.5**
Trends Affecting Marketing Communications

Emphasis on Accountability and Measurable Results

Company leaders expect advertising agencies to produce tangible outcomes. They spend promotional dollars carefully. Any coupon promotion,

Gulf Coast Seafood

▲ This app for Gulf Coast Seafood illustrates the rapid explosion of digital media.

contest, rebate program, or advertising campaign should yield measurable gains in sales, market share, brand awareness, customer loyalty, or other observable results to be considered successful.

The increasing emphasis on accountability and measurable results has been driven by chief executive officers (CEOs), chief financial officers (CFOs), and chief marketing officers (CMOs). According to Martyn Straw, chief strategy officer of the advertising agency BBDO Worldwide, corporate executives and business owners are tired of "funneling cash into TV commercials and glossy ads" that keep increasing in cost while appearing to do less and less.

Many companies rely less on 30-second television spots and instead pursue digital and alternative communication venues. Marketing messages can be tied to special events in which names, profiles, and addresses of prospective customers are collected and tracked. Straw suggests that marketing should not be viewed as an expense, but rather as an investment in which promotional dollars generate sales and profits.[5]

Explosion of Digital Media

Internet-based marketing communications have evolved from individual web advertisements to interactive websites, blogs, and social networks. Smartphones, tablets, and text-messaging systems have created a new landscape and, in some cases, nearly a new language. Ingenious digital marketing techniques seek to create experiences with a brand rather than mere purchases with little or no emotional attachment. Notice the advertisement for the smartphone app in this section. The app was created for Gulf Coast Seafood. It offers a recipe along with a GPS function that assists consumers in locating the nearest Wild Gulf Seafood.

Many companies have cut traditional media expenditures, moving the dollars to digital media. Procter & Gamble (P&G), AT&T, Johnson & Johnson, Kraft Foods, Verizon, and Toyota are a few of the many companies that have reduced company television advertising budgets to expand use of various forms of digital media. Unilever recently increased its digital spending by 15 percent.[6] As a General Motors executive noted, "Some 70 percent of consumers who shop for a new car or truck do web research."[7] The same holds true for many other products.

With social media and the internet, consumers enjoy access to a wealth of information about companies, products, and brands. They can communicate with each other, sending favorable or unfavorable ratings and information. Messages travel almost instantaneously. Digital marketing cannot be considered as an option for companies but rather as a mandatory ingredient. Marketers now seek to engage a brand with all current and prospective customers in order to achieve success.

Advances in digital technology allowed self-styled makeup maven Lauren Luke to sell cosmetics around the world. She started by offering them on eBay and then began posting videos that she recorded in her bedroom on YouTube. The videos have been viewed 50 million times. Her YouTube channel now contains more than 250,000 subscribers. It is not just entrepreneurs such as Lauren Luke who have taken advantage of the opportunities present in today's information and technology-rich environment. In just six months, Dell generated $1 million in sales from individuals who contacted the firm using Twitter.[8]

Integration of Media Platforms

Today's consumers spend an average of five hours and 16 minutes in front of a screen that does not involve television. When combined with television (which consumers watch for an additional four hours and 31 minutes per day), the total becomes more than 10 hours per day examining some kind of screen, whether it is a computer, tablet, mobile

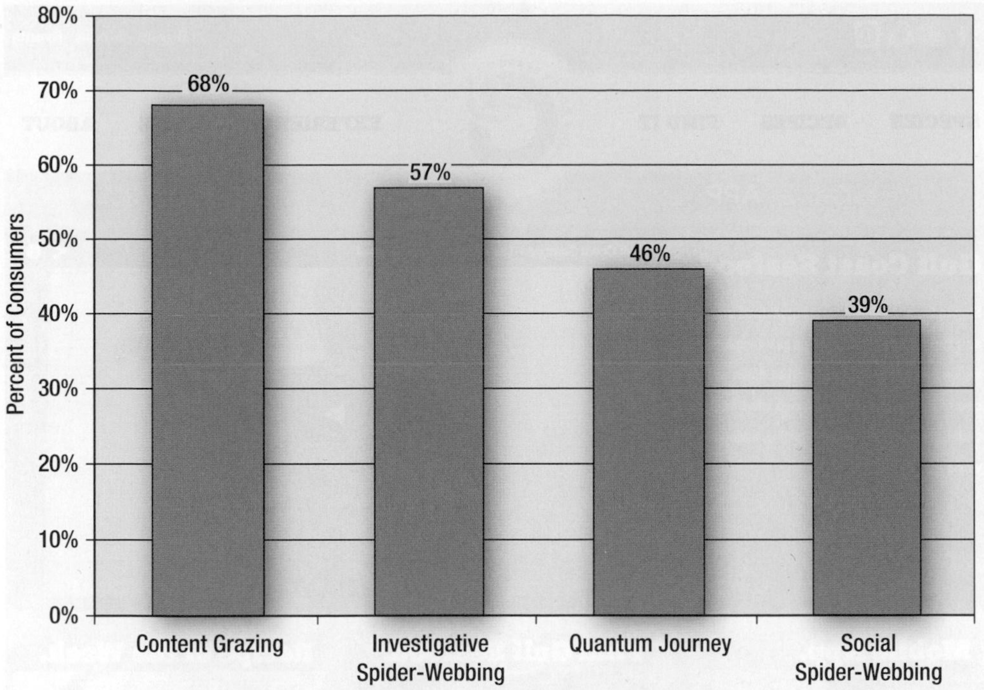

FIGURE 1.6
Pathways Consumers Use to Interact Across Media Devices

Source: Based on Mark Walsh, "Microsoft Highlights Usage Across Device Pathways," *Online Media Daily*, March 14, 2013, www.mediapost.com/publications/article/195786

phone, or television.[9] Understanding how consumers integrate these multiple devices into their daily lives is important to marketers as they devise ways to reach these individuals. Research by Flamingo Research and Ipsos OTX indicates four ways consumers interact across these multiple media formats (see Figure 1.6).[10]

Content grazing involves looking at two or more screens simultaneously to access content that is not related. It may be someone watching TV and texting a friend at the same time or checking on football game scores on his smartphone. *Investigative spider-webbing* occurs when a consumer pursues or investigates specific content across multiple platforms. It may be someone watching a football game and accessing stats for various players on her PC or mobile phone. *Quantam journey* focuses on completing a specific task, such as when a consumer looks for a Chinese restaurant using a PC to locate one in the area, then obtains consumer reviews of the units close by on a smartphone, and finally employs a map app to locate the restaurant or to place an order. The fourth pathway, *social spider-webbing*, takes place when consumers share content or information across multiple devices. Posting pictures on Facebook from a laptop then texting friends to go check them out would be an example.

To reach consumers, marketers understand that today's consumers use multiple devices in multiple ways. An individual television ad or banner ad will likely go unnoticed. Advertisers try to find ways to engage consumers with a brand through portals such as their tablets and mobile phones. That same ad or message delivered across all of the platforms in various formats increases the chances it will be heard and assimilated by consumers.

Changes in Channel Power

A marketing channel consists of a producer or manufacturer vending goods to wholesalers or middlemen, who, in turn, sell items to retailers who offer the items to consumers. Recent technological developments alter the levels of power held by various members of the channel.

Retailers seek to maintain channel power by controlling shelf space and purchase data that allows them to determine which products and brands are placed on store shelves. Through checkout scanners, retailers know which products and brands are selling. Many retailers share the data with suppliers and require them to ensure that store

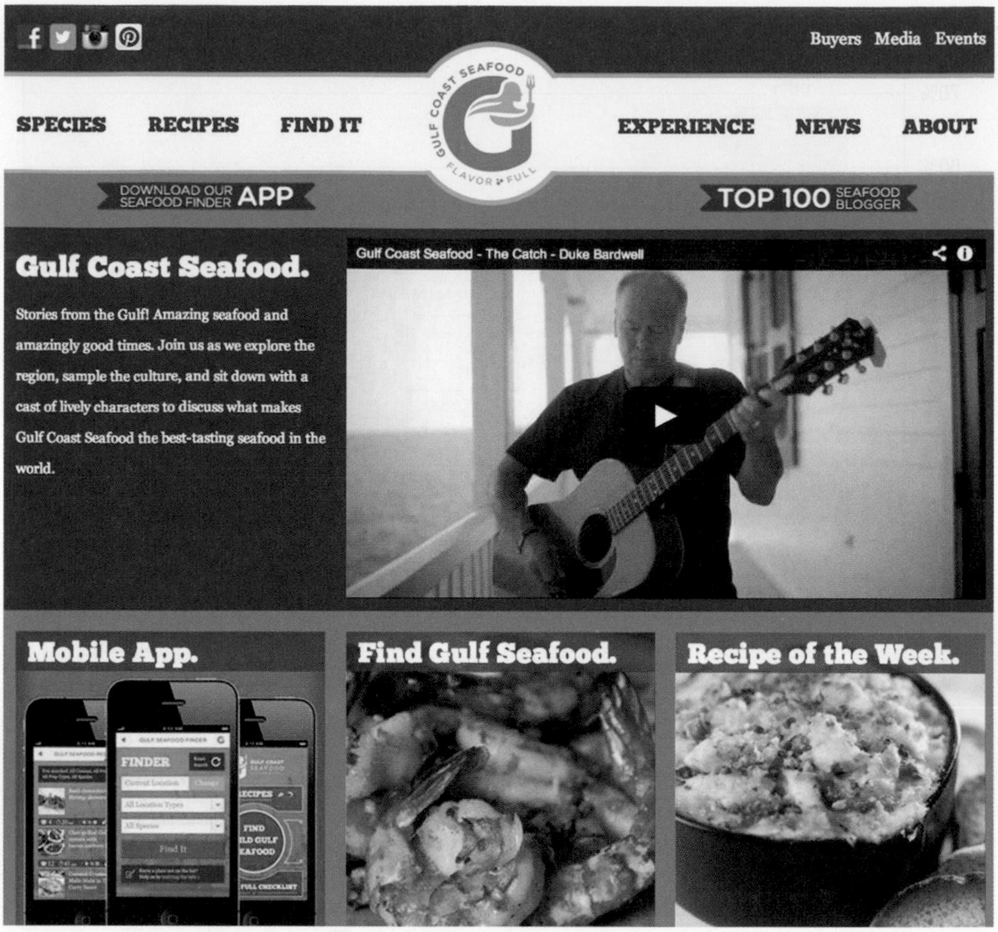

Gulf Coast Seafood

▲ In designing Gulf Coast Seafood's website, marketers for the brand understand that consumers integrate various media platforms and desire an experience with the brand.

shelves remain well stocked. The size and power of mega-retailers mean manufacturers and suppliers have no choice but to follow the dictates of "mega" stores.

At the same time, the growth of internet usage along with other methods of communication has shifted some channel power to consumers.[11] Consumers obtain information about goods and services and purchase them using the internet. Internet-driven sales have risen at a tremendous rate. According to Forrester Research, online retail sales have grown from $31 billion in 2001 to $252 billion in 2013 and are projected to reach $327 billion by 2016. Currently, online purchases account for about eight percent of all retail purchases.[12]

Consumer relationships with brands have changed. Individuals wield tremendous power. Social media allows dissatisfied customers to instantly vent about bad experiences to enormous audiences, where little forgiveness of mistakes takes place. Fifty-seven percent of consumers say they will not buy a particular brand after just one negative experience and 40 percent are likely to tell others not to purchase that brand.[13] Previously held positive feelings about a company are quickly forgotten.

The same principles apply to business-to-business purchasing activities. Buyers who shop on behalf of organizations and other company members seeking business-to-business products also are quick to use social media to lament about brands that did not deliver. Consequently, a similar shift in channel power has taken place in the business-to-business sector.

Fortunately, the environment is not completely negative. Approximately 50 percent of consumers share positive experiences with a brand. Consumers often seek the opinions of friends and relatives concerning products. As a result, approximately 70 percent of consumers say friends and families are a primary source of information regarding various brands.[14]

Understanding these shifts in channel power has become essential. Marketers know they cannot rely solely on mass media advertising. They must incorporate social media and engage consumers with their brands.

Ariwasabi/Fotolia

▲ Advances in information and communication technology have created global competition for goods and services.

Increases in Global Competition

Advances in information technology and communication means competition no longer takes place with just the company down the street—it may be from a firm 10,000 miles away. Consumers desire high quality along with low prices. The company that delivers the best value of quality and price makes the sale, often regardless of location. Advancements in delivery systems make it possible for purchases to arrive in a matter of days from anywhere in the world.

Doritos' marketing team recognized that new communication technologies and social media have made the world smaller. Consumers travel and communicate with each other. As a result, Doritos launched its first global campaign by updating packaging and the company's logo to give a consistent look across 37 countries in which its products are sold. Before this global effort, Doritos offered 25 different package designs and utilized a number of different marketing approaches. The global campaign, called "For the Bold," included digital and TV spots in the United States, Mexico, England, Canada, Spain, and Turkey as well as digital and social media initiatives. The global campaign provided a venue to connect fans worldwide, a consistent storyline, and the same look and feel for the Doritos brand across multiple countries. Today, Doritos remains the largest tortilla/corn chip brand in the world with a 39 percent market share.[15]

Increase in Brand Parity

Many currently available products offer nearly identical benefits. When consumers believe that various brands provide the same set of attributes, **brand parity** results. When it occurs, shoppers select from a group of brands rather than one specific brand.[16] Brand parity means quality becomes less of a concern because consumers perceive only minor differences between brands. Consequently, other criteria—such as price, availability, or a specific promotional deal—impact purchase decisions. The net effect becomes a steady decline in brand loyalty.[17]

A recent survey revealed that consumers are willing to switch brands in most product categories because they do not have one specific brand they must buy or believe is significantly superior.[18] In response to this trend, marketing teams have created messages that suggest the ways a company's products are different. Although these messages were designed to convince consumers that the company's brand was superior and not the same as the competition, they often did not move consumers from the perception of brand parity. As a result, some companies have changed to new and innovative marketing tactics to connect consumers with the brand.

Emphasis on Customer Engagement

The expanding number of available brands perceived to be roughly equivalent leads to another response. To build loyalty, many marketing efforts have been made to engage customers with the brand at every contact point. Any place where customers interact with or acquire additional information about a firm constitutes a **contact point**. Customer engagement programs often utilize digital and social media and have become part of the total integrated marketing approach.

Salvation Army of San Diego

▲ Nonprofits, such as the Salvation Army, must understand how to engage donors to ensure sufficient funds when disasters strike.

An effective contact provides a setting for two-way communication. Engagement can be built by offering incentives and reasons for the consumer to communicate with the company. For customers to take advantage of these initiatives, however, they must develop emotional commitments to the brand and have feelings of confidence, integrity, pride, and passion toward it.[19] The brand, in turn, must deliver on its promises and provide reasons for consumers to continue to interact with the company.

The Restaurant Industry

Technomic Consumer Brand Metrics monitors 120 restaurants across 60 attributes. The company published a white paper entitled "Perceptions of Restaurant Advertising." In the study, the researchers asked 78,743 respondents to evaluate restaurants on three advertising metrics:

- Has memorable advertising
- Has advertising I can relate to
- Has advertising that makes me hungry

The scores were then tabulated on a percent basis. Figure 1.7 presents the composite score of the top 10 restaurants. The study reveals that while some restaurants tended to scored high on the metric "advertising makes me hungry" they did not fare as well on "advertising I can relate to" and "memorable advertising."[20]

Subway's high score can be partially attributed to the organization's real-life spokesperson, Jared Fogle, who has been the face of the company for 15 years. Jared's weight gain of 40 pounds in 2010 was documented in the press and created a potentially

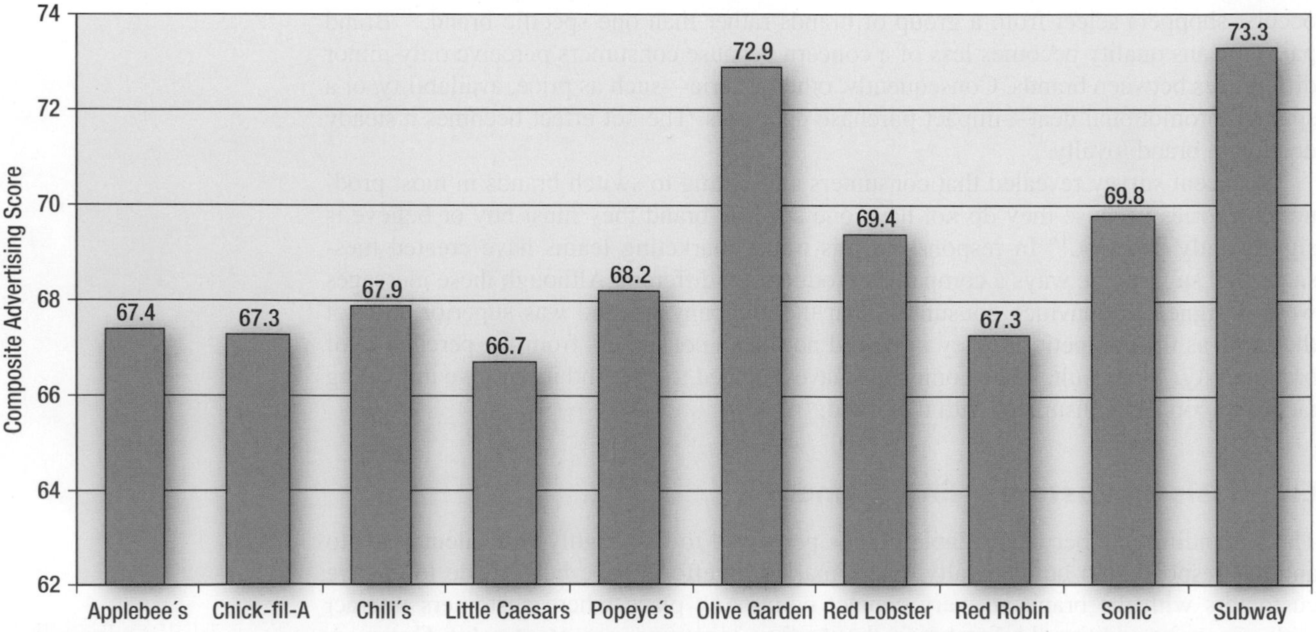

▲ **FIGURE 1.7**
Composite Scores of Top Ten Restaurants on Advertising Perceptions
Source: Based on Colleen Rothman and Gina Gapp, "Perceptions of Restaurant Advertising," *Technomic* white paper, Issue 3, September 2013.

damaging effect on Subway's advertising program. The company's marketing team learned, however, that Jared's struggle resonated with consumers because he represented what many real people face—difficulty with weight control. Subway's leaders remained loyal to Jared and encouraged him to train and enter the New York City marathon. Another factor contributing to Subway's top ranking was that the marketing messages were delivered in newer formats and social media. Subway features strong online content and has 24 million Facebook fans and 1.5 million Twitter followers. Subway was named a top brand in terms of social currency, which measures the extent to which consumers include a brand in their status updates, videos, and image posts.

Many of the examples of integrated marketing communications in this text will be drawn from the restaurant and food industries. These examples will help provide a better understanding of the concepts and theories presented.

IMC Components and the Design of this Text

objective 1.4
What are the components of an integrated marketing communications program?

Figure 1.8 presents an overview of the IMC approach featured in this textbook. As shown, the foundation of an IMC program consists of a careful review of the company's image, the buyers to be served, and the markets in which the buyers are located. Advertising programs are built on this foundation, as are the other elements of the promotional mix. The integration tools located at the peak of the pyramid help the company's marketing team make certain all of the elements of the plan are consistent and effective.

IMC Foundation

The first section of this text builds the foundation for an IMC program. Chapter 2 examines the elements of corporate image and brand management. Strengthening the firm's image and brand answers the question, "Who are we, and what message are we trying to send?" Branding includes the development of packages and labels that speak in the same voice as other marketing messages.

Chapter 3 describes buyer behaviors. The steps of the consumer purchasing process explain how individuals make choices. Marketers identify the motives leading to

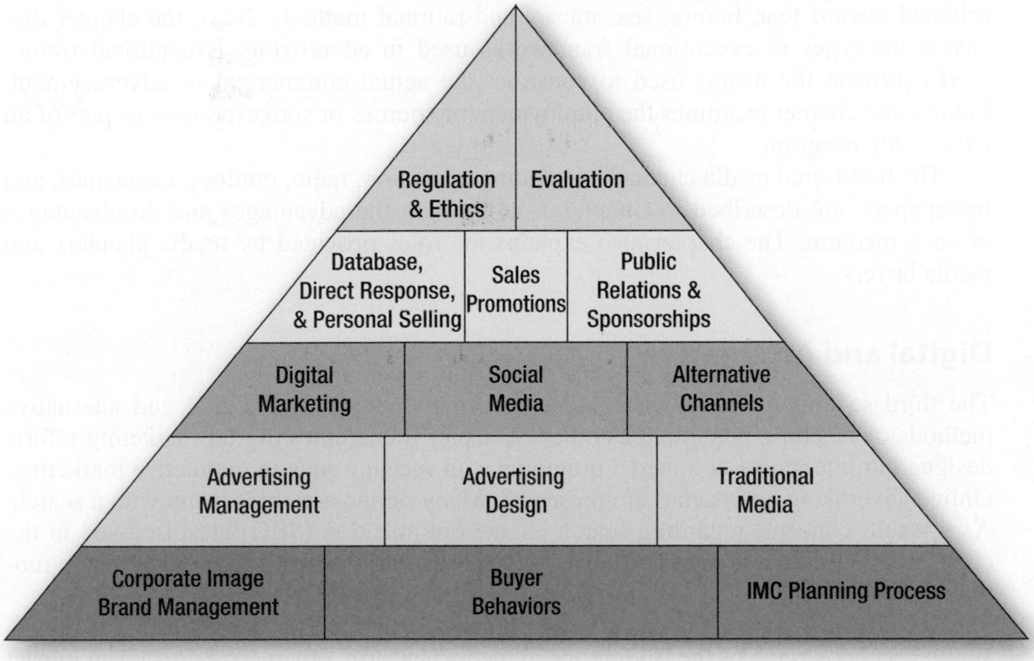

FIGURE 1.8
Overview of Integrated Marketing Communications

Interstate Batteries

▲ Advertising is an important integrated marketing component for Interstate Batteries.

purchases and factors affecting those decisions. Then, the IMC program can be designed to influence consumer thinking. The chapter also examines business-to-business (B2B) buyer behaviors. Discovering viable business-to-business marketing opportunities by reaching purchasing managers and other decision makers in the target business often plays a vital role in overall company success.

Chapter 4 explains the IMC planning program. This includes identifying all target markets, most notably consumer and business-to-business market segments. Then quality communications objectives can be set. The plan becomes complete when communications budgets have been developed and all appropriate media have been identified.

Advertising

Advertising issues are noted in the second section of this text. Chapter 5 describes advertising campaign management and addresses the major advertising activities, including the selection of an advertising agency. Campaign management identifies the general direction the company will take. Chapter 5 also explains various advertising theories and the general principles of advertising effectiveness. Advertising theories form the theoretical background used to design advertisements.

Chapter 6 begins with an analysis of the ingredients involved in creating effective message strategies. Then, various advertising appeals can be used, including those oriented toward fear, humor, sex, music, and rational methods. Next, the chapter discusses the types of executional frameworks used in advertising. Executional frameworks provide the means used to construct the actual commercial or advertisement. Finally, the chapter examines the employment of sources or spokespersons as part of an advertising program.

The traditional media channels, including television, radio, outdoor, magazines, and newspapers, are described in Chapter 7, along with the advantages and disadvantages of each medium. The chapter also explains the roles provided by media planners and media buyers.

Digital and Alternative

The third section of this book contains information regarding digital and alternative methods of reaching potential customers. Chapter 8 examines digital marketing efforts designed to integrate e-commerce programs with recent trends in interactive marketing. Online advertising approaches are presented. Many online activities begin with a search. As a result, concepts regarding search engine optimization (SEO) are discussed in the chapter. Due to the rise in smartphone use, the chapter also explores new trends in mobile advertising.

Social media has exploded in usage in recent years and is the topic of Chapter 9. While Facebook remains the leading social media platform, others have created an impact on both consumer and business markets. The chapter examines current trends in social media and how businesses are using these venues to encourage brand engagement.

Many communication channels are available beyond both the traditional networks and the internet. Chapter 10, titled "Alternative Marketing," describes methods such as buzz marketing, guerrilla marketing, product placements, branded entertainment, and lifestyle marketing. Brand communities are also featured.

Selling Components

The next level of the IMC pyramid adds database and direct response marketing programs, personal selling, trade promotions, consumer promotions, public relations efforts, and sponsorship programs. Each of these efforts helps to stimulate sales. When marketing managers carefully design all of the steps taken up to this point, the firm can integrate these activities. Messages presented in the advertising campaign can be reinforced through a variety of communication promotions.

Chapter 11 explains database programs, direct response marketing efforts, and personal selling tactics. The chapter first describes effective data collection and analysis. Then, the information gained can be used to develop data-driven marketing programs, including permission marketing, frequency programs, and customer relationship management (CRM) systems as well as personal selling activities. Personal selling involves contacts with retail customers and other businesses.

Chapter 12, which has the general title of "Sales Promotions," describes consumer and trade promotions. Trade promotions include trade incentives, cooperative advertising, slotting fees, and other promotions and discounts that help the manufacturer or channel member to push the product through the distribution channel. Consumer promotions are directed at end users and include coupons, contests, premiums, refunds, rebates, free samples, and price-off offers.

Chapter 13 explores public relations programs that connect with consumers in positive ways. This involves emphasizing positive events and dealing with negative publicity. In many cases, the marketing team utilizes public relations efforts to help a sponsorship program achieve the greatest impact.

Integration

The final level of an IMC program adds the integration tools needed to make sure the company effectively serves all customers. Chapter 14 begins with a presentation of the many legal and regulatory issues that are part of the advertising and promotions environment. The chapter discusses several ethical issues that emerge in marketing communications.

The final chapter of this textbook, Chapter 15, explains the evaluation of integrated marketing communications (IMC) programs. Evaluations can begin prior to any promotional campaign and continue during the campaign to post-campaign evaluations. These evaluations generate valuable information to alter campaigns before they are commercially introduced. They also provide input to modify programs that have already run. A promotions evaluation process holds everything together and drives the entire IMC process. Fully integrated marketing requires a well-defined linkage between planning and evaluation processes.

▼ Companies often utilize the expertise of marketing research firms such as ReRez to evaluate IMC programs.

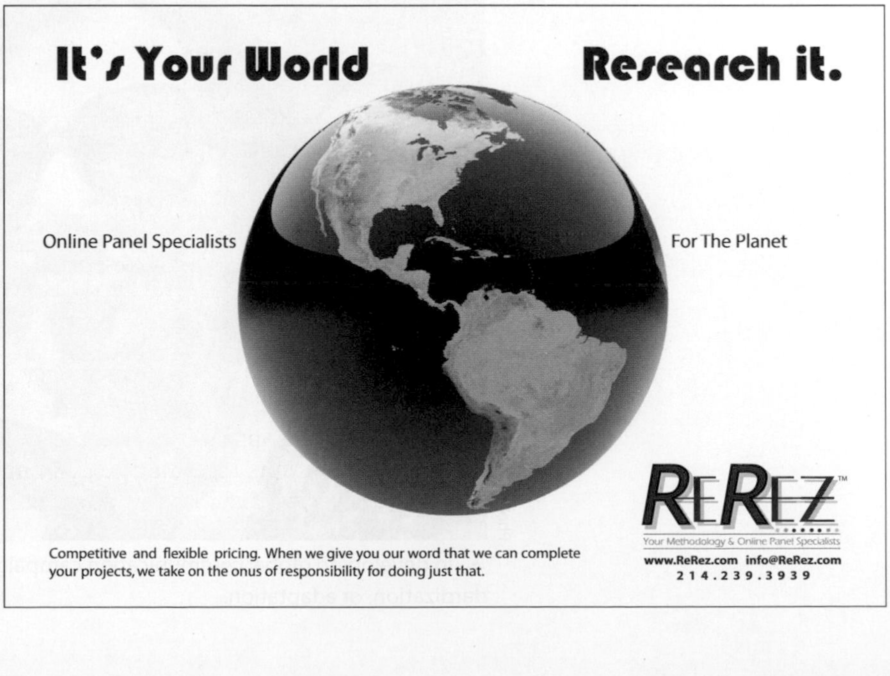

ReRez

International Implications

objective 1.5
What does the term *GMIC* mean?

The same trends that exist among advertising agencies in the United States occur in the international arena. Instead of IMC, international programs are called *GIMC*, or *globally integrated marketing communications programs*.[21] The goal remains the same: to coordinate marketing efforts across all platforms. The challenges become greater due to larger national and cultural differences in target markets.

Marketers employ two different strategies for global companies. **Standardization**, in which a company features a uniform product and message across countries, represents one option. The approach involves generating economies of scale in production while creating a global product using a more universal promotional theme. The language may be different, but the basic marketing message stays the same.

The second approach, **adaptation**, results in the creation of products and marketing messages designed for and adapted to individual countries. The manner in which a product is marketed in Mexico will differ from the methods used in Italy, India, or Australia.

The standardization method may be easier to apply; however, GIMC principles can and should be used with either adaptation or standardization.[22] To reduce costs, careful coordination of marketing efforts should occur across countries. Even when a firm uses the adaptation strategy, marketers from various countries learn from each other. Synergies take place between countries and regions. More importantly, learning can occur.

Recently, Adrian Hallmark, global brand director of Jaguar, commented that "for too many luxury consumers, there is awareness of the Jaguar brand, but not consideration and modern relevance." To restore its iconic status, Jaguar's marketing group launched a multinational ad campaign created by Spark 44, a London ad agency. The campaign debuted on websites JaguarUSA.com, Facebook, and YouTube with a 45-second version of a 30-second TV ad. Jaguar then introduced print, digital, and outdoor advertising in the United States, Austria, Spain, France, Germany, Italy, Russia, Korea, Japan, Australia, and South Africa. The campaign included an 18-city road show in the United States to allow prospective buyers to try the new Jaguar. The ads were adapted to individual markets in each country using the central theme of the campaign "How alive are you?" which was featured in every print, digital, outdoor, television, and video ad.[23]

Photocreo Bednarek/Fotolia

▲ In developing global communication campaigns, firms must decide the best approach, standardization, or adaptation.

INTEGRATED campaigns in action

In the upcoming sections of this book, various integrated advertising and marketing campaigns will be featured. The insights for the *Integrated Campaigns in Action* resulted from personal interviews by the authors with members of the advertising agencies and client companies. Featured brands include:

- Section 1: Progressive Bank (Chapter 4)
- Section 2: The Snoring Center (Chapter 7)
- Section 3: Interstate Batteries (Chapter 10)
- Section 4: Wayport Austintatious (Chapter 13)
- Section 5: Centric Credit Union (Chapter 15)

Each *Integrated Campaigns in Action* features a PowerPoint presentation that can be used as well as copies of collateral materials featured in the campaigns, such as print ads, photos, television ads, and radio spots. The *Integrated Campaigns in Action* can be found at the Pearson Instructor's Resource Center (www.pearsonhighered.com) and MyMarketingLab.

Pink Jacket Creative: A Creative Factory

▲ This advertisement for the Snoring Center seeks to capture attention while presenting its key message.

Summary

Communication consists of transmitting, receiving, and processing information. It represents a two-way street in which a sender establishes a connection with a receiver. Effective communication forms the basis for a solid and successful marketing program. The components of the communication process include the sender, an encoding process, the transmission device, the decoding process, and the receiver. Noise is anything that distorts or disrupts the flow of information from the sender to the receiver.

In the marketing arena, senders are companies seeking to transmit ideas to consumers, employees, other companies, retail outlets, and others. Encoding devices provide the means of transmitting information and include advertisements, public relations efforts, press releases, sales activities, promotions, and a wide variety of additional verbal and nonverbal cues sent to receivers. Transmission devices are the media and spokespersons that carry the message. Decoding occurs when the receivers (customers or retailers) encounter the message. Noise takes many forms in marketing, most notably the clutter of an overabundance of messages in every available channel.

Integrated marketing communications (IMC) takes advantage of the effective management of the communications channel. Within the marketing mix of products, prices, distribution systems, and promotions, firms that speak with one clear voice are able to coordinate and integrate all marketing tools.

The fields of advertising, promotions, and marketing communications have experienced several new trends. Marketing departments and advertising agencies, as well as individual account managers, brand managers, and creatives, encounter strong pressures. They are held accountable for expenditures of marketing communications dollars. Company leaders expect tangible results from promotional campaigns and marketing programs.

IMC plans are vital to achieving success. The explosion of digital media, new information technologies, and social media strongly influences IMC programs. Marketing professionals seek to find ways to integrate all media platforms together to present a consistent message. Channel power has shifted in many ways. Company leaders adjust in order to maintain a strong market standing, and IMC programs can assist in this effort. New levels of global competition drive marketers to better understand customers and be certain that those end users hear a clear and consistent message from the firm.

As consumers develop a stronger sense of brand parity, wherein consumers perceive no real differences in product or service quality, marketers seek to create situations in which a company or brand develops a distinct advantage over others. This may be difficult because consumers collect and integrate information about products from a wide variety of sources, including the internet and social media. Quality IMC programs help maintain the strong voice a company needs to ensure customers hear its message through an emphasis on customer engagement in all marketing activities.

When a firm conducts business internationally, a GIMC, or globally integrated marketing communications system, can be of great value. By developing one strong theme and then adapting that theme to individual countries, the firm conveys a message that integrates international operations into a more coherent marketing package.

This textbook explains the issues involved in establishing an effective IMC program. The importance of business-to-business marketing efforts is noted because many firms market items as much to other companies as they do to consumers. Successful development of an IMC program should help firms remain profitable and vibrant, even when the complexities of the marketplace make these goals more difficult to attain.

Key Terms

communication Transmitting, receiving, and processing information

senders The person(s) attempting to deliver a message or idea

encoding The verbal (words, sounds) and nonverbal (gestures, facial expressions, posture) cues that the sender utilizes in dispatching a message

transmission devices All of the items that carry a message from the sender to the receiver

decoding What occurs when the receiver employs any of his or her senses (hearing, seeing, feeling) in an attempt to capture a message

receivers The intended audience for a message

feedback The information the sender obtains from the receiver regarding the receiver's perception or interpretation of a message

noise Anything that distorts or disrupts a message

clutter What exists when consumers are exposed to hundreds of marketing messages per day, and most are tuned out

integrated marketing communications (IMC) The coordination and integration of all marketing communication tools, avenues, and sources in a company into a seamless program designed to maximize the impact on customers and other stakeholders

marketing mix The elements of a marketing program, including products, prices, places (the distribution system), and promotions

brand parity What occurs when there is the perception that most goods and services are essentially the same

contact point Any place where customers interact with or acquire additional information about a firm

standardization A program in which a firm features uniform products and market offerings across countries with the goal of generating economies of scale in production while using the same promotional theme

adaptation What takes place when products and marketing messages are designed for and adapted to individual countries

MyMarketingLab

Go to **mymktlab.com** to complete the problems marked with this icon ✪.

Review Questions

1-1. Define communication. How does it play a crucial role in marketing and business?

1-2. What are the parts of an individual communications model?

1-3. What pivotal role does communication play in all marketing and advertising programs?

1-4. Name the transmission devices, both human and nonhuman, that carry marketing messages.

1-5. Define clutter. Name some of the forms of clutter in marketing communications.

1-6. What is the expanded view of promotion?

1-7. What are the foundations of marketing strategies?

1-8. What are the key purposes of a SWOT analysis?

1-9. What trends were given to explain the growth in importance of IMC plans in this chapter?

1-10. How has the explosion of the digital arena impacted marketing communications?

1-11. Identify and describe the four ways consumers interact with multiple media formats.

1-12. Why is it vital for marketing professionals to check the marketing messages they send?

1-13. What is meant by the term "quality marketing communication"?

1-14. In the marketing process what does an advertiser hope for in customer feedback?

1-15. What are the components of an integrated marketing communications program, as outlined in this textbook?

1-16. What is a GIMC? Why is it important for multinational firms?

1-17. What is the difference between standardization and adaptation in GIMC programs?

Critical Thinking Exercises

DISCUSSION QUESTIONS

✪**1-18.** Do you use Miracle Whip? Ask five people how they feel about the product. Using YouTube and the website highlighted in this chapter, view the 2011 campaign. Evaluate its impact and explain whether you believe the campaign was a good idea. Defend your answer.

✪**1-19.** The marketing director for a furniture manufacturer is assigned the task of emphasizing the furniture's natural look in the company's integrated marketing communications program. Discuss the problems the director might encounter while developing this message and in ensuring that consumers understand the message correctly. Refer to the communication process outlined in the chapter for ideas. Explain how noise or clutter interferes with the communication process.

✪**1-20.** How many different forms of advertising are you exposed to over the course of a normal day? Do you recall any specific advertising that had relevance and resonance with you? Compare your observations with the other members of the class.

1-21. Why do advertisers ensure that they feature their marketing messages across multiple forms of media?

1-22. The use of social media has exploded during the last decade. Discuss your personal use of social media. Which social media platforms do you use? Why did you select those particular ones? How do you use social media?

1-23. Brand parity has become a major issue for companies. Identify three product categories where the brand you purchase is not very important. Why is the brand not important? Identify three product categories where the brand is important. What brand or brands do you typically purchase in each category?

1-24. The marketing director for a manufacturer of automobile tires has been asked to integrate the company's global marketing program. Should the director use a standardization or adaptation approach? How could the company be certain that its marketing program will effectively be integrated among the different countries in which it sells tires?

Integrated Learning Exercises

1-25. Data analysts Kantar rate Maggi as the number one global brand. Access their website at **www.maggi.com**. The other top five were Knorr (**www.knorr.com**), Lay's (**www.fritolay.com**), Oreo (**www.oreo.com**), and Bimbo (**www.grupobimbo.com**). Each is likely to have its own sites specifically for country or region. Compare and contrast the information available and the design of each company's website. Which website did you like the best or least? Why?

1-26. Figure 1.7 identified the top 10 restaurants based on a composite score of advertising perceptions from a survey by Technomic Consumer Brand Metrics. Pick one of the restaurants and access the company's website. Go to YouTube and locate at least three ads for the restaurant. Is the company's advertising effective? Why or why not? From the website, describe how the restaurant utilizes social media. In your opinion, does the restaurant integrate all of its marketing messages? Why or why not?

1-27. Information is one key to developing a successful integrated marketing communications program. Access each of the following websites. Describe the type of information and news available on each site. How would this information help in developing an integrated marketing campaign?

a. *Adweek* (**www.adweek.com**)
b. *Interbrand* (**www.interbrand.com**)
c. *Media Industry Today* (**www.media.einews.com**)
d. *Branding Asia* (**www.brandingasia.com**)

Blog Exercises

Access the authors' blog for this textbook at the URLs provided to complete these exercises. Answer the questions that are posed on the blog.

1-28. Chick-fil-A campaign, **http://blogclowbaack.net/2014/04/24/chick-fil-a-chapter-1/**

1-29. Subway advertising, **http://blogclowbaack.net/2014/04/24/subway-chapter-1/**

1-30. Integrated marketing, **http://blogclowbaack.net/2014/04/24/imc-chapter-1/**

Student Project

CREATIVE CORNER

Executives at Red Robin Gourmet Burgers have decided to open a restaurant near your campus. You have been chosen as a marketing intern to help the firm establish this restaurant. Examine the company's website at http://www.redrobin.com. Read the "About Us" section of the website in order to fully understand the Red Robin brand. When you have a good feel for Red Robin, prepare a newspaper ad for your student newspaper about a grand opening near your campus. Next, examine the company's social media presence on Facebook, Twitter, YouTube, and LinkedIn by accessing these pages from the restaurant's website. Write a report that discusses whether you believe social media will be effective in reaching students at your college. Cite specific examples from the company's social media pages.

CASE 1 WAKE UP CALL FOR 8:00

Any longstanding product runs the risk of becoming stale in the eyes of consumers. Eight O'Clock Coffee's marketing team recently decided that the company's entire brand and promotion program was in need of rejuvenation. The net result was an entire "refresh" marketing effort.[24]

Eight O'Clock Coffee has been available to consumers since 1859. To combat recent sluggish sales, company leaders began with a rejuvenation of the product itself, creating new flavors such as Dark Chocolate Cherry, Cinnamon Bun, and others. The new items were complemented with updated packaging that was slimmer and brandished a bright red color.

To launch these innovations, the marketing program began with a redesigned website that highlighted a major event. The campaign included a social-media driven sweepstakes that was incorporated into Fashion Week in New York. Participants in the fashion show were offered red bags. The theme, "The Red Bag Collection in Support of Dress for Success" was featured, which added a cause-related tie-in to the refresh rollout. Individuals involved in the fashion event were encouraged to "Spot the Red Bag" in order to win prizes. They accessed the company through the hash tag "#SpottheRedBag" to post photos of their discoveries. The photos of red bags were posted on the company's Facebook page.

Beyond the social media and fashion show elements, the company added more traditional advertising during the Emmy awards on television. The tagline "put coffee first" punctuated these messages. The campaign was then extended to other programs in many of the company's major markets.

These marketing efforts for Eight O'Clock Coffee stress the value of a multifaceted approach to enticing, exciting, and engaging customers and potential customers. Use of new methods such as social media combined with more traditional marketing programs (sweepstakes, television advertising) indicates the wave of the future for integrated marketing communications.

Michaeljung/Fotolia

▲ Eight O-Clock Coffee's marketing team understood that it must engage consumers with the brand to obtain long-term loyalty.

1-31. What coffee brands would constitute Eight O'Clock Coffee's primary competition?

1-32. Would you characterize coffee consumption as a situation in which brand parity or brand loyalty exists? Why?

1-33. Who is the target market for Eight O'Clock Coffee's brand refresh program? Will the campaign be effective in reaching the right audience? Why or why not?

1-34. Evaluate the value of using social media for this type of marketing communications effort. Is it necessary or helpful? Why or why not?

CASE 2 EMIRATES: TAKING THE IMC ROUTE

On October 25, 1985, Emirates flew its first routes out of Dubai with just two aircraft—a leased Boeing 737 and an Airbus 300 B4. Emirates' focus has always been on quality rather than quantity, and in the years since taking those first small steps onto the regional travel scene it has grown to become a major player in the global airline industry. Emirates has never had less than 20 percent annual growth, and it has generated a profit every year. It now has one of the fastest-growing and youngest fleets in the airline industry. The airline is committed to offering its customers the highest possible level of professional flight services, and it has earned more than 400 awards for excellence worldwide.

Companies have paid close attention to the IMC approach. Today, markets are cluttered with different advertising messages. Fragmentation of media and consumer markets, as well as recent developments in mass communication technologies, such as the Internet and smartphones, has meant that new marketing methods are needed to ensure the consistency and the effectiveness of messages targeted to various audiences. Emirates has embraced the IMC concept, which has enabled

John Foxx Collection/Imagestate

▲ IMC allows Emirates to ensure consistency of message across many marketing methods.

it to achieve an excellent market position and a positive image in the minds of its customers. The following examples demonstrate how Emirates uses different promotional tools to maximize its message exposure rate:

- Commercials and print advertisements in major media highlight the airline's new products, routes, and aircraft.
- For more than two decades, beginning with a boat race in 1987 in Dubai, Emirates has been a committed sponsor of both regional and international events. His Highness Sheikh Ahmad bin Saeed Al-Maktoum, Chairman of Emirates, sees the importance of sponsorship activities in the airline's marketing strategy. He believes that sponsorships are the best way to get in touch with passengers and to build a close relationship with them. Emirates is currently an official FIFA partner. The airline held the rights to all FIFA events from 2007 to 2014, and the Emirates brand name is on all official World Cup publicity material.
- Emirates publishes three in-flight magazines in order to reach readers during their flights.
- Emirates' onboard entertainment system has been highly recognized as a market leader, winning awards for its quality and variety and enabling the airline to show passengers commercials about it latest offers, partners, and services.
- Passengers are encouraged to donate to the Emirates Airline Foundation, which seeks to improve the quality of the life of children, regardless of their culture, religion, geographic location, or political boundaries.
- The Emirates has an official retail website from which customers can shop for Emirates-related merchandise and have it delivered to their doorstep.
- The airline is proudly developing an environmentally sustainable strategy that aims at protecting natural resources and reducing air pollution. Emirates is active in large-scale industrial recycling efforts and, more importantly, in selecting the most fuel-efficient aircraft.

Emirates uses a variety of marketing communication tools in an integrated way to deliver one message about the high quality of its services. It uses television commercials, print advertisements, sponsorships, charitable foundations, in-plane advertisements, Internet marketing, and trade promotion. All of these communication tools have helped Emirates to appeal to a large number of travelers all over the world and to create a solid, positive image about its services.[25]

1-35. Explain how Emirates' marketing strategy has been successful in creating a positive brand image with current and potential customers.

1-36. Classify the IMC tools used by Emirates.

1-37. Emirates flies all over the world. Should Emirates modify its messages and channels according to where it advertises? Explain.

MyMarketingLab

Go to **mymktlab.com** for the following Assisted-graded writing questions:

1-38. For years, Nike's advertising tagline was "Just do it." What meaning was conveyed by the tagline? Do you think this conveys a clear message about the company's operations?

1-39. Find each of the following companies on the internet. For each company, discuss how effective its website is in communicating an overall message. Also, discuss how well the marketing team integrates the material on the website. How well does the website integrate the company's advertising with other marketing communications?

a. Revlon (**www.revlon.com**)
b. J.B. Hunt (**www.jbhunt.com**)
c. JD Bank (**www.jdbank.com**)
d. Red Lobster (**www.redlobster.com**)

Chapter 2 Brand Management

Chapter Objectives

After reading this chapter, you should be able to answer the following questions:

2.1 How does a brand's image affect consumers, other businesses, and the company itself?

2.2 What elements are involved in identifying, creating, rejuvenating, or changing a brand's image?

2.3 What are the different types of brand names?

2.4 What are the characteristics of effective logos?

2.5 What different kinds of brands can firms offer?

2.6 How are brands developed, built, and sustained in order to build brand equity and fend off perceptions of brand parity?

2.7 What current trends affect private brands?

2.8 How can packaging and labels support an IMC program—domestically and in foreign settings?

2.9 How are brands managed in international markets?

Overview

Managing an organization's brand image constitutes a critical ingredient in the successful development of an integrated marketing communications plan. A corporation's brand image reflects the feelings consumers and businesses have about the overall organization as well as its individual products or product lines. Advertising, consumer promotions, trade promotions, personal selling, the company's website, and other marketing activities all affect consumer perceptions. A strong brand creates a major advantage for any good or service. When the image of an organization or one of its brands becomes tarnished, sales revenues and profits can plummet. Rebuilding or revitalizing the brand's image then becomes difficult.

The marketing team seeks to understand the firm's overall brand image and the strengths of individual brands in order to make solid connections with consumers and business-to-business customers. A strong integrated marketing communications (IMC) foundation combines an analysis of the firm's image and brands with assessments of consumer and business buyer behaviors. Marketers then can prepare consistent messages designed to reach every individual that might purchase a firm's products. At times, such a process involves rejuvenating or adjusting the image a brand conveys.

APPLEBEE'S

Brand Image Overhaul

The 2008 recession brought substantial challenges to the casual dining industry. Chains—including Applebee's Neighborhood Bar and Grill, T G I Fridays, Chili's, and others—experienced declining sales. Prior to these events, DineEquity, which owns IHOP (formerly the International House of Pancakes), approved the purchase of Applebee's.

IHOP CEO Julia A. Stewart labeled the Applebee's purchase, "Make the minnow swallow the whale." IHOP had only 1,400 locations where Applebee's maintained 2,000 units. Concerns were raised that Stewart and DineEquity were purchasing the Applebee's chain as an act of retribution. She countered, "Sweet vengeance? No. I would never borrow $2.3 billion for ego." Instead, Stewart pointed to her success at rejuvenating the IHOP brand, where she had concentrated efforts in two main areas: improving the employment experience and making the restaurants better.

Stewart employed much of the same model upon arriving at Applebee's, emphasizing product quality, pricing, promotion, the dining experience, and a quality employment environment. In the area of product quality, some food items were removed and others were added to the menu, including sliders and other dining innovations. In terms of pricing, Applebee's developed the "2 for $20" option, in which patrons received an appetizer and two full-sized entrees.

In the area of promotion, Applebee's launched a "Girl's Night Out" (GNO) social media campaign. The Applebee's Facebook Fan Page allowed guests to send a GNO invite with the time, date, Applebee's location—and a personalized message. The tool lets fans keep track of events they host, attend, or both.

Robert Kneschke/Fotolia

"Applebee's is convinced that girls STILL want to have fun, so we're doing all we can to make it easier to have 'girl time' happen at Applebee's," said Rebeca Johnson, senior vice president, marketing and culinary for Applebee's Services, Inc.

DineEquity changed advertising agencies in 2012. The Crispin Porter agency was retained. Rebeca Johnson noted that Crispin Porter's creative staff members "...really excel at retail, and they are knowledgeable about food and beverage and restaurant brands—big, iconic American brands that have large, loyal followings."

The success stories at IHOP and Applebee's indicate that brand building and rejuvenation are possible, even in difficult situations. Quality marketing communication programs, working in conjunction with other managerial efforts, can help a stagnant company turn the corner and once again become a major player in an industry.[1]

The first part of this chapter examines the activities involved in managing a corporation's brand image, including its name and logo. The second part addresses ways to develop and promote the various forms of brand names. Brand equity and brand parity are described. Finally, packages and labels, which should be included in any marketing communications program, are assessed. Ethical and international considerations are noted.

Corporate and Brand Image

objective 2.1
How does a brand's image affect consumers, other businesses, and the company itself?

A corporate or brand image summarizes what the company stands for as well as how it is known in the marketplace. Whether it is the "good hands" of Allstate Insurance or the "good neighbors" at State Farm Insurance, creating a specific impression in the minds

Kraft Foods, Inc.

▲ Kraft Foods created a strong, positive brand image through effective communications and high quality.

of clients and customers should be the goal of image management. Insurance companies often accomplish this by stressing helpfulness, safety, and security as elements of a strong image.

Consumer beliefs about a firm are more important than how company officials perceive the image. Corporate brand names such as Bank of America, Toyota, Kraft Foods, and BP (British Petroleum) create impressions in the minds of clients and customers. Although the specific version of the image varies from consumer to consumer or for each business-to-business buyer, the combined views of all publics determine the overall brand image, which can be positive or negative.

The same holds true for individual brands. Some companies, such as Kraft Foods, sell a large number of brands. While the corporate name Kraft Foods projects an image and identity, so do many of the individual brands offered by the company, including Oscar Mayer, Crystal Light, Maxwell House, Planters, and Miracle Whip. Other companies only feature one brand for the entire organization, which means the corporation's and brand image coincide. Therefore, with regard to the various concepts presented in this chapter, the ideas can refer to various brands sold by a company, such as Kraft Foods, or to an overall corporate brand such as State Farm, Allstate, or Wal-Mart.

Components of Brand Image

Brand images contain invisible and intangible elements (see Figure 2.1). Consumers encounter many elements as they interact with a company or brand. A recent study of the restaurant industry indicated that the quality of a company's goods and services ranked as the most important component of brand image. The willingness of a firm to stand behind its goods and services when something went wrong was second. Third were perceptions of how the firm dealt with customers, such as by being pleasant, helpful, or professional.[2]

Negative publicity can stain or damage consumer perceptions of a corporation's or brand's image. Examples include the damage to reputations of financial institutions, such as Bank of America, Toyota following quality control problems, and Domino's after poor customer evaluations of its pizza. Each organization undertook major efforts to help restore a more positive image.

Tangible Elements
- Goods or services sold
- Retail outlets where the product is sold
- Advertising
- Marketing communications
- Name and logo
- Package and labels
- Employees

Intangible Elements
- Corporate personnel
  - Ideals
  - Beliefs
  - Conduct
- Environment policies
- Corporate culture
- Country location
- Media reports

▶ **FIGURE 2.1**
Elements of Brand Image

A mechanic at a local Chevrolet garage can impact the image a consumer has of General Motors.

An image consists of a unique set of features. The corporate brand image of an automobile manufacturer such as Porsche, Mazda, Toyota, or General Motors might be based on the following: (1) evaluations of vehicles, (2) whether the company is foreign or domestic, (3) customer views of each company's advertisements, and (4) reactions to the local dealership. A corporation's image often includes consumer assessments of company employees. In fact, the mechanic trying to repair a vehicle at a local Chevrolet dealership garage might become the dominant factor that shapes a customer's perception of General Motors.

In the past decade, Wal-Mart faced criticisms regarding employee discontent, conditions at foreign factories, and bribery allegations in other countries. In an effort to boost the image of the brand, Wal-Mart's marketing team launched a multimillion dollar "American Success Story" campaign. The national campaign featured customers, store employees, and truck drivers sharing personal stories and warm feelings about Wal-Mart.[3] The campaign sought to show the public another side of the company by featuring positive aspects of Wal-Mart.

The Role of Brand Image—Consumer Perspective

From a consumer's perspective (or business customer perspective), brand image serves several useful functions, including those displayed in Figure 2.2. A well-known brand offers customers positive assurance about what to expect. A can of Coke or Pepsi purchased in Anchorage, Alaska, features a comparable taste to one purchased in Liverpool, England, or Kuala Lumpur, Malaysia. Products ordered online from Bed Bath & Beyond are the same as those purchased in the retail store.

Positive assurance generates greater value when customers purchase goods or services with which they have little experience. Consider families on vacation. A family visiting Brazil might normally not stay at the Holiday Inn, but the familiar name makes it a lower-risk option. Purchasing from a familiar corporation seems "safer" strategy than

- Provides confidence regarding purchase decisions
- Gives assurance about the purchase when the buyer has little or no previous experience
- Reduces search time in the purchase decision
- Provides psychological reinforcement and social acceptance of the purchase

FIGURE 2.2
Brand Image: Benefits to Consumers

Monkey Business/Fotolia

▲ Social acceptance can become one benefit of purchasing a well-known brand.

buying something from an unknown company. Taking a room at an unfamiliar hotel feels riskier than staying at one with a more a recognizable name.

Purchasing from a familiar firm reduces search time and saves effort. An individual or company loyal to Ford spends fewer hours searching for a new car than someone without such loyalty. The same may be true when purchasing low-cost items such as groceries or office products.

Purchasing from a highly recognized company often provides psychological reinforcement and social acceptance. Psychological reinforcement comes from feeling that a wise choice was made and the belief that the good or service will perform well. Social acceptance results from knowing that other individuals, such as family and friends, have purchased the same brand and are likely to accept the choice.

Interbrand produces a yearly list of the top 100 corporate brands. The list does not include companies offering portfolios of products and brands, such as Procter & Gamble. Also, privately-held companies, including VISA and those that operate under different names in different countries, such as Wal-Mart, are not considered. The list only notes corporations that provide products under one name. Using these criteria, Interbrand ranked Apple as the top global corporate brand, followed by Google and Coca-Cola.[4] Figure 2.3 provides a list of the top 10 brands along with each brand's value.

The Role of Brand Image—Company Perspective

From the viewpoint of the firm itself, a highly reputable image generates many benefits, as noted in Figure 2.4. A quality image provides the basis for the development of new goods and services. The introduction of a product becomes easier when potential customers are familiar with the brand name and image. Long-term patrons are willing to try new items and transfer trust in and beliefs about the brand to those products. A *brand alliance*, in which two companies use brand strength to develop and co-market a new product featuring both names, (such as Old Spice and Head & Shoulders) has recently begun to emerge.

Rank	Company	Brand Value (Billions)	Country
1	Apple	$98.3	United States
2	Google	$93.3	United States
3	Coca-Cola	$79.2	United States
4	IBM	$78.8	United States
5	Microsoft	$59.5	United States
6	General Electric	$46.9	United States
7	McDonald's	$41.9	United States
8	Samsung	$39.6	South Korea
9	Intel	$37.3	United States
10	Toyota	$35.3	Japan

▶ **FIGURE 2.3**

Top 10 Corporate Global Brands

Source: Based on "2013 Ranking of Top 100 Brands," *Interbrand*, www.interbrand.com/en/best-globa-brands/2013/top-100-list, accessed September 30, 2013.

◀ **FIGURE 2.4**
Brand Image: Benefits to Companies

- Extension of positive customer feelings to new products
- Ability to charge a higher price or fee
- Consumer loyalty leading to more frequent purchases
- Positive word-of-mouth endorsements
- Higher level of channel power
- Ability to attract quality employees
- More favorable ratings by financial observers and analysts

Many customers believe they "get what they pay for." Consumers often associate better quality with a higher price. A strong brand image allows a company to charge more for goods and services, which can lead to improved markup margins and profits for the firm.

Firms with well-developed brand images enjoy more loyal customers, which leads them to purchase products more frequently. Loyal customers are less inclined to make substitute purchases when other companies offer discounts, sales, and similar enticements.

Heightened levels of customer loyalty often result in positive word-of-mouth endorsements. Favorable comments help generate additional sales and attract new customers. Consumers and business buyers have more faith in personal references than other forms of advertising or promotion.

Positive customer attitudes create stronger positive feelings about the brand, which then provides greater channel power. Retailers stock the brands customers view positively and seek out brands that pull people into stores. A product or brand with a high positive image retains control and channel power when marketing items to retailers.

Attracting quality employees can become another advantage of a dominant brand image. Just as consumers are drawn to strong firms, potential workers apply for jobs at companies with solid reputations, thereby reducing recruiting and selection costs. Southwest Airlines holds the image of a great place to work, which assists in the recruiting process. A high-quality work force normally experiences lower turnover rates. The result is a stronger brand image to customers.

Interstate Battery System International, Inc.

▲ Interstate Batteries has accrued positive benefits from a strong brand name.

A strong reputation often leads to more favorable ratings by Wall Street analysts and other financial institutions, which can help a company raise capital. Legislators and governmental agencies tend to act in a more supportive manner toward companies with strong and positive reputations. Lawmakers might be less inclined to pursue actions that might hurt the business. Members of regulatory agencies may be less likely to believe rumors of wrongdoing.

Building a strong brand image provides tangible and intangible benefits. Both customers and organizations benefit from a well-known firm with an established reputation. Organizational leaders devote considerable amounts of time and energy to building and maintaining a positive brand image. Client companies expect advertising agencies to help design marketing programs that take advantage of the benefits of a strong brand image.

Identifying the Desired Brand Image

objective 2.2
What elements are involved in identifying, creating, rejuvenating, or changing a brand's image?

When creating a program to promote a desired image, the marketing team first evaluates the nature of the brand's current image. Brand managers study the brand's image in order to identify its strengths and weaknesses. A study of the external environment helps identify opportunities to pursue and the best positioning of the brand relative to competitors. The marketing team should try to discover how those outside of a company view the brand.

Once a team understands how various groups view the brand, decisions can be made regarding ways to correct any misperceptions and/or build on the image that customers currently hold. Marketers can then tailor future communications to promote the target image. These messages will be sent to every constituency, including customers, suppliers, and employees.

At one time Nokia was the market leader in the mobile phone industry. Recently, after years of declining sales and a lower market share, the company became more of an underdog and was forced act more like a challenger. As the market leader, the company's approach was simply to defend its share. The new goal of Nokia, according to CMO Tuula Rytila, was to reignite the brand by bringing meaning, relevancy, and emotion to it. The messages were created to resonate with customers in the United States, and also those in Europe, China, and India.[5]

Creating the Right Brand Image

The right image sends a clear message about the unique nature of an organization and its products. A strong image accurately portrays what the firm sells, even in large corporations that offer multiple brands, such as Kraft Foods. As an example, the top management team at Kraft developed the phrase "Make today delicious" in an effort to unite the corporation and its various brands by focusing its employees in a cohesive direction.[6]

▼ The goal of Scott Equipment's rebranding campaign was to present a consistent image to its customers across all 25 locations.

Scott Equipment

In a business-to-business operation, creating the right image can be challenging. Scott Equipment sells new and used construction, agricultural, and industrial equipment. The company was founded in 1939 and grew to 25 locations in five different states. Scott's management team faced a challenging circumstance in which each location took care of its own marketing and advertising, which had the effect of creating 25 different brand images. Recognizing the need to create a consistent image among all of its outlets, Scott Equipment hired New Orleans-based Peter Mayer advertising agency. The agency sought to unify communications promoting one common brand image while at the same time allowing each location some flexibility in how that image would be portrayed. As shown in the advertisement in this section, the Peter Mayer agency helped develop the tagline "Heavy-Duty Commitment" as an integral part of Scott's brand image. The key message to business buyers was that Scott was committed to providing quality "heavy-duty" equipment and support to its customers.[7]

Rejuvenating a Brand's Image

Rejuvenating an image helps a firm sell new products and can attract new customers. At the same time, reinforcing previous aspects of an image enables the company to retain loyal patrons and those who are comfortable with

- Help former customers rediscover the brand
- Offer timeless consumer value
- Stay true to original, but contemporize
- Build a community

FIGURE 2.5
Keys to Successful Image Rejuvenation

the original version. Quality image reengineering programs require companies to remain consistent with a previous image while at the same time incorporating new elements to expand each firm's target audience.

Successful rejuvenation includes attention to four key areas (see Figure 2.5).[8] First, former customers need to rediscover the brand. For these individuals, the brand experience will be nostalgia. For other consumers, usually the younger age groups, the brand represents a totally new experience. Connecting the nostalgic and new consumer groups requires attention to some timeless value such as authenticity, simplicity, or a compelling brand story or heritage. When making this connection, the message should stay true to what originally made the brand great. Then the brand can be contemporized. Successful rejuvenation involves building a brand community through social media, mobile, and other interactive marketing techniques. Energizing brand advocates and influencers to spread the word about the "new and improved" version of the brand becomes the goal. As was noted in the opening section of this chapter, both IHOP and Applebee's were able to rejuvenate brand images by focusing on numerous aspects of the marketing program that went beyond mere changes in advertising.

L'eggs represents a once highly-visible brand that recently achieved rejuvenation. Twenty years ago, the slogan "Nothing beats a great pair of L'eggs" was well known, as was the jingle that went with it. When the fashion industry changed and fewer females wore hosiery, L'eggs brand name and market share almost vanished. Angela Hawkins of HanesBrands (corporate owner of L'eggs), said, "We wanted to move on, contemporize, and modernize [the L'eggs brand]. We needed to speak to a new generation, [but] we wanted to stay true to our brand positioning and personality, which is fun and kind of flirty." In addition to a new website, L'eggs developed a strong presence in social media and developed a new slogan "You're in luck. You're in L'eggs." L'eggs also employed television and print advertising to reach its target market, women ages 18 to 34.[9]

Changing a Brand's Image

Completely changing the image people hold regarding a company or a brand may not be possible. Attempting to change an image becomes necessary when target markets have begun to shrink or disappear or when the brand's image no longer matches industry trends and consumer expectations. At that point, company leaders consider what they wish to change, why, and how they intend to accomplish it.

The retailer Target faced a unique situation when the companied tried to buy advertising space in *Vogue* magazine. Target was told "no." Tom Novak, president of Target's advertising agency (Peterson Milla Hooks), said the company received a letter from *Vogue* stating "We don't want your money because

▼ Target developed an aggressive advertising campaign designed to alter its brand image.

Olesiabilkei/Fotolia

Kraft Foods, Inc.

Kraft Foods, Inc.

▲ These Maxwell House coffee advertisements seek to change consumer perceptions by suggesting that they can purchase and enjoy gourmet coffee at home.

including a brand like Target would diminish the quality of our advertising." As a result, Target and its advertising agency realized that the company had an image of being a "dowdy Midwestern discounter." The Peterson Milla Hooks agency faced the challenge of designing an advertising and communications program that would change that image for media outlets such as *Vogue* as well as current and new customers.

Target attacked its image problem on two fronts. First, company leaders changed the product mix by including designer labels such as a collection from the Italian fashion house Missoni. Second, Target's advertising agency created a campaign entitled "Signs of the Times" that was designed to elevate the Target brand rather than sell merchandise. Marketers positioned Target as a place where consumers could purchase high-end designer lamps, clothes, and other merchandise for less. The Peterson Milla Hooks agency created the now famous red and white bull's-eye image that consumers instantly recognize as Target. The efforts changed the image of Target among consumers as well as with media outlets. In a recent issue, Target placed a 20-page insert as well as an advertisement on the back cover of *Vogue*.[10]

At times, changing an image requires trying to influence views of the product or service category. Notice the two advertisements for Maxwell House coffee in this section that were created by the mcgarrybowen agency. The campaign seeks to persuade individuals that gourmet coffee is available at grocery stores and not just from coffee shops.

Brand Names

A brand name provides the overall banner for operations. David Placek, president and founder of Lexicon, Inc., said, "The brand name is really the cornerstone of a company's relationship with its customers. It sets an attitude and tone and is the first step toward a personality."[11] Brand names can be divided into four categories based on their actual, implied, or visionary meaning (see Figure 2.6).[12]

- **Overt names.** Reveal what a company does.
- **Implied names.** Contain recognizable words or word parts that convey what a company does.
- **Conceptual names.** Capture the essence of what a company offers.
- **Iconoclastic names.** Represent something unique, different, and memorable.

FIGURE 2.6
Categories of Brand Names

- Google—name started as a joke about the way search engines search for information. The word googol is one followed by 100 zeros.
- Lego—combination of Danish phrase "leg godt" which means "play well" and Latin word lego which means "I put together."
- Reebok—alternative spelling of "rhebok" which is an African antelope.
- Skype—original name was "sky-peer-to-peer," which was changed to "skyper" then to "skype."
- Verizon—combination of Latin word "veritas" which means "truth" and horizon.
- Volkswagen—created by Adolph Hitler as a car for the masses that could transport 2 adults and 3 children at speeds up to 62 mph. Name means "people's car."
- Yahoo—word from Jonathan Swift's book *Gulliver's Travels,* which represented a repulsive, filthy creature that resembled Neanderthal man. Yahoo! founders, Jerry Yang and David Filo considered themselves to be yahoos.

FIGURE 2.7
Origins of Some Unique Brand Names

Overt names include American Airlines, Kraft Foods, and BMW Motorcycles USA. *Implied names* include FedEx and IBM. *Conceptual names*, such as Google, Twitter, and Krispy Kreme, take a different approach. The name "Google" evokes a vision of a place where an endless number of items can be found, and "Krispy Kreme" suggests confectionaries filled with tasty crème. Monster.com, Nabisco, and Calumet are examples of *iconoclastic names*.

objective 2.3
What are the different types of brand names?

Marketing the first two categories (overt and implied) should be easier because consumers more readily recall the name, which implies the type of good or service offered. The other two categories (conceptual and iconoclastic) necessitate greater marketing efforts to ensure that consumers connect the name with the product offered. Figure 2.7 provides backgrounds for some well-known brand names.

Pink Jacket Studio

▲ The Snoring Center is an overt name because it reveals what a company does.

Developing a brand name can generate a great deal of excitement and interest in a company. For example, approximately 1,000 Kraft employees from around the world submitted more than 1,700 names for a new high-growth snack business spun off by Kraft Foods. The conceptual name that was chosen, Mondelez, combines "monde" the Latin word for "world" with "delez," a new word that conveys "delicious." According to Kraft CEO Irene Rosenfeld, "we wanted to find a new name that could . . . reinforce the truly global nature of this business and build on our higher purpose—to make today delicious." She further suggests that the name Mondelez is "unique and captures a big idea—just the way the snacks we make take small moments in our lives and turn them into something bigger, brighter, and more joyful."[13]

Brand Logos

objective 2.4
What are the characteristics of effective logos?

A **brand logo** is the symbol used to identify a brand. It should be designed to be compatible with the brand's name. A logo can contribute an additional aspect to a brand's image. Organizations have spent millions of dollars selecting and promoting names and logos. A strong name featuring a well-designed logo helps consumers remember specific brands and company advertisements. Consumers can reduce search time when they look

▸ **FIGURE 2.8**
Four Tests of Quality Logos and Brand Names

- Recognizable
- Familiar
- Elicits a consensual meaning among those in the firm's target market
- Evokes positive feelings

for specific product names identified by effective logos. Quality logos and brand names should pass the four tests identified in Figure 2.8.[14]

Logos assist in-store shopping. The mind processes visuals faster than words. A logo may be more quickly recognized by shoppers. Logo recognition can occur at two levels. First, a consumer might remember seeing the logo in the past. An image stored in a person's memory will be jogged when it is seen at the store. Second, a familiar logo may remind the consumer of the brand or corporate name. This reminder can elicit positive (or negative) feelings regarding the branded item.

Successful logos elicit shared meanings across consumers, a process known as **stimulus codability**. Logos with high stimulus codability evoke consensual meanings within a culture or subculture (such as the Prudential Rock). Consumers readily recognize logos with high degrees of codability such as those used by Apple, McDonald's, and Pepsi. Companies that have logos with lower degrees of codability often spend more money on advertising. At first, Nike spent a considerable amount of funds to make the "swoosh" more recognizable, because at first the logo by itself did not conjure any specific image. Now, almost everyone recognizes the Nike swoosh. The brand name does not even have to be present.

Some companies modify logos as market conditions change. Others maintain the same logo for decades with only minor changes. John Deere holds a long-lasting logo, which was designed in 1876 and is still used today. Figure 2.9 identifies some of the oldest logos and when they were created.

Creating quality logos can be challenging. Logos that pass the test of time are even more difficult. Figure 2.10 lists tips for creating or changing logos. Logos are a reflection of a brand. Consequently, a cheap, poorly designed logo might suggest an inferior brand to consumers. Quality logos require careful thought, planning, and the expertise of designers who understand the principles behind creating or changing one into a version that will be effective.

Company/Brand	Year Company Founded	Year Logo First Used
John Deere	1837	1876
Coca-Cola	1886	1886
Johnson & Johnson	1886	1886
Union Pacific Railroad	1862	1888
Prudential Life Insurance	1875	1896
Campbell's Soup	1869	1898
General Electric	1892	1900
Goodyear	1898	1901
Sherwin-Williams	1866	1905
DuPont	1802	1907

▸ **FIGURE 2.9**
Some of the Oldest Logos
Source: Based on Samuel Weigley, Alexander Hess, and Paul Ausick, "The Oldest Company Logos in America," http://246wallst.com/2013/06/18/the-oldest-company-logos-in-america, June 18, 2013.

- The logo is a reflection of the brand
- Creating logos requires knowledge and expertise
- Use professional designers
- Make the logo simple
- Make the logo media transferrable

▸ **FIGURE 2.10**
Tips on Creating or Changing Logos

A logo does not have to be complex and contain every element of the brand's meaning. Simple logos can be valuable.[15] The Nike swoosh and McDonald's arches are simple but powerful logos. A logo should complement the brand name and not overpower it, the product's packaging, or the product itself. Effective logos are media transferrable, which means they can be used in all types of media from print ads to broadcast ads to the internet and social media. The best logos transcend cultures and can be featured around the world.

Water Institute of the Gulf

▲ This logo for The Water Institute of the Gulf was created by Zehnder Communications.

Changing logos does not always modify public opinion of a company. American Airlines may have discovered this the hard way when the company tweeted via social media the message that its new logo on the tail of its planes reflected the spirit of America—"innovative, progressive, and open to the world." The public saw it differently. One Twitter quote said, "… a new paint job [does not] make up for crappy service [and] operating model deficiencies." Another tweet predicted the new logo will be hated by everybody. The new logo design's impact is best summarized by the words of Massimo Vignelli when he said, "It seems to me that there was no need for American Airlines to undertake such a change…. but many people do not understand the difference between design and styling, and believe in a change for the sake of change."[16]

When completed properly, logo changes can trigger positive reactions and symbolize a positive change, as was the case with Pepsi. Vice president of Pepsi, Frank Cooper, noted that a change was needed as the company moved, "out of traditional mass marketing and mass distribution," and that a "more dynamic and alive" logo was needed to engage consumers. The new logo took five months to create and cost more than $1 million. Additional costs were incurred when the company placed the new logo on delivery trucks, vending machines, stadium signage, and point-of-purchase materials.[17]

Stanley tools marketing team recognized a similar situation—that the brand needed a modernized logo. The former logo placed the Stanley name stylized on tools that looked too much like a nameplate rather than a logo. The new logo has a tight "N" with an angular cut and an upward swoop designed to evoke an "Action" theme. The rationale behind the new logo design was to give the brand more of an action-oriented feel, to sustain the brand long-term, and to allow expansion into global markets.[18]

Types of Brands

objective 2.5
What different kinds of brands can firms offer?

Brands develop histories. They have personalities. In fact, one of the current trends in branding involves trying to create a human persona or personality for the brand. Key human traits that brands espouse include customer empathy, talking and acting like people, and empowering individuals to be the brand. Notice that the copy in the Maxwell House coffee ad in this section contains a play on words "stay grounded" by referring to both the coffee grounds and the human characteristic of staying grounded.

The powerful impact branding has on purchase behaviors means that marketers should make branding decisions thoughtfully. Figure 2.11 identifies several types of brands.

Family Brands

Many brands produce family trees. A **family brand** means a company offers a series or group of products under one brand name. The Campbell's brand applies to various lines of soups and other vegetable products. Consumers seeing the Campbell's brand expect a certain level of quality in existing products and any product line addition or modification,

▶ **FIGURE 2.11**
Types of Brand

- **Family brands.** A group of related products sold under one name.
- **Brand extension.** The use of an established brand name on products or services not related to the core brand.
- **Flanker brand.** The development of a new brand sold in the same category as another product.
- **Co-branding.** The offering of two or more brands in a single marketing offer.
- **Ingredient branding.** The placement of one brand within another brand.
- **Cooperative branding.** The joint venture of two or more brands into a new product or service.
- **Complementary branding.** The marketing of two brands together for co-consumption.
- **Private brands.** Proprietary brands marketed by an organization and sold within the organization's outlets.

such as Healthy Choice soups. These transfer associations occur as long as the new product remains within the same product category. When the additional products added that are not related to the brand's core merchandise, the transfer of loyalty does not occur as easily.

▼ This advertisement for Maxwell House uses a play on words to convey the human characteristic of staying grounded.

Kraft Foods, Inc.

Brand Extensions

Brand extension involves the use of an established brand name on new goods or services. The extension may not be related to the core brand. Nike has been successful in extending its brand name to a line of clothing. Black & Decker effectively extended its brand name to new types of power tools but did not succeed in extending the brand to small kitchen appliances.

Flanker Brands

As an alternative to brand extensions, a **flanker brand** is the development of a new brand by a company in a good or service category in which it currently has a brand offering. Procter & Gamble's primary laundry detergents are Cheer and Tide. Over the years, P&G introduced a number of additional brands such as Ivory, Dreft, and Gain. In total, P&G offers eight different brands of detergents in North America (see Figure 2.12). P&G's marketing team creates flanker brands to appeal to target markets a brand does not reach. This helps the company to offer a more complete line of products and reach a higher percentage of customers. It also establishes barriers to entry for competing firms.

A flanker brand may be introduced when company leaders believe that offering the product under the current brand name might adversely affect the overall marketing program. Several years ago, Hallmark's marketers created the flanker brand Shoebox Greetings to sell cards in discount stores as

Cosmetics
- Covergirl
- Max Factor

Body Wash & Soap
- Ivory
- Olay
- Old Spice
- Safeguard

Laundry & Fabric Care
- Bounce
- Cheer
- Downy
- Dreft
- Era
- Febreze Air Fresheners
- Gain
- Ivory
- Tide

Hair Care
- Aussie
- Head & Shoulders
- Herbal Essences
- Pantene

Dish Washing
- Cascade
- Dawn
- Ivory
- Joy

FIGURE 2.12
Select Brands Sold by Proctor & Gamble

well as Hallmark outlets. At first, the Hallmark brand was only sold in retail stores carrying the Hallmark name. The marketing team discovered that although Shoebox Greeting cards are lower priced, they allowed Hallmark to attract a larger percentage of the market, even in its own stores.

Firms operating in low-end or middle markets may use flanker brands to compete in high-end markets. Such was the case with Nestlé. Nestlé brands San Pellegrino and Perrier are more mainstream. Nestlé did not have a premium brand to compete with Smartwater, Fiji, and Evian until the firm introduced Resource. The target market was primarily females who are trendier, earn higher incomes, and are around age 35. The ad campaign promoted the concept that Resource offered more than hydration. The premium brand included total "electrolytenment" in bottles containing 50 percent recycled plastic content.[19]

Flanker brands are used in international expansion. Procter & Gamble sells Ariel laundry detergent in Latin America, Europe, the Middle East, Asia, and Africa but not in the United States. Offering different brands for specific markets helps a firm to operate in international markets.

Co-Branding

Co-branding, or **alliance branding**, is the combination or alliance of two brands and can take three forms: ingredient branding, cooperative branding, and complementary branding (see Figure 2.13). **Ingredient branding** involves the placement of one brand within another brand, such as Intel microprocessors in Dell computers or Nestlé chocolate in Pillsbury brownie mix. **Cooperative branding** is a joint venture in which two or more brands are placed in a new good or service, such as when Citibank combines American Airlines and VISA into a credit card. **Complementary branding** is the marketing of two brands together to encourage co-consumption or co-purchases, such as Velveeta cheese marketed with Rotel Tomatoes and Diced Green Chilies.

Co-branding succeeds when it builds brand equity in both brands. Wholly Guacamole formed brand alliances with several brands including Sonic, Disney, Schlotzksy's, and Jennie-O. According to Tracy Altman of Wholly Guacamole, the advertising and marketing budgets of many brands are stretched extremely thin and at the same time greater results are expected. One way to maximize advertising dollars is to develop alliances with other brands.[20]

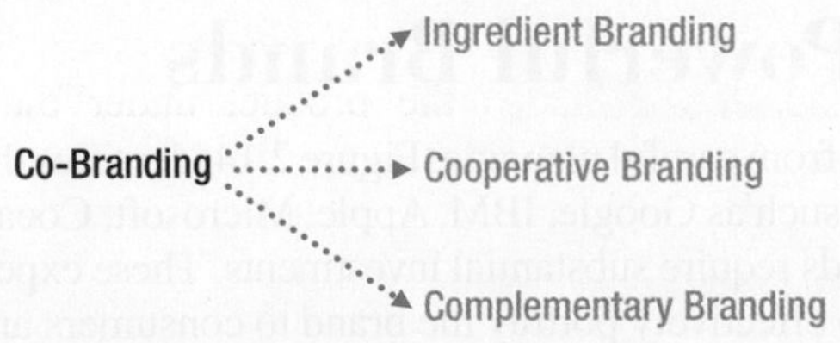

FIGURE 2.13
Forms of Co-Branding

Freshertized Foods

▲ Wholly Guacamole developed a brand alliance with Sonic.

When Monsanto created NutraSweet, consumer confidence in the product was generated by placing the NutraSweet logo on trusted brands, including Diet Coke, Wrigley's Chewing Gum (Wrigley's Extra), and Crystal Light. The strategy led NutraSweet to become the standard in the sweetener industry.[21]

Co-branding involves some risk. If the relationship fails to do well in the marketplace, both brands may suffer. If one brand suffers, it can impact the sales of the other. For instance, a few years ago reports surfaced that aspartame may contribute to certain types of cancer. Both NutraSweet and Equal contain aspartame. Sales of products containing aspartame (or Nutrasweet) such as Diet Coke saw sales slip. To reverse this trend, Diet Coke and other brands containing aspartame went on the offensive to convince consumers the product was safe to consume.

While risk cannot be eliminated, alliances between brands of goods and services that are highly compatible generally will be less risky. Ingredient and cooperative branding tend to be less risky than complementary branding because both companies have more at stake and devote greater resources to ensure success.

For small companies and brands that are not as well known, co-branding can be an effective strategy. Finding a well-known brand willing to create an alliance with a lesser-known product may be difficult. When such an alliance forms, the co-brand relationship often builds brand equity for the lesser-known brand more than the established brand.

Developing Brands

objective 2.6
How are brands developed, built, and sustained in order to build brand equity and fend off perceptions of brand parity?

Developing a strong brand begins with discovering why consumers buy a brand and why they rebuy the brand. In assessing a brand, marketing professionals ask questions such as:

- Where does your brand stand now?
- What are your objectives?
- What are you doing to build your brand and business?
- What are your brand's strengths? Weaknesses?
- Which opportunities should be pursued first? Where are the pitfalls?[22]

The answers to these inquiries assist the company's marketing team or its agency in developing a plan that cultivates a stronger brand position.

A primary feature that keeps a brand strong occurs when it contains something that is **salient** to customers, which can come from several sources. A product or brand that provides benefits consumers consider important and of higher quality than other brands enjoys salience. The view that the brand represents a good value also creates this advantage. The brand may be deemed superior to others because its image leads to customer loyalty based on such salient properties.[23]

Building Powerful Brands

Powerful brands result from careful planning. Figure 2.14 identifies the ingredients required to build powerful brands such as Google, IBM, Apple, Microsoft, Coca-Cola, and McDonald's. As shown, strong brands require substantial investments. These expenditures create the communications needed to effectively portray the brand to consumers and businesses.

- Invest in the brand
- Create awareness
- Offer authenticity uniqueness
- Build trust
- Deliver an experience
- Offer value
- Utilize social media
- Utilize mobile
- Act responsibly

◀ **FIGURE 2.14**
Building Powerful Brands

Branding begins with awareness, which may be achieved by featuring the brand name prominently in repeated advertisements. Repetition captures the buyer's attention. It increases the odds that a brand and the accompanying message will be stored in long-term memory and recalled later during a purchase process.

Brands should be authentic or unique in some manner. The brand name should be associated with the product's most prominent characteristic that makes it stand out from competitors. Many consumers connect Crest with "cavity prevention." Coca-Cola seeks to associate its name with a product that is "refreshing." For BMW, it is "performance driving," and for 3M it is "innovation." Marketers seek to identify the "one thing" the brand stands for, that consumers recognize, and that will be salient to them. When these are present, more powerful brand recognition occurs. In the marketplace for automotive suspension systems, the Skyjacker brand is well-known to many consumers, distributors, and automobile manufacturers.

Business and retail customers trust powerful brands. **Trust** represents the customer's belief in the efficacy and reliability of the brand. It can be established over time through personal experiences. Trust results from a brand performing consistently and fulfilling its promise, its authenticity, and its uniqueness. For decades, Tide has consistently kept its promise to consumers. To sustain that trust, the marketing team at Tide continues to pay attention to the brand's image. Recent advertisements note how well Tide cleans clothes, using themes such as "Tide knows fabrics best," "Dirt can't hide from Tide," "If it's got to be clean, it's got to be Tide," and "Style is an option. Clean is not." To make sure the message will be seen and heard, Tide employs traditional mass media advertising; alternative media, including YouTube and Facebook; signs known as *wild postings* in urban locations; and

▼ Skyjacker built a high level of brand equity through domination in the vehicle suspension market.

Skyjacker Suspensions

Gulf Coast Seafood

▲ Gulf Coast Seafood created an effective app as part of its mobile advertising campaign.

sponsorship of events in South Beach, Florida, and other resort areas. Tide also enhances its brand image by delivering cleaning products to victims in disaster areas such as those affected by tornadoes and hurricanes.[24]

Powerful brands go beyond delivering functional features. They focus on providing an experience that involves the opportunity to be customized and personalized. The iPhone, with more than 100,000 apps, allows users to customize the phone to fit their personalities. The brand becomes a central part of their lives and who they are. When delivered effectively, the experience creates a strong emotional bond between the consumer and the brand. Apple, Nike, Harley Davidson, and Jeep are brands that have built strong communities of followers.

Retailers can develop similar experiences. Tom Novak of Peterson Milla Hooks, the advertising agency for Target, states "A lot of retailers focus on the transaction, but we really believe that an emotional connection trumps selling. Because you like Target, you feel better buying your toothpaste there even though you could buy it at Wal-Mart."[25]

The 2008 recession caused many consumers and businesses to re-evaluate brands they purchased. "Value" became the buzz word in the marketplace. Consumers and businesses looked for brands that offer the best value, which is a balance between quality and price. Currently, only seven percent of consumers focus entirely on price while discarding quality considerations. Even fewer individuals focus on quality without any price considerations.

Building powerful brands includes the effective use of social media. It should be authentic and in-tune with the brand. Merely creating a Facebook page or posting videos to YouTube does not suffice. An effective social media strategy engages consumers and enriches their experiences with the brand.

Building brands incorporates the creative use of mobile advertising. Marketers for more powerful brands have discovered ways to use mobile to enhance the customer's experience through personalization and customization of content. Mobile advertising offers companies the opportunity to interact with customers anywhere at any time; however, the interaction must enhance the customer's experience and not be an intrusion. A text or an ad every time the user turns on his or her phone will quickly alienate even a brand loyal customer.

The final ingredient of a powerful brand results when the company acts ethically. Consumers want to purchase brands from companies that understand the importance of not harming the earth or people. Also, using sweat shops to produce products alienates customers. In essence, consumers tend to prefer brands sold by socially responsible companies.

Brand Loyalty

Brand loyalty constitutes the ultimate objective of building powerful brands. Brand loyalty occurs when customers purchase only one brand. They consider no other choice, regardless of price differences. The Brand Keys Customer Loyalty Engagement Index (CLEI) suggests that emotion and value are the core drivers of brand loyalty, rather than rational thought based on functional product attributes. Loyalty results from the consumer's experience with the brand and emotional connection she has with it. In essence, loyalty represents what a "brand stands for or means to the consumer on an emotional level."[26]

The degree to which the brand has established a clear unique or authentic proposition determines the value of the brand. Value depends heavily on the "delight factor," or the degree to which the brand exceeds basic expectations by delivering benefits or an emotional connection that enhances a consumer's day-to-day life. Using the Customer Loyalty Engagement Index, Brand Keys identified the top performing brands in 54 different product categories. Figure 2.15 identifies some of the top brands in select categories.

Category	Top Brand	CLEI Emotional Engagement
Athletic Footwear	Skechers	86%
Bank	JP Morgan Chase	79%
Car Insurance	State Farm	82%
Casual Dining	Applebee's	82%
Cosmetics	Clinique	93%
Gasoline	Shell	80%
Major League Sports	NFL	86%
Pizza	Domino's	84%
Quick Service Restaurant	Subway	95%
Soft Drinks (Diet)	Diet Coke	89%

FIGURE 2.15
Top Brands Based on Brand Keys Customer Loyalty Engagement Index (CLEI)

Source: Based on "Brand Keys 2013 Customer Loyalty Index Finds Seismic Shift I How Consumers Emotionally Engage with Products, Services," Press Release, http://brandkeys.com/wp-content/uploads/2013/02/2013-CLEI-Press-Release-FINAL-Overall.pdf

Brand Equity

Many companies encounter the **brand parity** problem, which occurs when consumers conclude that few tangible distinctions exist between competing brands in mature markets. Customers see only minor product differences and, in many product categories, even minor variations are difficult to identify.

In contrast, **brand equity** represents a set of characteristics that are unique to a brand. Equity helps to fight the brand parity problem. The perception of brand equity means that consumers view a good or service's given brand name as different, better, and one that can be trusted. In business-to-business markets, brand equity influences selections in the buying decision-making process. Products with strong brand equity are often selected over products with low brand equity or brands that firms know less about. The same scenario occurs in international markets. Brand equity opens doors to foreign firms, brokers, and retailers and provides privileges that products with low brand equity cannot obtain.

Brand equity dissuades consumers from looking for cheaper products, special deals, or other incentives. It prevents erosion of a product's market share, even when a proliferation of brands is coupled to promotional maneuvers by competitors.

Kraft enjoys a high level of brand equity, which produces brand loyalty.

Kraft Foods, Inc.

Measuring Brand Equity

Measuring brand equity can be difficult. To do so, marketing experts apply **brand metrics**, which measure of the return on branding investments.

- Financial value
- Stock market value
- Revenue premium
- Consumer value

▲ **FIGURE 2.16**
Methods of Measuring Brand Equity

According to Millward Brown Optimor, a strong brand constitutes one of the most valuable assets a company holds and accounts for about one-third of shareholder value.[27]

Unfortunately, no concrete, scientific, or quantitative method exists because brand equity is an abstract concept. In response, marketers have developed four different methods to measure it (see Figure 2.16). Arguments can be made in favor of each. The personal preference of the company's CEO or the one that yields the highest value for a particular brand often dictates method selection.

Brand equity based on *financial value* estimates the future cash flows of a brand based on its unique strength and characteristics, which will then be discounted to determine a net present value. With the *stock market* approach, the financial value of the company is determined through stock valuation. Then, an estimate of the portion of the value allocated to brand equity—not physical assets—can be made.

The third approach, *revenue premium*, compares a branded product to the same product without a brand name. To calculate a brand's revenue premium, the revenue generated by a particular brand will be compared to a private label brand. The difference is the revenue premium, or value of that brand, and would equate to the accrued brand equity.

The final method, *consumer value*, attempts to assess the value of a brand based on input from consumers. Typical measures include familiarity, quality, purchase considerations, customer satisfaction, and willingness to seek out the brand. The difficulty with this approach is that all of the measures are based on consumer attitudes. No concrete financial or accounting numbers are calculated.[28]

The CLEI index from Brand Keys described in the Brand Loyalty section of this chapter offers one example of the consumer value approach. Another is the "Most Beloved Brands" produced by APCO Worldwide from a survey of 70,000 consumers. The study measured eight emotional feelings consumers have toward a brand: understanding, approachability, relevance, admiration, curiosity, identification, empowerment, and pride.[29] Figure 2.17 displays the top 10 most loved brands using this methodology.

Private Brands

objective 2.7
What current trends affect private brands?

Private brands, private labels, and store brands are proprietary brands marketed by an organization and normally distributed exclusively within the organization's outlets. Private brands have experienced a roller-coaster ride in terms of popularity and sales. To some individuals, private brands carry the connotation of a lower price and inferior quality. Historically, the primary audiences for private labels were price-sensitive individuals and low-income families. This may no longer be the case. Retailers invest significant

Rank	Company	Emotional Index
1	Disney	74.7
2	Yahoo!	74.3
3	Google	74.2
4	Sony	74.1
5	Nestlé	73.3
6	Auchan	72.9
7	Netflix	72.8
8	Whole Foods	72.7
9	Apple	72.7
10	Lowe's	72.5

▲ **FIGURE 2.17**
Top 10 Most Loved Brands

Source: Based on Christopher Heine, "Check Out the Top 100 Beloved Brands," *Adweek*, www.adweek.com/news/advertising-branding/check-out-the-top-100-beloved-brands, October 10, 2013.

dollars to develop private brands, which now account for approximately 23 percent of all unit sales in the United States.[30]

Many consumers report that they cannot tell the difference in quality between national brands and private brands. In a Nielsen survey of consumers, two-thirds said private brands are equivalent to national brands. Another survey suggested that only 19 percent of consumers believe national brands are worth paying more money for.[31] These changes, as well as others that have occurred in the private-brand arena, are summarized in Figure 2.18.[32]

Private brands tend to fare better in recessions and slow economic times as consumers try to save money. Sales for national brands often decline during slow economic cycles. Retailers offering private brands can reduce the impact of slow economic times by offering store brands.[33]

bst2012/Fotolia

▲ Private labels are often displayed in retail store windows and made to look as attractive as manufacturers' brands.

Advantages to Retailers

Although private labels tend to be priced between five and 20 percent lower than national brands, they also generate higher gross margins than national brands because middlemen are not used. Higher margins enable retailers to earn higher profits on private brands or, alternatively, to reduce the prices of the private brands to make them more attractive to price-sensitive consumers. Retailers that maintain the higher markup on private labels have the opportunity to use some of the margin for advertising and promotions of the brands.

One emerging trend in retailing indicates that loyalty toward retail stores has been growing while loyalty toward individual brands has been on the decline. Rather than going to outlets selling specific brands, many shoppers visit specific stores and buy from the brands offered by those stores. The increase in loyalty to retailers has caused several stores to expand the number of private-brand products offered. This requires the retailer to develop private brands that are congruent with consumer images of the company.[34]

Savvy retailers recognize the value of private labels and how they can be used to differentiate the store from competing retailers and from national brands. These stores promote these labels as distinctive brands aimed toward specific market segments. Retailers can emphasize meeting consumer needs with a quality product rather than simply focusing on price.

JC Penney has been successfully utilizing private branding in apparel lines. JC Penney offers more than 30 private labels, accounting for more than 40 percent of sales.[35] Liz Sweeney of JC Penney stated, "We are dedicated to creating and managing winning private brands that develop customer loyalty. This means managing and marketing our key private brands as true brands versus labels."[36]

- Improved quality
- Perceived as a value purchase
- Higher loyalty toward retail outlets and lower loyalty toward specific brands
- Used to differentiate retail outlets
- Increased advertising of private brands
- Increased quality of in-store displays and packaging of private brands

◀ **FIGURE 2.18**
Changes in Private Brands

Art Allianz/Fotolia

▲ The Sears private label, Kenmore, is now advertised like a national brand.

Emerging trends in the use of private labels include retailers spending marketing dollars on improving the label, on designing noticeable in-store displays, and on packaging. Retailers without large national ad budgets rely more on displays and attractive packaging. A drab, cheap package does not convey the message that the private brand represents the equivalent or better alternative to a national brand. Many consumers blur the distinction between private labels and national brands. Unless a customer is familiar with the store's private brand labels, the individual might believe he is purchasing a national brand.[37]

Some retailers go one step further by designing the advertising of private brands apart from the store's regular advertising program. Recently, Sears launched a series of advertisements featuring its Kenmore and Craftsman brands. Sears was only mentioned in the context of being the place to purchase Kenmore and Craftsman products. A similar approach was used for Lands' End. Kmart's private labels include Martha Stewart, Jaclyn Smith, Route 66, Structure, and Joe Boxer. The company promotes these private brands separately in order to establish the names as bona fide brands, competing head-to-head with national brands and to distance the brands from the retail parent.

Responses from Manufacturers

Manufacturers respond to the inroads made by private labels in various ways. Figure 2.19 lists some common tactics.[38] A manufacturer can focus on a few core brands rather than split advertising dollars among a large number of brands. The core brands are advertised heavily, which helps the manufacturer maintain its brand name and reinforces the message that consumers are making the right decision when they purchase the manufacturer's national brand. Creating bonds with consumers both before and after purchases will be the goal.

▶ **FIGURE 2.19**
Tactics Used by Manufacturers to Combat Private Labels

- Focus on core brands
- Increase advertising
- Introduce new products
- Focus on in-store selling and packaging
- Use alternative methods of marketing

Manufacturers may attempt to reduce the impact of private labels on sales by expanding product offerings. Aggressively introducing new products and new versions of current products may help a manufacturer maintain the loyalty of its current customers and be seen as an innovator. To further combat the impact of private brands, manufacturers can focus on in-store selling to emphasize core brands. Also, alternative methods of marketing, such as brand communities and social networks, might increase loyalty to a brand rather than a private label.

Packaging

objective 2.8
How can packaging and labels support an IMC program—domestically and in foreign settings?

A product's package represents the final opportunity to make an impression on a consumer. Packaging constitutes a marketing activity as much as television advertising and social media. Marketing surveys reveal that only 31 percent of purchases are planned prior to reaching a retail outlet. This means 69 percent of consumers make purchase decisions while in the store. Other research indicates that when an individual walks within 10 to 15 feet of a product, the item has as little as three seconds to catch the person's attention.[39]

The primary purposes of packaging are shown in Figure 2.20. Now, however, packages and labels are increasingly viewed as a key part of a company's integrated marketing communications program. It makes little sense to spend millions of dollars on advertising only to lose the sale in the store because of a lackluster, unattractive, or dull package.

Most retail purchase decisions are made based on familiarity with a brand or product at a retail store. Consequently, a unique and attractive package that captures the buyer's attention increases the chances the product will be purchased, sometimes as an impulse buy. In the grocery market, customers prefer foods that are fast, convenient, portable, and fresh. A consumer who experiences inferior packaging will be more likely to switch to another brand the next time.[40]

Not long ago, the marketing team at Alcoa Rigid Packaging watched consumers as they purchased groceries and stocked refrigerators. The team noticed that the standard 3-by-4-can (12-pack) beverage box was too large for the refrigerator, and consumers would only take out a few cans at a time to cool. It seemed logical that if more cans were cold, consumers might drink more. This observation led to the design of a box that was easier and more convenient to use, the longer and slimmer 6-by-2-can box. The newly designed self-dispensing 12-pack fits into the refrigerator door or on a shelf. As an individual takes out a can, a new one automatically slides down to the front of the box. The innovation improved sales for both Alcoa and soft-drink manufacturers, who embraced the new package.[41]

Monkey Business/Fotolia

▲ Packaging represents the final opportunity to make an impression on consumers that will result in a purchase.

Sometimes packaging changes are necessitated by adverse market conditions. The popularity of Proctor & Gamble's Tide Pods surged as soon as it hit the market

- Protect product
- Provide for ease of shipping and handling
- Provide for easy placement on shelves
- Prevent or reduce theft
- Prevent tampering (drugs and food)
- Meet consumer needs for speed, convenience, and portability
- Communicate marketing message

◀ **FIGURE 2.20**
Primary Purposes of Packaging

because of ease of use. The pods were placed in clear containers. Unfortunately, children accidentally consumed some of the packets of concentrated detergent thinking it was candy. To correct this problem, P&G switched to opaque containers and added a double-latch lid.[42]

Labels

Labels on packages serve several functions. First, they must meet legal requirements. This includes identifying the product contained in the package and any other specific information about content, such as nutritional information on foods. The Food and Drug Administration (FDA) regulates food labels in the United States. Many companies print warranties and guarantees on product labels.

The label represents another marketing opportunity. It can make the difference in whether a particular brand is purchased. Simple, yet powerful, changes can be made to influence purchasing behaviors. For Honest Tea, it was a matter of the label for the peach tea showing the peach cut open rather than a whole peach. The same approach was applied to pomegranate tea; a picture of a cut pomegranate instead of a whole one was featured on the label.[43]

A typical label contains the company's logo and the brand name. Labels may reveal special offers and other tie-ins such as a box of cereal with a toy contained inside. Labels often carry terms designed to build consumer interest and confidence in making the purchase. Words such as "gourmet," "natural," "premium," "adult formula," and "industrial strength" help make the product appear to be a better buy. A company's image, brand, logo, and theme extend to the design of the package and label, which allows the marketing team the opportunity to make the sale when the consumer is in the store making a purchasing decision.

Labels with QR Codes

The placement of QR codes for consumers to access with mobile devices represents a new trend in packaging and labeling. Figure 2.21 identifies the various ways companies use QR codes on packages and labels. Consumers use the codes to access product information as well as videos or instructions about how to use the product. While in a retail store, consumers can access via the QR code information about the product to see if it fits their particular needs. The information can help assure customers that they are purchasing the kind of product, size, or style that will satisfy their desires.

When showing how to use a product, videos can be helpful. They may be posted on YouTube or on the manufacturer's website. Either way, consumers can access information from the QR code for food information. QR codes take consumers to sites providing nutritional information, which can be valuable to people on special diets or those with allergies to certain foods such as peanuts or shellfish.

Shoppers can also access product reviews and ratings of various brands via QR codes, including the brand being considered. The danger in using QR codes for these two purposes is that they could lead consumers to choose an alternative brand; however, it may also strengthen the relationship with a customer who views the brand as honest and not afraid to share information, both good and bad.

The final two uses for QR codes are strictly for marketing purposes. By linking to social media sites such as Facebook, marketers hope the consumer will "like" the brand on

FIGURE 2.21
Ways QR Codes Are Used on Packaging

- Access product information
- Access videos on product use
- Access recipes and nutritional information
- Compare sizes, brands, and styles
- Access to product reviews and ratings
- Provide links to social media and entertainment sites

Facebook and follow it on Twitter or other social media sites. Realizing the power of word-of-mouth and peer-to-peer recommendations, the goal is to have consumers help spread the word about the brand.

At other times, the QR code links to an entertainment site. Taco Bell developed a campaign around placing QR codes on its cups and boxes that took customers to MTV content. The content changed every week to keep it fresh to encourage customers to revisit. Ten days into the campaign, the scans of the QR code were into the six-figure range, according to David Javitch, vice president of marketing at Scanbuy, the agency used by Taco Bell for the QR campaign.[44]

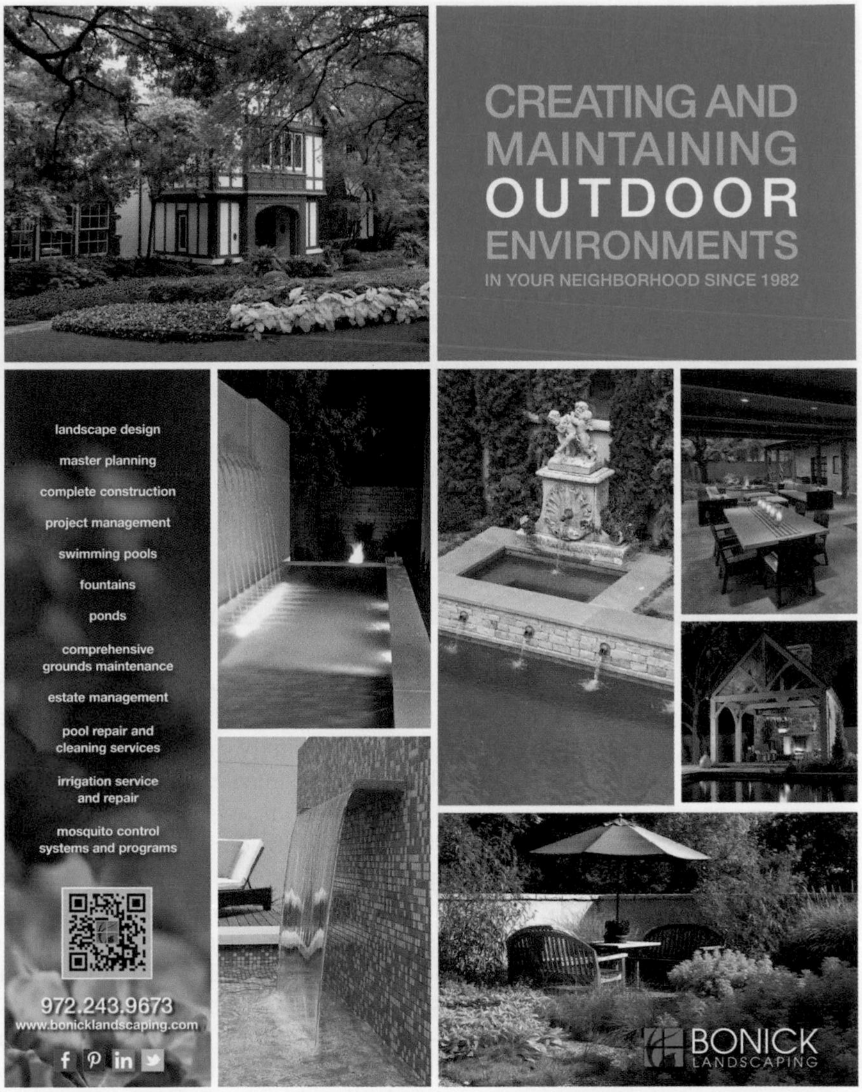

Bonick Landscaping

▲ This advertisement for Bonick Landscaping contains a QR code consumers can access for more information.

Ethical Issues in Brand Management

A variety of ethical issues are associated with brand management. For years, the most common problem, *brand infringement*, occurred when a company created a brand name that closely resembled a popular or successful brand, such as Korrs beer. In that case, the courts deemed the brand an intentional infringement on the Coors brand, and the name was abandoned. Another brand-infringing company that was forced by the courts to give up its name was Victor's Secret.

Brand infringement becomes more complex when a brand becomes so well-established that it may be considered a generic term, such as a Kleenex tissue or a Xerox copy. Band-Aid encountered the problem in the 1970s, forcing the marketing team to make sure the product was identified as "Band-Aid Brand Strips" rather than simply "band aids," to prevent the competition from using the name. The most vulnerable new brand names might be Google and Twitter because the names have entered everyday conversation, as in "I googled myself" or "I tweeted you."

According to many sources, *cyber squatting*, or *domain squatting*, constitute another form of unethical behavior. The practice involves buying domain names (e.g., barnesandnoble.com, kohls.com, labronjames.com, etc.) that are valuable to specific people or businesses in the hopes of making a profit by reselling the name. Any new company trying to build a presence in the online marketplace might find itself stifled by domain squatters. Names matter. Cyber squatters take advantage of that to make profits at someone else's expense.

International Implications

objective 2.9
How are brands managed in international markets?

In international markets, product development, branding, and maintaining an image are more complex. As noted previously, firms employ either an *adaptation* strategy or a *standardization* strategy in promotional programs. These two approaches apply to the products as well as to brand names. With standardization, the same brand name and product are sold in all countries. With adaptation, the brand and/or the actual product may be

OutdoorPhoto/Fotolia

▲ A market in Hong Kong.

different in each country or region. This can mean a product may be viewed as a local brand. Mr. Clean uses the adaptation brand approach for the same products. Items are sold under the names of Mr. Proper and Maestro Limpio as well as other names in various countries.

Using a standardized global brand reduces costs. Instead of advertising each local brand with a separate communication strategy, one standardized message can be sent. Standardized global brands also allow for the transference of best practices from one country to another. Further, purchasing a standardized global brand may be viewed as a better choice than buying a local brand. The global brand might have a higher perceived quality. The consumer's self-concept of being cosmopolitan, sophisticated, and modern can be enhanced when buying a global brand. As the world continues to shrink through advances in telecommunications, consumers are becoming increasingly similar, displaying comparable consumer characteristics and purchase behaviors. This may lead to greater use of standardized global brands.

Recently, Banana Republic moved to a global brand-management structure across its 700 stores worldwide. The goal was to establish a single brand voice and consistent brand experience worldwide. The challenge was to create a brand voice that resonated with longtime customers as well as new customers. In analyzing Banana Republic's customer base, Catherine Sadler (chief marketing officer) was "struck by the common customer profile that I see in all of our stores around the world." She described this customer as fashion aware and tech-savvy.[45]

A common global integrated marketing communications (GIMC) strategy is to "think globally, but act locally." This approach applies to branding. Developing global brands might be the ultimate goal; however, the marketing team still considers each local market's unique features and should be sensitive to supporting and developing local brands. The success of global brand largely depends on the brand's ability to adapt to local needs and tastes or as Eileen Campbell, CEO of Millward Brown Group, noted, "Cultural relevance is important." For example, the "Real Beauty" campaign developed by Ogilvy and Mather for Unilever's Dove featured images of women in underwear in Western countries, but was modified to reveal a face behind a woman's veil for the Middle East.[46]

Packaging and labeling issues are complex for global firms. The label must meet legal requirements of the country in which the product is sold. An attractive label can be an attention-getting device that draws the consumer to the product. Labels remain vitally important ingredients in the United States as well as Asian countries where purchases, in part, are driven by the appeal of the label.[47] At the same time, some culturally-sensitive items, such as lingerie and other personal products, carry labels that basically disguise or hide the contents. Packages must also be able to withstand the rigors of long-distance shipping, meet any legal restrictions, and be as cost-effective as possible.

Summary

An effective integrated marketing communications program emphasizes a strong and positive brand image. A brand's image consists of the feelings consumers and business-to-business customers have toward the organization and each individual brand. The image contains both tangible and intangible components. Tangible elements include products, advertisements, names, logos, and services provided. Intangible elements consist of policies and practices that change or enhance the brand's image in the consumer's mind.

A brand name provides the overall banner under which all other operations occur. The logo accompanying the name is the symbol used to identify a brand, helping to convey the overall image. The brand's name and image are important to general customers as well as other firms that might purchase from or conduct business with a manufacturer or service provider.

Brands are names given to goods or services or groups of complementary products. Effective brands present the firm with an advantage, especially in mature markets containing fewer actual products or where service differences exist. Strong brands convey the most compelling benefits of the product, elicit proper consumer emotions, and help create loyalty. Various versions of brands include family brands, flanker brands, and co-brands. In each, marketers build brand equity through domination or the recognition that the brand has one key advantage or characteristic.

Creating an effective image constitutes a difficult task. It requires understanding of how various publics view the firm before seeking to build or enhance an image. Rejuvenating the image involves reminding customers of their previous conceptions of the company while at the same time expanding into a closely related area of concern. A strongly established image becomes difficult, if not impossible, to change.

Private brands, or private labels, have become important components in the success of both producers and retailers. Consumers now view private brands as having quality equal to or close to that of more famous manufacturer brand names. At the same time, customers expect price advantages in private label products. Effective brand management includes creating a mix of offerings that both end users and retailers recognize as a beneficial range of choices.

Company leaders remain aware of legal and ethical brand challenges. Brand infringement remains both a domestic and international problem. The generic problem may also influence a new generation of products and services.

International marketers utilize both standardization and adaptation tactics with regard to brands and products. Packages and labels must meet the legal and cultural needs of individual countries.

Key Terms

brand logo The symbol used to identify a brand, helping to convey the overall brand image

stimulus codability Feelings attached to items that evoke consensually held meanings within a culture or subculture

family brand A strategy in which a company offers a series or group of products under one brand name

brand extension The use of an established brand name on goods or services not related to the core brand

flanker brand The development of a new brand by a company in a good or service category in which it currently has a brand offering

co-branding/alliance branding The marketing or alliance of two or more brands in a single marketing effort

ingredient branding A form of co-branding in which one brand is placed within another brand

cooperative branding A form of co-branding in which two firms create a joint venture of two or more brands into a new good or service

complementary branding A form of co-branding in which the marketing of two brands together encourages co consumption or co-purchases

salient A situation in which consumers are aware of the brand, have it in their consideration sets (things they consider when making purchases), regard the product and brand as a good value, buy it or use it on a regular basis, and recommend it to others

trust A customer's belief in the efficacy and reliability of a brand

brand parity View of consumers that few tangible distinctions exist between competing brands in mature markets

brand equity The perception that a good or service with a given brand name is different, better, and can be trusted

brand metrics Measures of returns on brand investments

private brands (also known as *private labels* and *store brand*) Proprietary brands marketed by an organization and normally distributed exclusively within the organization's outlets

MyMarketingLab

Go to **mymktlab.com** to complete the problems marked with this icon ✪.

Review Questions

2-1. Describe the concept of brand image. What are the tangible aspects of a brand image? What are the intangible aspects?

2-2. What aspects or inferences would be ideal in the corporate or brand image of a bank or other financial institution?

2-3. How will company leaders know when they have created the desired brand image?

2-4. What does positive assurance mean in relation to brand image and what is its value?

2-5. What is a brand logo? What are the characteristics of an effective logo?

2-6. What is meant by the term "psychological reinforcement"?

2-7. What elements of brand images are ideal for retailers?

2-8. Why would you want to change a brand image?

2-9. Distinguish between overt, conceptual, and iconoclastic names with some examples.

2-10. Explain the role of trust in creating a strong brand.

2-11. What is the difference between brand equity and brand parity?

2-12. What methods can be used to measure brand equity?

2-13. How has private branding, or private labeling, changed in the past decade?

2-14. What role does a product's package play in the marketing program?

2-15. How can a label support an IMC program or advertising campaign?

2-16. What ethical issues are associated with brand management?

2-17. How do the concepts of standardization and adaptation apply to products, brand names, and marketing strategies?

Critical Thinking Exercises

DISCUSSION QUESTIONS

2-18. Identify a business in any market based in your country that has seemed to defy modernization. This could be a traditional form of business that has not embraced marketing, the Internet, or other forms of marketing communication. Perhaps until this point in time the business has not needed to look beyond its regular customer base, but perhaps it has lost market share to more forward-looking competitors. Look at the business with fresh eyes and create a company or brand image for it. Reinforce the image with a list of key attributes that should be pushed in any marketing communications in the future.

2-19. Henry and Becky Thompson plan to open a new floral and gift shop in Orlando, Florida. They want to project a trendy, upscale, and fashionable image. They are trying to decide on a name and a logo. What should be the name of the company? What kind of logo should be developed?

2-20. Find an example of a brand or corporation that has undergone a complete rejuvenation in recent years. Now look for one that seems to have failed to capture the imagination of its existing customers while also failing to attract new customers. What did they do to reverse things?

2-21. Identify five different brands for which you have a high level of brand loyalty. Describe your level of loyalty and discuss why you are loyal. Explain whether brand equity plays a major role in your loyalty.

2-22. What is your opinion of private brands or labels? Compare your purchase behavior of private labels in contrast to national or manufacturers' brands. What private labels do you purchase regularly? Why do you purchase those particular private labels instead of national or manufacturers' brands?

2-23. Go to a local retail store. Choose five packages that are effective. Describe why they are effective. Choose five labels that are effective at capturing attention. What are the attention-getting aspects of each label?

2-24. Go to a local retail store. Look at packaging and locate five packages with QR codes. Access the code through a smartphone. Which of the purposes discussed in the chapter does the QR code serve? Evaluate the QR code and the information or site that was accessed.

Integrated Learning Exercises

2-25. Websites constitute an essential element of a brand's image. Access the websites of the following brands to get a feel for the image each brand tries to project. Is the image projected on the website consistent with the image portrayed in the brand's advertisements?

a. Bluenotes (**www.blnts.com**)
b. Portillo's Restaurants (**www.portillos.com**)
c. BMW Motorcycles (**www.bmwmotorcycles.com**)
d. Maxwell House Coffee (**www.maxwellhousecoffee.com**)
e. Sony (**www.sony.com**)

2-26. A leading consulting firm that has been a leader in extending marketing knowledge and in the area of brand development is the Boston Consulting Group. Other companies that have actively been involved in brand development include Lexicon Branding and Corporate Branding. Access each firm's website. Describe the services provided by each firm.

a. Boston Consulting Group (**www.bcg.com**)
b. Lexicon Branding, Inc. (**www.lexicon-branding.com**)
c. Corporate Branding (**www.corebrand.com**)
d. Brand Keys (**www.brandkeys.com**)

2-27. Brand extension and flanker branding are common strategies for large corporations. Access the following websites. Identify the various brand extension strategies and flanker brands used by each company.

a. Marriott Hotels (**www.marriott.com**)
b. Procter & Gamble (**www.pg.com**)
c. VF Corporation (**www.vfc.com**)
d. Kraft Foods (**www.kraftfoods.com**)

2-28. Private labels provide a significant source of revenue for many retail stores and manufacturers. The Private Label Manufacturers' Association promotes manufacturers that produce private labels. Visit the organization's website at **www.plma.com**. Access each item on the menu. Summarize the information provided for each item.

2-29. Go to each of these global brands' websites. What is the image that they are trying to portray? What is their positioning strategy? Are the sites specifically designed for a global market or are you looking at a regional variation?

a. Apple (**www.apple.com**)
b. Samsung (**www.samsung.com**)
c. Coca Cola (**www.coca-cola.com**)
d. BMW (**www.bmw.com**)
e. McDonald's (**www.mcdonalds.com**)

Blog Exercises

Access the authors' blog for this text at the URLs provided to complete these exercises. Answer the questions posed on the blog.

2-30. Kenmore, Craftsman, and Diehard: **http://blogclowbaack.net/2014/05/07/private-brands-sears-chapter-2/**

2-31. Target: **http://blogclowbaack.net/2014/05/07/target-chapter-2/**

2-32. Branding: **http://blogclowbaack.net/2014/05/07/branding-chapter-2/**

Student Project

CREATIVE CORNER

The brand name and logo constitute critical elements a marketing manager considers when introducing a new product. Pick one of the products from the following list. Assume you are the product manager and your company has introduced a new brand within the product category. Your first task is to choose a brand name. Using the internet, identify three key competitors and make a case for how the brand name you select will help the item stand out in the marketplace. Once you have created your brand name, create a logo that will fit well with the brand name and will be distinctive on your product or the product's packaging.

PRODUCTS

2-33. A new brand of skis for recreational boating
2-34. A new line of eyeglasses
2-35. A new chocolate candy bar
2-36. A new line of jeans
2-37. A new energy drink
2-38. A new perfume or cologne

CASE 1 MALAYSIAN BREAD WARS

In 1986, the first Gardenia loaf was produced in Malaysia. By 1990, the brand had become the leading supplier in Malaysia, prompting the business to open its own fully automated factory the following year. The incredible demand had to be met with a huge increase in production. In 1991, the new factory line could produce 6,000 loaves an hour. By 1994, this had increased to 10,000. Today, there are six fully automated lines producing 900,000 loaves each day. This makes Gardenia the biggest fresh bread producer in South East Asia.

One of Gardenia's primary suppliers was the Federal Flour Mills (FFM). In 2012, with Gardenia switching suppliers, FFM responded by promoting their own rival brand Massimo. At the same time, an online campaign was launched to urge Malaysians to switch brands from Gardenia to Massimo. FFM was quick to point out that they were not behind the Facebook and email campaign. The other factor made clear in the campaign was the fact that Massimo was significantly cheaper than Gardenia. The standard-sized white loaf was the same price, but whilst Gardenia's longer white was RM0.05 cheaper, their wheat germ was RM0.70 more expensive. Behind the pricing and the commercial competition, there was another angle. Gardenia was accused of terminating their purchases from FFM on the grounds of race, an accusation that was impossible to prove and one that Gardenia strenuously denied. Whatever the reason for the change, Malaysian consumers found themselves faced with a clear choice for the daily loaf. Ultimately it would be a decision based on taste, not race or any advertising messages.

Gardenia is associated with quality and freshness. It is a brand that is very important in Malaysia. One of the key brand values is to ensure quality and at the same time reliability in its distribution channels. This is important as Gardenia is a staple food product and consumers have come to rely on its availability.

Strangely, Gardenia can actually trace its history back to America and not Malaysia. In 1969, Horatio Sye Slocumm arrived in Malaysia to open a bakery for the International Executive Service Corps. Slocumm was an accomplished baker with 35 years of experience behind him. The ultimate result was Gardenia and to this day, the brand proudly states that their bread is still made to the original recipe.

What is particularly interesting about the bread wars is Robert Kuok. Kuok owns FFM. When Gardenia switched flour suppliers to the Malayan Flour Mills and the Prestasi Flour Mills, he was left with the stark realization that his largest customer was lost. Kuok responded by acquiring the Italian-based Massimo franchise in order to create his own bread company using his own flour. According to Forbes, Kuok is the richest man in Malaysia. He has a commodities background.

Certainly, until the end of 2011, Gardenia had a 90 percent market share in Malaysia. It was a position that had taken many years to achieve. Over the decades, they had changed the perceptions and taste of the consumer to accept, in essence, a mass produced product.

Karianphotography/Shutterstock

▲ Tough competition in the Malaysian bread market is heavily based on brand image.

What is clear is that Massimo is here to stay and has a battle on its hands to win market share. Armed with the advantage of using the very same flour which was a constituent part of Gardenia for so many years, it is already winning support. Gardenia has seen a drop in its market share; understandable in the circumstances when the full weight of Kuok's business empire and commercial knowledge has been thrown behind FFM.[48]

2-39. Provide an analysis of the Gardenia brand. What factors shape perceptions of the brand in the eyes of Malaysian consumers?

2-40. What brand problems did the Massimo brand create for the Gardenia brand?

2-41. How might social media affect perceptions of both the Gardenia and Massimo brands?

2-42. Do you think the efforts made by Robert Kuok were the most effective ways to launch the brand? Defend your answer.

2-43. Going forward, what tactics would you use to maintain and build the Massimo brand?

CASE 2 ARÇELIK: FROM "FAMILY" TO "INNOVATIVE" BRAND

Arçelik A.Ş, which is part of the Turkish family conglomerate Koç Holding, was founded in Istanbul in 1955. The company's core business is the production of consumer appliances and electronics. Arçelik offers products and services around the world with over 22,000 employees and fourteen different production facilities located in Turkey, Romania, Russia, China, and South Africa. It offers products under its 10 brand names including Arçelik, Beko, and Grundig.

By the mid-1990s Arçelik felt the strong need to change its strategy. Despite high recognition, the brand was not perceived as a young, dynamic, modern company with sophisticated technology, nor was it perceived as desirable by young consumers. In May 2002, the decision was made for a new communication strategy aiming to improve the credibility and viability of the brand by focusing on "innovativeness." Advertisements were created with the promise of innovation, which were communicated by a robot character as the spokesman. Thus, the "Robot SteelÇelik," later joined by a girlfriend "Çeliknaz," was created and the characters appeared in the advertisements. Besides the advertisements, Arçelik's logo was redesigned to address customers' expectations and also shows the flexibility, determination, and readiness of the brand for the new millennium. The company started using new slogans such as "Arçelik Means Innovation," "Arçelik Designs Innovations with Love," and "With Arçelik There is Always Time for Love." The dealer shops were redesigned and redecorated according to the new concept. Arçelik increased its presence on the Internet by selling products on its redesigned website and using social media. Its Facebook account updates allow for strong brand communication with consumers. By December 2012 the company had over 112,000 fans, and fan growth each month is around 2,000.

The effects of this successful marketing communication were seen shortly after the implementation of the new strategy. Consumer research showed that the brand awareness of Arçelik achieved the highest levels of all times. At the end of 2012 Arçelik won "The Most Innovative Company" award as part of "Turkish Innovation Week," for the first time.[49]

Anthony Berenyi/Shutterstock

▲ The youth market can be especially difficult for some brands to reach, but Arçelik's revised innovative strategy seem to have managed it.

2-44. What are the image issues in this case?

2-45. Do you think that such a strategy change of Arçelik was risky? If you were the manager in charge of the new strategy what would you do?

2-46. Do you think that this new strategy would be successful in all the markets the company operates? Would you advise any changes for various markets?

2-47. What other types of activities could Arçelik pursue to build a strong and positive corporate image?

MyMarketingLab

Go to **mymktlab.com** for the following Assisted-graded writing questions:

2-48. Brand image affects purchase decisions. What brands do you consider to hold a positive image? Why? Which brands should attempt to change brand images? Why? Explain how to accomplish this task. Which brands do you believe need rejuvenation? How can it be accomplished for each brand?

2-49. Look up each of the following brands on the internet. Discuss the image conveyed by each brand's website. What positioning strategy is used? Justify your selection. What changes or improvements could these brands make to their website to enhance its appeal?

a. Canyon Beachwear (**www.canyonbeachwear.com**)
b. Union Pacific Railroad (**www.uprr.com**)
c. Bicycle Museum of America (**www.bicyclemuseum.com**)
d. Applebee's (**www.applebees.com**)
e. Cheerios (**www.cheerios.com**)

Chapter 3 Buyer Behaviors

Chapter Objectives

After reading this chapter, you should be able to answer the following questions:

3.1 What elements are involved in internal and external information searches by consumers, as part of the purchasing process?

3.2 What three models explain how individuals evaluate purchasing alternatives?

3.3 What trends are affecting the consumer buying environment?

3.4 How do the roles played by various members of the buying center and the factors that influence them impact business purchases?

3.5 What types of business-to-business sales are made?

3.6 What are the steps of the business-to-business buying process?

3.7 How does dual channel marketing expand a company's customer base and its sales?

3.8 How can a company overcome international differences when adapting to buying processes?

Overview

One primary goal of many integrated marketing communications programs continues to be enticing people to buy goods and services. Understanding how buyers make purchase decisions helps the marketing team achieve this goal. Two types of buyer behaviors—consumer buyer behaviors and business-to-business buyer behaviors—receive attention in this chapter. Comprehending the steps consumers use to make purchase decisions assists the marketing team in creating quality communications.

This chapter first examines consumer purchasing processes. Two stages of the process are the keys to marketing communications. In the *information search* stage, the customer reviews previous memories and experiences looking for acceptable ways to meet a need by buying a product. During the *evaluation of alternatives* stage, the individual compares various purchasing possibilities. An effective IMC program targets potential buyers involved in these activities. This chapter provides a review of the traditional factors affecting consumers, along with discussion of the newer trends present in the consumer buying environment.

SECRET RECIPE CAKES & CAFÉ

In the complex and competitive market for traditional food, a new option has emerged—Secret Recipe Cakes & Café—the lifestyle café chain. Teenagers and adults in Malaysia are gaining a taste for Western food with ethnic flavors. For food lovers, the sight of a red, square-shaped paper bag printed with the words "Secret Recipe" in gray conjures up the image of a cake. That is the "secret recipe" of the brand's founder, Datuk Steven Sim, who made the brand popular over a decade ago. As the leading café chain in Malaysia, Secret Recipe outlets offer more than 20 types of fusion food, 40 types of cakes and pastries, and a flavorful range of ice creams and beverages. Secret Recipe locations offer a simple, uncluttered setting, featuring dark wooden tables and chairs, where customers can enjoy the pleasant, relaxed vibe.

According to Sim, the brand was designed to be acceptable and adaptable to a wide market. Secret Recipe has successfully established itself in Malaysia, Singapore, Indonesia, Thailand, China, the Philippines, Pakistan, Brunei, and Australia. The café's concept is flexible so that different menu items can be offered in different countries. That's why one can find Malaysian favorites in some of the overseas outlets, too. In all countries, customers can order cakes and cookies online. Secret Recipe has experienced rapid growth over the past decade, opening 250 cafés throughout the region.

The company focused on brand building early on. It created its own logo, corporate color, marketing strategies, uniforms, menu layout, interior design, and customer service standards. The success and growth of the chain suggest a well-designed creative strategy manifesting in an integrated marketing communications program.[1]

Business-to-business buyer behaviors are the focus of the second part of this chapter. First, a review of the five major roles played in the buying center takes place. Next, the chapter notes the types of purchases companies make, along with the steps involved in the purchasing process. Finally, dual channel marketing, which involves selling the same product to both consumers and business buyers, is discussed. Effective IMC programs identify potential customers from both markets. This leads to increased sales and helps a company maintain a strong presence in the marketplace.

Consumer Purchasing Process

objective 3.1
What elements are involved in internal and external information searches by consumers, as part of the purchasing process?

Finding ways to influence the consumer purchasing process continues to be a vital marketing communications activity. Figure 3.1 models the consumer buying decision-making process. Two of the stages are the most directly related to integrated marketing communications: the information search, and the evaluation of alternatives. Discovering how customers seek out product information and then the manner in which they evaluate the information are keys to creating effective marketing messages.

The first step of the buying decision-making process displayed in Figure 3.1 occurs when the consumer experiences a need or want. A problem or gap exists between an individual's current state and desired state. The need can be physical, such as hunger or thirst. It can be social, such as when a consumer visits a friend's apartment and sees his new HDTV and wants one as a result. Needs may be psychological in nature, including the desire for love or protection from fear.

▶ **FIGURE 3.1**
Consumer Decision-Making Process

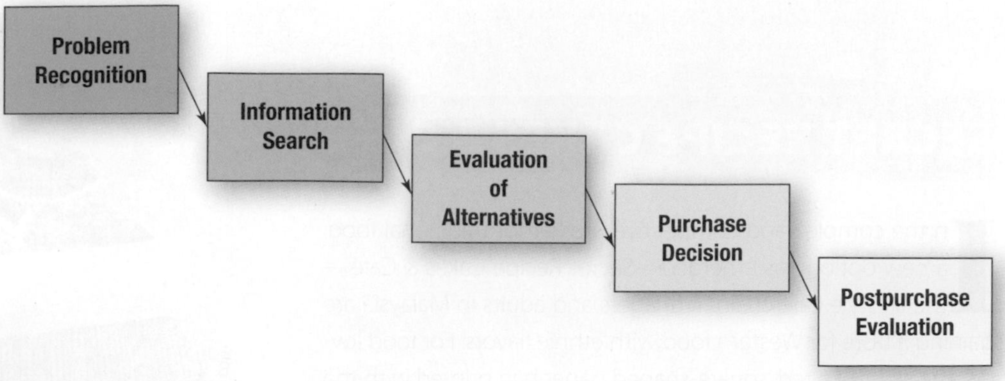

▼ This advertisement for Skyjacker might trigger a search for additional information about truck suspensions and lift kits.

Skyjacker Suspensions

Consumer needs can also be triggered by marketing communications. The advertisement for Skyjacker suspensions in this section may act as a catalyst for an individual to want a lift kit for his vehicle. Once this occurs, consumers enter the next phase of the process.

Information Search

After a need emerges, the consumer begins an internal search, mentally recalling products that might satisfy it. Often, the individual remembers how the need was met in the past. If a particular brand was chosen and the experience was positive, the consumer repeats the purchase decision, and the information search ends. When a previous purchase did not work out, or the consumer wishes to try something else, a more complete internal search may commence.

Internal Search

During an internal search, the consumer thinks about the brands she is willing to consider. This group may not contain every brand the consumer has experienced, because she removes brands associated with negative experiences. Brands she knows little about are also eliminated. In other words, the consumer quickly reduces the number of potential brands.

Making sure a company's brand becomes part of the consumer's set of potential purchase alternatives in an internal search constitutes a key marketing communications objective. A product with a high level of brand awareness or brand equity will likely be included in the consumer's set of alternatives. The Kraft Singles advertisement on the next page uses appealing visuals coupled with compelling copy to persuade consumers it should be the first and only choice when it comes to sliced cheese. Kraft wants to be seen as the solution when the internal search process occurs.

External Search

Following an internal search, the consumer makes a mental decision regarding an external search. When the customer has sufficient internal information, he moves to the next step of the decision-making process: evaluating the alternatives. A consumer who remains uncertain about the right brand to purchase undertakes an external search.

Individuals gather external information from a variety of sources, including friends, relatives, experts, books, magazines, newspapers, advertisements, in-store displays, salespeople, the internet, and social media. The amount of time a consumer spends on an external search depends on three factors: ability, motivation, and costs versus benefits (see Figure 3.2).[2]

Kraft Foods, Inc.

▲ A Kraft Singles advertisement designed to convince consumers that the Kraft brand should be the first choice when selecting cheese to make a "new kind of burger."

Ability to Search The extent to which an information search will be undertaken is partially determined by the ability to search. Ability consists of a person's educational level combined with the specific knowledge he has about a product and the brands in a given category. Educated individuals are more inclined to spend time searching for information. They are often more willing to visit stores or search online prior to making decisions. Consumers possessing extensive knowledge about individual brands and product categories are better able to conduct a more involved external search. Thus, someone who knows a great deal about digital cameras has a more sophisticated ability to examine information than someone who knows little about the technology. In addition, a person with more comprehensive knowledge of a product area often collects additional information, even when she is not in the market for the product.[3]

In terms of the amount of time an individual devotes to the external search process, an unusual phenomenon occurs. Although extensive product category knowledge means an individual has greater ability to search for external information, the consumer will normally spend less time on the external search process because of the extensive knowledge he already possesses. Consumers at the other end of the spectrum also spend less time in the external search process—but for the

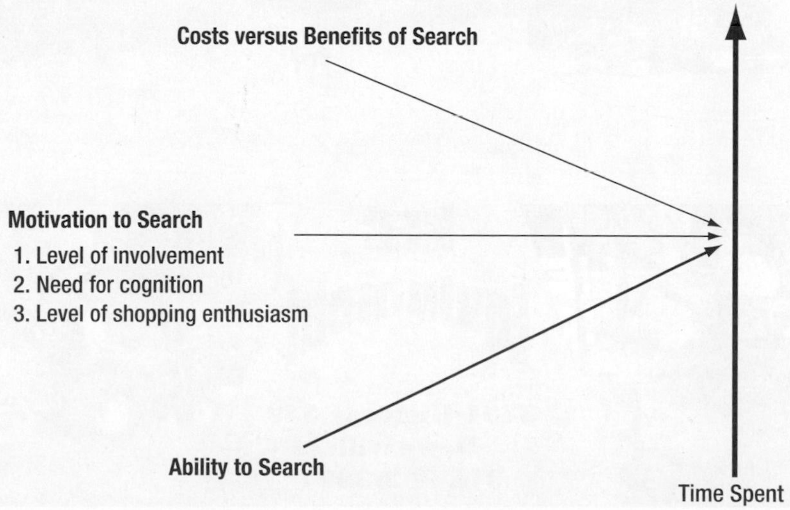

◀ **FIGURE 3.2**
Factors that Affect the Amount of Time a Consumer will Spend Conducting an External Search

opposite reason. They do not have knowledge about the product category and do not know what type of information to ask for or what type of information would be useful, which means they lack the ability to search for information. Individuals in the middle, who have some knowledge of a product category but require additional information in order to make intelligent decisions, typically spend the most time searching for external information.

Level of Motivation The degree to which an external search takes place further depends on the customer's level of motivation. The greater the motivation, the more time spent on an external search. Motivation is determined by the consumer's

- Level of involvement
- Need for cognition
- Level of shopping enthusiasm

Individuals experience greater motivation to search for information when involvement levels are high. **Involvement** summarizes the extent to which a stimulus or task is relevant to a consumer's existing needs, wants, or values. When a consumer deems a product to be important, it becomes more likely she will engage in an external search. The amount of involvement is based on factors such as the *cost* of the product and its *importance*. The higher the price, the more time an individual spends searching for information.

The same holds true for importance. Choosing clothes might not be an important decision to some young males, which suggests their clothing purchases typically have low involvement. Picking a tuxedo for the high school prom, however, may spur greater involvement and a higher level of information search due to the social ramifications of dressing poorly at such an important event. The higher level of involvement emerges from the addition of a new element—a major occasion in the person's life.

The **need for cognition** personality characteristic identifies individuals who engage in and enjoy mental activities. Mental exercises have a positive impact on the information search process. People with high needs for cognition gather more information and search more thoroughly. The search also depends on a person's **enthusiasm for shopping**. Customers who enjoy shopping undertake more in-depth searches for goods and services.[4]

Kenneth Clow

▶ A utility tractor is a high-involvement purchase that would trigger an external search process.

Costs versus Benefits Two final factors that influence an information search are the perceived costs versus the perceived benefits of the search. Higher perceived benefits increase the inclination to search.

The ability to reduce purchase risk becomes a benefit that many consumers seek while examining external information. Additional information lowers the chances of making a mistake in the purchase selection. The cost of the search consists of several items:

- The actual cost of the good or service
- The subjective costs associated with the search, including time spent and anxiety experienced while making a decision
- The opportunity cost of foregoing other activities to search for information (e.g., going shopping instead of playing golf or watching a movie)

Yellowj/Fotolia

▲ Enthusiasm for shopping has an impact on the amount of time spent on an external search.

Higher perceived subjective costs associated with collecting external information search decrease the likelihood that the consumer will conduct a search.[5]

Consumers normally consider the three factors that make up an external search (ability, motivation, costs versus benefits) simultaneously. When the perceived cost of a search is low, and the perceived benefit is high, a consumer has a higher motivation to search for information. A consumer with a minimal amount of product knowledge and a low level of education will be less likely to undertake an external search, because the consumer lacks the ability to identify the right information.

From a marketing communications perspective, the search process represents an important time to reach the consumer. The consumer's objective during an external search is to acquire information leading to a better, more informed decision. The marketing team provides information that leads consumers to the company's products. One ideal time to attempt to influence the decision-making process occurs when the consumer has not yet made up his mind. Marketing experts utilize three models of the information search process: attitudes, values, and cognitive mapping.

Consumer Attitudes

Effective marketing communications influence consumer attitudes. An **attitude** is a mental position taken toward a topic, a person, or an event that influences the holder's feelings, perceptions, learning processes, and subsequent behaviors.[6] Attitudes can drive purchase decisions. A consumer holding a positive attitude toward a brand becomes more likely to buy it. Someone who enjoys an advertisement will also be more inclined to purchase the product.

Attitudes consist of three components: affective, cognitive, and conative.[7] The *affective* component contains the feelings or emotions a person has about the object, topic, or idea. The *cognitive* component refers to a person's mental images, understanding, and interpretations of the person, object, or issue. The *conative* component holds an individual's intentions, actions, or behavior. One common sequence of events that takes place in attitude formation is:

Cognitive → Affective → Conative

Advertisement for Centric Federal Credit Union furnished by Emogen Marketing

▲ This advertisement for Centric Federal Credit Union is designed to influence a person's beliefs (cognitive component of attitude) about the financial institution's fees and rates.

Advertisement of The Salvation Army furnished by The Richards Group

▲ What emotions does this advertisement for the Salvation Army elicit?

Most of the time, a person first develops an understanding about an idea or object. In the case of marketing, these ideas center on the benefits of the good or service. Thoughts about the product emerge from watching or reading advertisements. Other thoughts may result from exposures to information from other sources, such as the internet, social media, or a friend's referral. Eventually, these ideas become beliefs the consumer holds about a particular product. A consumer seeing the Centric Federal Credit Union advertisement might notice the emphasis on fewer fees and better rates for banking.

The affective part of the attitude carries the general feeling or emotion a person attaches to the idea. In the case of goods and services, the product, its name, and other features can all generate emotions. Consider your emotional reactions to the following goods and services:

- Cough medicine
- Diapers
- Motorcycles
- Children's toys made in China
- *Sports Illustrated*'s annual swimsuit issue
- Condoms

Some emotions or attitudes about particular goods and services are relatively benign. Others are more strongly held. Cough medicine does not typically evoke an emotional response; however, the swimsuit issue or condoms may generate stronger reactions.

What emotions and thoughts do you associate with the Salvation Army advertisement on the previous page? The image in the ad and the headline "Invest in Futures" attempt to instill sympathetic and caring feelings, which will then lead to donations to the Salvation Army.

Decision and action tendencies constitute the conative parts of attitudes. Therefore, when a person feels strongly enough about the swimsuit issue, she might cancel a subscription to *Sports Illustrated*. Most attitudes are not held that strongly. Some people might feel favorably about a topic, such as green marketing, but this does not necessarily change their purchasing behaviors.

Attitudes develop in other ways. An alternative process is:

Affective → Conative → Cognitive

Advertisements and other marketing communications can first appeal to the emotions or feelings held by consumers in order to move them to "like" a product and make the purchase (the conative component). Cognitive understanding of the product comes after the purchase. A woman viewing the ad for Platinum Motorcars in this section may be drawn to the idea of being "pampered" in a luxury car. Emotionally, she has a desire to rent the car and takes action. Cognitive reasoning about renting the luxury car follows the emotional experience.

Courtesy of Platinum Motorcars

▲ This advertisement for Platinum Motorcars focuses on the affective component of an attitude.

Some attitudes result from a third combination of the components, as follows:

Conative → Cognitive → Affective

Purchases that require little thought, have a low price, or do not demand a great deal of emotional involvement might follow this path. For instance, while shopping for groceries, a customer may notice a new brand of cookies on sale. The person may have never seen the brand or flavor before; but, because it is on sale, decides to give the cookies a try. As the consumer chews them, he develops a greater understanding of the product's taste, texture, and other qualities. Finally, the consumer reads the package to learn more about contents, including how many calories were present in each bite. He finally develops feelings toward the cookies that affect future cookie purchases.

No matter which path a consumer takes to develop attitudes, each component will be present, to some extent. Some attitudes are relatively trivial (e.g., "I like ping pong, even though I hardly ever get to play"). Others are staunchly held, such as "I hate cigarette smoke!" Both are associated with feelings toward things, including products in the marketplace.

Consumer Values

Attitudes reflect an individual's personal values. **Values** are strongly held beliefs about various topics or concepts. Values frame attitudes and lead to the judgments that guide personal actions. Values tend to endure. They normally form during childhood, although they can change as a person ages and experiences life.

FIGURE 3.3
Personal Values

- Comfortable life
- Equality
- Excitement
- Freedom
- Fun, exciting life
- Happiness
- Inner peace
- Mature love
- Personal accomplishment
- Pleasure
- Salvation
- Security
- Self-fulfillment
- Self-respect
- Sense of belonging
- Social acceptance
- Wisdom

Figure 3.3 identifies some common personal values. People hold them to differing degrees. Factors that affect a person's values include the individual's personality, temperament, environment, and culture. By appealing to these elements, marketers try to convince prospective customers that the company's products align with their values.

In terms of consumer decision-making processes, both attitudes and values carry influence. A good or service tied to a relatively universal value, such as patriotism, helps the firm take advantage of the linkage and present the product in a positive manner. In a survey of 4,500 consumers, Brand Keys found that Jeep was regarded as the most patriotic brand followed by Hershey's, Coca-Cola, Levi-Strauss, and Walt Disney. According to Brand Keys, patriotism remains an emotionally-engaged and ingrained value that can become part of a brand's equity. Figure 3.4 lists the top 10 most patriotic brands.[8]

Cognitive Mapping

The manner in which individuals store information further affects decisions, because it impacts recall. Knowing how people store, retrieve, and evaluate information assists the company's marketing team in developing advertisements and marketing communications. Understanding how various thought processes and memories work constitutes the first step.

Cognitive maps simulate the knowledge structures and memories embedded in an individual's brain.[9] These structures contain a person's assumptions, beliefs, interpretation of facts, feelings, and attitudes about the larger world. Such thought processes interpret new information and determine a response to fresh information or a novel situation. Figure 3.5 depicts a simplified hypothetical cognitive map of an individual thinking about a Ruby Tuesday restaurant.

Based on the cognitive structures illustrated, when this customer considers Ruby Tuesday, she connects images of it with other restaurants offering fast food and others providing dine-in services. The individual recognizes Ruby Tuesday as a dine-in

FIGURE 3.4
Top 10 Most Patriotic Brands
Source: Based on "Jeep Leads List of 25 Most Patriotic Brands," *USA Today*, www.usatoday.com/story/driveon/2013/07001/most-patriotic-brands-jeep/2481337, July 1, 2013.

Rank	Company	Patriotic Emotional Engagement Score
1	Jeep	98%
2	Hershey	97%
3	Coca-Cola	97%
4	Levi-Strauss	95%
5	Walt Disney	95%
6	Colgate	94%
7	Zippo	93%
8	Wrigley's	92%
9	Ralph Lauren	91%
10	Kodak	90%

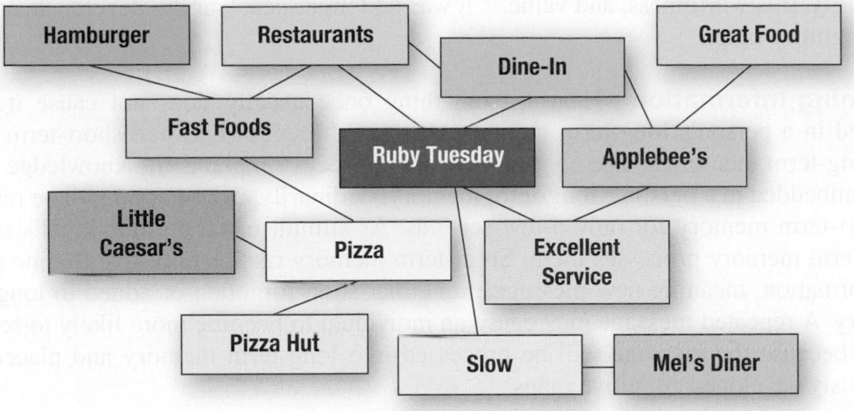

◀ **FIGURE 3.5**
A Cognitive Map for Ruby Tuesday

establishment. The consumer believes that Ruby Tuesday offers excellent food, but that the service is slow. Next, when the customer thinks about slow service, her thoughts turn to Mel's Diner. When she thinks of excellent service, she recalls Applebee's.

Cognitive Linkages Cognitive structures contain many linkages and exist on several levels. For instance, one level of cognition may be the map shown in Figure 3.5. At another level, a cognitive map becomes more spatial and conjures images of the actual physical location of Ruby Tuesday and the surrounding businesses. A third cognitive level related to Ruby Tuesday may be the person's recall of the interior of the restaurant along with other linkages that occur at that level. The consumer may have thoughts about Ruby Tuesday that focus on employees, including a relationship she had with a friend who was a server. Therefore, cognitive processing occurs on several levels using highly complex mechanisms.

Processing New Information In terms of cognitive mapping, when a consumer receives information or sees an advertisement, it can be processed in two primary ways. New information that stays consistent with current information tends to strengthen an existing linkage. A different response occurs when a message has no current linkages. The customer creates a new linkage between the new information and brand.

When the marketing team at Esurance observed individuals engaged in an online purchasing process, the marketers discovered that when potential customers arrived at the end of the process they were not pushing the purchase button. Thus, conversions (sales) were not occurring. Additional research indicated that consumers felt uneasy or unsure about the company, primarily because no linkages for the Esurance brand existed in the minds of many potential customers. This was true especially for the older, multicar, higher income individuals that Esurance was trying to reach.

As a result, company leaders had a choice: They could spend millions of dollars on establishing a brand name and linkages in the cognitive map of consumers or partner with an established brand that was already present in peoples' cognitive maps. The dilemma was solved when Allstate purchased Esurance in 2011. The company could then focus on current linkages consumers had with Allstate insurance through a campaign with the tagline "insurance for the modern world." Allstate gave the Esurance brand instant linkages to

▼ This advertisement tries to create a linkage between the Wholly Guacamole brand and Sonic.

Freshertized Foods

credibility, trustworthiness, and value.[10] It was no longer necessary to develop an entirely new cognitive map.

Retaining Information Hearing something once usually does not cause it to be retained in a person's long-term memory, due to differences between short-term recall and long-term memories. The cognitive mapping process explains the knowledge structures embedded in a person's long-term memory. Ordinarily, information will be retained in short-term memory for only a few seconds. As stimuli reach an individual's senses, short-term memory processes them. Short-term memory retains only five to nine pieces of information, meaning new messages are either soon forgotten or added to long-term memory. A repeated message may cause an individual to become more likely to remember it, because the message will be processed into long-term memory and placed into previously developed cognitive maps.

As a result, when a company attempts to introduce consumers to a new brand, advertisements and other marketing messages repeat the name of the brand several times during the presentation. The repetition improves the chances of recall at a later time. To illustrate how this works, consider what happens when a person gives a phone number to a friend. To help remember it, the individual repeats the number several times.

▼ This advertisement seeks to create linkages between "Your City, Your News" and *The Times-Picayune* and NOLA.com.

NOLA Media Group

New Concepts Another way a consumer can process information is to link the message to a new concept. For example, if a consumer sees an advertisement from Ruby Tuesday emphasizing that it has great food but has never thought about the restaurant in terms of quality food, that linkage does not currently exist. If the advertisement persuades the consumer, she might construct a linkage between Ruby Tuesday and good food without even traveling to the restaurant. If she does not believe the message, she will ignore or forget the information, and no new linkage results. A third possibility is that the consumer recalls the advertisement at a later time and decides to try Ruby Tuesday. If the food is great, then the link becomes established at that point. If it is not, the consumer continues thinking that Ruby Tuesday does not offer good food.

Marketing Messages From a marketing perspective, strengthening linkages that already exist will be easier. Adding new linkages or modifying linkages will be more difficult (see Figure 3.6). Regardless of how marketers present information, repetition remains important due to the limitations of short-term memory. Consumers experience hundreds of marketing messages daily. Only a few will be processed into long-term memory.

Cognitive mapping and persuasion techniques designed to change attitudes or tap into strongly held values represent two key ingredients of any IMC program. When the marketing team

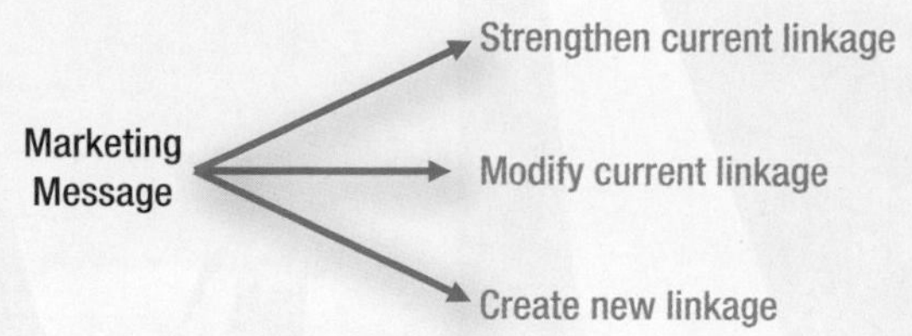

FIGURE 3.6
The Role of Marketing Messages in Cognitive Mapping

understands the needs and attitudes of the target market, messages can be structured to meet them. A message should capture the consumer's attention by exposing him to concepts that travel effectively through a core mental processing channel or peripheral channels, either through logic or alluring emotional appeals.

Creatives attempt to design ads that reach the linkages consumers have already made between a product and other key ideas. For instance, for a long time, a linkage existed between Cadillac and quality, as witnessed by the advertising and promotional phrase "This product is the *Cadillac*…[of all products in the market]." Common linkages exist between products and ideas such as quality, value, low cost, expense, fun, sex, danger, practicality, exoticness, and others. Carefully planned marketing campaigns identify linkages that entice the consumer to buy a brand and to believe in or be loyal to that brand in the future. This advantage remains as the consumer considers various purchasing alternatives.

Evaluation of Alternatives

objective 3.2
What three models explain how individuals evaluate purchasing alternatives?

Evaluation of alternatives constitutes the third step in the consumer buying decision-making process (see Figure 3.7). Three models portray the nature of the evaluation process: the evoked set approach, the multiattribute approach, and affect referral. Understanding how consumers evaluate choices helps the firm's marketing team develop more effective materials.

The Evoked Set Method

A person's **evoked set** consists of the brands the individual considers in a purchasing situation. An evoked set might be reviewed during both the information search and evaluation stages of the buying decision-making process. Two additional brand sets become part of the evaluation of purchase alternatives: the inept set and the inert set. The **inept set** contains the brands that are part of a person's memory that are *not considered* because they elicit negative feelings. These negative sentiments are normally caused by a bad experience with a vendor or particular brand. They can also originate from negative comments made by a friend, by seeing an advertisement that the potential customer did not like, or comments made in one of the social media outlets.

The **inert set** holds the brands that the consumer is aware of, but the individual has neither negative nor positive feelings about them. Using the terms from cognitive mapping, these brands have not been entered into any map, or they only have weak linkages to other ideas. The lack of knowledge about these brands usually eliminates them as alternatives. In other words, in most purchase situations a consumer only considers brands in her the evoked set.

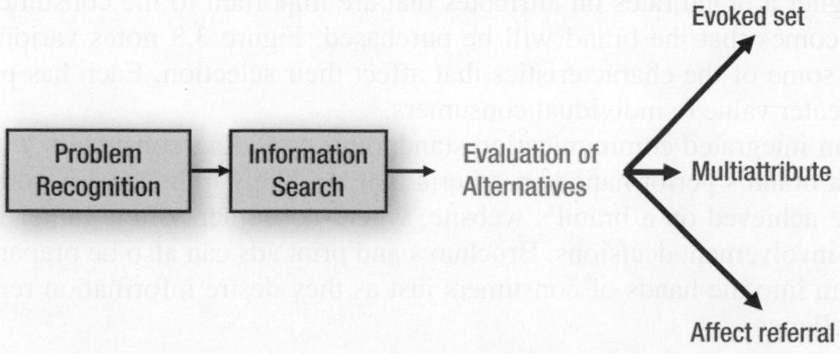

FIGURE 3.7
Methods of Evaluating Alternatives

▶ This advertisement for Visit South Walton seeks to make the area part of a consumer's evoked set as she considers vacation spots.

Visit South Walton

Placing a brand name in the evoked sets of consumers may be the primary goal of a marketing message. Doing so requires promoting the brand name and that brand's primary benefit extensively and consistently using multiple media and other venues. The consumer should see the brand name frequently in as many locations as possible. Then, to make sure the name becomes part of an evoked set, the concepts described related to cognitive mapping can be employed. By tying the brand with its primary benefit, the marketing team seeks to embed the brand's name in the consumer's long-term memory. The message establishes or reinforces linkages between benefit and the brand name. When a consumer evaluates alternatives using his evoked set and the company's brand becomes the part of the set being considered, the advertisement succeeds.

The Multiattribute Approach

The multiattribute approach may be most useful for understanding high-involvement types of purchases. Consumers often examine sets of product attributes across an array of brands. The multiattribute model suggests that a consumer's attitude toward a brand is determined by:[11]

- The brand's performance on product or brand attributes
- The importance of each attribute to the consumer

The higher a brand rates on attributes that are important to the consumer, the more likely it becomes that the brand will be purchased. Figure 3.8 notes various products, along with some of the characteristics that affect their selection. Each has potentially a lesser or greater value to individual consumers.

From an integrated communication standpoint, providing consumers with information about a brand's performance on criteria that are likely to be used becomes the key. This can be achieved on a brand's website, where consumers often gather information about high-involvement decisions. Brochures and print ads can also be prepared; thereby placing them into the hands of consumers just as they desire information represents the greatest challenge.

FIGURE 3.8
The Multiattribute Model

Product	**Characteristics**				
Computer	Price	Style	Service contract	Software	Memory storage
Telephone	Price	Style	Speed dial	Caller ID	Cordless feature
Car	Price	Style	Safety	Room	Other features
T-bone steak	Price	Age	Fat content	Degree cooked	Seasonings
Sunglasses	Price	Style	UV protection	Durability	Prescription lenses
Sofa	Price	Style	Foldout bed	Stain resistance	Color
Credit card	Interest rate	Fees	Billing cycle	Access to ATM	Credit limit

Consider each item. Which characteristic is most important to you personally? Least important?

In advertising, creatives often feature a product with multiple benefits by designing a series of messages. Advertisements highlight price, style, service contracts, software, memory, storage, or other product features. Only one or two of these benefits should be presented in each message. Otherwise, the advertisement becomes overloaded. Consumers who see commercials featuring one or two benefits are able to learn about a brand's characteristics. Over time, consumers obtain sufficient information to evaluate the product.

Affect Referral

The concept of **affect referral** suggests that consumers choose brands they like the best or the ones with which they have emotional connections. The individual does not evaluate brands or think about product attributes. Instead, the consumer buys the brand he likes the best or the one that incites positive feelings. Toothpaste, chewing gum, soft drinks, and candy are some of the products consumers normally select in this way. These purchases typically have low levels of involvement. They also tend to be frequently purchased products.

The affect referral model may apply to the use of artificial sweeteners such as Splenda, Equal, and Sweet'N Low. Previously, many consumers gave little thought to brand selection when choosing sweeteners. Recent negative publicity about the health impact of some products may have changed those perceptions. As a result, the Truvia marketing team modified its advertising to focus on consumer education. The messages suggest the brand as being a "natural sweetener" for consumers, who have a choice. Those with concerns about health and wellness might then switch to Truvia. In essence, a new affect referral model in which Truvia represents the first and best choice may be cultivated.[12]

The affect referral model explains three things. First, using this approach to product evaluation saves mental energy. Making a quick choice will be easier than going through the process of evaluating every alternative. Some purchases do not deserve much effort, and the affect referral model fits those situations.

Second, a multiattribute model approach might have been used previously when making a

The multiattribute model explains the process a consumer uses in the purchase of high-involvement products such as furniture sold by Scott + Cooner.

Scott and Cooner Inc.

JackF/Fotolia

▲ Customers often use affective referral when purchasing clothes.

purchase. The person already spent a great deal of time considering various product attributes, deciding which are most critical, and reaching a decision. Going through the process again would be "reinventing the wheel." A teenager buying jeans may have already spent considerable time evaluating styles, prices, colors, durability levels, and "fit" of various brands. After making the purchase, the teen continues to purchase the same brand as long as the experience remains positive. The affect referral model explains this buying behavior. Making a repurchase based on positive feelings becomes simple and convenient.

Third, consumers often develop emotional bonds with brands. In terms of the purchase decision, an emotional bond with a product can be the strongest and most salient factor in the decision.[13] It can be more important than any attribute or benefit the product can offer. Successful brands establish emotional bonds with consumers. A bond generates brand loyalty, enhances brand equity, and reduces brand parity. Consequently, consumers do not evaluate alternatives because of the bond with the brand. Harley-Davidson has developed such a bond with many of its customers. These individuals hold feelings toward Harley-Davidson that are so strong they would not even consider other alternatives. Jeep and Apple are two other brands that have obtained strongly emotional brand followers. Affect referral explains this phenomenon.

Trends in the Consumer Buying Environment

objective 3.3
What trends are affecting the consumer buying environment?

Studying the steps consumers take while making purchasing decisions helps create effective marketing communications. The environment in which consumers make purchases continually changes and evolves. Several trends in the consumer buying environment affect purchasing patterns (see Figure 3.9).

Age Complexity

Technology has changed the way children grow up. Children are bombarded with advertisements, video games, television shows, movies, and a myriad of other images from an early age. Most become fashion conscious as preteens. Many social observers believe children "grow up" at a much earlier age.

- Age complexity
- Gender complexity
- Active, busy lifestyles
- Diverse lifestyles
- Communication revolution
- Experience pursuits
- Health emphasis

▶ **FIGURE 3.9**
Trends Affecting Consumer Buying Behavior

At the other end of the spectrum, some adults refuse to grow old. They wear fashions that resemble those worn by college students. They drive sports cars or convertibles. Many middle-aged adults apparently do not want to grow old, acting like younger people and buying products normally purchased by them. This trend challenges marketers to create messages that reflect these behaviors but do not offend or confuse more traditional middle-aged persons.

Gender Complexity

Gender complexity means that the traditional roles, lifestyles, and interests of men and women have become blurred. Many women attend college, delay marriage, and wait to start families. Some choose to focus on moving up the corporate ladder instead of other options.

Men have become more likely to play an active role in parenting, help with household chores, and do more of the shopping. Since 1985, a shift in the number of men who are the primary household shopper has occurred. Almost one-third of men are now the principal shopper. Males spend 38 percent of all grocery dollars.[14] The percentage of men who do the household cleaning is almost as high, 31 percent. Men are using more makeup and grooming products traditionally thought of as female, such as skin care and foundation. Traditional female fashions, including a man bag and leggings, are now being accepted by men.[15] Figure 3.10 highlights the acceptance rate of both female grooming products and female fashions by millennial men. According to Alexandra Smith, editor of Mintel Inspire, "The next generation of men is coming of age in an era when gender roles are less rigidly defined."[16]

Active, Busy Lifestyles

Active lifestyles impact consumer behaviors. In one survey, 47 percent of respondents stated that they would prefer additional free time over more money. The 2008 recession may have caused many individuals to work longer hours in order to protect their jobs. Many people concentrate less on material possessions and more on experiences with friends and family.[17]

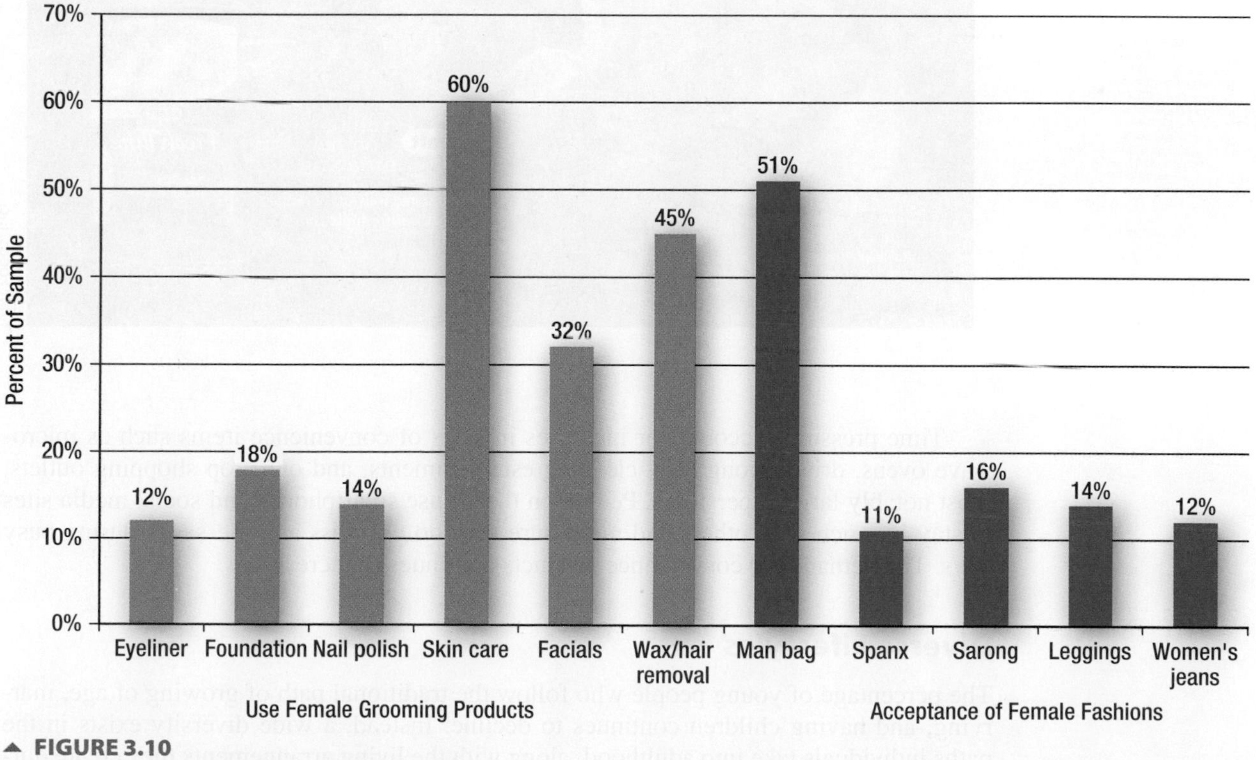

▲ **FIGURE 3.10**
Acceptance of Female Products by Millennial Men

Source: Based on Lucia Moses, "Millennial Guys Are Turning to Makeup," *Adweek*, www.adweek.com/news/advertising-branding/millennial-guys-are-turning-makeup-150313, June 19, 2013.

▶ This advertisement for Kraft Fresh Taste provides "endless inspiration" for individuals with active, busy lifestyles.

Kraft Foods, Inc.

Time pressures account for increases in sales of convenience items such as microwave ovens, drive-through dry-cleaning establishments, and one-stop shopping outlets, most notably large superstores. People on the go use smartphones and social media sites to stay in touch with others and make sure they do not miss any messages during busy days. The demand for convenience products continues to increase.

Diverse Lifestyles

The percentage of young people who follow the traditional path of growing of age, marrying, and having children continues to decline. Instead, a wide diversity exists in the paths individuals take into adulthood, along with the living arrangements they create during that time. More college kids are moving home to live with parents. Those that do not may live with roommates of mixed genders and ethnicities. Many put off marriage until later in life or choose to remain single or simply live with a partner.

Divorce and remarriage alter many family units. Remarried divorcees represent about 10 percent of the population. Divorcees tend to develop a new outlook on life. This group, called *second chancers*, is usually between the ages of 40 and 59 and has a higher household income. Second chancers are more content with life than average adults. They tend to be happy with their new families but also have a different life focus. Second chancers spend less time trying to please others and more time seeking fuller, more enriching lives for themselves and their children or spouses. Although the home and family continue to be a major emphasis, entertainment and vacation services also appeal to this group.[18]

The number of openly lesbian, gay, bisexual, and transgender (LGBT) people has grown to approximately five percent to 10 percent of the population. These consumers tend to favor products and companies that feature gay themes in advertising and support causes that are important to them. Wes Combs, President of Witeck-Combs Communication, notes that "LGBT consumers express an unmistakable and stronger sense of brand loyalty to companies that support their communities." Digital ads may be especially effective with this group, because they have a higher than average ownership of smartphones.[19]

Poggenpohl

▲ Second chancers and families who want to invest in their home's kitchen are the target for this ad for Poggenpohl.

Communication Revolution

Advances in telecommunications, primarily social media and smartphones, have influenced consumers all over the world and have created significant changes in the way individuals communicate with each other, with brands, and with companies. Social media and smartphones have also created cultural changes. Many people now communicate with one another through Facebook or Twitter rather than talking in person or by telephone. Someone in Florida can communicate with a friend in Alaska or in Japan instantaneously. Smartphones allow these individuals to take the internet with them, which means they do not even have to phone someone to talk. Instead, they can send text messages or access the internet and correspond through email, Skype, or other social media platforms.

Emerging technologies have changed the way brands and firms are influenced by word-of-mouth communication. If a consumer has a bad experience with a brand, he is not limited to telling just a few of their friends and family members. An individual who is dissatisfied can use social media and Twitter and instantly be "heard" by thousands of consumers all over the world within hours and many times within minutes. The potential for negative word-of-mouth can be devastating to a brand.

These same technologies can be used to engage consumers and stimulate positive endorsements. Many companies now monitor social media. Marketers listen to what consumers say and respond to them. Social media offers a pathway to engage consumers in two-way communication, at the point of purchase in a retail store, in their homes, or at their place of business.

Experience Pursuits

Some people handle the stress of a hectic, busy lifestyle through occasional indulgences or pleasure binges such as expensive dinners out and smaller luxury purchases. Pleasure pursuits include getaway weekends in resorts and on short cruises. These self-rewarding activities make the consumer feel that all the work and effort is "worth it." Instead of

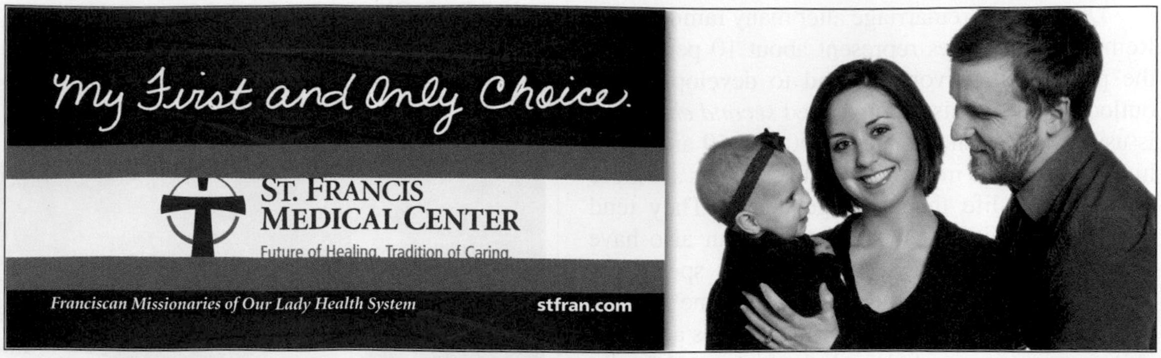

Advertisement for St. Francis Medical Center furnished by Newcomer, Morris, and Young

▲ With the emphasis on health, St. Francis Medical Center promotes itself as the first and only choice for medical care.

buying "things," the current trend is to purchase "experiences," which can vary from theme parks to virtual reality playrooms. It may be visiting a gambling establishment or taking an exotic vacation.

Recognizing that consumers often prefer experiences over things, companies can provide customers with moments to remember rather than more things to put in their homes. Ritz-Carlton presented the theme "Let us stay with you" in a recent campaign to emphasize the memories of staying in a Ritz-Carlton luxury property rather than the usual campaign requesting consumers to "Please stay with us." Orient-Express Hotels created a similar campaign featuring the theme "Embark on a journey like no other." The commercial emphasized a positive and memorable consumer experience.[20]

Health Emphasis

The U.S. population continues to age, leading to two trends: a blossoming interest in health and maintaining youthful appearance. Many consumers try to develop a balanced lifestyle with an emphasis on nutrition, exercise, and staying active.[21]

Recently, Reebok launched a global marketing campaign called "Live with Fire" that reflected the holistic benefits of exercise. The messages featured ordinary people rather than millionaire celebrities and athletes. Instead of focusing on the solitary battles individuals face when exercising, the commercials showed communities and groups of people exercising together. TV spots highlighted a running club doing sprints, a Latin Dance class, two women on an early morning walk, two men racing each other to the top of a stadium, and a yoga class. In addition to TV spots, Reebok developed print, digital, and out-of-home campaign components. Marketers created Reebok Fitness apps for Apple and Android phones that had workouts for walking, running, dance, yoga, and training. The objective of the campaign was to encourage individuals to transform their lives through fitness and community support.[22]

The desire for healthier foods, with less sodium and less sugar content, suggests another aspect of healthy lifestyles. At the same time, consumers do not want to sacrifice convenience. Busy lifestyles mean consumers are less willing to cook from scratch. They prefer prepared foods that can be assembled easily and cooked quickly. Products that combine health attributes with convenience sell well.

In sum, these new trends in the consumer buying environment create several challenges for marketing experts, as shown in Figure 3.11. Company leaders continue to monitor changes so their organizations are not surprised by them. Also, companies can create goods and services that match changing values. Then, marketing messages can be designed to reflect and build on the values people express. Incorporating new trends into the marketing program may be undertaken while at the same time being careful not to alienate any current customers who might not like those trends.

▶ FIGURE 3.11
Marketing Responses to Changing Trends in the Consumer Buying Environment

- Monitor consumer environment for changes
- Create goods and services that are compatible with the changes
- Design marketing messages that reflect the changes

Business-to-Business Buyer Behaviors

objective 3.4
How do the roles played by various members of the buying center and the factors that influence them impact business purchases?

In business-to-business purchases, *people* still make the decisions. At the same time, when selling to a business organization, the marketing team knows that normally several individuals will be involved. Further, corporate policies create restrictions and decision rules that affect purchasing activities. Factors such as costs, quality, and profit considerations also influence the final choice.

The **buying center** consists of the group of individuals making a purchase decision on behalf of a business. This complicates buying decisions. The buying center contains five different purchasing roles shown in Figure 3.12. The roles are:

- **Users**—Members of the organization who actually use the good or service
- **Buyers**—Individuals given the formal responsibility of making the purchase
- **Influencers**—People who shape purchasing decisions by providing the information or criteria utilized in evaluating alternatives such as engineers
- **Deciders**—Individuals who authorize the purchase decisions
- **Gatekeepers**—Individuals who control the flow of information to members of the buying center

These roles often overlap. Also, several individuals can occupy the same role in a buying center, especially for large or critical purchases. A variety of members of the organization may serve as influencers, because the roles usually are not fixed and formal.

The purchasing process will be unique in each organization. It also varies within an organization from one purchase decision to the next. Salespeople calling on a business seek to locate members of the buying center and understand their roles in the process. When these roles change from one purchase situation to another, the marketing and selling task becomes more complicated.[23]

Factors Affecting Business Buying Centers

A series of organizational and individual factors influence the behaviors of members in the buying center.[24] These influences change the manner in which decisions are made and affect the eventual outcome or alternative chosen.

Organizational Influences

Several organizational factors may have an impact on the ways employees make purchasing decisions for a company. The factors include the company's goals and its operating environment (recession, growth period, lawsuits pending, etc.). Decisions are further

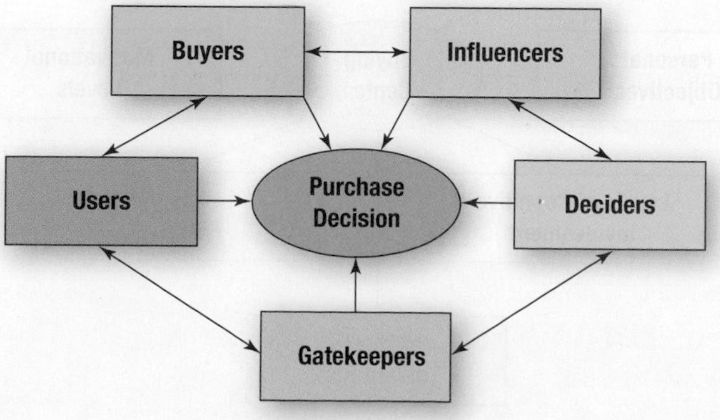

FIGURE 3.12
The Buying Center

constrained by the organization's finances, capital assets, market position, the quality of its human resources, and the country in which the firm operates.

Studies of organizational decision making indicate that employees tend to adopt *heuristics*, which are decision rules designed to reduce the number of viable options to a smaller, manageable set. Company goals, rules, budgets, and other organizational factors create heuristics. One decision rule often employed is *satisficing*, which means that when an acceptable alternative has been identified, it is taken and the search ends. Rather than spending a great deal of time looking for an optimal solution, decision makers tend to favor expedience.[25]

Individual Factors

At least seven factors affect each member of the business buying center (see Figure 3.13).[26] Each has an impact on how the individual interacts with other members of the center.

Personality Numerous personality facets exist. A decisive person makes purchase decisions in a manner different from someone who vacillates. Confidence, extroversion, shyness, and other personality traits influence both the person performing the various buying-center roles. An aggressive "know-it-all" type affects the other members of a decision-making team. Such a personality feature does not always benefit the organization. An extrovert tends to become more involved in the buying process than a more introverted individual. The extrovert spends more time talking while the introvert spends more time listening. The introvert might be too timid with salespeople and other members of the buying center and consequently does not ask important questions.

Roles An individual's age, heredity, ethnicity, gender, cultural memberships, and patterns of social interaction influence the roles the person plays. Roles are socially constructed, which means people define how they intend to play roles as part of a negotiation process with others. A person's perception of how the role fits into the buying center process and the overall organization affects how the individual becomes involved in the purchase.

A buying center member who views his role as merely giving approval to decisions made by the boss (the decider) does not actively participate. Members who believe their inputs are valued and are being solicited become more active. One person might think providing information constitutes her role. Another might perceive her role as being the person who synthesizes information provided by vendors and then relating the information to the buying center to save time. Roles and perceptions of roles are crucial factors that determine how members of the buying center engage in the decision.

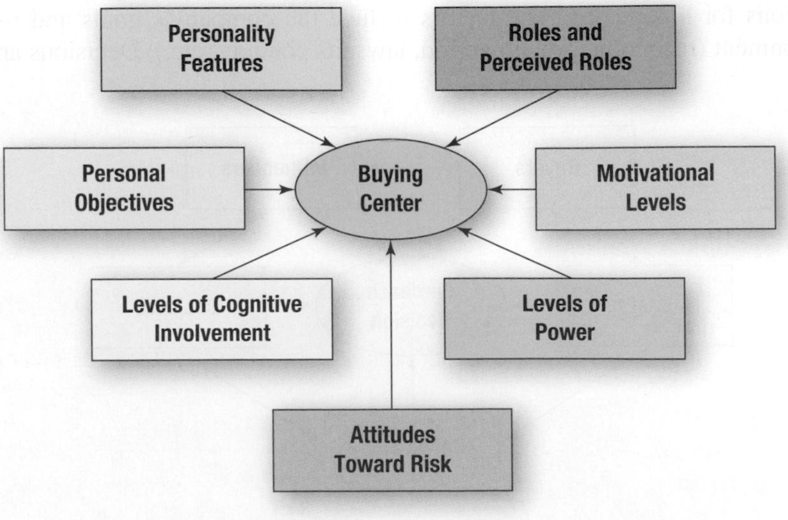

FIGURE 3.13 Individual Factors Affecting Members of the Buying Center

Gaedeki Group

◀ This advertisement for Gaedeke Group illustrates the importance of personality in the decision for a firm's office location

Motivation A person's degree of motivation depends on the match of the individual's goals to the organization's objectives. A factory foreman with a personal goal of becoming the vice president of operations will be more likely to become involved in the purchasing decisions that affect his performance and that of his department. A purchasing agent who has been charged by the CEO to reduce expenses will take a more active role to ensure that cost-cutting selections are made. The need for recognition motivates many individuals. Then, the goal of making successful purchasing decisions becomes to ensure that others recognize the effort, because the person believes a link exists between recognition and promotions or pay raises.

Level of Power A person derives her level of power in the buying process from the role in the buying center, official position in the organization, and the impact of the purchase decision on a specific job. When a particular purchase decision directly affects an employee, she may try to gain more power through the buying process. For instance, a factory foreman has greater power within the buying center in the purchase of raw materials, whereas the maintenance foreman has more power in the purchase of maintenance supplies. In these situations, each strives to influence the decision that affects his or her area and job performance.

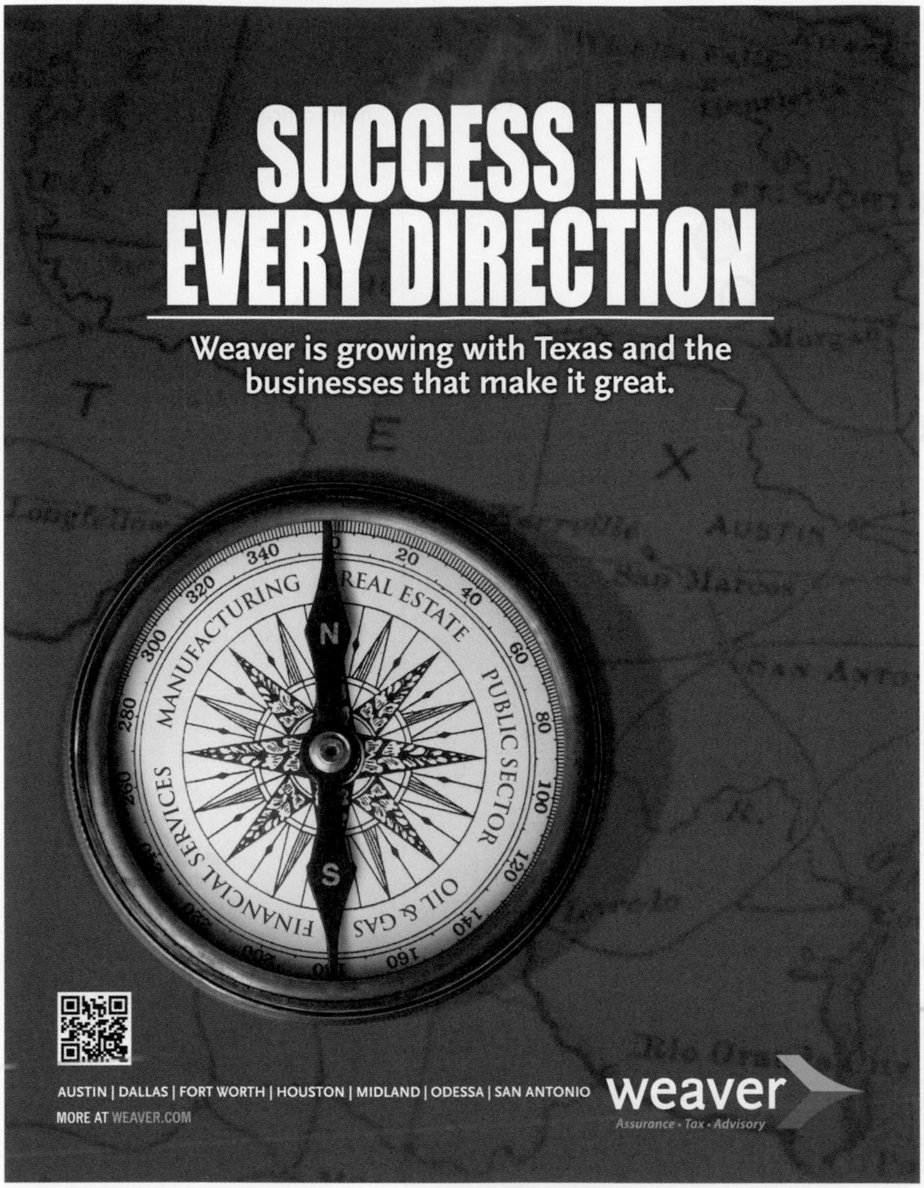

Weaver and Tidwell L. L. P.

▲ A business-to-business ad by Weaver offering assurance, tax, and advisory services.

Risk Oftentimes, vendors are chosen because buyers believe the choice represents the lowest risk. Risk avoidance often leads buyers to stay with current vendors rather than switching. In marketing to businesses, reducing risk remains a priority, especially when signing large contracts or when a purchase might affect company profits. People tend to believe that taking risks, especially when a failure follows, affects performance appraisals, promotions, and other outcomes.

Levels of Cognitive Involvement Both consumer and business buying behaviors are influenced by levels of cognitive involvement. Individuals with higher levels of cognitive capacity seek more information prior to making decisions. They ask more questions when interacting with a salesperson. They spend more time deliberating prior to making decisions. Clearly-stated message arguments help persuade both consumers and business buyers with higher cognitive levels.

Personal Objectives Motives, personality types, perceptions of risk, and the other individual factors shape personal objectives. These objectives can lead buyers to make purchases that help them politically in the organization, even when they are not the best choice. For example, if someone knows his boss is friends with a particular vendor, the buyer might choose that vendor even when others offer higher quality, lower prices, or both. Personal objectives in buying decisions can be tied to obtaining promotions, making rivals look bad, "brown-nosing" a boss, or the genuine desire to help the organization succeed.

In sum, a buying center consists of a complex set of relationships. Members can serve different roles and may play more than one role. Understanding these dynamics helps when marketing to businesses. The marketing team identifies who will make the decision, how the decision will be made, and any forces or factors that might affect the decision-making process. Examining the organizational and individual influences makes it possible to design a communications program that reaches the key people at the right time.

Types of Business-to-Business Sales

objective 3.5
What types of business-to-business sales are made?

Business buyers make different types of purchasing decisions. The marketing team adapts to the type of decision being made. The three categories of buying activities include a straight rebuy, a modified rebuy, and a new task.[27]

A **straight rebuy** occurs when the firm has previously chosen a vendor and places a reorder. This routine process normally involves only one or a few members of the buying center. Often the purchasing agent (buyer) and the users of the product are the only ones aware of a rebuy order. The user's role in this purchase situation is to ask the buyer to replenish

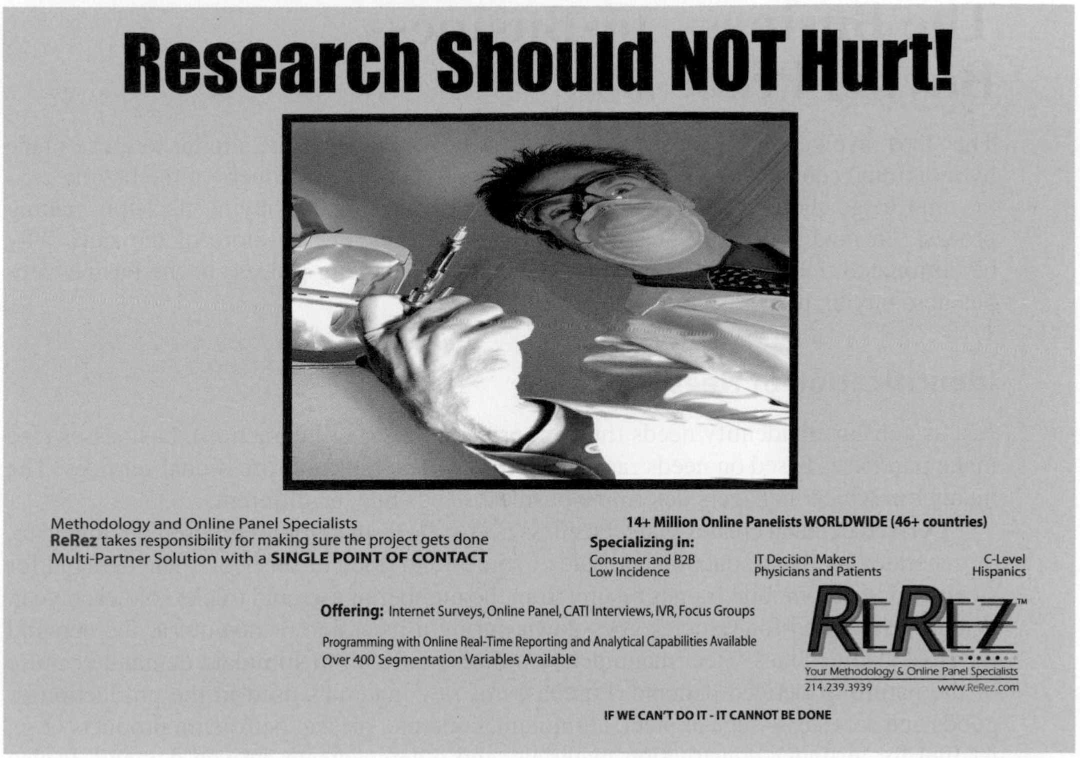

ReRez

◀ This advertisement for ReRez is designed to influence members of a buying center who are evaluating a marketing research firm.

the supply. The buyer then contacts the supplier and places the order. Little or no evaluation of alternatives or information takes place. These purchases often take place electronically.

When making a **modified rebuy**, the buying team considers and evaluates alternatives. As identified in Figure 3.14, a modified rebuy purchase can be made for four different reasons. First, when a company's buyers are *dissatisfied with the current vendor*, they look for new options. A greater level of dissatisfaction creates a strong enticement to examine new possibilities. Second, if a new company offers what is perceived by a member of the buying center to be a *better buy*, the purchase decision may be revisited.

A third type of modified rebuy occurs at the *end of a contractual agreement*. Many organizations, as dictated by corporate policy, must ask for bids each time a contract is written. This situation often occurs when governmental and nonprofit organizations make purchases. The final reason for a modified rebuy is that the people in the company assigned to make the purchase might have only *limited or infrequent experience with the good or service*. When a company purchases delivery trucks, the typical time between decisions may be 5 to 7 years. This creates a modified rebuy situation, because many factors change over that amount of time. Prices, product features, and vendors (truck dealerships) change rapidly. Also, in most cases, the composition of the buying group will be different. Some may have never been part of the decision to purchase delivery vehicles.

In **new task** purchasing situations, the company considers a good or service for the first time or it has been a long time since the last purchase. Further, the product involved is one with which organizational members have no or extremely little experience. This type of purchase normally requires input from a number of buying center members. A considerable amount of time will be spent gathering information and evaluating vendors. In many cases, purchasers ask vendors to assist in identifying the required specifications.

- Dissatisfaction with current vendor
- A different vendor makes an attractive offer
- End of contractual arrangement with current vendor
- Individuals involved in decision process have no or little experience with the product

◀ **FIGURE 3.14**
Reasons to Make a Modified Rebuy

The Business-to-Business Buying Process

objective 3.6
What are the steps of the business-to-business buying process?

The steps involved in the business-to-business buying process are similar to those made by individual consumers. In new task purchasing situations, members of the buying center tend to go through each of the seven steps as part of the buying decision-making process. In modified rebuy or straight rebuy situations, one or more of the steps may be eliminated.[28] Figure 3.15 compares the consumer buying process to the business-to-business buying process.

Identification of Needs

Just as consumers identify needs (hunger, protection, social interaction), businesses also make purchases based on needs ranging from raw materials to professional services. The manner in which managers determine business needs may be different.

Derived demand creates many business needs. **Derived demand** is based on, linked to, or generated by the production and sale of some other good or service.[29] The demand for steel used in automobile frames results from the number of cars and trucks sold each year. When the demand for vehicles goes down during a recession or downturn, the demand for steel also declines. Steel manufacturers find it difficult to stimulate demand because of the nature of derived demand. Purchases of raw materials used in the production of goods and services—such as steel, aluminum, concrete, plastic, petroleum products (e.g., jet fuel for airlines), construction materials, and others—create derived demand. It also exists for services. Most of the demand for mortgages depends on housing sales.

Once a need has been recognized, the order will be placed with the current vendor in a straight rebuy situation. When the purchase constitutes a modified rebuy or new task, members of the buying center move to the next step.

Establishment of Specifications

In a new task purchase, the most complete specifications are spelled out. Many times, various vendors assist the buyer in developing clear specifications. In modified rebuy situations, managers examine specifications to ensure they are current and still meet the company's needs. While they occasionally change, normally most are minor alterations.

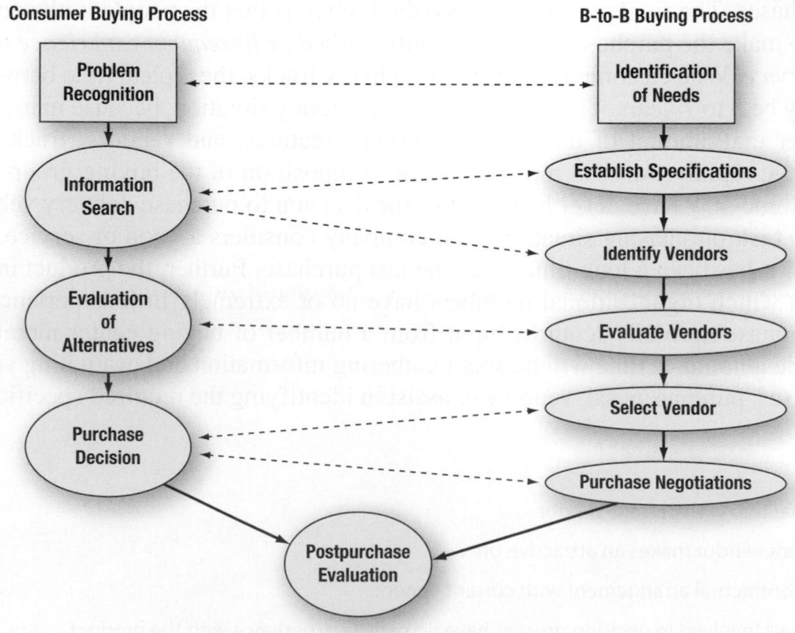

FIGURE 3.15
A Comparison of the Business-to-Business Buying Process to the Consumer Buying Process

Identification of Vendors

Once specifications have been identified, potential vendors are located and asked to submit bids. In most business situations, written, formal bids are required. A vendor's ability to write a clear proposal often determines whether the company will present a successful bid. Effective proposals spell out prices, quality levels, payment terms, support services, and other conditions requested by the company.

Vendor Evaluation

Evaluations of vendors normally occur at two levels. The first, an *initial screening* of proposals, narrows the field of vendors down to three to five competitors. The number of people from the buying center involved in the initial screening depends on the dollar value of the bid and whether the product is critical to the firm's operation. As dollar values increase and the product becomes more critical, the number of individuals from the buying center involved also rises. Managers often delegate minor choices to a single individual.

The second level of evaluation occurs as the firm undertakes a *vendor audit*. An audit becomes especially important when members of the company seek to develop a long-term relationship with a supplier. Vendors that are the primary sources for critical components or raw materials recognize that long-term bonds benefit both the vendor and the purchasing firm. Members of the audit team often include an engineer, someone from operations, a quality-control specialist, and members of the purchasing department. An audit serves several purposes, including an evaluation of each potential supplier's ability to meet demand, provide the level of quality needed, and deliver the product on time.

Vendors are people, just as members of the buying center are people. Attitudes, values, opinions, and first impressions influence evaluations made about vendors. All messages, including bids and proposals, should be designed to create favorable impressions.

Vendor Selection

Once company officials have studied all of the vendors and the bids have been considered, the final choice can be made. In the decision-making process, members of the buying center experience the individual and organizational pressures presented earlier. The selection criteria used include quality, delivery, performance history, warranties, facilities and capacity, geographic location, technical capability, and per-dollar value.[30] The team rarely deems a single vendor as superior across all selection criteria. Consequently, the marketing team for each seller emphasizes the company's specific strengths as part of its presentation. In reality, however, politics and other similar forces often have an impact on the final decision.

Negotiation of Terms

In most purchasing situations, negotiation of terms will be a formality because the conditions have already been worked out. Occasionally, however, changes are made at this point in a contract or purchase. These tend to be minor and are normally negotiated by the purchasing agent. When the final agreement is set, goods are shipped or services provided. Assuming no further complications, the buying process is complete until the next cycle begins.

Scott Equipment

▲ This internet banner ad is designed to encourage firms looking to purchase heavy equipment to consider Scott Equipment as a vendor.

Postpurchase Evaluation

In the business-to-business arena, the postpurchase phase represents a marketing opportunity. Vendors that provide high-quality products, make follow-up calls, and offer additional services often move into a straight rebuy situation. They avoid going through the process again because they are the chosen vendor—unless something changes. Even for products purchased occasionally, the firm that gives attention to the postpurchase component of the selling process gains an edge the next time the company makes a purchase.

Dual Channel Marketing

objective 3.7
How does dual channel marketing expand a company's customer base and its sales?

Firms sell virtually the same goods or services to both consumers and businesses in **dual channel marketing**.[31] The approach fits several situations. The most common scenario occurs when a product sold in business markets is then adapted to consumer markets. New products often have high start-up costs, including R&D expenditures, market research, and other tasks. Businesses tend to be less price-sensitive than retail consumers, which makes it logical to approach them first.

As sales grow, economies of scale emerge. Larger purchases of raw materials combined with more standardized methods of production make it possible to enter consumer markets. The benefits of economies of scale entice manufacturers to sell products previously supplied to the business sector in the retail markets. Products including digital cameras, calculators, computers, fax machines, and mobile phones were first sold to businesses and then later to consumers.

To make the move to the retail arena possible, prices must be lower and products need to be user-friendly. For example, consumers often have their photos put on a CD rather than obtaining prints. The imaging technology developed by Kodak and Intel was first sold to various businesses and now is offered to retail customers. By forming an alliance with Intel, Kodak brought the cost down and developed the economies of scale necessary for consumer markets.

Spin-Off Sales

Another type of dual channel marketing—spin-off sales—occurs when individuals who buy a particular brand at work have positive experiences and, as a result, purchase the same brand for personal use. This situation often takes place with computers and computer software. Favorable feelings about more expensive items can also result in spin-off sales. A salesperson who drives a company-owned Buick for work might like it so well that she purchases one for personal use. Holiday Inn's marketing team discovered that

Monkey Business/Fotolia

▶ Digital cameras were first sold to businesses because of the high cost but are now owned by most consumers.

many of its private stays come from business-related spin-offs. Approximately 30 percent of Holiday Inn's business customers also stay with the chain on private vacations.[32]

Marketing Decisions

In dual channel marketing, a primary decision will be made about how to represent the product in each channel. The firm can either emphasize similarities between the two markets or focus on differences. Consumers and businesses looking for the same benefits and product features receive similar marketing messages. When consumers and business buyers value different product attributes or desire different benefits, the marketing strategy team customizes messages for the separate markets. Figure 3.16 identifies three approaches companies can use in marketing products to dual channels.

- Use different communication messages
- Create different brands
- Use multiple or different channels

▲ **FIGURE 3.16**
Dual Channel Marketing Strategies

In some instances, the product's attributes are the same, but the value or benefit of each attribute differs. Messages then focus on the benefits each segment derives from the product. Mobile phones marketed to businesses stress area coverage and service options. For consumers, mobile phone marketing messages may center on the fashionable design of the product, ease of use, or price.

To avoid confusing individuals who might see both messages from the same producer, companies may apply dual branding. For instance, when Black & Decker launched a professional line of power tools, the DeWalt brand name was chosen. This avoided confusion with the Black & Decker name.

In most cases, business customers and consumers seek the same basic benefits from products. In these situations, a single approach for both markets will be used. Tactics include:

- Integrating communications messages
- Selling the same brand in both markets
- Scanning both markets for dual marketing opportunities

In addition to creating economies of scale, integrating consumer markets has another advantage: the potential to create the synergies that arise from increased brand identity and equity. An image developed in the consumer market can then be used to enter a business market, or vice versa. Using one brand makes it easier to develop brand awareness and brand loyalty. A business customer who uses a company-owned American Express card may obtain a card from the company for personal use.

Monkey Business/Fotolia

▲ Quicken discovered a dual channel opportunity for its accounting software with both consumers and small business owners.

Scanning both types of customers for new opportunities is part of dual channel marketing. For example, the firm Intuit, which sells Quicken software, discovered that individuals who use Quicken at home were willing to use a similar version for their small businesses. Capitalizing on this advantage, Quicken added features including payroll and inventory control to its business software package while maintaining the easy-to-use format. By identifying business use for a consumer product, Quicken adapted the product and captured 70 percent of the small-business accounting software market.[33]

Dual channel marketing can create a major competitive advantage as products are sold in both markets. A complete IMC planning process includes the evaluation of potential business market segments as well as consumer market segments. Firms that integrate messages across these markets take major steps toward reaching every potential customer.

International Implications

objective 3.8
How can a company overcome international differences when adapting to buying processes?

Selling to consumers and businesses requires the marketing team to understand cultural differences related to products, messages, and selling techniques. A *cultural assimilator* will be a valuable member of the marketing team in international projects. Individual buyers and members of companies from other countries exhibit cultural differences as they consider purchasing alternatives.

Understanding the nuances of the purchasing process for transactions that take place in foreign countries can be helpful. For example, at domestic U.S. trade shows, actual purchases are normally not finalized. Instead, information is collected and transferred between the buyer and the seller. At international trade shows, however, sales are often completed. Higher-ranking members of the purchasing company attend the shows and want to complete transactions. Knowing these kinds of differences helps a company succeed in international trade.

Building a powerful brand represents an important activity in any IMC program. A strong brand means the product becomes part of the consumer's initial set of brands to consider when making a purchase. A powerful brand crosses national boundaries and becomes part of an effective globally integrated marketing communications program. Successful global brands are built over time. It takes a combination of high-quality products and effective marketing communications to reach that point.

In business-to-business marketing, a visible global brand presence is equally crucial. The existence of multiple vendors, increasing perceptions of brand parity, and growing use of the internet make it impossible for a company to succeed using only price differentiation. To combat such situations, a strong brand is a necessity in the global environment. A strong brand increases the chances of being selected. As Robert Duboff writes, "It is no longer sufficient to be a great company; *you must be a great brand*."[34]

Summary

Buyer behaviors are part of the purchasing process in both consumer markets and business-to-business transactions. An effective IMC program accounts for the ways in which goods and services are purchased in both markets. The consumer buying decision-making process consists of five steps. Marketing experts are aware of each step and prepare effective communications that lead most directly to the decision to buy. For the purposes of creating effective marketing communications, the information search stage and the evaluation of alternatives stage will be the two most important.

After recognizing a want or need, a consumer searches for information both internally and externally. Marketing messages attempt to place the product or service in the consumer's evoked set of viable prospects. Three factors that influence search behaviors include involvement, needs for cognition, and enthusiasm for shopping. Customers consider the benefits and costs of searches and make decisions regarding how extensively they will seek information. Evoked sets, attitudes and values, and cognitive maps explain how an individual evaluates various purchasing choices.

Marketers face an evolving buying decision-making environment. New cultural values and attitudes, time pressures, and busy lifestyles influence what people buy, how they buy, and the manner in which they can be enticed to buy. Many consumers try to escape through indulgences and pleasure binges, by finding excitement or fantasy, and by planning to meet social needs. An aging baby boom population concentrates more on lasting values and on health issues. Social media has affected the ways in which consumers communicate with one another. Marketing experts can address these needs and lead customers to purchases based on them.

By understanding business buyer behaviors, the marketing team constructs a more complete and integrated marketing communications program. Business purchases are driven by members of the buying center. These members include users, buyers, influencers, deciders, and gatekeepers. Members of the buying center are influenced by both organizational and individual factors that affect various marketing decisions.

Business-to-business sales take three forms. A straight rebuy occurs when the firm has previously chosen a vendor and intends to place a reorder. A modified rebuy occurs when the purchasing group is willing to consider and evaluate new alternatives. This decision is usually based on dissatisfaction with a current vendor. A new task purchase takes place when a company buys a good or service for the first time, and the product involved is one with which organizational members have no experience.

The business-to-business buying process is similar to the consumer purchase decision-making process. A more formal purchasing process includes formal specifications, bids from potential vendors, and a contract finalizing the purchasing agreement.

Dual channel marketing means that the firm sells virtually the same goods or services to both consumers and businesses. Dual channel marketing creates both economies of scale and synergies for the vendor company. It also enhances the chances that a product will be sold to every available customer. The challenge to the marketing team is to create strong and consistent marketing messages to every potential buyer, accounting for how buyer behaviors are present in purchasing processes.

Key Terms

involvement The extent to which a stimulus or task is relevant to a consumer's existing needs, wants, or values

need for cognition A personality characteristic an individual displays when he or she engages in and enjoys mental activities

enthusiasm for shopping Customers who like to shop will undertake a more in-depth search for details about goods and services

attitude A mental position taken toward a topic, person, or event that influences the holder's feelings, perceptions, learning processes, and subsequent behaviors

values Strongly held beliefs about various topics or concepts

cognitive maps Simulations of the knowledge structures embedded in an individual's brain

evoked set Consists of the set of brands a consumer considers during the information search and evaluation processes

inept set The part of a memory set that consists of the brands held in a person's memory but are *not considered* because they elicit negative feelings

inert set The part of a memory set of brands that hold the brands the consumer has awareness of but has neither negative nor positive feelings about

affect referral A purchasing decision model in which the consumer chooses the brand for which he or she has the strongest liking or feelings

buying center The group of individuals who make a purchase decision on behalf of a business

straight rebuy What occurs when the firm has previously chosen a vendor and intends to place a reorder

modified rebuy The company buying team considers and evaluates new purchasing alternatives

new task A purchase in which the company buys a good or service for the first time or the product involved is one with which organizational members have no experience

derived demand Demand based on, linked to, or generated by the production and sale of some other good or service

dual channel marketing Selling virtually the same goods or services to both consumers and businesses

compensatory heuristics A purchasing decision model that assumes no single brand will score high on every desirable attribute and that individual attributes vary in terms of their importance to the consumer

conjunctive heuristics A purchasing decision model that establishes a minimum or threshold rating that brands must meet in order to be considered

phased heuristics A purchasing decision model that is a combination of the compensatory and conjunctive heuristics models

MyMarketingLab

Go to **mymktlab.com** to complete the problems marked with this icon ✪.

Review Questions

3-1. What is the first step in the information search when a consumer decides that they need to make a purchase and there are alternatives open to them?

3-2. What is "level of motivation" and what are the three factors that determine it?

3-3. Distinguish between cognitive and conative components as part of an assessment of consumer attitudes. Give examples of each.

3-4. What are the key factors that are said to affect a person's values?

3-5. Define the term "opportunity cost."

3-6. Why is repetition so important for marketing messages? Would they work without repetition?

3-7. In relation to an individual's evoked sets, distinguish between inept and inert sets.

3-8. What is meant by affect referral? When is a person likely to rely on such a cognitive approach to evaluating purchasing alternatives?

3-9. What new trends in the consumer buying environment affect consumer purchasing decisions?

3-10. Name and describe the five roles played in a buying center.

3-11. What organizational and individual factors affect members of the business buying center?

3-12. Describe the three main forms of business-to-business sales.

3-13. Name the steps in the business-to-business buying process.

3-14. Describe dual channel marketing and explain why it is important to a company's well-being.

Critical Thinking Exercises

DISCUSSION QUESTIONS

3-15. For college students and other individuals with compulsive buying behaviors, a primary influence is the family. Often one or both parents are compulsive shoppers. Families that display other forms of dysfunctional behaviors—such as alcoholism, bulimia, extreme nervousness, or depression—tend to produce children who are more inclined to exhibit compulsive shopping behaviors. Why do dysfunctional behaviors among parents produce compulsive shopping behavior among children? Another component of compulsive buying behaviors is self-esteem. Again, self-esteem is partly inherited, but it also develops in the home environment. How would self-esteem be related to compulsive shopping behaviors? What influences other than family might contribute to compulsive shopping behaviors? If an individual has a tendency to be a compulsive shopper, what can (or should) be done?

3-16. Think about the ways you purchase products and consider a recent purchase that involved an external search. Discuss your ability to search, the need for cognition, your personal level of shopping enthusiasm, and the perceived costs versus the perceived benefits of the search. How much time did you spend in the external search, and what was the outcome?

3-17. Study the list of personal values presented in Figure 3.3. Identify the five most important to you. Rank them from first to last. Beside each value, identify at least one product you have purchased to satisfy those values. Explain how that good or service satisfied that value.

3-18. Identify the last brand of clothing you purchased. Create a cognitive map similar to the one illustrated in the text for Ruby Tuesday in Figure 3.5. Discuss the linkages. Identify which linkages are strong. Which linkages are loosely held?

3-19. Review the three methods of evaluating alternatives. For each method, discuss a recent purchase you made using that method. Which method did you tend to use the most? Why?

3-20. Pick one of the product categories below. Identify brands in your evoked set, inept set, and inert set for that product category. Explain the rationale for the placement of each of the brands.

- **a.** Quick service restaurants
- **b.** Retail clothing stores
- **c.** Grocery stores
- **d.** Cell phone service providers

3-21. What are the discernible consumer buying trends in your own country? Choose a product or service category and examine how trends have changed over the past few years. What has influenced these changes? Are the changes consumer-led, marketing-led, or technological?

3-22. As a business and marketing advisor to a medium-sized business that tends to favor traditional forms of communication with their customers, outline how they could benefit from the communications revolution and how technology could have a positive impact on their sales and image. Take into account the fact that they may not even use email to a great extent. You should also assume that they do not have a website and cannot take payments electronically.

3-23. A purchasing agent for a clothing manufacturer is in the process of selecting a vendor (or vendors) to supply the materials to produce about 30 percent of its clothes. The clothing manufacturer employs about 300 people. As the audit nears completion, what factors are most important to the purchasing agent?

3-24. Identify four brands you have used in a work environment that you also have purchased in your personal life. Discuss the dual channel marketing approach each of the brands use. Discuss the process that occurred in purchasing the product for personal use and the influence using the brand in the work environment had on the purchase, or the reverse if you used it personally first.

Integrated Learning Exercises

3-25. Consumers and businesses conduct external searches when they lack sufficient internal knowledge to make a wise decision. Assume you have $100,000 to $150,000 to spend on a sailboat. Locate four websites that sell sailboats. Select one in your price range. Discuss the external search process you used to arrive at a decision. Relate this process to the concepts of external search, consumer attitudes, and consumer values presented in this chapter. Which method of evaluation did you use? Explain why.

3-26. Almost everyone has an opinion about tattoos. Some attitudes are positive whereas others are negative. Few are neutral. Go to **www.tattoos.com** and examine the material there. Did this information modify your attitude toward tattoos? What factors on the website influenced your attitude? Find at least one additional website of a company that offers tattoos. Provide the URL for the site and discuss the components of the website in terms of which components of attitude it is trying to influence: cognitive, affective, or conative.

3-27. United Raw Material Solutions, Inc. is a business-to-business marketplace that brings together buyers and sellers of textiles, petrochemicals, plastics, and electronics. Access the website at **www.urms.com**. Which members of the buying center would be most interested in this site? What services and benefits do you see for buyers? For suppliers?

3-28. Look at the following websites and identify the component of attitude that they are aiming to affect. Are several components of attitude under influence at the same time?

a. China Mobile (**www.chinamobileltd.com**)
b. Intel (**www.intel.com**)
c. Honda (**www.honda.com**)
d. Huawei (**www.huawei.com**)
e. SK Group (**www.sk.com**)

3-29. A member of the buying center has been asked to gather information about possible shipping companies for international shipments. Visit the following websites. What companies have the most appealing websites? Beyond online materials, what additional information do they need to supply to the buying center in order to win the contract?

a. ABC India Limited (**www.abcindia.com**)
b. SR International Logistics, Inc. (**www.srinternational.com**)
c. Allison Shipping International (**www.allisonshipping.com**)
d. Shipping International (**www.shippinginternational.com**)

Blog Exercises

Access the authors' blog for this textbook at the URLs provided to complete these exercises. Answer the questions posed on the blog.

3-30. Jeep: **http://blogclowbaack.net/2014/05/07/jeep-chapter-3/**

3-31. Olive Garden: **http://blogclowbaack.net/2014/05/07/olive-garden-chapter-3/**

3-32. Consumer behavior, buying process: **http://blogclowbaack.net/2014/05/07/consumer-behavior-chapter-3/**

Student Project

CREATIVE CORNER

A local travel agency decides to advertise in the student newspaper on your campus to promote spring break packages. The company hires you to perform the creative work. The marketing department is not sure which type of advertising approach to use. The agency knows that attitude consists of three parts: cognitive, affective, and conative. They also know that an advertisement can appeal to any one of the attitude components. The agency's management team is also not sure which component to use. Consequently, they have asked you to design three advertisements, with one designed to appeal to the cognitive component of attitude, the second to the affective component, and the third to the conative component. After you have finished designing the ads, discuss the pros and cons of each and make a recommendation to the travel agency about which one to use. The ads should be for a 5-day spring break vacation on the beach in Fort Lauderdale, Florida.

CASE 1 CHOOSING A PHONE COMPANY: OPTIONS AND ALTERNATIVES

The past two decades have witnessed a dramatic shift in the ways people can talk on the phone. Landline phones, while still in common use, are challenged by new and different technologies. AT&T, a major landline provider, has expanded to compete in areas such as mobile phones, texting, and internet access using handheld devices.

Also, a new type of telephone technology has emerged, Voice over internet Protocol (VoIP). This new technology allows a customer to make voice calls using a broadband internet connection instead of a regular (analog) phone line.

Some VoIP services allow users to make calls to people who use the same service. Others allow users to call anyone who has a telephone number, including local, long-distance, mobile phone, and international numbers. Some VoIP services only work over a computer or a special VoIP phone. Others can be used with a traditional phone connected to a VoIP adapter. In addition, wireless "hot spots" in locations such as airports, parks, and cafes allow callers to connect to the internet and use VoIP service wirelessly.

A customer owning a special VoIP phone or a regular telephone connected to a VoIP adapter will have a phone that rings like a traditional telephone. If the person's VoIP service requires him to make calls using a computer, the software supplied by the service provider alerts the user when he has an incoming call.

VoIP services do have some disadvantages. First, some VoIP services do not work during power outages unless the service provider offers backup power. Second, not all VoIP services connect directly to emergency services through 911. Third, VoIP providers may not offer directory assistance or white page listings.

nyul/Fotolia

▲ VoIP services can work with just a computer or with traditional phones.

The two major VoIP providers are Skype and Vonage. Skype allows customers to make calls to other Skype members free of charge. The service includes free text messaging and video calls as well. Skype offers low rates for calls of other types. A customer can use Skype on a computer or on a mobile device. Skype works on a wide range of mobile phones and on devices such as PlayStation Portable. Instant messages can be directed at individuals or group chat rooms. Skype users can also make conference calls. Skype offers customers pay-as-you-go or monthly payment options. No special equipment purchase is required in order to use Skype.

Vonage emphasizes that it provides lower-cost options when compared to AT&T. The company features international calling at greatly reduced rate. Vonage does require users to install special hardware. After signing up for an account, Vonage ships an adapter or other equipment to the customer who must then install it and set it up. Complete instructions are provided, and setup is relatively simple. Vonage service can be purchased at Best Buy, Wal-Mart, and Target. The systems offer unlimited local and long-distance calling, call waiting, call forwarding, automatic redial, and voice mail for a single monthly fee.

Kelli is evaluating the two VoIP services and two mobile phone services. Figure 3.15 provides the multiattribute evaluation approach she has developed. She is considering the attributes of sound quality, special services available, access to mobile devices, and difficulty in set up. Each attribute receives a score on a scale of 1 to 10 in terms of importance to Kelli, with 10 being the most important and 1 the least important. The four companies are then evaluated with a 10-point scale for each attribute, with 10 indicating the highest performance.

Using a **compensatory heuristics** method, Kelli assumes that no single brand scores high on every attribute and that individual attributes vary in importance. With this model, Kelli will purchase the brand with the highest compensatory score, which is calculated by multiplying each attribute score by its importance and then summing the total, as shown at the bottom of Figure 3.15.

Using the **conjunctive heuristics** method, a threshold or minimum rating is established. A brand is eliminated if an important attribute is rated lower than a certain number. For example, Kelli has rated "sound quality" as very important (rating of 10). She may decide any service with a rating lower than 8 will be eliminated. In her situation, Skype would be eliminated because it scored only a 5. This process is followed until one brand is left.

The **phased heuristic** approach combines the two methods. Any brand with a low score on any criterion is eliminated first. Then, if a tie exists, the conjunctive heuristics method is used to decide between the two remaining contenders.

Consumers make purchase decisions using one of these methods, or some other approach. Each competitor seeks to highlight the advantages of its approach in order to maintain current customers and attract new ones.

3-33. Use Figure 3.17 to explain the purchase decision Kelli will make using the following methods: (a) conjunctive heuristics, (2) compensatory heuristics, and (3) phased heuristics. Elaborate on which brand is chosen and which brands are not and explain why.

3-34. Create a similar table for two of the following products you have recently purchased. Explain which method of evaluation could be used for each purchase decision.

a. An automobile
b. A dinner at a high-end restaurant
c. A life insurance policy
d. A new pair of jeans

3-35. How would the multiattribute model be expanded to include paging services?

3-36. If a customer bases a purchase on affect referral rather than a multiattribute method for mobile phone service, which of the companies may have an advantage? Why?

Attribute	Importance	AT&T	Vonage	Skype	Verizon
Sound quality	10	10	8	5	8
Special services	9	6	9	8	9
Mobile device access	8	8	8	5	6
Setup difficulty	6	7	5	2	8
Phone style	5	8	4	9	4
Compensatory score		300	275	219	277

FIGURE 3.17
Example of a Multiattribute Evaluation Approach for a Phone Service

CASE 2 YEMEKSEPETI.COM—"MEAL BASKET"

Yemeksepeti.com, founded in 2001 by Nevzat Aydin, is the first online food delivery portal in Turkey based on a business style similar to that of waitersonwheels .com in the United States. The company works with local restaurants and big food chains throughout Turkey to offer various cuisine options to consumers. Yemeksepeti currently has more than 6,500 contracted delivery restaurants across 41 cities in Turkey. Consumers benefit from a large choice of restaurants, the convenience of online ordering, and the customer service that ordering from Yemeksepeti.com guarantees; restaurants access a much broader customer base. When assessing the situation, regarding the options of a new advertising campaign, four teams within the buying center participate: IT, marketing, finance, and the board of directors.

The IT team is directed by a young technology innovator. This department is keen on experimenting with new technologies, especially those surrounding the smartphone. It manages the advertising function as follows: more technology to keep up with the young audience. Augmented reality, QR codes, and 3D imaging are high on their agenda linked with location-aware technologies. The IT team attempts to leverage the debate for the new advertising campaign to gain more power and is willing to use political tactics to achieve its personal and organizational goals.

The marketing department is more grounded and claims to understand better the geodemographic behavior of consumers. Marketing believes access is important and fancy technology may put off some users. Its motto is "simplicity in a few clicks," together with fun, viral marketing videos and buzz on social networks. It has a strong experience of the practice acquired over the years and is up-to-date with the latest Web analytics backing its views. Marketing does not back down easily in a disagreement, even with higher-ranking management employees.

The finance department is traditionally more conservative and carries strong weight in influencing decision-making. However, over the years it has learned that successful advertising involves risk, testing, and investment. A deep understanding of growth drivers is what is required to convince the finance team. Still, it listens, seldom takes a stand, and tries to get unanimous group consensus in decision-making. If not, it normally goes with the lowest risk solution—which in this case would be replicating past successful advertisements on tested technologies and media platforms.

The board of directors is composed of an eclectic mix of individuals—some local, some international—including the founders. The board combines a collaborative global approach, sector-specific expertise, and a long-term investment horizon. It strongly supports the internal development of new product offerings. The board sees its role as analyzing information and thinking strategically about profitability and growth. Yet, it strongly supports the voicing of options, especially counterintuitive ones, and makes the final decision.

fotolistic/Shutterstock

▲ **Many different areas of a company must be involved in planning and execution in order to produce a successful food delivery portal.**

Having reviewed the company structure, a new challenge faces its key decision makers. Three options are being discussed regarding the strategy for their next marketing campaign. Only one option can be selected:

Option 1: Carry on the traditional and ongoing social media effort within the "fan club" on Facebook and Twitter. This is acceptable as the previous TV campaign received awards but does not really address the need for growth and new consumers. The cost for this option was $123,000.

Option 2: Begin immediate testing of new technology via smartphone including augmented reality, 3D design, and location-aware services with QR code technology from third party providers. It is argued that the effort will attract new consumers and cut through the current advertising clutter. In Turkey, 25% of the population already has a smartphone. The cost for this option is $339,000. Questions remain about the adaptability/understanding of novel technologies as well as third party technologies.

Option 3: If no internal agreement is found, a reputable global advertising agency has proposed a campaign. It is a traditional mix of television, print, radio, basic social media, and ambient marketing in Istanbul. Yemeksepeti has never worked with that agency. It bids $250,000 and the campaign will be ready within 2 months.

Nevzat Aydin is now opening the final meeting before a choice is made.[35]

3-37. Discuss the reasoning behind each team's choice based on the information provided and the individual factors outlined in this chapter.

3-38. Identify the factors that favor each team and the factors that are a challenge for the company.

3-39. How should Nevzat Aydin make the final choice, given such a great divergence in opinion exists?

3-40. What should Nevzat Aydin say to the team members whose preferred option is not chosen?

This case solely provides material for class discussion. The author does not intend to illustrate effective or ineffective handling of a managerial situation.

MyMarketingLab

Go to **mymktlab.com** for the following Assisted-graded writing questions:

3-41. Consumers and businesses conduct external searches when they lack sufficient internal knowledge to make a wise decision. Assume you have $80,000 to $100,000 to spend on a sailboat. Locate four websites that sell sailboats. Select one in your price range. Discuss the external search process you used to arrive at a decision. Relate this process to the concepts of external search, consumer attitudes, and consumer values presented in the chapter. Which method of evaluation did you use? Explain why.

3-42. United Raw Material Solutions, Inc. is a business-to-business marketplace that brings together buyers and sellers of textiles, petrochemicals, plastics, and electronics. Access the website at www.urms.com. Which members of the buying center would be most interested in this site? What services and benefits do you see for buyers? For suppliers?

Chapter 4 The IMC Planning Process

Chapter Objectives

After reading this chapter, you should be able to answer the following questions:

4.1 What makes marketing research critical to the IMC planning process?

4.2 What categories are used to identify consumer target markets or market segments?

4.3 What categories are used to identify business-to-business market segments?

4.4 How do the various approaches to positioning influence the IMC planning process?

4.5 How do the marketing communications objectives interact with the other elements of an IMC planning process?

4.6 How are communications budgets established?

4.7 What elements are considered in developing an IMC program?

Overview

An integrated marketing communications planning process requires careful oversight by the company's marketing personnel and any agency the firm employs. Decisions are made with regard to matching products to marketing messages and communications tactics. Successful marketing efforts occur when the company's marketing team identifies every opportunity to make quality contacts with customers or potential customers. An example of this type of work may be found in the case of Motel 6.

IMC PLANNING AND MOTEL 6

Pix by Marti/Fotolia

In an interview with Stan Richards, founder of The Richards Group, he talked about a "perfect example" of the value of marketing communications research in IMC planning. "We've worked with Motel 6 for 24 years," he said, "and the beginning of that relationship was a remarkable insight."

"The insight came out of our research. We sat behind a glass window in a focus room setting. Our account planner sat at the head of the table, moderating the session. We'd gotten a dozen people in the room whom we recruited by phone. They don't know why they're in the room. We know that they all use Motel 6. The moderator asks, 'Where do you stay when you're on the road?' They go around the table and nobody says, 'Motel 6.'"

"The moderator pushes further and says, 'Well, where else do you stay?' They go around the table again, and nobody says, 'Motel 6.' Now, why is that? They didn't know who the other people in the room were, and they didn't want to be perceived as being poor or cheap."

"Now, finally, you get somebody, by going around the table again, to say, 'You know, if it's late at night, I'll stop at a Motel 6, and I can save enough money to buy a tank of gas.' And then, somebody else across the table would say, 'I do the same thing, and I save enough money to bring a gift home to the grandkids.' And all of a sudden, the character of the room changed, because everybody had a story like that. What happened was a move from embarrassment to pride in the benefits of frugality.

"That's what the insight was all about. I am a frugal person, and if my eyes are closed, all hotel rooms look alike. I don't see any reason to overspend for lodging, when I can find a perfectly good place like Motel 6. " From this insight, The Richards Group developed the theme, tagline, and advertising approach for Motel 6 that are still used today. Richards noted that the phrase, "'A clean, comfortable room, at the lowest price of any national chain,'" appears in every spot."[1]

This chapter describes the nature of the IMC planning process. As illustrated in Figure 4.1, it begins with communications research. This allows the marketing team to identify potential target markets and positioning strategies that match the brand. Next,

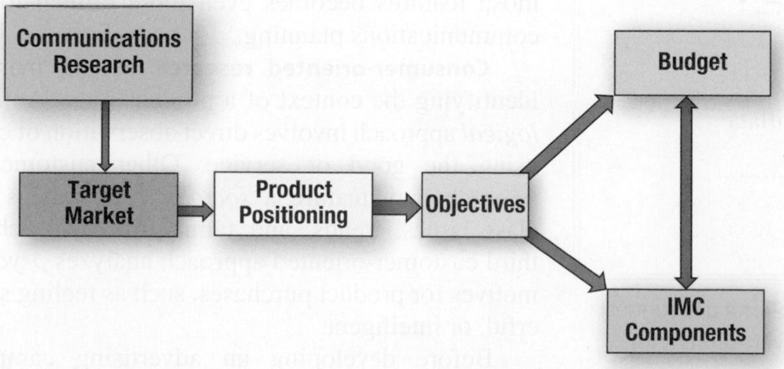

FIGURE 4.1
The IMC Planning Process

objective 4.1
What makes marketing research critical to the IMC planning process?

communications objectives are specified. Finally, a budget designed to achieve the communications objectives is designed with the IMC components to be employed in mind. In addition, any international considerations are taken into account.

Communications Research

The communications planning process begins with research. Those individuals involved in designing a communications campaign must thoroughly understand the product being sold and the consumers (or businesses) who are potential buyers.

▼ Through product-specific research, it was determined that trust is an important consideration in the selection of a financial institution.

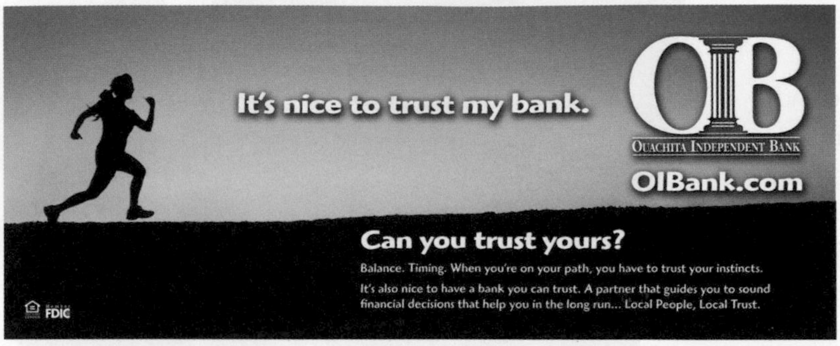

Newcomer, Morris and Young Inc.

More than basic product attributes influence purchase decisions. Customers consider the benefits a product provides. Individuals purchasing makeup, cologne, perfume, and other beauty products may not be concerned about the specific ingredients but care a great deal about how the items will make them look or smell. Communication research goes beyond identifying demographic profiles or target markets. Key insights about how products are used, when they are used, and why can emerge from effective research. Three primary research approaches include product-specific research, consumer-oriented research, and target-market research.

Product-specific research involves identifying key product characteristics that become selling points. For example, the marketing team might try to discover the most desirable "app" features for a cell phone. The team may find that consumers use certain apps when they are bored and passing time, whereas others provide specific functional information, such as the location of a restaurant while the person drives to dinner. One feature or the other becomes the focal point of a commercial or marketing message.

To be effective, product-specific research goes beyond understanding attributes or characteristics. It includes an understanding of benefits that a product provides. A smartphone provides multiple benefits, such as a means of communicating with other people through the phone feature or through social media. It can be used to access product information through a QR code at a retail store. It offers entertainment through watching TV shows or consumer-posted videos on YouTube. While understanding the features of a smartphone will be important, discovering the types of benefits customers derive from those features becomes even more critical to effective communications planning.

Daniel Taylor Clothier

▲ Consumer-oriented research might reveal that colorful ties suggest a person is fun-loving, such as is portrayed in this advertisement for Daniel Taylor Clothier.

Consumer-oriented research assists marketers in identifying the context of a product's use. An *anthropological* approach involves direct observation of consumers using the good or service. Other customer-oriented research may feature a *sociological* analysis of social class issues, trends, and family life cycle changes. A third customer-oriented approach analyzes *psychological* motives for product purchases, such as feeling sexy, powerful, or intelligent.

Before developing an advertising campaign for Scotts Miracle-Grow lawn fertilizer, The Richards Group engaged in consumer-oriented marketing research. The Richards team interviewed 4,000 consumers and gained the valuable insight that "people would change their behaviors if an expert spoke to them about lawn care." The research revealed that many people reported that usually someone in the neighborhood is "knowledgeable about lawn care." Using this information, The Richards Group's advertising team created the expert spokesperson "Scottish." His name is a mnemonic play on the Scotts brand. Early evaluations of the campaign indicated that it resonated well with consumers.[2]

Target-market research identifies who will be the recipient of the planned communications campaign. For instance, product-oriented research may determine that one benefit of joining a fitness center can be improved heart health. Consumer-oriented research might indicate that elder individuals and those who have developed some type of heart trouble would be the most likely to want this particular benefit. Thus, target-market research looks at the best market for a particular benefit of a good or service.

Sometimes, a company's marketing team becomes so close to products and customers that they do not see these issues. Consequently, agencies often seek out more information from clients. One common approach used by agencies to understand a client's customers is a focus group, such as the one described in the Motel 6 story at the beginning of this chapter. A **focus group** consists of consumers who talk about a particular topic, product, or brand in front of a moderator or panel who tracks consumer comments and ideas. The insights gained become crucial elements in the IMC planning process.

Kraft Foods, Inc.

▲ Through target-market research, individuals who love chocolate were identified as a viable audience for this Philadelphia Cream Cheese advertisement.

Market Segmentation by Consumer Groups

objective 4.2
What categories are used to identify consumer target markets or market segments?

Communications research identifies the target markets a company seeks to serve. Target markets exist in two areas: consumer markets and business-to-business markets, which are also known as market segments. A **market segment** consists of a set of businesses or group of individual consumers with distinct characteristics. For a market segment to be viable, it should pass the following tests:

- The individuals or businesses within the market segment should be similar in nature, having the same needs, attitudes, interests, and opinions. This means that persons or businesses within the segment are *homogenous*.
- The market segment differs from the population as a whole. Segments are distinct from other segments and from the general population.
- The market segment must be large enough to be financially viable to target with a separate marketing campaign.
- The market segment must be reachable through some type of media or marketing communications method.

Market researchers spend considerable resources and time working to discover viable market segments. The process, known as **market segmentation**, consists of identifying the specific consumer and business groups that are the most likely to purchase the brand based on their needs, attitudes, and interests.

FIGURE 4.2
Methods of Segmenting Customer Markets

- Demographics
- Psychographics
- Generations
- Geographic
- Geodemographics
- Benefits
- Usage

Consumers, or end users, represent one primary target market for a firm's offerings. Effective IMC programs identify sets of consumers who are potential buyers. Figure 4.2 lists the most common consumer market segmentation approaches.

Segments Based on Demographics

One primary method of segmentation employs **demographics**, or population characteristics. Typical demographic variables include gender, age, education, income, and ethnicity. Companies create goods and services to meet the needs of individual demographic segments.

Gender Men and women purchase different products, buy similar products with different features (e.g., deodorants), desire products for dissimilar reasons (stereos, televisions), and buy the same products after being influenced by different kinds of appeals through different media. For example, both genders use deodorant. Degree deodorant was introduced as a unisex brand in 1990. Then, in 2005, the product was divided into two forms, Degree Men and Degree Women, featuring different advertising approaches. Ads for Degree Women emphasized that the deodorant left no marks on clothing and that it would hold up as she worked and socialized. For men, the focus was more on physical feats such as riding mountain bikes or snowboarding.

Today, both brands have been placed under one agency with a single campaign and shared strategy and tagline. The new ads feature famous athletes, both male and female, training in a sport other than their primary sport. The voiceover promises "Degree won't let you down" and the tagline is "Do More." The concept suggests that Degree, whether for men or women, provides the same benefit and works in all situations that create sweat.[3]

Other products focus on a specific gender. A recent study suggested that women control 66 percent, or $12 trillion, of the world's annual consumer spending. Women now influence or make purchases in product categories that were traditionally controlled by men.[4] For instance, in the United States:

- 96 percent of women are involved in purchasing high-priced electronics.
- 90 percent of women deal with financial advisors.
- 80 percent of women buy and sell stocks to make money.
- 70 percent of women are their household's primary "accountant."

Some companies that have done well include Olay, Paige Premium, and OfficeMax. Olay advertises skin care products for females and tells women that the company wants to help them enjoy beautiful skin. Paige Premium encourages women to love their bodies and places a card in each pair of denim jeans that reads "I want you to love your body. Feel comfortable in your skin. Feel comfortable in your jeans. Thanks for believing in our product." OfficeMax has created a fashion brand of office products targeted specifically at women.[5]

Mothers represent an increasingly attractive target audience for marketers. This segment contains the fastest-growing buyers of iPhones. They tune in more often and for longer periods of time to media websites such as Pandora. They are more likely to share photos and news on Facebook via a smartphone as well as a computer. Moms represent 20 percent of online users and an even higher percentage of mobile device users.

They are the biggest web spenders either directly through a mobile app or researching a product online, then purchasing it later at a retail store. Many moms now use smartphones to access product and brand information rather than calling a relative or friend.[6]

Other marketing programs target men. Researchers have discovered that men are shopping more, whether for their own clothes or for groceries. To reach males shoppers, marketers seek to understand how males differ from females. Males tend to focus on product performance. Dyson has been effective in reaching men using this approach by focusing on a design that creates a powerful suction in the company's vacuum cleaners.

Men enjoy doing things that they can do well and dislike things they cannot. They do not enjoy browsing and instead prefer looking for specific information. Amazon.com meets both of these needs by helping men purchase books and music online. Consumer lists, reviews, and suggestions provide concise information that males desire in order to feel confident about their purchases. Men favor products reflecting their status and those that demonstrate "I have good taste." As a result, males tend to purchase well-known brand names and look for other indicators of quality.[7]

Gender presents the opportunity to match a product with a large category of individuals. Careful thought should be given as to whether it should be aimed at only one sex, because gender roles have shifted over the past half-century.

Age Marketing programs often concentrate on persons of a certain age, such as children, young adults, middle-age adults, and senior citizens. Age can be combined with another demographic, such as gender. Consequently, older women may be primary targets for specific types of vitamins and medical products such as those that combat osteoporosis. Young working women with children are more likely to notice advertisements for conveniences, including ready-made foods and snacks and oil and lube facilities. The advertisement for JD Bank on the next page highlights retirement and investment services and targets senior men.

Infants to 3-year-olds are an attractive market for companies. A study by the Campaign for Commercial-Free Childhood revealed that by six months of age babies form mental images of brand logos and mascots. Other studies indicate by the time children reach three years of age they recognize as many as 100 brand images. Reaching babies has become easier now than ever before, primarily because of technology and parent use of technology. A Joan Ganz Cooney Center study indicates that 80 percent of children age five and under use the internet weekly and 60 percent of children three and younger watch online videos. One in four parents allows children to interact with a mobile phone or iPad by the age of two.[8]

Despite criticisms from parental and other watchdog groups, advertising to children (even babies) generates big business. If brand loyalty can be obtained at a young age, a company might retain a customer for a lifetime.

Newcomer, Morris and Young Inc.

▲ A St. Francis advertisement targeted to mothers making health care provider choices.

JD Bank

▲ This advertisement for JD Bank uses both gender and age segmentation.

Tweens represent an additional age-based market segment. Figure 4.3 presents some interesting information about tweens. As shown, tweens influence household purchases. They are online and have already started making purchases using the internet.[9]

The marketing push to reach young consumers continues through the teen years. At the same time, recent research indicates that marketers may need to modify the ways they have been seeking to reach this target group. Teens have switched a substantial amount of shopping from specialty and department stores to online. Value has become more important than brand names. The digital world takes up more of their time and has become the primary source of product and brand information. For this group, Facebook has declined in popularity; however, use of Twitter, Instagram, and other social media venues has risen.[10]

Income A family's level of income and educational attainment are often closely related. Members of lower-income homes, often with less education, primarily purchase *necessities* such as food, clothing, and housing needs; however, members of these households also buy cell phones, automobiles, and other, more costly products. As income and educational attainment increase, household members purchase from a greater selection of expensive items. The products, or *sundry* items, include vacations, more expensive automobiles, more fashionable clothes, and meals at higher-end restaurants. These items are purchased occasionally by those who can afford them, but not on a routine basis. At the extreme, *luxury* products such as yachts and private planes target the wealthy.

Companies in the furniture industry often use income segmentation to create products and advertisements. One demographic group that receives attention is the

▶ **FIGURE 4.3**
Influence of Tweens

Source: Based on Lucia Moses, "Tweens Have a Big Say in Household Spending," *Adweek*, www.adweek.com/news/advertising-branding/tweens-have-big-say-household-spending-150570, June 26, 2013.

Influence/Opinion	Percent
Want instant gratification	56%
Want customized product	59%
Want what others have	41%
Sometimes visit online stores	31%
Shop online	28%
Influence on household purchases	
Movies	55%
Food	29%
Personal care products	26%
Family vacation destination	27%
Technology	23%

"exhausted affluent." Individuals in this group generate household incomes from $100,000 to $150,000. They are affluent but identify with the working class. They bridge the gap between, "the haves and the have nots." In furniture, they desire style and quality rather than something overly fancy. Members of this segment want furniture to be right for them, that lets them stand out, but not so much that it says "I've been too extravagant and spent money foolishly."[11] In contrast, many furniture sellers focus on price, appealing to lower-income consumers, while another group offers high-end furniture to the wealthy.

Joplin Globe

▲ The "Exhausted Affluent" market segment is an excellent target for home furnishings.

Ethnicity The United States is becoming increasingly diverse. Ethnic minorities now represent $2.5 trillion in buying power. This growth represents both an opportunity and a threat: an opportunity for companies able to adapt their messages to other cultures and heritages. It threatens those that do not. Seventy percent of ethnic minorities state that ethnicity constitutes a significant part of their personal identities. Ethnic marketing succeeds in some, but not all, product categories. Sixty-two percent of African Americans want health and beauty products marketed specifically to them; 53 percent of Hispanics said ethnicity is important for consumer packaged goods, entertainment, and clothing; and 50 percent of Asians stated that ethnicity was important for entertainment services.[12]

Chrysler Group LLC created a campaign targeted toward Hispanics that included television, radio, print, newspaper, and digital media ads in the top 15 Hispanic markets. The campaign spots were not transcreated or translated from English ads. Instead they were produced for the Hispanic audience, although the ads were in Spanish and English. Large pick-up trucks are historically one of the best-selling vehicles among Latinos. As a result, the campaign focused on the Ram 1500 and Ram 2500. The creative focused on unscripted, real-life testimonies from Hispanic truck owners talking about the values that are essential to them and how the Ram truck is an extension of their lives. The campaign theme "A Todo Con Todo," which translates as "To everything, with everything," captured the consumer mindset and "true essence" of the Ram truck for the Hispanic target market.[13]

▼ Hispanics are a viable ethnic group for market segmentation.

Monkey Business/Fotolia

Similar approaches were used by Kraft's marketing team in developing ads for Kraft Mac & Cheese as well as by the advertising group for Domino's pizza. Rather than focus on the product, both brands focused on people. Kraft sent the message that eating an American food (Mac & Cheese) does not make a Latino less Latino. A graphic popup states, "Mantente 100%," which means "Stay 100% Latino." The Domino's spots featured Mauricio Arroyave who was born in Colombia and now owns ten franchises. The messages told his story and that of other Hispanic employees. Both approaches were well-received by the Hispanic segment.[14]

In recent years, the ways in which marketing professionals approach ethnic marketing have changed. Rather than create separate campaigns for each ethnic group, agencies take a more holistic approach that incorporates insights into various ethnic groups to help create stronger campaigns.

Psychographics

Demographics are relatively easy to identify. They do not, however, fully explain why people buy particular products or specific brands or the type of appeal that works to reach them. To assist in the marketing effort while building on demographic information, psychographic profiles have been developed. **Psychographics** emerge from patterns of responses that reveal a person's activities, interests, and opinions (AIO). The measures can be combined with demographic information to supply marketers with a more complete understanding of the target market.[15]

Strategic Business Insights provides a popular classification of lifestyles using psychographic segmentation. The VALS typology categorizes respondents into eight different groups based on resources and on the extent to which they are action-oriented.[16] The VALS typology includes the following segments:

- **Innovators**—Successful, sophisticated, and receptive to new technologies. Their purchases reflect cultivated tastes for upscale products.
- **Thinkers**—Educated, conservative, practical consumers who value knowledge and responsibility. They look for durability, functionality, and value.
- **Achievers**—Goal-oriented, conservative consumers committed to career and family. They favor established prestige products that demonstrate success to peers.
- **Experiencers**—Young, enthusiastic, and impulsive consumers who seek variety and excitement and spend substantially on fashion, entertainment, and socializing.

▼ An advertisement for Visit South Walton (Florida) targeted to the "Experiencers" VALS group.

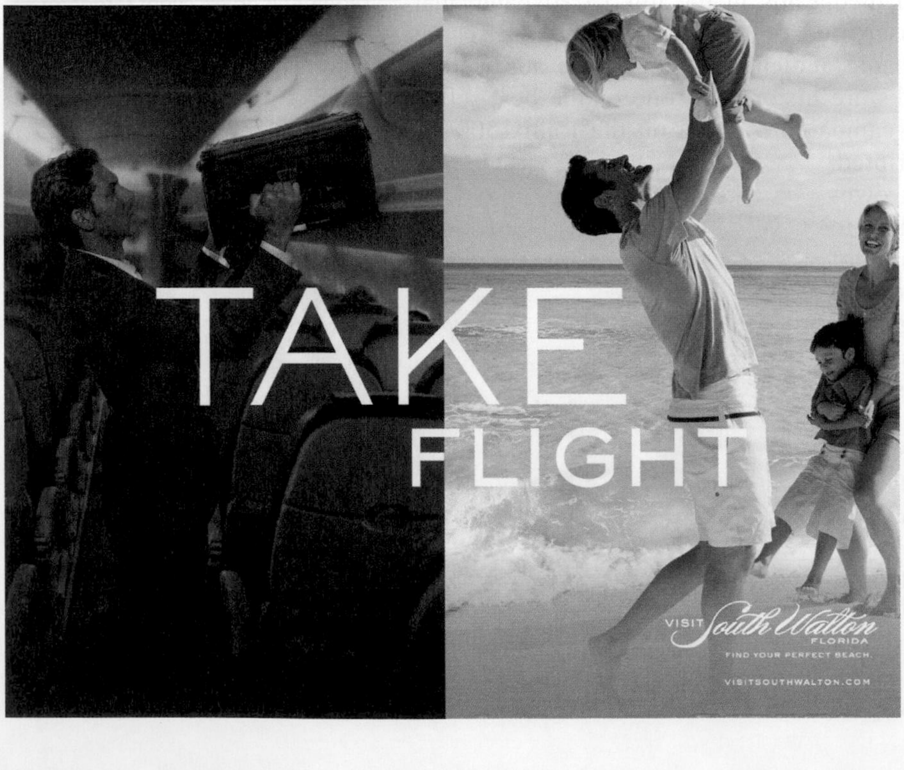

Visit South Walton

- **Believers**—Conservative, conventional consumers who focus on tradition, family, religion, and community. They prefer established brands and favor American-made products.
- **Strivers**—Trendy, fun-loving consumers who are concerned about others' opinions and approval. They demonstrate to peers their ability to buy.
- **Makers**—Self-sufficient consumers who have the skill and energy to carry out projects, respect authority, and are unimpressed by material possessions.
- **Survivors**—Concerned with safety and security, focus on meeting needs rather than fulfilling desires. They are brand loyal and purchase discounted products.

This type of information helps marketers design more effective communications. For instance, reaching Strivers requires advertisements that convey fun and trendy products. Ads for Believers should focus more on traditional and patriotic values.

Revel, the $2.4 billion resort casino in Atlantic City, developed an advertising campaign aimed at the VALS "experiencer" group. The target market was defined as "leisure and lifestyle consumers among the 47 million people age 21 and over who live within a 5-hour drive of Atlantic City." The emphasis of the campaign was not on gambling, but on "elevationism," which according to Revel meant "when you go to Revel, you experience something you've never experienced before—you feel elevated as a result of it. The TV, radio, print, and digital ads focused on presenting an elevated experience and featured the resorts, concerts, cabanas, beaches, and bonfires—all of the amenities except gambling. The campaign and resort was built "on the belief that the more fun we have, the more fun we have!"[17]

Segments Based on Generations

Many marketing efforts target generational cohorts, because the approach does not require the use of psychographic information but does possess some of the richness of psychographics. Marketing to generational cohorts relies on the common experiences and events that create bonds between people who are about the same age.

Generational segmentation proponents suggest that people experience significant events during late adolescence or early adulthood. These events create an impact on social values, attitudes, and preferences based on shared experiences. This may lead to common preferences for music, foods, and other products. A cohort group may respond favorably to the same type of marketing appeal. Figure 4.4 identifies six generational cohorts along with basic characteristics.

Millennials offer an attractive market segment. Some of the brands that have successfully reached millennials include Subway, Chick-fil-A, Chipotle, Panera Bread, Target, Gap, Playtex, and Hanes. Marketers for these brands understand the common characteristics of this segment. Millennials constitute a compassionate generation that prefers brands which support causes and the environment. Millennials enjoy connecting with brands through social media. Engagement and interaction are important. They want to be active participants with their favorite brands, not just passive customers. Being different is acceptable. These individuals tend to be more accepting of persons from every race, social class, and sexual orientation than those from any other generation. This acceptance transfers to brands. Brands can be different too, but should incorporate the multiculturalism now present in society.[18]

Segmentation by Geographic Area

Marketing appeals made to people in a geographic area or region is **geo-targeting**. Retailers often seek to limit marketing communications programs to specific areas where primary customers live in order to maximize the impact of advertising dollars. The increased ownership

FIGURE 4.4
Characteristics of Generation Segments

Name of Segment	Year of Birth	Characteristics
Millennials	1978–2002	Spend money on clothes, automobiles, college, televisions, and stereos. Ninety percent live at home or in a dorm or rent an apartment.
Generation X	1965–1977	Focus on family and children. Spend on food, housing, transportation, and personal services.
Younger Boomers	1954–1964	Focus on home and family. Spend on home mortgage, pets, toys, playground equipment, and large recreational items.
Older Boomers	1952–1953	Spend on upgrading homes, ensuring education and independence of their children, and luxury items, such as boats.
Seniors	Up to 1951	Most have fixed incomes. Spend heavily on health care and related medical items.

of smartphones with built-in GPS devices allows marketers to expand geo-targeting programs. For instance, during a snow storm along the East Coast, consumers in that area can receive Home Depot ads related to snow removal while other areas of the country get ads related to fall lawn care or other topics of relevance. With geo-targeting, advertisements can be aimed to specific regions with messages that fit consumers, the region, and specific events.

French Creative

▲ Med Camps of Louisiana can use geo-targeting to increase support for its work with disabled children.

Geodemographic Segmentation

Geodemographic segmentation identifies potential customers using demographic information, geographic information, and psychographic information. Geodemographic segmentation may be beneficial for national firms conducting direct-mail campaigns or using sampling promotions. Mailing a sample to every household in a geographic area can be expensive and unproductive. Through geodemographics, samples are only sent to households matching the profile of the target market. For instance, colleges and universities use geodemographics to locate ZIP codes of communities that match particular student profiles.

One firm, PRIZM (Potential Rating Index by Zip Marketing) specializes in geodemographics. PRIZM has identified 66 different market segments in the United States. The company has categorized every ZIP code in the United States. The PRIZM concept suggests that ZIP codes contain neighborhoods of people with relatively uniform characteristics. Consumers tend to be attracted to neighborhoods consisting of people who are similar to them. Recognizing that more than one market segment might live within a ZIP code, however, PRIZM identifies the top market segments within each ZIP code.[19]

A PRIZM-coded map of downtown Jackson, Mississippi, identifies two primary clusters. The more predominant is the "Southside City" residents. This cluster contains mainly young and elderly African Americans employed in low-paying blue-collar jobs. They tend to have lower levels of formal education, rent apartments, and read sports and fashion magazines. The second cluster within downtown Jackson holds the "Towns and Gowns" neighborhoods. Towns and Gowns inhabitants also rent apartments, but members tend to be college graduates with better-paying white-collar jobs. This group likes to ski, reads beauty and fitness magazines, and frequently uses ATM cards.[20]

Benefit Segmentation

Benefit segmentation focuses on the advantages consumers receive from a product rather than the characteristics of consumers themselves. Demographic and psychographic information can be combined with benefit information to identify viable segments.

Benefit segmentation appears in the fitness market. Regular exercisers belong in one of three benefit segments. The first group, "Winners," do whatever it takes to stay physically fit. This segment tends to be younger, upwardly mobile, and career-oriented. The second group, "Dieters," exercise to maintain their weight and enhance physical appearance. This group tends to contain females over the age of 35. They are primarily interested in reliable wellness programs offered by hospitals and weight-control nutritionists. The third group, "Self-Improvers," exercise to feel better and to control medical costs.[21] The understanding that individuals exercise for different reasons provides excellent material for designing marketing programs.

Usage Segmentation

The final type of consumer segmentation examines groups based on usage or purchases, including the company's best customers or heavy users, average users, casual or light customers, and nonusers. Marketers try to provide the highest level of service to the best customers while promoting the company to the other two usage groups in the attempt to move them up to the next usage group.

Marketing teams can identify heavy users through internal databases. Bar-code scanners; point-of-sale systems; and data from credit, debit, and in-house transaction cards provide marketers a wealth of information about customers. Many companies experience a situation in which 10 to 30 percent of a company's customers generate 70 to 90 percent of total sales. Instead of using firms such as PRIZM to create customer clusters, marketers develop customer clusters from in-house databases. Customers are then placed in clusters based on common attitudes, lifestyles, and past purchase behaviors. This technique offers a business the following advantages:[22]

Rheagan Sutton

▲ The fitness industry is often segmented based on the benefit each segment seeks from exercise.

1. A meaningful classification scheme to cluster customers based on a firm's various levels of users.
2. The ability to reduce large volumes of customer data down to a few concise, usable clusters.
3. The ability to assign a cluster code number to each customer in the database. Each number is based on the customer's actual purchases and other characteristics (e.g., address, amount spent, spending potential, demographics, etc.).
4. The capacity to measure the growth and migration of customers over time and from one cluster to another, which allows for the evaluation of marketing programs.
5. The ability to develop different marketing programs for each cluster that matches the characteristic of the clusters.

Instead of heavy users, Dairy Queen developed a campaign aimed at light users who visited only once a month and saw the brand as merely an ice cream stand. The tagline "Fan food, not fast food" was developed to encourage individuals to visit Dairy Queen instead of a competing fast-food restaurant. The idea behind the campaign was to bump that once-per-month visit to two or three visits per month. The messages featured ice cream as the bonus to great food.[23]

Occasionally, a company's marketing team will create a communications program for nonusers. For instance, a Carnival Cruise Lines campaign targeted the 76 percent of Americans who had never taken a cruise. A dozen humorous ads were prepared featuring the theme of "land versus sea." Scenes compared disastrous land vacations to peaceful and calm moments on the cruise ship. Along with the humorous scenes, the ads pointed out the prices were competitive with the costs of land vacations, seeking to dispel the belief that cruises are expensive. Passengers were shown in roomy cabins and

▼ Carnival Cruise Line created a campaign targeting the 76 percent of Americans who have never taken a cruise.

Andy Dean/Fotolia

relaxing on deck to change the perception that cruise rooms are small and cramped as well as that schedules were too structured to just relax and enjoy some private time.[24]

Business-to-Business Market Segmentation

objective 4.3
What categories are used to identify business-to-business market segments?

Another set of target markets may be found by identifying business-to-business market segments (see Figure 4.5). The primary goals of business segmentation efforts are to group similar organizations into meaningful clusters in order to provide better service.

- Industry (NAICS code)
- Size of business
- Geographic location
- Product usage
- Customer value

▲ **FIGURE 4.5**
Methods of Segmenting Business-to-Business Markets

Segmentation by Industry

When segmenting by industry, many marketers use the NAICS (North American Industry Classification System) coding system. NAICS allows the marketing team to examine specific industries such as construction (23) or wholesale trade (42). There are also segments within specific categories. For example, NAICS codes health care and social assistance services as 62. A manufacturer of health-related products may find four segments, based on these subsections:

621	Ambulatory Health Care Services
622	Hospitals
623	Nursing and Residential Care Facilities
624	Social Assistance

The segments can be broken down into smaller subcomponents. For example, Ambulatory Health Care Services includes physicians, dentists, chiropractors, and optometrists.

The NAICS system divides the economy into 20 broad sectors using a six-digit code. The six-digit code allows for stratification of industries and provides flexibility in creating classifications. The federal government records corporate information and data using the NAICS, making it a useful system for identifying market segments.

Segmentation by Size

Some market segments may be based on a company's sales volume or number of employees. Large firms with 100,000 employees experience needs that differ from mid-size firms and smaller companies employing 100 or fewer individuals. Marketing approaches vary based on the size of a target prospect. For instance, for a large prospect firm, a selling company may utilize the outside sales staff to make sales calls. For mid-size corporate prospects, outside sales people make contact after a company has shown initial interest through digital and telephone inquiries. For smaller firms, email and surface mail may be combined with inbound telemarketing. A salesperson would not make a sales call on the customer, because the revenue generated would be too small to warrant the expense.

▼ Scott Equipment's advertising team can use the NAICS code to target this advertisement to specific industries.

Scott and Cooner Inc./French Creative

Segmentation by Geographic Location

Identifying market segments by geographic location can be a successful tactic. The approach benefits businesses with customers concentrated in geographic pockets, such as the Silicon Valley area of California. It works for other firms as well.

When the Applied Microbiology firm developed a new antimicrobial agent, the goal was to market the product to dairy farmers. The traditional agricultural marketing and distribution channel required for a national launch was estimated to be $3 million. Such a traditional marketing plan involved national advertising in agriculture magazines plus recruiting sales agents and brokers to introduce the product. Instead, Applied Microbiology used geodemographics. The marketing team identified areas with dairy herds consisting of 1,000 or more cows per ranch. These farmers were contacted for two reasons. First, large dairy farmers who adopted the product would purchase greater quantities. Second, the company's leaders believed the larger farmers were the opinion leaders who could influence smaller farmers, thereby causing them to adopt the product as well.

Several separate direct-response pieces offering discounts for and samples of Applied Microbiology's new product were sent to larger farms. After sales started rising, the marketers asked farmers for testimonials. The most powerful testimonials were incorporated into new direct-marketing pieces. One brochure contained three testimonials and validation of the product by Cornell University. After a dairy farmer adopted the product, the company sent direct-marketing pieces to farmers in the surrounding area. The method yielded excellent sales figures and reduced marketing costs to one-third of the traditional approach. Using geodemographics, marketing costs were $1 million rather than the proposed $3 million, and sales increases were substantially higher.[25]

Courtesy of Reynolds Protection

▲ An advertisement for Reynolds Protection targeted to businesses requiring protection services.

Segmentation by Product Usage

Business markets can be segmented based on the manner in which companies use the good or service. Some services (financial, transportation, shipping, etc.) offer a variety of uses for distinct customers. For example, many times companies require protection services for various individuals. The Reynolds Protection advertisement featured in this section provides services for three different situations: hostile meetings, workplace threats, and employee terminations. The company also provides protection services in other circumstances. By segmenting the market based on the specific service needed, Reynolds can prepare marketing materials for the various client types.

Segmentation by Customer Value

One final method of business segmentation examines the value associated with each customer. Business-to-business firms are more likely to use this approach than consumer-oriented businesses due to the availability of in-depth data about each business customer. A more precise value can be assigned to each individual business through sales records and other sources of data and information, placing them into low-, medium-, and high-value groups.

In summary, consumer and business-to-business market segments can be identified in many ways. In choosing market segments to approach, a marketer looks for groups that best match the company's goods and services as well as the firm's overall message. The message can be structured to meet the needs of the various market segments and should be aligned with the company's positioning strategy.

Product Positioning

objective 4.4
How do the various approaches to positioning influence the IMC planning process?

Each target market or market segment will be selected, in part, because the company, product, or brand position matches the segment. **Product positioning** summarizes the perception in the consumer's mind of the nature of a company and its products relative to competitors. Positioning features variables such as the quality of products, the price, methods of distribution, packaging, image, and other factors. Typically, two elements stand out—customer perceptions of the product and the product's standing relative to the competition.

Consumers ultimately determine the position a product holds. Marketing programs attempt to help position the product or brand effectively. Marketing communications either reinforce what consumers already believe about a product and the brand or try to shift consumer views. The first outcome will be easier to accomplish. It also facilitates selection of target markets. When attempting to reposition a product, the marketing team considers whether the new position continues to match existing market segments.

Positioning enables companies such as Procter & Gamble, VF Corporation, Sara Lee Corporation, and Campbell's Soups to prevent cannibalism among various brands within a product category. Campbell's produces five different types of V8 juice. Each one targets a different market segment. Celestial Seasonings offers several types of tea, each one designed for a different set of consumers.

Approaches to Positioning

Effective positioning can be achieved in seven different ways (see Figure 4.6). Although companies might try two or three approaches, such efforts generally only manage to confuse customers. Normally, staying with one approach achieves the best results.

Product Attributes Any product trait or characteristic that sets a brand apart from other brands may be considered an attribute. Advertising for Dove Men+Care emphasized this concept by noting that the deodorant line contains moisturizers, which led to the tagline "Tough on sweat, not on skin." The Chickme advertisement shown on the next page features the idea that hummus comes in seven different flavor combinations.

Competitors Using competitors to establish position can be accomplished by contrasting the company's product against others. For years, Avis ran advertisements comparing itself to Hertz. Avis admitted it was not number one, but turned that position into an advantage because Avis was willing to "try harder" for business.

Use or Application Positioning that involves creating a memorable set of uses for a product emphasizes the use or application approach. Arm & Hammer has employed this approach for many years, seeking to convince consumers to use baking soda in other ways, such as a deodorizer in the refrigerator. Arm & Hammer is a co-brand in toothpaste, creating another use for the product and enhancing its position. Tide also employed this method with its revolutionary Tide pods. The pods took the guess work out of how much detergent to use. Consumers simply toss a pod into the washing machine.

Price–Quality Relationship Businesses that offer products at the extremes of the price range may position by price–quality relationships. At the high end, quality becomes the emphasis. At the low end, price or value is emphasized. Hallmark cards cost more but are for those who "only want to send the very best." Other firms seek to be a "low-price

FIGURE 4.6
Product Positioning Approaches

- Attributes
- Competitors
- Use or application
- Price–quality relationship
- Product user
- Product class
- Cultural symbol

leader," with no corresponding statement about quality. Instead of focusing solely on low prices, Wal-Mart's tagline "Save Money, Live Better" highlights the importance of price and how it can improve the customer's quality of life.

Product User Another positioning strategy distinguishes a brand or product by specifying who might use it. GoDaddy has shifted its approach in an effort to reach small-business owners. For these users, GoDaddy focuses on its products and services and seeks to create the image of being a helpmate. Swanson's marketers chose this positioning strategy for the company's line of broths. The messages focused on the cooking process rather than the end result. The goal was to reach the growing number of individuals who like to spend time in the kitchen cooking.[26]

Product Class Position can also be based on product class. In the beverage category, soft drinks compete with energy drinks and others, such as breakfast drinks. Recently, Denny's repositioned its restaurants as diners, because focus groups did not consider Denny's a family restaurant. According to Frances Allen, chief marketing officer for Denny's, "People think of the brand as a diner, with great comfort food at a great price, and they feel that incredible warmth and connection to the servers. There's a soul to a diner that is very authentic, very warm, and very accepting."[27]

Occasionally, a company creates a new brand in a product class designed to stress superiority such as was the case with Swiffer. The

Taylor Kemp

▲ This advertisement for Chickme hummus features a product attribute positioning approach.

Fiesta Nutrition Center

◀ This advertisement for Fiesta Nutrition Center focuses on health conscious consumers by using a product user positioning approach.

Swiffer Sweeper provides an alternative to traditional mopping of floors, sweeping floors with brooms, and dusting with feather dusters. Marketers identified the "Quick Clean" category and positioned Swiffer as the best brand within that category.

Cultural Symbol Positioning a product as a cultural symbol will be difficult. When the company successfully achieves such a position, it holds a strong competitive advantage. For many years, Chevrolet enjoyed such status. General Motors advertised Chevrolet with the theme of being as American as baseball and apple pie. A slight variation was recently utilized in a campaign for the Chevrolet Silverado pickup. The messages focused on American patriotism and values such as independence and commitment. The campaign was launched during baseball's All-Star game.

Other Elements of Positioning

A brand's position is never completely fixed. It can be altered if market conditions change over time or a brand's target market shrinks. Competitors can enter a market and usurp a brand's position. Company leaders must then decide whether to fight for the position through strong advertising or seek an alternate position.

International Positioning In the international arena, effective positioning remains vitally important. Marketers make plans to establish an effective position when the firm expands into new countries. Often the positioning strategy presented in one country will not work as well in another. Marketing experts investigate the competition as well as the consumers or businesses that are potential customers. Following this analysis, the marketing team chooses a positioning approach. Although the positioning strategy might need to be modified for each country, the company's overall theme and brand image should stay as consistent as possible.

Marketing Communications Objectives

objective 4.5
How do the marketing communications objectives interact with the other elements of an IMC planning process?

An effective IMC planning process requires quality communications objectives. These objectives tie the organization's context, target markets, and positioning approaches to the ultimate selection of budget figures and IMC components, as depicted in Figure 4.1. Further, communications objectives guide account executives and advertising creatives in designing the actual advertising messages.

Communications objectives are derived from overall marketing objectives. Marketing objectives tend to be general because they are for the entire company. Some examples of marketing objectives include:

- Sales volume
- Market share
- Profits
- Return on investment

In contrast, a communications plan may emphasize a specific communications objective. Figure 4.7 identifies some common objectives. A large firm may establish

▸ FIGURE 4.7
Communications Objectives

- Develop brand awareness
- Increase category demand
- Change customer beliefs or attitudes
- Enhance purchase actions
- Encourage repeat purchases
- Build customer traffic
- Enhance firm image
- Increase market share
- Increase sales
- Reinforce purchase decisions

Newcomer, Morris and Young Inc.

◀ Benchmark measures can provide Ouachita Independent Bank's marketing team with an indication of the success of the advertising campaign.

different objectives for each brand within a product portfolio. Oftentimes, a communications plan for an individual brand emphasizes a single objective.

Some advertising message programs can accomplish more than one communications objective at a time. This occurs when logical combinations of communications objectives are identified. For example, the same advertisement can develop brand awareness and enhance a brand's image. Increasing sales can be accomplished through price changes, contests, or coupons. Matching the objective to the medium and the message remains the key.

Many marketing professionals believe that benchmarks are helpful tools. A **benchmark measure** establishes a starting point to be compared with the degree of change following a promotional campaign. In other words, the benchmark constitutes the baseline from which future outcomes can be assessed.

When market research revealed that a dry cleaning company's name was only known by 20 percent of the community's population and that the company held a three percent share of the city's total market, a benchmark was present. In response, the primary communications objective for the next advertising cycle became to increase awareness and market share to 30 percent awareness and a five percent share. Then a campaign featuring advertisements, coupons, and discounts for certain days of the week (Tuesday specials) and to senior citizens was designed by establishing a budget that matched these IMC components. If the company achieved the desired target, it would indicate a level of success based on the previously specified benchmarks.

Types of Budgets

objective 4.6

How are communications budgets established?

A communications budget can be prepared in a number of different ways. Figure 4.8 provides a list of the various methods.[28]

- Percentage of sales
- Meet the competition
- "What we can afford"
- Objective and task
- Payout planning
- Quantitative models

▲ **FIGURE 4.8**
Methods of Determining a Marketing Communications Budget

Percentage of Sales

In a **percentage-of-sales budget**, allocations are derived from either sales from the previous year or anticipated sales for the next year. This method offers simplicity in preparing the budget.

The approach also encounters problems. First, it tends to change in the opposite direction of what is typically needed; that is, when sales go up, so does the communications budget. When sales decline, the communications budget also declines. In most cases, when sales decline, the communications budget should be increased to help reverse the trend. Further, during growth periods, the communications budget may not need to be increased. The method also experiences the disadvantage of failing to allocate money for

FIGURE 4.9
Ad Spending, Brand Recognition, and Market Share of Top Auto Insurance Companies

Auto Insurer	Ad Spending (millions)	Brand Recognition	Market Share
Geico	$600	98%	8.2%
Progressive	$506	92%	7.5%
State Farm	$455	76%	18.6%
Allstate	$369	63%	10.5%
Farmers	$203	59%	6.4%

special needs or to combat competitive pressures. Therefore, many marketing experts believe the disadvantages of the percentage of sales method tend to outweigh its advantages.

Meet the Competition

A **meet-the-competition budget** seeks to prevent loss of market share. Companies raise or lower expenditures to match those of the competition. This format may be found in highly competitive markets in which intense rivalries exist between competitors.

The potential drawback to meet-the-competition budgeting is that marketing dollars might not be spent efficiently. Matching the competition's spending does not guarantee success. Market share can still be lost. Rather than *how much* is spent, *how well* money has been allocated and how effectively the marketing campaign works at retaining customers and market share is the key.

Expenditures for advertising in the auto insurance industry have grown dramatically in the last decade and now exceed $5 billion per year. Each company encounters pressures to increase its advertising budget to match the competition, because the level of brand recognition often corresponds with the level of spending. Market share, however may not be affected quite as much since exposure and recognition of an insurance brand do not always equate to purchases. It takes time. Figure 4.9 displays the level of spending of the top five insurance companies, the level of brand recognition, and the market share.[29]

"What We Can Afford"

A **"what we can afford" budget** sets the marketing allotment after all of the company's other budgets have been established or while determining other budgets. Company leaders allocate money based on what they feel can be spent. Use of this method suggests that management may not fully recognize the benefits of marketing communications. Instead, company leaders view marketing expenditures as non-revenue-generating activities. Newer and smaller companies with limited finances often employ the "what we can afford" approach.

Objective and Task

To prepare an **objective-and-task budget**, management identifies the communications objectives to pursue during the year and then calculates the cost of accomplishing each objective. The communications budget represents the cumulative sum of the estimated costs for all objectives.

Many marketing experts believe that the objective-and-task method represents the best budgeting approach, because it relates dollar costs to achieving specific objectives; however, a large company, such as Procter & Gamble, may find it difficult to apply. With hundreds of products on the market, producing a budget based on objectives for each brand and product category is time consuming. Despite these challenges, about 50 percent of major firms use some form of the objective-and-task method.[30]

Payout Planning

With a **payout-planning budget**, management establishes a ratio of advertising to sales or market share. This method normally allocates greater amounts in early years to yield payouts in later years.[31] Allocating larger amounts at the beginning of a new product introduction helps build brand awareness and brand equity. As the brand becomes accepted and sales build, a lower percentage of advertising dollars will be required in order to maintain a target growth.

Quantitative Models

In some instances, computer simulations can be developed to model the relationship between advertising or promotional expenditures with sales and profits. These models are far from perfect. They do offer the advantage of accounting for the type of industry and product in the model. In most cases, quantitative models are limited to larger organizations with strong computer and statistics departments.

Therefore, as the marketing team constructs a budget, the assumptions that drive the process should be considered. The newness of the product, the economy, and other complicating factors should be reviewed when attempting to tie budgeting expenditures to marketing and communications objectives. A budget becomes finalized when the company marketing team specifies how funds will be spent on each of the major communications tools.

Communications Schedules After establishing the total amount of dollars to be allocated to marketing communications, the next step is to choose the proper schedule approach to reach the communications goal. Marketers emphasize one of three basic tactics to allocate communication funds:

- Pulsating schedule
- Flighting schedule
- Continuous schedule

A **pulsating schedule** involves continuous advertising and communications during the year with bursts of higher intensity at specific times (more ads in more media). Companies can also select a **flighting schedule** or approach, whereby communications are presented only during peak times and not at all during other times of the year.

Firms often advertise more during peak seasons such as Christmas, seeking to send messages during the times when customers are most inclined to buy, or when they are *on the hot spot*. Weight Watchers, Diet Centers, and others advertise heavily during the first weeks of January. Many New Year's resolutions include going on a diet.

Marketing communications during slow sales seasons focuses on "drumming up business" when people do not regularly buy. In retail sales, slow seasons occur during January and February. Some companies advertise more during these months to sell merchandise left over from the Christmas season and to encourage customers to shop. Manufacturers also realize that many retailers are not advertising and hope that the ads will capture greater attention as a result.

Many marketing experts believe spending in level amounts keeps the brand name repetitively in front of consumers, which is a **continuous campaign schedule**. Consumers purchase durable goods, such as dishwashers and refrigerators, on an "as needed" basis. A family ordinarily buys a new dishwasher only when the old one breaks down or when they build or remodel a home. Level

▼ A pulsating advertising schedule might be used to promote dark chocolate Philadelphia Cream Cheese, with a burst during the Christmas season.

Kraft Foods, Inc.

advertising increases the odds that the buyer will see an advertisement or remember a given name (Kenmore, Whirlpool, or General Electric) at the right time.

Matching the pacing of communications with the message, the media, and the nature of the product should be the objective. Some media make it easier to advertise for longer periods of time. Contracts for billboards are normally for a month or a year. They can be rotated throughout a town or city to present a continuing message. At the same time, budgetary constraints can influence the strategies and tactics deployed in any advertising or communications program.

IMC Components

objective 4.7
What elements are considered in developing an IMC program?

As has been noted, marketing communications consists of much more than traditional advertising. In fact, advertising expenditures may not make up the major portion of a marketing communications budget. In terms of dollars spent, media advertising normally accounts for about 41 percent of a marketing communications budget. Trade promotions receive about 28 percent and consumer promotions average about 28 percent of overall marketing expenditures (see Figure 4.10).[32] These percentages vary considerably from industry to industry. Consumer product manufacturers spend more on trade promotions directed toward retailers. Service companies tend to favor media advertising.

Budgets also vary by product type. For example, for dolls and stuffed toys, the average expenditure on media advertising as a percentage of sales is 11.2 percent, whereas for men's clothing, expenditures on media advertising represent only 3.3 percent of sales.[33]

Selecting IMC components and media takes place in conjunction with preparation of the budget. Figure 4.11 highlights the ways global advertising dollars are allocated among various media. Television ranks first, primarily because of the high cost of advertising time. Although digital expenditures represent only 4.3 percent of total global ad spending, they are the fastest-growing component.[34]

Choosing the best IMC components remains a challenge. A company's marketing personnel will work with its external agencies to analyze the firm's target audience, communications objectives, and budget to determine the optimal media mix.

International Implications

Globally integrated marketing communications (GIMC) programs are vital for international firms. Each message should fit a country's language and culture. Brand names, marketing ideas, and advertising campaigns designed for one country do not always

▶ **FIGURE 4.10**
Breakdown of Marketing Communications Expenditures

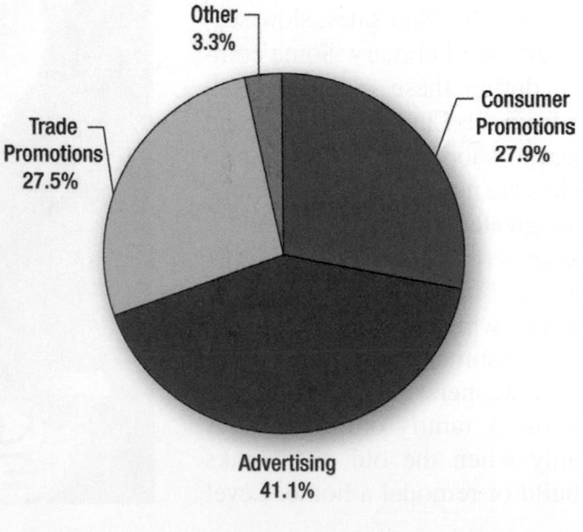

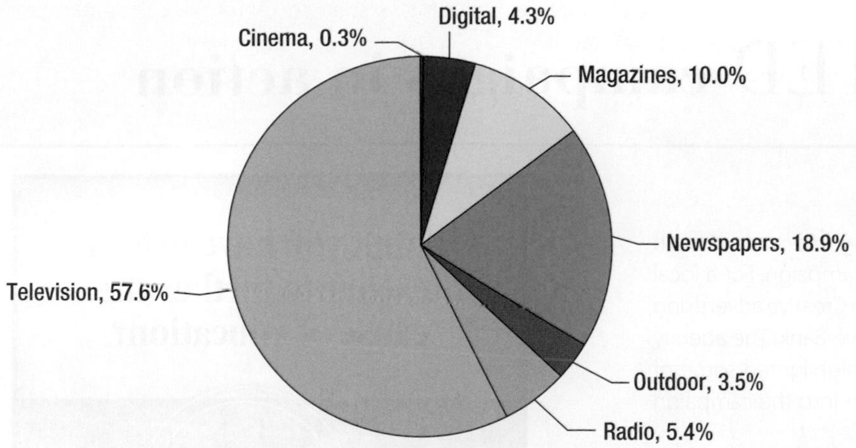

FIGURE 4.11
Global Ad Spending by Media

translate correctly to another. Consequently, understanding the international market is essential. Figure 4.12 highlights the ingredients of successful GIMC plans.

Marketing campaigns do not necessarily require a unique program for each country and every cultural group within a country. Marketers try to make sure the company's products and marketing messages will be *understood in the region*. When needed, the message can be tailored to an individual area. The goal is to *create a borderless marketing plan* that uses the same basic marketing approach for all of a company's markets. This allows each subsidiary the freedom to determine how to implement that marketing plan, in essence, to *think globally but act locally*. It also presents the opportunity to maintain a theme while targeting the message to a given region.

Another key to a successful GIMC is developing *local partnerships*. Local partners can be marketing research firms or advertising firms that are familiar with the local language and culture. *Communication segmentation* means creating a communications package that effectively reaches all possible target markets in another country. Many times, both consumer and business-to-business segments are present. A well-designed *market communications analysis* begins with the marketing team identifying strengths and weaknesses of local competitors and places in which opportunities exist. They must also develop an understanding of how the firm is perceived in the international marketplace.

Finally, *solid communications objectives* should be established. Linguistics represents one major hurdle. Translating an English advertisement into another language requires expertise, because exact word translations often do not exist. For example, the slogan of Ruth's Steak House, "We sell sizzle as well as steaks," could not be translated into Spanish, because there is no equivalent word for "sizzle." Therefore, the translator found a Spanish idiom conveying a similar meaning in order to solve the problem.

The IMC planning process becomes more complicated in international settings; however, it is crucial in creating an effective GIMC. Language, culture, norms, beliefs, and laws are all taken into consideration. Literal translation of a commercial's tagline might not be acceptable within a given culture. Laws concerning advertising and promotions vary by country. Cultures view ideas and objects differently. These differences should be considered when designing a communications program.

- Understand the international market
- Create a borderless marketing plan
- Think globally but act locally
- Local partnerships
- Communication segmentation strategies
- Market communications analysis
- Solid communications objectives

FIGURE 4.12
Successful Globally Integrated Marketing Tactics

INTEGRATED campaigns in action

Progressive Bank

Banks operate in a competitive market. Making one standout can be difficult, especially through an advertising campaign. For a local bank, it becomes even more challenging. French Creative advertising agency accepted this challenge with Progressive Bank. The agency developed a unique campaign that not only highlighted some of the bank's strengths but also brought a human into the campaign to make the bank personal.

Information about the Progressive Bank campaign is available at the Pearson Instructor's Resource Center (www.pearsonhighered.com). The campaigns feature PowerPoint presentations outlining the details of the campaigns and examples of the collateral developed by each of the advertising agencies.

Newcomer, Morris and Young Inc.

Summary

A marketing communications planning program will often be based on information derived from communications research. Product-specific, customer-oriented, and target market research assist marketers in understanding the ways in which products are viewed and purchased. When the analysis is complete, target markets may be selected in conjunction with product-positioning tactics.

Market segmentation identifies sets of business or consumer groups with distinct characteristics. Segments must be clearly different, large enough to support a marketing campaign, and reachable through some type of media. Consumer groups that can be segmented include those identified by demographics, including gender, age, income, and ethnicity. Markets can also be identified using psychographic, generational, and geographic delineations. Geodemographic segmentation combines demographic, psychographic, and geographic information together. Other ways to categorize consumers are by the benefits they receive from goods or services and by the ways they use products.

Business-to-business segmentation can be accomplished by targeting business customers by industry, business type, the size of the company, geographic location, usage, and customer-value calculations. Marketing managers specify the company's consumer and business market segments. All other promotions opportunity analysis processes are tied to the identification of key customers.

Product positioning represents the perceptions in consumer minds of the nature of a company and its products relative to the competition. Positioning may be based on product attributes, competitors, product uses or applications, the price–quality relationship, product class, or through the association with a cultural symbol.

Marketing objectives lead to the development of communications objectives that are matched to the product, target market, and product positioning. These objectives form the basis for developing communications budgets and selecting IMC components for actual marketing campaigns.

Globally integrated marketing communications efforts are guided by the IMC planning process. National differences, cultural concerns, language issues, and other challenges must be viewed in light of the target markets an individual company intends to serve.

Key Terms

product-specific research A form of communications research that seeks to identify key product characteristics that become selling points

customer-oriented research A form of communications research that seeks to discover the context of a product's use through anthropological, sociological, or psychological analysis

target-market research A form of communications research that identifies the recipients of a planned communications campaign

market segment A set of businesses or group of individual customers with distinct characteristics

market segmentation Identifying specific groups (target markets) based on their needs, attitudes, and interests

demographics Population characteristics such as gender, age, educational levels, income, and ethnicity

psychographics Patterns of responses that reveal a person's activities, interests, and opinions (AIO)

geo-targeting Marketing appeals made to people in a geographic area or region

product positioning The perception in the consumer's mind of the nature of a company and its products relative to the competition

benchmark measures Starting points that are studied in relation to the degree of change following a promotional campaign

percentage-of-sales budget A form of communications budgeting in which budgeting is based on sales from the previous year or anticipated sales for the next year

meet-the-competition budget A communications budget in which expenditures are raised or lowered to match the competition

"what we can afford" budget A communications budget that is set after all of the company's other budgets have been determined or while the other budgets are set and communications money is allocated based on what company leaders feels they can afford to spend

objective-and-task budget A communications budget in which management first lists all of the communications objectives to pursue during the year and then calculates the cost of accomplishing those objectives

payout-planning budget A budgeting method that establishes a ratio of advertising to sales or market share

pulsating schedule An advertising program that is continuous throughout the year with bursts of higher intensity at specific times

flighting schedule An advertising schedule in which communications are present only at peak times during the year

continuous campaign schedule An advertising schedule that involves level amounts of spending and messages throughout the year

MyMarketingLab

Go to **mymktlab.com** to complete the problems marked with this icon ✪.

Review Questions

4-1. What three forms of market research are used to develop marketing communications?

4-2. What is involved in product-specific research? How can it be used?

4-3. Define market segment and market segmentation.

4-4. What are the three approaches for consumer-orientated research?

4-5. In marketing terms, how do male preferences differ from female preferences?

4-6. What does a "homogenous segment" mean?

4-7. How does income and education link together in segmentation?

4-8. List all of the segments of the VALS typology.

4-9. What are the views of generation segmentation supporters?

4-10. Describe usage segmentation and benefit segmentation.

4-11. What are the common business-to-business market segments?

4-12. Describe the NAICS approach to business market segmentation.

4-13. Describe a usage segmentation approach in a business-to-business setting.

4-14. Describe a segmentation approach based on company size.

4-15. Define product positioning and identify the types of positioning approaches that can be used in the IMC planning process.

4-16. What is a benchmark measure?

4-17. What common marketing communications objectives do firms establish?

4-18. Describe the methods that can be used to establish a communications budget.

4-19. Describe the three types of advertising schedules that may be used during the course of a year.

4-20. Which IMC components are more likely to be used in business-to-business marketing communications programs, as compared to consumer markets?

Critical Thinking Exercises

DISCUSSION QUESTIONS

4-21. Think about your regular purchases. Are all of them targeted at consumers of your age and with your general profile? Are some of the products atypical for your profile?

4-22. In some societies traditional forms of entertainment still thrive and attract new generations of fans and followers. In other societies these forms of entertainment have all but died out. Conduct some research amongst your friends and fellow students and find out whether traditional entertainment still appeals to them. It may be the case that the traditional forms of entertainment have been modernized and that they still have a broader relevance than would be expected.

4-23. Make a list of five consumer goods or services segmented on the basis of gender but sold to both genders. Are there any differences in the product or service attributes? Are there differences in how they are marketed? What are those differences? Do you think using a different marketing approach has worked?

4-24. Make a list of five consumer goods or services segmented on the basis of age. Are there actual differences in the product or service attributes? Are there differences in how they are marketed? What are those differences? Do you think using a different marketing approach has worked?

4-25. Examine the list of demographic segmentation variables. For each demographic variable listed in the text, identify two products that are marketed to a specific demographic segment. Identify the specific demographic segment and explain why the product is aimed at that particular market segment. Identify one brand that has been especially successful at reaching a specific demographic segment.

4-26. For each of the following goods or services, identify the various benefits that consumers may derive from the good or service. Can you think of an advertisement or marketing communication that has featured the benefit as the central part of the appeal?

a. Seafood restaurants
b. Auto insurance
c. Optometrist or eye-care clinics
d. Soft drinks
e. Aspirin or other pain relievers

4-27. Usage segmentation targets heavy users, average users, light users or nonusers. Describe campaigns for each of the usage segments by tanning salon. In your discussion, identify the best communications objective for each of the campaigns and the product positioning strategy that you would use for each segment. Justify your decisions.

4-28. For each of the product-positioning strategies discussed in this chapter, identify two brands that feature the strategy and explain how the strategy is used to successfully market the brand.

4-29. Locate five ads in a magazine. Either tear out the ads or scan them. For each ad, identify the target market of the ad, the communications objective, and the product-positioning strategy you think is being used.

Integrated Learning Exercises

4-30. Use a search engine to locate five companies on the internet that sell swimwear. For each company, discuss the types of products sold, the types of promotional appeals used, and the types of special offers used to entice buyers. From looking at each website, describe the target market you think the company is trying to reach. Of the five companies, which one do you think does the best job of marketing itself? Why?

4-31. A brand's product positioning strategy should be an integral part of the company's advertising and marketing strategy, including its website. Examine the following websites and identify the product-positioning strategy you think is being used. Explain your answer.

a. Polaris (**www.polaris.com**)
b. Edgewater Beach & Golf Resort (**www.edgewaterbeachresort.com**)
c. Celestial Seasonings (**www.celestialseasonings.com**)
d. Sony (**www.sony.com**)
e. Stetson cologne (**www.stetsoncologne.com**)

4-32. VALS psychographic segmentation can be a valuable tool for marketers as they prepare their marketing materials. Access VALS through the Strategic Business Insights (SBI) website at **www.strategicbusinessinsights.com/vals** and examine the characteristics of each of the groups. Then take the test to determine which group you belong to. How can VALS help marketers develop advertising messages?

4-33. Global websites with local content are essential for global organizations. Each country or region not only has its own distinctive language or culture, but it may also favor a specific mix of the organization's products and services. This issue becomes even more complex when several languages are spokcn in the same country or region. Investigate these Malaysian organizations and comment on how they have handled it.

a. Lelong (**www.lelong.com.my**)
b. Citizen Infonet (**www.cari.com.my**)
c. Air Asia (**www.airasia.com**)

4-34. Choose two of the following companies. Examine the company's website to determine what segmentation strategy the firm uses. Describe the intended target market for the website. What communications objective(s) do you think the company is trying to accomplish? What product-positioning strategy is being used? Explain your responses.

a. Sports Spectrum Greeting Cards (**www.sportsgreetingcards.com**)
b. Ty Beanie Babies (**www.ty.com**)
c. Sara Lee Desserts (**http://saraleedesserts.com**)
d. Skeeter boats (**www.skeeterboats.com**)
e. Gold Bond (**www.goldbond.com**)

Blog Exercises

Access the authors' blog for this textbook at the URLs provided to complete these exercises. Answer the questions posed on the blog.

4-35. Motel 6: **http://blogclowbaack.net/2014/05/05/motel-6-chapter-4/**

4-36. Carnival Cruise Line: **http://blogclowbaack.net/2014/05/05/carnival-cruise-line-chapter-4/**

4-37. Segmentation and positioning: **http://blogclowbaack.net/2014/05/05/segmentation-and-positioning-chapter-4/**

Student Project

CREATIVE CORNER

A number of companies and advertising agencies use the VALS typology to create marketing materials. Your task is to design two advertisements for Yamaha boats. Pick one of the following pairs of VALS segments and design an advertisement promoting Yamaha for each segment. When you are finished, write a paragraph explaining how the ads you created will appeal to their respective VALS segment and how the two ads are different. Before you begin work on the ads, go to the Strategic Business Insights (SBI) website at **www.strategicbusinessinsights.com/vals** to obtain more information about the two segments you will be targeting with your ads.

Pair 1: Innovators and Survivors
Pair 2: Thinkers and Makers
Pair 3: Believers and Achievers
Pair 4: Strivers and Experiencers

CASE 1 THE JAPANESE STEAKHOUSE EXPERIENCE

Hiroaki Rocky Aoki founded the first Benihana restaurant in New York in 1964. His innovative approach to dining featured an authentic Japanese farmhouse interior. Food preparation took place in front of customers on steel cooking grills. Chefs were taught to be entertaining, engaging employees with fascinating knife skills and a flair for the dramatic, including the use of fire as part of the show. A famous restaurant critic at the time, Clementine Paddleford wrote a raving, positive review in a local newspaper and the business grew dramatically as a result. Soon after, a second location was added in New York.

By 1972, six Benihana locations were opened across the United States. Currently more than 70 restaurants are active, with franchising possibilities offered to others. The chain has expanded to include locations in other countries as well and has acquired three other restaurant chains, HARU, RA Sushi, and Rudy's Restaurant Group.

The success of the original Benihana concept can be explained in part by the unique dining experience the company was first to offer. Groups of up to eight individuals are combined in each serving area, which means smaller sets, such as couples, often share the food preparation activities with other guests.

Lester120/Fotolia

▲ Benihana offers diners a unique dining experience.

Benihana currently holds the title of the longest running dinner show in the world.[36]

Not surprisingly, a series of entrepreneurs has jumped on the bandwagon and created similar dining programs. Some have developed chains of restaurants while others offer single locations in various cities in the United States.

The concept of combining food preparation, dining, and entertainment is not limited to Japanese steakhouse-type organizations. A series of restaurants features singing waiters. Missouri-based Lambert's Café sells "throwed rolls" that the servers literally toss at patrons. To achieve success, one key appears to be creating a logical combination of the entertainment program with the food to be served.

At the same time, other elements deserve attention, including the colors chosen for the restaurant's décor. For example, the Logo Company states that green suggests something "natural, organic, youth, nurturing, (and) instructional…" among others. Green fits with medicine, science, government, and ecology, but maybe not food (think mold). Orange generates cheerfulness, red creates excitement, gold conjures images of warmth, and blue suggests dependability and strength.[37]

Colors combine with music, furniture, server outfits, and many other ingredients in order to construct a total dining experience. Then, marketing communications can be added to the mix. Focus groups and other forms of research help the marketing team discover if all of the elements work together. Eventually, a company name, logo, and an advertising program can be designed to entice patrons to try something new and different.

4-38. Which consumer market segments best match with Benihana?

4-39. Explain the positioning approach used by Benihana.

4-40. If you were assigned to create a competitor restaurant that prepared and served Japanese-style hibachi meals, which colors would you choose for the restaurant? What type of music should be played? What other features should be key parts of the interior of the restaurant? How would you differentiate the restaurant from Benihana and other similar chains?

4-41. For the same competitor restaurant, assume that it has only one location in Seattle, Washington. Design an advertising campaign and identify the types of media that would reach your target market and create the right positioning.

4-42. The color red holds special meaning in Asian culture as a symbol of celebration. Consequently, red is featured in much of Benihana's marketing materials. Which colors would match other restaurant types such as fried chicken, fast food hamburgers, or pizza parlors? Would your answer be different if the food were to be sold in other countries? Why or why not?

CASE 2 PLATINUM MOTORCARS: MARKET SEGMENTATION AND REPEAT PURCHASES

Benny Black drove up to his Platinum Motorcars location to begin another day's work in his 1997 Mercury Sable with 198,000 miles on the odometer. He calls the car, which he purchased on craigslist, "Goldie." Benny doesn't believe in using his own money to buy and drive fancy cars.

At the same time, he wore a high-end black suit. As he explained, "I'm always going to be dressed to the nines. I always have the matching pocket square with the same color tie. I'm letting you know where my brand is. I'm not going to be cheap. You know that right from the get-go. You know it's going to be expensive, but you're going to get the value in what it is that you're trying to do."

Platinum Motorcars grew out of a unique entrepreneurial experience. Benny said, "I had 2 years of experience in the limo business. I told the wife one day that I wanted to start a limo company. I always had the affinity for wanting to serve people of wealth, with means, because I thought, 'If you can serve the masses, great, but if you can find a niche, and just reach a certain type of clientele, I always thought the easy one would be people with money.' My motto has always been 'a rich man will always be rich.' That's the ones you want to try to get to."

He continued, "I had that (limo service) for 2 years. I had already built a clientele base, but I thought there was too much competition, because I wasn't using my own limousine. What I was doing was borrowing a limo from my friends, pay them for the limo, get paid for my time, and then just try to give that great service to the client.

"I had to figure out a different way. I could utilize the same clientele but in something that nobody else is doing. So that's

Courtesy of Platinum Motor Cars

▲ Benny Black turned his vision into a lucrative exotic car rental business.

where I had the idea that I needed to figure out how I can drive nice cars and not have to pay for them.

"My biggest catalyst for that was that I got a call from one of the larger hotels, and they had a ballplayer in town that wanted to be driven around in a limousine. I picked him up, and while I was driving I actually said to him, 'If you ever need a nice car while you're in Dallas, let me see what I can do for you.'

"And he said, 'Can you get me a Bentley tomorrow after the game?' This was in 2000.

"So I said, 'Yeah, I think I can make that happen.' I just got on the phone with some of the clients I'd been servicing, I called one client in particular and I said, 'I need to borrow one of your Bentleys.'

"They said, 'What have you got going on?'

"I said, 'I've got an athlete that wants to rent one to drive tomorrow after the game.'

"He said, 'What will you give me?'

"I said, 'I'll give you a thousand.'

"He said, 'Give me a thousand and an autographed jersey, and it's yours.'"

Benny completed the deal, making a handsome profit.

From there, Black developed the business model that has expanded to include rental services for high-end luxury vehicles, chauffeur services, and sales/leasing arrangements. His exotic rental cars include Aston Martin, Bentley, Rolls Royce, Ferrari, and Lamborghini. Sports cars are also available with Mercedes, BMW, Porsche, and Maserati vehicles for rent.

Renters must meet high standards, including a $1,000 hold on a credit card, a $250 nonrefundable reservation fee, proof of insurance, and a significant charge for cancellation. Drivers must be 25 years old for some cars and over 30 for others. Platinum Motorcars serves an impressive client list, including major sports stars, celebrities, local business leaders, and even foreign dignitaries and tourists. As Black puts it, "I became 'The Exotic Car Guy.' I'm the guy you call when you come into Dallas. My tagline is 'We provide the lifestyle you deserve.'"

Bennie noted that several similar auto rental businesses had come and gone in the Dallas area. His explanation was that the businesses catered to people who would drive a luxury car as a "once in a lifetime experience" such as for a prom, wedding, or some other major event. Instead, his company focuses on individuals who might desire a luxury driving experience on an ongoing (even if sporadic) basis. These customers, rather than buying a single car, are able to rent from a wide selection for various events during the course of the year, including simply taking a weekend to drive a luxury vehicle.

Through connections with a variety of people of wealth, including the "new" and the "old" rich, and effective combinations of the internet, social media, word-of-mouth, and exciting events and offers, the future looks bright for Benny Black and Platinum Motorcars. Most recently, the company expanded to a second location using the same marketing and business model.[38]

4-43. Define the consumer market segments served by Platinum Motorcars. Define the potential business-to-business market segments Platinum Motorcars could serve.

4-44. Explain the product positioning of the Platinum Motorcars rental service.

4-45. Using the internet, locate Platinum Motorcars. What new businesses has the company entered? Do these make sense given the company's target markets and product positioning? Defend your answer.

4-46. Consider Benny's target market of individuals who could afford to purchase one of his exotic cars but realizes the investment is not wise for the few times they would drive it. Design a print ad for the Dallas magazine aimed at individuals with incomes of $300,000 plus.

MyMarketingLab

Go to **mymktlab.com** for the following Assisted-graded writing questions:

4-47. Pick a product you have recently purchased and that you have considerable knowledge about. Conduct a context analysis. Examine the customers, competition, and communications of the product and brand.

4-48. Use a search engine to locate five companies on the internet that sell swimwear. For each company, discuss the types of products sold, the types of promotional appeals used, and the types of special offers used to entice buyers. From looking at each website, describe the type of customer you think the company is trying to reach. Of the five companies, which one do you think does the best job of marketing itself? Why?

Part 2

IMC ADVERTISING TOOLS

Chapter 5 Advertising Campaign Management

Chapter Objectives

After reading this chapter, you should be able to answer the following questions:

5.1 Why is an understanding of advertising theories important in the advertising management process?

5.2 What is the relationship of advertising expenditures to advertising effectiveness?

5.3 When should a company employ an external advertising agency rather than completing the work in-house?

5.4 How do companies choose advertising agencies?

5.5 What are the primary job functions within an advertising agency?

5.6 What are the advertising campaign parameters that should be considered?

5.7 How does a creative brief facilitate effective advertising?

5.8 What are the implications of advertising management in the global arena?

Overview

The average person encounters more than 600 advertisements per day, delivered by an expanding variety of media. Television and radio have long been the advertising staples, along with newspapers, magazines, and billboards. More recently, internet advertisements, social networks, and mobile phones apps offer additional venues to contact and interact with customers.

Today's marketers face several challenges. A company simply cannot afford to prepare advertisements for every medium. Further, each message should create a marketing advantage in a highly cluttered world in which people are increasingly adept at simply tuning ads out. **Advertising campaign management** is the process of preparing and integrating a specific advertising program in conjunction with the overall IMC message. One advertising agency that has achieved success in advertising campaign management is Zehnder Communications. Some of the agency's ads are featured in this textbook.

ZEHNDER COMMUNICATIONS

Courtesy of Zehnder Communications

▲ Lobby of Zehnder Communications.

Zehnder Communications provides a variety of services, including strategic planning, creative, web and application development, media, public relations, and social media. The company also provides research and analytics services for clients. As stated on the company's website, "We have a unique situation at Zehnder in that we are a full-service agency that continually challenges traditional thinking."

Zehnder's client list includes Visit South Walton (Florida), Visit Baton Rouge, Burger King, Community Trust Bank, Gulf Seafood Marketing Coalition, NOLA.com/The Times Picayune, along with many others. The firm specializes in the Advocacy, Attractions/Entertainment, Automotive, Energy Services, Financial Services, Food and Beverage, Healthcare, Hospitality/Tourism, and Insurance industries.

Zehnder states, "As experts, it's not enough that we remain well versed in new media trends. We owe it to our clients to remain at the forefront of innovation, dedicated to developing new ways to reach the consumer. That's what it all comes down to—connecting with your audience through all available means. Innovation and campaign integration mean nothing unless you can make that connection which changes perception and ultimately behavior."

Zehnder has been listed as a "best place to work" in the area for more than 12 consecutive years. One innovation developed by founder Jeffrey Zehnder is the VAN ("Vacation as Needed") system. The firm allows employees to take time off when they feel it is appropriate, so long as doing so does not interfere with or slow down the activities of other employees. The sense of freedom and empowerment that results helps build morale over time.

Zehnder Communications provides a quality example of the nature of advertising in today's complicated marketplace. This section of the textbook describes the role advertising plays in an integrated marketing communications program. Figure 5.1 portrays the overall IMC approach. The three chapters in this section focus on developing an effective integrated advertising program. This chapter explains advertising management, which lays the groundwork for the total advertising campaign program. Chapter 6 reviews advertising design issues including the message strategy, appeals, executions, and the use of spokespersons. Chapter 7 presents traditional media that can be used for advertising. While the use of social media and digital media are growing, traditional media remain vital for the advertising of most brands.

▼ Zehnder has been listed as a "best place to work" for more than 12 consecutive years.

Courtesy of Zehnder Communications

Advertising management consists of several important activities. First, those involved decide on an advertising

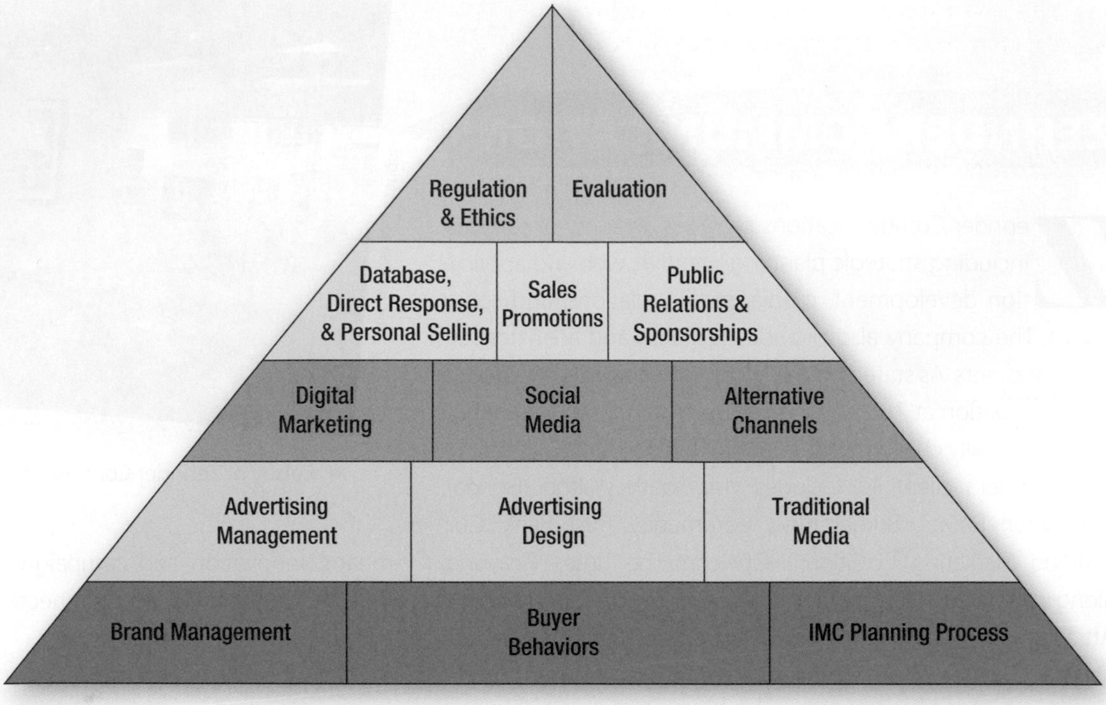

▲ **FIGURE 5.1**
Overview of Integrated Marketing Communications

theory or approach to guide the process. Next, company leaders develop guidelines that help everyone understand the relationship of advertising to eventual success. Then, the company's management team decides whether to complete advertising work as an in-house activity or in conjunction with an advertising agency. Advertising parameters are generated to help control the process. A creative brief will then be prepared to direct the actual design of the advertising campaign. This chapter concludes with an examination of the international implications of these activities.

Advertising Theory

objective 5.1
Why is an understanding of advertising theories important in the advertising management process?

In developing an advertising campaign, two theoretical approaches provide a solid foundation. The hierarchy of effects model and a means–end chain can assist in developing effective campaigns. Advertisers also consider the mix of visual and verbal elements in a commercial or advertisement.

Hierarchy of Effects

The **hierarchy of effects model** helps to clarify the objectives of an advertising campaign. The model outlines six steps a consumer or a business buyer moves through when making a purchase:

1. Awareness
2. Knowledge
3. Liking
4. Preference
5. Conviction
6. The actual purchase

These steps are sequential. The model suggests that a consumer spends a period of time at each one before moving to the next. Thus, before a person develops a liking for a product, she must first know about the product. Once the individual has the knowledge and develops liking for the product, the advertiser tries to influence the consumer to favor a particular brand or company.

The hierarchy of effects approach enjoys the benefit of allowing marketers to identify common steps consumers and businesses take when making purchases. Building brand loyalty requires all six steps. Logically, a customer cannot be loyal to a brand without first being aware of it. The customer typically will not develop loyalty to a brand without sufficient knowledge. Then, the purchaser must like the brand and build a strong preference for it. Finally, the customer experiences the conviction that the particular brand is superior to the others on the market. The components of the hierarchy of effects approach highlight the responses that advertising or marketing communication should stimulate in both consumers and business-to-business customers.

Kadmy/Fotolia

▲ When making high-involvement purchases, such as with a 35 mm digital camera, consumers will typically go through all six hierarchy of effects steps.

The hierarchy of effects model features similarities with theories regarding attitudes and attitudinal change, including the concepts of cognitive, affective, and conative elements. As presented in Chapter 3, the cognitive component refers to the person's mental images, understanding, and interpretations of the person, object, or issue. The affective component contains the feelings or emotions a person has about the object, topic, or idea. The conative component consists of the individual's intentions, actions, or behavior. The most common sequence that takes place when an attitude forms is:

Cognitive → Affective → Conative

The sequence parallels the six-step hierarchy of effects process. As a general guideline, cognitive-oriented ads work best for achieving brand awareness and brand knowledge. Affective-oriented advertisements are better at inspiring liking, preference, and conviction. Conative ads are normally best suited to facilitating product purchases or other buyer actions.

Although the hierarchy of effects approach may help a creative understand how a consumer reaches a purchase decision, recent literature suggests that some of the theory's assumptions may be questioned. For one, these six steps might not always constitute the route taken by a consumer. A person may make a purchase (such as an impulse buy) and then later develop knowledge, liking, preference, and conviction. Also, a shopper could purchase products with little or no preference involved, because a coupon, discount, or purchase incentive caused him to choose one brand instead of another. The introductory

▼ This introductory price may spur a consumer to make a purchase without going through the first five steps of the hierarchy of effects model.

Taylor Kemp

FIGURE 5.2
Personal Values

- Comfortable life
- Equality
- Excitement
- Freedom
- Fun, exciting life
- Happiness
- Inner peace
- Mature love
- Personal accomplishment
- Pleasure
- Salvation
- Security
- Self-fulfillment
- Self-respect
- Sense of belonging
- Social acceptance
- Wisdom

price of $3.59 in the newspaper ad for Chickme hummus on the previous page may spur a consumer to purchase the product with no prior knowledge of or preference for the brand. At other times, the individual might not even remember the name of the brand purchased previously. This may be the case with commodity products such as sugar or flour or even some clothing purchases such as socks and shirts. Even with these criticisms, however, the framework remains as a popular approach to the development of advertising messages and campaigns.

▲ A milk advertisement based on the means–end chain.

Means–End Theory

The second theoretical approach available to creatives, a **means–end chain**, suggests that an advertisement should contain a message, or *means*, that leads the consumer to a desired end state. These *end* states are personal values (see Figure 5.2). A means–end chain should start a process in which viewing the advertising message leads the consumer to believe that using the product will help achieve a personal value.

Means–end theory forms the basis of the **Means–End Conceptualization of Components for Advertising Strategy (MECCAS)** model.[1] The MECCAS model explains ways to move consumers from product attributes to personal values by highlighting the product's benefits. Advertisers can link the attributes of the product to specific benefits consumers can derive. These benefits, in turn, lead to the attainment of a personal value. Using the elements in Figure 5.3, the product attribute calcium found in milk connects to the benefit of healthy bones. The personal value the consumer obtains from healthy bones may be feeling wise for using the product or a comfortable life. The milk ad shown in this section highlights the use of a means–end chain.

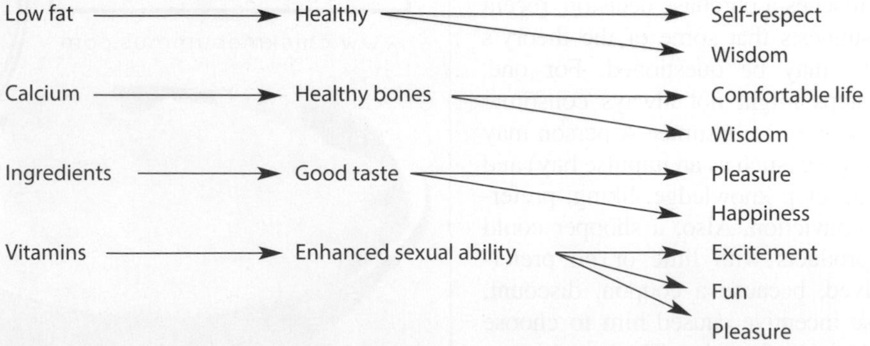

FIGURE 5.3
Means–End Chain for Milk

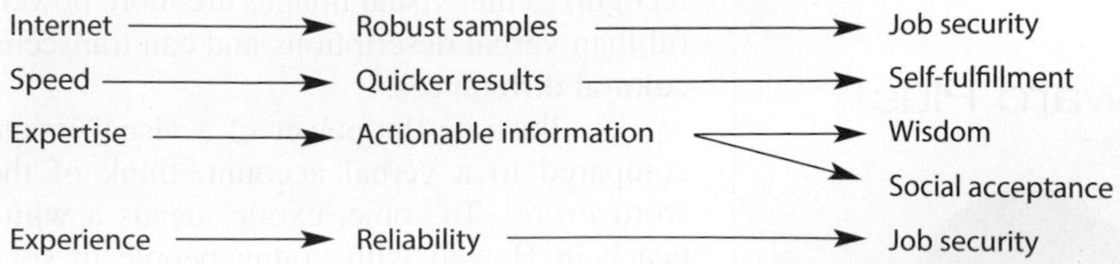

FIGURE 5.4
B-to-B Means–End Chain for Marketing Research Services

The MECCAS approach can be applied to business-to-business advertisements. Members of the buying center may be influenced by personal values, organizational values, and corporate goals. Consider the advertisement for ReRez shown in this section and the means–end chain provided in Figure 5.4. Each attribute in the ad leads to the benefits business customers can obtain. Although not explicitly stated, the personal values of members of the buying center choosing ReRez might include job security for making good decisions, self-fulfillment, wisdom, and social acceptance by other members of the buying group that believe ReRez offers quality marketing research.

ReRez

▲ A ReRez business-to-business advertisement for marketing research that illustrates the use of the means–end chain.

Verbal and Visual Images

Most major forms of advertising contain visual and verbal or written elements. A visual ad places the greatest emphasis on a picture or the optical element of the presentation. A verbal or written ad places more emphasis on the copy. Visual and verbal elements should work together to create an advertisement that meets the desired stage of the hierarchy-of-effects model or the attribute-benefit-personal value chosen from a means–end chain.

Visual images often lead to more favorable attitudes toward both the advertisement and the brand. Visuals tend to be more easily remembered than verbal copy. They are stored in the brain as both pictures and words. This dual-coding process makes it easier for people to recall the message. Further, verbal messages tend be stored in the left side of the brain only; images are usually stored in both the left and right sides of the brain. The advertisement for OIB Reward Plus on the next page illustrates the power of visual imagery. Created by the Newcomer, Morris and Young advertising agency, the visual image of the child immediately garners attention and is more likely to be remembered than an ad that only uses copy.

Visual images range from concrete and realistic to highly abstract. A concrete visual displays something recognizable such as a person, place, or thing. In an abstract image, the subject becomes more difficult to recognize. Concrete pictures instill a higher level of recall than abstract images because they allow the image to be stored in the brain with both visual and verbal elements. Viewers process an advertisement with a picture of spaghetti as both a picture and as a verbal representation of the restaurant. Ads with concrete images also tend to lead to more favorable attitudes than those with no pictures or abstract pictures.[2]

Radio advertisers often seek to create visual images for the audience. Pepsi produced a radio commercial in which listeners could hear a can being opened, the soft drink being poured, and the sizzle of the carbonation—an excellent example of creating a visual image. If consumers visualize a picture in their imaginations, the effect may be greater than actually viewing a visual. A visual image requires less brain activity than using one's imagination. The secret is getting the person to think beyond the advertisement and picture the scene being simulated.

Visual Esperanto Advertisers often use visual imagery in international marketing. Global advertising agencies try to create ***visual Esperanto***, the universal language that makes global advertising possible for any good or service. *Visual Esperanto* advertising

Newcomer, Morris and Young Inc.

▲ An advertisement for OIB (Ouachita Independent Bank) with a strong visual image.

recognizes that visual images are more powerful than verbal descriptions and can transcend cultural differences.[3]

To illustrate the power of a visual image compared to a verbal account, think of the word *exotic*. To some, exotic means a white beach in Hawaii with young people in sexy swimsuits. To others, it may be a small cabin in the snow-capped mountains of Switzerland. To others still, exotic may be a close-up of a tribal village in Africa. The word "exotic" can vary in meaning. At the same time, a picture of a couple holding hands in front of Niagara Falls has practically the same meaning across all cultures, because the image conveys a similar emotional experience in multiple settings.

Finding the appropriate image constitutes the most important challenge in creating *visual Esperanto*. The creative looks for the image that conveys the intended meaning or message. Brand identity can be emphasized using visuals rather than words. Then the creative uses words to support the visual image. For example, the creative may decide that a boy and his father at a sports event illustrate the priceless treasure of a shared family moment. In Mexico, the setting could be a soccer match instead of a baseball game in the United States. The specific copy (the words) can then be adapted to another country. Identifying an image that transcends cultures represents the most difficult part of inspiring *visual Esperanto*. Once a universal image has been found, creatives in each country represented take the image and modify it to appeal to the local target audience.

Luliia Sokolovska/Fotolia

▶ While the meaning "exotic" may vary across cultures, the visual created in this photo can transcend cultures through *visual Esperanto*.

Business-to-Business In the past, creatives designing business-to-business advertisements relied heavily on the verbal or written element rather than on visuals. The basis of this approach was the belief that business decisions are made in a rational, cognitive manner. In recent years, more business ads have incorporated strong visual elements to heighten the emotional aspects of making purchases.

In summary, the two theoretical models, along with concepts regarding visual and verbal messages, provide useful ideas for the advertising creative. Each suggests key concepts to be followed in developing an advertising campaign. The endpoint will be reached when the viewer remembers the products, thinks favorably about it, and looks for that product when making a purchase decision.

The Impact of Advertising Expenditures

objective 5.2
What is the relationship of advertising expenditures to advertising effectiveness?

In developing advertising campaigns, unrealistic assumptions concerning the relationship of advertising budgets to effectiveness may occur. For instance, a manager may believe that a direct relationship exists between expenditures on advertising communications and subsequent sales revenues. A common concept was that a 10 percent increase in advertising would lead to a two percent increase in sales. Unfortunately, recent studies indicate that the increase might be closer to one percent, although the actual amount varies widely.[4] Figure 5.5 displays a more realistic conceptualization of the relationship between marketing expenditures and advertising. The factors present in the relationship include:

- The communications goal
- Threshold effects
- Diminishing returns
- Carryover effects
- Wear-out effects
- Decay effects

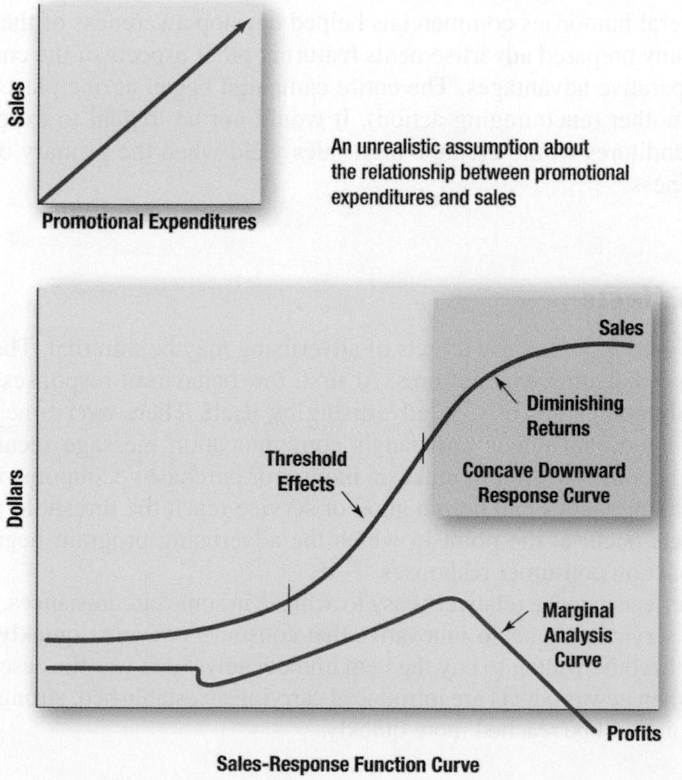

FIGURE 5.5
Relationships between Advertising and Marketing Expenditures and Sales and Profit Margins

▶ By offering a $50 appreciation bonus, the impact of this advertisement will be different than if the objective was to create awareness of the Cub Cadet brand with no bonus offered.

Alliance One Advertising

Communications goals differ depending on the stage in the buying process. The hierarchy of effects model suggests that prior to making a purchase, a consumer goes through the stages of awareness, knowledge, liking, preference, and conviction. The communications objective and stage in the hierarchy of effects model influence the advertising goal, budget, and message to be sent. For example, an early advertising campaign for the Sun Life Financial company highlighted the fact that people had not heard of the company, but would. Several humorous commercials helped develop awareness of the brand. Over time, the company prepared advertisements featuring other aspects of the company's services and comparative advantages. The entire campaign began at one place (awareness) and ended at another (encouraging action). It would not be logical to expect that early marketing expenditures would create a high sales yield when the primary objective was to create awareness.

Threshold Effects

As shown in Figure 5.5, the early effects of advertising may be minimal. The same holds true for all communication expenditures. At first, few behavioral responses occur, especially when only companies rely on advertising by itself. Then, over time, a consumer who is exposed repeatedly to a company's communication message recalls the brand and eventually becomes willing to make an inquiry or purchase.[5] Coupons, free samples, and other marketing tactics can help a good or service reach the threshold point sooner. **Threshold effects** occur at the point in which the advertising program begins to have a significant impact on consumer responses.

Threshold effects may be relatively easy to achieve in some circumstances. For instance, a new good or service may be so innovative that consumers become quickly aware of its advantages and become willing to buy the item immediately. Such was the case with the first iPhone. Also, when new products are introduced carrying an established, strong brand name, the threshold point will be reached more quickly.

Diminishing Returns

Eventually, a circumstance will be reached in which a promotional campaign has saturated the market, which indicates a point of **diminishing returns**. At that instant, further expenditures produce a minimal impact. The S-shaped curve displayed in Figure 5.5 represents a *sales-response function curve* and the diminishing returns from additional advertising expenditures. Diminishing returns are part of the *concave downward function*, in which incremental increases in expenditures in advertising result in smaller and smaller increases in sales. A *marginal analysis* reveals that further advertising and promotional expenditures adversely affect profits, because sales increases are less than what the company spends on the marketing or advertising.

Carryover Effects

Consumers purchase many products only when they are needed, such as washing machines and refrigerators. Promotions for these products should be designed to create brand recall. Recall occurs when the consumer has been exposed to the company's message for so long that when the time comes to buy, the individual remembers the key company, which indicates the presence of **carryover effects**. In other words, when a washing machine breaks down and requires a replacement, remembering Maytag brand will be the company's goal. Consequently, the consumer remembers Maytag's products and the advertisements have effectively carried over.

Wear-Out Effects

An additional complication to the advertising campaign may emerge. At a certain point, an advertisement or particular campaign simply becomes "old" or "boring." Consumers tend to ignore the advertisement or tune it out.[6] Some consumers may even develop negative attitudes toward the brand if they become annoyed at the marketing communication and believe the advertisement should be discontinued. This indicates **wear-out effects**.

Research regarding advertising campaigns over the last 50 years indicates that about half of all campaigns last too long and experience wear-out effects. On the other hand, the same research suggests that the long-term effect of advertising remains twice as high as the short-term effect. As a result, marketers try to continue a campaign long enough to capture that long-term effect but not so long that wear-out sets in.[7] Discovering the balance between wear-out and long-term impact remains challenging.

Decay Effects

When a company stops advertising, consumers begin to forget the message, which indicates **decay effects** (see Figure 5.6). In some instances, a dramatic degree of decay takes place. In others, the carryover effects are strong enough that some time can lapse before the brand drops out of the consumer's consciousness. The presence of decay effects means that companies should continue to engage in some form of marketing communications to keep the brand in people's minds.

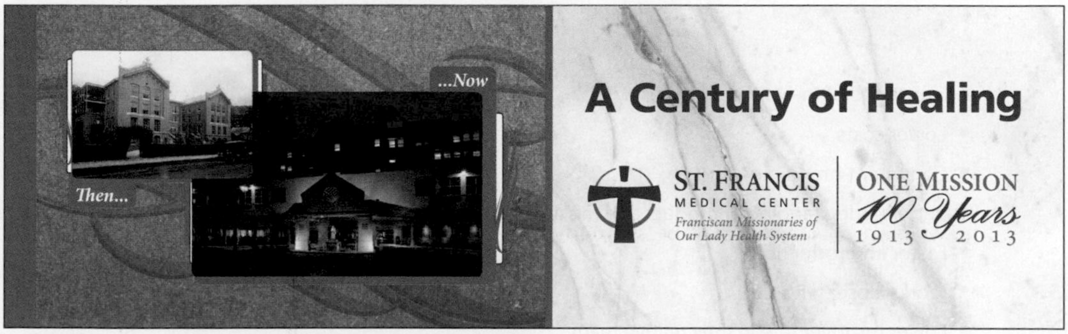

Newcomer, Morris and Young Inc.

◀ The concept of carryover effects applies to this advertisement for St. Francis Medical Center.

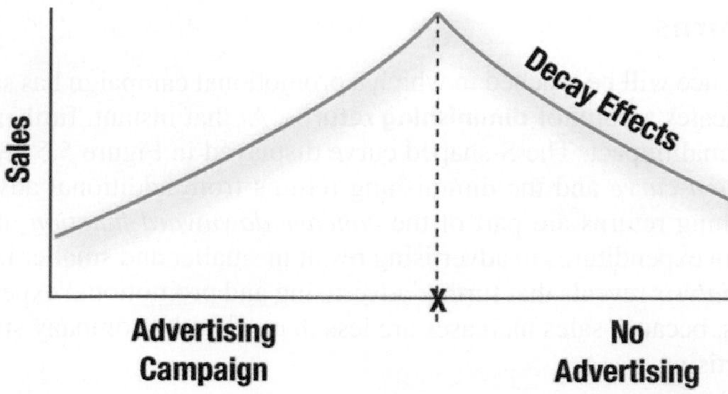

▶ FIGURE 5.6
A Decay Effects Model

In-House Versus External Advertising Agencies

objective 5.3
When should a company employ an external advertising agency rather than completing the work in-house?

When beginning an advertising program, deciding whether to use an in-house advertising group or an external advertising agency constitutes the first issue. Figure 5.7 compares the advantages of an in-house facility to an outside agency.

With tightening marketing budgets, more companies are deploying in-house advertising resources. Recently, Apple significantly expanded its in-house department from 300 to more than 500 employees. A study conducted by the Association of National Advertisers revealed that 58 percent of the association's members now utilize in-house advertising resources, compared to 42 percent five years ago.[8]

In-house advertising may help create several advantages. First, marketing managers may believe the approach lowers costs and retains better control of the message, which can be aligned with the brand and other company communications. The CEO can work closely with the marketing team to make sure this occurs. Consequently, members of the marketing department may conclude they have a better understanding of the firm's products and mission and more quickly produce advertisements. An in-house program will be more consistent, because of a lower turnover rate in the creative team.

While companies may use in-house resources, many will outsource specific functions such as writing, filming, recording, and editing advertisements. Most utilize media companies to plan and purchase media time (on television and radio) and space (in magazines, in newspapers, and on billboards).

An outside agency often reduces costs when compared to less efficient in-house facilities. This occurs when in-house employees spend more time on campaigns and ad designs than an agency would. The agency provides greater expertise and may have access to top talent in the industry. Advertising agencies offer an outside perspective not influenced by internal corporate politics and personal biases. Agency professionals often have a better understanding of consumers and trends because they work with a number of clients over an array of products. Knowledge gained from one product can often be transferred to other, even unrelated products.

Advantages of In-House
- Lower costs
- Consistent brand message
- Better understanding of product and mission
- Faster ad production
- Works closer with CEO
- Lower turnover rate in the creative team

Advantages of Outside Agency
- Reduce costs
- Greater expertise
- Outsider's perspective
- Access to top talent

▶ FIGURE 5.7
Advantages of In-House Versus External Agencies

Advertising agencies provide a variety of options. All sizes and types of agencies exist. At one end of the spectrum, highly specialized, boutique-type agencies offer one specific service (e.g., making television ads) or serve one type of client. G+G Advertising of Albuquerque, New Mexico, specializes in advertising to Native Americans—a market of an estimated 10 million people.[9]

At the other end of the spectrum, full-service agencies such as mcgarrybowen, Zehnder Communications, and The Richards Group provide every type of advertising and promotional activity. These companies offer advice and assistance in working with other components of the IMC program, including consumer and trade promotions, direct-marketing programs, digital programs, and alternative media (see Figure 5.8).

Some agencies provide specialized services. For instance, *media service companies* negotiate and purchase media packages (called *media buys*) for companies. *Direct-marketing agencies* handle every aspect of a direct-marketing campaign through telephone orders (800 numbers), internet programs, and direct mail. Some companies focus on *consumer promotions, trade promotions*, or both. These companies assist in developing promotions such as coupons, premiums, contests, and sweepstakes. A new group of agencies specializes in developing *digital services*. Boxcar Creative designs *interactive websites* and widgets that can be used on multiple sites. Other companies offer *social media services* to reach consumers and businesses through a wide array of social media techniques. *Public relations* firms provide experts to help companies and brands develop positive public images and for damage control responses when negative publicity arises.

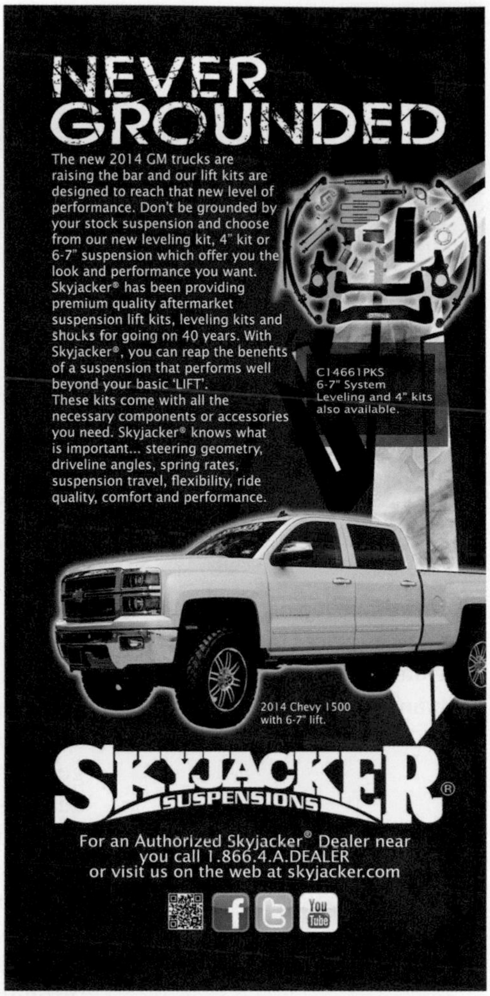

Skyjacker Suspensions

▲ Skyjacker is one of a number of firms that perform all advertising functions in-house.

Budget Allocation Considerations

The size of the account affects the choice between an in-house team versus an external advertising agency. A small account may not be attractive to an advertising agency, because it generates lower revenues. If the agency charges a higher fee to compensate, it becomes too costly for the small firm. Smaller accounts create other challenges. Less money can be spent on media time and space purchases because the company spends the majority of the advertising budget on production of the advertisement.

One rule of thumb marketers consider, the 75–15–10 breakdown, suggests that 75 percent of the money to be spent on advertising should be used to purchase media time or space, 15 percent to the agency for the creative work, and 10 percent for the actual production of the ad. In contrast, for smaller accounts, the breakdown may be 50–30–20. Only 50 percent of expenditures are for media purchases; the other 50 percent of the funds goes to the creative and production work.

Unless the majority of the company's advertising budget can be used to pay for media purchases, it may be wise either to perform the work in-house or to develop contracts with smaller specialty firms to prepare various aspects of an advertising campaign.

- Advice about how to develop target markets
- Specialized services for business markets
- Suggestions about how to project a strong company image and theme
- Assistance in selecting company logos and slogans
- Preparation of advertisements
- Planning and purchasing media time and space

◀ **FIGURE 5.8**
Services Provided by Full-Service Agencies

Stakhov/Fotolia

▲ Crowdsourcing of creative materials involves fans and can generate considerable buzz for the brand.

Crowdsourcing

Crowdsourcing involves outsourcing the creative aspect of an advertisement or campaign to the public. It offers an alternative to creating commercials in-house or hiring an external advertising agency. Crowdsourcing can create a viral buzz as users view advertisements online, recommend or send favorites to friends, and post links.

Doritos has used crowdsourcing to create Super Bowl ads. Fans were invited to submit ideas for ads. Doritos ads have been voted as some of the best of the Super Bowl. Although it may seem that crowdsourcing would be a cheaper method of creating a Super Bowl commercial, in reality the total cost stays about the same as for hiring a professional agency. The costs of running the contest, paying prize money, creating the microsite to host the contest, and producing the commercial combined with the time spent by Doritos and the agency in choosing from the thousands of entries are nearly equal to what would have been spent on an agency. Crowdsourcing, however, yields the advantage of involving fans and generating the subsequent buzz that surrounds the contest for the consumer-generated advertisement.[10]

Harley-Davidson employs an extreme approach to crowdsourcing. The company obtains all creative work through crowdsourcing with agencies only responsible for producing the ads. According to Harley-Davidson CMO Mark-Hans Richer, "We made a decision to turn over the major creative to owners because we have a passionate customer base who wants to engage with us." The creative comes through Facebook. Harley-Davidson has about 3 million Facebook fans. About 8,000 signed up to be part of the Fan Machine, the creative forum for Harley. The Fan Machine group reviews advertising briefs, submits ideas, and votes on ideas from members. While the company offers some branded products, according to Richer "it's really about the spirit and creativity and passion of the brand than the financial reward." A recent project received 300 idea submissions, with 20,000 votes for the best ideas. "What really shocked me was how good the ideas actually were. There were a lot of surprising insights. It's like a focus group and creative wrapped into one," he said.

Recent research regarding consumer-generated advertising produced several key findings. First, consumer-generated advertising works best when targeted to current customers and customers who have high levels of brand loyalty. Consumers with lower levels of brand loyalty are likely to be more skeptical of the ad creation and the campaign overall. Second, sharing background information about the ad creator increases the persuasiveness of the consumer-generated ad by establishing credibility and showing similarities between the ad creator and consumers. The social media and public relations components of crowdsourcing constitute important ingredients in successfully using this approach to advertising. Consequently, while consumer-generated ads may be effective at generating customer retention, they are not as successful for increasing a customer base.[11]

Critics of crowdsourcing argue that while the approach may lead to innovative and eye-catching advertisements, no consistent message or theme results over time. The commercials may or may not reinforce the brand's major selling points or elements. Stan Richards of The Richards Group suggests that without a strategic approach, key components of the overall communications effort can be lost.

Choosing an Agency

objective 5.4
How do companies choose advertising agencies?

Choosing an agency begins with the development of quality selection criteria. The choice of an agency represents a key component of the advertising management process for many companies. Figure 5.9 lists the steps involved in selecting an agency.

Goal Setting

Prior to making any contact with an advertising agency, company leaders identify and prioritize corporate goals. The goals provide a sense of direction and prevent personal biases from affecting selection decisions. Goals guide company leaders by providing a clear idea of what the company seeks to accomplish. They also help the marketing team as they make requests for proposals for campaigns.

Kraft Foods recently changed agencies for 20 of the company's iconic brands, including Maxwell House, Crystal Light, Kraft Singles, Cadbury, Fig Newtons, Planters, Oreo, and Kraft Macaroni & Cheese. Dana Anderson, Senior VP of Marketing Strategy and Communications stated that, "More than ever, we're focusing on contemporizing and making our iconic brands more relevant to today's consumers. We're raising the bar with our agencies in order to deliver more creative and engaging campaigns. Our ultimate goal is to heighten the profile and performance of Kraft Foods brands." By determining the goal in advance, Kraft's marketing team was able to select the best agency for each of the brands under review.[12]

Selection Criteria

Even firms with experience set selection criteria in advance in order to reduce any biases that might affect decisions. Emotions and other feelings can lead to poor choices. Figure 5.10 identifies some of the major issues to be considered during the process. The list can be especially useful during the initial screening, when the field narrows to the top five (or fewer) agencies.

Agency Size As noted earlier, the size of the agency should be considered, most notably as it compares to the size of the company hiring the agency. A good rule of thumb to follow is that the account should be large enough for the agency so that it is important to the agency but small enough that, if lost, the agency would not be badly affected.

Relevant Experience When an agency has experience in a given industry, the agency's employees are better able to understand the client firm, its customers, and the

1. Set goals.
2. Select process and criteria.
3. Screen initial list of applicants.
4. Request client references.
5. Reduce list to two or three viable agencies.
6. Request creative pitch.

FIGURE 5.9
Steps in Selecting an Advertising Agency

- Size of the agency
- Relevant experience of the agency
- Conflicts of interest
- Creative reputation and capabilities
- Production capabilities
- Media purchasing capabilities
- Other services available
- Client retention rates
- Personal chemistry

FIGURE 5.10
Evaluation Criteria in Choosing an Advertising Agency

Orkin Pest Control advertisement furnished by The Richards Group

Orkin Pest Control advertisement furnished by The Richards Group

▲ Orkin Pest Control is just one of the many accounts handled by The Richards Group.

structure of the marketing channel. At the same time, the client company makes sure the agency does not have any *conflicts of interest*. An advertising firm hired by one manufacturer of automobile tires would experience a conflict of interest if another tire manufacturer attempted to hire the agency.

An advertising agency can have relevant experience without representing a competitor. Such experience can be gained when an agency works for a similar company operating in a different industry. For example, when an agency has a manufacturer of automobile batteries as a client, the experience will be relevant to selling automobile tires.

The agency should also have experience with the business-to-business program, so that retailers, wholesalers, and any other channel party are considered in the marketing and advertising of the product. A number of advertisements in this textbook were created by The Richards Group. In addition to the Orkin advertisements in this section, The Richard's Group's clients include Motel 6, Home Depot, Sub-Zero, and Bridgestone. Note that the list does not include competing firms within the same industry.

Creative Reputation and Capabilities

One method of assessing an agency's creativity would include asking for a list of awards the company has received. Although awards do not always translate into creating effective advertisements, in most cases a positive relationship exists between winning awards and writing effective ads. Most creative awards are given by peers. As a result, they represent effective indicators of what others think of the agency's creative efforts.

Production and Media-Purchasing Capabilities Agency capabilities should be examined when production and media-purchasing services are needed. A firm that needs an agency to produce a television commercial and also buy media time should check on these activities as part of the initial screening process. Many agencies either employ subsidiary companies to perform the media work or subcontract it to a media firm. The advertising agency does not necessarily need to make media buys, but it should have the capacity to make sure they are made to fit with the ads being designed.

Other Criteria The final three selection criteria—*other services available, client retention rates*, and *personal chemistry*—are utilized during the final steps of selection. These criteria help make the final determination in the selection process.

Creative Pitch

Monkey Business/Fotolia

▲ During a creative pitch, an agency presents ideas on the problem or campaign posed by the potential client.

When the company reduces the list to two or three finalists, the selection team asks each for a creative pitch. The advertising agencies chosen to compete provide a formal presentation that addresses a specific problem, situation, or set of questions—a process also called a *shootout*. The presentations reveal how each agency would deal with specific issues that might arise during preparation of a campaign. The process helps a client company choose the agency that best understands the issues at stake and offers a comprehensive approach to solving the problem or issue. For instance, after Bank of America suffered several years of corporate crises and publicity missteps, it put its $380 million account up for review. Agencies were asked "to create a new positioning for Bank of America" that would signal to its audiences that the bank was addressing its challenges.[13]

Preparing a pitch takes time and creates expenses for advertising agencies; therefore, they only want to prepare pitches that have a decent chance of acceptance. When an agency spends time preparing a presentation only to find out later that the company had no desire to switch agencies, but were told by upper management to solicit pitches, it becomes frustrating.[14] A company seeking to retain an advertising agency should provide sufficient time for the competing finalists to prepare the pitch. Pink Jacket Creative's Bill Breedlove reports, "I would prefer at least 30 days to prepare a pitch. Even 45 to 60 days would be wonderful sometimes, and for some companies."

Recently, Oscar Mayer, a brand under the Kraft umbrella, sought ways to unify its portfolio of products and contemporize its image with consumers. The mcgarrybowen agency demonstrated how Oscar Mayer could contemporize the brand and build emotional ties with customers. The agency's ideas were fresh, contemporary, and had the emotional spark the organization desired.[15]

When Kraft launched its Oscar Mayer Deli Creations sandwiches, the initial print ad developed by the brand's previous agency depicted a woman in a suit, standing with her arm bent eating one of the Deli Creation sandwiches. Karen Adams, senior director of advertising at Kraft Foods, stated, "People don't eat sandwiches that way." Instead, new ads were created showing real people in real-life situations eating sandwiches.[16]

Successful creative pitches result from hard work and thorough planning. Figure 5.11 highlights some of the "do's" and "don'ts" for advertising agencies in making pitches.

- Do listen. Allow the client to talk.
- Do your preparation. Know the client and its business.
- Do make a good first impression. Dress up, not down.
- Do a convincing job of presenting. Believe in what you are presenting.
- Don't assume all clients are the same. Each has a unique need.
- Don't try to solve the entire problem in the pitch.
- Don't be critical of the product or the competition.
- Don't overpromise. It will come back to haunt you.
- Don't spend a lot of time pitching credentials and references.

◀ **FIGURE 5.11**
Pitching Do's and Don'ts

Agency Selection

During the presentation phase, company marketers meet with agency creatives, media buyers, account executives, and other people who will work on the account. *Chemistry* between employees of the two different firms becomes critical. The client company's leaders should be convinced that they will work well together. Chemistry can break or make the final decision.[17]

After completing the selection process, the agency and the company will work together to prepare the advertising campaign. Those who did not win the account are also notified, in order to maintain more positive relations with them over time. The account executive, account planner, and advertising creative all play key roles in the process.

Roles of Advertising Personnel

objective 5.5
What are the primary job functions within an advertising agency?

Advertising agency employees perform a wide variety of roles. In small agencies, an individual may carry out multiple roles. In a large agency, multiple individuals will be employed in the various departments and perform similar functions. The primary roles within the agency consist of the account executives, creatives, traffic managers, and account planners.

Account Executives

The account executive serves as the go-between for the advertising agency and the client company. In some agencies, the executive will be actively involved in soliciting the account, finalizing details of the contract, and working with personnel within the agency to make sure the advertisements meet the client's specifications. In other agencies, especially larger firms, account executives do not solicit accounts, but rather manage the relationship and work that the agency performs for the brand. The account executive often helps the company define the theme of the overall IMC program and how advertising fits into the brand's marketing strategy.

Creatives

Creatives develop and design advertisements. They are either members of advertising agencies or freelancers. Some smaller agencies provide only creative advertising services without becoming involved in other marketing programs and activities. Creatives may appear to hold the "glamour" jobs in agencies, because they get to actually create ads and marketing materials. At the same time, creatives work long hours and face enormous pressures to design effective advertisements that produce tangible results.

▼ Account executives work with creatives, traffic managers, and account planners to develop advertising campaigns for clients.

Monkey Business/Fotolia

Traffic Managers

The traffic manager works closely with the advertising agency's account executive, creatives, and production staff. The manager's responsibilities include scheduling the various aspects of the agency's work to make sure it is completed on time. During production, the traffic manager assumes the responsibility of making sure props, actors, and other items needed have been ordered and are in place at the time of the filming or recording.

Account Planners

The account planner provides the voice and serves as the advocate for the consumer within the advertising agency. The planner makes sure the creative team understands the consumer (or business). Account planners interact with the account executive and the client to understand the target audience of the ad campaign. The planner then works to make sure creative messages reach the right customers.

The account planner assists the client in developing long-term communication strategies and provides direction for individual advertising campaigns. In small agencies, the role may be performed by the account executive. Larger firms employ separate individuals and/or departments to conduct the account planning role.

Kraft Foods, Inc.

▲ The account planner represents the consumer's viewpoint so that a creative can design effective advertisements such as this one for Maxwell House coffee.

Advertising Campaign Parameters

Producing effective advertising campaigns requires the joint efforts of the account executive, creative, account planner, and media planner. Working independently might produce some award-winning ads, but often they may not achieve the client's objectives. Advertising agencies seek to produce campaigns that stand out among the competing messages. Creating effective campaigns requires attention to the advertising campaign parameters listed in Figure 5.12.

objective 5.6
What are the advertising campaign parameters that should be considered?

- Advertising goals
- Media selection
- Tagline
- Consistency
- Positioning
- Campaign duration

▲ **FIGURE 5.12**
Advertising Campaign Parameters

Advertising Goals

Advertising goals are derived from the firm's overall communication objectives that were presented in Chapter 4. Figure 5.13 identifies the most common advertising goals. These goals should be consistent with the marketing communication objectives and other components of the integrated marketing communications plan.

Build Brand Awareness A strong global brand often constitutes a key advertising goal, especially for larger companies. Building a brand's image begins with developing brand awareness. *Brand awareness* means the consumers recognize and remember a particular brand or company name when they consider purchasing options. Advertising offers an excellent venue to increase brand awareness.

Successful brands possess two characteristics: the top of mind and the consumer's top choice. When consumers are asked to identify brands that quickly come to mind from a product category, one or two particular brands are nearly always mentioned. These names are the **top-of-mind brands**. For example, when asked to identify fast-food hamburger restaurants, McDonald's and Burger King almost always head the list. The same may be true for Nike and Reebok athletic shoes and may be the case in the United States as well as in other countries.

The term **top choice** suggests what the term implies: A top-choice brand is the first or second pick when a consumer reviews her evoked set of possible purchasing alternatives. Many products become top-of-mind or top choice due to brand equity. Advertising can strengthen brand equity.

Provide Information Advertising can achieve other goals such as providing information to both consumers and business buyers. Typical information for consumers includes

▼ FIGURE 5.13
Advertising Goals

- To build brand awareness
- To inform
- To persuade
- To support other marketing efforts
- To encourage action

a retailer's store hours, business location, or sometimes more detailed product specifications. Information may make the purchasing process appear to be simple and convenient, which can entice customers to travel to the store to finalize a purchase.

Persuasion When an advertisement convinces consumers of a particular brand's superiority, persuasion has taken place. Changing consumer attitudes and convincing them to consider a new purchasing choice can be challenging. Advertisers can utilize several persuasion methods. One involves showing consumers the negative consequences of failing to buy a particular brand. Persuasive advertising more often targets consumers rather than business-to-business prospects.

Supporting Marketing Efforts Advertising supports other marketing functions. Manufacturers use advertising to accompany trade and consumer promotions such as theme packaging or combination offers. Contests, such as the McDonald's Monopoly game, require additional advertising to be effective.

Taylor Kemp

▲ This advertisement supports a brand alliance between Wholly Guacamole and Disney.

Retailers also advertise to support marketing programs. Any type of special sale (white sale, buy-one-get-one-free, pre-Christmas sale) requires effective advertising to attract customers to the store. Manufacturers and retail outlets both run advertisements in conjunction with coupons or other special offers. The advertisement for Wholly Guacamole in this section features a brand alliance with Disney along with a coupon on any Wholly product plus a rebate for Disney's *The Lion King* movie.

Encouraging Action Many firms set behavioral goals for advertising programs. A television commercial encouraging viewers to take action by dialing a toll-free number to make a quick purchase serves as an example. Everything from ShamWow to Snuggies has been sold using action tactics. Infomercials and home shopping network programs rely heavily on immediate consumer purchasing responses.

Action-oriented advertising can be used in the business-to-business sector. Generating leads becomes the primary goal. Many business advertisements provide web addresses or telephone numbers buyers can use to request more information or make a purchase.

The five advertising goals of building image, providing information, being persuasive, supporting other marketing efforts, and encouraging action are not separate from each other. They work together in key ways. For instance, awareness and information are part of persuasion. The key is to emphasize one goal without forgetting the others.

Media Selection

Selecting the appropriate media requires an understanding of the media usage habits of the target market and then matching that information with the profile of each medium's audience. Volkswagen positioned the Tiguan crossover as a fun vehicle aimed at young, active individuals who love the outdoors. Although the campaign featured television commercials, the more unique component of the campaign was the outdoor segment. The theme "people want an SUV that parks well with others" was featured in a series of outdoor ads placed at bike racks and trail heads at 150 national parks and resorts. Brian Martin, CEO of Brand Connections Active Outdoor, which placed the ads, noted that more than 30 million impressions were made with hikers, bikers, and other outdoor lovers.[18]

The advertising team identifies the media favored by a target market. Teenagers surf the web and watch television. Only a small percentage reads newspapers and news magazines. Various market segments exhibit differences in when and how they view various media. Older African Americans watch television programs in patterns that differ from those of older Caucasians. Males watch more sports programs than females, and so forth.

In business-to-business markets, knowing the trade journals or business publications that various members of the buying center most likely read assists in the development of a print advertising campaign. Engineers, who tend to be the influencers, often have different media viewing habits than vice presidents, who may be the deciders.

Although media buys are guided by the advertising agency and the client company, media companies typically make the purchases. A trend toward involving media companies at an earlier stage in the campaign process has evolved in recent years. Previously, most media companies were contacted after a campaign became ready or was nearly complete, with the specific task of purchasing media space or time. Now, companies such as Procter & Gamble, Johnson & Johnson, Clorox, Kimberly-Clark, Verizon, and HP enlist media companies as strategic partners in developing advertising and marketing campaigns.[19] Agencies invite media companies to participate in the strategy development stage because many have quality insights regarding the target audience. They are able to provide valuable information to the creative staff about how to best reach the client's target market employing the primary media that target consumers favor.

Advertisement for Progressive Bank furnished by French Creative

▲ Selecting the right media ensures that the consumers who are the most likely to use Progressive Bank for trust and wealth management will see this advertisement.

In some cases, media companies actually create commercials. Joe Kuester, senior brand manager for Kimberly-Clark, stated, "It doesn't matter to us where the idea comes from or who champions that idea." That statement was in response to Kimberly-Clark's media company, Mindshare Entertainment, creating a series of webisodes involving Whoopi Goldberg for its Poise brand. Another media company, MEC Entertainment, worked with its client Ikea to produce a campaign for A&E called "Fix this Kitchen." This trend to involve media companies in all facets of advertising campaign development is quickly gaining momentum with companies.[20]

Taglines

The key phrase in an advertisement, the **tagline**, should be something memorable that identifies the uniqueness of a brand or conveys some type of special meaning. "Just Do It" has been Nike's tagline for many years. Figure 5.14 identifies other well-known taglines.

- American Express—"Don't leave home without it."
- Avis—"We try harder."
- Bounty—"The quicker picker-upper."
- Capital One—"What's in your wallet?"
- CNN—"The most trusted name in news"
- Energizer—"It keeps going, and going, and going."
- Hallmark—"When you care enough to send the best."
- John Deere—"Nothing runs like a Deer."
- Maxwell House—"Good to the last drop."
- Nokia—"Connecting people"
- Office Depot—"Taking care of business."
- Target—"Expect more. Pay less."
- UPS—"What can Brown do for you?"
- Wal-Mart—"Save money. Live better."

◀ **FIGURE 5.14**
Taglines Used by Various Brands

Taglines provide consistency across various advertising platforms. Consumers often remember taglines and identify them with specific brands. A catchy tagline identifies a brand and then stays with it over successive campaigns. In order to bring freshness to a campaign, company marketers occasionally tweak or modify a tagline every few years. With shorter attention spans, taglines have been shrinking from short sentences to just two or three words. L'Oreal Paris has used the shortened tagline "Because I'm Worth It" for more than 40 years. Other taglines that have been shortened include BMW's "ultimate driving machine," Lucozade"s (British energy drink) "Yes" and Wal-Mart's "Save money, live better."

In other instances, a completely new version may be developed. To make the Oscar Mayer brand more contemporary, the company's marketing personnel and its agency, mcgarrybowen, created a new tagline. Oscar Mayer was known for trust, nostalgia, heritage, jingles, bologna, hot dogs, and kids. The image needed to be freshened, made more contemporary, and reach adults as well as kids. The Oscar Mayer marketing team wanted to take the brand to a place that was energetic, culturally relevant, and that captured the spirit of everyday food making people feel good. Real joy, real moments, real friendship, real emotion, and real people were at the forefront. The idea was that Oscar Mayer is "good mood food." One Oscar Mayer ad conveys the good mood feeling that resulted from marketing brainstorming sessions and music collaborations and led to the campaign tagline "It doesn't get better than this."[21]

▼ This advertisement for JD Bank, combined with the one on the next page, use variability theory concepts to create consistency within the campaign.

JD Bank

Consistency

Repeatedly seeing a specific visual image, headline, copy, or tagline helps to embed a brand into a person's long-term memory. Visual consistency becomes especially important because most customers spend very little time viewing an advertisement. In most cases, an individual makes just a casual glance at a print advertisement or a cursory glimpse at a television commercial. Visual consistency leads the viewer to move the message from short-term to long-term memory. Logos, taglines, and headlines that remain consistent across ads and campaigns aid in this process.

Repetition helps increase consumer ad recall as well as brand recall. While mere repetition of the same ad may accomplish this goal, varying the ad appears to have better results. Some advertisers emphasize the principles present in **variability theory**,[22] which suggests that variable encoding occurs when a consumer sees the same advertisement in different environments. These varied environments increase recall and effectiveness by encoding it into the brain through various methods. Creatives can generate the effect by varying the situational context of a particular ad. For example, Capital One campaigns use various settings to convey the same basic message, "What's in your wallet?" Changing the context of the ad increases recall and offers an effective method for overcoming competitive ad interference.[23]

Selecting two media to convey a message generally can be more effective than repeating an advertisement in the same medium. An advertisement placed in more than one medium reduces competing ad interference. In other words, a message presented on television and in magazines works better than one that appears only on television. Consumers seeing an advertisement in a different medium are more likely to recall the ad than when it appears in only one medium.

Whether across different media or modifications of ads within the same media, consistency constitutes the key to effectiveness. Consistency reduces wear-out effects and maintains interest in the advertising campaign. It aids in providing carryover effects when the consumer is in the purchase state.

JD Bank

Positioning

Maintaining consistent product positioning throughout a product's life makes it more likely that a consumer will place the product in a cognitive map. When the firm emphasizes quality in every advertisement, it becomes easier to tie the product into the consumer's cognitive map than if the firm stresses quality in one ad, price in another, and convenience in a third campaign. Inconsistency in positioning makes the brand and company more difficult to remember. Consistent positioning avoids ambiguity, and the message stays clear and understandable.

Campaign Duration

The length or duration of a campaign should be identified. Using the same advertisement for an appropriate period of time allows the message to embed in the consumer's long-term memory. Account executives consider how long to run an advertisement. It should be changed before it becomes stale and viewers lose interest; however, changing ads too frequently impedes retention. Creating new campaigns also increases costs.

Typical campaigns last about six months, but there are exceptions. Some last for years. The criterion that typically determines when it is time to change a campaign is the wear-out effect. When consumers ignore ads and it no longer is producing results, it becomes time to launch a new campaign.

The Creative Brief

objective 5.7
How does a creative brief facilitate effective advertising?

When an advertising agency prepares a document to guide in the production of an advertising campaign or for a specific commercial, the document is called a *creative strategy* or **creative brief**. Although various forms exist, the basic components of a standard creative brief are displayed in Figure 5.15. The creative takes the information provided to produce

▼ **FIGURE 5.15**
The Creative Brief

- The objective
- The target audience
- The message theme
- The support
- The constraints

advertisements and use it to convey the desired message. A quality creative brief, when prepared properly, saves the agency considerable time and effort and results in a stronger advertising campaign for the client.

Ineffective communications between agencies and clients sometimes occurs when those involved do not properly prepare a brief. A survey of senior executives of advertising agencies indicated major problems with creative briefs, and most agencies voiced some level of frustration. The most common problem cited was a lack of focus. Fifty-three percent of the executives said the briefs were complete, but lacked focus and 27 percent said they were both incomplete and inconsistent. Only 20 percent said they were complete and focused most of the time. Not one, zero percent, said they were complete and focused all of the time.[24]

The Objective

A creative brief identifies the objective of the advertising campaign such as those common objectives noted in the previous section. The creative reviews the main objective (or goal) before designing specific ads or the advertising campaign. The objectives guide the advertising design and the choice of execution. For instance, for an increased brand awareness goal, the name of the product will be prominently displayed in the advertisement or repeated several times in a television ad. Building brand image normally results in the actual product being more prominently displayed in the ad.

▼ An advertisement targeted to human resource individuals within businesses.

LUBA Workers' Comp

The Target Audience

A creative then examines the target audience. An advertisement designed to persuade a business to inquire about new computer software differs from a consumer advertisement created for the same company. The business advertisement focuses on the type of industry and a specific member of the buying center. The more detail available regarding the target audience, the easier it becomes for a creative to design an effective advertisement. The LUBA Worker's Comp ad in this section targets individuals who work in human resource departments within companies.

Overly general target market profiles are not helpful. Rather than specifying "males, ages 20 to 35," more specific information will be needed, such as "males, ages 20 to 35, college educated, and professionals." Other information, including hobbies, interests, opinions, and lifestyles, make it possible to more precisely develop an advertisement.

The Message Theme

The message theme presents an outline of key idea(s) that the advertising program conveys. The message theme represents the benefit or promise the advertiser uses to reach consumers or businesses. The promise, or unique selling point, describes the major benefit the good or service offers customers. A message theme for an automobile could be oriented toward luxury, safety, fun, fuel efficiency, or driving excitement. A message theme for a hotel could focus on luxury, price, or unusual features, such as a hotel in Paris, France, noting the ease of access to all of the nearby tourist attractions. The message theme matches the medium selected, the target market, and the primary IMC message.[25]

Message themes can be oriented toward either rational or emotional processes. A "left-brain" advertisement oriented toward the logical, rational side informs individuals using numbers, letters, words, and concepts. Left-brain advertising features a logical, factual, rational appeal. A number of logical features (size, price, special features) influence the decision to buy a car. At the same time, many consumers purchase cars for emotional reasons. The right side of the brain contains emotions. It works with abstract ideas, images, and feelings. An automobile may be chosen for its color, sportiness, or other less rational reasons.

Most advertising targets either the right brain or the left brain. Advertising can also be effective by balancing the two sides. Rational, economic beings have difficulty defending the purchase of an expensive sports car such as a Porsche. Many product purchases are based on how a person feels about the good or service, combined with rational information.[26]

The Support

Support should be provided in the fourth component of the creative strategy. **Support** takes the form of facts that substantiate the message theme. When Aveeno products won "Best of Beauty" awards from *Allure* magazine, its "Best of Beauty" seal was placed on the company's products. Company advertising mentioned the award to support Aveeno's claims of superiority.

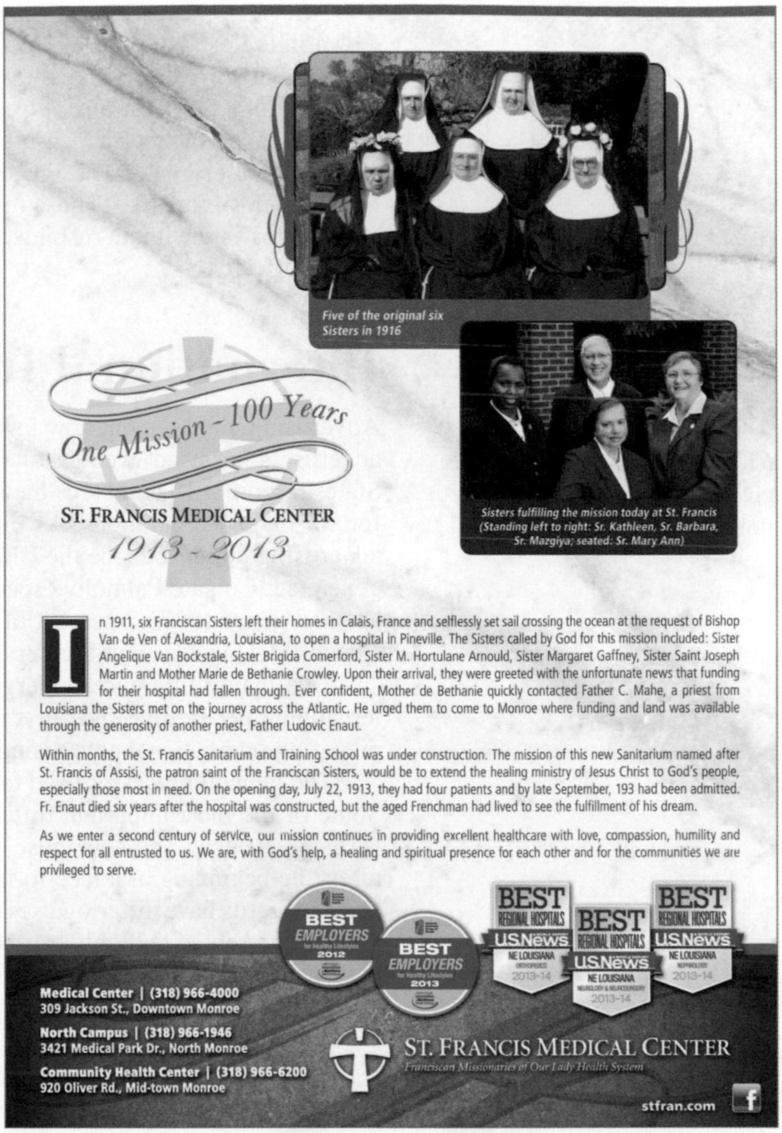

Newcomer, Morris and Young Inc.

▲ An advertisement for St. Francis Medical Center showing the awards the institution has received.

In this section, the advertisement for St. Francis Medical Center shows three Best Regional Hospital awards by *US News* and two Best Employers awards. This type of support indicates to patients the high quality of care they will receive from St. Francis.

The Constraints

Constraints include any legal and mandatory restrictions placed on advertisements. Constraints spell out legal protections for trademarks, logos, and copy registrations. Constraints also establish all disclaimers about warranties, offers, and claims. For warranties, a disclaimer specifies the conditions under which they will be honored. Tire warranties, for example, often state that they apply under normal driving conditions with routine maintenance. A person cannot ignore tire balancing and rotation and expect to get free new tires when the old ones quickly wear out. Disclaimer warranties notify consumers of potential hazards associated with products. Tobacco advertisements contain statements and images regarding the dangers of smoking and chewing tobacco. Disclaimers about marketing offers specify the terms of financing agreements as well as when bonuses or discounts apply. Claims identify the exact nature of the statement made in the advertisement. This includes nutritional claims as well as statements about serving sizes and other information describing the product.

After these steps have been completed, the creative brief is ready. From this point forward, the message and the media match, and actual advertisements can be produced. Effective creative briefs take the overall IMC message and tailor it to a specific advertising campaign. This, in turn, gives the company a better chance of reaching customers with messages that return measurable results and help guarantee success. Recent research suggests that campaigns designed in two months or less have the greatest likelihood of being "highly effective." Those that take longer tend not to be as effective. Marketers try to move forward without rushing. A campaign designed in two weeks or less is also likely to be ineffective.[27]

International Implications

objective 5.8

What are the implications of advertising management in the global arena?

Advertising management now involves major expenditures overseas. The top 100 global advertisers spent an average of 62 percent of advertising budgets outside the United States. Figure 5.16 compares the non-U.S. advertising budget to non-U.S. sales revenue for six major corporations. As illustrated, Coca-Cola spends 83.5 percent of company advertising dollars outside the United States, where 74.9 percent of its total revenues are generated. Colgate-Palmolive spends 85.6 percent of its advertising dollars on non-U.S. ads and generates 76.7 percent of its revenues outside the United States. Data for Ford, Mattel, McDonald's, and Procter & Gamble are also provided.[28]

Two major differences emerge when considering advertising management in an international perspective. The first is in regard to the process itself. The second concerns preparing international advertising campaigns.

The general processes used to prepare advertising campaigns remain fairly uniform. Some of the most important differences are in the areas of availability of qualified advertising agencies and how those agencies are selected. For example, in many Asian cultures, the beginning of a face-to-face meeting would include an exchange of gifts. Also, business cards have differing uses and meanings across cultures. In some countries, cards are only presented to highly trusted allies. In others, they are freely passed out. The marketing team in any company should carefully study the nuances of business meetings,

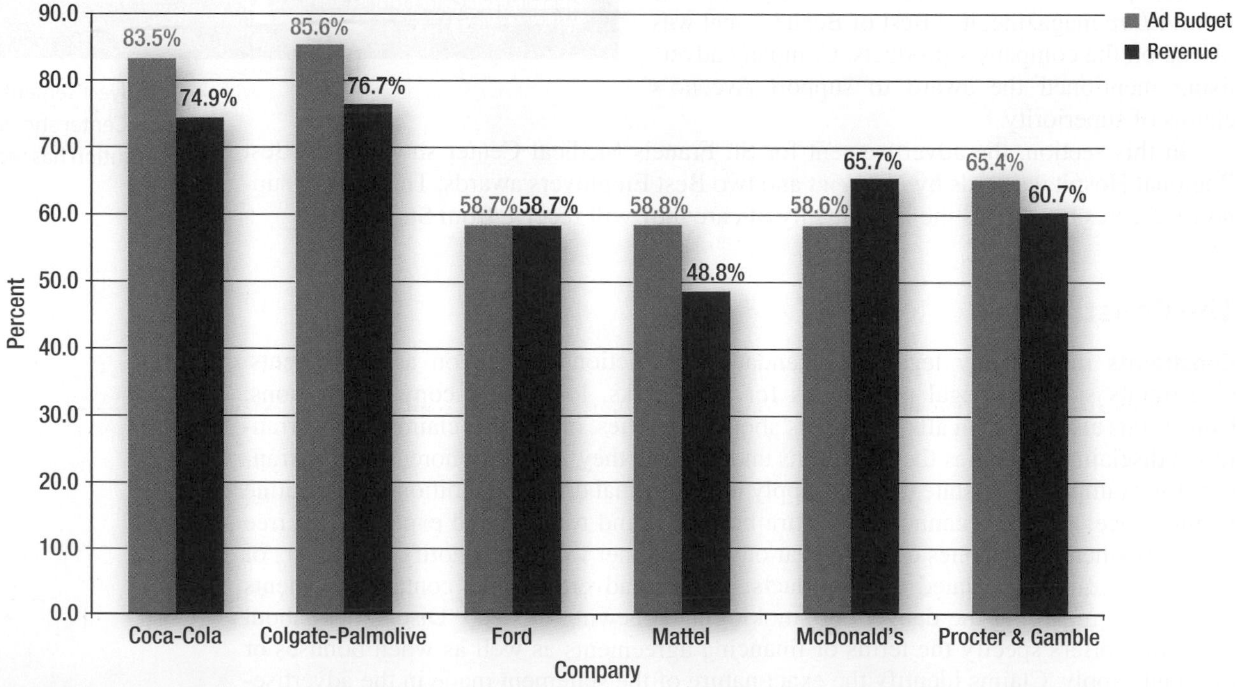

▲ **FIGURE 5.16**

Non-U.S. Ad Budgets and Sales Revenue Comparisons for Major Brands including the use of formal titles, eye contact, who speaks first, and other variables, before beginning a relationship with an advertising agency in another country.

Agencies in other countries might not follow typical procedures such as a shootout or the preparation of a creative brief. Forms of preplanning research may also vary. In some countries, it is not possible to conduct the same types of research as in the United States and other Western cultures.

Advertising campaigns designed for an international audience require an understanding of the various languages and cultures that might be involved. In Europe, French, Spanish, Portuguese, Italian, and other languages need translation and back-translation of advertising themes and messages to make certain the idea can be clearly presented in various countries. Media selection processes may also require adjustment; some countries have state-run television networks and others place restrictions on what can be shown in an advertisement.

Summary

This chapter reviews the advertising campaign management process. Effective advertising occurs when the firm has a well-defined mission statement and targets its energies in the direction of creating goods or services to meet the needs of a target market.

Quality advertising begins with an understanding of various advertising theories that explain consumer purchasing processes. The hierarchy of effects model, a means–end analysis or MECCAS model can be combined with an analysis of the visual and verbal elements needed to create an effective method provide marketers with quality guidelines for creating marketing messages. *Visual Esperanto* is a universal language that makes global advertising possible.

Advertisers should also understand the impact of advertising expenditures. The relationships between marketing expenditures and eventual success can be modeled using concepts such as threshold effects, diminishing returns, carryover effects, wear-out effects, and decay effects. Such an analysis assists in the design of advertisements as well as in assessing levels of effectiveness.

Advertising management continues with the decision to employ an in-house department to develop advertisements or whether an external advertising agency should be retained. When choosing an external agency, the company's leaders establish clear steps to lead to the selection of the optimal agency. The steps include spelling out and prioritizing organizational goals, establishing quality selection criteria, screening firms based on those criteria, requesting references from firms that are finalists, requesting creative pitches, making on-site visits to get to know those in the agencies, and offering and finalizing a contract.

Common selection criteria used in selecting agencies include the size of the agency matching the size of the company, relevant experience, no conflicts of interest, production capabilities, quality creative capabilities, suitable media-purchasing skills, other services that can be rendered as needed, client retention rates, and a good chemistry between those in the company and those in the agency. Carefully utilizing these criteria increases the odds of a successful match between the company and the agency, which increases the chance of success.

Within the advertising agency, the account manager performs the functions of soliciting accounts, finalizing contracts, and selecting creatives to prepare advertising campaigns. Account executives are go-betweens who mediate between the agency and the client company and aid client organizations in refining IMC messages and programs. Traffic managers help to schedule various aspects of the agency's work. Account planners serve as the voice and advocate for the consumer within the advertising agency.

Creating effective advertising campaigns requires attention to various parameters. Advertising goals are derived from the firm's overall communication objectives and include building brand awareness, providing information, generating persuasion, supporting other marketing efforts, and encouraging action. Then media selection can commence. Advertisers seek to develop quality taglines that express something memorable and unique about the brand or convey a special meaning. Another key advertising parameter, consistency, assists in recall of the advertisement. Variability theory suggests that variable encoding can help build strong campaigns. Advertisers also pay attention to quality positioning and seek to understand the best duration for the campaign.

Creatives who prepare advertisements are guided by the creative brief. The document spells out the objective of the promotional campaign, the target audience, the message theme, the support, and the constraints. The message theme presents an outline of the key idea(s) that the program seeks to convey. The constraints include logos, warranties, disclaimers, or legal statements that are part of various advertisements. These processes are carried out by domestic U.S. agencies as well as by advertisers around the world.

Key Terms

advertising campaign management The process of preparing and integrating a company's advertising efforts with the overall IMC message

hierarchy of effects model A method advertisers use to help clarify the objectives of an advertising campaign

means–end chain A conceptual model that shows how a message, or means, can lead consumers to a desired end state

Means–End Conceptualization of Components for Advertising Strategy (MECCAS) A model that explains ways to move consumers from product attributes to personal values by highlighting the product's benefits

visual Esperanto A form of universal language that makes advertising possible for any good or service

threshold effects What occurs at the point in which an advertising program begins to have a significant impact on consumer responses

diminishing returns A point at which a promotional campaign has saturated the market and further advertising and promotional expenditures adversely affect profits

carryover effects An instance in which an individual becomes ready to buy a product and remembers a key company due to the effectiveness of its marketing program

wear-out effects An instance in which consumers ignore or even develop negative attitudes toward a brand because the campaign has become "old" or "boring"

decay effects What occurs when a company stops advertising and consumers begin to forget the message

crowdsourcing The process of outsourcing the creative aspect of an advertisement to the public

top-of-mind brands The brands that quickly come to mind when consumers are asked to identify brands from a product category

top choice The first or second pick when a consumer reviews his or her evoked set of possible purchasing alternatives

tagline A key, memorable phrase in an advertisement that conveys some type of special meaning

variability theory A theory that suggests variable encoding will be more effective as consumers view advertisements in differing environments

creative brief A document that guides in the production of an advertising campaign or for a specific commercial

support The facts that substantiate the unique selling point of a creative brief

constraints The company, legal, and mandatory restrictions placed on advertisements which include legal protection for trademarks, logos, and copy registrations

MyMarketingLab

Go to **mymktlab.com** to complete the problems marked with this icon ✪.

Review Questions

5-1. Define advertising campaign management.

✪ **5-2.** What are the six stages of the hierarchy of effects model? Do they always occur in that order? Why or why not?

5-3. Distinguish between cognitive, affective, and conative advertisements. What are each useful in achieving?

5-4. What is meant by the Means–End Conceptualization of Components for Advertising Strategy (MECCAS) model?

✪ **5-5.** Why are visual elements in advertisement important? What is the relationship between visual and verbal elements? Can there be one without the other?

5-6. Outline the range of visual images.

5-7. Why do business-to-business ads tend to be verbal or written?

5-8. Why do communication goals differ at various stages of the buying process?

5-9. What are the advantages of using in-house advertising resources that make it suitable for those involved in the process?

5-10. How do you build brand loyalty?

5-11. What is crowdsourcing? What are its advantages and disadvantages?

5-12. What steps should be taken in selecting an advertising agency?

5-13. What evaluation criteria should be used in selecting an advertising agency?

5-14. What is a creative pitch?

5-15. Describe the various roles within an advertising agency.

5-16. What advertising campaign parameters were described in this chapter?

5-17. Describe the terms top-of-mind and top choice.

5-18. What is a tagline, and what role does a tagline play in an advertisement?

✪ **5-19.** Explain how variability theory can be used to create consistency in an advertising campaign.

5-20. What elements are included in a creative brief?

Critical Thinking Exercises

DISCUSSION QUESTIONS

5-21. Identify five recent commercials that you have seen or watched that you believe are effective. Identify the part of the hierarchy of effects model that the advertisement targets, noting the specific step in the model. Explain your answer.

5-22. Pick one of the following brands. Develop a means–ends chain similar to the two that are shown in this chapter.

a. St. Francis Medical Center
b. JD Bank
c. Orkin Pest Control
d. Maxwell House Coffee

5-23. Think about recent advertisements you have seen or watched. For each of the concepts listed, give an example of an advertisement you believe illustrates the concept. Explain why you believe the ad fits the category.

- Threshold effects
- Diminishing returns
- Carryover effects
- Wear-out effects
- *Visual Esperanto*

5-24. What is it that personally appeals to you in an advertisement? What attracts and maintains your attention? Ultimately, does the advertisement work as far as the business is concerned? Are you influenced enough to base a purchasing decision on the advertisement alone? Does the stimulus change?

5-25. How do you think you would fit into an advertising agency environment? What aspects of the work best suit your skills and interests?

5-26. Choose one of the following products. Use the information in this chapter to prepare a creative brief. You can pick a brand from within the product category.

a. Energy drink
b. Frozen apple juice
c. Fast-food restaurant
d. Museum
e. Dress shoes

Integrated Learning Exercises

5-27. Making the decision to use an external advertising agency as opposed to an in-house program for advertising or some other aspect of the advertising function can be difficult. Access the American Association of Advertising Agencies website at **www.aaaa.org**. What type of information is available at this website? How would it benefit companies looking for an advertising agency? Explain your answer. How would it benefit advertising agencies? Explain your answer.

5-28. A number of agencies assist business organizations with integrated marketing communications programs. Whereas some firms try to provide a wide array of services, others are more specialized. Access the following association websites. What type of information is available on each site? How would the information provided be useful in building an IMC program?

a. International Social Media Association (**www.ismaconnects.org**)
b. Brand Activation Association (**www.bbalink.org**)
c. Outdoor Advertising Association of America (**www.oaaa.org**)
d. Direct Marketing Association (**www.the-dma.org**)
e. Digital Marketing Association (**www.digitalmarketingassoc.com**)

5-29. Prior to getting involved with social media platforms in China, a global provider decides to monitor trends at the excellent China Internet Watch (**www.chinainternetwatch.com/category/social-media**). Over the course of a few days assess the value of this website and comment on whether you feel that the information is dependable and independent. How could you go about verifying the data on the site? Where could you double-check and make sure it is correct?

5-30. Many advertisers direct ads toward the right side of the brain and develop advertisements based entirely on emotions, images, and pictures. Companies often advertise auto parts and tools with a scantily clad woman to attract the attention of men. The woman has nothing to do with the product, but garners attention. The rationale for using a sexy woman is that if consumers like her, they will like the product and then purchase that brand. Effective advertisements integrate elements from both the left side of the brain as well as the right. They contain elements that appeal to emotions but also have rational arguments. A laundry detergent can be advertised as offering the rational benefit of getting clothes cleaner but also contain the emotional promise that your mother-in-law will think of you more favorably. For each of the following websites, discuss the balance of left-brain versus right-brain advertising appeal.

a. Pier 1 Imports (**www.pier1.com**)
b. Pig O' My Heart Potbellies (**www.potbellypigs.com**)

c. Volkswagen of America (**www.vw.com**)
d. Popeyes Louisiana Kitchen (**www.popeyes.com**)
e. Backcountry.com (**www.backcountry.com**)

5-31. You have been asked to select an advertising agency to handle an account for Red Lobster, a national restaurant chain. Your advertising budget is $30 million. Study the websites of the following advertising agencies. Follow the selection steps outlined in the chapter. Narrow the list down to two agencies and justify your decision. Then choose between the two agencies and justify your choice.

a. The Richards Group (**www.richards.com**)
b. Leo Burnett (**www.leoburnett.com**)
c. DDB (**www.ddb.com**)
d. Lucas Design & Advertising (**www.aladv.com**)
e. mcgarrybowen (**www.mcgarrybowen.com**)
f. Zehnder Communications (**www.z-comm.com**)

5-32. A marketing manager has been placed in charge of a new sporting goods chain of stores to be introduced into the market. The company's corporate headquarters are in Atlanta, and the firm's management team has already decided to use one of the local advertising agencies. The primary objective in choosing an agency is that the firm must have the capability to develop a strong brand name. Type "advertising agencies in Atlanta" into a search engine. Identify an initial list of six ad agencies. Follow the steps outlined in the chapter to narrow the list to two agencies. Discuss the steps you used in choosing the two agencies and why you selected them. Then design a project for the agencies to prepare as part of an oral and written presentation to the company's marketing team.

Blog Exercises

Access the authors' blog for this textbook at the URLs provided to complete these exercises. Answer the questions that are posed on the blog.

5-33. Oreo Cookies: **http://blogclowbaack.net/2014/05/07/oreo-cookies-chapter-5/**

5-34. John Deere: **http://blogclowbaack.net/2014/05/07/john-deere-chapter-4/**

5-35. Advertising Agencies: **http://blogclowbaack.net/2014/05/07/advertising-agencies-chapter-5/**

Student Project

CREATIVE CORNER

Use the following creative brief for this exercise.

Product:	Porsche
Objective:	To change consumers view that the Porsche can be driven every day
Target Audience:	30- to 55-year-old consumers, slightly more male, college educated, with annual incomes of approximately $100,000. Psychographically, the targeted market is a group known as individualists. They tend not to buy mainstream products. In automobile selection, they place greater emphasis on design elements, distinctiveness, and utility. Social status is important.
Background Information:	Market research found that potential customers balked at the idea of buying a car just to sit around. When asked what kept them from driving the car every day, they said, "I don't feel comfortable driving in city traffic. It doesn't have the technology that I need to manage my everyday life. It doesn't have space for passengers."
Message Theme:	The Porsche can be driven every day for normal activities. It does not have to sit in the garage and be driven only on weekends. It has the newest technology and can comfortably carry passengers.
Constraints:	All ads must contain the Porsche logo.

5-36. As an account executive for an advertising agency, discuss the creative brief in terms of the completeness of the information provided and whether the objective is realistic. What additional information should Porsche provide before a creative can begin working on the account?

5-37. The media planner for the Porsche account suggests a media plan consisting of cable television, print advertising, internet ads, and network advertising on *Family Guy, CSI, Monday Night Football, Big Bang Theory*, and *American Idol*. Evaluate this media plan in light of the creative brief's objectives. Can these shows reach the target audience? What information does a creative and the account executive want from the media planner before starting work on actual commercials?

5-38. Using the information provided in the creative brief, prepare a magazine advertisement. Which magazines might match the target audience? Why?

CASE 1 CLASSIC CRYSTAL

Every day, most people in developed countries will use a glass or cup as part of their routines. Glassware is sold in a variety of stores, from large discount retailers such as Wal-Mart and Target to small specialty stores. Customers purchasing glassware range from individuals seeking the simplest, most economical versions to brides making choices at various registries, to bars, restaurants, and hotels requiring vessels to hold drinks of all types.

Glasses can be made from plastic, actual glass, crystal, and other elements. Designs can be nonexistent to exotic. Some glasses are round; others square or in more unusual shapes. Some are dishwasher safe and even designed for heavy-duty use. Arcoroc sells "drinkware" in conjunction with flatware and silverware, giving various businesses such as restaurants the option of purchasing an entire dinner setting that meshes together. In its marketing materials, Arcoroc stresses the durability of it products. At the other extreme, heavy duty glassware can also be found in some Army surplus stores.

Other glassware forms are dainty and can only be hand washed or should at least be handled with a great deal of care. Novica offers hand-blown drinkware that the company describes as "our artisan crafted treasures." Two popular products include "Amber Feast" with a light amber tint and "Night Sky," which is a dark, cobalt blue.

Glassware is often designed to match the fluid it will hold and the setting it will serve. Wine glasses tend to have stems and seek to enhance the aroma of the drink. Some are created to generate "snob appeal." Beer mugs tend to be sturdy and feature handles. Milk glasses for children are short, round, and stout. Dinner glasses assume a variety of forms.

Advertising campaign management for glass manufacturers would feature all of the elements described in this chapter. Advertising theories would help explain how a product is chosen and why. Advertising expenditures should be managed to achieve the highest levels of effectiveness. The manufacturer will decide on an in-house or agency-based approach to marketing. When an agency is chosen, the campaign parameters will be outlined and a creative brief should be developed to guide the advertising process.

Nataliya Dvukhimenna/Fotolia

▲ Drinkware comes in a variety of shapes and sizes.

5-39. Using the internet, identify a glassware brand and/or manufacturer that interests you. Based on the information provided for the brand, choose a particular type of glassware. Explain why you chose this particular brand. In your explanation, include the brand's website address and a screenshot of its main page.

5-40. Develop a means–end chain that explains the purchasing process for the brand's specific products.

5-41. Using the internet, identify five advertising agencies in your area. Evaluate each advertising agency in terms of its ability to handle an advertising campaign for your company. Choose one of the five to handle your account and explain why it was chosen. (Include each agency's URL in your response).

5-42. Develop a creative brief for an advertising campaign that you believe would best fit your glassware company.

5-43. Design a print ad that fits the creative brief you developed.

CASE 2 ADVERTISING JEANS TO TEENS

If there is one nearly common denominator among teens around the world, it may be the desire to impress peers and potential romantic partners. A variety of enticing adornments assist in the process, including choices regarding hair style, cosmetics, jewelry, and clothing. In many cultures, designer jeans allow younger consumers to look sleek and sassy.

In the United States, top name designer jeans include Citizens of Humanity, Rockstar, Bluelab, Superfine, Dylan George, Stitch's, Current/Elliot, Red Engine, Rich and Skinny, Chip & Pepper, Mavi, Monarchy, HA-67, and Diesel. These companies compete with more established Lee and Levi jeans. In Brazil, Butt Lift products have gained an edge in the marketplace, competing with Moleton and Blue Monster. French products include 2Leep and German companies sell Trewano.

The market for jeans remains lucrative. Teens with disposable income may spend a great deal of time and effort choosing the brand they will wear. Influences include the price and fit, but also social and peer pressure, jeans worn by celebrities, and parental limitations. Social media allows them to consider a variety of brands, discussing the options with friends while seeking to discover the most popular new hot item.

Each year, jean styles change. The elements in jeans may move from looking old and torn, to those stitched with special designs, and then to multifabric entries. Length can be Capri, full, straight-legged, or flared. Pockets may be small or large. They may be closed using zippers or buttons. Trendsetters dictate the new fads and fashions.

To complicate matters further, jeans may be worn for style or for work. Besides teenagers, young children and older adults also buy these items. Some marketers, such as Levi and Lee, try to develop brands and lines with staying power. Others focus solely on one segment such as young women or work jeans for older men.

Jason Stitt/Fotolia

▲ Teens are an attractive market for brands of jeans.

5-44. Select one of the brands of jeans in this case or another brand you like. Access the brand's website. Explain why you chose this particular brand. In your response, include the brand's website address and a screenshot of its main page.

5-45. Develop a means–ends chain that explains the purchasing process for the brand of jeans.

5-46. Using the internet, identify five advertising agencies in your area. Evaluate each advertising agency in terms of its ability to handle an advertising campaign for your company. Choose one of the five to handle your account and explain why it was chosen. (Include each agency's URL in your response).

5-47. Develop a creative brief for an advertising campaign that you believe would best fit the brand of jeans you selected.

5-48. Design a print ad that fits the creative brief you developed.

MyMarketingLab

Go to **mymktlab.com** for the following Assisted-graded writing questions:

5-49. Look through the ads in this chapter. Which ad to you like the best? Why? Which ad is the least appealing to you? Why? Discuss what makes a print ad appealing and what creates the opposite effect.

5-50. You have been asked to select an advertising agency to handle an account for Red Lobster, a national restaurant chain. Your advertising budget is $30 million. Study the websites of the following advertising agencies. Follow the selection steps outlined in the chapter. Narrow the list down to two agencies and justify your decision. Then choose between the two agencies and justify your choice.

a. The Richards Group (**www.richards.com**)
b. Leo Burnett (**www.leoburnett.com**)
c. DDB (**www.ddb.com**)
d. Lucas Design & Advertising (**www.aladv.com**)
e. mcgarrybowen (**www.mcgarrybowen.com**)
f. Zehnder Communications (**www.z-comm.com**)

Chapter 6 Advertising Design

Chapter Objectives

After reading this chapter, you should be able to answer the following questions:

6.1 How are message strategies used in designing effective advertisements?

6.2 What are the seven main types of advertising appeals?

6.3 What role does the executional framework play in advertising design?

6.4 How are sources and spokespersons decisions related to advertising design?

Overview

Which advertising message made the biggest impression on you in the past five years? Was it funny, sexy, or emotional? Did it appear during the Super Bowl? In a recent *Adweek* Media and Harris Interactive survey, the majority of consumers (55 percent) said that advertisements were somewhat or very interesting. Only 13 percent replied that ads were not interesting at all. When making purchase decisions, six percent of the respondents reported that advertisements were "very influential" and 29 percent viewed them as "somewhat influential." Contrary to popular belief, advertising does influence younger consumers. Nearly half of 18- to 34-year-olds in the survey stated that they were influenced in some way by advertising, compared to 37 percent for 35- to 44-year-olds and 28 percent for consumers age 45 and older.[1]

This poll emphasizes the importance of designing a compelling and influential advertising campaign. Doing so can be one of the most challenging elements of an integrated marketing communications program. A successful advertising campaign results when people do more than merely enjoy what they see; it also changes their behaviors and attitudes. At the least, viewers should remember the good or service. One advertising agency with a strong track record of success in advertising design is mcgarrybowen.

MCGARRYBOWEN

In 2002, three partners came together to form a new competitor in the advertising and communications world, the mcgarrybowen agency. John P. McGarry, Jr., Gordon Bowen, and Stewart Owen designed a company that would be "gracious" and "tenacious" at the same time. Instead of one distinct style with a predetermined media solution, the agency delivers a strategic approach focused on the client's business and brand.

Mcgarrybowen Chicago

Mcgarrybowen Chicago

Mcgarrybowen Chicago

◀ Chicago office of mcgarrybowen.

The agency's impressive client list includes Chevron, Canon, Disney, J. P. Morgan, Kraft, Marriott, Oscar Mayer, Pfizer, Sharp, *The Wall Street Journal*, and Verizon. Specific products advertised and marketed through mcgarrybowen include 7UP, Advil, Miracle Whip, Snapple, and Viagra. Most recently, the firm recaptured the Reebok account and added several new clients, including Sears, Burger King, United Airlines, and Bud Light. *Advertising Age* named mcgarrybowen Agency of the Year in 2009, #2 on its A-List in 2010, and Agency of the Year in 2011.

The mcgarrybowen agency's full service approach covers nearly every marketing and communications activity. Among them, advertising, brand strategies, digital messages, mobile, social networks, data analytics, direct marketing, sponsorships, entertainment marketing, media planning, and multicultural marketing are featured. Company leaders emphasize collaboration. The net result is a motivated and inspired work force that delivers high-quality, creative solutions for clients.

A creative at mcgarrybowen noted, "We pride ourselves on storytelling. The foundations of those stories come out as a product truth." Another employee noted, "Our account planning has more fluidity. Planning becomes most crucial when strategy is the first chapter of the story. The premise of our brand strategy is how we are going to connect the brand story on a human level." In essence, storytelling involves "getting to a single insight that interprets the brand and makes a personal connection."

Chapter 5 described the overall advertising management program, such as the approach used by mcgarrybowen. As noted in that chapter, account executives lead advertising agencies by working with creatives, media planners, and media buyers. This chapter turns the focus to message design. The work will be completed by the agency's staff based on the creative brief that was prepared by the client in conjunction with the account executive.

The first three topics in this chapter are message strategies, appeals, and executional frameworks. These elements of advertising design are similar to what takes place when developing a movie or television program. The message strategy resembles what the actor says—the verbal message. The appeal represents the manner in which a message is conveyed; through a serious tone, laughter, or sexual cues. The executional framework is comparable to the plot or story of the movie in which the action takes place.

The final topic in the chapter is a discussion of sources or spokespersons. These individuals present the message verbally and visually through the various media used in the advertising program. Agencies and companies carefully consider who will become the "face" of the company and its products.

Message Strategies

objective 6.1

How are message strategies used in designing effective advertisements?

The message theme outlines the key idea in an advertising campaign and becomes the central part of the creative brief, as described in Chapter 5. The message theme helps the advertising team derive a **message strategy**—the primary tactic or approach used to deliver the message theme. The three broad categories of message strategies include cognitive, affective, and conative approaches.[2] The categories represent the components of attitudes, as noted in the previous chapter. Figure 6.1 identifies the various forms or approaches from each category.

- Cognitive
  - Generic
  - Unique selling proposition
  - Hyperbole
  - Comparative
- Affective
  - Resonance
  - Emotional
- Conative

FIGURE 6.1
Message Strategies

Cognitive Message Strategies

A **cognitive message strategy** presents rational arguments or pieces of information to consumers. The ideas require cognitive processing. The advertising message seeks to describe the product's attributes or benefits customers can obtain by purchasing the product.[3]

A cognitive message strategy advertisement influences a person's beliefs and/or knowledge structure by suggesting one of a variety of potential product benefits. Foods may be described as healthy, pleasant tasting, or low calorie. Marketers can depict a tool as durable, convenient, or handy to use. The five major forms of cognitive strategies are generic messages, preemptive messages, unique selling propositions, hyperbole, and comparative advertisements.

▲ An advertisement for Community Trust Bank featuring a cognitive message strategy stating checks can be deposited anytime and anywhere.

Trust Bank, Community

Generic Messages An advertisement that directly promotes the product's attributes or benefits without any claim of superiority transmits a **generic message**, which works best for a brand leader firm or one that dominates the industry. A generic message makes the brand synonymous with the product category. Campbell's can declare "Soup is good food" without making any claim to superiority. The company leads the industry. When most consumers think of soup, they think of Campbell's, which sells 69 percent of all cans sold each year.[4] Nintendo employs a similar approach because the company dominates the game-console category with a 47 percent market share.[5] In the business-to-business arena, Intel can deploy the generic message strategy "Intel inside" because it controls 80 percent of the microchip market.[6]

Generic message strategies help stimulate brand awareness. The advertiser may try to develop a cognitive linkage between a specific brand name and a product category, such as Sketchers and sporty footwear. The advertisement might contain little information about the product's attributes. Instead, it attempts to place the brand in a person's cognitive memory and cognitive map.

Preemptive Messages A claim of superiority based on a product's specific attribute or benefit with the intent of preventing the competition from making the same or a similar statement is a **preemptive message**. Crest toothpaste's reputation as "the cavity fighter" preempts other companies from making similar claims, even though all toothpastes fight cavities. An effective preemptive strategy occurs when the company states the advantage first. Competitors saying the same thing become viewed as "me too" brands or copycats.

Unique Selling Proposition An explicit, testable claim of uniqueness or superiority that can be supported or substantiated in some manner is a **unique selling proposition**. In the advertisement for P & S Surgical Hospital shown in this section, the company claims to have the best smaller-sized hospital. Substantiation of these claims comes through being rated #1 in Louisiana by CareChex and receiving a 5-star rating by HealthGrades.

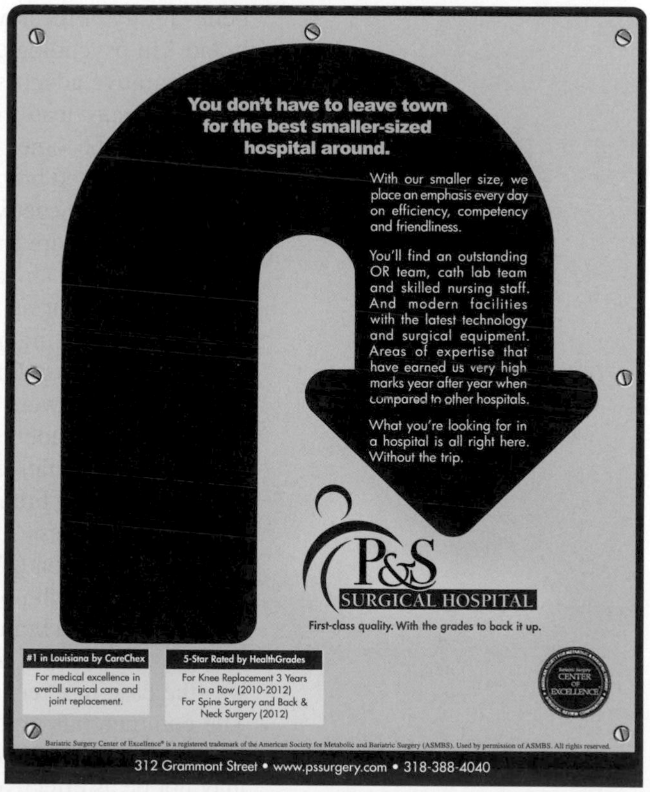

▲ An advertisement for P & S Surgical Hospital using a unique selling proposition message strategy.

French Creative

Karns Quality Foods

▲ This advertisement for Karns Quality Foods features a hyperbole message strategy.

Hyperbole An *untestable* claim based on some attribute or benefit is **hyperbole**. When NBC states that it has America's favorite comedies, the claim is hyperbole. It does not require substantiation, which makes this cognitive strategy quite popular. The hyperbole approach often uses puffery terms, such as *best* or *greatest* such as in the ad for Karns Foods shown here.

Comparative Advertising The final cognitive message strategy, a **comparative advertisement**, allows an advertiser to directly or indirectly compare a product to the competition on some product attribute or benefit. The advertisement may or may not mention the competitor by name. An advertiser can simply present a make-believe competitor with a name such as "Brand X."

Comparative ads offer the advantage of capturing the consumer's attention. When comparisons are made, both brand awareness and message awareness increase. Consumers tend to remember more of what was said about a brand than when a non-comparative format presents the same information.

Low believability and negative consumer attitudes represent the potential downside of comparative ads. Many consumers consider comparative ads to be less believable. They view the information about the sponsor brand as exaggerated and conclude that the advertisement probably mis-states information about the comparison brand to make the sponsor brand appear superior. This in turn can lead to negative consumer attitudes toward a brand.

Another danger with comparative ads occurs when consumers experience negative attitudes toward the advertisement, which can then transfer to the sponsor's product. This becomes more likely when the sponsor runs a *negative comparative ad* about the competition's product. Research suggests that negative comparative ads typically result in lower believability of the advertising claim and may result in less favorable attitudes toward the brand.[7] In psychology, the concept of *spontaneous trait transference* suggests that when a comparative advertisement criticizes the competition's brand based on a particular attribute, it may lead viewers to also attribute the deficiency to the sponsor brand. The transference becomes more likely when the consumer purchases the comparative brand, not the sponsored brand.[8]

At times, negative ads can succeed. One negative comparative campaign that achieved the desired results was the "Scroogled" campaign by Microsoft's search engine, Bing. The campaign presents negative information about Google, such as invasive ads in Gmail, sharing data with app developers, and exploiting private data to maximize Google's advertising profits. Most of the ads do not mention Bing until the very end when the voiceover says "For honest results, try Bing." Ad effectiveness research indicated that 53 percent of viewers said they would look at Bing after viewing the ads.[9]

Company leaders carefully choose an appropriate comparison firm and use caution when using a negative comparison format. The comparison brand must be viewed as a viable competing brand. Comparisons consisting of hype and opinion with no substantial differences are less likely to succeed. Misleading comparisons may cause the Federal Trade Commission (FTC) to investigate. The majority of complaints filed with the FTC are concerned with potentially misleading comparison advertisements.

Comparing a brand with a low market share to the market leader works well, because viewers concentrate more carefully on the advertisement's content and message. Such was the case in a recent campaign for the Kindle Fire, which was compared to the iPad. The commercials argue that the Kindle Fire has better quality product attributes and a lower price. Comparing a high-market share brand with another high-market share brand may not be as effective. In these cases, a better strategy may be to simply make the comparison without naming the competitor.

The five cognitive message strategies are based on rational logic. Advertisers design messages that lead consumers to pay attention to the ad and take the time to cognitively process the information. In terms of attitudes as described in Chapter 5, the sequence of *cognitive* → *affective* → *conative* represents the rational approach. The cognitive message strategy first presents consumers with rational information about a good, service, or company and then leads them to develop positive feelings about the same product or company.

Affective Message Strategies

Advertisements trying to evoke feelings or emotions and match those feelings with the good, service, or company feature **affective message strategies**. These messages attempt to enhance the likeability of the product, recall of the appeal, or comprehension of the advertisement. Affective strategies should elicit emotions that in turn lead the consumer to act, preferably by buying the product and subsequently by affecting the consumer's reasoning process.

Resonance Connecting a brand with a consumer's experiences in order to develop stronger ties between the product and the consumer is resonance affective advertising. The use of music from the 1980s takes Echo Boomers back to that time. Any strongly held memory or emotional attachment becomes a candidate for resonance advertising.

Subaru's advertising team designed a resonance approach for an online marketing effort that attempted to tap into a person's nostalgia for his first car. The program included an animation generator at a microsite called FirstCarStory.com where consumers could recreate the look and feel of their first cars. The program's technology transferred words into custom images. Alan Bethke, director of marketing communications at Subaru, noted, "The First Car Story campaign provides a creative outlet for reliving those unique, funny, unforgettable experiences anyone who had a first car can relate to."[10]

A new form of resonance advertising, **comfort marketing**, emerged when marketers looked for ways to encourage consumers to purchase branded products rather than generic versions. The approach reassures consumers looking for value that a branded product stands the test of time. Comfort marketing involves bringing back vintage

◀ This advertisement for visit South Walton (Florida) presents an affective message strategy through the headline "Make Connections."

Visit South Walton

Kraft Foods, Inc

▲ An advertisement for Philadelphia Cream Cheese using an emotional message strategy through the image and tagline "pheel the moment."

characters, themes, and jingles from the past to evoke fond memories when times were better. To ensure the brand does not look old-fashioned, most refresh the mascot, music, taglines, and other aspects of the ad to the twenty-first century. Brands that have employed this approach include StarKist, Alka-Seltzer, Bacardi, Doritos, Dr. Pepper, Pepsi-Cola, and Planters. Robert Furniss-Roe of Bacardi North America, said, "People, particularly in this environment, are looking for substance and authenticity."[11]

Emotional The **emotional affective approach** attempts to elicit powerful emotions that lead to product recall and choice. Many emotions can be connected to products, including trust, reliability, friendship, happiness, security, glamour, luxury, serenity, pleasure, romance, and passion. Companies incorporate emotional appeals into both consumer-oriented and business-to-business advertisements. Members of the buying center in a business are human. They make purchasing decisions based on more than simple rational thought processes. Emotions and feelings also affect choices. When an advertisement presents products' benefits in an emotional framework, it will normally be more effective, even in business-to-business ads.[12]

Many creatives believe affective strategies help build a stronger brand name. Affective advertisements guide consumers to like the brand, develop positive feelings toward it, and eventually purchase the item. Cognitive beliefs about the brand then follow. This approach relies on the attitude development sequence of *affective* → *conative* → *cognitive*. For some products, affective advertisements succeed because few real tangible differences among brands actually exist. The St. Francis Medical Center advertisement in this section features an affective strategy by depicting a warm mother/daughter relationship.

Conative Message Strategy

Conative message strategies seek to lead directly to a consumer response. They can support other promotional efforts, such as coupon redemption programs, cash-back rebates, or encourage consumers to access a website. Advertisements that seek to persuade viewers to call a toll-free number to purchase DVDs or other merchandise contain the goal of

▶ An advertisement for St. Francis Medical Center featuring an emotional message strategy.

Newcomer, Morris and Young

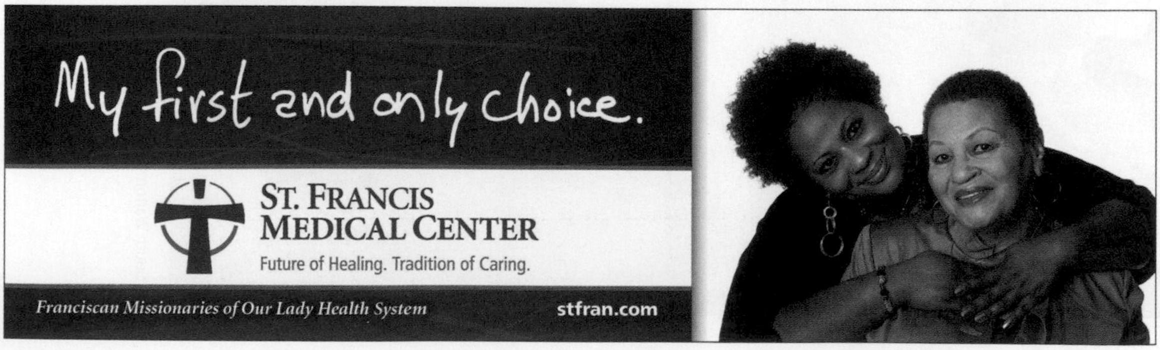

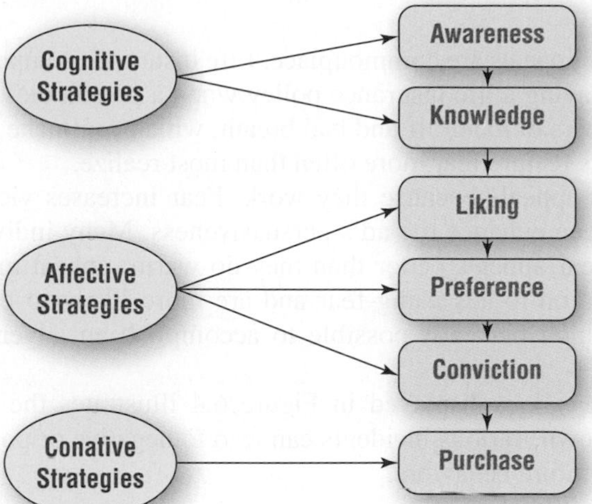

◀ **FIGURE 6.2**
The Hierarchy of Effects Model and Message Strategies

eliciting behaviors. Conative ads typically encourage quick action by stating that the item cannot be purchased in stores and will be available for only a limited time.

With conative advertising, cognitive knowledge of the brand or affective liking of the product may come later (after the actual purchase) or during product usage. For instance, a point-of-purchase display can be designed (sometimes through advertising tie-ins) to cause people to make *impulse buys*. Making the sale constitutes the goal, with cognitive knowledge and affective feelings forming as the product is used. The attitude sequence for conative message strategies becomes *conative → cognitive → affective*.

Cognitive, affective, and conative strategies can be matched with the hierarchy of effects approach, which as noted in the previous chapter, suggests that consumers pass through a series of stages, from awareness to knowledge, liking, preference, conviction, and, finally, to the purchase. As shown in Figure 6.2, each message strategy highlights a different stage of the hierarchy of effects model that was first described in Chapter 5.

Choosing the right message strategy remains a key ingredient in creating a successful advertising program. To be effective, the message strategy should match the message to the appeal and executional framework. These should mesh with the media to be utilized. The creative and the account executive remain in constant contact throughout the process to be certain all of these advertising ingredients remain consistent.

▼ This advertisement for Skyjacker Suspensions offers a cash-back rebate.

Skyjacker Suspensions

Types of Advertising Appeals

Throughout the years, advertisers have employed numerous advertising approaches. Of these, seven **advertising appeals** have achieved the most success. Normally, one or a combination of these types of appeals will be featured in an advertisement (see Figure 6.3).

The type of appeal chosen will be based on a review of the creative brief, the objective of the campaign, the means–end chain to be conveyed, and the message strategy. Advertisers consider a number of factors, including the product being sold, the target market of the campaign, and the personal preferences of the advertising agency and client.

objective 6.2
What are the seven main types of advertising appeals?

- Fear
- Humor
- Sex
- Music
- Rationality
- Emotions
- Scarcity

▲ **FIGURE 6.3**
Types of Appeals

Fear Appeals

Advertisements featuring fear appeals are commonplace. Life insurance companies focus on the consequences of not having a life insurance policy when a person dies. Shampoo and mouthwash ads invoke fears of dandruff and bad breath, which can make a person a social outcast. Advertisements feature fear more often than most realize.

Advertisers employ fear appeals because they work. Fear increases viewer interest in an advertisement and can enhance the ad's persuasiveness. Many individuals remember commercials with fear appeals better than they do warm, upbeat messages.[13] Consumers pay greater attention to ads using fear and are more likely to process the information they present, which makes it possible to accomplish an advertisement's main objective.

The *behavioral response model* displayed in Figure 6.4 illustrates the ways fear works in advertising.[14] As shown, various incidents can lead to negative or positive consequences, which then affect future behaviors.

Severity and Vulnerability When developing fear advertisements, the creative includes as many aspects of the behavioral response model as possible. A business-to-business advertiser offering internet services tries to focus on the **severity** of downtime if a company's internet server goes down or is hacked. Another ad describes the firm's **vulnerability** by showing the probability that a company's server will crash or can be hacked into and customer data stolen. The ReRez advertisement for marketing research services shown on the next page features a picture of a man hanging to illustrate the danger of poor marketing research. The advertisement attempts to cause business leaders to believe low quality decisions would result from inadequate research. ReRez can help them identify these potential problems before they turn into disasters.

Rewards to Response Efficacy To further understand the behavioral response model, consider a young smoker who sees an ad for the Nicoderm CQ patches, which help a person quit. The man considers three things in evaluating the advertisement and making a decision to purchase Nicoderm CQ.

Intrinsic and extrinsic rewards are the first factor. Intrinsic rewards come from gaining social acceptance by quitting and feeling healthier. Extrinsic rewards may include savings on the cost of cigarettes as compared to the price for Nicoderm CQ.

The smoker then considers the second factor, *response costs.* When smoking leads to peer acceptance it becomes rewarding, which means there is a lower incentive to quit,

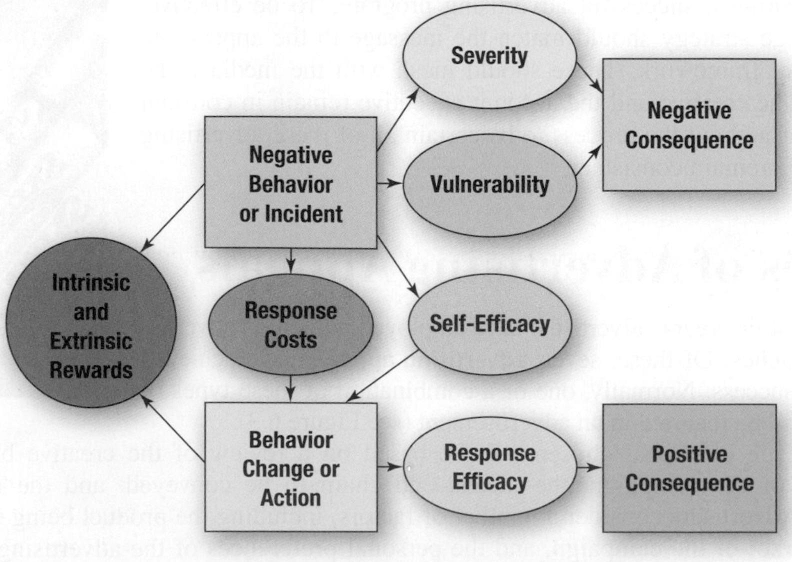

▶ **FIGURE 6.4**
The Behavioral Response Model

◀ This business-to-business advertisement for ReRez features a fear appeal.

ReRez

because smoking creates intrinsic value, making quitting more difficult. A man who quits smoking becomes more likely to gain weight and lose the friends who continue to smoke. The higher the perceived costs, the less likely the decision to quit smoking becomes.

Self-efficacy constitutes the third factor. In this situation, self-efficacy relates to the man's confidence in his ability to stop smoking. Many individuals have tried and failed. Thus, they have little hope Nicoderm CQ will work. The smoker must believe that Nicoderm CQ can truly help him quit before he will purchase it.

The combination of intrinsic and extrinsic rewards, response costs, and the degree of self-efficacy contribute to the smoker's *response efficacy*. The decision to purchase Nicoderm CQ with the idea of stopping smoking will be based on the conclusion that doing so will lead to net positive consequences. The person concludes he will fit in with family and friends, feel better, improve his health, and believe that he is capable of quitting smoking.

Appeal Strength When using fear, the strength of the appeal constitutes another key factor. Most advertisers believe a moderate level of fear will be the most effective. A low level of fear may not be noticed and the fear level may not be convincing in terms of severity or vulnerability. An advertisement containing a fear level that is too strong can also backfire, because the message only generates feelings of anxiety. This leads the viewer to avoid watching the commercial by changing the channel or muting the sound.[15] Consequently, a fear appeal should be powerful enough to capture a viewer's attention and to influence her thinking but not so scary that she avoids the advertisement.

Humor Appeals

Clutter presents a significant problem in every advertising medium. Capturing a viewer's attention continues to be difficult. Even after grabbing the audience's attention, keeping it becomes even more challenging. Humor has proven to be one of the best

Himchenko/Fotolia

▲ Marketers use humor in advertising because people like to laugh.

techniques for cutting through clutter, by getting attention and keeping it. Consumers, as a whole, enjoy advertisements that make them laugh. A funny message offers intrusive value and attracts attention.[16]

Humor appears in about 30 percent of television and radio advertisements.[17] Humorous ads often win awards and tend to be favorites among consumers. In a *USA Today* consumer survey of the most likeable advertising campaigns, humor was a key ingredient.[18]

Humorous ads achieve success for three reasons. Humor causes consumers to: watch, laugh, and, most important, remember. In recall tests, consumers most often recall humorous ads. The best results occur when the humor connects directly with the product's benefits. The advertisement should link the product's features with the advantage to customers and personal values in a means–end chain.

Advertising research indicates that humor elevates people's moods. Happy consumers often associate a good mood with the advertiser's products. In essence, humor helps fix the brand in the consumer's cognitive structure with links to positive feelings. Figure 6.5 summarizes the primary reasons for using humor.

Although a funny advertisement can capture the viewer's attention, cut through clutter, and enhance recall, humorous ads can also go wrong. A Snickers commercial that ran during a recent Super Bowl featured two mechanics eating from opposite ends of the same candy bar until they accidentally ended up kissing. The two men responded in disgust by ripping out their own chest hairs. The outcry from some groups was loud enough that it was immediately pulled.[19]

Advertisers should not allow the humor to overpower the message. Humor fails when consumers remember the joke but not the product or brand. In other words, the advertisement was so funny that the audience forgets or does not catch the sponsor's name.

Using humor with global campaigns can create difficulties. Humor rooted in one culture may not transfer to another. Further, not all audiences experience a humorous ad in the same way. To avoid these potential problems, the humor in an advertisement should focus on a component of the means–end chain. The humor can relate to a product's attributes, a customer benefit, or the personal value obtained from the product. The most effective ads are those in which the humor incorporates all three elements.

FIGURE 6.5
Reasons for Using Humor in Ads

- Captures attention.
- Holds attention.
- Often wins creative awards.
- High recall scores.
- Consumers enjoy ads that make them laugh.
- Evaluated by consumers as likeable ads.

Sex Appeals

Advertisers use sexual appeals to break through clutter. Advertisements in the United States and other countries contain more visual sexual themes than ever. Nudity and other sexual approaches are common. Sexual themes in ads, however, do not always work. Sex no longer has shock value. Today's teens grow up in societies immersed in sex. One more sexually-oriented ad captures little attention. Currently, many advertisers prefer more subtle sexual cues, suggestions, and innuendos.[20] Figure 6.6 lists the ways marketers employ sexuality in advertisements.

- Subliminal techniques
- Sensuality
- Sexual suggestiveness
- Nudity or partial nudity
- Overt sexuality

▲ **FIGURE 6.6**
Sexuality Approaches Used in Advertising

Subliminal Approach Placing sexual cues or icons in advertisements in an attempt to affect a viewer's subconscious is the subliminal approach. In an odd paradox, truly subliminal cues are not noticed, which means they do not create any effects. Consumers already pay little attention to ads. A subliminal message that registers only in the viewer's subconscious will not be effective. If it worked, there would be no need for stronger sexual content in advertising.

Sensuality Some women respond more favorably to a sensual suggestion than an overtly sexual approach. An alluring glance across a crowded room can be sensual and draw attention to a product. Many view sensuality as being more sophisticated, because it relies on the imagination. Images of romance and love can be more enticing than raw sexuality.

Sexual Suggestiveness A sexually suggestive advertisement hints that sex is about to take place. Recently, Pine-Sol included suggestiveness to advertise a household cleaner. In several television ads, shirtless, muscular men are shown mopping the floor while the female watches or fantasizes. Diane Amos, who has been featured in Pine-Sol ads for the last 16 years and appears in this new series of ads featuring men, says, "We would all like our husbands to mop. It can be fun, it can be sexy, and women like it clean."[21]

Nudity or partial nudity Products that contain sexual connotations or elements, such as clothing, perfume, and cologne, may feature a degree of nudity. Some ads are designed to solicit a sexual response. Others are not. In 1987, underwear companies were first allowed to use live models in television advertisements. The first commercials were modest and informational, emphasizing the design or materials used in the undergarment. The first Playtex bra commercials with live models drew strong criticism from organizations such as the American Family Association. Currently, advertisements for undergarments go much further and involve superstars, such as actress Jennifer Love Hewitt who appeared in television and print ads for the Hanes All-Over Comfort Bra and the Perfect Panty. The campaign even included an online element with footage from the photo shoots, a "bad bra toss" game, and a blog about bad bra moments.[22]

▼ A milk advertisement using a sex appeal.

Tuzyra/Fotolia

▲ Live models are now featured in lingerie ads with sexual appeal.

Overt Sexuality Using overt sexuality in ads for sexually-oriented products is normally accepted, but it often becomes controversial when used for other types of products. When Procter & Gamble launched a television advertising campaign for Dentyne, eyebrows were raised. The commercial showed two teens in a living room. The girl pops a piece of Dentyne Fire bubble gum into her mouth and then rips off her blouse and jumps on her boyfriend. At first, the parents stare in shock. Then, the mom tries a piece of Dentyne Fire and promptly jumps on the dad. The controversy centered on whether the ad promoted teenage sexuality by suggesting that parents should openly display sexual feelings and desires.[23]

Decorative Models One common sexual approach involves placing **decorative models** into advertisements. These individuals adorn products as sexual or attractive stimuli. They serve no other purpose than to attract attention. In the past, commercials for automobiles, tools, and beer often used female models dressed in bikinis standing by the products. Marketers conducted a number of studies in order to determine the effectiveness of decorative models. Figure 6.7 provides some basic conclusions regarding this tactic.[24]

Effectiveness of Sex Appeals Numerous studies have examined the effectiveness of sexual appeals and nudity in advertising. Almost all of them conclude that sex and nudity do increase attention. At the same time, brand recall tends to be lower than advertisements with other types of appeals. It appears that although people watch the advertisement, the sexual theme distracts them from noticing the brand name.[25]

Observers often rate sexually-oriented advertisements as more intriguing. Both males and females rate ads deemed to be highly controversial in terms of sexual content as more interesting. The paradox, however, is that although such ads are more interesting, they fail to increase the transmission of information. Respondents are less likely to remember any more about the message.[26]

Advertisements featuring overt sexual stimuli or containing nudity produce higher levels of physiological arousal responses. These arousal responses have been linked to

▶ **FIGURE 6.7**
Factors to Consider Before Using Decorative Models

- The presence of female (or male) decorative models improves ad recognition, but not brand recognition.
- The presence of a decorative model influences emotional and objective evaluations of the product among both male and female audiences.
- Attractive models produce a higher level of attention to ads than do less attractive models.
- The presence of an attractive model produces higher purchase intentions when the product is sexually relevant than if it is not sexually relevant.

the formation of both affective and cognitive responses. If the viewer is male and the sexual stimulus is female, such as a nude female in an ad for cologne, then the viewer tends to develop a strong feeling (affective) toward the ad based on the arousal response his body experiences. Female viewers of male nudity in an advertisement often experience the same type of response, although the arousal response may not be as strong. The cognitive response depends on whether the viewer sees the advertisement as pleasant or offensive. When the viewer likes the ad, it results in a positive impression of the brand. When the viewer thinks the ad exhibits poor taste, negative feelings and beliefs about the brand often emerge.[27]

Coka/Fotolia

▲ Sexually-oriented images in advertisements stimulate physiological responses in both males and females.

Societal Trends When an advertising team determines the level of sex appeal to feature in an advertisement, they consider society's views and prevalent levels of acceptance.[28] Just as economies go through cycles, attitudes toward sex in advertising experience acceptance fluctuations.

The use of and approval of sexual themes in advertising had swung to a high level of tolerance in the early part of the 2000s, until the Super Bowl of 2004. The public reaction to Janet Jackson's breast-baring halftime show sent ripples all the way to Madison Avenue. Shortly afterward, Victoria's Secret dropped its TV lingerie fashion show. Abercrombie & Fitch killed the company's quarterly catalog, which had been strongly criticized for featuring models in sexually suggestive poses. Anheuser-Busch dropped some of its risqué ads.[29]

The pendulum has now begun swinging back toward greater acceptance of sexually-oriented ads, but it has not reached the pre-2004 level yet. A recent Calvin Klein ad featuring actress Eva Mendes in the nude in a provocative pose for its Secret Obsession fragrance was rejected by the major networks in the United States but accepted by television stations in Europe. A less-provocative version was created for the United States, although it was not shown until after 9:00 p.m.[30]

Criticisms of Sex Appeals One common criticism of sexually based advertising is that it perpetuates dissatisfaction with one's body. Often, thin females adorn print and television advertisements. The prevailing idea seems to be "the thinner the better." As advertising models have gotten thinner, body dissatisfaction and eating disorders among women have risen. Research indicates that many women feel unhappy about their own bodies and believe they are too fat after viewing advertisements showing thin models. Dove's recent "Campaign for Real Beauty" included a series of advertisements and social media posts highlighting this criticism. Still, ads featuring thin models are more likely to convince women to purchase a product.[31] With men, the reverse is true. Many men worry they are not muscular enough and are too thin or too fat to buy the item. It does not make any difference whether the male views a male model or a female model in advertisements.[32]

▲ One of the criticisms of sex appeals is that they perpetuate dissatisfaction with one's body.

Music Appeals

Music often adds an important ingredient to an advertisement. A musical theme connects with emotions, memories, and other experiences. Music can be intrusive; it gains the attention of someone who previously was not listening to or watching a program. It may provide the stimulus that ties a particular musical arrangement, jingle, or song to a certain brand. As soon as the tune begins, consumers recognize the brand being advertised because they have been conditioned to tie the product to the music.

Music gains attention and increases the retention of information when it becomes intertwined with the product. Even when a consumer does not recall the ad message argument, music can lead to a better recall of an advertisement's visual and emotional aspects. Music can increase the persuasiveness of an argument. Subjects who compared ads with music to identical ads without music almost always rated those with music higher in terms of persuasiveness.[33] Several decisions are made when selecting music for commercials, including the following:

- What role will music play in the ad?
- Will a familiar song be used, or will something original be created?
- What emotional pitch should the music reach?
- How does the music fit with the message of the ad?

Music plays a variety of roles in advertisements. Sometimes music will be incidental. In others, it becomes the primary theme. An important decision involves selecting a familiar tune as opposed to creating original music. Writing a jingle or music specifically for the advertisement occurs more often and has become the current trend. Background or mood-inducing music is usually instrumental, and advertisers often pay musicians to write music that matches the scenes in the ad. A number of advertising agencies have formed in-house recording labels for the sole purpose of writing jingles, songs, and music for ads.[34]

In the 2000s, using a well-known song in an advertisement was common. A popular, well-known song creates certain advantages. The primary benefit is that consumers already have developed an affinity for the song. Brand awareness, brand equity, and brand loyalty become easier to develop when consumers are familiar with the music. This occurs when consumers transfer an emotional affinity for the song to the product. Some companies purchase an existing song and adapt the ad's verbiage to the music.[35] Using popular songs may be expensive. The price for the rights to a popular song can be in the range of six to seven figures.[36] The internet company Excite paid $7 million for the rights to Jimi Hendrix's song "Are You Experienced," and Microsoft paid about $12 million for the Rolling Stones' "Start Me Up."[37]

An alternative method of developing music has emerged, primarily because of the internet. Greater cooperation now exists between musicians and marketers. Some musicians view advertisements as a way to get their songs heard. Marketers see an opportunity to tie a new, exciting song to a product.

When a commercial only plays part of a song, many firms place entire tunes on company websites or on YouTube so that individuals can download them. Occasionally, a song written for a commercial will crack Billboard's Top 100 list. Jason Wade, a singer in the band Lifehouse, had never written a song for a commercial before. After viewing a copy of the 60-second commercial for Allstate Insurance produced by Leo Burnett Agency, Wade wrote a song entitled "From Where You Are." The commercial promoted Allstate's safe-driving program for teenagers. After the commercial aired, the song was made available on iTunes. Within two weeks, sales were high enough for the song to reach number 40 on Billboard's charts.[38]

Jessmine/Fotolia

▲ Music can be an integral part of a broadcast advertisement.

Rational Appeals

A rational appeal follows the hierarchy of effects stages of awareness, knowledge, liking, preference, conviction, and purchase. A creative designs the advertisement for one of the six steps. An ad oriented to the knowledge stage transmits basic product information. In the preference stage, the message shifts to presenting logical reasons that favor the brand, such as the superior gas mileage of an automobile. A rational advertisement should lead to a stronger conviction about a product's benefits, so that the consumer eventually makes the purchase.

Rational appeals rely on consumers actively processing the information presented in the advertisement. The consumer must pay attention to the commercial, comprehend the message, and compare the information to knowledge embedded in a cognitive map. Messages consistent with the current concepts in a person's cognitive map strengthen key linkages. New messages help the individual form cognitive beliefs about the brand and establish a new linkage from her current map to the new product. As a result, print media and the internet offer the best outlets for rational appeals. Television and radio commercials are short, which makes it harder for viewers to process message arguments.

Marketers feature rational appeals in many business-to-business advertising campaigns. A business customer who sees a Kinko's advertisement about videoconferencing services already may have the company in his cognitive structure. The customer may have used Kinko's in the past but was not aware that the company offers videoconferencing. When Kinko's has been established in this person's cognitive map, creating a new linkage to entice the customer to try its videoconferencing services becomes easier.

In general, rational appeals succeed when potential customers have high levels of involvement and are willing to pay attention to the advertisement. Message arguments, product information and benefits should be placed in the copy. A rational appeal works best when individuals have a particular interest in the product or brand. Otherwise, people tend to ignore rational appeal ads.

Crowe Horwath

▲ This advertisement for Crowe Horwath features a rational appeal targeting the construction industry.

Emotional Appeals

Emotional appeals are based on three ideas (see Figure 6.8). First, consumers ignore most advertisements. Second, rational appeals go unnoticed unless the consumer is in the market for a particular

- Consumers ignore most ads.
- Rational appeals generally go unnoticed.
- Emotional appeals can capture attention and foster an attachment.

▲ **FIGURE 6.8**
Reasons for Using Emotional Appeals

product at the time it is advertised. Third and most important, emotional advertising can capture a viewer's attention and create an emotional attachment between the consumer and the brand.

Most creatives view emotional advertising as the key to brand loyalty. Creatives want customers to experience a bond with the brand. Visual cues in advertisements are key components of many emotional appeals. The visual elements in the ad for Colorado shown in this section help contribute to a feeling or mood of serenity. Although individuals develop perceptions of brands based largely on visual and peripheral stimuli, this does not happen instantly. With repetition, perceptions and attitudinal changes emerge. Figure 6.9 displays some of the more common emotions presented in advertisements.

Godiva employed an emotional appeal in its latest advertising campaign entitled "the golden moment." Created by Lipman Agency, the campaign focused on the emotional appeal of giving, sharing, or eating Godiva chocolates. Laurie Len Kotcher, Chief Marketing Officer and Senior Vice President for Global Brand Development of Godiva Chocolatier, said, "When you give the gold box, receive the gold box, eating something from the gold box, there is something special about that moment."[39]

Colorado Tourism Office

▲ This advertisement for Colorado features visual elements that create the emotional appeal of serenity and peace.

While advertisements for many consumer products feature emotional appeals, the approach has begun to appear more frequently in business-to-business advertising. In the past, only five to ten percent of all business-to-business ads featured emotional appeals. Today, the figure has risen to nearly 25 percent. A magazine advertisement created by NKH&W Advertising Agency for a product to treat racehorses switched from a rational appeal to an emotional appeal. The target market was veterinarians. In the past, an advertisement would have opened with such ad copy as "For swelling in joints use…" The emotional ad shows the horse thinking, "I will prove them wrong. I will run again. I will mend my spirits."[40]

Television remains one of the best medium to present emotional appeals, because it offers advertisers intrusion value and can utilize both sound and sight. Models in the ads can be real people. Facial expressions convey emotions and attitudes. Consumers learn about a particular brand and develop attitudes based on these experiences. Television ads also are more vivid, lifelike, and often create dynamic situations that pull viewers in. Music can be incorporated to make the commercial more dramatic. Peripheral cues constitute important components of emotional appeals. The cues, such

- Trust
- Reliability
- Friendship
- Happiness
- Security
- Glamour-luxury
- Serenity
- Anger
- Protecting loved ones
- Romance
- Passion
- Family bonds
  - with parents
  - with siblings
  - with children
  - with extended family members

▶ **FIGURE 6.9**
Emotions Used in Advertisements

as music and background visuals, help capture the viewer's attention.

Emotions are often tied with humor, fear, music, and other appeals to make a compelling case for a product. The same ad can influence a consumer both emotionally and rationally. The creative selects the most appropriate emotional appeal for the product and company.

Scarcity Appeals

Scarcity appeals urge consumers to buy a particular product because of a limitation. It can be a limited number of the products available or that the product will be made available for only a limited time. When consumers believe only a finite supply of a product will be available, the perceived value of the product might increase. For the Olympics, General Mills introduced USA Olympic Crunch cereal and Betty Crocker Team USA desserts for a limited time.[41] McDonald's, Wendy's, and Burger King offer sandwiches (McRib, Hot N' Spicy Chicken, Dollar Whoppers) for limited-time periods throughout the year. The scarcity concept applies to musical compilations, encouraging consumers to buy a CD because of its restricted availability. By making sure it is not available in retail stores, marketers increase its scarcity value. Notice in the advertisement for Wholly Guacamole shown in this section that the company's guacamole is only free on one day, March 20, and only at Schlotzsky's.

DuPage Medical Group

▲ This advertisement for DuPage Medical Group utilizes an emotional appeal.

Executional Frameworks

An **executional framework or execution** signifies the manner in which an ad appeal will be presented and a message strategy conveyed. Figure 6.10 displays the various frameworks. Each will be matched with the type of appeal and message strategy as part of the overall advertising design process.

Animation Executions

Animation has become an increasingly popular executional framework, and its use has risen dramatically. The growing sophistication of computer graphics programs makes new and exciting animation technologies available. Successful animated movie films such as *Up*

- Animation
- Slice-of-life
- Storytelling
- Testimonial
- Authoritative
- Demonstration
- Fantasy
- Informative

▲ **FIGURE 6.10**
Executional Frameworks

Fresherized Foods

▲ This advertisement uses a scarcity appeal because Wholly Guacamole is free at Scholotzky's only on March 20.

objective 6.3
What role does the executional framework play in advertising design?

and *Dr. Seuss' The Lorax* continue to generate interest in animation advertising, which can be featured in television spots, on the internet, and in movie trailers. Single shots of animated characters, such as *Dora the Explorer*, are placed in print ads.

The *rotoscoping* process facilitates digitally painting or sketching figures into live sequences, which makes it possible to present both live actors and animated characters in the same frame.[42] The creative can also merge or modify various live scenes. Advertising executive Stan Richards noted, "The opportunities are great, because we are at a point where anything that we can think of, we can do. We've never had that before. There is a cost consequence. A lot of that digital production is expensive, but those costs are coming down. Within a few years, those costs will be half of what they are now."[43]

Pink Jacket Creative: A Creative Factory

▲ This advertisement created by Pink Jacket Creative for the Snoring Center uses animation combined with a slice-of-life execution.

For years, marketing professionals rarely used animation in business-to-business advertisements. Many marketers viewed it negatively, believing animation appealed to children but not to businesspeople. These opinions have changed. Business ads shown on television now take advantage of high-quality graphics to illustrate a product's uses with animation.

Slice-of-Life Executions

In slice-of-life commercials, advertisers provide solutions to the everyday problems consumers or businesses face. Proctor & Gamble made this format famous during the early days of television advertising in the 1950s. Slice-of-life commercials depict the common experiences, especially the problems people encounter, and introduce the brand to solve the problem. The most common slice-of-life format contains four components: encounter, problem, interaction, and solution (see Figure 6.11). In some ads, the actors portray the dilemma or problem and solve the problem themselves. In others, a voiceover explains the benefits or solution to the problem that the good, service, or company provides.

Business-to-business advertisements often utilize the slice-of-life method because it allows the advertiser to highlight the ways a brand can meet business needs. A typical business-to-business ad begins with a routine problem, such as a sales manager making a presentation to the board of directors. Then, a projector being used does not have a clear picture. The ad offers the solution: a projector from Sony. The presentation resumes with great clarity, and the board of directors accepts the

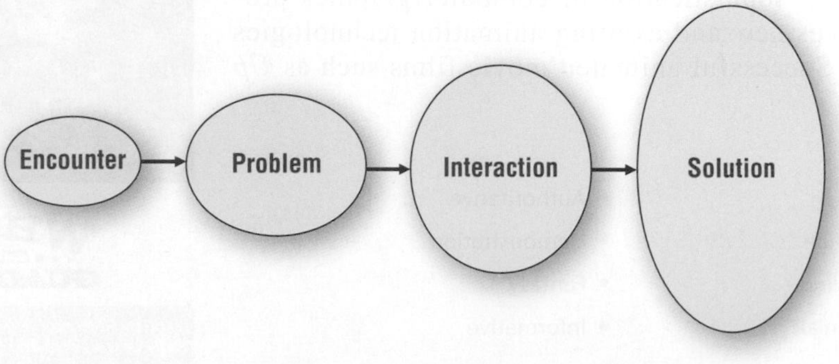

▶ **FIGURE 6.11**
Components of a Slice-of-life Execution

customer's bid for the account. As with all slice-of-life commercials, a disaster has been avoided and a happy ending results instead.

Storytelling Executions

Many advertisers use a new execution format: storytelling. Storytelling does not include an encounter where a brand solves a problem faced by a consumer or business, such as in the slice-of-life approach. Instead, a storytelling execution resembles a 30-second movie with a plot or story suggesting the brand is more at the periphery rather than at the center of the ad. In contrast to a "hard-sell" approach in which the ad directly presents a brand's benefits or features; the storytelling format allows the viewer to draw his own conclusions about the product. In a recent ad for Subaru, the commercial depicts a loving dad handing his daughter the car keys for the first time. He still sees her as his little girl, but now she is a teenager. The Subaru brand does not appear in the ad until the end. The story focuses on a little girl growing up and the dad trusting his beloved daughter with a Subaru. Many of the Super Bowl ads now feature the storytelling approach. Budweiser developed ads showing a small calf and colt growing up together and developing a strong bond. Another Budweiser ad features a dog that keeps returning to a farm because he developed a relationship with one of the horses.

Testimonial Executions

Advertisers have achieved success with a testimonial type of execution for many years, especially in the business-to-business and service sectors. A customer relating a positive experience with a brand offers a testimonial. In the business-to-business sector, testimonials from current customers add credibility to the claims. Most buyers believe what others say about a company more than they believe what a company says about itself. Testimonials generate greater credibility than self-proclamations.

Testimonials offer an effective method for promoting services. Services are intangible; they cannot be seen or touched and consumers cannot examine them before making decisions. A testimony from a current customer provides a succinct description of the benefits or attributes of the service. Choosing a dentist, an attorney, or an automobile repair shop employee often leads customers to ask friends, relatives, or coworkers. A testimonial advertisement simulates this type of word-of-mouth recommendation.

Testimonials can enhance company credibility. Endorsers and famous individuals do not always have high levels of credibility, because consumers know they are being paid for their endorsements. The same holds true for paid actors who look like everyday consumers. The most believable testimonies come from everyday people, actual customers. Retailer Stein Mart featured real customers talking about their favorite merchandise in a recent TV campaign. Marketers recruited customers through the company's Facebook page. The TV spots encouraged customers to create videos about their favorite merchandise at Stein Mart and upload them to the website. The goals

▼ An advertisement featuring a testimony execution.

© Andres Rodriguez/Fotolia

were to reach a younger target market, women between 35 and 55, and to create an online community of avid customers who found something they love at Stein Mart.[44]

Authoritative Executions

When using the authoritative execution, the advertiser seeks to convince viewers regarding a brand's superiority. *Expert authority* constitutes one form. The ads employ a physician, dentist, engineer, or chemist to state the particular brand's advantages compared to other brands. Firms also can feature less recognized experts such as automobile mechanics, professional house painters, and aerobics instructors. These individuals talk about the attributes or benefits of the product that make the brand superior.

Many authoritative advertisements include scientific or survey evidence. Independent organizations such as the American Medical Association undertake a variety of product studies. Quoting the results generates greater credibility. Survey results may be less credible. Stating that four out of five dentists recommend a particular toothbrush or toothpaste may not be as effective, because consumers do not have details about how the survey was conducted or even how many dentists were surveyed (5 or 500). In contrast, an American Medical Association statement that an aspirin a day reduces the risk of a second heart attack will be highly credible. Bayer can take advantage of the finding by including the information in the company's ads. The same holds true when a magazine such as *Consumer Reports* ranks a particular brand as the best.

The authoritative approach assumes consumers and business decision makers rely on cognitive processes when making purchase decisions and that they will pay attention to an ad and carefully think about the information conveyed in it. The approach works well in print ads, because buyers take the time to read the claim or findings presented in the advertisement.

Demonstration Executions

▼ This advertisement for Biltmore uses a fantasy execution of an escape to a romantic castle.

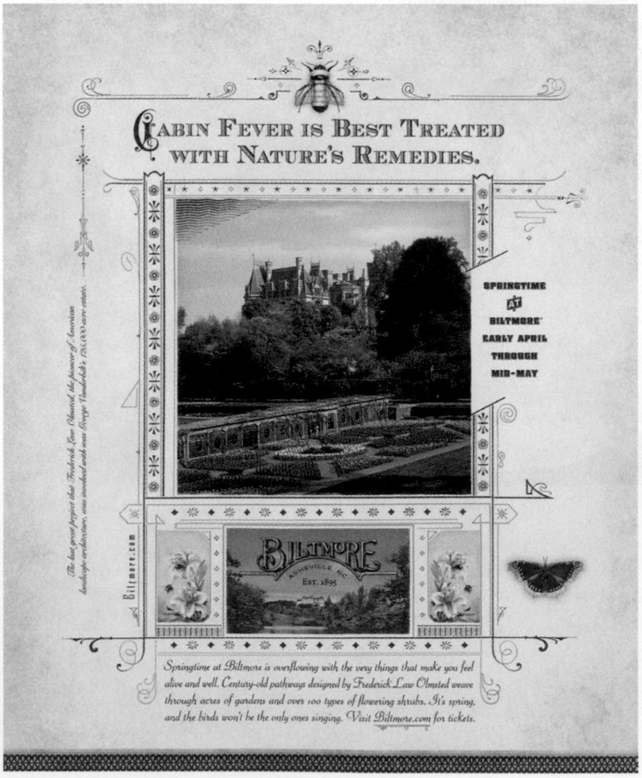

The Richards Group

A demonstration execution displays how a product works. It provides an effective way to communicate the product's benefits to viewers. Recent advertisements for Swiffer demonstrated the product's multiple uses by cleaning a television screen, a wooden floor, a saxophone, and light fixtures. Consumers were shown how to use the product while at the same time hearing about its advantages.

Business-to-business ads often present demonstrations. These allow a business to illustrate how a product meets the specific needs of another business. For example, GoldTouch, Inc. can demonstrate the InstaGold Flash System, which deposits a bright and uniform gold surface finish on products, such as jewelry, through a nonelectrical current process of immersion plating. Such demonstrations can be presented via television ads or flash media ads on the internet.

Fantasy Executions

Fantasy executions lift the audience beyond the real world to a make-believe experience. Some are meant to be realistic. Others are completely irrational. Viewers often more clearly recall the most irrational and illogical ads. Fantasies can deal with anything from a dream vacation spot or cruise ships to a juicy hamburger or an enticing DiGiorno pizza.

Common fantasy themes include sex, love, or romance. Some marketing experts believe sex and nudity in advertising have lost their impact. Instead, advertisers feature a softer, more subtle presentation. Fantasy fits with target audiences that have a preference for a tamer presentation. Instead of raw sexuality, fantasy takes them into a world of romantic make-believe.

The perfume and cologne industries often employ fantasy executions. In the past, a common theme was that splashing on the cologne caused women to flock to a man. For women, the reverse was suggested. Although used extensively, these ads were not particularly effective because people did not believe them. Currently, perfume advertisers tend to portray the product as enhancing a couple's love life or making a man or woman feel more sensuous.

Informative Executions

Informative advertisements present information to the audience in a straightforward manner. Agencies prepare informative messages extensively for radio commercials, where only verbal communication takes place. Informative ads are less common in television and print, because consumers tend to ignore them. With so many ads bombarding the consumer, it takes more than just the presentation of information to capture someone's attention. The Philadelphia Cream Cheese ad shown here has an excellent chance of being noticed for two reasons: it utilizes an eye-catching image, and it provides a recipe with instructions on how to prepare the cheesecake bars.

Kraft Foods, Inc.

▲ An advertisement for Philadelphia Cream Cheese using an informative execution.

Consumers who are highly involved in a particular product category pay attention to an informational ad. Business buyers in the process of gathering information for either a new buy or a modified rebuy will notice an informative commercial. When a business does not need a particular product, buying center members often pay less attention to the advertisement. Thus, informative ads tend to work best in high-involvement situations. Many advertisers believe that business buyers desire detailed information in order to make intelligent buying decisions. As a result, the informative framework continues to be a popular approach for business-to-business advertisers.

Correct placement of an informative advertisement is vital. An informative advertisement about a restaurant placed on a radio station just before noon will be listened to more carefully than one that runs at 3:00 p.m. An informative ad about a diet product in an issue of *Glamour* that has a special article on weight control or exercising will be noticed more than if it is placed in the fashion section of the magazine. An informative business ad featuring a new piece of industrial equipment works well next to an article about the capital costs of equipment.

Beyond these executional frameworks, the creative selects the other ingredients, including music, copy, color, motion, light, and the size of a print ad. Almost any of these executions can be used within the format of one of the various appeals and message strategies. A slice-of-life can depict a fear appeal and cognitive message strategy. Informative ads may be humorous, but so can animations. Testimonials or demonstrations are rational or emotional, and can deploy any of the three message strategies. As the advertising campaign comes together, one element remains, finding the face or voice for the product.

Sources and Spokespersons

objective 6.4
How are sources and spokespersons decisions related to advertising design?

When creating a commercial or ad, the final issue facing the creative, the company, and the account executive will be the choice of the **source or spokesperson**, who delivers an advertising message visually and/or verbally. Selection of this individual often constitutes a critical choice. Consider, for example, the impact of the spokesperson Flo in

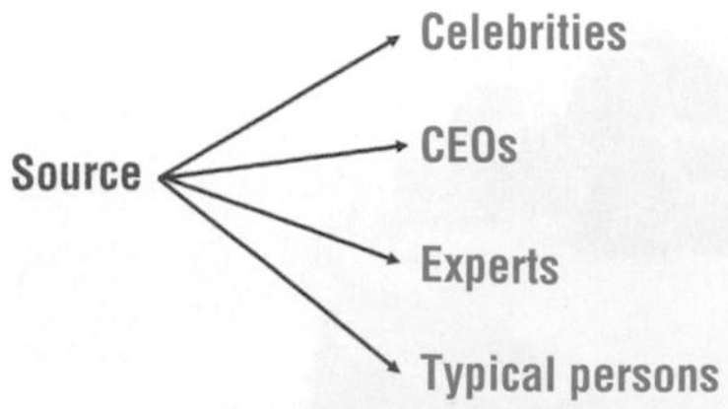

▲ **FIGURE 6.12**
Types of Sources and Spokespersons

Progressive Insurance ads, or The Most Interesting Man in the World in commercials for Dos Equis beer. Both have greatly enhanced the visibility of the products they represent. Figure 6.12 identifies four types of sources and spokespersons.

Celebrity Spokespersons

Of the four types, celebrity spokespersons are the most common, even though their appearances in ads have been declining. The research firm Millward Brown noted that only around six percent of advertisements feature celebrity endorsements.[45] The high cost of celebrity endorsements represents a primary reason for the decline. Many ask for millions of dollars and want multiyear deals. Others may sign on for only one campaign. It cost the high-end fashion label Louis Vuitton $10 million for actress Angelina Jolie's appearance in a single advertising campaign.[46]

An advertiser employs a celebrity endorser when the person's stamp of approval enhances the brand's equity. Celebrities can also help create emotional bonds with brands. Transferring the bond that exists between the celebrity and the audience to the product being endorsed is the objective. A bond transfer will often be more profound for younger consumers. A MediaEDGE survey revealed that 30 percent of 18- to 34-year-olds would try a brand promoted by a celebrity. The survey also indicated that younger people are 50 percent more likely than older consumers to recommend a celebrity-endorsed product to others. Older consumers are less likely to be influenced by celebrity endorsements. Fewer than 14 percent reported that they would try a celebrity-endorsed product. Still, many advertisers believe that celebrity endorsements improve brand awareness and help define the brand's personality.[47]

Athletes constitute a significant component of the celebrity endorsers. Some, such as Danica Patrick, earn more from endorsements than they do from their sports. Top athletic endorsers include Phil Mickelson, Roger Federer, Lebron James, David Beckham, Cristiano Ronaldo, Alex Rodriguez, and, until recently, Tiger Woods. The top two female athletic endorsers are Danica Patrick and Maria Sharapova.[48]

Agencies also feature celebrities to help establish a brand "personality." The objective is to tie the brand's characteristics to those of the spokesperson. A brand personality

▶ Interstate Batteries features NASCAR driver Kyle Busch in some advertisements.

Interstate Battery Systems International, Inc.

emerges after the brand has been established. The celebrity helps to define the brand more clearly. Using celebrities for new products does not always work as well as it does for established brands.

Additional Celebrity Endorsements Four additional variations of celebrity endorsements include unpaid spokespersons, celebrity voiceovers, dead person endorsements, and social media endorsements. *Unpaid spokespersons* are celebrities supporting a charity or cause by appearing in advertisements. These types of endorsements are highly credible and can entice significant contributions to a cause. Politicians, actors, musicians, and athletes all appear in these ads. A few years ago, a campaign featured a number of musicians plus former Presidents Bush and Clinton in an effort to raise money for Haiti after its devastating earthquake.

Celebrities may provide *voiceovers* for television and radio ads without being shown or identified. Agencies may use a voiceover because the celebrity provides a quality voice to the advertisement, even when individuals listening to the ad do not recognize the voice. Advertising executive Stan Richards noted, "We use Hollywood actors quite a bit. It's largely not for their celebrity; we're not interested in that. Our voice for Home Depot is Ed Harris, who is a terrific actor. I don't think anybody in the world knows it's him, but he can take a script and bring it to life."[49] One negative of voiceovers is that they can be a distraction if the consumer becomes focused on identifying the speaker rather than hearing the content of the ad.

A *dead person endorsement* occurs when a sponsor uses an image or past video or film featuring an actor or personality who has died. Dead person endorsements are somewhat controversial but are becoming more common. Bob Marley, Marilyn Monroe, John Wayne, John Lennon, Elvis Presley, and many others have appeared in ads and have even become spokespersons for products after dying.

The newest form of endorsements is through *social media*. Firms now pay celebrities to send promotional tweets for them. Most of these tweets are not cheap, costing between $200 and $10,000 per message. Snoop Dog was recently paid to tweet about the Toyota Sienna, which he called a "swagger wagon." Kathy Ireland has been hired by Therapedic International to endorse the company's mattresses through social media and Twitter.[50]

CEO Spokespersons

Instead of celebrities, advertisers can employ a CEO as the spokesperson or source. Michael Dell has appeared as the spokesperson for Dell. A highly visible and personable CEO can become a major asset for the firm and its products. Many local companies succeed, in part, because their owners are out front in small-market television commercials. They then begin to take on the status of local celebrities.

Experts

Expert sources include physicians, lawyers, accountants, and financial planners. These experts are not celebrities or CEOs. Experts provide backing for testimonials, serve as authoritative figures, demonstrate products, and enhance the credibility of informative advertisements.

▼ Showing the partners, Ronquillo and Godwin, in this advertisement for litigation services adds credibility.

Gosdwin Ronquillo PC

Courtesy of Alliance One Advertising

▲ An advertisement for Richland State Bank using typical persons.

Typical Persons

Typical persons are one of two types. The first includes paid actors or models that portray or resemble everyday people. The second is actual, typical, everyday people. Wal-Mart has featured store employees in freestanding insert advertisements. Agencies also create "man-on-the-street" types of advertisements. For example, PERT shampoo recently prepared ads showing an individual asking people if they would like to have their hair washed. Dr. Scholl's interviews people about foot problems that might be resolved with cushioned shoe inserts.

Real people sources are becoming more common. One reason may be the overuse of celebrities. Many experts believe that consumers have become bored by celebrity endorsers and that the positive impact today will be less than in the past. One study conducted in Great Britain indicated that 55 percent of the consumers surveyed reported that a famous face was not enough to hold their attention.[51]

Source Characteristics

In evaluating sources, most account executives and companies consider several characteristics. The effectiveness of an advertising campaign that utilizes a spokesperson depends on the degree to which the person has one or more of the characteristics listed in Figure 6.13.

Credibility The composite of attractiveness, similarity, likeability, trustworthiness, and expertise creates credibility, which in turn affects the receiver's acceptance of the spokesperson and message.[52] People believe credible sources. Most sources do not score highly on all five attributes, yet they need to score highly on multiple characteristics to be viewed as credible. Celebrities may be more likely to possess at least an element of all characteristics. A CEO, expert, or typical person probably lacks one or more of them.

Attractiveness Two forms of attractiveness include physical and personality characteristics. Physical attractiveness contributes an important asset for an endorser. Advertisements with physically attractive spokespersons fare better than advertisements with less attractive people, for both male and female audiences. The attractiveness of the spokesperson's personality will also be important to many consumers, because it helps viewers form emotional bonds with the spokesperson. When the spokesperson exhibits a sour personality, even if physically beautiful, consumers become less likely to develop an emotional bond with the individual and the product.

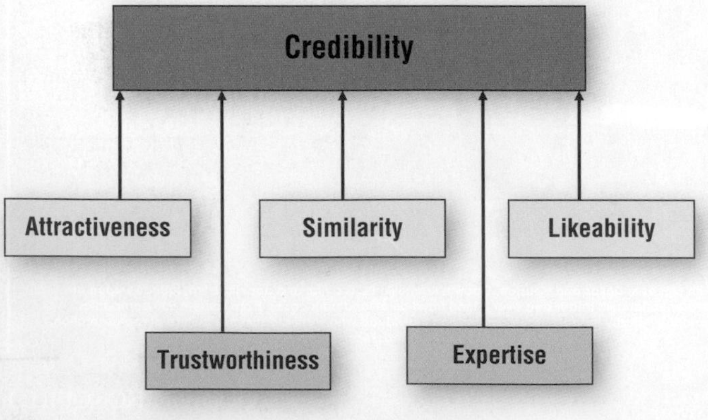

▲ **FIGURE 6.13**
Characteristics of Effective Spokespersons

Similarity Closely related to attractiveness is similarity. Consumers are more inclined to be influenced by a message delivered by a similar person. A "stay-at-home" mom may be more influenced by an advertisement that starts out with a woman saying, "Since

Newcomer, Morris and Young Inc.

◀ Attractiveness remains an important source characteristic even for children in ads, such as this one for Ouachita Independent Bank.

I made the decision to stop working and care for my family full-time…." Similarity leads the viewer to identify with the spokesperson. Dove recently launched a series of ads featuring male athletes, but the focus was on them and their families, not sports. Individuals such as Magic Johnson, Drew Brees, and Shaquille O'Neal talk about being "comfortable in their own skin."

At other times, *identification* comes from the belief that the source has similar beliefs, attitudes, preferences, or behaviors or faces the same or a similar situation as the customer. Female fans are able to identify with female jockey Anna Roberts as the "new face of horse racing" because many females have enjoyed horseback riding and have dreamed of winning a famous horse race. Identification was also gained because most jockeys are males. Anna Roberts immediately gained similarity and identification with female fans.

Likeability Attractiveness and similarity are closely linked to likability. Consumers respond positively to spokespersons they like. Viewers may like an actor or the character played by the actor in a movie. La-Z-Boy signed a multiyear agreement with Brook Shields to serve as its celebrity spokesperson. The campaign targeted females ages 35 to 64 who report a high degree of likeability for her.[53] Terry Bradshaw is one the most well-known and well-liked retired athletes and hosts of football telecasts.

▼ Terry Bradshaw's high degree of likeability makes him an excellent choice to be the spokesperson for Community Trust Bank.

Community Trust Bank

1. Betty White
2. Denzel Washington
3. Sandra Bullock
4. Clint Eastwood
5. Tom Hanks
6. Harrison Ford
7. Morgan Freeman
8. Kate Middleton
9. Will Smith
10. Johnny Depp

▲ **FIGURE 6.14**
The 10 Most Trusted Celebrities

Choosing him as a spokesperson for Community Trust Bank was easy, because he is also one of the bank's customers.

Consumers who do not like a particular spokesperson are inclined to transfer that dislike to the brand. This explains why many companies who retained Tiger Woods quickly dropped him as an endorser in 2010 after his extramarital affairs became public. The worry was that his endorsement would result in a negative impact on attitudes toward the brand. In other situations, it may not be an automatic transfer because consumers recognize that endorsers are paid spokespersons.

Trustworthiness A celebrity may be likeable or attractive but may not be viewed as trustworthy. Trustworthiness represents the degree of confidence or the level of acceptance consumers place in the spokesperson's message. A trustworthy spokesperson helps consumers believe the message. Likeability and trustworthiness are connected. People who are liked tend to be trusted, and people who are disliked tend not to be trusted. A Reuters/Ipsos survey revealed that celebrities ranking the highest in terms of trustworthiness included Betty White, Denzel Washington, Sandra Bullock, and Clint Eastwood (see Figure 6.14 for a complete list). The most unpopular personalities included Paris Hilton, Charlie Sheen, Britney Spears, Arnold Schwarzenegger, and Tiger Woods.[54]

▼ Willie Robertson, star of reality TV show *Duck Dynasty*, has a high level of expertise for truck suspension and lift kits.

Skyjacker Suspensions

Expertise Spokespersons exhibiting higher levels of expertise become more believable. Kyle Bush and Jeff Gordon are experts when advertising automobile products and lubricants. Willie Robertson, star of reality TV show *Duck Dynasty*, is viewed as an expert for off-road vehicles.

Often when a commercial requires expertise, the advertising agency opts for the CEO or a trained or educated expert in the field. American Express features Maria Barraza, a small-business owner and designer, to promote its Small Business Services. Expertise can be valuable in persuasive advertisements designed to change opinions or attitudes. Spokespersons with high levels of expertise are more capable of persuading an audience than someone with zero or low expertise.[55]

Matching Source Types and Characteristics

The account executive, ad agency, and corporate sponsor, individually or jointly, may choose the type of spokesperson. They can choose a celebrity, CEO, expert, or typical person, and the specific individual should have the key source characteristics.

In terms of trustworthiness, believability, persuasiveness, and likeability, celebrities tend to score well. These virtues increase when the match between the product and celebrity consists of a logical and proper fit. Phil Mickelson endorsing golf merchandise offers a good fit. Some celebrities have become almost as famous for their advertising appearances as for an acting or athletic career. Danica Patrick has signed endorsement contracts with Honda, Secret, Boost Mobile, Pepsi, and Go Daddy, possibly gaining as much notoriety from endorsements as she has from competing in races.[56]

Two dangers exist when using celebrities. First, any negative publicity about a celebrity caused by inappropriate conduct may damage credibility. Michael Vick's arrest and conviction for dog fighting created considerable negative press. A second danger of using celebrities occurs when they endorse too many products. Advertising research indicates that when a celebrity endorses multiple products, it tends to reduce likeability as well as consumer attitudes toward the brand.[57]

A CEO or other prominent corporate official may or may not possess the characteristics of attractiveness and likeability. CEOs should, however, appear to be trustworthy, have expertise, and maintain a degree of credibility. A CEO is not a professional actor or model. It might be difficult for the CEO to come across well in a commercial.

First and foremost, experts should be credible. The advertising agency seeks an attractive, likeable, and trustworthy expert. Experts are helpful in promoting health care products and other high-involvement types of products. Recent research indicates that experts are more believable than celebrities for high-technology products. As a result, the use of an expert reduces a consumer's level of perceived risk in purchasing the brand, which means they are the most helpful when consumers or businesses perceive high levels of risk involved in a purchase.[58]

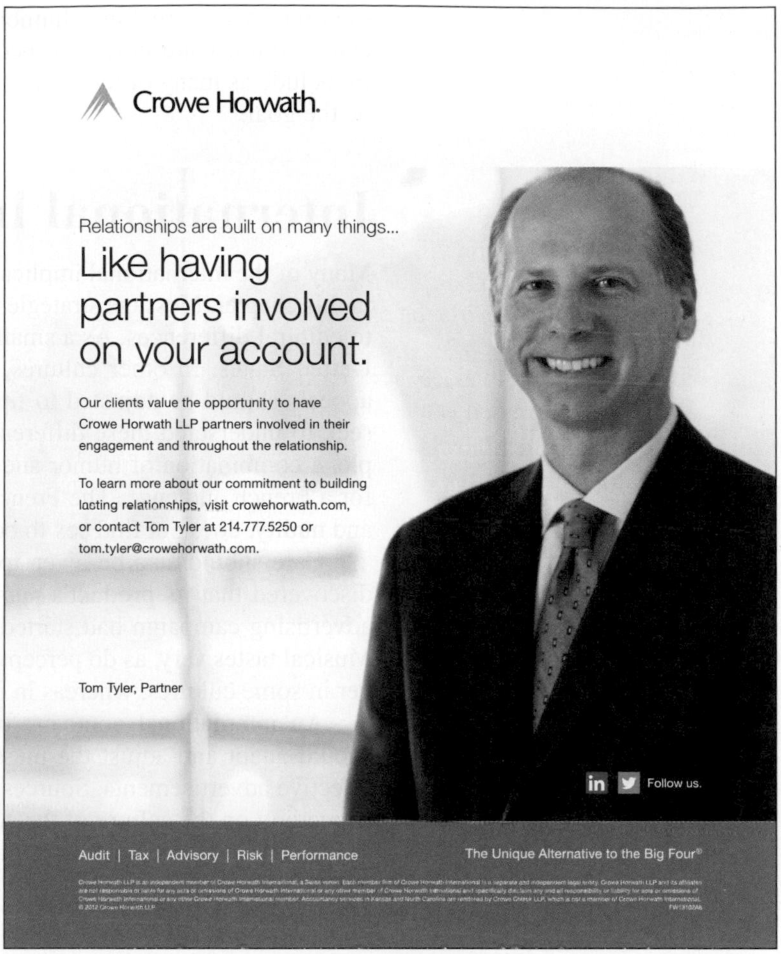

Crowe Horwath

▲ Showing Tom Tyler, a partner in the firm, presents the source characteristics of trustworthiness, expertise, and credibility.

Advertisements with typical persons are sometimes difficult to prepare, especially when they employ real persons. Typical person sources do not have the name recognition of celebrities. Consequently, advertisers often feature multiple sources within one advertisement to build credibility. Increasing the number of sources makes the ad more effective. Hearing three people talk about a good dentist will be more believable than hearing it from only one person. By using multiple sources, viewers are motivated to pay attention and process its arguments.[59]

Real person ads present a double-edged sword. On the one hand, trustworthiness, similarity, and credibility rise for a bald or overweight source or someone with other physical imperfections. This can be especially valuable when the bald person promotes a hair replacement program or the overweight source talks about a diet program. On the other hand, attractiveness and likeability may be lower.

For the first time in its history, Pizza Hut decided to go with servers, bartenders, and franchise executives in their advertisements rather than celebrities. Dan Howard, a marketing professor at Southern Methodist University, noted, "With an actor, there's an inherent loss of persuasiveness because they are paid. Employees are not viewed in the same way as paid actors. They have greater credibility." One of the employees, 28-year-old Ashlie Marquez, who was featured in an ad further stated, "We're real employees who know what the customer likes and we can talk more passionately about it." Many viewers see employees as credible. Featuring employees in ads has also generated a positive effect on the company's culture, because the company recognizes that employees make a difference and celebrates their work.[60]

In general, the advertising agency wants to be certain that the source or spokesperson has the major characteristics the advertisement requires. Likeability would be important when creating a humorous appeal. In a rational or informational ad, expertise and credibility are crucial, especially in business-to-business ads. In each case, trying to include as many of the characteristics as possible when retaining a spokesperson will be the goal.

International Implications

Many of the international implications of advertising design have already been described in this chapter. Message strategies, advertising appeals, and executions should be adapted to cultural differences. As a small example, fear of body odor often sells products in the United States. In other cultures, body odor does not carry the same meaning. Sexual appeals should be adjusted to fit the laws and customs of a region. Advertisers should seek to understand these differences before designing advertising messages. For example, a combination of humor and sex would not be advisable in a commercial designed for a French audience. The French culture, while quite comfortable with overt sexuality and nudity, does not find sex to be funny.

Care should also be given to language and translation. For example, Sega recently discovered that its product's name is slang for "masturbation" in Italian, after a major advertising campaign had started. Marketers make great efforts to avoid such mistakes. Musical tastes vary, as do perceptions of rationality and scarcity. Emotions may be stronger in some cultures, whereas in others people are much more reserved.

An international company or a firm seeking to expand into additional countries should adapt and adjust the message strategy, appeal, and execution in order to create effective advertisements. Sources and spokesperson may have differing levels of success, depending on the culture of the country involved. Finally, finding universal themes, such as *visual Esperanto*, as described in Chapter 5, may be of great help to the international advertising creative.

Summary

A message strategy represents the primary tactic or approach used to deliver an advertisement's message theme. Three categories of message strategies include cognitive, affective, and conative approaches. Cognitive message strategies present rational arguments of pieces of information to consumers. Cognitive approaches include generic messages, preemptive messages, unique selling propositions, hyperbole, and comparative advertisements. Affective message strategies seek to invoke feelings or emotions that match those feelings with a good or service. Affective approaches include resonance advertising, comfort marketing, and emotional methods. Conative message strategies seek to lead directly to a consumer response. Each message exhibits specific advantages and disadvantages. Marketing teams seek to match the strategy with the message to be delivered.

Advertising creatives form advertising messages using one (or more) of the seven major appeals: fear, humor, sex (through sensual, suggestive, nudity-based, or overt formats), music, rationality, emotions, or scarcity. Logical combinations of these appeals for various messages can be utilized. Often, music provides the backdrop for messages invoking fear, humor, sex, and emotions. Humor can be linked with sex, music, rationality (by showing how being illogical is silly or funny), and scarcity. Rationality combines with fear in many commercials. Creatives seek to design message arguments that take advantage of the various characteristics of these appeals, break through clutter, and convince the audience to buy the item.

Executional frameworks constitute the manner in which an advertising appeal will be presented and the message strategy will be conveyed. Executions include animation, slice-of-life, testimonial, authoritative, demonstration, fantasy-based, and informative approaches. These methods can be used to enhance the effectiveness of an advertisement.

Sources or spokespersons present the advertising message visually and/or verbally. Celebrities, CEOs, experts, and typical persons can serve as sources. Advertisers seek to enhance the quality of the message by relying on the credibility, attractiveness, similarity, likeability, trustworthiness, and expertise of the spokesperson.

The process of designing ads for international markets is similar to that for domestic ads. The major difference is careful consideration of local attitudes and customers, with due care given to the language, slang, and symbols of the area.

Key Terms

message strategy The primary tactic or approach used to deliver a message theme

cognitive message strategy A strategy used to present rational arguments or pieces of information to consumers

generic message An advertisement that directly promotes a product's attributes or benefits without any claim of superiority

preemptive message An advertising claim of superiority based on a product's specific attribute or benefit with the intent of preventing the competition from making the same or a similar statement

unique selling proposition An explicit, testable claim of uniqueness or superiority in an advertisement

hyperbole An untestable advertising claim based on some attribute or benefit

comparative advertisement The direct or indirect advertising comparison with a competitor based on some product attribute or benefit

affective message strategies Advertisements trying to evoke feeling or emotions that match those feelings with the good, service, or company

comfort marketing A form of resonance advertising designed to encourage consumer to purchase branded product rather than generic versions because the branded product has stood the test of time

emotional affective approach An advertising method that attempts to elicit powerful emotions that will lead to product recall and choice

conative message strategy An advertising approach designed to lead directly to a consumer response

advertising appeals Advertising approaches to reaching consumers with ads, featuring an element of fear, humor, sex, music, rationality, emotions, or scarcity

severity The part of the fear behavioral response model that leads the individual to consider how strong certain negative consequences of an action will be

vulnerability The part of the fear behavioral response model that leads the individual to consider the odds of being affected by the negative consequences of an action

decorative models Individuals in advertisements whose primary purpose is to adorn the product as a sexual or attractive stimulus without serving a functional role

source or spokesperson The individual who delivers an advertising message visually and/or verbally

MyMarketingLab

Go to **mymktlab.com** to complete the problems marked with this icon ✪.

Review Questions

6-1. What is a message strategy?

6-2. What are the important and wholly necessary components of a unique selling proposition?

6-3. What is a preemptive message?

6-4. Describe an affective message strategy and identify the primary forms it can take in an advertisement.

6-5. What is hyperbole and why should it be avoided?

6-6. Why might it be advantageous to the business to create resonance between a product and the consumer?

6-7. What are the seven most common types of advertising appeals?

6-8. What is the emotional affective approach?

6-9. When does humor work in an ad? What pitfalls should companies avoid in using humorous appeals?

6-10. Why do retail stores tend to have point-of-purchase displays?

6-11. What are the key stages of the hierarchy of effects?

6-12. Name the different ways music can play a role in an advertisement. Explain how each role should match individual appeals, media, and other elements in the design of the ad.

6-13. Compare the advantages and disadvantages of rational appeals to emotional appeals.

6-14. What types of execution frameworks can be used when developing an advertisement?

6-15. Describe how each of the executional frameworks can be used in ad development.

6-16. What four types of sources or spokespersons can be used by advertisers?

6-17. What are the most desirable characteristics of a source or spokesperson?

Critical Thinking Exercises

DISCUSSION QUESTIONS

6-18. Advertisements can often be a matter of taste. An ad might appeal to some but will annoy other people. Choose an advertisement that got it all wrong from execution to message. What went wrong with it?

6-19. Studies involving comparative advertisements versus noncomparative ads produced the following findings. Discuss why you think each statement is true. Try to think of comparative ads you have seen that substantiate these claims.

- **a.** Message awareness was higher for comparative ads than for noncomparative ads if the brands are already established brands.
- **b.** Brand recall was higher for comparative ads than for noncomparative ads.
- **c.** Comparative ads were viewed as less believable than noncomparative ads.
- **d.** Attitudes toward comparative ads were more negative than toward noncomparative ads.

6-20. Watch one of your favorite television shows. Record all of the television commercials in one commercial break (at least seven ads). Identify the appeal used in each one. Were the ads effective? Why or why not?

6-21. Locate a print ad or television ad that features a fear appeal. Using the behavioral response model shown in this chapter, identify various elements in the ad that correspond with the components in the model. Some of the elements will require thinking beyond what is visually or verbally present in the ad itself.

6-22. Find examples of advertisements that attempt to use the stereotypical image of the close-knit family to sell products and services. Is this type of appeal and setting likely to work in today's market? Why is it used?

6-23. Identify an advertisement that uses each of the following executional frameworks. Evaluate the advertisement in terms of how well it is executed. Also, did the appeal and message strategy fit well with the execution? Was the ad memorable? What made it memorable?

- a. Animation
- b. Slice-of-life
- c. Testimonial
- d. Authoritative
- e. Demonstration
- f. Fantasy
- g. Informative

6-24. Find a copy of a business journal such as *Business Week* or *Fortune* or a trade journal. Also locate a copy of a consumer journal such as *Glamour, Time, Sports Illustrated*, or a specialty magazine. Look through an entire issue. What differences between the advertisements in the business journal and consumer journals are readily noticeable? For each of the concepts listed below, discuss specific differences you noted between the two types of magazines. Explain why the differences exist.

- a. Message strategies
- b. Appeals
- c. Executional frameworks
- d. Sources and spokespersons

6-25. A manager from a resort in Florida wants to develop an advertisement highlighting scuba diving lessons. The target market will be college students. Identify the best combination of message strategy, appeal, and execution. Justify your choice. What message strategy, appeal, and execution would you use if the target market was families with children? Justify your choice. Choose one of the target markets. Design a print ad using the design combination you selected.

6-26. Name three influential spokespersons. For each one, discuss the five characteristics used to evaluate spokespersons and their overall level of credibility. Next, make a list of three individuals who are poor spokespersons. Discuss each of the five evaluation characteristics for each of these individuals. What differences exist between an effective and a poor spokesperson?

Integrated Learning Exercises

6-27. Current as well as past Super Bowl ads are available at **www.superbowl-ads.com**. Access the site and compare Super Bowl ads over the last several years. What types of message strategies were used? What types of appeals were used? What types of executions were used? Who and what types of endorsers or spokespersons were used? Compare and contrast these four elements of ads over the last three years of Super Bowl ads.

6-28. Most advertising agencies provide examples of advertisements on company websites. The goal is to display the agency's creative abilities to potential clients. Using a search engine, locate three different advertising agencies. Locate samples of their work. Compare the ads produced by your three agencies in terms of message strategies, appeals, executions, and spokespersons. What similarities do you see? What differences do you see? Which agency, in your opinion, is the most creative? Why?

6-29. Visit the following top five South African websites. In the past, South Africans favored international sites, but now they prefer and trust home-grown ones. Do the websites use spokespersons? Who are they meant to appeal to? Do you perceive the sites to be international ones or do they appear to be distinctly South African?

a. Gumtree (**www.gumtree.co.za**)
b. News 24 (**www.news24.com**)
c. Bid or Buy (**www.bidorbuy.co.za**)
d. First Rand Bank (**www.fnb.co.za**)
e. Standard Bank (**www.standardbank.co.za**)

6-30. Visit the following websites. Identify the primary message strategy, appeal, and execution used. Evaluate the quality of the website based on message strategy, appeal, and execution. Do the sites utilize a spokesperson? If so, who is it and which type is he or she? Evaluate the spokesperson in terms of the components of credibility.

a. Ruby Tuesdays (**www.rubytuesday.com**)
b. Bonne Bell (**www.bonnebell.com**)
c. MessageMedia (**www.message-media.com**)
d. Jantzen (**www.jantzen.com**)
e. Jockey International (**www.jockey.com**)

Student Project

CREATIVE CORNER

It is time to try your creativity with a television advertisement. Borrow a camcorder and develop a 30- or 45-second television spot for one of the following products, using the suggested appeal. Before designing the ad, decide on the message strategy and execution you will use. Justify your decision. If you do not have access to a camcorder, then develop a magazine advertisement.

a. Denim skirt, sex appeal
b. Tennis racket, humor appeal
c. Ice cream, emotional appeal
d. Vitamins, fear appeal
e. Golf club, rational appeal
f. Spring break trip package, scarcity appeal
g. Restaurant, music appeal

Blog Exercises

Access the authors' blog for this textbook at the URLs provided to complete these exercises. Answer the questions that are posed on the blog.

6-31. Television ads, set 1 - **http://blogclowbaack.net/2014/05/08/television-ads-set-1-chapter-6/**

6-32. Television ads, set 2 - **http://blogclowbaack.net/2014/05/08/television-ads-set-2-chapter-6/**

6-33. Television ads, set 3 - **http://blogclowbaack.net/2014/05/08/television-ads-set-3-chapter-6/**

6-34. Television ads, set 4 - **http://blogclowbaack.net/2014/05/08/television-ads-set-4-chapter-6/**

CASE 1 SOUTH AUSTRALIAN FOOD MARKETING

The South Australia (SA) Food Center was established by the South Australian government in 2008 to provide practical advice to food businesses in the state. Approximately 300 businesses have already taken advantage of the agency's expertise. South Australia's major export markets are Japan, the United States, and Hong Kong. Its main exports are products meat, seafood, fruit, and cheese. The SA Food Center aims to promote South Australia's food businesses through *Food Talk* (an online magazine), Food-e-News (email news updates), and the Premier's Food Awards (awards for South Australian food producers).

South Australian food producers work hard to make sure that their brand is exciting to consumers, focusing on factors such as packaging and labeling. However, like many businesses, they fall short in effectively marketing their products. SA Food Center encourages food producers to promote their brands by not only informing consumers about their availability, but also highlighting what is special about a particular product. The key aim of the SA Food Center is to create a collaborative partnership with industry and government, in order to ensure a thriving South Australian food industry. One such result of this work came from Charlie's Group Limited.

South Australian fruit growers received a considerable boost from Charlie's Group Limited, the manufacturers of Charlie's and Phoenix Organics (smoothies and organic beverages). Charlie's, which was established in 1999, operates in New Zealand, Australia, Asia, the Pacific, the Middle East, and India. It has a major production facility in South Australia. Charlie's was able to gain entry into 750 Coles supermarket stores across Australia. Eleven Charlie's drinks are offered, including the brand-leading Spirulina Smoothie. The deal with the supermarket was so big that Charlie's needed to squeeze an additional 4 million lemons each year, a 300 percent increase, just to meet the demand. Coles supported the new brand rollout with in-store marketing programs, and Charlie's launched a new advertising campaign. All of this was great news for South Australia's fruit growers.

Marie C. Fields/Shutterstock

▲ Thanks to the SA Food Centre, the South Australian mushroom industry has seen a boost in sales.

Even foods such as mushrooms are not forgotten when the SA Food Center promotes South Australian produce. The SA Food Center promotes many events, including annual food festivals and shopping appearances alongside celebrity chefs and media personalities. The South Australian mushroom industry has three major campaigns a year. Mushroom Madness recognizes the best mushroom retailer in each state in Australia. The Mushroom Mania program involves some 2,000 restaurants across Australia in an effort to promote mushrooms as a healthy eating option when dining out. BBQ Mushrooms, fronted by the enthusiastic TV chef Fast Ed, encourages consumers to use mushrooms for outdoor meals. The industry also runs major advertising campaigns, targeting families, grocery buyers, and chefs. Growers also support the Mushroom Lovers' Club, which sends out regular newsletters to consumers, and Mushroom Farm Walks, where South Australian chefs are encouraged to visit mushroom farms to understand the mushroom-growing process. This well-supported program is indicative of the activities of the SA Food Center.[61]

6-35. What type of message strategy should SA Food Center utilize? Should it be the same for all of the brands and in all of the markets (will there be strength in the unity of a South Australia brand)?

6-36. What leverage point makes the most sense for South Australian food producers' advertising?

6-37. What type of executional framework should be used in traditional advertisements aimed at consumers?

6-38. What type of executional framework should be used for print advertisements aimed at business-to-business sales? Why might it differ from ads aimed at consumers?

6-39. Should the SA Food Center use a spokesperson? If so, which one of the four types should be used?

CASE 2 MAVI JEANS: DESIGNING THE COMMUNICATION STRATEGY

Mavi, which means "blue" in Turkish, is known for high quality, great fitting, and fashion-forward premium denim. Time magazine chose Mavi as one of the top 16 jeans brands worldwide. The company was founded in Istanbul in 1991 and designs a full collection of denim clothing for young women and men. In addition to being Turkey's leading jeans brand for the past 16 years, it is also sold at 4,000 sales points, in 285 stores and across 50 countries.

Mavi believes that "design carries the product to the brand" and has multicultural design teams based in Istanbul, New York, Vancouver, and Sydney. Although Turkish companies usually start their overseas expansion in neighboring countries, Mavi did the opposite and started in the homeland of jeans, in the USA. Mavi's first international advertising campaign was "Made in Maviland" in 2001, which was broadcast on TV channels in the USA, Canada, and Germany, and was supported by outdoor and magazine ads. Following that campaign, in 2002 "Mavi Fit" was launched with Maroon 5's first single, "This Love".

In 2007, Mavi collaborated with Italian fashion photographer Oliviero Toscani in the "Mavi Fits" local campaign where the brand's "Mediterraneanness" was elaborated in a bold way. Jeans, the core product of Mavi, were styled as headwear, and Mediterranean objects were used in an prominant way—big evil eyes used as a necklace—to show the soul and courage of the brand.

In 2008 Mavi again collaborated with well known creatives, this time Serbian film director Emir Kusturica, in a local campaign entitled "Emir Kusturica for Mavi". Reflecting again the

Veniamin/Shutterstock

▲ Mavi have distinguished their brand from competitors' by emphasizing the "Mediterraneanness" of their jeans.

roots of Mediterraneanness, the campaign was inspired by the spirit of Kusturica's famous film *Underground*.

Mavi launched another global campaign in 2011 to celebrate its 20th year, featuring the slogan "The Jean is Mavi." The photographs, taken by Mert and Marcus, fashion photographers who were named by *Industrie* magazine among the fifty most influential and inspirational creative working in fashion in 2011, spread throughout global media.

Mavi's 2012 global ad campaign with world famous model Adriana Lima has been a huge success that once more proved the brand's world-wide strength. In the TV ad, Adriana Lima visits the Mavi store in New York and the entire store turns to a Mavi-Adriana Lima catwalk. The global pillar of the campaign is an outdoor campaign where Adriana Lima is pictured together with Jon Kortajarena, a globally recognized male model. The worldwide campaign has had phenomenal success in Turkey and across Europe, conveying the message that Mavi is a global, attractive fashion brand.[62]

6-40. Do you think a brand should have a rigid brand philosophy that should be applied wherever it goes?

6-41. Where does a brand stand in using a celebrity where the celebrity is not shadowing the brand and the brand message is conveyed in a right way? Could you think of other examples where celebrity usage is a success or a failure and why?

6-42. If you were assigned to prepare the next international advertisement campaign for the company, what would be your ideas for the campaign?

6-43. What do you think about the choice of "Mediterraneanness" in the advertisement campaigns? Would you prefer an adaptation strategy? Why?

MyMarketingLab

Go to **mymktlab.com** for the following Assisted-graded writing questions:

6-44. Watch one of your favorite television shows. Record all of the television commercials in one commercial break (at least seven ads). Identify the appeal used in each one. Were the ads effective? Why or why not?

6-45. Hardee's and Carl's Jr. recently used a television commercial featuring a schoolteacher dancing on top of her desk while a room full of guys performed a rap song entitled "I Like Flat Buns." The song seemed appropriate because the ad was for the Patty Melt on a flat bun. Instead, the ad received considerable flack because the sexy blonde schoolteacher was wearing a short, tight skirt. Teachers' associations complained that it was inappropriate because it was a "sexually exploitive assault" on teachers, students, and schools. Which type of sex appeal is being used? Discuss the appropriateness of this ad in terms of the concepts presented in the chapter in the "Sex" appeal section. What makes it effective? What makes in ineffective?

Chapter 7 Traditional Media Channels

Chapter Objectives

After reading this chapter, you should be able to answer the following questions:

7.1 What is a media strategy?

7.2 What elements and individuals are involved in media planning?

7.3 How do the terms used to describe advertising help the marketing team design effective campaigns?

7.4 What are some of the primary advertising objectives?

7.5 What are the advantages and disadvantages associated with each traditional advertising medium?

7.6 How can the marketing team use the media mix to increase advertising effectiveness?

7.7 What are the key issues associated with media selection for business-to-business markets?

7.8 What issues are associated with media selection in international markets?

Overview

If a tree falls in the forest and no one is present, does it make a sound? This philosophical question has been posed for many years and even recently appeared in a Geico Insurance commercial. Unfortunately, in the world of advertising, far too many "trees" fall as unheard and unseen advertisements. Successful marketing involves identifying target markets and finding the media that reach the members of those markets. Once the advertising team identifies the right media, creatives can design clever, memorable, exciting, and persuasive advertisements. When an advertising campaign succeeds, it may not only reach customers in traditional ways (television, magazines, radio), but in the new world of digital media it will be passed along and shared via the internet and in other ways.

UEFA CHAMPIONS LEAGUE

It has been estimated that the total global value of sports television rights reached $27 billion in 2010. That is an amazing number, but consider that the value of sports sponsorships and other commercial revenues generated by teams is now a staggering $54 billion. Soccer plays a big part in these numbers. In May 2009, the UEFA Champions League final had an estimated audience of 109 million. Including those viewers who watched just a part of the TV coverage, the figure rises to 206 million. In 2010, approximately 170 million viewers tuned in to the final played in Madrid.

First held in 1992, the Champions League allows eight brands to sponsor soccer matches. Each sponsor is allocated advertising boards around the pitch perimeters, logo placement for interviews, and priority for television advertisements during matches. The matches are broadcast in 70 countries, and commentary is available in 40 different languages.

The main target market for the brands is the elusive 16- to 34-year-old male demographic. The cost of advertising during a soccer game is some 40 percent higher than for other televised sports. The cost of advertising during the Champions League finals has gradually increased as television audience figures have grown. A Champions League sponsorship is usually on a rolling 3-year contract.

During the final in 2010, Nike ran a staggering 3-minute specially commissioned advertisement simultaneously in 32 countries. The cost to air the advertisement during the final was estimated to have cost $2.4 million in the UK alone. Nike is not an official sponsor, but used its financial muscle to create more buzz and media coverage than the official sponsors.

In light of Nike's advertising blitz, UEFA now controls all advertising time during its matches, allotting time to its sponsors alone. Sponsors are obliged to buy additional advertising to better leverage their investment. UEFA's proactive policy seems to be working well. Companies have shown enormous interest in the well-protected 3-year sponsorship packages for the Champions League (believed to be $220 million per sponsor). There is even a waiting list to become a sponsor.[1]

The Media Strategy

objective 7.1
What is a media strategy?

A **media strategy** involves analyzing and choosing media for an advertising and marketing campaign. The average consumer examines only nine of the more than 200 consumer magazines on the market. A radio listener usually tunes in to only three of the stations available in an area. Television viewers on average watch fewer than eight of the stations available via cable or satellite. Network prime-time ratings have declined by more than 30 percent over the last decade. Consequently, choosing the optimal media to speak to potential customers creates challenges.

To make the account executive and media buyer's jobs more difficult, prices for advertising time and space have risen. Client budgets for advertising have not gone up as quickly, even as stronger demands for results and accountability emerged. The marketing team faces difficulties in locating cost-effective media outlets. After developing a media strategy, other aspects of media selection can proceed.

Media Planning

objective 7.2
What elements and individuals are involved in media planning?

Media planning commences with an analysis of the target market. It involves understanding the processes customers use in making purchases and what influences their final decisions. One method of addressing media planning starts with a study of the media choices that members of a specific, defined target market might make at different times during the course of a day (see Figure 7.1).

Details of the type shown in Figure 7.1 become valuable when developing a media strategy. Demographics such as age, sex, income, and education do not explain the media habits of consumers. Information about the listening and viewing patterns of groups helps the marketing team design appealing messages. These can then be shown at the best times and in the best places. No two media plans are alike. The components of a media plan include the elements identified in Figure 7.2.

A marketing analysis provides a comprehensive review of the marketing program. It includes a statement about current sales, current market share, and prime prospects to be solicited (by demographics, lifestyle, geographic location, or product usage). These elements should reflect a compatible pricing strategy based on the product, its benefits and distinguishing characteristics, and an analysis of the competitive environment.

An advertising analysis states the primary advertising strategy and budget to be used to achieve advertising objectives. The media strategy spells out the media to be used and the creative considerations. The media schedule notes when ads will appear in individual vehicles. The justification and summary outlines the measures of goal achievement. It also explains the rationale for each media choice.[2]

▼ Understanding consumer media choices is important for newspapers, such as *The Times-Picayune* of New Orleans.

NOLA Media Group

Several individuals take part in media planning. In addition to account executives, account planners, and creatives, most agencies utilize media planners and media buyers. In smaller agencies, the media planner and media buyer may be the same person. In larger companies, they are usually different individuals. Some agencies employ media firms to handle media planning and buying or hire a subsidiary agency.

Media Planners

The **media planner** formulates a media program stating where and when to place ads. Media planners work closely with creatives, account executives, account planners, agencies, and media buyers. The creative should know which media will be used to help design effective messages. Creatives construct television ads in different ways than for radio or newspaper.

Media planners provide valuable services and are in high demand. The issue of accountability for advertising results combined with the need to create a return on investment on marketing dollars has led the media buying side of an agency to hold greater power.

- A favorite wake-up radio station or one listened to during the commute to work
- A favorite morning news show or newspaper
- Trade or business journals examined while at work
- A radio station played during office hours at work
- Favorite computer sites accessed during work
- Favorite magazines read during the evening hours
- Favorite television shows watched during the evening hours
- Internet sites accessed during leisure time
- Shopping, dining, and entertainment venues frequented

◀ **FIGURE 7.1**
Examples of Times Consumers Are Exposed to Advertisements

- Marketing analysis
- Advertising analysis
- Media strategy
- Media schedule
- Justification and summary

▲ **FIGURE 7.2**
Components of a Media Plan

Media planning has an impact on strategic planning. Marketing experts at companies such as Procter & Gamble and Unilever consider media planning to be at the heart of a communications strategy. In both companies, setting brand priorities and objectives constitutes the first step.[3] The task media buyers in this environment undertake, according to Carl Fremont of the media services company Digitas, will be "to integrate marketing messages across a range of media, and sometimes this involves working with several agencies to accomplish the client's goals."[4]

The media planner conducts research to help match the product with the market and media. If JD Bank's executives decide to run a print campaign directed to farmers who may need loans for tractors, the media planner researches the best media to place the ads. The media planner matches the target market with the venues that farmers would most likely watch or view.

The media planner gathers information about various media. This includes newspaper and magazine circulation rates along with the characteristics of those who read them. The audience for a television show may be different from those of a radio station or a magazine. Quality research improves the chances of selecting the appropriate media.

▼ The media planner will locate the best medium for this advertisement for JD Bank.

JD Bank

Media Buyers

After the media are chosen, the **media buyer** purchases the space and negotiates rates, times, and schedules for the ads. Media buyers remain in contact with media sales representatives. They know a great deal about rates and schedules. Media buyers watch for special deals and tie-ins between media outlets (e.g., radio with television, magazines with the same owner, etc.).

Placement in a television show or magazine continues to be an important consideration, both in terms of price and effectiveness. Recently, the Pink Jacket Creative advertising agency purchased magazine space for The Snoring Center consisting of the outer sides of adjacent pages containing an article. The slender ads on the edges of the two pages bracketed the article. As individuals read the article, they first noticed the ad on the left side of the article and the second half on the right side as they held the magazine open. The cost of the ad space was lower and it turned out to be more effective in conveying the two-part message.

Courtesy of Pink Jacket Creative: A Creative Factory

Some research indicates that little connection exists between the size of an advertising firm and the prices it can negotiate. Differences in media costs are based on the time of the actual purchase (closer to the day the ad is to run) rather than the size of the agency.[5] A media plan costing one firm $10 million can cost another $12 million. Other major factors in cost differences are knowledge of the marketplace and the ability to negotiate package deals.

A **spot ad** is a one-time placement of a commercial in a medium. Rates are negotiated individually by the number of times the ads appear. Spot television prices fluctuate by as much as 45 percent for the same time slot. Radio time slot prices vary by as much as 42 percent and national print ads by as much as 24 percent.[6] Negotiation skills affect media purchase outcomes.

The quality of media choices, creativity, financial stewardship, the agency's culture and track record, and the relationship between the agency and the medium's sales representative lead to differences in the effectiveness of various advertising campaigns. The quality of the media selections made combined with the advertisement's content determines eventual levels of success.

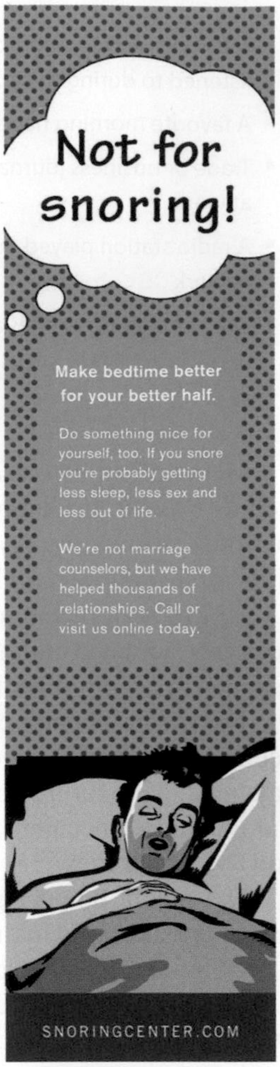

Courtesy of Pink Jacket Creative: A Creative Factory

▲ These ads for the Snoring Center were placed strategically on a two-page article spread on the outer edges.

Advertising Terminology

As with many subjects, advertising has its own unique set of terms and measures (see Figure 7.3). **Reach** represents the number of people, households, or businesses in a target audience exposed to a media vehicle or message schedule at least once during a given time period, which normally consists of four weeks. In other words, how many targeted buyers did the ad reach at least once during a four-week period?

objective 7.3
How do the terms used to describe advertising help the marketing team design effective campaigns?

Frequency

The average number of times an individual, household, or business within a particular target market is exposed to a particular advertisement within a specified time period, again, usually four weeks, constitutes **frequency**. It specifies how many times the person encountered the ad during a campaign. A regular viewer will see the same ad shown daily on *Wheel of Fortune* more frequently than she views an ad shown once on *CSI*, even though the *CSI* program has a greater reach.

Opportunities to See

In media planning, instead of frequency, buyers can use **opportunities to see (OTS)** or the cumulative exposures achieved in a given time period. When a company places two ads on a weekly television show, eight OTS (four shows × two ads per show) occur during a four-week period.

- Reach
- Frequency
- Opportunities to see (OTS)
- Gross rating points (GRP)
- Cost per thousand (CPM)
- Cost per rating point (CPRP)
- Ratings
- Continuity
- Gross impressions

▶ **FIGURE 7.3**
Advertising Terminology

Gross Rating Points

Gross rating points (GRPs) measure the impact or intensity of a media plan. Advertisers calculate gross rating points by multiplying a vehicle's rating by the OTS, or number of insertions of an advertisement. GRPs provide the advertiser with a better idea of the odds that members of the target audience actually viewed the commercial. By increasing the OTS or frequency, the chances of a magazine reader seeing the advertisement rise. An advertisement featured in each weekly issue of *People* during a four-week period is more likely to be seen than one appearing in a monthly periodical.

Cost

Cost measures the overall expenditures associated with an advertising program or campaign. To see how cost-effective one medium or ad placement is compared to another, the **cost per thousand (CPM)** figure can be calculated. CPM identifies the dollar cost of reaching 1,000 members of the media vehicle's audience. Marketers calculate CPM using the following formula:

$$\text{CPM} = (\text{Cost of media buy} / \text{Total audience}) \times 1{,}000$$

Figure 7.4 displays cost and readership information for a campaign for a 35 mm digital camera. The first three columns of the figure provide the name of the magazine, the cost of a four-color full-page advertisement, and the magazine's paid and verified circulation. The fourth column contains a measure of the CPM of each magazine. The CPM for *Better Homes and Gardens* is $66.21 and has a circulation of 7.6 million. *Sports Illustrated* has a smaller circulation, 3.2 million, but the CPM is $122.69. In terms of cost per thousand readers, *Reader's Digest* offers the best buy, at $26.04 per thousand.

Philadelphia Cream Cheese

▲ Opportunities to see measures the number of times consumers have an opportunity to see this advertisement for Philadelphia Cream Cheese.

				Target Market (20 Million)			
Publication	4C Base Rate	Total Paid & Verified Circulation	CPM	Percent of Readers Fit Target Market	Number of Readers Fit Target Market	Rating (Reach)	Cost per Rating Point (CPRP)
Better Homes and Gardens	$506.380	7,648,600	$566.21	13.51%	1,033,000	5.2	$97,381
Glamour	$219,190	2,320,325	$94.47	24.65%	572,000	2.9	$76,640
Good Housekeeping	$387,055	4,652,904	$83.19	10.81%	503,000	2.5	$153,899
National Geographic	$225,455	4,495,931	$50.15	26.96%	1,212,000	6.1	$37,204
Reader's Digest	$185,300	7,114,955	$26.04	18.62%	1,325,000	6.6	$27,970
Southern Living	$198,800	2,855,973	$69.61	10.57%	302,000	1.5	$131,656
Sports Illustrated	$392,800	3,201,524	$122.69	16.77%	537,000	2.7	$146,294
Time	$320,100	3,376,226	$94.81	18.60%	628,000	3.1	$101,943

▲ **FIGURE 7.4**
Hypothetical Media Information for a 35 mm Digital Camera

Ratings and Cost per Rating Point

Consider the target market's profile when a company seeks to advertise a 35 mm digital camera. The number of readers that fit the target market's profile becomes the key goal. **Ratings** measure the percentage of a firm's target market exposed to a television show or the number of readers of a print medium. In order to compare media, a measure called the **cost per rating point (CPRP)** may be used. The cost per rating point formula that measures the relative efficiency of a media vehicle relative to a firm's target market is:

$$\text{CPRP} = \text{Cost of media buy}/\text{Vehicle's rating}$$

Assume there are 20 million potential buyers of 35 mm digital cameras. The figure shows the rating for *Better Homes and Gardens* is 5.2, which means that 5.2 percent of the defined target market for 35 mm digital cameras read *Better Homes and Gardens.* Backing up a step, 13.51 percent, or 1.033 million, of *Better Homes and Gardens'* readership fits the target profile for the 35 mm digital camera. The 5.2 rating is then obtained by dividing the 1.033 million *Better Homes and Gardens* readers that fit the target profile by the 20 million total for the target market. The CPRP for *Better Homes and Gardens* becomes $98,041. It specifies the average cost for each rating point, or of each 1 percent of the firm's target audience (35 mm digital camera buyers) that can be reached through an advertisement in *Better Homes and Gardens.* Not all readers of a magazine are part of the firm's target market. The CPRP more accurately measures an advertising campaign's efficiency than does CPM. Notice that the CPRP is the lowest for *National Geographic* and *Reader's Digest.* It is the highest for *Good Housekeeping.*

CPRP provides a relative measure of reach exposure in terms of cost. It costs $37,204 to reach 1 percent, or 200,000, of the 20 million in this firm's target market using *National Geographic.* It costs $146,294 to reach 1 percent, or 200,000, using *Sports Illustrated.* To reach 1 percent, or 200,000, using *Reader's Digest* costs only $27,970. *Reader's Digest* is the most efficient, which raises the question, "Why wouldn't a media planner just do all of the advertising in that magazine?" The answer lies in *Reader's Digest*'s rating. Advertising in only that magazine reaches just 6.6 percent (or 1,325,000) of the target audience; 93.4 percent of the target market does not read *Reader's Digest* and would not see the ad. Another magazine or media outlet is needed to reach them. This explains why diversity in media is essential to reach a large portion of a firm's target market.

An alternative method of determining whether an ad has reached the target market efficiently is a **weighted (or demographic) CPM** value, which can be calculated as:

$$\text{Weighted CPM} = \frac{\text{Advertisement cost} \times 1{,}000}{\text{Actual audience reached}}$$

Referring to Figure 7.5, the cost of an advertisement in *Good Housekeeping* is $387,055. Although it has a circulation of 4,652,904, only 503,000 of the readers fit the target profile for the 35 mm digital camera. Using the formula for weighted CPM, the

▼ FIGURE 7.5
Calculating Weighted (or Demographic) CPM

				Target Market (20 Million)		
Publication	**4C Base Rate**	**Total Paid & Verified Circulation**	**CPM**	**Percent of Readers Fit Target Market**	**Number of Readers Fit Target Market**	**Weighted (Demographic) CPM**
Better Homes and Gardens	$506,380	7,648,600	$66.21	13.51%	1,033,000	$490.20
Glamour	$219,190	2,320,325	$94.47	24.65%	572,000	$383.20
Good Housekeeping	$387,055	4,652,904	$83.19	10.81%	503,000	$769.49
National Geographic	$225,455	4,495,931	$50.15	26.96%	1,212,000	$186.02
Reader's Digest	$185,300	7,114,955	$26.04	18.62%	1,325,000	$139.85
Southern Living	$198,800	2,855,973	$69.61	10.5%	302,000	$658.28
Sports Illustrated	$392,800	3,201,524	$122.69	16.77%	537,000	$731.47

cost to reach 1,000 readers of *Good Housekeeping* that fit the target profile is $769.49. As with CPRP, marketers can compare the various magazines to determine which offer the best buy in terms of reaching the target demographic. The difference in the numbers is that CPRP measures the cost of reaching 1 percent of the target market, whereas the weighted CPM measures the cost of reaching 1,000 members of the target market.

Continuity

The exposure pattern or schedule used in a campaign signifies its **continuity**. The three types of patterns are continuous, pulsating, and discontinuous. A *continuous campaign* uses media time in a steady stream. Home construction companies such as Buford Hawthorne would use a continuous schedule, because individuals making decisions to build homes do not follow any consistent time frame for when they will be ready to buy. Consequently, media buyers would look for ad space in specific magazines for a period of one to two years. By using different ads and rotating them, readers will not get bored, because they will see more than one advertisement for the same product.

A retailer such as JCPenney might feature a *pulsating schedule* by placing ads in various media throughout the entire year, but then increasing the number of advertisements in small, short bursts around holidays, including Christmas, Thanksgiving, Memorial Day, Labor Day, Mother's Day, Father's Day, and Easter. Pulsating advertising should reach consumers when they are most likely to make purchases or buy special merchandise, such as during the holidays. A Barnes & Noble advertisement just prior to Christmas can encourage consumers to purchase gift cards.

A *flighting* (or *discontinuous*) *campaign* schedule, in which advertisements run at only certain times of the year, differs from the first two approaches. It would be more likely to be used by a ski resort that runs ads during the fall and winter seasons but none during the spring and summer.

Buford Hawthorne

▲ In terms of continuity, a continuous schedule is a logical choice for home construction firm Buford Hawthorne.

Impressions

The final advertising term is impressions. The number of **gross impressions** represents the total exposures of the audience to an advertisement. It does not account for the percentage of the total audience that sees the advertisement. Figure 7.5 indicates that *National Geographic*'s total circulation is approximately 4.6 million. If six insertions were placed in *National Geographic*, multiplying the insertions by the readership would yield a total of 27.6 million impressions.

Achieving Advertising Objectives

objective 7.4
What are some of the primary advertising objectives?

Advertisers consider the number of times a person will be exposed to an advertisement before it creates an impact. Most agree that a single exposure will not be sufficient. The actual number inspires a great deal of debate. Some argue it takes three. Others say as many as 10 or more.

Scott and Cooner Inc.

▲ Based on recency theory, a person looking for designer home furnishings would be more likely to notice this advertisement.

The Three-Exposure Hypothesis

Most media planners believe an advertisement requires a minimum of three exposures for an advertisement to be effective. The three-exposure hypothesis, as developed by Herbert Krugman, states that an advertisement can make an impact on an audience regardless of individual needs or wants.[7] Further, the **intrusion value** of an advertisement represents the ability of a medium or an advertisement to capture the attention of a viewer without her voluntary effort. This reasoning suggests that it takes at least three exposures to capture a viewer's attention.

Recency Theory

Currently, many advertisers believe that clutter has diminished the viability of the three-exposure hypothesis. Another concept, **recency theory**, notes that a consumer exhibits selective attention and focuses on personal needs and wants as he considers advertisements.[8] When a consumer pays attention to messages that might meet his needs or wants, the closer an exposure to a commercial is to the purchase decision, the more powerful the ad becomes. Further, when a consumer contemplates a future purchase of the product being advertised, the consumer becomes more likely to notice and react favorably toward an ad. A member of a buying center from a business in the market for a new copier will more readily notice copier advertisements. Someone who is not in the market for a copier ignores the same ad. The same holds true in consumer markets: An individual desiring a new pair of jeans notices clothing ads, especially ones that feature jeans.

Recency theory proposes that *one ad exposure* may actually be enough to affect an audience when that person or business needs the product being promoted. Additional exposures may not be necessary. Therefore, companies should advertise almost continually to ensure an advertisement reaches a buyer when she thinks about making a purchase.

The advertising approach that matches recency theory would be to spread the message around using a variety of media, each type providing limited exposure per week or time period. In the case of selling supplemental health insurance to the elderly, magazines such as *Senior Living*, television spots on local news and weather programs, and newspaper ads can quickly reach the target audience in a cost-effective manner. This method, which maximizes reach, accomplishes more than increasing frequency.

In the business-to-business arena, recency theory suggests that advertisements should appear in a number of outlets and over a longer period of time rather than running a series of ads in one trade journal. Many times, buying centers consist of several members, each with differing responsibilities. Making sure each one sees an advertisement would mean placing ads in every journal that might be read by buying center members. To facilitate the purchasing process for a company seeking to acquire an audio-conferencing system, the media buyer purchases space in trade journals, human resource journals, sales journals, and business journals. This increases the odds that the message will reach buying center members. One exposure might be enough for each, because the member actively looks for information and is ready to make a decision.

Effective Reach and Frequency

Seeking to discover the minimum number of exposures needed to be effective may be based on two concepts: effective frequency and effective reach. **Effective reach** identifies the *percentage of an audience* that must be exposed to a particular message to achieve a specific objective. **Effective frequency** refers to the *number of times* a target audience

◀ Effective reach and effective frequency are important considerations in reaching the target market for Office Furniture.

must be exposed to a message to achieve a particular objective. The effective frequency concept implies that a minimum number of exposures will be needed.

Effective frequency and effective reach provide crucial guidelines. Too few exposures means the advertiser might fail to attain its intended objectives. In contrast, too many exposures waste resources. Discovering the optimal reach and frequency mix to accomplish the intended objectives without experiencing diminishing returns from extra ads should be the goal. The optimal mix for an objective dealing with brand recognition will be different than when brand recall serves as the objective.

Other elements can also enhance effective frequency and effective reach. They include the size and placement of an advertisement. A small magazine advertisement does not create the same impact as a larger ad. If a firm uses 15-second television ads, effective frequency may require six exposures. In comparison, a longer 45-second spot may require only four exposures to be remembered. In television advertising, a spot in the middle of an ad sequence usually has less of an impact than the ads shown at the beginning and end of the series.

The number of different media used in an advertising campaign also influences effectiveness. In general, a campaign featuring ads in two types of media, such as television and magazines, will generate greater effective reach than a campaign in only one medium, such as magazines only.

In recent years, numerous media companies have designed computer models to optimize reach and frequency, including Nielsen SAVE and Adware. These programs are based on probability theory. They help a marketing team effectively allocate advertising dollars. The interaction between an attention-getting television commercial and a magazine ad with copy explaining the product's features may create a more potent synergistic effect than either ad would generate by itself.

Brand Recognition

Brand recognition requires an emphasis on the visual presentation of the product and/or logo. Strengthening or creating links between the brand and other nodes of information that exist in the person's knowledge structure becomes the goal. Rather than leading the individual to recall the brand name from memory, the advertiser wants the person to recognize the brand name and logo at the retail store or in the advertisement. Media that are effective at maximizing reach include television, billboards, magazines, the internet, and direct mail.[9]

▶ Billboards offer an excellent medium for achieving brand recognition objectives for Ouachita Independent Bank.

Newcomer, Morris and Young Inc.

▶ **FIGURE 7.6** Brand Recognition Versus Brand Recall

Objective	Brand Recognition	Brand Recall
Goal	Create or strengthen mental linkages	Place brand in evoked set
Method	Increase reach	Increase frequency (repetition)
Best media	Television	Television
	Billboards	Radio
	Magazines	Newspapers
	Internet	Internet
	Direct mail	

Brand Recall

To increase brand recall, frequency becomes more important than reach. Repetition helps embed a brand in the consumer's cognitive memory. Repetition makes it more likely that a particular brand will come to mind. When a 30-second commercial repeats the name of a restaurant seven times, it becomes easier to remember than when it is stated only once or twice. In terms of media selection, television, radio, newspapers, and the internet offer the potential for higher frequency.[10] Figure 7.6 compares brand recall with brand recognition.

Once the media buyer, media planner, account executive, and company leaders agree to basic objectives of the advertising campaign, they select the actual media, seeking to identify logical media combinations. The next section examines traditional advertising media.

Media Selection

objective 7.5
What are the advantages and disadvantages associated with each traditional advertising medium?

Effectively mixing advertising media constitutes a vital element in the design of a quality advertising campaign. To do so, marketing professionals consider the advantages and disadvantages of each individual medium.

Television

Deloitte Research recently noted that 71 percent of Americans still rate television as their favorite medium. In terms of impact on buying decisions, 86 percent stated that TV advertising exerts the greatest influence.[11] While the power of television has declined,

▶ This banner advertisement for "Visit Baton Rouge" should help increase brand recall.

Visit Baton Rouge

Advantages	Disadvantages
• High reach	• High level of clutter
• High frequency potential	• Low recall due to clutter
• Low cost per contact	• Channel surfing during ads
• High intrusion value	• DVRs skipping ads
• Quality creative opportunities	• Short amount of copy
• Segmentation through cable	• High cost per ad

FIGURE 7.7
Television Advertising

for many brands and companies it remains a viable advertising option. At the same time, advertisers should be aware that television viewing has changed. It now occurs on a tablet or laptop computer rather than a regular television screen. Figure 7.7 lists the pros and cons of television advertising.

Advantages of Television Advertising Television provides the most extensive coverage and highest reach of any medium. A single advertisement can reach millions. Television offers a low cost per contact, which justifies spending as much as $4 million for a 30-second spot on the Super Bowl, where a vast audience of more than 110 million households and nearly one billion people may be watching. The cost per person reached by the commercial is low.

Television provides intrusion value. Commercials featuring a catchy musical tune, sexy content, or humor can quickly capture a viewer's attention. Television offers opportunities to be creative in designing advertisements. Visual images and sounds can be incorporated in a commercial. Advertisers are able to demonstrate products and services on television in a manner not possible in print or using radio advertisements. Segmentation may be achieved by targeting specialty shows and networks such as *The Food Channel* or *ESPN*.

Disadvantages of Television Advertising Clutter continues to be the primary problem for television advertising. Many programs include 31 commercials per hour and they take as long as 19 minutes to run. Four- and five-minute commercial breaks are common.[12] As a result, many viewers switch channels during commercial breaks. Often, low recall exists, especially for commercials placed in the middle of an advertising segment. Messages at the beginning or near the end of the break have a better chance to be recalled. Also, ads near the beginning of a television show or during the last commercial break have a higher recall, because individuals want to catch the start of the show and make sure they see the last part of a show for its climax or conclusion.

Some viewers cope with clutter by using a DVR, recording favorite programs and watching them later. Advertisers fear the DVR users will skip over the commercials. Recent research indicates, however, that fewer than half fast-forward through commercials. Also, the majority watches the television show the same day it is recorded, and 75 percent have viewed it by the end of the next day. This means that time-sensitive ads are seen close to when they first were run. Consequently, the fear that DVRs cause viewers to skip commercials may be somewhat unjustified.[13]

Television airtime is expensive, as are the costs of producing ads. The average cost of production for a 30-second national ad is $358,000. Production fees account for the largest portion of the cost, an average of $236,000. Other costs include director fees ($23,000), fees for editing and finishing the ad ($45,000), and creative/labor fees and music ($34,000).[14]

Ratings To gain a sense of how well an advertisement fared in terms of reaching an audience, a given program's rating can be calculated. The typical ratings formula is:

$$\text{Rating} = \frac{\text{Number of households tuned to a program}}{\text{Total number of households in a market}}$$

▶ A storyboard illustrating a television commercial for Interstate Batteries.

Interstate Battery Systems International, Inc.

In the United States, approximately 109.7 million households own television sets. To calculate the rating of an episode of *American Idol*, if the number of households tuned to the season finale was 17.8 million, the rating would be:

$$\text{Rating} = \frac{17{,}800{,}000}{109{,}700{,}000} = 16.2$$

Next, if the advertiser were interested in the percentage of households that actually were watching television at that hour, the program's share could be calculated. Assuming 71 million of the 109.7 million households had a television turned on during the hour in which *American Idol* aired, the share would be:

$$\text{Share} = \frac{\text{Number of households tuned to } \textit{American Idol}}{\text{Number of households with a television turned on}} = \frac{17{,}800{,}000}{71{,}000{,}000} = 25$$

▼ Ratings measure how many households are tuned to a particular television program.

Tatyana Gladskih/Fotolia

A 16.2 rating would mean that 16.2 percent of all televisions in the United States were tuned to *American Idol*. A 25 share means 25 percent of the households with a television actually turned on were watching the program. Ratings do not guarantee viewers saw the commercial. Ratings and shares only indicate of how well the television program fared.

C3 Ratings Some advertisers have began to adopt a new system—the commercial C3 rating—which calculates a rating for the actual commercial time slot rather than the television program. It computes a commercial's rating plus any viewing of the commercial three days after the original ad ran. Many firms now use the C3 rating to determine national television

American Idol	$467,617
Sunday Night Football	$415,000
Glee	$272,694
Family Guy	$259,289
The Simpsons	$253,170
House	$226,180
Grey's Anatomy	$222,113
The Office	$213,617
Desperate Housewives	$210,064

FIGURE 7.8
Cost of 30-second advertisements based on C3 Ratings

advertising rates. Marketers calculate the C3 rating by computing the average rating of all commercials within a particular pod or commercial segment. Various advertisers have criticized the system, claiming that not all ads within a pod receive equal exposure. For instance, the first position in a pod generates 28 percent higher awareness than ads in the middle of the commercial sequence. Thus, the position of a particular ad in the commercial break and the length of the pod have no impact on the rates being charged.

Nielsen intends to expand the C3 rating system to correct this problem. Called "On Demand C3" the new system will produce a rating for each commercial. It will include the show's live telecast viewing along with three-day post viewing period via DVRs.[15]

Figure 7.8 provides the costs of 30-second ads using the C3 system. The higher a show's rating over time, the more that can be charged. The highest costs are for *American Idol* at $467,617 and *Sunday Night Football* at $415,000.[16]

Ratings Providers ACNielsen continues to be the primary organization that calculates and reports ratings and shares. The company provides information regarding shares of stations in local markets known as *designated marketing areas* (DMAs). Data-gathering techniques used by ACNielsen include diaries written by viewers who report what they watched, audience meters that record what is being shown automatically, and people meters that track the viewing habits of individual members of families. Nielsen augments TV ratings with information about viewing from tables and smartphones, because the number of individuals using these alternative screens to watch television programming continues to grow, especially among younger consumers.

These numbers can be further refined to help advertisers understand whether an advertisement reached a target market. Within rating and share categories, viewers can be subdivided by certain demographics, such as age, income, gender, educational level, and race or ethnic heritage. Organizations that prepare this information include Nielsen Media Research; Starch INRA; Hooper, Inc.; Mediamark Research, Inc.; Burke Marketing Research; and Simmons Market Research Bureau. Psychographic information can be then be added, such as whether outdoor enthusiasts watch certain programs. This gives the advertiser a sense of whether the program provides the best audience for an advertisement or campaign.

Local and Regional Television Advertising For local and regional companies, spot TV may be the best television advertising option. In many cases, national brands supplement national commercials with spot TV purchases in select markets. Media planners use this approach primarily due to the high cost of national ad time and because 75 to 80 percent of prime-time slots are sold out during the spring, shortly after they go on the market. By selecting local early news, late news, and local prime access, a media planner generates higher GRP at a lower cost than if only national ad time has been purchased.

Denver local pizza operation Anthony's Pizza & Pasta switched from 90 percent out-of-home billboard advertising to 90 percent television. The company used a concentrated flighting schedule during the first and fourth quarters to build awareness and

Monkey Business/Fotolia

▲ Through dynamic advertising, DirecTV targeted Spanish-speaking consumers in select markets.

drive traffic to the restaurants. Spots were run in Denver on all of the national broadcast networks and 14 cable channels including ESPN, Comedy Central, Cartoon Network, Food Network, and AMC. The spots featured the key message/tagline "authentic, New York-style pizza." Five spots focused on the crafting of the pizza, and six spots utilized humor. During the six months when no ads were run, the company used social media, especially Facebook, to maintain contact with customers.[17]

Dynamic Advertising TV networks, cable, and satellite TV companies have introduced a new technology that helps advertisers zero in on specific target markets. **Dynamic advertising** allows a company such as DirecTV to obtain consumer information from marketing research firms and combine it with the company's data to send targeted ads to its subscribers that meet specific criteria and live in targeted areas. It can be Spanish-speaking consumers, individuals who want to lose weight, or who are early adopters of technology. Toyota used dynamic advertising to target ads to DirecTV customers who were identified as tech-savvy early adopters who live in San Francisco, Los Angeles, and San Diego. No other DirecTV subscribers saw the ads.[18]

Social Media and Television The rise of social media and the internet has led some advertisers to become concerned that television provides less of an impact. While many consumers watch less TV as they spend more time online, for others the opposite takes place. Social media, mobile, and the internet can be used to enrich television viewing experiences and actually drive consumers to watch more programs. Individuals who spend considerable time with social media tend to watch more TV, although some of it may be on tablets and other portable devices. Adam Rossow of iModerate notes that these individuals "love the social interaction and frequently add shows to their viewing lineup due to social chatter. More time is spent on social networks and more hours watching television." A Deloitte Research study revealed that 75 percent of consumers multitask while watching TV—42 percent are online, 29 percent are talking on phones, and 26 percent are sending text messages.[19] Research by Nielsen's SocialGuide service suggests that the heaviest Twitter activity occurs during television shows, not during commercial breaks.[20]

The interaction between social media and television viewing caused the marketing team for Bluefin Labs to examine online buzz about brands and television shows. People who commented online about Wal-Mart also tweeted or commented about television shows *America's SuperNanny, Dallas Cowboys Cheerleaders, Wife Swap, Cell Block 6: Female Lockup*, and *America's Most Wanted*. In contrast, social media comments about Target were tied to online comments and tweets about *Top Secret Recipe, My Yard Goes Disney, HGTV'd, Fashion Hunters*, and *Free Agents*.[21]

As people spend greater amounts of time on social media, the amount of online buzz about television shows will also rise. By monitoring this type of online chatter, advertising professionals and their clients can gain better perspectives regarding the television shows that provide the best matches for placing ads.

YouTube and Television Many companies and advertising agencies post television commercials on YouTube. Some of the ads are placed on the site simultaneously with the TV launch (called *in-stream*) while others are be submitted to YouTube prior to the national launch (called *pre-roll*). For the Super Bowl, part of the ad, a teaser, appears on YouTube prior to the game.

Google and Ipsos research indicates that YouTube pre-roll of TV ads as well as in-streaming of TV ads result in higher recall. Individuals who watched the commercial on

YouTube and on TV had a 200 percent higher recall than individuals who saw the ad only on TV. Those who saw the ad online on YouTube only had a 150 percent higher recall. More than 3 billion consumers watch videos on YouTube daily.[22]

Richard Kane/Fotolia

▲ The Super Bowl has become a showcase for advertisers.

Super Bowl Advertising The Super Bowl offers the biggest television advertising event of the year. Many of the 110 million viewers tune in to see new ads as much as to watch the game. Recent research indicated that 39 percent of the viewers stated the new commercials were their favorite part of the game, and 73 percent consider Super Bowl advertisements to be entertainment. These findings reinforce the statement by Paul Chibe, vice president of marketing at Anheuser-Busch, that, "the Super Bowl is a huge brand-building opportunity."[23]

In the past, ads were kept under wraps until the moment they appear during the game. The rise of social media changed this approach. Many Super Bowl commercials first appear on YouTube, Facebook, the company's website, or on the agency's site prior to the game. As noted, pre-roll teaser ads entice viewers to watch the entire commercial during the game. Prerolling ads generates excitement and allows viewers to see, share, and discuss the ads before, during, and after the game. Many companies and agencies now spend as much time developing a marketing plan for the preroll as they do for the actual Super Bowl commercial. Further, another new approach involves the release of extended versions of advertisement with more content or additional information about the ad spot on the website.

One pre-roll teaser ad for Volkswagen released to YouTube three weeks prior to the Super Bowl was viewed 11 million times. Then, an extended version of the sequel was uploaded to YouTube the week prior to the Super Bowl and was viewed over 1.3 million times. A Super Bowl commercial for the Chevrolet Camaro went online 17 days before the Super Bowl. Brian Sharpless, chief executive of HomeAway, stated that, "Because social media can build buzz for Super Bowl commercials before, during, and after the game, if you don't take advantage of all that, you're not getting the most bang for your buck."[24]

Super Bowl advertising results in nearly immediate feedback. A number of companies run various types of ad meters during the game and monitor social media buzz to determine the best ads and those that missed the mark. Stan Richards of the Richards Group commented, "You get quick feedback. I have to tell you, when you go to bed right after the Super Bowl, your last thought is, 'What is it going to say in *USA Today* tomorrow morning?'"[25]

Radio

Despite CDs, iPods, audio books, and other types of audio devices, the vast majority of Americans, approximately 80 percent, still listen to the radio daily.[26] Adverting professional Mary Price stated that, "Right now, on a weekly basis terrestrial radio still reaches 93 percent of everybody. It used to be 96 or 97, but it's still up there. As long as they can create a following for local personalities and local events, you can't get that off an iPod. If you want some kind of commentary about the music you're listening to … you can't get that on a pre-recorded iPod."[27]

While radio may not seem as glamorous as television, it remains an effective advertising medium (see Figure 7.9). A well-placed, clever commercial results in a one-on-one message (announcer to driver in a car stuck in traffic). Many smaller local companies rely heavily on radio advertising. Most radio ads are produced locally and with small budgets.

FIGURE 7.9
Radio Advertising

Advantages	Disadvantages
• Recall promoted	• Short exposure time
• Narrower target markets	• Low attention
• Ad music can match audience	• Difficult to reach national audiences
• High segmentation potential	• Target duplication with several stations using the same format
• Flexibility in making ads	• Information overload
• Modify ad to local conditions	
• Intimacy with DJs	
• Mobile – listen anywhere	
• Creative opportunities with sound and music	

Advantages of Radio Advertising Quality radio advertisements cause the listener to remember the message by creating powerful images to visualize and by employing repetition. These actions move the information from the consumer's short-term to long-term memory. Sound effects and lively tunes can assist in the process. Through repetition a person hears an advertisement often enough to generate recall.

A radio station reaches definable target markets based on its format, such as talk radio, lite mix, oldies, or country. A firm can advertise on a specific type of station across the country. Radio advertisers can examine the rating and share of a program as well as the estimated number of people listening. Arbitron calculates these numbers for local stations. Radio's All-Dimension Audience Research (RADAR) reports ratings for national radio networks.

Radio can create intimacy. Listeners often feel personally close to DJs and radio personalities. The attachment grows over time. Listening to the same individual becomes more personal and intimate, especially if the listener has a conversation with the DJ during a contest or when requesting a song. The bond or intimacy level gives the radio personality a higher level of credibility and an edge to goods and services the radio celebrity endorses.

▼ Radio is an important component of an integrated advertising campaign.

Fotolia/ra2 studio

Beachbody, a fitness brand based in Santa Monica, California, used radio as the prime medium to promote its P90X, a home exercise system that promised total body improvements within 90 days. Robinson Radio from Virginia was contracted to develop and manage the radio campaign. Robinson realized the best approach was to use "radio's secret weapon," the DJs, who used the product, documented their successes, and then described their progress on the air. The DJs also posted their photos on the company's website, created chat rooms for listeners, and asked listeners to share their success stories. Early in the campaign, it became clear that the micro website was a key component of the radio campaign, because it allowed communications between the listeners, customers of the product, and the DJs. The other advantage of emphasizing radio was that it was easy and inexpensive to make changes to ads as the campaign progressed. The campaign was highly successful in California. Beachbody expanded the campaign nationally within a few months.[28]

© WavebreakmediaMicro/Fotolia

▲ Radio enjoys the advantage of intimacy with the local DJ.

Disadvantages of Radio Advertising Short exposure time creates one problem for radio. Most commercials last 15 or 30 seconds. Listeners involved in other activities, such as driving or working on a computer, may not pay attention. Further, people often use radio as a background to drown out other distractions, especially at work.

For national advertisers, covering a large area with radio advertisements can be difficult. To place a national advertisement requires contacting a large number of companies. Few large radio conglomerates means contacts must be made with multiple stations. Negotiating rates with individual stations based on volume may be difficult. Local businesses can often negotiate better rates than national advertisers because of the local company's relationships with the radio stations.

The four main national radio networks in the United States are Westwood One, ABC, CBS, and Unistar. These are joined by a few other strong networks, such as ESPN radio and CNN. Nationally syndicated programs such as those on the Fox radio network offer some opportunities to national advertisers.

In large metropolitan areas, duplication presents another problem. Several radio stations may try to reach the same target market. Chicago has several rock stations. Advertising on each one may not be financially feasible, yet reaching everyone in that target market might not be possible unless all rock stations are included.

Opportunities for Radio Radio advertising offers a low-cost option for a local firm. Ads can be placed at ideal times and adapted to local conditions. Careful selection of stations, times, and quality construction of the advertisement will be the keys. Radio allows local businesses to present remote broadcasts. Remotes may be used to attract attention to a new business (restaurants, retail stores, etc.) or to a company trying to make a major push for immediate customers. Advertisers often combine radio promotions with other media (local television or newspapers) to send more integrated messages.

For business-to-business advertisers, radio provides the opportunity to reach businesses during working hours, because many employees listen to the radio during office hours. Radio often reaches businesspeople while in transit to or from work. Both radio and television usage has increased for business-to-business marketing.

Out-of-Home Advertising

Billboards along major roads continue to be the most common form of out-of-home (OOH) advertising; however, there are others. Signs on cabs, buses, park benches, and fences of sports arenas are other types of outdoor advertising. A blimp flying above a major sporting event constitutes another form of out-of-home advertising.

▼ This billboard was part of a highly successful campaign for the Snoring Center.

Courtesy of Pink Jacket Creative: A Creative Factory

▶ **FIGURE 7.10**
Expenditures on Out-of-Home Advertising

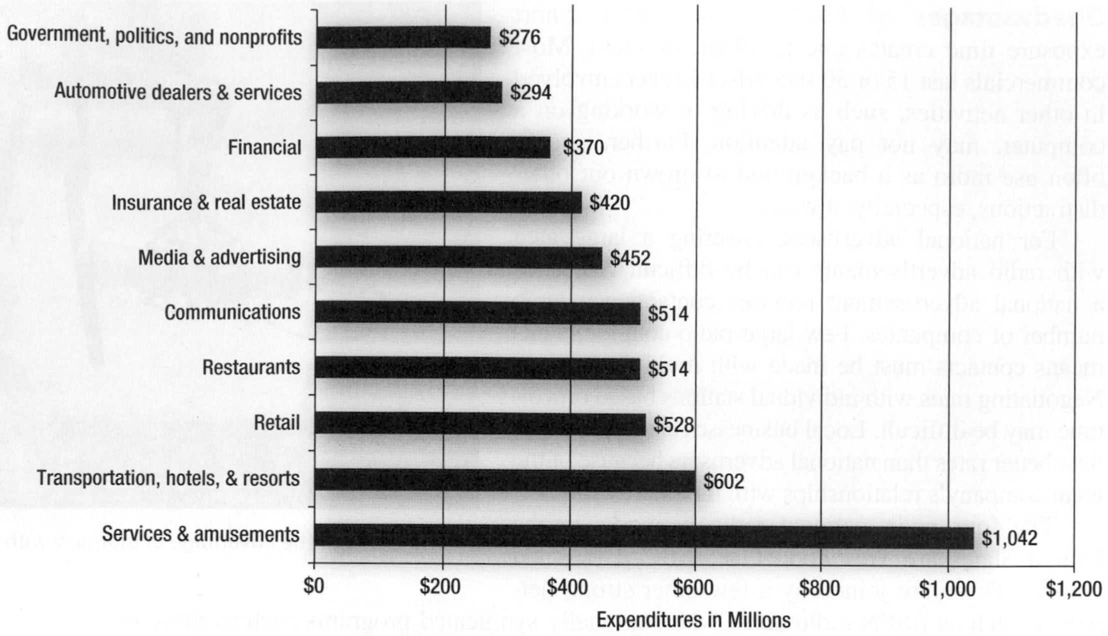

In the past, many company leaders seldom considered outdoor advertising as part of the planning process for an integrated marketing communications program or the development of the media plan; however that has now changed. Advances in technology have dramatically improved OOH advertising. Annual expenditures on outdoor advertisements total more than $5.5 billion. Global positioning systems, wireless communications, and digital display technology have transformed outdoor advertising. LED technology creates animated videos in locations such as Times Square in New York and the Strip in Las Vegas. It can present static messages and visuals that change electronically. Figure 7.10 provides a breakdown of outdoor spending by categories.

The Firehouse Agency of Dallas created a unique billboard campaign for Stripes Convenience Stores. The signs invited customers of Stripes to tweet about tacos sold at the convenience stores. The tweets were then streamed into digital billboard displays located near traffic lights in eight different Texas cities where vehicles would stop for a red light. According to Ian Dallimore of Lamar Advertising, "Stripes wanted to do something more than just change the copy a few times a day. It wanted to create the sense of a conversation, and make people feel involved. The idea is to get people more engaged with outdoor advertising and arouse curiosity about the tacos." The tweets ran from lunchtime until midnight daily.[29]

Advantages of Out-of-Home Advertising Billboard advertising offers long life. For local companies, billboards can be an excellent advertising medium, because the message will primarily be seen by residents. It also provides a low-cost medium in terms of cost per impression. Out-of-home advertising features a broad reach and a high level of frequency when advertisers purchase multiple billboards or venues. Every person who travels past a billboard or sees an advertisement on a taxi has been exposed to the message. Many out-of-home companies feature rotation packages in which an ad moves to different locations throughout an area during the course of the year, thereby increasing its reach. Digital boards and signs deliver higher resolution graphics as well as capabilities of changing messages on demand or on a routine schedule. Figure 7.11 lists the advantages and disadvantages of out-of-home ads.

Disadvantages of Out-of-Home Advertising Short exposure time remains the major drawback of out-of-home advertising. Drivers must pay attention to the traffic as they travel by a billboard. As a result, advertisers keep messages short. Pedestrians often

Advantages	Disadvantages
• Select key geographic areas	• Short exposure time
• Accessible for local ads	• Brief messages
• Low cost per impression	• Little segmentation possible
• Broad reach	• Clutter
• High frequency on major commuter routes	
• Large visuals possible	
• Digital capabilities	

◀ **FIGURE 7.11**
Out-of-Home Advertising

get only a quick look at an advertisement placed on a vehicle. Most either ignore outdoor ads or give them just a casual glance. Ironically, in large cities along major arteries the cost of billboard spots has increased. The reason: traffic jams. People stuck in slow-moving traffic spend more time looking at billboards. Another option is to purchase billboard locations where traffic stops for signals or at stop signs.

Print Media

Printed outlets remain an important component of traditional media. A growing number of print magazines and newspapers have developed digital versions of materials that can be viewed on computers, tablets, and smartphones. In some cases, the digital format will be identical to the print version. In others, the site includes additional or different content. Just as websites became essential for businesses, print media companies now must develop digital components to compete effectively. This chapter covers traditional print media. The next chapter describes the digital component.

▼ Print advertising is a valuable IMC component for LUBA Workers' Comp.

LUBA Workers' Comp

Magazines

For many advertisers, magazines represent a secondary choice in media buying. Recent research indicates, however, that magazines often deliver a quality option. An Affinity Research study suggests that half of readers either take action, such as accessing a website, after seeing an ad in a magazine. Others develop more favorable opinions about magazine advertiser companies. Several studies conclude that magazines are a strong driver of purchase intentions and boost the effectiveness of other media.[30] Figure 7.12 identifies some potential advantages and disadvantages of magazines.

Advantages of Magazine Advertising Magazines create high levels of market segmentation by topic area. Even within certain market segments, such as automobiles, a number of magazines exist. High audience interest constitutes another advantage. An individual who subscribes to *Modern Bride* has an attraction to weddings.

FIGURE 7.12
Magazine Advertising

Advantages	Disadvantages
• High market segmentation	• Declining readership
• Targeted audience by magazine	• Clutter
• Direct-response techniques	• Long lead time
• High color quality	• Little flexibility
• Long-life	• High cost
• Read during leisure—longer attention to ads	
• Availability of special features	

People reading magazines also tend to view and pay attention to advertisements related to their needs and wants. Often, readers linger over an ad for a longer period of time because they read magazines in waiting situations, such as in a doctor's office, or during leisure time. The high level of interest, segmentation, and differentiation, when combined with high-quality color, are ideal for products with well-defined target markets.

Trade and business journals represent the primary choice for business-to-business marketers. Businesses target advertisements to buying center members. The ad's copy can deliver a greater level of detail about products. Interested readers take more time to study the information provided in the advertisement. Ads often contain toll-free telephone numbers and website addresses so that interested parties can obtain further information.

▼ Magazines offer an excellent medium for GE Café to reach its target audience.

GE Café

Magazines have long lives that reach beyond an immediate issue. An avid magazine reader may examine a particular issue several times and spend a considerable amount of time with each issue. Advertisers know the reader will be exposed to the ad more than once and might be more likely to pay attention. Other individuals may also review the magazine. In the business-to-business sector, trade journals are often passed around to several individuals or members of the buying center. As long as the magazine lasts, the advertisement is still available to be viewed.

In addition to the standard sniff-patches that can be placed in magazines for perfume and cologne, advertisers can now add QR codes or special mobile apps. DirecTV partnered with *Sports Illustrated* to create a free Android and IOS app for *SI*'s annual swimsuit edition. Individuals who downloaded the app to their smartphones could hold the phone over the swimsuit models in the *SI* magazine and watch videos of the model's picture shoot. The magazine had 19 embedded videos, each approximately 30 seconds in length.[31]

Disadvantages of Magazine Advertising

While overall readership of magazines has declined, the trend is less evident among "influential Americans." Individuals with incomes of $100,000 or more read an average of 15.3 publications, and individuals with incomes over $250,000 read an average of 23.8.[32] Magazine advertisements require a great deal of lead time and are expensive to prepare. They may be less viable for more general consumption products such as basic necessities.

At the same time, magazines still provide an effective advertising medium. In both consumer and business markets, it appears that magazines, used in conjunction with other media, can enhance the effectiveness of an advertising campaign.

Baxter Painting, Inc.

▲ Newspapers provide an ideal medium for advertising local businesses, such as Baxter Printing, which offers high-end home and commercial painting and decorating.

Newspapers

When *USA Today* was launched, few believed a national daily newspaper could succeed. At the same time, news reporting has changed. Many small local papers no longer exist and conglomerates, such as Gannett, own most major city newspapers. Still, daily readership continues in some segments.

For many smaller local firms, newspaper ads, billboards, and local radio programs provide the most viable advertising options. Newspapers are distributed daily, weekly, or in partial form as the advertising supplements found in the front sections of grocery stores and retail outlets.

Advantages of Newspaper Advertising As noted in Figure 7.13, many retailers rely on newspaper because it offers geographic selectivity (local market access). Promoting sales, retail hours, and store locations is easier. Short lead time permits retailers to quickly change ads and promotions. Such flexibility presents the advantage of allowing advertisers the ability to keep ads current, and the ads can be modified to meet competitive offers or to focus on recent events.

Newspapers retain high levels of credibility. Readers rely on newspapers for factual information. Newspaper readers hold high interest levels in the articles as well as advertisements. Greater audience interest permits advertisers to provide more copy detail in ads. Newspaper readers take more time to read copy unless an advertiser jams too much information into a small space. A recent survey of shoppers revealed that newspapers were the most trusted source of information for purchase decisions.[33]

Recognizing a match between newspaper readers and its customer base, Starbucks launched a unique newspaper campaign designed by the agency Wieden + Kennedy

Advantages	Disadvantages
• Geographic selectivity	• Poor buying procedures
• High flexibility	• Short life span
• High credibility	• Clutter
• Strong audience interest	• Poor quality reproduction
• Longer copy	• Internet competition
• Cumulative volume discounts	• Aging readership
• Coupons and special-response features	

◀ **FIGURE 7.13**
Newspaper Advertising

Fiesta Nutritional Center

▲ Newspapers remain an excellent medium for local businesses to advertise, such as Fiesta Nutrition Center.

of Portland, Oregon. Starbucks invited coffee drinkers to stop at a local Starbucks for a free cup of coffee on March 15. Four-page full-color ads were placed in daily newspapers of 11 major markets, including New York, Los Angeles, Chicago, Boston, and Dallas. The ads were placed in the newspapers the week before the giveaway and again the day before. Then, on the day of the giveaway, Starbucks hired street vendors to pass out free copies of the newspapers that contained the Starbucks ad. The newspapers were banded with the distinctive Starbucks' coffee cup sleeve. The campaign cost $545,000, but resulted in a half-million customers going into a Starbucks store. Lines wrapped around the block in some locations. Starbucks estimated the newspaper campaign resulted in 12 million impressions.[34]

Disadvantages of Newspaper Advertising

Newspapers cannot be easily targeted to specific market segments, although sports pages carry sports ads, entertainment pages contain movie and restaurant ads, and so forth. Newspapers have short lives. Once read, a newspaper will be cast aside, recycled, or destroyed. If a reader does not see an advertisement during the first pass through a newspaper, it may go unnoticed. Readers rarely pick up papers a second time. When they do, it is to continue reading, not to reread or rescan a section that has already been viewed.

Newspaper readers continue to age. Younger consumers obtain news either through the internet or from television; few read a print newspaper. The average age of those who read printed papers is 51 compared to 44 for those who read the digital version. Digital readers are younger, better educated, and are often more affluent than the print readers.[35]

Media Mix

objective 7.6

How can the marketing team use the media mix to increase advertising effectiveness?

Selecting the proper blend of media outlets for advertisements is crucial. As they prepare campaigns, advertisers make decisions regarding the appropriate mix of media. Media planners and media buyers are excellent sources of information regarding the most effective type of mix for a particular advertising campaign. Figure 7.14 displays the media mix in the United States for Coca-Cola. Total U.S. spending for advertising by Coca-Cola was $752 million; 63.4 percent went to television advertising. Coca-Cola spent far less on the other media.[36]

Recent studies by Millward Brown and ACNielsen highlight the benefits of combining media.[37] The Millward Brown report indicates that ad awareness became strongest when consumers were exposed to an advertisement on television and in a magazine. Ad awareness was considerably lower for only those who read the magazine ad and even less for those who only saw the television commercial.

The **media multiplier effect** suggests that the combined impact of using two or more media will be stronger than using either medium alone. The British insurance company Churchill discovered that 62 percent of consumers who saw the company's TV commercial and heard its radio ad planned to look into Churchill Insurance, compared to 49 percent who only saw only the television advertisement.[38]

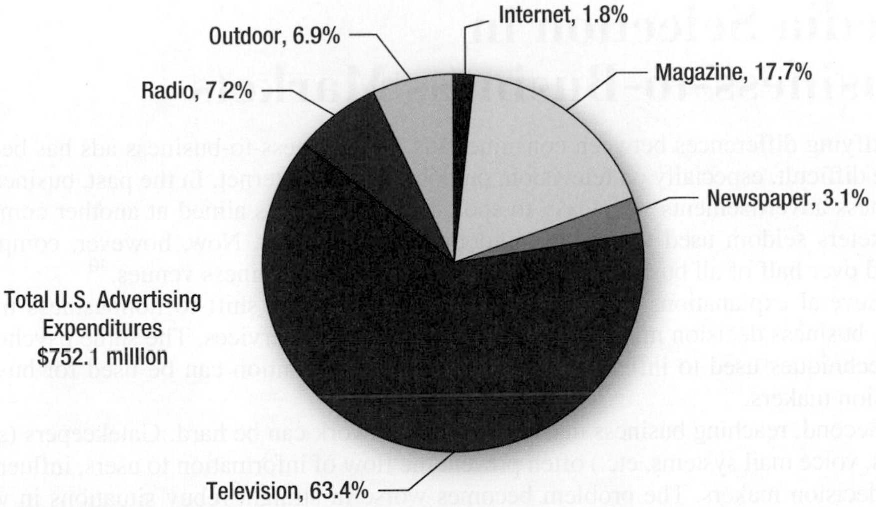

◀ **FIGURE 7.14**
U.S. Advertising Expenditures by Media for Coca-Cola

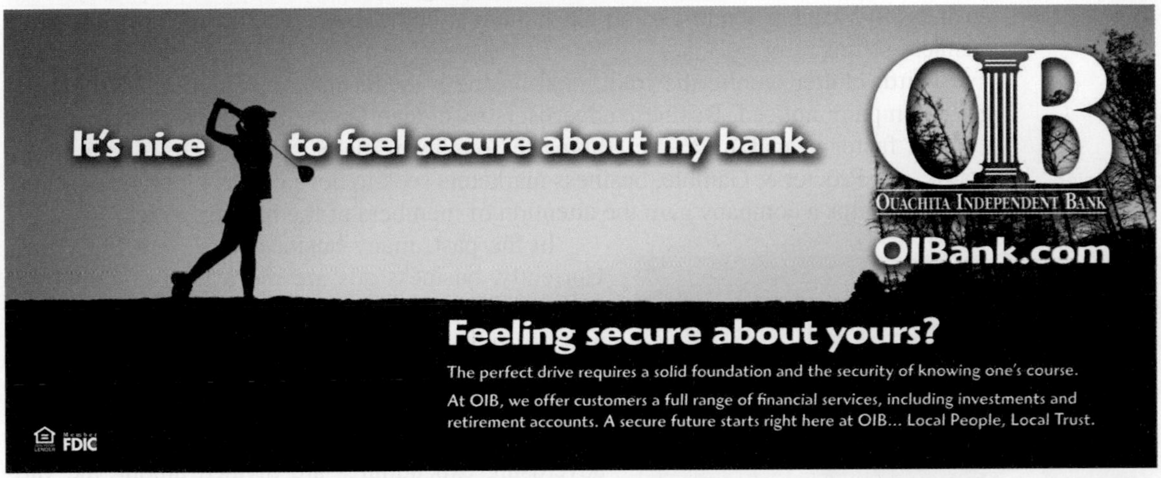

Newcomer, Morris and Young Inc.

▼ The campaign for Ouachita Independent Bank utilized multiple media, such as television, radio, newspapers, internet, and billboards.

The media multiplier effect is equally useful for business-to-business advertisers. In a survey conducted by American Business Media, 89 percent of the business respondents indicated that an integrated marketing approach raised their awareness of a company or brand. Seeing advertisements in more than one medium led the company or brand name to become top-of-mind. It also resulted in more businesses making purchases.[39] Finding effective combinations of media will be the key to utilizing the media multiplier effect. Figure 7.15 displays the process for choosing the best media for a particular advertising message. Media experts decide which go best together for individual target markets, goods and services, and advertising messages.

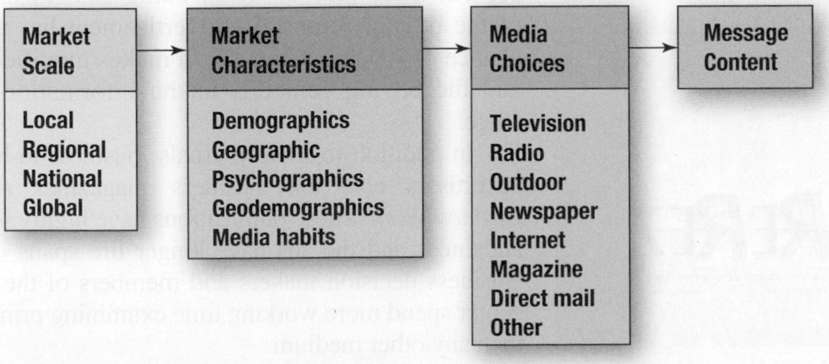

◀ **FIGURE 7.15**
Developing Logical Combinations of Media

Media Selection in Business-to-Business Markets

objective 7.7

What are the key issues associated with media selection for business-to-business markets?

Identifying differences between consumer ads and business-to-business ads has become more difficult, especially on television, outdoor, and the internet. In the past, business-to-business advertisements were easy to spot. The content was aimed at another company. Marketers seldom used television, outdoor, or the internet. Now, however, companies spend over half of all business advertising dollars on nonbusiness venues.[40]

Several explanations have been offered regarding the shift to nonbusiness media. First, business decision makers also consume goods and services. The same psychological techniques used to influence and gain consumer attention can be used for business decision makers.

Second, reaching business decision makers at work can be hard. Gatekeepers (secretaries, voice mail systems, etc.) often prevent the flow of information to users, influencers, and decision makers. The problem becomes worse in straight rebuy situations in which orders are routinely placed with the current vendor. Any company other than the chosen vendor finds it difficult to make contact with buying center members. Consequently, some business-to-business vendors try to reach them at home, in the car, or in some other nonbusiness setting.

Third, clutter among the traditional business media makes it more challenging to get a company noticed. Business advertisers recognize that a strong brand name can be a major factor in making a sale. Taking lessons from major giants such as Nike, Kraft Foods, and Procter & Gamble, business marketers seek to develop strong brands because the name helps a company gain the attention of members of the buying center.

▼ In business-to-business advertising, print remains an important medium for companies such as ReRez.

ReRez

In the past, many business ads were fairly dull. Currently, business ads are more likely to resemble those aimed at consumers. Ads feature creative appeals and the use of music, humor, sex, and fear. The boldest business ads sometimes include nudity or other more risqué materials.

Figure 7.16 identifies the ways business-to-business advertising expenditures are divided among the various media. In the past, business publications accounted for most of the expenditures, often half of the dollars. Business publications now represent about one-fourth of the more than $14 billion spent annually on business-to-business advertising. As more dollars are shifted to nonbusiness types of media, the amount being spent on television, newspapers, and consumer magazines has steadily increased.[41]

Although the use of business publications has decreased, trade journals still present an excellent opportunity to contact members of the buying center whom salespeople cannot reach. Gatekeepers do not prevent trade journals from being sent to members of the buying center. An advertisement has the best chance of success when a firm makes modified rebuy and the buying center is in the information search stage.

In addition to trade journals, business-to-business advertisers also use business magazines such as *BusinessWeek*. These publications have highly selective audiences and the ads have longer life spans in print. Business decision makers and members of the buying center spend more working time examining print media than any other medium.

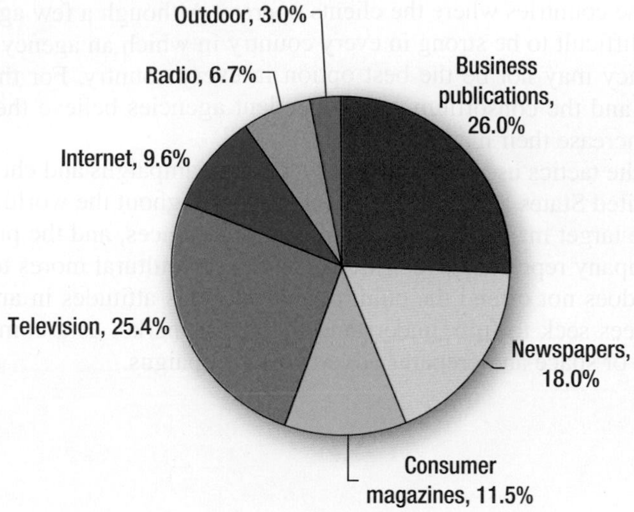

◀ **FIGURE 7.16**
Business-to-Business Advertising Expenditures

Many goals in business-to-business advertisements are the same as those devoted to consumers. Most of the variables shown in Figure 7.15 apply equally well to business advertising.

International Implications

objective 7.8
What issues are associated with media selection in international markets?

Understanding media viewing habits in international markets constitutes an important part of a successful advertising program. In Japan, television provides a major advertising tool; in other countries, it is not as prevalent. In Europe, a good way to reach consumers is through print media, such as magazines and newspapers.

For several years, reports have surfaced that teenagers are watching less TV and spending more time on the internet. A Forrester Research study contradicted that notion, at least in Europe. Thousands of teenagers in Europe were surveyed about their media usage.[42] The general conclusions of the Forrester study are that:

- European teens spend more time watching TV than they do with any other medium, averaging 10.3 hours per week.
- Average personal time on the internet is 9.1 hours per week.
- Europeans ages 10 to 17 spend less time on the internet than individuals 18 and older.
- Only 41 percent of European teens visit social networks at least once a week.
- Teenagers like to multitask—watching TV while texting friends or playing video games while listening to music or TV.
- Younger European teens love video games, playing twice as much as individuals 18 and older.
- Most teenagers do not read the paper. They get news from TV or the internet.

Although a large number of media buying agencies operate throughout the world, nearly three-quarters of all media buying is conducted by only six large global agencies or their holding agencies. The largest global media company is the WPP Group, which holds 22 percent of the market share.[43] To combat these large media networks, a global media consortium has been formed. The consortium consists of a number of smaller independent agencies and offers services in Europe, North America, the Russian Federation, and Asia. Central offices are located in New York and London to serve business clients and to pitch for regional and national accounts.[44]

Large global media agencies have faced some criticism in recent years from marketing managers. They complain about the inability to provide effective media buys throughout all the countries where the clients operate. Although a few agencies do cover the world, it is difficult to be strong in every country in which an agency has a presence. The global agency may not be the best option in every country. For this reason, local media agencies and the consortium of independent agencies believe they have a better opportunity to increase their market shares.

In general, the tactics used to develop advertising campaigns and choose appropriate media in the United States apply to other countries throughout the world. What differs is the nature of the target markets, consumer media preferences, and the processes used to buy media. Company representatives carefully attend to cultural mores to make sure the buying process does not offend the cultural and religious attitudes in any given region. Agency employees seek to fully understand the target market as a company purchases advertising time or space and prepares advertising campaigns.

INTEGRATED campaigns in action

The Snoring Center

In the past decade, the Pink Jacket Creative advertising agency, led by co-owners Bill Breedlove and Elena Baca, helped develop a highly successful advertising program for a medical company—The Snoring Center. According to Breedlove, "When we first started working with The Snoring Center, a physician had an office here in Dallas. He decided he wanted to start treating snoring and sleep apnea. Did you know that 46 percent of adults snore? 25 percent snore habitually? Of that, 23 percent of married couples regularly sleep apart because of sleep apnea."

To develop brand awareness for The Snoring Center, the central component of the advertising program was billboards, with television and print ads as support media. Bill Breedlove recalls, "It was a really simple outdoor campaign. We put up branded billboards that said simply, 'Snoring Kills …,' and then underneath it would have something that it kills, such as 'it kills careers' or 'it kills your love life,' or 'it kills your mojo,' or 'your morning quickies,' or 'your afternoon delight,' and so on.

Within a year and a half, the physician shut his ENT practice down and had two locations of The Snoring Center. Within 24 months, The Snoring Center became the world's leading provider of minimally invasive snoring treatment. The company now performs more procedures than any other provider in the world.[45]

The Snoring Center campaign is located at the Pearson Instructor's Resource Center (www.pearsonhighered.com). The campaign has a PowerPoint presentation outlining the details of the campaigns and examples of the collaterals developed by Pink Jack Creative. Also available is video of the creative minds behind the campaign, Bill Breedlove and Elena Baca.

Courtesy of Pink Jacket Creative: A Creative Factory

Billboard ads were the central component of the campaign for The Snoring Center.

Summary

In traditional advertising, the roles of media planners and media buyers have grown in importance. Bob Brennan, chief operating officer of Chicago-based Leo Burnett Starcom USA, stated that in the past "Ninety-five percent of your success was great creative and 5 percent was great media. Now it's much closer to 50–50."[46]

A media strategy is the process of analyzing and choosing media for an advertising and promotions campaign. Media planners and buyers complete much of this work. The media planner formulates a program stating where and when to place advertisements. Media planners work closely with creatives and account executives. Media buyers purchase the space, and they negotiate rates, times, and schedules for the ads.

The goals of reach, frequency, opportunity to see, gross rating points, effective rating points, cost, continuity, and gross impressions drive the media selection process. Reach identifies the number of people, households, or businesses in a target audience exposed to a media vehicle or message schedule at least once during a given time period. Frequency represents the average number of times an individual, household, or business within a particular target market is exposed to a particular advertisement within a specified time period. Gross rating points (GRPs) measure the impact or intensity of a media plan. Cost per thousand (CPM) is one method of finding the cost of the campaign by assessing the dollar cost of reaching 1,000 members of the media vehicle's audience. Cost per rating point (CPRP), a second cost measure, assesses the efficiency of a media vehicle relative to a firm's target market. Ratings measure the percentage of a firm's target market exposed to a show on television or an article in a print medium. Continuity sets the schedule or pattern of advertisement placements within an advertising campaign period. Gross impressions are the number of total exposures of the audience to an advertisement.

The three-exposure hypothesis suggests that a consumer must be exposed to an ad at least three times before it has the desired impact; other experts believe even more exposures are necessary. In contrast, recency theory suggests that ads truly reach only those wanting or needing a product and that the carryover effects of advertising diminish rapidly. It is necessary, therefore, to advertise on a continuous basis to ensure that the message is noticed by consumers as they make purchase decisions.

In addition to these basic concepts, advertising experts often utilize the concepts of effective frequency and effective reach. Effective frequency states the number of times a target audience must be exposed to a message to achieve a particular objective. Effective reach identifies the percentage of an audience that must be exposed to a particular message to achieve a specific objective.

In seeking advertising goals, marketing experts, account executives, and others assess the relative advantages and disadvantages of each individual advertising medium. Thus, television, radio, out-of-home, magazines, and newspapers should all be considered as potential ingredients in a campaign. Other new media can be used to complement and supplement the more traditional media outlets. Logical combinations of media should be chosen.

In business-to-business settings, companies can combine consumer media outlets with trade journals and other business venues (trade shows, conventions, etc.) to attempt to reach members of the buying center. In many cases, enticing ads using consumer appeals such as sex, fear, and humor have replaced dry, dull, boring ads with an abundance of copy.

International advertising media selection is different in some ways from that which takes place in the United States, because media buying processes differ as do media preferences of locals in various countries. At the same time, the process of media selection is quite similar. Marketing experts choose media they believe will reach the target audience in an effective manner.

Key Terms

media strategy The process of analyzing and choosing media for an advertising and promotions campaign

media planner The individual who formulates the media program stating where and when to place advertisements

media buyer The person who buys the media space and negotiates rates, times, and schedules for the ads

spot ad A one-time placement of a commercial on a local television station

reach The number of people, households, or businesses in a target audience exposed to a media vehicle or message schedule at least once during a given time period

frequency The average number of times an individual, household, or business within a particular target market is exposed to a particular advertisement within a specified time period

opportunities to see (OTS) The cumulative exposures to an advertisement achieved in a given time period

gross rating points (GRPs) A measure of the impact or intensity of a media plan

cost per thousand (CPM) The dollar cost of reaching 1,000 members of the media vehicle's audience

ratings A measure of the percentage of a firm's target market exposed to a show on television or an article in a print medium

cost per rating point (CPRP) A measure of the efficiency of a media vehicle relative to a firm's target market

weighted (or demographic) CPM A measure used to calculate whether an advertisement reached the target market effectively

continuity The schedule or pattern of advertisement placements within an advertising campaign period

gross impressions The number of total exposures of the audience to an advertisement

intrusion value The ability of media or an advertisement to intrude upon a viewer without his or her voluntary attention

recency theory A theory suggesting that consumer attention is selective and focuses on individual needs and wants and therefore has selective attention to advertisements

effective reach The percentage of an audience that must be exposed to a particular message to achieve a specific objective

effective frequency The number of times a target audience must be exposed to a message to achieve a particular objective

dynamic advertising A research method that allows a company to obtain consumer information from marketing research firms and combine it with the company's data to send target ads to consumers

media multiplier effect The combined impact of using two or more media is stronger than using either medium alone

MyMarketingLab

Go to **mymktlab.com** to complete the problems marked with this icon ✪.

Review Questions

7-1. What is a media strategy? How does it relate to the creative brief and the overall IMC program?

7-2. What is a spot ad?

7-3. What is the role of a media planner, and who do they work with?

7-4. What determines the success or failure of an ad campaign?

7-5. What is OTS? How is it used as a tool in advertising campaign planning?

7-6. In advertising campaign terms, what does cost measure?

7-7. What is the formula for weighted or demographic CPM?

7-8. What is a discontinuous campaign?

7-9. Describe the three-exposure hypothesis.

7-10. How does recency theory differ from the three-exposure hypothesis?

7-11. What is effective frequency? Effective reach?

7-12. What are the major advantages and disadvantages of television advertising?

7-13. What are the major advantages and disadvantages of radio advertising?

7-14. What are the major advantages and disadvantages of outdoor advertising?

7-15. What are the major advantages and disadvantages of magazine advertising?

7-16. What are the major advantages and disadvantages of newspaper advertising?

✪ **7-17.** Is the strong intrusion value of television an advantage? Why or why not?

7-18. What special challenges does media selection present for businesses? What roles do gatekeepers play in creating those challenges?

7-19. What special challenges does media selection present for international advertising campaigns? What differences and similarities exist with U.S. media selection processes?

Critical Thinking Exercises

DISCUSSION QUESTIONS

✪ **7-20.** To be effective, multiple media should be chosen and integrated carefully. Individuals exposed to advertisements in combinations of media selected from television, radio, magazines, newspapers, and outdoor are more inclined to process the information than when a message appears in only a solitary medium. For each of the media, what is the probability of being exposed to an advertisement? The percentages should add up to 100 percent. Discuss which media are most effective in reaching you.

7-21. What is the most lucrative form of advertising in your country? Identify some of the major spenders in that media and suggest reasons why they choose to invest so much in advertising and promotion. What is the main point of their advertising? Can you work out the purpose of the campaigns? Find out how much they spend and compare this to two or three competitors.

7-22. The Super Bowl is the most watched program on television. Many tune in just to watch the ads. Discuss the concepts of effective reach, effective frequency, ratings, gross rating points, brand recognition, brand recall, and opportunities to see as it relates to Super Bowl advertising. What are the advantages for a brand to advertise on television during the Super Bowl? What are the disadvantages?

7-23. Xerox offers a color printer that sells for $1,200. The goal is to market it to business buyers. What media mix would you suggest for a $5 million advertising campaign? Justify your answer.

7-24. Complete the following table by calculating the missing values. Based on the values you calculated, identify two magazines and two television shows for advertising sports equipment. Support your answer with specific data from the table.

Publication	4C Base Rate or 30-second Ad	Circulation or Audience	CPM	Percent of Readers Fit Target Market	Number of Readers Fit Target Market	Rating (Reach)	Cost per Rating Point (CPRP)	Weighted (Demographic) CPM
					Target Market (30 million)			
				Magazines				
Allure	$165,554	1,080,000		12.2%				
Ebony	$81,167	1,170,000		16.1%				
Men's Health	$215,850	1,900,000		22.7%				
Road & Track	$119,421	720,000		28.4%				
Sports Illustrated	$412,500	3,170,000		7.8%				
				Television Shows				
NCIS	$180,264	19,700,000		6.3%				
2 Broke Girls	$175,506	9,000,000		4.2%				
Big Bang Theory	$316,912	20,000,000		10.8%				
Criminal Minds	$119,052	10,400,000		12.5%				
Modern Family	$281,961	9,100,000		17.8%				

▲ **FIGURE 7.17**

7-25. Using a TV guide or the internet, compile a comprehensive list of TV stations that are broadcast in your own country. How many of them are commercial stations in the sense that they carry advertising? What are these TV stations' key target markets? How is this reflected in both the programming and the type of advertisers that feature on the station?

7-26. As you drive to school (or home) make a list of all of the billboards and outdoor advertising you see. Which are the most effective? Why? Which are the least effective? Why? How effective are billboards at reaching you with an advertising message?

7-27. Pick three different magazines on a wide range of topics. For each, describe the types of ads and the number of ads in the issue. Did you see any business-to-business ads? What similarities did you see in the ads across the five magazines? What differences did you notice? Which would be most effective at reaching people in your demographic?

Integrated Learning Exercises

7-28. Find out what the top ten best-selling music tracks were last week in your country. How are the results compiled? What other information about the artists is available on the same sites? Are they local or international?

7-29. In Canada, a valuable source of information is BBM (Bureau of Broadcast Measurement). Access this website at **www.bbm.ca**. What type of information is available on the site? What media does the BBM cover? How can it be used to develop a media plan for Canada?

7-30. A trade organization for magazines is the Magazine Publishers of America. Access the association's website at **www.magazine.org**. What type of information is available? How could it be used by a company wanting to advertise in magazines?

7-31. Two websites important for radio advertising are the Radio Advertising Bureau at **www.rab.com** and the top 100 radio sites at **www.100topradiosites.com**. Access both sites. What information is available on each site? Discuss how the information can be used to develop an advertising plan using radio.

7-32. A major company for outdoor advertising is Lamar Advertising Company. Access its website at **www.lamar.com**. Access the outdoor advertising component of the company and locate the rates for your area or another area of interest to you. What type of outdoor advertising is available? What other products does Lamar offer? What services does Lamar offer? Write a short report on what types of advertising Lamar can provide for a company.

7-33. An excellent source of information for business advertisers is at *Entrepreneur*. Access the advertising section of *Entrepreneur* at **http://www.entrepreneur.com/advertising**. What type of information is available at this website? How can it be used by a small business?

7-34. The Newspaper Association of America is a trade association for newspaper. Access the website at **http://www.naa.org**. What type of information is available? How could this information be used by your local newspaper to increase business?

Blog Exercises

Access the authors' blog for this textbook at the URLs provided to complete these exercises. Answer the questions that are posed on the blog.

7-35. Duracell Batteries - **http://blogclowbaack.net/2014/05/08/duracell-chapter-7/**

7-36. Geico Insurance - **http://blogclowbaack.net/2014/05/08/geico-chapter-7/**

7-37. Media-**http://blogclowbaack.net/2014/05/08/media-chapter-7/**

Student Project

CREATIVE CORNER

Horse racing has struggled to maintain attendance at some race tracks. The majority of serious fans of horse racing are older, white males. One challenge in drawing new fans to horse racing is to help them understand this complex sport. Recognizing which horse won a race is easy; however, after that it becomes very complex and difficult to grasp horse racing stats. A steep learning curve that requires thoughtful and complex analysis is needed. Many potential fans do not want to invest the time or energy to learn. According to Tim Capps, a professor at the University of the Louisville College of Business, horse racing "has been run more for itself than for its fans. One thing racing has to do is make participation in our sport easier for fans, because the fan has not come first in our industry." He further adds "people don't want to go to school. They want to be entertained."

While all agree there is a need to attract new fans, wide disagreement exists regarding the type of fan it should be. Do you market to the individuals who are already going to the track, or do you go after new individuals? Do you go after young people, middle-age individuals, or work harder to reach baby boomers? Which gender—male or female—do you seek?

First, choose the target audience for an advertising campaign. Defend your choice. Second, select the media that would be most appropriate. Third, design a magazine ad for the target market chosen. Fourth, develop a billboard or outdoor ad to accompany the magazine ad.

CASE 1 TRUST YOUR POWER

Designing television commercials that will be powerful and create a long-lasting impact is a key goal for many companies and advertising agencies. At times, inspiration comes from unusual places and circumstances. The New York-based Saatchi and Saatchi agency recently developed an inspiring advertisement for Duracell batteries.

Professional football player Derrick Coleman is the first legally deaf person to make an NFL roster, the Seattle Seahawks. Coleman made the team even though he was not a draft pick. His ability to read lips combined with new hearing aid technology helped in the process. In 2014, he was asked to tell his story as part of a commercial for Duracell. As fortune would have it, the Seahawks moved into the NFC Championship game just as the spot was aired.[47]

As reported by *Adweek*, "Bravely narrating the ad himself, Coleman tells his own story of being picked on as a kid, being told he could never make it—and being passed over by the NFL draft. 'They didn't call my name, told me it was over,' he says. 'But I've been deaf since I was 3, so I didn't listen.' That's a great line. The tagline: "Trust the power within.'"

The buzz was immediate. Within a short period of time, the commercial had been viewed by more than 2 million people on YouTube. Yahoo! asked, "Want goosebumps? Watch this commercial." The site adds: "That might just be another victory Coleman adds to his amazing list.[48] Other sites, such as BleacherReport, chimed in with similar praise and a story about the ad appeared in *USA Today*. Twitter and other social media outlets also picked up on the story. Coleman's response was, "I just hope to inspire people, especially children, to trust the power within and achieve their dreams."[49]

SUDIO 1ONE/Fotolia

▲ Derrick Coleman's ad and story are an inspiration to many youth that they can succeed.

7-38. Go to Duracell's YouTube channel (**www.youtube.com/user/OfficialDuracell**) and watch the advertisement for Durcell featuring Derrick Coleman. What was your reaction? Do you think Coleman's story could overpower the brand being advertised? Why or why not?

7-39. As a media planner, how would you evaluate this type of advertisement? In which television shows would you place this ad? Why?

7-40. Explain the roles that reach, frequency, and opportunities to see would play in the release of this ad. For Durcell, which would be more important—brand recognition or brand recall? Justify your answer.

7-41. Besides television, which media would support this message and campaign? Explain why.

7-42. Explain the media you would choose to present this advertisement to men. Explain which media you would choose to present this advertisement to women. Provide support for your answers.

CASE 2 AFTER UNLEASHING

Dog owners constitute a large target market. Most members share something in common: the desire to let the pet run free and unfettered. If other friendly dogs are nearby and want to play—all the better. The Unleashed Dog Park was created to meet this need.

Out-of-home advertising can be the critical component of an IMC program and, in some cases, the primary medium. To help launch the new business venture, The Pink Jacket Creative advertising agency created a feeling of expectancy and mystery with its "Unleashed Dog Park" campaign, which featured the three successive billboards shown in this section.

The first billboard displays a dog on a leash. The unfinished nature of the image helps capture interest. Next, the dog, now with an unfastened leash, moves to the center of the billboard, and "unleash" appears in the top-right corner. In the final billboard, the dog is on the right side of the billboard, the leash is gone, and the message "Unleashed indoor dog parks" appears. It also displays the services offered, the website address of the park, and the location of the facility. In addition to billboards, street kiosks and bus wraps were used to get the message out.

The early results of the campaign were positive. Many dog owners became aware of the new indoor dog park. What followed represent common challenges in marketing communications: sustaining initial interest, moving consumers to action, and building repeat business.

In this next phase, dog owners needed to be encouraged to try the facility. They should be led to believe that the price of entry was a value. Then, over time, they can be enticed to make return visits and to offer word-of-mouth referrals to other pet owners. Only if these objectives can be attained will the initial success of the Unleashed campaign become validated.

7-43. Define the marketing goals for the second phase of the Unleashed Dog Park promotional efforts.

7-44. How would the three-exposure hypothesis or recency theory apply to this advertising program in its initial stages? What about the second campaign after consumers are aware of the dog park?

7-45. Which traditional advertising media should the marketing team use for the second campaign? Discuss the pros and cons of each in terms of the Unleashed Dog Park campaign and the desire to stimulate trial usage.

7-46. How could social media and nontraditional media be used to supplement a traditional media campaign in this circumstance?

7-47. Design a newspaper ad and an outdoor ad that will be placed at little league baseball parks in the area.

Pink Jacket Studio

▲ A series of ads for the Unleashed Dog Park was created by Pink Jacket Creative to gain the attention of motorists, causing them to wonder what the total message would be.

MyMarketingLab

Go to **mymktlab.com** for the following Assisted-graded writing questions:

7-48. The Super Bowl is the most watched program on television. Many tune in just to watch the ads. Discuss the concepts of effective reach, effective frequency, ratings, gross rating points, brand recognition, brand recall, and opportunities to see as it relates to Super Bowl advertising. What are the advantages for a brand to advertise on television during the Super Bowl? What are the disadvantages?

7-49. An excellent source of information for business advertisers is at *Entrepreneur*. Access the advertising section of *Entrepreneur* at **http://www.entrepreneur.com/advertising**. What type of information is available at this website? How can it be used by a small business?

Part 3

DIGITAL AND ALTERNATIVE MARKETING

Chapter 8 Digital Marketing

Chapter Objectives

After reading this chapter, you should be able to answer the following questions:

8.1 What is digital marketing?

8.2 How has the transition to Web 4.0 affected the field of marketing communications?

8.3 How can e-commerce programs and incentives build a stronger customer base and overcome consumer concerns at the same time?

8.4 How do mobile marketing systems enhance digital marketing programs?

8.5 What digital strategies do marketing professionals employ?

8.6 What types of web advertising can companies use to reach consumers?

8.7 What is a search engine optimization strategy?

8.8 How can companies successfully conduct digital marketing programs in international markets?

Overview

Developing quality advertising and communications programs has become increasingly complex over the past decade. The previous section of this textbook reviewed what had been considered to be the essential ingredients of a marketing communications program: traditional media programs working in combination with other elements of the promotions mix. Thus, a television–radio—magazine campaign would incorporate coupons, discounts, personal selling techniques, sponsorships, and other ingredients to create a strong, coherent message.

Today's marketers and advertising professionals recognize that these efforts, while necessary, do not constitute a complete program. This section of the textbook explains the additional elements needed to fully reach a target market and all potential customers. The activities to be added include the digital marketing programs detailed in this chapter; social media messages, which are the subject of Chapter 9; and the additional alternative marketing channels described in Chapter 10. Companies and marketers that effectively combine these ingredients with other communications efforts have the best chance at succeeding in today's complex and challenging marketing environment.

Digital marketing combines all of the components of e-commerce, internet marketing, and mobile marketing. It includes anything with a digital footprint. Today's consumers and businesses rely on the internet to research products, make comparisons, read comments by other consumers, interact with other consumers and businesses, and make product purchases. One such company that helps create effective digital marketing programs is Marketing Zen.

PHB.cz (Richard Semik)/Shutterstock

TOUCAN

Getting Tobago on the Tourism Map

In October 2008, Toucan Limited, a Dubai-based interactive advertising agency, set up offices in Port of Spain, Trinidad, and Kingston, Jamaica. Toucan's strengths lie in internet advertising, online consumer engagement, Web design, and search engine optimization.

The agency recognized that in the Caribbean the majority of businesses and organizations had a restricted online presence consisting of a standard, passive online brochure. With its experience in campaign management and with businesses in emerging markets, Toucan felt well placed to transform these static websites into something more dynamic and effective.

One of the Toucan's first commissions came from Tobago, which has a far lower profile as a tourist destination than many of the other more popular Caribbean islands. The Division of Tourism & Transportation of The Tobago House of Assembly asked Toucan to redesign its website. The client's goal was simple—to ensure that website visitors make Tobago their next vacation destination. The Republic of Trinidad and Tobago, a former British colony, is in a unique position in the Caribbean. With vast reserves of gas and oil, it is the largest supplier of liquefied gas to the United States; because of this, the islands have the advantage of being able to take a longer view on their tourism industry.

Warren Solomon, the Director of Tourism for Tobago, recognized that the time was right to use the internet as the island's primary advertising and marketing channel. Increasing broadband penetration worldwide and the trend towards consumers researching their own vacations and booking online were also key determinants. The opportunity for Tobago to establish a one-to-one relationship with customers was an exciting challenge.

Douglas Ames, Toucan's managing director, knew that social networking would also be vital in supporting the country's interactive strategy. Any online marketing campaign would have to harness the power of viral marketing, specifically social networking, so that the website could engage with customers on multiple levels. Timing was also a key issue, because the redesign would have to be achieved before the winter season, when the bulk of vacations are booked.

One of the key issues regarding the promotion of Tobago was the very nature of the organization of tourism promotion and development in Trinidad and Tobago. Before the creation of the Tobago House of Assembly in 1980, all tourism policy was coordinated and controlled in Trinidad. In July 2008, the catalyst of change came with the new tourism statement released by the Ministry of Tourism. The Ministry's goal was sustainable development. It knew that it would have to be innovative. The focus on marketing Tobago would need to be on the fact that it was unlike other Caribbean destinations. The Ministry needed to develop a strong and recognizable brand image and work with the private sector in the development of tourism.

Aggressive promotion of the islands was a key part of the new strategy, and the redesign of the tourism websites was viewed as a vital part of its implementation. Tobago has always been in the position of competing with more successful islands from the outset, which meant it had to convince tour operators to include the island in their tourism offerings. It then had to support the companies' promotional efforts to drive sales towards Tobago.

In offering a one-stop Web-based service, the hope was that traditional marketing and advertising channels could be replaced with a direct online service. The new website offers a portal through which Tobago was able to sell itself as a vacation destination. It also provides consumers the tools they need to make the necessary travel arrangements via an online booking engine.

Statistically, the initiative has shown signs of success. In 2008, the total number of cruise visitors to Tobago was over 22,000. By 2009, the number had risen to 70,000, and by the end of the second quarter of 2010 the island had already seen over 40,000 cruise visitors. The number of international air passengers to Tobago painted a more mixed picture. In 2008, 56,517 international air passengers landed in Tobago, dropping to 38,336 in 2009. The first two quarters of 2010 saw just 17,624 international air passengers. Innovative advertising and marketing remains a key tool in Tobago's ambition to use tourism as one of the drivers to attain developed nation status by 2020. More broadly, the island had also begun to recognize that future investment policy needed to focus on ensuring that SMEs on the island should have access to Web designers to improve online presence.[1]

objective 8.1
What is digital marketing?

Clearly, the internet has changed the ways individuals communicate and how the world conducts business. It presents an open environment. A buyer can locate numerous sellers offering practically the same merchandise at comparable prices and with similar offers at any time. Currently, the internet offers more than a method to conduct business transactions: It serves as a communication highway.

This chapter presents the various concepts related to digital marketing. The first section of the chapter examines the evolution to Web 4.0. Next, e-commerce programs, including the incentives used to attract customers as well as consumer concerns with internet shopping, are presented. Then, the explosion in the use of smartphones also leads to an examination of mobile marketing techniques. Digital strategies designed to maximize a company's reach are described. Also, web advertising programs receive attention along with search engine optimization (SEO) techniques. Finally, international implications of these activities are drawn.

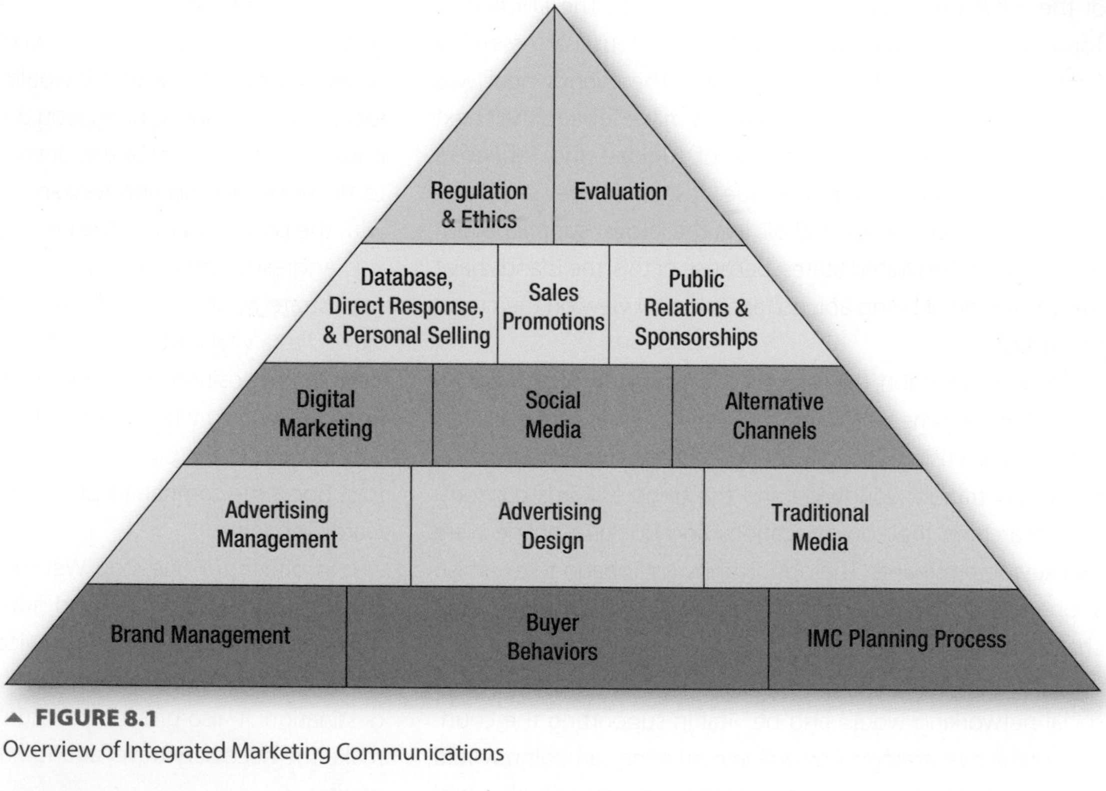

▲ **FIGURE 8.1**
Overview of Integrated Marketing Communications

objective 8.2
How has the transition to Web 4.0 affected the field of marketing communications?

Web 4.0

A recent study revealed that many companies have slashed traditional media marketing budgets and moved the funds to online communications. Many marketing experts believe that online searches, email, social media conversations, digital

- Web 1.0
  - Static content provided by creator
  - Dominated by institutions and businesses
  - Commercially and technically based
- Web 2.0
  - Content is socially based and audience generated
- Web 3.0
  - Content driven by online metrics
  - Integration of content and communications
  - Instant real-time communications
- Web 4.0
  - Customer engagement
  - Cloud operating systems
  - Web participation a necessity

◀ FIGURE 8.2
Primary Characteristics of Web 1.0 to 4.0

ads, and mobile marketing will soon constitute a significant portion of marketing expenditures. The transition from Web 1.0 to Web 4.0 changed the ways consumers communicate and interact with companies. Figure 8.2 displays the characteristics of Web 1.0 to Web 4.0.

In the 1990s, the internet (Web 1.0) was typified by static content provided by a site's creator. Businesses and institutions included little consumer involvement on websites. These commercially and technically based organizations created sites that were crude, simple, and designed to accomplish one specific function.

As Web 2.0 dawned, content became more socially based and audience-oriented. Social networking sites such as Facebook and MySpace emerged. People wrote blogs. E-commerce expanded and consumers could purchase almost anything online. Sites became more appealing and customer-focused as competition drove web designers to create customer-friendly experiences.

Integration, online metrics, and real-time instant communications characterize Web 3.0. As marketers realized the wealth of online metrics available and the ability to track browser behavior on the web, content on sites became metric driven. Individuals searching on a site for hiking supplies found that the next time they logged onto the site, hiking-related supplies would be prominently promoted on the main page. With online metrics came integration of the web with every aspect of a company's marketing program, both online and offline. The things consumers viewed online matched what they encountered offline.

Web 3.0 online channels pushed companies into "real-time" communications. Instant communication meant consumers demanded improved customer service through live chats and instant messaging. Consumers also expect immediate responses to negative events. When an internet video showed two Domino's employees doing disgusting things to food, Twitter lit up with chatter and demands that the company address the matter. When Ford's legal department sent a legal notice to a Ford Ranger blogger to surrender his URL, Scott Monty, Ford's social media leader, jumped in and quickly resolved the issue before it went viral.[2]

Now Web 4.0 has emerged, with key characteristics of customer engagement, cloud operations, and web participation as necessities. Companies cannot just sell products to individuals and then allow customers to post reviews. Engagement constitutes the primary business model for Web 4.0. Companies that succeed use the web to connect customers with the brand through various venues such as social media, blogs, and Twitter. With the rise of smartphones and tablets, consumers have access to thousands of apps and ability to operate using the cloud. They can access brands anywhere, at any time.

▶ This Visit Baton Rouge website encourages interaction and engagement with site visitors.

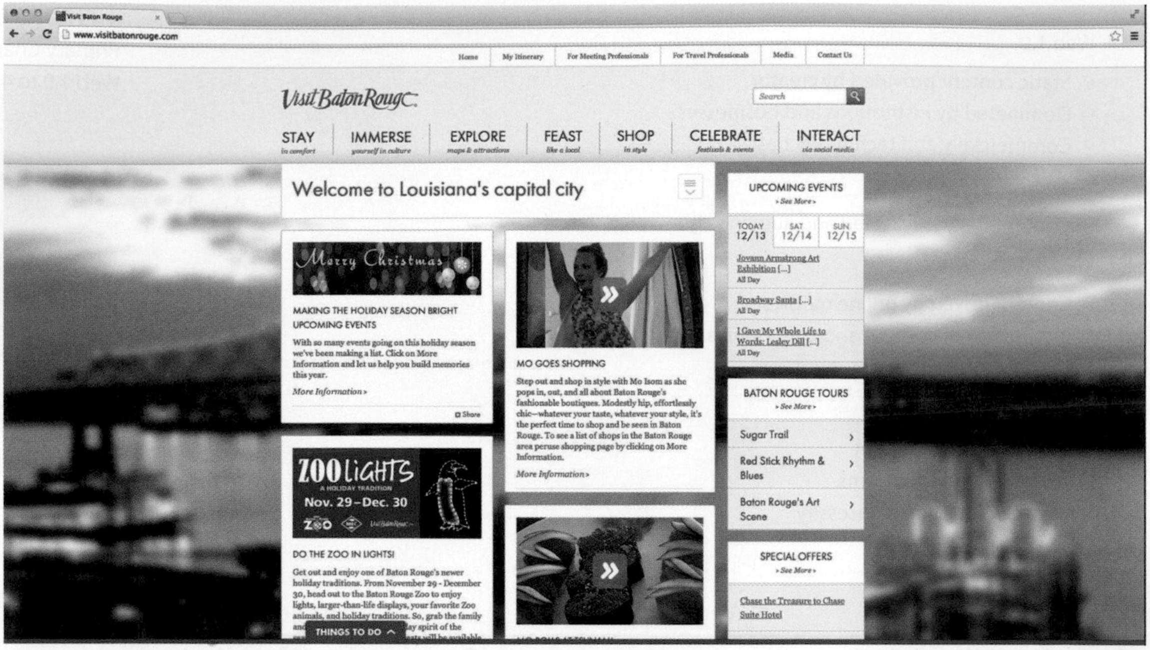

Visit Baton Rouge

E-Commerce

objective 8.3

How can e-commerce programs and incentives build a stronger customer base and overcome consumer concerns at the same time?

E-commerce focuses on selling goods and services over the internet. Many types of e-commerce businesses exist, ranging from click-only operations that sell entirely online to bricks-and-clicks that supplement physical store operations with an online presence. E-commerce involves both businesses selling to consumers (B2C) and businesses selling to other businesses (B2B). Mega-retailers such as Wal-Mart as well as mom-and-pop operations offering merchandise from home engage in e-commerce. Online sales account for nearly eight percent of all retail activity.[3]

Many consumers that make purchases at retail stores first use the internet to collect information or read reviews. A Pew Research Center survey revealed that 80 percent of Americans have researched a product online before making a purchase.[4] In Australia, half of the consumers first conduct online research.[5]

Building a Successful E-Commerce Site

E-commerce includes real-time communication and engagement with customers necessitated by Web 4.0. Figure 8.3 offers suggestions for developing successful e-commerce sites.

Effective e-commerce sites feature customer-centric designs in which individuals can easily locate merchandise. The marketing team arranges and indexes items using terms customers typically use rather than professional or technical language. If a large number of items are sold, then the site provides a drill-down search function that features customer-friendly terms and allows individuals to find items within one or two clicks.

- Customer-centric design
- Consistent customer experience
- Drill-down search
- Channel integration
- Brand engagement
- Customer interaction
- Customization and personalization
- Online and offline marketing
- Search engine optimization (SEO)
- Shopping cart abandonment strategies

▶ **FIGURE 8.3**
Characteristics of Successful E-Commerce Sites

Consistent Customer Experiences Today's consumers expect a consistent positive experience every time they access a website, whether it is from a desktop computer, tablet, or mobile device. Consumers have nearly a zero tolerance for poor website performance. Poor experiences translate into dissatisfaction and lost sales, as evidenced by a number of studies:[6]

- Wal-Mart saw a sharp decline in conversion rate when its website load time increased from one second to four seconds.
- Amazon discovered that for every 100-millisecond decline in site load time, revenue increased one percent.
- Research by Torbit revealed that as load time increased, so did the bounce rate (individuals leaving the site without exploring other pages).
- Of consumers who were dissatisfied with a website's performance, 40 percent were unlikely to ever visit the site again and 25 percent were less likely to purchase the brand again.

▲ Channel integration is an important feature of Skyjacker's website.

Skyjacker Suspensions

These studies highlight the importance of a positive, consistent customer experience and the impact of load-time of pages, especially the front page, has on visitor actions.

Channel Integration Channel integration becomes essential when the business sells through additional channels beyond the web. A company that offers a printed catalog or has a retail store should match the printed catalog with its web catalog. Victoria's Secret features a "catalog quick order" system that allows customers to enter the product number from the print catalog and then go straight to checkout. The program saves considerable time in trying to find and buy a product on the web.[7] The Skyjacker website shown in this section features an extensive line of products. The site is also integrated with channel partners to ensure customers can find the right part, whether from Skyjacker's website or from their local parts store.

Sears Holdings developed the online shopping experience "Shop Your Way" that assists customers by letting them shop in the manner they feel most comfortable. The customer can access Sears.com, Kmart.com, LandsEnd.com, TheGreatIndoors.com, or the new mobile application site Sears2Go. Each gives the consumer the ability to select a product from any retail operation in the manner desired.[8]

Brand Engagement E-commerce sites create opportunities for brand engagement and customer interaction. Blogs, feedback applications, and customer reviews provide ways for e-commerce sites to encourage customers to interact with the website. Facebook and Twitter allow customers to "like" a brand and become fans. Involvement in social causes that involve customers enhances brand engagement.

Many company leaders remain hesitant about adding reviews and feedback options to websites due to the potential for negative comments;

▼ Wholly Guacamole encourages individuals to engage with the brand through Twitter, Facebook, Pinterest, YouTube, Google Plus, and Instagram.

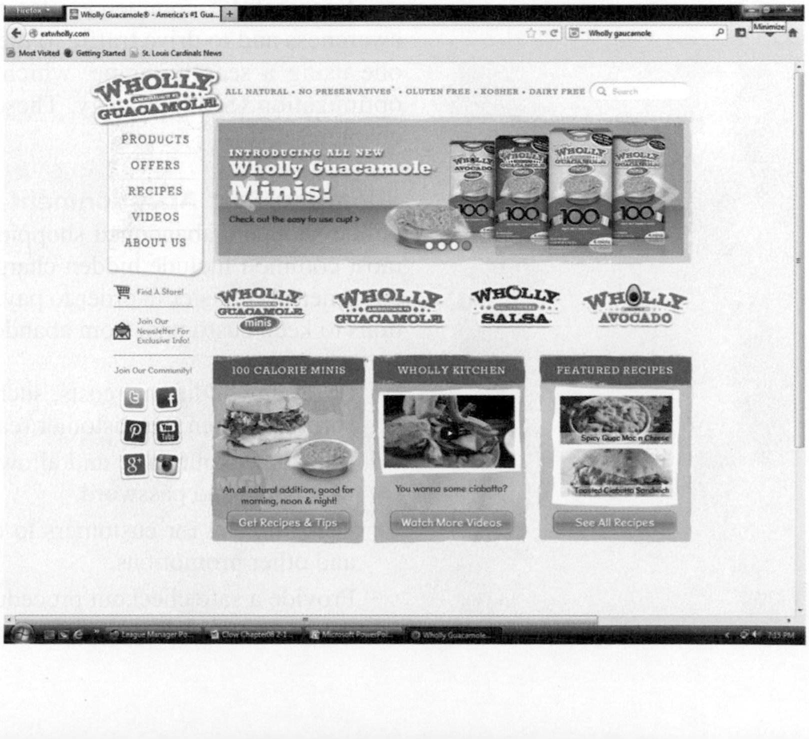

Fresherized Foods

Community Trust Bank

▲ This magazine advertisement for Community Trust Bank encourages individuals to visit the bank's website at ctbonline.com.

however, customer reviews represent an emerging trend in the Web 4.0 environment. These venues present opportunities for active interactions with customers and generate more honest relationships. They encourage customers to become brand advocates and provide a company with insights into customer thoughts and lifestyles.[9] Review and feedback pages also generate confidence for new customers visiting the site. Some e-commerce sites have also added "tell a friend" functions encouraging positive word-of-mouth recommendations.

Part of brand engagement involves personalization and customization. Personalization welcomes individuals by name as they access a site. After an individual registers, cookies deposited on the visitor's computer recall the person's name and browsing records each time the individual accesses the site. The browsing and purchase records allow the page to be customized to fit the person's history. Software can suggest additional items based on basket purchases of other customers. For instance, when someone buys a romance mystery novel, the next time she returns to the site, it suggests additional titles based on what other customers have purchased.

Most customers enjoy the convenience customization provides. Shoppers do not want to take time to sift through details. They favor the sites that remember them and the merchandise they prefer. Customization features also include the ability to:

- Locate the nearest retail store on a website or via mobile phone.
- Print coupons or other promotions from the website or use a mobile phone to access discounts at the retail store.
- Access information on the website or via a mobile phone noting that an item is in stock prior to making a purchase.[10]

Successful e-commerce sites require both online and offline marketing to build awareness and to drive traffic to the website. Most product purchases begin with someone using a search engine, which means e-commerce sites require a search engine optimization (SEO) strategy. These topics are discussed in greater detail later in this chapter.

Shopping Cart Abandonment Online retailers experience a high percentage of online shoppers abandoned shopping carts prior to checkout. The reasons vary, but the most common include hidden charges, difficulty in checking out, and sites that require customers to register in order to pay. Greg Hintz of Yahoo! Shopping offers these suggestions to keep customers from abandoning a shopping cart:

- Show any additional costs, such as shipping and handling, up front, so there are no surprises when the customer reaches checkout.
- Make checkout easy, and allow customers to make purchases without registering a user name and password.
- Make it easy for customers to enter discount codes from coupons, gift certificates, and other promotions.
- Provide a safe checkout procedure that the customer believes can be trusted.[11]

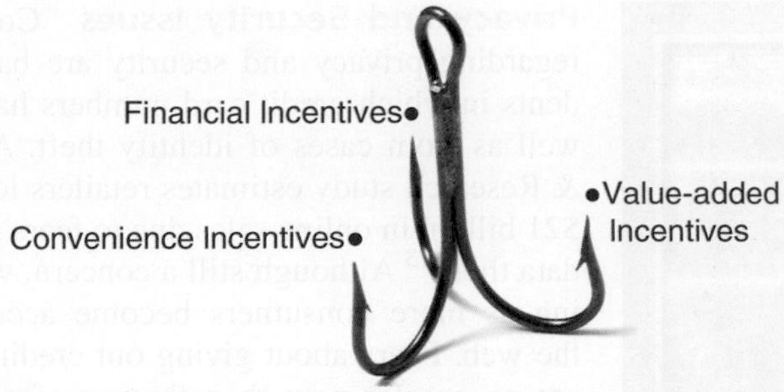

FIGURE 8.4
Common Forms of Cyberbait

Fotolia/johnsroad7

E-Commerce Incentives **Cyberbait** includes any lure or attraction that brings people to a website. The most common forms of cyberbait include financial incentives, convenience incentives, and value-added incentives (see Figure 8.4).

Financial incentives help persuade an individual or business to make a first-time purchase via e-commerce and encourage customers to return. These incentives may take the form of a reduced price, free shipping, or an e-coupon. Financial enticements can be offered because conducting business online provides cost savings through reduced shipping and labor costs. Once the individual or company takes advantage of a financial incentive and makes the switch, continuing it may not be necessary. At that point, the convenience and added-value features help retain the customer.

Typically, the most effective financial incentives offer something free or at a discount. A BizRate Research survey suggests that free shipping remains the most popular online promotion.[12] Financial incentives require two ingredients. First, they should be meaningful to individuals visiting the site. Second, they should be changed periodically to entice new visitors to buy and to encourage repeat purchases by current visitors.

Making the shopping process easier creates a convenience incentive that can encourage customers to visit a website. Instead of traveling to a retail store, a consumer can place the order in the office, at home, or while traveling by using a smartphone or app. The order can be made at any time, day or night. The convenience and speed of purchasing merchandise online drives many consumers to e-retailers.

Value-added incentives lead consumers to change purchasing habits over the long term. They can make the difference between an ordinary and an exemplary site. The added value may be customized shopping, whereby the software system recognizes patterns in customers' purchasing behaviors and makes offers matched to past purchasing behaviors or search patterns. The Gulf Coast Seafood website shown in this section offers information about species of fish, a seasonality chart, the recipe of the week, and the top 100 seafood bloggers. It includes engagement tools such as Facebook, Twitter, and Pinterest. Visitors can download the seafood finder app and search for locations. These features add significant value to the website.

Combining incentives offers the best strategy to lure customers to a website. Cyberbait may include a discount or special price on a pair of jeans (financial-based incentive) and at the same time offer the freedom to place an order at 3:00 a.m. (convenience-based incentive). The same site may feature a game or offer a weekly fashion tip on some topic (value-added incentive). This combination entices consumers and businesses to return to the site. E-shoppers find it easy to surf the internet and search competing sites. When they do, brand names and particular websites are not as important. Consumers need reasons to regularly return to sites.

▼ The website for Gulf Coast Seafood offers a number of value-added incentives.

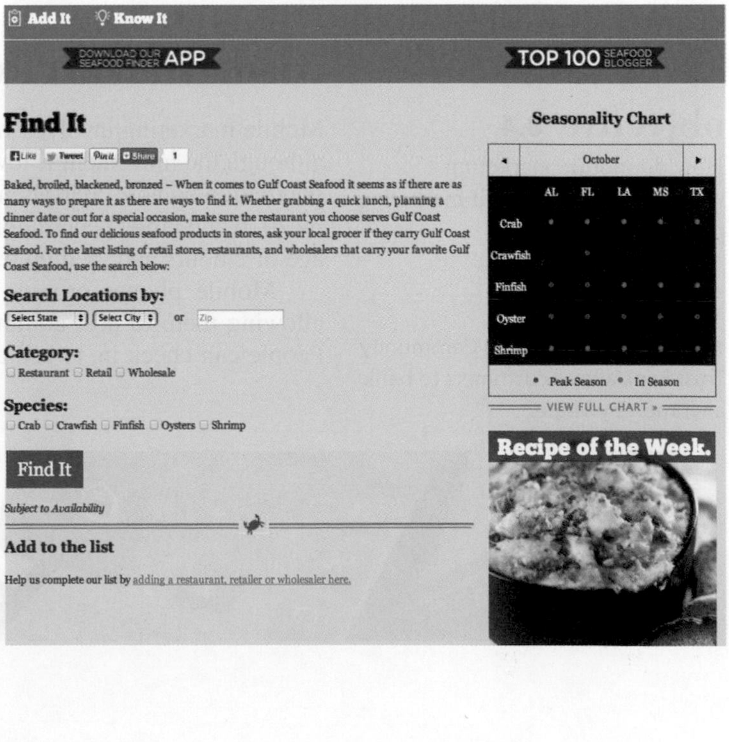

Gulf Coast Seafood

French Creative

▲ An advertisement for Progressive Bank promoting "Remote Banking" convenience.

Privacy and Security Issues Consumer concerns regarding privacy and security are based on past incidents in which credit card numbers have been stolen as well as from cases of identity theft. A Javelin Strategy & Research study estimates retailers lose approximately $21 billion in online sales due to fears about identity and data theft.[13] Although still a concern, worries are declining as more consumers become accustomed to using the web. Fears about giving out credit card information are no greater now than they are for telephone orders or in-store credit card sales. Consumer confidence in e-commerce website security has risen. A recent survey revealed that three-fourths of online shoppers express faith in web security.[14]

Beyond apprehensions about identity theft and fraud are concerns that firms will sell personal information. Once this information becomes readily available, the individual loses control over who sees it and how it is used. A person might not wish to have his shopping patterns known, especially when the individual buys personal care products such as those for baldness, sexual dysfunction, weight loss, or other private matters. Further, many consumers become frustrated by being bombarded with advertising and marketing messages. Consumers also strongly express the desire to maintain control over personal information. They believe they should decide who should use it and how it should be used.

Trust remains the key to concerns about privacy and security of personal information. A KPMG survey indicates that 62 percent of consumers do not mind being tracked as long as they perceive a benefit in the form of reduced costs or free content. Consumers also want to know what a company does with the information it collects. If information is sold, then consumers want the company to request their permission first. Most consumers hate feeling spied on without permission. Tudor Aw of KPMG Europe notes, "People are happy to be tracked, but you have to be upfront and explain it."[15]

Mobile Marketing

objective 8.4

How do mobile marketing systems enhance digital marketing programs?

Mobile marketing involves various forms of marketing on all mobile cell phone devices, although the movement is toward smartphones and tablets. Forty-four percent of the U.S. population owns a smartphone. Estimates suggest the figure will rise to almost 60 percent by 2016 and tablet penetration will increase to 49 percent. Individuals now spend an average of 2 hours and 21 minutes per day using some type of mobile device.[16]

Mobile phones provide a device linking individuals to social networks, thereby allowing them to post comments, pictures, and videos and read the thoughts of others. People can check in, tweet, and update their status at any time and anywhere. They can

▼ The mobile app from Community Trust Bank allows customers to bank anytime, anywhere.

Community Trust Bank

- Display ads
- Search ads
- Video advertising
- Text messages
- In-app advertising
- QR codes, digital watermarks, 2D barcodes
- Geo-targeting

FIGURE 8.5
Types of Mobile Marketing

download deals from companies, read reviews, check prices, and share information. Further, a mobile device offers a method for shopping. Purchases can be made with a mobile phone. Product information can be obtained. Consumers are able to check store hours, obtain directions to a business, and compare prices. These activities take place anywhere, including the retailer's store.

Effective mobile marketing involves understanding thc social and shopping nature of mobile phones and incorporates it into the firm's mobile marketing strategy. Figure 8.5 identifies various types of mobile marketing. Forms of advertising used on the internet can be played on smartphone mobile devices such as display ads, search ads, and video ads, as will be discussed later in this chapter in the online advertising section.

Companies take advantage of mobile phones by sending text message ads to consumers. While these may be annoying, they can also be effective when created properly. A text message near lunch or dinner by a restaurant offering a special deal might entice a consumer to visit the restaurant. Two keys to text message advertising include gaining the permission of the mobile phone owner and careful timing when sending messages.

▼ This advertisement for Philadelphia Cream Cheese includes a QR code that provides consumers access to the recipe for cheesecake.

Used with permission of Kraft Foods

In-app advertisements offer a popular new type of mobile advertising. Globally, people download 32 billion apps to smartphones each year. Advertisers spend $2.9 billion on in-app advertising while consumers spend $26.1 billion buying apps. These apps include games, songs, and those that check weather, stocks, and current events. Advertising in this area becomes more effective when the message relates to the app's content. For instance, weather-related products should be promoted on a weather app.

QR codes, watermarks, and 2D barcodes directing consumers with a smartphone to a website now appear in magazines. Almost every magazine features some type of action code. The codes are especially popular in magazines that focus on home, family, beauty, health, travel, and fashion. The QR code placed in the Philadelphia Cream Cheese advertisement in this section offers recipes to shoppers.

Engaging customers constitutes the primary purpose of action codes in magazines. A Nellymoser study revealed that the greatest usage was for videos (35 percent). These videos may provide a behind-the-scenes look, product demonstrations, a how-to video, or entertainment. Action codes help the marketing team collect data and build opt-in lists for permission marketing. Figure 8.6 displays other uses for action codes.[17]

▶ FIGURE 8.6
Marketing Uses for Action Codes

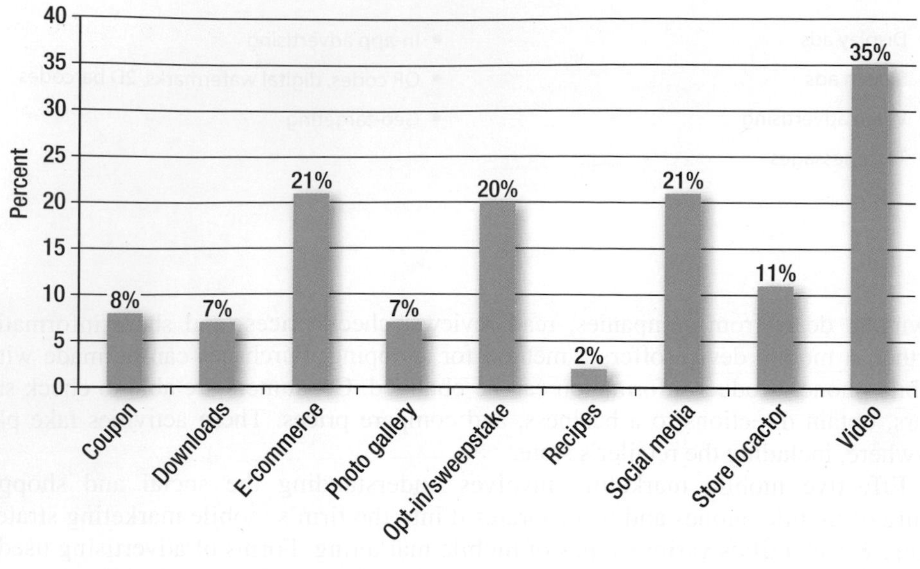

Digital Strategies

objective 8.5
What digital strategies do marketing professionals employ?

As society has shifted from desktop computers to laptops, tablets, and smartphones, marketers have adapted to these multiscreen formats. Advances in technology create new digital marketing opportunities along with the need to develop campaigns that can be viewed from any type of screen. Figure 8.7 identifies the primary digital marketing strategies brands feature today.

Interactive Marketing

The drive to engage consumers with a brand has led to an increase in **interactive marketing**, or the development of marketing programs that create interplay between consumers and businesses. The programs feature two-way communication and customer involvement.

The internet offers the ideal medium for interactive marketing due to the ability to track browser activities and translate the information into instant reactions. Software such as the Relationship Optimizer and Prime Response by NCR provides a powerful data analysis technique to personalize marketing messages. The NCR software analyzes customer interactions such as click-stream data traffic—any type of customer interaction with the firm—and combines it with demographic information from external or internal databases. As the data are processed, the software can launch complex interactive and personalized marketing materials in real time.

Interactive marketing emphasizes two primary activities. First, it assists marketers in targeting individuals, specifically potential and current customers, with personalized information. Second, it engages the consumer with the company and product. The consumer becomes an active participant in the marketing exchange rather than a passive recipient. Figure 8.8 lists online interactive tactics used by companies and the percentage of companies that utilize each method.

- Interactive marketing
- Content marketing
- Location-based advertising
- Behavioral targeting
- Video tactics
- Blogs and newsletters
- Email marketing

▶ FIGURE 8.7
Digital Marketing Strategies

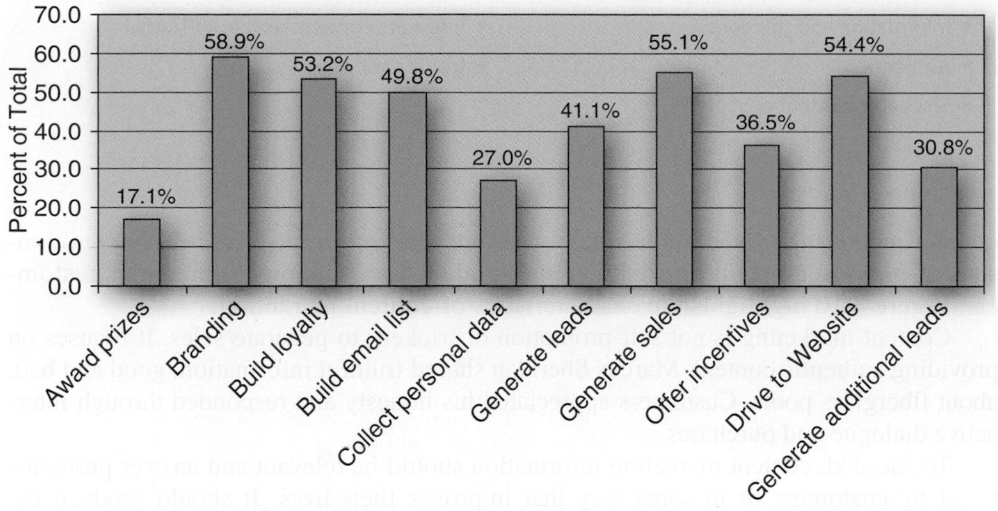

◀ **FIGURE 8.8**
Online Interactive Marketing Tactics

Marketing Zen's Shama Kabani describes the steps in developing an effective interactive marketing strategy (see Figure 8.9).[18] It starts with cultivating an attitude of giving. Consumers should believe they will receive something in exchange for their involvement. Both sides need to receive something of value. A free gift, such as merchandise or information about some other valuable item, will be the quickest way to capture consumer attention.

The second step in gaining trust involves understanding customers, empathizing with them, and providing solutions to their problems. Consumers engage with companies and brands they trust. The company should be honest, upfront, and cannot pull surprises or use trickery to gain a sale. Otherwise, it becomes a one-time transaction.

Shama suggests that marketers should synthesize the company or brand down to one or two words that best describe what the firm offers or stands for. It might be "feminine" or "quality" or "communication" or "innovator" or "passionate." Tied closely with the one-word brand is an ultimate vision. What outcome does the company deliver? FedEx provides "overnight delivery." Gatorade delivers "energy and refreshment."

Choosing the best communication channels to present messages and to interact with customers and prospects constitutes the next step. As Figure 8.8 shows, several options are available. The best choice depends on the target audience and the message. Evaluation and adjusting make up the final step. These activities are especially important for digital marketing programs, because the field changes rapidly. Current channels may not exist in five years, or even by next year. Different—and perhaps better channels—may arise.

Content Marketing

Orders for in-ground fiberglass pools at River Pools and Spas declined from an average of six per month to barely two. Four customers who had made deposits during the winter requested their money back because they had changed their minds. Marcus Sheridan, owner of River Pools and Spas, was spending $250,000 a year on radio, television, and pay-per-click web advertising. He reduced the budget to $25,000 and focused on providing useful information through blog posts and videos. He answered questions about costs from potential customers.[19] This approach, called

1. Cultivate an attitude of giving	**4.** Define your ultimate vision
2. Gain trust	**5.** Choose your communication channels
3. Identify your one-word brand	**6.** Evaluate and adjust

▲ **FIGURE 8.9**
Steps in Developing an Interactive Marketing Strategy

▶ FIGURE 8.10
Content Marketing

- Information and solutions
- Authentic
- Shareable content
- Integrate content, search, and social
- Update consistently

content marketing, saved his business. **Content marketing**, or *branded content*, consists of providing useful information and product-use solutions to potential customers. Figure 8.10 highlights the characteristics of content marketing.

Content marketing is not self-promotion or trickery to generate sales. It focuses on providing authentic content. Marcus Sheridan shared truthful information, good and bad, about fiberglass pools. Customers appreciated his honesty and responded through interactive dialogue and purchases.

To succeed, content marketing information should be relevant and answer problems faced by customers or in some way that improves their lives. It should produce the information and solutions that site visitors will want to share with friends and relatives. Integrating content with the search and social strategies creates synergy. Using key search words in the content and providing content consumers consider to be valuable enhances the chance that a visitor seeking a solution to a problem will share the site with friends and relatives through social media.

▼ Philadelphia Cream Cheese has been successful with the branded website *realwomenofphiladelphia.com*.

courtesy of Kraft Foods

Frequency constitutes one key to obtaining search engine results. Also, the content should be updated consistently. Most experts believe two to three changes per week will be necessary. Marketers should avoid the temptation to drift into self-promotion and sales talk over time. Staying true to the mission of the branded content, providing information and solutions, is vital.

An alternative to branded content is **sponsored content**, whereby a brand sponsors the content of a blogger or related website. A YouTube video showing how to get prefect curls included references to the Remington curling iron brand embedded in the video. Spectrum Brands, which owns Remington, pays bloggers to create stories, articles, and videos for the web. An article and video entitled "Get the Right Swimsuit for Your Body" featured references to Remington embedded in the content. The goal was for the article and video to be shared through social media venues such as Twitter and YouTube.[20]

Sponsored content and content marketing share the same keys to success. The difference is that the company pays bloggers or website owners to promote content. Marketing professionals hope that potential customers will perceive the information to be valuable, share it with others, and most important, purchase the sponsored brand. The potential downside is that consumers will view it as advertising and self-promotion and not respond. Also, the company has limited control over the content and what people say. Negative comments or behaviors that do not represent the brand well might create a potentially negative or embarrassing situation that then must be addressed.

Location-Based Advertising

Mobile phones allow marketers to create location-based mobile advertising campaigns, often called geo-targeting. **Geo-targeting** involves reaching customers where they are located by contacting their mobile communication devices. Geo-targeting represents a unique and attractive feature of mobile marketing. By downloading an app, a fast-food restaurant can identify a person's location, show him how far he is from the nearest outlet, and then provide walking or driving directions to that unit. Many smartphone owners have check-in services at Foursquare, Gowalla, Facebook Places, and Twitter geolocation. Starbuck's, McDonald's, Chipotle, and Burger King provide the largest number of restaurant check-ins. When someone checks in, software instantly sends a special promotion and information about the nearest locations. Marketing experts believe this location-based marketing approach will grow in use in the future. Businesses can harness the ability to drive consumers to retail outlets near where they are located, which can be an effective method to engage consumers with a brand on a one-to-one basis.

McDonald's recently ran a campaign through radio streaming on iTunes and Pandora. As the audio plays the song, copy encourages consumers to tap on the ad for the nearest McDonald's location. A map pops up and consumers can either type in a zip code or let the mobile phone's GPS find the closest locations, which are typically marked with a flag on the map. Tapping on a flag produces the restaurant's address and phone number. A click-to-call feature embedded in the ad enables the consumer to call the McDonald's with just another tap on the phone. Another version helps consumers access driving or walking directions via using the GPS feature.[21]

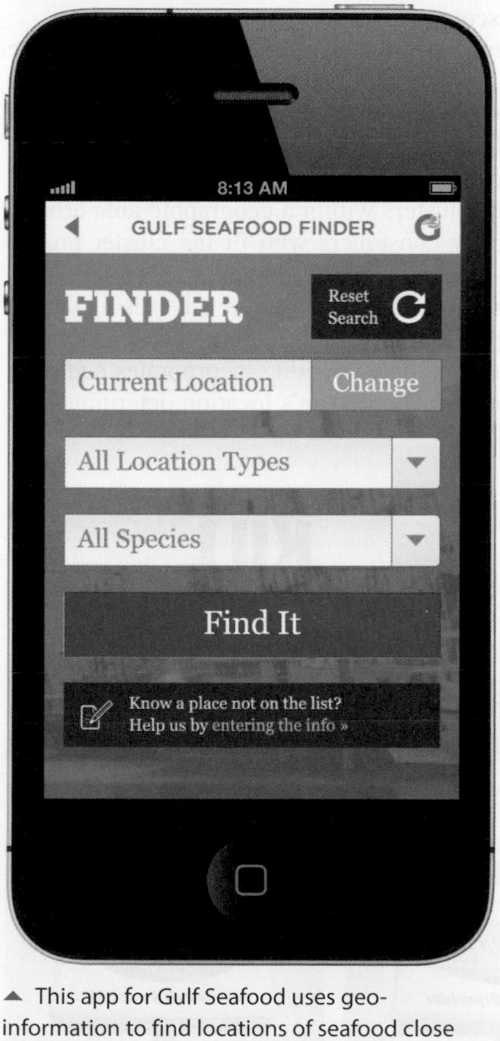

Gulf Coast Seafood

▲ This app for Gulf Seafood uses geo-information to find locations of seafood close to where an individual is located.

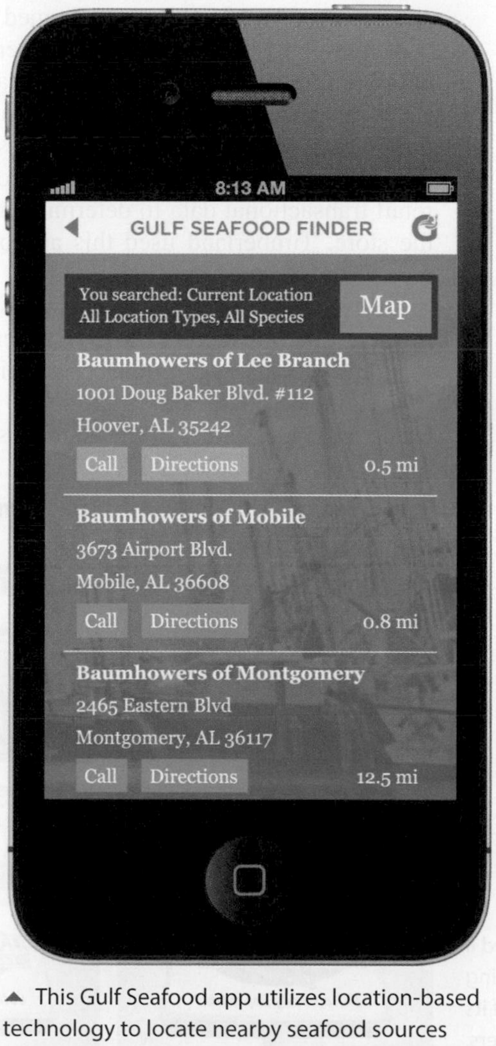

Gulf Coast Seafood

▲ This Gulf Seafood app utilizes location-based technology to locate nearby seafood sources with a click-to-call option as well as directions.

FIGURE 8.11
Location-Based Advertising

Source: Based on Mark Walsch, "Location-Based Mobile Ads Deliver Best Engagement, Performance," *Online Media Daily*, www.mediapost.com/publications/article/192780, February 6, 2013.

- Targeting by DMAs (designated marketing areas), 30%
- Geo-fencing, 27%
- Audience-data targeting, 24%
- Geo-aware advertising, 14%
- City or zip code, 5%

Applebee's restaurant also employs location-based targeting. The brand's mobile banner ad reads "See You Tomorrow. Applebee's." When a consumer taps on the mobile ad, the content asks if it can access the person's current location through the phone's GPS. If the person responds "yes," then he is taken to a mobile landing page that provides the nearest Applebee's location, menu items, and specials. Through the app, consumers are able to purchase gift cards and receive them through Facebook, Twitter, or other social media venues.

According to Shuli Lowy, marketing director at Ping Mobile, "Mobile is no longer an option for restaurants." A study by Nielsen revealed that 95 percent of smartphone users conduct restaurant searches on their mobile device and 90 percent of those convert within a day. Sixty-four percent convert within an hour.[22]

Other brands also feature geo-targeting. Nissan, Procter & Gamble, Pepsi, Macy's, Kenneth Cole, and Timberland have conducted successful geo-targeted campaigns. Swirl is a mobile app used by retailers such as Timberland. Shoppers who agree to download the Swirl app and let it track their locations are notified of a 20 percent discount on merchandise. The app provides a consumer with a store's location and the individual has one hour to take advantage of the special. A clock within the app begins the time countdown. According to the VP of retail and digital commerce at Timberland, "Because it's opt-in ... you're receptive to it." According to Shadrin, 75 percent of recipients checked out the special offer, and 35 percent redeemed the discount.[23]

Figure 8.11 displays the different forms of location-based advertising and the approximate percentage quantity of each.[24] Targeting by demographic marketing areas (DMAs) is the most common approach. Everyone within the DMA that has granted permission receives the targeted message. Geo-fencing targets consumers near a specific retail location. Usually, the location is coupled with third-party demographic data or retail transactional data to determine audience clusters within a geographic area around the store. Timberland used this approach. Only consumers who fit the cluster profile receive the targeted message.

Restaurants including McDonald's and Applebee's use geo-aware advertising targeting real-time locations to deliver advertising messages based on the person's proximity to a unit's location. For other companies, audience-data targeting incorporates audience behaviors and characteristics to reach individuals. The person's location determines the exact brand and nature of the ad to be sent.

Interstate Batteries launched a geo-targeted online advertising campaign to build awareness of its Battery Centers.

Interstate Batteries

Creating successful geo-targeting campaigns requires two actions. First, consumers should be in control of the engagement. They opt-in for the app. Second, the brand should provide a discount or something of value to consumers. Campaigns that follow these principles routinely yield engagement and performance measures that are higher than any other type of digital advertising.

Stanislav Komogorov/Fotolia

▲ Behavioral targeting can be used to target fishing-related digital advertisements to fishermen who are most likely to make purchases.

Behavioral Targeting

Marketers for some brands can target the individuals who are most likely to purchase the item rather than merely placing ads on websites. **Behavioral targeting** utilizes web data to identify these potential customers. Behavioral targeting occurs in three different ways. It can be based on

- Pages a person visits on the internet
- Keyword searches or content read
- Past visitors to a site

The most common form of behavioral targeting involves tracking a person's movements on the internet. Cookies placed on the individual's computer track the data points as she moves from site to site. They record the types of sites visited, the information read, the searches conducted, and the products she purchased. Based on this information, ads will be placed on the websites that match her browsing history. If she has visited a number of websites about fishing, the screen will display advertisements for fishing supplies, boats, or other fishing-related products. Marketers can place a coupon or other form of cyberbait on the ad to encourage the consumer to click on it.

The second form of behavioral targeting examines an individual's search behavior. It identifies keywords typed into search engines and the content read based on keyword searches. If an individual has used a search engine to locate articles and information about new cars, then he may see an advertisement for Toyota or another car brand. If he has been reading about SUVs, then the ad may actually be for an SUV rather than a sedan or other type of vehicle. These ads typically appear on the search engine being used.

The final form is behavioral targeting based on past visitors. Amazon uses this method to suggest books and movies that may interest a person shopping on the company's website. The behavioral marketing program is triggered when an individual places a book or movie in a shopping basket or on a wish list. An ad will be generated that says "Others who purchased this book have also purchased these books." Several suggestions are made based on combinations of purchases of other customers.

Behavioral targeting takes place in seconds without a person even realizing it has occurred. Algorithms can be written to trigger these ads as the page loads. The brand being advertised may rotate or change based on the bidding process for display advertising. In the above example with keyword behavioral targeting, instead of a Toyota ad, it may be for a Ford, Nissan, or Chevrolet ad, depending on the winner of the bidding process that took place.

Video Tactics

Online video viewing has exploded over the last few years. Approximately 58 percent of the U.S. population watches digital videos, and 75 percent of internet users watch them. As shown in Figure 8.12, video tactics include advertising on videos, posting broadcast video ads, producing informational and cause-related videos, and product reviews.

Video ad spending has risen to $4.6 billion annually and is currently growing 20 percent to 40 percent per year, a rate much faster than any other form of advertising. Research indicates that consumers are more receptive to online video ads. The average time consumers view online video ads is 21.4 seconds, compared to 13.6 seconds for

- Advertising on videos
- Posting broadcast video ads
- Producing informational videos
- Producing cause-related videos
- Product reviews

▲ **FIGURE 8.12**
Video Tactics

▶ **FIGURE 8.13**

Online Ads Versus Television Ads

Source: Based on Lucia Moses, "Online Video Ads Have Higher Impact Than TV Ads," *Adweek*, www.adweek.com/news/advertising-branding/online-video-ads-have-higher-impact-than-tv-ads-148982, May 1, 2013.

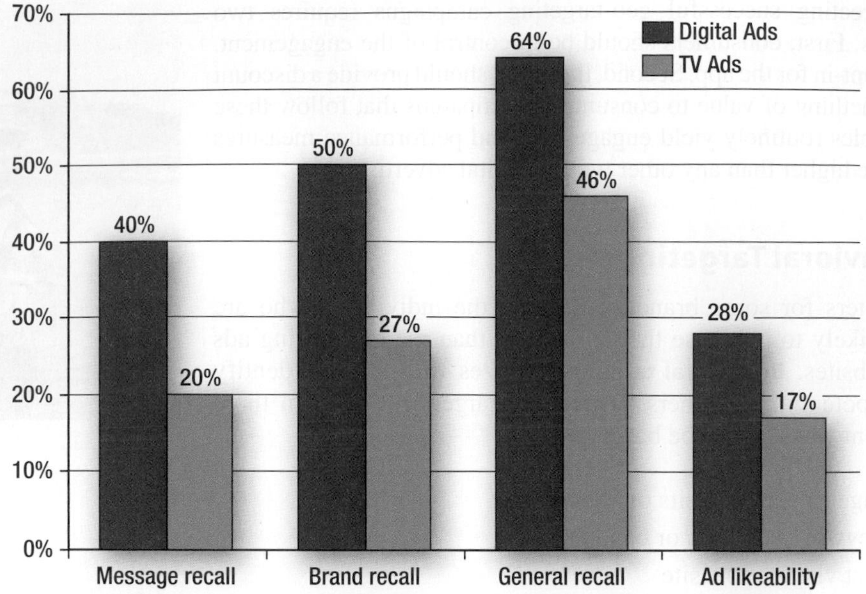

television. The completion rate for online video ads is 88 percent versus 79 percent for TV. Recall and ad likability are also higher for digital video ads (see Figure 8.13).[25]

Video ads can be pre-roll (before the video starts), mid-roll (in the middle of the video content), or post-roll (at the end of the content). Advertisements placed at the end of a video have a better click-through rate, because the individual has finished watching the video content. Ads at the beginning of the video have more impressions while those in the middle have the highest completion rate. Therefore, if the goal of the video ad campaign is to create impressions or enhance recall, then advertisers should front-load the ads. If the company seeks to increase brand recognition or enhance brand image, then mid-roll ads represent a better option, because viewers tend to watch the entire ad. Post-roll ads best match direct response-type of advertising with some type of call to action.

▼ Television advertisements for Community Trust Bank featuring Terry Bradshaw have also been posted on YouTube.

Community Trust Bank

Most brands now have a YouTube channel where the company can share various types of videos. Ads prepared for television are now posted to video websites, such as YouTube. Many Super Bowl advertisers post a commercial or a snippet of it on YouTube prior to the game. Often, the digital ad will be viewed by more people than those who see the actual commercial during the Super Bowl. In addition to ads, advertisers post background scenes or videos explaining how the ad was produced. Viewers find these interesting, and this approach can increase engagement with the brand.

In addition to broadcast ads, many companies produce two other types of videos for posting online. Informational or instructional videos are the first method, using a strategy similar to the branded content approach described earlier in this chapter. Companies strive to provide useful information to consumers and answer questions they may have about the brand or product. Providing instructions on how to use a product, especially a complex item, can be useful. As with branded content, advertisers should ensure the videos will be perceived as authentic and useful—and not a sales gimmick.

Another approach involves posting videos with public relations or cause-related marketing messages. Duracell produced a video about firefighters and emergency personnel telling their personal stories. Advil produced a video featuring Melissa Stockwell, who lost her leg in Iraq. John Deere produced a video about a Mexican immigrant who came to the United States with nothing and now owns his own business. This type of video seeks to generate goodwill toward a brand.

Currently, numerous consumers use videos to conduct product research. Rather than visiting various websites, Amazon.com, or brand sites to obtain reviews, consumers turn to YouTube. An increase in the popularity of YouTube as a source of product information may be due to the following reasons:[26]

- Any product can be reviewed on video, and almost any product a person can think of has been reviewed on YouTube.
- Videos are more engaging because they provide both visual and spoken content.
- Videos represent the best place for early adopters to learn about a new product.

An Eyeblaster study revealed that online videos performed best when they appear next to online content or in an email, as compared to social network or gaming sites. Eyeblaster examined two metrics: dwell rate and dwell time. **Dwell rate** measures the proportion of impressions that result in users clicking an ad or mousing over it. **Dwell time** indicates the amount of time individuals spend engaged with an advertisement. Dwell rate and dwell time were both higher for video ads placed beside content or in an email rather than when they accompanied social networks and gaming sites. Ariel Geifman of Eyeblaster explains, "What we found is that people browse social networks really quickly. People spend a lot of time in social networks, but it's not on the same web page." In terms of gaming sites, Geifman said, "People are more focused on the game" and, as a result, less interested in watching a video ad.[27]

▼ Blogs and newsletters can be used effectively by fashion retailers to engage customers with the store.

Captblack76/Fotolia

Blogs and Newsletters

Blogs are online musings that cover a wide range of topics. Some permit visitors to post comments; others do not. Company-sponsored blogs can emulate word-of-mouth communication and engage customers with a brand. Fashion retailers entice customers to visit the company's blog to enjoy postings on new styles, upcoming designers, and fashion *faux pas*. In the past, customers may have relied on magazines such as *Vogue* for fashion information. Now, company blogs allow them to obtain information quicker, and, more important, interactively. This helps the marketing team engage with customers and establishes a two-way communication channel.

A company-sponsored blog provides a number of potential benefits; however, analysts stress the importance of identifying a specific reason for the blog before launching it. The goal may be to make the company more open (Dell), to humanize the organization (Microsoft), or to show a fun-and-happy company (Southwest Airlines).[28] When Coca-Cola acquired 40 percent of Honest Tea, many customers became unhappy about the move and voiced opinions on the Honest Tea blog. Honest Tea CEO Seth Goldman answered each one. While some customers still did not like the idea, "The blog at least helps people see how we think about it," Goldman said.[29]

Company leaders carefully select methods to respond to negative comments. CEO Bill Marriott of Marriott International hosts a blog for customers and employees. About 20 percent of the blog's readership consists of employees. Marriott employees monitor the comment section. No comment will be posted until it has been approved. The company does not remove comments simply because they are negative. Only those not germane to the discussion or blog are taken down. Those remaining are left up and addressed by Bill Marriott, which provides credibility to the blog through his willingness to listen to negative feedback.

For small businesses, blogs provide a relatively inexpensive way to communicate with customers. Robb Duncan began a blog for his Georgetown gelato shop, Dolcezza. When a second store was opened in Bethesda, Maryland, he announced an ice cream giveaway on opening night through the blog. More than 1,000 individuals showed up.[30]

The Thrillist (thrillist.com) and UrbanDaddy (urbandaddy.com) websites are designed to take advantage of the power that newsletters can provide. Newsletters are sent via email to approximately 1.1 million subscribers. Most subscribers are college graduates with median incomes of $88,000. The UrbanDaddy newsletter emphasizes an exclusive and luxurious approach, advising men about where to shop and how to fit in. The Thrillist newsletter features a fun and relaxed tone. Both organize free, heavily-sponsored events for subscribers of the newsletters. The newsletter becomes a means of engaging the subscribers with the websites.[31]

Both blogs and newsletters should follow the same principles as those pertaining to content marketing. The information provided should be useful and present solutions to the problems customers face. Authentic messages offering something individuals want to share receive more positive attention. They should be integrated with the brand's web content, search strategy, and social media outreach.

Effective blogs and newsletters are consistently updated. For blogs, this normally involves entries three times per week. For newsletters, publication frequency depends on the industry, content, target audience, and purpose of the newsletter. At a minimum, marketers need to add new materials once each month. A lower frequency sends the message that the company does not have anything interesting or new to provide. It also conveys the hidden message of, "We are doing this only to get your business, to increase sales."

Email Marketing

Email can become an important part of a company's digital marketing strategy. To be successful, companies integrate the email marketing program with other channels. It cannot simply be a program where addresses are purchased and mass emails are sent to individuals on the list. Most people resent spam, and response rates are extremely low, in addition to damaging the brand's reputation.

Response rates increase when an email message resembles the information presented on the company's website and in its advertisements and direct mail messages. When Data Inc. introduced new project management software, the marketing team integrated email with its webinar, direct mail, social media, and telemarketing programs. The webinar explained how the new software tool worked. Direct mail, telemarketing, and email were used to reach 600 influential decision makers. For emails that were returned undeliverable, Data, Inc. used LinkedIn to locate the contact's correct information. The email integrated approach resulted in a three percent response rate.[32]

▼ Targeted emails can be used to contact individuals who abandon shopping carts.

Alistair Cotton/Fotolia

Web analytics allow a company to develop email campaigns that offer the greatest chance of response. Emails can be based on the browsing history of an individual on a particular website. They identify those who made past purchases or items placed in the "wish" list but never purchased.

Email campaigns may be directed at consumers who abandon shopping carts without making purchases. About 40 percent of online

- Be upfront, honest with subscribers
- Build list for quality, not quantity
- Give subscribers what they want
- Be familiar to your audience
- Keep emails neat and clean
- Be eye-catching
- Integrate social media
- Test, test and test

FIGURE 8.14
Developing Successful Email Campaigns
Source: Based on interview with Holly Betts, Marketing Zen, February 12, 2014.

shoppers abandon the shopping cart just prior to the checkout. Only about 30 percent of these shoppers return to complete the transaction. The IT department can identify individuals who abandon a shopping basket. Sending an email to them offering free shipping, a discount if they complete the order, or a simple reminder that they have items in their shopping basket can lead to greater sales. Converting these individuals to customers is much easier and more lucrative than sending mass emails. Targeted emails experience a conversion rate five to ten times higher than mass emails sent to the firm's customers. In addition, revenues from these follow-up emails are three to nine times higher than other approaches.[33]

In Figure 8.14 Holly Betts, an email expert with Marketing Zen, offers a number of suggestions for developing successful campaigns. It starts with individuals opting-in to the program. She emphasizes being upfront and honest with subscribers. Companies should tell recipients what they can expect, when they can expect it, and then deliver on those promises. As with branded content, emails should offer subscribers something useful that meets their needs or interests.

Marketing professionals make sure all emails come from the same source. Subscribers then instantly recognize the source and understand that it is an email they gave permission to receive. The messages should be short, neat, and eye-catching. They can include links to all of the brand's social media outlets so that recipients can increase their engagement with the brand if they wish. Email advertisers should test every campaign and keep records of what worked and what did not. This information makes it possible to build a file of best practices, based on previous results.

Web Advertising

objective 8.6
What types of web advertising can companies use to reach consumers?

Online advertising presents a highly effective method for reaching today's consumers, especially the younger, affluent, and internet-savvy market. Budgets for online advertising have steadily increased and are now more than $500 billion annually. Online advertising is the fastest-growing medium with annual growth rates exceeding 20 percent. Part of the growth has been fueled by multiscreen advertising, which involves media buys across the various platforms such as the web, mobile, and tablets.[34]

Figure 8.15 indicates the percentage of online advertising dollars allocated to each of the primary formats. Banner, media/video, and classified advertising will be presented in this section. Search spending will be described in the next section.

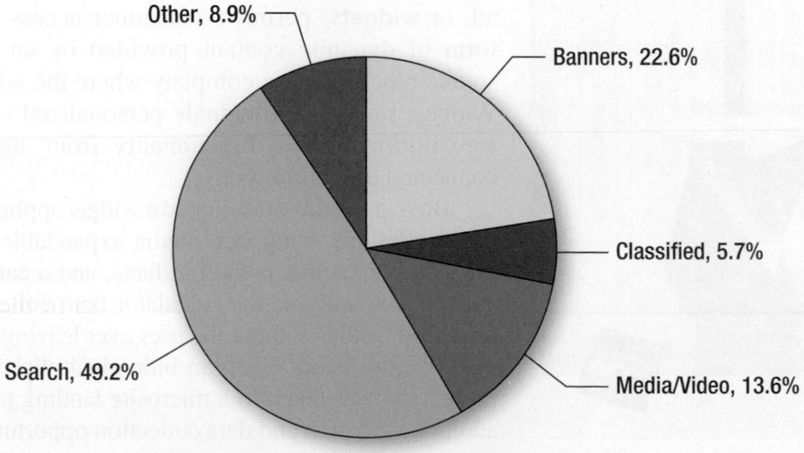

FIGURE 8.15
U.S. Online Ad Spending by Format

Newcomer, Morris and Young Inc.

▲ A banner advertisement for Ouachita Independent Bank featuring images that were also used in print and outdoor ads, thereby creating continuity in the promotions program.

Banner Advertising

The first form of online advertising involved the use of a display, or banner, ad. In 1994, AT&T ran one carrying the message "Have you ever clicked your right mouse here? You will." This very basic form of advertising generated billions of dollars in advertising revenues. Today, banner ads account for 22.6 percent of online advertising.[35]

Currently, banner ads can be embedded with videos, widget applications, or targeted display ads that increase the chances viewers will see and click the icon. The newest online technology, which has been taken from paid search auction systems, allows advertisers to display a banner ad only to individuals the company chooses. The system is built on a vast warehouse of user internet data and automated auction advertising exchanges such as Google's Double-Click, Yahoo!'s Right Media ad exchange, and Microsoft's AdECN. Advertisers develop messages for specific audiences. Prices can be set to entice the members of the audience who will see the banner ad.

▼ Google's Double-Click technology can target advertisements to consumers who are browsing the web for stylish modern furniture.

Scott and Cooner, Inc.

When a consumer, such as a 20- to 25-year-old female, accesses a website featuring paid search auction technology, in a microsecond the software searches the auction exchange for advertisers that match the profile of the individual who logged onto the page. Once an advertiser has been located, a banner ad instantly flashes on the computer screen. It may be an advertisement for L'Oreal or Liz Claiborne. If a male with an interest in hunting logs on, an advertisement for hunting supplies or hunting attire may appear. The automated exchange system grants precise targeting of ads to specific consumers.[36]

Widgets Mini-applications embedded in a banner ad, or **widgets**, permit a consumer access to some form of dynamic content provided by an external source other than the company where the ad resides. Widgets provide individuals personalized access to web information or functionality from any device connected to the internet.

Boxcar Creative developed a widget application for ConocoPhillips using rich media expandable banners to create interactive polls, fun facts, and a carbon calculator. The poll and the calculator both collected and produced results without the user ever leaving the banner advertisement. When an individual clicked "learn more," she was taken to a microsite landing page with additional content and data collection opportunities.

Scott Equipment

◀ A Scott Equipment banner ad with a call-to-action "Learn More" icon.

Location-based widgets can be placed in banner ads. These ads are presented only to individuals who log on to a website in a particular region. The technology can be ideal for retailers, restaurants, and smaller businesses seeking to reach a specific region around a retail outlet.

Impact of Online Advertising

As more dollars shift to online advertising, concerns have arisen about the impact of the ads. Web users, just like television viewers, are becoming immune to advertisements. The percentage of people who respond to banner ads steadily shrinks. The click-through rate on major web destinations has declined to less than one percent. A recent measurement resulted in a response rate of 0.27 percent.[37]

To improve response rates, advertisers have created increasingly complex targeting campaigns that utilize various web metrics. MediaMind survey results indicate that the number of digital ads with two or more third-party tags increased 267 percent over the last two years. These third-party tags track items such as ad interactions, brand impact, and browsing behavior in order to optimize a campaign. Brands that utilize geo-targeting, behavioral targeting, and third-party demographic data tend have the most tags attached to the ads.[38]

According to comScore Inc., 54 percent of display ads on thousands of websites were not seen. That means almost $6 billion in display advertisements were wasted. Technical issues cause some of the problems, such as the ad appearing below the fold on a screen. The "below the fold" term describes the part a website that is not visible on a computer or smartphone screen that can only be seen by scrolling down. Unless the individual scrolls down the website, the ad will not be viewed. Another technical problem occurs when the ad loads so slowly that the web visitor either switches off the ad or goes to another site. Blocking software also prevents web ads from being visible. An increasing number of consumers has purchased software that blocks all forms of advertising. This is true especially for tech-savvy individuals.[39]

The final reason for ads not being seen is fraud. A significant number of ad impressions that brands pay for are never seen because the impressions are based on fake traffic. Malicious software makes a website record that a person is visiting the site and is viewing the ads being displayed. While both unethical and illegal, these scams generate millions of ad views and dollars for the scammers and are difficult for companies to detect.

The diminishing impact of online advertising and the high percentage of ads that are never viewed have led many advertisers to bank on new technologies designed to increase response rates and detect fraud. Advertisers are also spending more time and dollars in planning integrated campaigns that incorporate digital advertising with social media and traditional advertising.

Offline Advertising

To build a brand's reputation and brand loyalty, online advertising should be integrated with offline branding tactics that reinforce each other to speak with one voice. This

▼ Off-line advertising is an important part of building an online presence for brands such as JD Bank.

JD Bank

process, **brand spiraling**, involves the use of traditional media to promote and attract consumers to a website. Marketers design television, radio, newspapers, magazines, and billboards that encourage consumers to visit the firm's website in an effort to maintain a uniform brand presence and advertising message.

One recent study indicated that, after viewing a magazine advertisement, nearly half of the consumers polled said they might access a website or conduct an online search for the product. More than 40 percent were more inclined to visit a website after seeing a television or newspaper advertisement.[40] Traditional media can be the driving force behind online branding efforts.

Currently, tailor-made websites accompany many direct and email campaigns. These sites are accessed through **personalized URLs**, called **PURLs**, such as the hypothetical www.kenclow.offer.officedepot.com. A PURL contains a personalized preloaded web page that contains the customer's personal data, contact information, purchase behavior, and previous interactions with the company. A company such as Ford could display the customer's current vehicle, maintenance record, and other interactions with the company. The PURL creates a one-on-one dialogue with a customer and engages her with the company and provides messages, offers, and incentives tailored to her past data and history.[41]

Search Engine Optimization (SEO)

objective 8.7
What is a search engine optimization strategy?

The largest category of online expenditures is for spots on search engines. Funds devoted to search engines constitute nearly 50 percent of online advertising expenditures. About 80 percent of all web traffic begins at a search engine.[42] Therefore, making sure that a company's name or brand becomes one of the first ones listed when a person performs a search becomes a key marketing goal. **SEO**, or **search engine optimization**, is the process of increasing the probability of a particular company's website emerging from a search.

Optimization can be achieved in one of three ways. First, a *paid search insertion* comes up when certain products or information are sought. Companies can speed this process by registering with various search engines in order to have the site indexed and by paying a higher placement fee for top positions. The placement of the ad on a search page depends on the price the company pays and the algorithm a search engine used to determine the advertisement's relevance to a particular search word or phrase.

Second, a company can increase identification through the *natural* or *organic emergence* of the site. This method involves developing efficient and effective organic results that arise from a natural search process. Each search engine uses a slightly different set of algorithms to identify key phrases that match what was typed into the search box. To be listed first in an organic search requires time and effort. Normally, a new website will probably not emerge at the top of the search results. It takes time for the search engine to locate the site.

▼ The goal of search engine optimization is to increase the chances a company's brand will emerge when individuals type in particular search words.

nyul/Fotolia

Some studies suggest that the impact of organic listings can be impressive. For sites that come up on the first page of a search or within the top ten, web traffic increases nine fold. For second- and third-page listings, web traffic increases six fold. In terms of sales, being a top ten listing has resulted in a 42 percent increase in sales the first month and a 100 percent increase the second month.[43]

The third optimization method, *paid search ads*, includes small text boxes that pop up when a particular word is typed in or it can be paid to link boxes at the top or side of a search result. A comScore study suggests that search ads have a strong positive impact on brand awareness, perception, and purchase intentions—even when consumers do not click the paid search ad.[44] The study revealed that for brands in the top search positions:

- The paid search ads generated a 160 percent increase in unaided awareness.
- Consumers were 20 percent more likely to have a positive perception of the brands.
- Consumers were 30 percent more likely to consider purchasing the brand.

Companies spend large amounts on search engine optimization. The typical click-through rate for online advertising remains around 0.2 percent; for search advertising, it is around five percent.[45] Although the early results are impressive, marketers should remember that search engine optimization represents a long-term investment. The effects do not occur quickly. Moving to the top ten listings of a search can take months or years. It requires optimizing content, programming, and finding the codes that will be picked up by search engines.

Search ads can be effective for local businesses. Barbara Oliver owns a boutique jewelry store in Williamsville, New York. She spent $50 per month in Google search ads targeted to an 80-mile radius of her store. It resulted in more customers than all of her offline advertising. With Google Places local directory, someone typing in the keywords designated by Oliver within an 80-mile radius of Williamsville was likely to see the search ad. Its effectiveness can be enhanced by smartphones and their GPS capabilities as well as Facebook and Foursquare where people sign in with their locations, which means visitors to the Williamsville area may see Oliver's search ad.[46]

International Implications

objective 8.8

How can companies successfully conduct digital marketing programs in international markets?

The ability to reach customers worldwide constitutes one of the major advantages that e-commerce holds over brick-and-mortar retail stores. Some online companies are still forced to turn away international orders because they do not have processes in place to fill them. This means that while the internet makes it possible to sell items in an international marketplace, some companies are not prepared to go global. Obstacles to selling across national boundaries include global shipping problems due to a lack of sufficient structure, communication barriers, and other technological barriers.[47] Also, internet companies must follow local exporting and importing laws.

Shipping Issues

One key to the effective launch of a global e-commerce site is preparing to make international shipments. Air transport may be affordable for smaller products; DHL Worldwide Express, FedEx, and UPS offer excellent shipping options. Larger merchandise normally can be shipped by a freight forwarder that finds the best mode of delivery, from ships to trucks to rail. Air transport companies and freight forwarders both offer specialized logistics software and provide the proper documentation and forms to meet importing and exporting regulations in every country served.

▼ International shipping is an important component of a global e-commerce business.

il-fede/Fotolia

Communication Issues

Developing a website that appeals to the audience in each country will be a key task. It includes adding information that someone in another country would require, such as the country code for telephone numbers. It also requires removing or changing colors, words, or images that might offend a particular group of people in another country.

New globalization software has been developed for companies expanding into other countries. One software package translates an English-language website into a large number of foreign languages. Another valuable feature that the software offers is "cultural adaptation," which adjusts a website's terminology, look, and feel to suit local norms. The software also has a feature in which the content developed in one location can easily be deployed to all sites around the world. This provides a more consistent look to the websites, without someone spending time modifying each foreign site. The software makes it easier to prepare a website in the proper native language and conform to local customs.[48]

Technology Issues

The technical side of international e-commerce remains challenging. Software compatibility continues to present unresolved technical issues. Ideally, these various technologies will eventually be merged into a single system. Currently, the bandwidth for handling internet traffic varies considerably. Information technology staff members are involved in every step of an internationalization process in order to overcome the potential technical glitches.

A coherent IMC strategy utilizes local input from the various countries involved. The brand on an internet site should stay consistent from one country to the next and present the company's primary marketing message. For IBM, this meant using local companies in each country to design individual websites and provide the information used on each site. To ensure consistency, IBM designs the main marketing messages at its central office, but then local companies translate the messages and add reseller contact and pricing information.

In the future, the growth of international e-commerce will continue to rise. Firms that get in on the ground floor are likely to enjoy a major marketing advantage.

Summary

Digital marketing combines all of the components of e-commerce, internet marketing, social media, and mobile marketing. Digital marketing includes anything with a digital footprint. An effective IMC program incorporates these new elements into the advertising and promotions plan.

The transition from Web 1.0 to Web 4.0 changed the ways in which consumers communicate and interact with companies. The key characteristics of Web 4.0 include customer engagement, cloud operations, and web participation.

An e-commerce website includes a catalog, a shopping cart, a payment collection method, and a store locator. Customers should believe the process is secure and be enticed to change buying habits. Effective e-commerce programs seek to engage customers who have abandoned shopping carts prior to making purchases. Three incentives that help people alter buying patterns are financial incentives, greater convenience, and added value. Quality programs overcome consumer concerns about privacy and security when using websites.

Digital marketing strategies begin with interactive marketing, which is the development of marketing programs that create interplay between customers and businesses. It assists the marketing department in targeting potential customers with personalized information and engages the consumer with the product and company. Content marketing can be used to provide useful information and product-use solutions to customers. Location-based advertising, or geo-targeting, involves reaching customers where they are located by contacting their mobile communication devices. Behavioral targeting utilizes web data to identify the individuals who are most likely to purchase an item. Video tactics involve placing marketing messages on various forms of video content. Further, customer engagement can take place through the distribution of blogs and newsletters. Blogs create a new form of word-of-mouth advertising. Blogs can be company-sponsored or posted by individual internet users.

Email can supplement an integrated program. Web analytics assist in directing email blasts to the most viable markets. Email newsletters help create brand awareness, drive traffic to a website, and spur sales.

Online web advertising tends to reach younger, more internet-savvy consumers. It includes banner advertising, classified and media/video advertising, search engine optimization, and paid search ads. Offline advertising can be used to build a brand's reputation and brand loyalty. Brand spiraling may be used to combine the internet program with advertising in traditional media. Tailor-made websites accompany many direct and email campaigns using personalized URLs or PURLs.

Search engine optimization (SEO) is the process of increasing the probability of a particular company's website emerging from a search. Paid search insertions, natural or organic emergence, and paid search ads can help achieve this goal.

International markets may also be served by e-commerce enterprises, especially when cultural differences, shipping problems, and internet capability problems can be solved. Information technology departments play a key role in solving the internet problems. Shipping issues and language differences also require attention in this lucrative and growing marketplace.

Key Terms

digital marketing Marketing that incorporates the components of e-commerce, internet marketing, mobile marketing, and social media

e-commerce Selling goods and services on the internet

cyberbait A type of lure or attraction that brings people to a website

interactive marketing The development of marketing programs that create interplay between consumers and businesses

content marketing (or *branded content*) Providing useful information and product use solutions to potential customers

geo-targeting Advertising designed to reach customers where they are located based on contacting their mobile communication devices

behavioral targeting Using web data to identify and target individuals most likely to purchase an item

dwell rate Measures the proportion of ad impressions that resulted in users clicking an ad or mousing over it

dwell time Measures the amount of time individuals spend engaged with an advertisement

blogs The online musings of an individual or group; the term is derived from "web logs"

widgets Mini-applications embedded in a banner ad that permit a consumer access to some form of dynamic content provided by an external source other than the company where the ad resides

brand spiraling The practice of using traditional media to promote and attract consumers to a website

personalized URLs (PURLs) A personalized web page preloaded with the customer's personal data, contact information, purchase behavior, and previous interactions with the company

search engine optimization (SEO) The process of increasing the probability of a particular company's website emerging from a search

MyMarketingLab

Go to **mymktlab.com** to complete the problems marked with this icon ✪.

Review Questions

8-1. Is the internet an open environment?

8-2. What stage of internet development saw the arrival of social networks?

8-3. What is e-commerce?

8-4. In what circumstances is channel integration vitally important to a business?

8-5. Why is shopping cart abandonment so common for online retailers?

8-6. How do you avoid shopping cart abandonment?

8-7. What is interactive marketing?

✪ **8-8.** Describe content marketing.

8-9. What is geo-targeting, or location-based, advertising?

8-10. What is behavioral targeting?

✪ **8-11.** What is a blog? How can blogs be used in marketing communication programs?

8-12. Identify and describe the elements of an effective email campaign in marketing.

8-13. What primary forms of online or web advertising are used by marketing teams?

8-14. How can magazines utilize smartphone use?

8-15. Can traditional media help online branding?

8-16. What is a personalized URL or PURL?

✪ **8-17.** What is meant by the term search engine optimization (SEO)? How can it be accomplished?

8-18. What challenges must be overcome to establish an international e-commerce operation?

Critical Thinking Exercises

DISCUSSION QUESTIONS

8-19. Examine the characteristics of Web 1.0 to Web 4.0. Discuss how the internet affects your daily life. Interview individuals in each of the following age categories about their use of the internet: 30–39, 40–59, 60+. Relate their conversations to Web 1.0, Web 2.0, Web 3.0, and Web 4.0.

✪ **8-20.** What types of goods or services have you purchased online during the past year? Have your parents or grandparents purchased anything online? If so, compare your purchases and attitudes toward buying via the internet with theirs. If neither you, your parents, nor your grandparents have used the internet to make purchases, why not?

8-21. Which form of cyberbait might best help solve the problem of shopping cart abandonment? Would any form of cyberbait help alleviate consumer concerns about privacy and security? Defend your answers.

8-22. Look through the digital marketing strategies identified in Figure 8.7. Discuss each strategy as it relates to your online experience. Which strategies are the most successful at reaching you? Why? Which are the least effective? Why?

8-23. Accepting cookies means that sites can make personalized offers to you. The cookies remain until the cache is deleted. What products or services have you been offered in this way?

8-24. Do businesses have your mobile phone number to make sales calls or to send text message offers? How did they get the number? How would you go about removing your number from their call lists? How do you avoid giving out your number?

8-25. Interview five individuals of different ages about blogs. What percent have read, launched, or participated in blogging on the internet? What was each person's motivation? What is your experience with blogs? If you have never read or contributed to a blog, why not?

8-26. A high percentage of internet traffic begins with someone conducting a search. Compare and contrast the concepts of paid search insertions, organic search results, and paid search ads from the perspective of a consumer wanting to locate websites that provide information and products on camping. Compare and contrast paid search insertions, organic search, and paid search ads from the viewpoint of Coleman, a company that sells camping supplies and equipment.

Integrated Learning Exercises

8-27. Best Buy was a late e-commerce entrant, but has developed a strong e-commerce component. The key to Best Buy's success, according to Barry Judge, vice president of marketing, is, "We do a lot of one-to-one marketing. We're not overly focused on where the consumers buy." The website carries every product that Best Buy stocks. It offers personalized services, along with convenient pick-up and fair return policies to entice consumers to shop. Consumers can purchase items on the internet and either have them shipped directly to them or pick them up at the closest store. Shoppers can use the internet to see if Best Buy stocks a particular item, to determine what the item costs, and to gather product information. What is the advantage of this strategy? Access the website at **www.bestbuy.com**. Evaluate it in terms of ease of use and product information, and then locate the Best Buy closest to you. Next, access Tiger Direct's website at **www.tigerdirect.com**. Compare it to Best Buy's site. Select a product, such as a camcorder, to compare the two websites.

8-28. Pick one of the following product categories and access the websites of two companies that sell the product. What types of financial incentives are offered on each company's website to encourage you to purchase? What about the other two types of incentives, greater convenience and added value? What evidence do you see for them? Compare and contrast the two companies in terms of incentives offered.

a. Contacts or eyeglasses
b. Water skis
c. Clothes
d. Cameras
e. Camping supplies

8-29. Find the websites of the five most popular companies that provide package delivery services in your own country. How do they differentiate themselves? What are their reputations, particularly in terms of reliability and customer service? Are the sites easy to navigate? Do they address any specific customer concerns or issues with their services?

8-30. Pick two of the following e-commerce sites. Discuss each of the characteristics of Web 4.0 e-commerce sites listed in Figure 8.2. Compare and contrast the two sites for each of the characteristics.

a. Travelocity (**www.travelocity.com**)
b. Wells Fargo Bank (**www.wellsfargo.com**)
c. **WeddingChannel.com** (**www.weddingchannel.com**)
d. Bluefly (**www.bluefly.com**)
e. Diesel (**www.diesel.com**)
f. Quiznos (**www.quiznos.com**)

8-31. Blogs provide opportunities for individuals and businesses to share information, thoughts, and opinions. Go to Google Blog Search at **www.google.com/blogsearch**. Type in a topic you are interested in that is related to advertising and marketing communications, such as "advertising to children." Locate three blogs on the topic you chose. Discuss who initiated the blog and the value of the information on the blog.

8-32. Access each of the following search engines. For each one, discuss how it handles paid search advertising when you type in a search, such as "running shoes." What ads do you see as display ads, and what ads are part of the search results? Discuss the differences among the five search engines. Which one do you like the best? Why?

a. Google (**www.google.com**)
b. Yahoo! (**www.yahoo.com**)
c. AOL Search (**http://search.aol.com**)
d. Bing (**www.bing.com**)

8-33. Use a search engine to locate three digital advertising agencies. For each agency, describe what type of digital marketing services the agency provides. If you owned a small restaurant chain, which agency would you hire for your digital marketing program? Why? (Provide the URL for each agency in your response.)

8-34. Access the internet and locate five banner ads. Copy and paste the banner ads in a Word document. Evaluate each banner ad in terms of design and appeal. Access each banner ad by clicking on it. Discuss the result of clicking on the banner ad. Of the five banner ads, which yielded the best results in terms of providing useful information? Why?

Blog Exercises

Access the authors' blog for this textbook at the URLs provided to complete these exercises. Answer the questions that are posed on the blog.

8-35. Advil - **http://blogclowbaack.net/2014/05/12/advil-chapter-8/**

8-36. Digital Marketing Strategies - **http://blogclowbaack.net/2014/05/12/digital-marketing-strategies-chapter-8/**

8-37. Search Engine Optimization - **http://blogclowbaack.net/2014/05/12/seo-chapter-8/**

Student Project

CREATIVE CORNER

Bluefly's marketing team wants to enhance the company's brand name and internet presence. They have asked you to be an internet advertising consultant. Access the Bluefly website at **www.bluefly.com**. Once you feel comfortable with the company, prepare a banner ad that can be used on the internet. Design a magazine ad that can be used with the banner advertisement. Then, design an email promotion that can be sent to customers who purchased from **Bluefly.com**, but it has been at least 90 days since that purchase.

CASE 1 BLACK FRIDAY AND HONG KONG CYBER SALES

Each year, as the United States undergoes the traditional Thanksgiving to Christmas holiday season, businesses across the country hope for strong sales. The term "Black Friday" resulted from the realization that the Friday following Thanksgiving was the day many retailers moved from the "red" (loss) to the "black" (profit).

Black Friday has evolved over the years. From the traditional rush to shop, retailers began seizing the opportunity by offering special discounts on limited amounts of merchandise, opening stores in the early morning. Bargain hunters lined up in the middle of the night, and patrons regularly fight over the last item on a sales rack. In 2011, some stores actually opened at midnight on Thanksgiving evening, trying to optimize sales.

According to an eCommerce Tracker Survey, some 96 percent of all Hong Kong residents browsed online for a variety of products and services over the course of 2012. The survey also found that 84 percent made an online transaction and that 87 percent would do so in the following year. The most popular online products were electronics and cosmetics. Although Black Friday can be considered as a uniquely American phenomenon, businesses such as the credit card company Visa have been quick to note the potential for business by making it easier for Hong Kong online shoppers to take advantage of U.S. Black Friday sales. Visa's partnership with com-Gateway made it possible for U.S. retailers to accept non-U.S. credit cards and, for many that had not done it before, to ship to Hong Kong. In this way Hong Kong residents could take advantage of discounts of up to 80 percent.

Hong Kong residents are not alone in wanting the big global brand names—comGateway also provided Chinese language support.

According to data compiled by Fiftyone, a global e-commerce solutions provider, online spending on Black Friday by international consumers was twice as high in 2012 than it was in 2011. U.S. retailers were actually marketing their sales internationally and this included Hong Kong, Australia, and the United Kingdom. Hong Kong was in the top five as far as international sales were concerned. Sales figures leapt by at least 300 percent compared to an average day.

Across China, Black Friday has still some catching up to do. Singles Day on the November 11 each year, a version of Valentines Day, generated sales revenue of $3 billion. Black Friday online sales managed $1.042 billion. China has 193 million online shoppers—the United States has 170 million—so the potential for growth is enormous.[49]

8-38. Describe the differences between individuals who shop in retail stores on Black Friday and individuals who buy online. Are they the same individuals or different? Justify your answer.

8-39. Discuss for your personal view of Black Friday. Do you participate? Why or why not? Do you think retailers take advantage of consumers on this day? Why or why not?

8-40. How can retailers integrate shopping in the store with shopping online?

8-41. What types of advertising and promotions should be sent out to consumers immediately preceding the Black Friday event?

8-42. As some companies now begin Christmas advertising as early as mid-October, how will the role of Black Friday be affected?

8-43. Design a magazine ad for an electronics product encouraging consumers to make an online purchase on Black Friday. You must use an incentive other than a steep price discount.

CASE 2 ONLINE GROUP BUYING SERVICES: COMPETING IN THE MIDDLE EAST

The e-commerce space is just developing in the Middle East region, with still considerable wariness on the part of consumers across the Arab world to buy goods and services online. Market research results nevertheless reveal a small but growing segment, which is keen on online purchases. Most common purchases included cinema tickets, flight tickets, books, and CDs.

Group Buying Services (GBS), where businesses partner with a group buying site to offer a limited time deal with the site's members, has taken off in the region with the growth of e-commerce, with several group buying sites established in recent years. GBS enables local companies to promote their business to a large group of "opt-in" buyers. Interested businesses offer users a discount of 50 percent or more in the form of a for-purchase deal or coupon. Each group buying site typically offers only a primary deal and one or two "side" deals per market per day, guaranteeing the local business significant reach among a user base that has already opted to receive the promotions. Businesses pay a relatively high price for the advertising/promotion, considering both the 50 percent discount on the deal and the fee of 50 percent of the deal proceeds a GBS typically takes.

The first group buying website to cater to the Middle East market was GoNabit, a local startup that was launched on May 2011. GoNabit first offered deals in Dubai, and then in Abu Dhabi a month later. Over its first year, the company claims hundreds of thousands of Middle Eastern users have saved more than US$5 million. GoNabit has since expanded operational websites to Lebanon, Jordan, and Egypt.

Second in the Middle East region was another local startup, Cobone, launched in September 2011 in the UAE and emerging as the number one player in this space. Currently the company

▲ Group buying sites have helped customers in the Middle East to overcome their reservations about shopping online.

is present in Lebanon, Jordan, Saudi Arabia, Bahrain, and Qatar. Cobone claims monthly growth of up to 50 percent and a 70 percent share market in the Middle East and North Africa, and more than 500,000 Cobone users have saved $10 million over 10 months.

Both Cobone and GoNabit have grown very quickly and hired many employees in 2011. The small success of these startups attracted their Western counterparts to the Middle East. Groupon launched a UAE website with much fanfare. Headquartered in Washington, LivingSocial—a global GBS provider—entered the Middle East market in 2011 through the acquisition of GoNabit. For GoNabit, this was the opportunity to be sustained by a larger company, a key factor enabling long-term survival with this business model.

However, LivingSocial was unable to get its Middle East operations on a path to sustained profitability and closed down its Middle East operations in August 2012, exiting the market after just one year of operation.

At the beginning of 2012, LivingSocial laid out its strategic plan. They decided to continue to focus aggressively on areas with the greatest opportunity for growth and profitability. As a result, LivingSocial suspended its Middle East operations and direct company resources to other regions.

The companies struggle to distinguish themselves for the same pool of potential customers. Global companies had to compete with local group discount services, where the local first mover has a significant advantage in the daily deals space.

Another factor that every GBS and internet retailer will have to overcome in the Middle East is the reluctance on the part of shoppers to make online purchases. According to a recent research study, 18–28 percent of respondents in UAE and Kingdom of Saudi Arabia have used websites which offer discounts for limited periods (similar to GBS providers). This percentage is significantly lower in Egypt (6 percent) and Morocco (8 percent). However, in the Gulf, another challenge is that the market in each individual country is small, and so the key is to have a presence in the whole Arab world as opposed to being in only one or two countries.[50]

8-44. Describe the difference between traditional vouchers such as voucher books and GBS websites.

8-45. Discuss your personal view of GBS. Do you participate in them? Why or why not? Do you think retailers take advantage of consumers on these sites? Why or why not?

8-46. What types of advertising should be sent out to consumers promoting deals on GBS websites?

8-47. In your opinion what are the main factors that led to the failure of LivingSocial in the Middle East? What could they have done to survive and get sustained profits?

8-48. Design an email ad for some type of electronics encouraging consumers to make a purchase on a GBS website. You must use some other incentive other than a steep price discount.

MyMarketingLab

Go to **mymktlab.com** for the following Assisted-graded writing questions:

8-49. A high percentage of internet traffic begins with someone conducting a search. Compare and contrast the concepts of paid search insertions, organic search results, and paid search ads from the perspective of a consumer wanting to locate websites that provide information and products on camping. Compare and contrast paid search insertions, organic search, and paid search ads from the viewpoint of Coleman, a company that sells camping supplies and equipment.

8-50. Blogs provide opportunities for individuals and businesses to share information, thoughts, and opinions. Go to Google Blog Search at **www.google.com/blogsearch**. Type in a topic you are interested in that is related to advertising and marketing communications, such as "advertising to children." Locate three blogs on the topic you chose. Discuss who initiated the blog and the value of the information on the blog.

Chapter 9 Social Media

Chapter Objectives

After reading this chapter, you should be able to answer the following questions:

9.1 What constitutes a social network?

9.2 What are the unique characteristics of the primary social media websites?

9.3 What is the nature of social media marketing?

9.4 Which social media marketing strategies do companies employ?

9.5 What social media measurement metrics are available to marketers?

9.6 How can marketers use social media strategies in international operations?

Overview

The previous chapter explained the evolution from Web 1.0 to Web 4.0. A major social and technological change facilitated that progression. The emergence of social media networks has altered the ways individuals interact with families, friends, businesses, and even strangers on a routine basis. The continual growth of social network websites presents opportunities and challenges to marketing departments from the smallest single family business to major corporations. Instant communication creates the potential to create buzz and excitement in a short period of time. Marketers are able to develop more sophisticated interactions with customers. At the same time, negative word of mouth and other developments may quickly damage a brand across a wide range of customers and the general public. Marketing communications experts understand the need to quickly adapt to this exciting new world. One firm that has been able to benefit from the possibilities that social media networks offer is Wholly Guacamole.

WHOLLY GUACAMOLE

The biggest problem with an avocado may be that, as soon as one is cut open, it begins to brown. Wholly Guacamole's founder, Don Bowden, sought to solve this problem. He discovered the process of High Pressure Processing, which was quickly marketed as "fresherized" guacamole. It results in a "100% all natural, fresh tasting product." Pre-made guacamole can be sold in grocery stores and in food markets. It has become a staple for many companies featuring the ingredient in sandwiches and other menu items. Wholly Guacamole's website indicates that, "We always use real Hass avocados and natural ingredients that never include preservatives (except Wholly Salsa Avocado Verde Dip), artificial flavoring or fillers."[1]

Wholly Guacamole's marketing team understands the potential impact of social media on a product's success. The company successfully leveraged it to create brand awareness, develop a strong brand, and boost sales. While social media played a significant role in recent campaigns, the messages were fully integrated with traditional advertising media channels as well as digital components in order to achieve the greatest impact.

WONG SZE FEI/Fotolia

▲ Guacamole has become a staple for many individuals to use on sandwiches.

Marketers at Wholly Guacamole increased the power of the company's limited advertising budget by creating alliances with several organizations, including *The Biggest Loser* television program, Sonic Drive-in, Disney, and the Disney movie, *Wimpy Kid*. The marketing and social media efforts designed for the co-brands led to a more powerful impact. For instance, the social media component of the alliance with *The Biggest Loser* produced 111,000 Facebook fans; 3,000 Twitter followers; comments from 200+ bloggers; more than 1,350 likes; 2,140 comments; and almost 1.6 million impressions. The connection with *Wimpy Kid* resulted in more than 46 million Facebook impressions, resulting in 3,700 new Wholly Guacamole fans. The Sonic program generated more than 1,200 tweets and 20 million impressions.

These efforts illustrate the power of social media. While the term has multiple meanings, in this context, **social media** is defined as any digital tool or venue that allows individuals to socialize on the web. A **social network** is a social structure of individuals and/or organizations that are tied together in some manner. **Social media marketing** is the utilization of social media and/or social networks to market a product, company, or brand.

Fresherized Foods

▲ A digital banner advertisement featuring the tie-in between Wholly Guacamole and the television show *The Biggest Loser*.

This chapter first explains the basics of social networks and their relationships with marketing programs. Next, popular websites are briefly described, along with examples of how companies incorporated them into marketing and advertising programs. The third section explains the basics of social media marketing in greater detail. Social media marketing tactics are explored. A brief discussion of the additional issues associated with international social media marketing programs concludes the chapter.

Social Networks

objective 9.1
What constitutes a social network?

Numerous popular social networking sites currently operate (see Figure 9.1). **General social networking sites** are broadly based and are designed to appeal to all demographics, regardless of gender, age, race, income, or education. General sites provide venues for interpersonal communication. Individuals can stay in touch, learn what others in their networks are doing, share events in their lives, and make new friends. Facebook is the most well-known general social networking site.

A **niche social networking site** focuses on a specific interest, hobby, or demographic group. Some, such as LinkedIn, offer interactions between businesspeople. Dating sites provide an outlet to meet potential mates including target groups on sites such as OurTime, ChristianMingle, and FarmersOnly. Others cater to family or lifestyle interests such as single parents, gays, and lesbians. Special interest and hobby sites vary widely and include sites that focus on a sport such as skiing; a hobby such as photography; or special interests such as gardening. Shopping networks provide venues for individuals to share product reviews and information about brands and products. These are not e-commerce sites but rather provide a meeting place that enables individuals to share information with others about product or brand along with comments about their shopping experiences.

- General social networking sites
- Niche social networking sites
  - Business
  - Family and lifestyle
  - Dating
  - Special interests and hobbies
  - Shopping
- Social bookmarking sites

▲ **FIGURE 9.1**
Types of Social Networking Sites

Social bookmarking sites allow individuals to share bookmarks of websites. While most people bookmark their favorite sites on computers, social bookmarking sites make these public. They can be organized in a wide variety of ways and accessed at any time by anyone. Individuals may also provide comments about sites they have bookmarked and encourage comments by others.

Social Media Sites

objective 9.2
What are the unique characteristics of the primary social media websites?

The social media landscape rapidly evolves. Marketers recognize the importance of examining the major social media sites and who uses them. Some differences in the audiences of each of the major social media sites can be identified, as shown in Figure 9.2. Overall, females utilize social media more than men and approximately 42 percent of online consumers use multiple sites.[2] The most widely visited sites currently are Facebook, Twitter, YouTube, Instagram, and Pinterest. Facebook outpaces all other sites. Two-thirds of internet users have a Facebook page compared to between 13 percent and 16 percent for Instagram, Pinterest, and Twitter.[3]

The demographic makeup of each social media network's visitor group differs. Each site appeals to varying types of people. While the social networking sites continually change, marketers find it worthwhile to examine each one in terms of its usefulness to a brand in a social media marketing program. A brief review of the most often-visited sites follows.

Social Networking Site	Percent of Internet Users	Primary Users
Facebook	67%	Adults 18–29 Females
Twitter	16%	Adults 18–29 African-Americans Urban residents
Pinterest	15%	Adults under 50 Females Caucasians Some college
Instagram	13%	Adults 18–29 Females African-Americans, Latinos Urban residents

▶ **FIGURE 9.2**
Social Media Users
Source: Based on Maeve Duggan and Joanna Brenner, "The Demographics of Social Media Users – 2012," *Pew Research Center*, www.pewresearch.org, February 14, 2013.

Facebook

Facebook, the largest social media site, houses more than 1.2 billion users worldwide. It presents the largest source of display ads of all social networks, with a 17.7 share.[4] According to *AdWeek*, Facebook's popularity comes from a blend of "sheer size of fan base, record of publishing useful content, and the extent of consumer interaction that is offered."

Facebook generates almost $2 billion in annual advertising revenues. In addition to brands being advertised on its pages, Facebook recently expanded its advertising services to allow marketers to target customers on mobile devices based on an individual's activity outside of the Facebook site. This behavioral targeting tool—called "custom audiences"—allows marketers to gather information from the company's websites and applications, and then use that data to target individuals when they visit Facebook, whether on a mobile phone, tablet, or desktop computer.[5]

Michaeljung/Fotolia

▲ Females tend to use social media more than men; blacks trend toward using Twitter and Instagram.

Although Facebook remains the largest social media network, the number of teen users has declined by more than 25 percent in the last three years. At the same time, the number of older consumers, individuals 55 years old or older, increased 80 percent to 28 million. Part of the reason why teens leave Facebook may be the presence of their parents and grandparents. Many teens prefer the private messaging that is available on Twitter or Snapchat.

In addition to the changing demographic profile of Facebook users, only a small percentage now share details of their lives on a daily basis. Only ten percent update their status daily and only four percent update it more than once a day. Approximately 15 percent comment on photos once or more a day. Many believe Facebook has peaked in terms of number of users and frequency of use. While this may be true, the site still has more than 1.2 billion users, which makes it an attractive social network for marketers.[6] According to Brad Kim, vice president of research firm Curebit, compared to Twitter, Facebook generates ten times the number of shares, 20 times the amount of site traffic, and 20 times the number of new customers acquired. According to Kim, the reason for this vast difference in effectiveness is that Twitter tends to be a one-way message whereas Facebook features two-way communication between friends.[7]

The companies with the most successful Facebook presence, according to *Adweek*, are Starbucks, Coca-Cola, Best Buy, and Microsoft. Starbucks has 3.7 million fans, compared to 3.5 million for Coke.[8] An independent study by WetPaint and the Altimeter Group notes that these companies and others that have high levels of social media activity tend to increase revenues more than companies that lack a social media presence.[9]

Twitter

The Twitter microblogging service allows individuals and companies to send out tweets with a maximum of 140 characters per message. Twitter's users are more racially diverse than the internet as a whole or Facebook. Approximately 41 percent of the 54 million Twitter users come from a minority race. While a large number of users are Hispanics, Twitter's primary strength is among African Americans. About 18 percent of Twitter users are African American, which is almost double that of internet users. Among those in this group ages 18–29, the percentage is close to 40 percent. For companies that target minorities, especially African Americans, Twitter can be an effective social media network.[10]

▼ An advertisement for Wholly Guacamole and Sonic appearing on Facebook.

Fresherized Foods

Twitter offers an effective method of reaching customers. Marketers may monitor what customers

Michaeljung/Fotolia

▲ Starbucks utilized Twitter for a successful campaign entitled "Tweet-a-Coffee".

say about a company or brand. Software, such as Tweetscan or Summize, locates a brand or company name mentioned in tweets. Company officials are able to respond or gather the information for future use or evaluation. It provides valuable information regarding customer perceptions of the brand and what they are saying.

JetBlue, Starbucks, Comcast, H&R Block, and Southwest Airlines utilize Twitter. Starbucks launched a Twitter campaign entitled "Tweet-a-Coffee," which allowed individuals to give a $5 gift card to a friend by putting both the hashtag @tweetacoffee and the person's Twitter handle in the tweet. Within two months, the campaign generated $180,000 in purchases. In addition to the revenue generated by the program, Starbucks collected 54,000 Twitter IDs along with additional information on the Starbucks account each customer had to set up to utilize the Twitter gift card function.[11]

For small local businesses, Twitter can be an effective means of marketing. Three weeks after Curtis Kimball opened his crème pastry cart in San Francisco, he noticed a stranger who had lined up to purchase some of his desserts. When quizzed, the man said he heard about the pastry cart from Twitter. Kimball created a Twitter account and now has a fan base of 5,400 customers who wait for him to post the flavor of the day at his store.[12]

YouTube

The fastest-growing area of social media networking involves posting videos, especially on YouTube. Experts forecast that by 2017, YouTube will have more views, likes, and shares than either Facebook or Twitter. Consumers create their own videos with mobile devices; and, as a result, the number of videos produced grows dramatically every year. This proliferation of videos has led to a new venue for fans to interact with brands. They are no longer passive customers but passionate fans using videos to share their thoughts. Figure 9.3 highlights the ways consumers share videos online through YouTube as well as other video sharing social networks.

A large number of consumers have a YouTube channel where they post their favorite videos. They create some; others are videos they like. One type of video that has seen a sharp increase is broadcast ads produced by brands. These may be television ads or digital ads produced for the internet. Passionate fans who see an advertisement they like re-post the ad on their channels or on YouTube for their friends to see. The vast majority of ads posted by individuals are positive responses to commercials they liked. There are instances in which individuals post ads for some negative reasons. When this occurs, brand managers must be quick to react.

A second trend includes video reviews of products. Rather than write a review and post it on a blog or a website, consumers create videos in which they talk about the brand and their experiences. Most are made by positive and passionate fans praising a product, although some are negative. In one circumstance, Covergirl had 251 million total views on YouTube. 249 million of them (99 percent) were consumer-created videos talking about the brand. Similar statistics apply to other brands, such as Oreos, where 92 percent of the views are fan-created messages and Revlon, with 99 percent consumer-created videos.

Closely tied with consumer video reviews is the re-creation of broadcast ads. Swiffer has encountered an explosion of interest in the brand on YouTube. Many of the company's ads have been posted and re-posted by fans, along with a large number of product reviews. Recently, however, 150 people have re-created one of the television ads and posted their versions on YouTube. They are shown mopping the floor with a Swiffer mop or dusting with a Swiffer product, just as in the agency-produced ad in which the actor breaks out into a dance. The total number of views for all three types of Swiffer fan-created videos exceeds 10.5 million, compared to only 225,000 views of the videos produced by Swiffer. Clearly the popularity of fan-produced material exceeds company-produced materials.[13]

- Uploading broadcast ads
- Video reviews of products
- Re-creation of ads
- Creating consumer produced how-to videos
- Capturing real-time events
- Creating branded videos

▲ **FIGURE 9.3**
Trends in Consumer Video Sharing

In the past, when consumers wanted to know how to use a product, fix a product, or repair it, they would visit the brand's website or contact technical support. Now, many turn to YouTube. Consumers post how-to videos that show ways to use a particular product and how to fix or repair a particular item. Seeing a demonstration on video makes it easier to understand than reading a reference manual or the step-by-step instructions presented on a blog or website.

Built-in video features and still cameras in cell phones allow consumers to capture events as they occur. Many products become part of the event, either in the video or mentioned by the consumer starring in the video. Occasionally, these go viral. For instance, after Charles Ramsey rescued a captured Amanda Berry, in his interview he mentioned McDonald's. The Ramsey video resulted in more than 11 million views in less than 24 hours. McDonald's was mentioned more than 6,000 times as consumers shared the video with friends. Reacting to the buzz, McDonald's marketing team sent a tweet supporting Ramsey and gave him free hamburgers for one year. Such positive buzz can only occur when marketers actively listen to social media and quickly take advantage of real-time events.

Community Trust Bank

▲ Popular advertisements, such as the ones with Terry Bradshaw produced for Community Trust Bank, are often posted and shared on YouTube.

One final marketing approach involves creating branded videos. Devin Graham is a 30-year-old filmmaker with the YouTube handle of "devinsupertramp." He creates stunt videos such as the "World's Largest Rope Swing," which had 22 million views; "Human Slingshot Slip and Slide" had 13 million views. He has almost 2 million subscribers to his YouTube channel. His popularity drew the interest of several firms. He now makes daredevil-type branded videos through sponsorships by Mountain Dew and Ford.[14]

Marketing professionals recognize that YouTube presents unique opportunities and challenges. Consumers are sharing videos, producing videos, and talking about videos. Fans create most of them, which means individual companies cannot control the content. Monitoring these videos becomes important because it allows the marketing department to support those that favor the brand and its desired image. For negative videos, company leaders must creatively respond to show they are listening. The negative reviews or posts can also be used to improve the company's products, services, and the image it seeks to project.

Instagram

Instagram, a mobile photo and video social sharing network owned by Facebook, has enjoyed an explosion in popularity during the past few years, with more than 200 million users. Instagram users tend to be young, wealthy, and female. Almost 60 percent visit Instagram every day.

Among the brands that have established a presence on Instagram, the largest is lingerie retailer Victoria's Secret with 4 million followers. Of note, Chanel has no official presence on Instagram but has attracted 5 million photos using the hashtag #chanel. Other brands with a strong presence on Instagram include Ben & Jerry's, Bloomingdale's, Lipton, Macy's, Gucci, and Michael Kors.[15]

Amyinlondon/Fotolia

▲ Bloomingdale's developed a contest encouraging fans to submit selfies along with their favorite beauty or styling tips.

Instagram's recent emergence into social media has caused marketers for various brands to explore the best options to use on the site. Currently, the two most popular tactics are contests and crowdsourcing for photos. Bloomingdale's and Lipton held contests on Instagram. In the Bloomingdale's contest, users were asked to submit selfies with details about a favorite beauty or styling tip. To encourage participation and social sharing, Bloomingdale's posted the photos on a score board where fans could vote for their favorites. Individuals who submitted photos were encouraged to get their friends to vote for them by sharing the link through Instagram and other social media networks. In Lipton's contest, Instagram users were invited to submit "uplifting moments" via Instagram's image-sharing platform to one of four hashtags.[16]

The crowdsourcing of photos followed YouTube's pattern, except the photos were submitted through Instagram. Macy's, West Elm, and Coach recently encouraged fans to submit photos, which were placed on each brand's website, often alongside professional models.

A closely related trend in retailing involves individuals uploading personal pictures wearing a particular brand of clothing, which provides a consumer-to-consumer recommendation. Katherine Lin uploaded photos of herself with friends at the Coachella music festival on Twitter and Instagram. She was wearing a Dannijo necklace she had purchased online. Dannijo marketers saw the photo and posted it on the company's website. Lin was thrilled and instantly shared the posting with friends. Retailers realize the power of word-of-mouth communications. Some retailers post the photos on company websites; others provide a link to the photos, and another group encourages customers to upload photos directly to the company's website. Regardless of the method used, showing consumers wearing the brand's fashions is the objective. It helps consumers connect with the brand through social media and keeps them on the website longer. As a result, sales increase.[17]

▼ Pinterest is a popular social media site for food items, such as recipes by Gulf Coast Seafood.

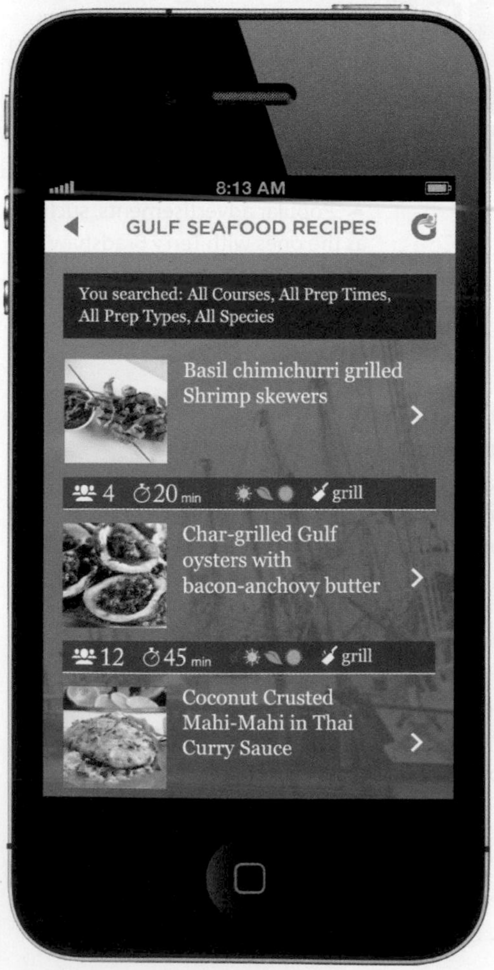

Gulfcoast Sea Food

Pinterest

Pinterest is a bulletin-board style social site that allows users to post photos and image-based articles about events, special interests, or hobbies. Currently, 70 million people use Pinterest, and 70 percent are female. Fashion and food are the two most featured topics on the site, which means retailers and food manufacturers find it to be an attractive outlet.

Land O' Lakes recently offered a promotion on Pinterest entitled "Pin a Meal, Give a Meal." Each time a meal or recipe from Land O' Lakes was pinned on Pinterest, the company donated $1 to the Feeding America foundation. Other companies active on Pinterest include Amazon, Wal-Mart, Apple, QVC, Staples, Best Buy, Netflix, and Sears. QVC and Wal-Mart currently have the most followers, but Amazon and Apple have the most pins on user pinboards.[18]

Social Media Marketing

Brand managers develop social media marketing campaigns for a variety of reasons. Figure 9.4 identifies some of the more common.[19] Two frequently reported rationales are to stay engaged with customers and increase brand exposure to potential customers. To do so, most brands utilize multiple social media networks.

- Engage fans
- Increase brand exposure
- Avenue for customer interaction
- Increase traffic
- Generate leads
- Enhance brand image
- Improve search rankings
- Gather customer intelligence
- Develop loyal fans
- Increase sales

FIGURE 9.4
Reasons for Social Media Marketing
Source: Based on "Social Strategies for 2014," *Wildfire by Google Whitepaper, Ad Age Content Strategy Studio*, October 2013; Michael A. Stelzner, "2013 Social Media Marketing Industry Report," *Social Media Examiner*, www.socialmediaexaminer.com, 2013.

objective 9.3
What is the nature of social media marketing?

As an example, on its 30th anniversary, Hooters of America launched a brand overhaul aimed at winning over female customers while maintaining its predominantly male customer base. Social media provided an integral part of the brand rejuvenation. Prior to the social media launch, Hooters revamped its menu to include more "female-friendly" items, remodeled many of its restaurants, and developed a TV and radio advertising campaign. The heart of the campaign, however, was social media. Hooters fans were urged to share their experiences on Facebook, Twitter, Instagram, YouTube, and other social media platforms. Within 30 days of the launch, consumers had posted 10,000 photos. During the campaign, Hooters' Instagram account grew to more than 25,000 followers, its Facebook page produced more than 2.5 million likes, and it garnered almost 54,000 Twitter followers. The social media campaign pushed Hooters' ranking in the Nation's Restaurant News Social 200 Index from #56 to #12.[20]

When Wholly Guacamole hosted a Lion King DVD giveaway, the program generated 95,301 impressions on Facebook with more than 600 individuals making comments. It also led to an increase of 4,000 followers on Twitter.[21] Giveaways or promotions are not always needed to engage fans through social media or to gain brand exposure, but they can generate additional interest in a brand. In addition, engaging fans with a brand often creates increased customer interactions. These connections take place among fans (or customers) or between fans and the brand. Customer interactions are especially beneficial because they provide word-of-mouth endorsements for the brand. A customer relating her experience with a product carries considerably more weight with other consumers than a company touting its own merits.

▼ Hooters used social media in an effort to win over more female customers while retaining its male customer base.

Monkey Business/Fotolia

Increase Traffic and Enhance Brand Image Social media can also drive traffic, normally to the brand's website. Visitors can click on a URL embedded in a social media contact or message. Companies also take advantage of social media to drive traffic to a retail location such as a restaurant. For business-to-business programs, social media generates leads to be followed up by members of sales staff, including field salespeople, telemarketers, or the email sales force.

Social media may help enhance a brand's image. To achieve this goal, it should become more than just a sounding board for customers. It should offer a venue for solving problems, gathering useful information, and gaining insights. Research by J.D. Power and Associates revealed that, among highly satisfied customers of a brand, 87 percent said their online interactions with the brand positively impacted their perceptions of the brand and their likelihood to purchase a product. Individuals with low satisfaction scores indicated social communications negatively impacted their likelihood of purchasing the item in the future.[22]

Improve Search Rankings Social media can boost organic search rankings with search engines. These increased rankings occur for two reasons. First, individuals more frequently mention the brand name on social media networks, because most algorithms on search engines examine numbers of mentions. Second, if content or comments made about the brand fit the search terms, then the quality of those interactions are increased and various search engines assign greater credibility to the brand.

Fresherized Foods

▲ Wholly Guacamole's marketing team used social media to engage fans with a Lion King DVD giveaway.

Customer Intelligence **Social listening**, or listening to social chatter, often provides enlightening information to marketing professionals. Comments may be negative or positive, but in most cases visitors render honest opinions. Occasionally, social media buzz creates a situation in which the marketing team should react immediately. For instance, when General Mills launched a television advertisement for Cheerios featuring a family with parents from different races, the ad also ran on YouTube. Some of the social media response was immediate, fierce, and unfortunately racist and negative. Within days, the ad had been viewed more than 1.7 million times. Part of the language and views posted on the comment section of YouTube were not family-friendly, which led officials at General Mills to disable the comment function. Although individuals could not make comments about the ad, it could still be viewed.

Despite the negative reactions present on social media, General Mills' management team did not back down. Company leaders believed the ad reflected current American society. According to Camille Gibson, vice president of marketing for Cheerios, "There are many kinds of families, and Cheerios celebrates them all. Despite some serious, negative responses online, it's been a very positive response overall."[23] The Cheerios example illustrates one outcome of gathering customer intelligence. Seldom do marketing employees have to react as quickly as those at General Mills.

Figure 9.5 displays other functions related to social listening. Marketers detect potential problems with its products or some other aspect of a company before it becomes a larger issue. In listening to comments of social media, brand managers avoid reacting to a small number of individuals who may not represent the majority of brand users. Typically, those who express a view over social media are passionate about the topic. It can be a bad experience they want others to know about, or it can be a good experience they want to share. Thus, before deciding to alter a product or take action, marketers try to determine whether the view being expressed represents a small subset of its customer base or the views of a larger segment. In the case of Cheerios, General Mills decided those who expressed negative opinions on social media did not stand for the majority of the population.

Social listening provides an excellent source of ideas for branded content. Problems consumers face, along with the information they seek, can be presented on branded content pages. By listening, the company appears to be in tune with consumers and seen as striving to meet consumer needs. New software packages often have bugs that users detect. These bugs and how they can be solved can be posted on the software creator's blog or website in advance of the majority of users experiencing the problem.

Sparks and Honey is a digital agency that monitors social chatter for various brands. In addition to counting mentions for a brand, the company produces a sentiment score that indicates the level of positive or negative chatter. The agency also employs predictive analytics to estimate how quickly a trend might take effect and have an impact on its clients. The firm produces what it calls a "burst quotient." The figure tells a client how quickly or slowly they might need to respond to a trend occurring in society or whether a response will be necessary.

A trend being examined by marketing professionals involves wearable devices, such as mobile wallets and eye glasses that also serve as cameras. Listening to social interactions among consumers provides valuable information regarding what consumers think of this trend and how soon it will become part of American culture—or rather that it is a fad that will hit and then disappear.

- React to negative feedback
- Detect problems
- Gather topics for branded content
- Predict trends
- Detect patterns or shifts in views
- Identify brand advocates

▲ **FIGURE 9.5**
Functions of Social Listening

In addition to identifying trends, marketers take advantage of social listening to detect patterns or shifts in views of consumers. In the case of the Cheerios ad featuring parents from different races, Sparks and Honey research discovered that the views expressed on YouTube were from a minority and not those of the overall society. Further, the agency detected younger consumers are more open to mixed race marriages than older consumers. Seeing this pattern and the reaction to the Cheerios ad, Sparks and Honey suggested that Gerber produce a video featuring children and young people talking about biracial couples. Rather than being reactive, the agency recommended a proactive approach.[24]

Eurobanks/Fotolia

▲ Through social listening, the research firm Sparks and Honey discovered younger consumers were open to interracial marriages.

Social listening patterns assist in identifying customer advocates. According to social media marketing platform EngageSciences, 4.7 percent of a brand's fans generate nearly all of its social buzz. While other companies argue the figure should be 20 percent of a brand's fans, a small percentage of a company's customers create most of its buzz. The vast majority remains silent or seldom says anything on social media. Consequently, this small set of individuals, whether 4.7 percent or slightly more, offers great value to a brand if the members in the group can be identified. When examining social interactions, brand advocates often exhibit three characteristics:

- Behavioral commitment
- Emotional connection
- Quality communication skills

Advocates often demonstrate behavioral commitment to the brand. They make regular, frequent purchases of the brand. A company with customer purchase data in its database can track actual purchase behaviors. Individual customers can be identified, and those with emotional connections will demonstrate the ties through compliments and praise of the brand. To these consumers, the brand is the best in the world and no other brand is even worth consideration. As a result, they are willing to take extraordinary measures to purchase the item. Although advocates exhibit emotional and behavioral commitments, to be useful to marketers they also should exhibit quality communication skills.[25] They need the ability to effectively express their thoughts, feelings, and emotions. When located, brand managers are able to recruit these individuals to be advocates. Their recommendations can be extremely valuable in recruiting other brand loyalists.

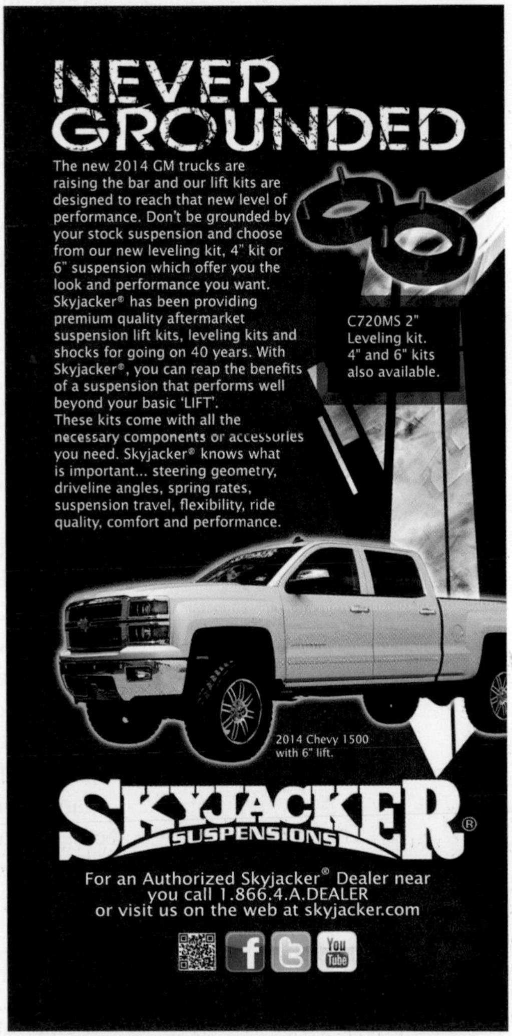

Skyjacker Suspensions

▲ Placing icons for Facebook, Twitter, and YouTube on ads encourages fans of Skyjacker to interact with the brand via social media.

Increase Sales and Build Brand Loyalty Developing brand loyalty and increasing sales are the ultimate goals of any marketing program, including social media marketing. At the same time, if customers view a social media outreach program as merely a masquerade for selling, they might be alienated by such efforts. Instead, marketers should set the primary objective of a social media program to engage consumers with the brand. Increasing sales should be viewed as a by-product of social media marketing.

A recent study conducted by Coca-Cola suggests that online buzz, or talk on social media about the brand, did not have any measurable impact on sales. This finding stunned many outsiders because Coca-Cola has more than 61 million Facebook fans—a total more than any other brand.[26] The researchers concluded that what cannot be determined by just counting social comments or even looking at the sentiment (whether positive or negative)

Foxy_A/Fotolia

▲ L'Oreal developed a successful social media marketing strategy.

is the impact on brand image and brand loyalty. Further, the researchers asked, "If Coca-Cola was not involved with social media, would the impact be negative on sales?" For megabrands such as Coca-Cola, social media marketing cannot be considered as an option. Instead, marketers use this valuable new tool to more deeply engage fans with the brand.

Although Coca-Cola did not find a positive relationship between sales and social buzz, a study by McKinsey & Co. revealed a relationship between sales and negative buzz. A telecom client of McKinsey's suffered a drop in sales of eight percent as a result of negative comments made about the brand on social media.[27]

L'Oreal L'Oreal provides an excellent example of successful social media marketing. According to L'Oreal social media chief Rachel Weiss, "The whole point for us with our social strategy is you can touch a customer at any point within the customer's decision journey." Weiss and others at L'Oreal created a three part strategy designed to maximize the impact of the company's social media efforts.

First, the company employs differing marketing strategies and unique Facebook pages for each country in which products are sold. Georges Edouard-Dias, senior vice president of digital business for L'Oreal, argues that, "This takes us back to the roots of marketing, which is about intuition, intelligence and feeling the market, not about reading or statistics or replicating best practice." In essence, each country is unique and consequently each social media program should be tailored to suit the situation present in each region.

Second, the company seeks to create content that will lead to social conversation. As Rachel Weiss says, "Women love to talk about what lipstick they're wearing, what lipstick was Sofia Vergara wearing from the Emmys. Beauty is always part of the social conversation. Women are always interested in what other women are wearing, doing, and beauty tips." To generate conversations, the L'Oreal Facebook page asks questions, provides beauty advice, and seeks to lead customers to share stories with each other.

Third, social media works best when customers encounter it before and after a purchase. L'Oreal's strategy includes providing "how-to" instructions for consumers in the store prior to any purchase. Then, follow up and tracking takes place on social media such as YouTube, Facebook, and Twitter.[28] For instance, recently the company launched the premium hair color Casting Creme Gloss in India. To achieve the maximum impact of social media, the marketing team integrated offline sales with a Facebook app that required the user to fill in a unique code found on the pack. The app allowed the customer to upload an image with her two best friends to enter a contest to appear in an ad starring Sonam Kapoor. The combination of offline and online promotions led to a 45 percent surge in sales.[29]

Social media may not be always be linked directly to sales from clicking on a link embedded on a site or social media message, but it can still exert a positive influence on other factors, including brand exposure, fan engagement, and enhanced brand image. The quality of fans and their levels of engagement with the brand remain far more important than a company's sales figures or its overall number of Facebook fans or Twitter followers. Social media provides a unique venue for businesses to connect with loyal customers while positively influencing others.

Social Media Marketing Strategies

objective 9.4
Which social media marketing strategies do companies employ?

Social interaction should be the fundamental basis for social media. It involves one consumer talking to another or to many others. The primary difference is that social media facilitates these interactions rather than face-to-face engagement. Skilled marketers recognize the potential inherent in such exchanges. The newness of this type of communication means that company leaders are still developing ideas regarding the best approaches to utilize these venues. Figure 9.6 offers some of the current strategies.

- Content seeding
- Real-time marketing
- Interactive blogs
- Consumer-generated reviews
- Viral marketing

▲ **FIGURE 9.6**
Social Media Strategies

Content Seeding

Farmers, gardeners, and homeowners plant seeds into the ground believing they will germinate and grow into a living plant that bears fruit or flowers. The same concept applies to social media marketing. **Content seeding** involves providing incentives for consumers to share content about a brand. The incentive does not have to be financial, although financial incentives tend to be the most frequently used. An incentive can be information, uniqueness, novelty, or anything that engages consumers with the brand and motivates them to share with others.

A common method of seeding is offering a coupon, rebate, contest, or other financial incentive to share content. Wholly Guacamole posted the following on Facebook about a contest in its alliance with *The Biggest Loser* television show:[30]

WHOLLY IS FOR LOSERS

Wholly Guacamole

BIG APRIL CONTEST. want to go to the live finale of TBL? stay for a week at TBL resort? check out our crazy april contest eatwholly.com/thebiggestloser.com that gives away over 80 prizes.

WIN SOMETHING TODAY HERE. giving away 10 free coupon prize packs w/ wholly,jennie-o turkey products & food should taste good chips.to enter, post your guilty eating pleasure below. be honest, we won't judge (well, maybe a little).

http://eatwholly.com/thebiggestloser.com
eatwholly.com

31,950 Impressions · 0.62% Feedback

Most people like to compete, especially if they believe they can win. When Microsoft launched Windows 7, the company asked high schools to submit videos for a computer lab makeover. The "School Pride" campaign invited visitors to vote on the best video submission. To add intrigue and to encourage sharing, Microsoft used a social graph that allowed web visitors to have friends go to the site and vote for the best entry, thereby increasing a school's chances of winning. The contest generated an increase of almost 75 percent in traffic to the website.[31]

▼ Microsoft used a content seeding contest entitled "School Pride" when it launched Windows 7.

Diego Cervo/Fotolia

One contest that generated a great deal of social buzz was created for Esurance. Rather than spending $4 million on a Super Bowl ad, the company purchased the first ad slot after the game ended, at a cost of $2.5 million. The ad announced that one lucky viewer would win the difference, about $1.5 million, who tweeted the hashtag #EsuranceSave30 within 36 hours of the ad airing.

The ad created a tremendous burst of Twitter shares. Leo Burnett, Esurance's agency, reported the following statistics from the campaign:[32]

- 5.4 million tweets with the #EsuranceSave30 hashtag
- More than 200,000 entries within the first minutes of the television ad
- 2.6 billion social impressions on Twitter
- 332,000 views of Esurance commercial that had been posted to YouTube
- 261,000 new followers on the official Esurance Twitter account
- A 12-fold spike in the visits to the Esurance website within the first hours of the television ad

Occasionally a mistake, or what appears to be a snafu, can create social buzz. JCPenney was the most-mentioned brand on social media that was not part of Super Bowl advertising. The retailer was mentioned 118,201 times, which is 25 times greater than its 30-day average. A typo-laden tweet from JCPenney read "Toughdown Seadawks!! Is sSeattle going toa runaway wit h this???" The tweet mystified Twitter land and was re-tweeted 40,000 times. While some thought it was a mistake or a JCPenney employee who had enjoyed too much to drink, the company revealed the jumbled message was the result of #TweetingWithMittens, a pair of Team USA mittens sold at JCPenney.[33]

A value-added incentive marketers can incorporate into a seed-sharing program is offering customers something exclusive to make them feel special. Sony artist Pitbull generated awareness for a new album prior to its launch through social media. If a person shared a message from Pitbull's website on Facebook or Twitter, it allowed that individual to listen to the CD online before the music went public. If the person got three of his friends to come back to the website, then it unlocked three bonus tracks. The idea of feeling special and offering something unique drove awareness of the album before it launched.[34]

Appealing to consumer altruism, such as a campaign to donate blood in the wake of a tragedy, offers an additional content-seeding approach. Recent storms in the United States created shortages of blood for the Red Cross. The organization used the internet to inspire individuals to share. The organization created a badge announcing the shortage and encouraged individuals to share the badge on their social networks and with their friends.

Humane societies often use social media to get word out about their work and the need for donations. Various companies may use this same tactic but must be extremely careful in how the program is announced and promoted. A brand that supports the Red Cross, a local human society, or other not-for-profit organization might encourage fans to share the information. The approach will only succeed when it appears genuine and not a gimmick to push sales by running a pseudo-advertisement.

▼ Oreo used real-time marketing to send out a tweet that it is okay to dunk Oreo cookies in the dark.

Jaimie Duplass/Fotolia

Real-Time Marketing

The idea of real-time marketing existed prior to the 2013 Super Bowl, but it was the infamous blackout during the game in the New Orleans Superdome that legitimized it as a feasible social media strategy. Oreo sent a message via Twitter that it is okay to dunk an Oreo cookie "in the dark." The message was placed on an image of an Oreo cookie, set in light, shadow, and darkness. That message became a viral hit and was re-tweeted 15,000 times within the first 14 hours.

Real-time marketing is the creation and execution of an instantaneous marketing message in response to—and in conjunction with—an occurrence during a live event. Marketers conceived and produced the Oreo tweet in just five minutes. Such a rapid reaction was possible because marketers from Oreo's parent company, Mondelez, and its agency were assembled at a "social media command center" in New York during the game. With creative and technical staff present and in place, the team was quickly able to create a response to the blackout, produce the message, and then send it.[35]

The instant success of Oreo led marketers for other brands to set up "war rooms" during major live events. These war rooms contain top marketing executives, creatives, digital technicians, and attorneys. The group seeks to strike instantly with an approved message when an opportunity occurs. During the 2014 Super Bowl, Adobe had 15 people assembled in its war room. The team employed Adobe's digital analytic tools to listen to social media chatter to determine what buzz was resonating with consumers and then congratulate whatever organization or company had initiated the buzz. Adobe's message was not for consumers but rather for businesses. It was designed to acquaint other companies with Adobe's digital analytical tools.[36]

© goodluz/Fotolia

▲ Brand managers now deploy teams to "war rooms" prior to a live event to devise and launch reactions to occurrences during the event.

Effective real-time marketing does not occur on the fly without any thought. The approach requires upfront strategic planning before assembling a war room and prior to any live event. While seeking to display human emotions and reactions to live events, those actions must be carefully planned to ensure they resonate with consumers (or businesses) and remain consistent with the brand's overall brand image and integrated marketing communications plan. The tone featured in a real-time marketing message becomes the key. It should correlate with what is presented in other company advertisements and other social media efforts. During these preplanning sessions, company leaders discuss and sometimes even prepare messages and ads to be used for various situations that might occur during a live event. While it may seem the message was a quick reaction, it may have been talked about and designed weeks earlier.

In addition to upfront strategic planning, rules, procedures, and processes must be in place that allows the team to react quickly. Individuals with authority to approve marketing messages, advertising, and media allocation have to be present. In today's litigious society, this means that individuals from the legal team will be involved with the decision prior to initiating the message. Without prior planning, such real-time marketing does not occur.

Real-time marketing can be utilized in places other than live sporting events. During a recent snowstorm in the Northeast, Starbucks' marketing department put together a social media plan for Facebook and Twitter that focused on conversations about the anticipated blizzard. Snow-themed ads appeared on Facebook and Twitter with the focus on an image of a warm cup of java. The Twitter ads appeared when individuals clicked on #blizzard, #snowstorm, and other related hashtags.[37]

McDonald's deploys real-time marketing messages, but at a slower pace. Marketers track 2.5 million to 3 million conversations each month listening to what consumers say about McDonald's, quick-service restaurants, and other topics relevant to the company's operations. The team watches for trends that the company can feature on its social media pages. When the company launched its Cheddar Bacon Onion burger, the ads highlighted various attributes of the product; however, the chatter was about the bacon. In response, the marketing team quickly changed its promotional effort in social media to focus more on the bacon rather than other aspects of the sandwich.[38]

Interactive Blogs

The power of a blog comes from the new landscape it creates in which one consumer dissatisfied with a particular brand can now tell thousands, and in some cases millions, of people. Previously, a bad shopping experience meant that 12 to 15 people would hear

Jinga80/Fotolia

▲ Discontented consumers can now express their unhappiness through blogs and other forms of social media to thousands or even millions.

about it. Now, an individual's complaint can be sent to more than just friends and family. A discontented consumer speaks to anyone willing to listen (or read about it) via the internet. The reverse can also occur. A satisfied customer can rave about a brand and have her comments read by thousands.

Interactive blogs permit visitors to send comments or posts, making them another important component of social media. Chapter 8 covered the basic concept of blogging as primarily a one-way communication device. While effective, blogs that allow and encourage active participation often become more powerful. Such interactions present a higher level of risk, because the blogging company surrenders some control over content. While employees can squelch and/or delete negative comments, doing so destroys the blog's credibility and damages its reputation. A better approach is for the company's marketing team to face any criticism honestly and humbly and react by seeking a solution to the problem or cause of the dissatisfaction.

Companies may feature three different types of interactive blogs (see Figure 9.7). The first occurs when a company or brand creates a blog. Blogs owned and operated by businesses find it more difficult to solicit honest interactions with consumers who may be more suspicious of their intentions. Also, company personnel operating the blog may be more sensitive to negative content and how it may be viewed by customers.

A blog sponsored by a company or brand constitutes the second form. New regulations passed by the Federal Trade Commission require an individual who is being paid by an organization with merchandise or money, or is compensated in any other way, to report that information on the blog. While these individuals have more freedom to express personal opinions, they will likely have to remain positive about the brand in order to maintain its sponsorship. Visitors to the site have more freedom to comment as well, but recognizing that a business sponsors the blog's author often tempers their views.

The third type of blog involves individuals who speak about a brand but have no financial connection to it. They truly like the brand. They take pleasure in talking about it. They enjoy interacting with others about the brand. When a brand has no affiliation with a blog, visitors feel comfortable in making comments and relating their honest opinions. These blogs can be valuable, because the marketing team learns what consumers really think about a product or service. Marketers use this type of blog to ask questions and seek opinions, if permission is granted by the blog's author.

- Brand blog
- Individuals sponsored by a brand
- Individual speaking about a brand

▲ **FIGURE 9.7**
Types of Interactive Blogs

Consumer-Generated Reviews

Word-of-mouth endorsements have changed. Many companies that vend multiple goods or services solicit consumer-generated reviews of those products. Amazon.com stands at the forefront of this approach. Each book offered online holds a space where individual customers can write reviews, with words and a one- to five-star rating. The site informs the shopper of the number of reviews, the average star rating, and notes if the reviews are written by anonymous critics or those who provide their real names. A person wishing to place his name on a review must authenticate it by presenting Amazon.com with a credit card number. Customers benefit by reading the reviews before making purchases. The system may not be perfect, because an author may use a pseudonym to write a highly favorable review and encourage friends and family members to do the same. At the same time, the author cannot control posts of outside reviews.

Best Buy incorporated consumer feedback into online retailing. The company hosts a blog section for consumers to read about and discuss various topics. In each product category, such as cameras, Best Buy provides a discussion forum on a variety of related topics. In the digital camera discussion forum, consumers post photos they have taken with various cameras. Best Buy posts customer reviews of each product, both positive and negative. The reviews may influence the brands consumers consider and eventually purchase. By providing blogs, discussion forums, and consumer reviews, Best Buy offers consumers methods to search for and evaluate products and to make purchase decisions without leaving the company's website.

The growing use of online reviews by consumers has led to an increase in websites devoted to providing them, such as TripAdvisor, Zagat, Edmunds, Yelp, and Foursquare. An online panel study of 3,404 individuals revealed that 75 percent think the information presented on rating sites is generally fair and honest; however, 25 percent still believe the information is biased or unfair. The larger and more established rating sites, such as TripAdvisor, Zagat, Open Table, Edmunds, Urbanspoon, and Yelp, tend to be the most trusted.[39]

Marketers carefully study customer-generated reviews because they provide important information about how customers evaluate brands and how the brand compares to the competition. This information becomes critical when developing marketing plans,

DuPage Medical Group

▲ Blogs can be a valuable source of information for patients looking for medical care as well as to the staff of DuPage Medical Group.

Visit Baton Rouge

◀ Consumer-generated reviews are important in tourist decisions for visiting Baton Rouge.

product modifications, and service strategies. As the usage of consumer-generated reviews continues to rise, the marketing challenge will be managing this aspect of consumer word-of-mouth endorsements in ways that enhance brand equity and increase sales.

Viral Marketing

Preparing a marketing message to be passed from one consumer to another through digital means, or **viral marketing**, takes the form of an email or a video posted to a personal blog and passed to other blogs or websites such as YouTube. It can evolve into a form of advocacy or word-of-mouth endorsement. The term "viral" derives from the image of a person being "infected" with the marketing message and then spreading it to friends, like a virus. The difference is that the individual voluntarily sends the message to others.

Viral marketing messages may include advertisements, hyperlinked promotions, online newsletters, streaming videos, and games. For instance, about a dozen videos were posted on YouTube of a man claiming to be the "world's fastest nudist." He streaks through various locations in New York City wearing only tennis shoes, tube socks, and a fanny pack positioned strategically in front. The links to the videos were emailed from individual to individual. They were posted on popular blogs such as The Huffington Post and Gawker. One appeared on CNN's *Anderson Cooper 360*. The campaign turned out to be a viral video campaign for Zappos.com, an online shoe and apparel store. The viral campaign highlighted that Zappos was selling clothes because additional videos were posted that showed a van screeching up to the "fastest nudist" and several people jumping out wearing Zappos T-shirts. As the van leaves, the video shows the nudist dressed in pants and a shirt.[40]

Figure 9.8 provides some suggestions on how to create successful viral campaigns. The viral message should focus on the product or business. In the Zappos.com videos, the nudist receives clothes from a Zappos team. The marketing team determines why an individual would want to pass the message along or tell friends about it.

Viral campaigns do not always succeed or yield positive benefits. Most brand managers would be thrilled to have three viral videos within one year, as Kmart did. The first YouTube video that went viral was "Ship My Pants," an advertisement created by Kmart. The video was viewed 20 million times. A short time later, an advertisement posted to YouTube—"Big Gas Savings"—based on a milder naughty double entendre was viewed more than 6 million times. Then "Show Your Joe" was a holiday ad that featured men playing *Jingle Bells* with their privates, viewed more than 15 million times. Despite all three ads going viral and being viewed more than 40 million times in total, sales fell 2.1 percent for the retailer.

Research regarding the impact of viral messages suggests that 61 percent of individuals exposed to a viral message or video had favorable opinions about the brand. Purchase intentions increased around five percent but were greater if the viral message was recommended by a friend via social media rather than a company.[41]

Individuals should receive an incentive to pass the message along. A message containing entertainment value offers one type of incentive. Others may be financial, such as free merchandise or a discount for messages passed along to friends that lead to purchases, logging onto a website, or registering for an e-newsletter. The incentive should be unique. A personalized message has a greater chance of being passed along.

- Focus on the product or business
- Determine why individuals would want to pass along the message
- Offer an incentive
- Make it personal
- Track the results and analyze the data

▶ **FIGURE 9.8**
Keys to Successful Viral Marketing

- Keep up with activities
- Learn about products or services
- Sweepstakes or promotion
- Provide feedback
- Join community of fans
- Make purchases
- To complain

▲ **FIGURE 9.9**
Why Consumers Follow Brand
Source: Based on Lenna Garibian, "Digital Influence: Blogs Beat Social Networks for Driving Purchases," *MarketingProfs*, www.marketingprofs.com/charts/print/2013/10336, March 18, 2013.

- Retail sites (56%)
- Brand sites (34%)
- Blogs (31.1%)
- Facebook (30.8%)
- Groups/Forums (28%)
- YouTube (27%)
- LinkedIn (27%)
- Google+ (20%)
- Online magazines (20%)
- Pinterest (12%)
- Twitter (8%)
- Instagram (3%)

▲ **FIGURE 9.10**
Internet Sites Most Likely to Influence Purchases
Source: Based on Lenna Garibian, "Digital Influence: Blogs Beat Social Networks for Driving Purchases," *MarketingProfs*, www.marketingprofs.com/charts/print/2013/10336, March 18, 2013.

The many forms of digital marketing mean that viral marketing has lost some of its luster. Some consumers have lost enthusiasm and are less willing to resend messages. Still, the marketing team can take advantage of the ability to track the results of a viral campaign and analyze the results to determine whether such a program will be effective.

Following Brands on Social Media

Figure 9.9 highlights reasons consumers follow brands in social media. Although they vary by social media site, the two top reasons tend to be to keep up with activities of the brand and to learn about the product or service. Typically, individuals do not follow a brand with the goal of making a purchase. Typically, they have purchased a brand, like the brand, and then become a fan or follower. If they are dissatisfied with a brand, they are not likely to follow it on social media. They may use social media to lodge the complaint but will not become a fan or follower.

In summary, company leaders have become involved in social media because it does influence purchase behaviors, as shown in Figure 9.10. Retail sites and the brand sites have the greatest online impact on purchase behaviors. Blogs rank third in terms of influence. Of the social media sites, Facebook was viewed as having the most influence, cited by 31 percent of the respondents in the survey.[42]

▼ Individuals follow brands, such as Kraft, on social media because they truly like the brand and use it regularly.

Kraft Foods, Inc

Social Media Metrics

objective 9.5
What social media measurement metrics are available to marketers?

Evaluating integrated marketing campaigns will be covered in Chapter 15. This chapter includes a discussion of social media metrics because digital platforms provide comprehensive feedback, often instantaneously, that can be used to modify social media marketing strategies. Figure 9.11 provides the primary social media metrics used by organizations.

A number of social media and digital research firms specialize in providing a **buzz score (or brand buzz)**, which measures the number of times a brand receives

FIGURE 9.11
Social Media Metrics

- Brand buzz (total mentions)
- Reach (number of fans)
- Facebook likes
- Twitter tweets and re-tweets
- Traffic from social media
- Click-through rate to Website

JD Bank

▲ A sentiment score can be used by marketers at JD Bank to determine whether the mentions received on various social media sites were positive or negative.

a mention on social network within a specific time frame. While counting the number of mentions provides an indicator of the popularity of a brand in social media, examining the sentiment score will be important. "Sentiment" refers to whether the buzz was negative or positive. Marketers recognize that both are important to monitor. When positive buzz takes place, employees can join the conversation and thank fans for their support and even reward them in some way. With negative buzz, the marketing team should be prepared to react quickly to prevent the buzz from growing exponentially and going viral.

Reach measures the number of fans, friends, or followers a brand has in social media. While the quantity will be important, it does not tell the whole story. The marketing team needs to know whether those fans are active or passive. They identify whether fans merely follow the buzz or share brand stories and information with their friends. Most important however, will be, "What is the trend?" Company leaders want to know whether the number of fans is growing, stagnant, or declining. This information assists in understanding the impact of the reach of a social media marketing campaign.

While many companies try to push their customers to like them on Facebook through ads, videos, and other social media, merely liking a brand does not necessarily translate into sales, as has been noted. Many marketing professionals have started to conclude that sharing represents a better metric than likes. A passive customer may click like, but a passionate customer will share the coupon, the promotion, or brand message. Sharing grows revenue and builds loyalty.

With Twitter, tweets and especially re-tweets reflect customer passion. Seeing a brand tweet may create a mental image, but retweeting that brand message conveys a word-of-mouth recommendation from one customer to another.

Technology allows company leaders to track how individuals got to a website. To determine the effectiveness of social media, marketers determine the percentage of visits that came through social media. If contests, coupons, or other promotions are sent via social media, a company's marketing team can determine the click-through rate, which is the number of individuals who clicked on a brand message and was taken directly to the brand's website. This, in turn, reflects the value of the social media advertising or marketing program.

▼ Scott Equipment can measure the effectiveness of this banner ad through the click-through rate.

Scott Equipment

International Implications

objective 9.6
How can marketers use social media strategies in international operations?

Social media interactions are a worldwide phenomenon. Most Facebook users are located outside the United States. Various social networks have been involved in social movements and political revolutions. They have helped widen the worldwide marketplace for a variety of goods and service while changing the landscape of shopping and purchasing patterns in numerous companies.

Marketing professionals understand that the social network environment creates additional complexities. Among the more notable, language differences, social norms, and technological issues represent three of the greatest challenges to individual companies.

As is the case in any marketing program, language differences complicate the ways in which messages can be constructed and transmitted. In countries where internet systems allow the free flow of messages, a marketing piece designed for viewers in Spain might quickly appear in China or Greece. Consequently, the viewer cannot decipher the intent of the message. Trying to present a consistent theme across languages presents a great deal of difficulty: Language differences enhance the dilemma. One tactic used to combat the problem is an emphasis on *visual Esperanto*, a more universal, emotionally-based approach designed to tap into feelings all citizens experience.

Social norms create a significant test for marketers. Norms regarding sexuality, modes of dress, attitudes toward women and minorities, and other differences become more readily noticeable when a tweet or Facebook post is sent across national boundaries. Companies seeking to establish an international presence carefully vet all messages to make sure they do not offend the norms or sensitivities of individuals in countries where the messages or advertisements will be shown.

Technological challenges can be presented by governments or by the nature of a country's infrastructure. Many national governments try to censor various websites from appearing within their boundaries. In other settings, poor internet service creates sporadic access at best. Marketing professionals account for these issues as they design social media programs.

Summary

Social media includes any digital tool or venue that allows individuals to socialize on the web. A social network is a social structure of individuals and/or organizations that are tied together in some manner. Social media marketing is the utilization of social media and/or social networks to market a product, company, or brand.

General social networking sites are broadly designed to appeal to all demographics, regardless of gender, age, race, or education. The most common include Facebook, Twitter, and YouTube. Niche social networking sites focus on a specific interest, hobby, or demographic group. Marketing professionals can target both types of sites. The objective involves determining the message that best resonates with individuals who frequently visit the site. The recent explosion of video productions by individuals is changing the landscape of social networking.

Social media marketing traditionally seeks to keep customers engaged with a brand and to increase the brand's exposure. It can also drive traffic to a desired site or place, enhance a brand's image, boost organic search rankings, and collect customer intelligence through social listening systems. A quality program identifies customer advocates who exhibit behavioral commitment, emotional connections with the brand, and quality communication skills. Social media marketing can help increase sales and enhance brand loyalty.

Social media marketing strategies include content seeding, which involves providing incentives for customers to share content about a brand. Effective real-time marketing efforts involve careful planning and preparation in order to provide an instantaneous marketing message in response to a live event. Interactive blogs allow visitors to make comments or posts on the site, including those created by the company, sites sponsored by the company, and those prepared by independent fans or advocates. Customer-generated review programs, when correctly managed, provide authenticity and engagement with those who use the systems to gather information about products. Viral marketing helps a company garner interest when a message is sent along via email or a re-post by consumers. Many consumers follow brands on social media.

Social media metrics include a buzz score, reach, likes on a site, re-posts and re-tweets, and click-through rates. These measures help marketers discover whether social media programs effectively reach their audiences.

International challenges in social media include language differences, social norms, and technological complications. Effective marketing teams monitor and respond carefully to these issues.

Key Terms

social media Any digital tool or venue that allows individuals to socialize on the web

social network A social structure of individuals and/or organizations that are tied together in some manner

social media marketing The utilization of social media and/or social networks to market a product, company, or brand

general social networking sites Websites that are broadly based and designed to appeal to all demographics, regardless of gender, age, race, income, or education

niche social networking site A website that focuses on a specific interest, hobby, or demographic group

social bookmarking sites Websites that allow individuals to share bookmarks of websites

social listening A social media marketing strategy that involves listening to social chatter

content seeding A social media marketing strategy that involves providing incentives for consumers to share content about a brand

real-time marketing The creation and execution of an instantaneous marketing message in response to—and in conjunction with—an occurrence during a live event

interactive blogs A marketing strategy in which a blog allows visitors to make comments or posts

viral marketing An advertisement tied to an email or other form of online communication in which one person passes on the advertisement or email to other consumers

buzz score (or brand buzz) A measure of the number of times a brand receives a mention on a social network within a specific time frame

MyMarketingLab

Go to **mymktlab.com** to complete the problems marked with this icon ✪.

Review Questions

9-1. What is the primary function of social media?

9-2. What value could a niche social network have for a business?

9-3. What makes Twitter radically different to Facebook?

✪ **9-4.** How has video posting changed the nature of social media networking?

9-5. Describe Instagram and the typical user of the service.

9-6. List the characteristics of brand advocates.

9-7. How can social media boost the organic search engine rankings for a business?

9-8. For businesses, social media is just about selling. Comment on this statement.

9-9. Describe content seeding.

9-10. Describe real-time marketing.

9-11. What three types of interactive blogs support social media marketing programs?

9-12. Describe viral marketing.

9-13. List the reasons why consumers follow brands on social media.

9-14. What social media measurement metrics are available to marketing professionals?

9-15. What issues complicate international social media marketing programs?

Critical Thinking Exercises

DISCUSSION QUESTIONS

9-16. Discuss the current trends of consumer video-sharing. Examine reasons brands have become involved in social media marketing. For each of the trends you identify, elaborate on ways brands can use social media marketing to reach video-sharing consumers. Be sure to justify your choices of social media marketing.

✪ **9-17.** Are you on Facebook? Why or why not? If you are on Facebook, how much time do you spend online at Facebook? Do you use Twitter? Why or why not? Based on your experience with Facebook and Twitter, how can companies use them to reach you? Are you a fan of any company on Facebook or Twitter? If so, why did you become a fan? If not, why did you choose not to become a fan?

9-18. YouTube has gained considerable popularity in recent years. Why do you think this is so? How often do you use YouTube? What types of videos do you watch? Do your friends and relatives access YouTube? If so, how often and why? If not, why not?

9-19. Do you follow brands on social media? What is the reason for this? What types of brands are better suited to following on social media and why? What about the brands that you don't like or have fallen out of favor, do you still follow them? Carry out research and ask ten other people whether they do, or ever have, followed a brand on social media. What were their reasons for doing this? From your findings, what seems to be the trend and why?

9-20. Have you made brand purchases based on comments made on social media? Why or why not? Provide specific details. Have you decided against purchasing a particular brand based on comments on social media? Why or why not? Provide specific details.

9-21. What exactly is viral marketing? Find an example of it from your own country or region. Why was it so effective? How did it become viral? Share your findings.

9-22. Do you use consumer-generated reviews in making purchase decisions? Why or why not? How valuable do you think they are to consumers?

9-23. Brand managers often become excited when something the company posts on the internet goes viral and spreads like wildfire among consumers. What factors contribute to a brand's posting going viral? Discuss how the social media strategies of content seeding, real-time marketing, interactive blogs, and consumer-generated reviews lead to a successful viral marketing attempt or unsuccessful viral marketing.

Integrated Learning Exercises

9-24. Choose one of the following Middle Eastern brands. Are they active on social media platforms? Are their social media links specific to the Middle East or are they global? How many fans or followers do they have? How active is the social media? Is there interaction? Is social media just being used as another sales platform?

- **a.** Al Arabiya (**www.alarabiya.com**)
- **b.** Al Jazeera (**www.aljazeera.com**)
- **c.** Pepsi Arabia (**www.pepsi.com**)
- **d.** KFC Arabia (**www.kfc-arabia.com**)
- **e.** Emirates Airline (**www.emirates.com**)

9-25. Pick a brand you really like and for which you have a high level of loyalty. Access the brand's website, Facebook page, Twitter page, YouTube Channel, and Instagram page. Discuss the information provided on each. Based on the reasons brands use social media shown in Figure 9.4, discuss what you think is the reason for each social media network. Evaluate how successful you think the brand is with social media.

9-26. Choose one of the following product categories, then select three prominent brands in that category. Access each of the brand's Facebook page, Twitter page, Instagram page, and YouTube Channel. Compare and contrast what information is provided for each brand. Which brand has the best social media presence? Why?

- **a.** Sports equipment
- **b.** Clothing
- **c.** Restaurants
- **d.** Beverage

9-27. Examine the reasons brands use social media shown in Figure 9.4. Pick three of the reasons and identify from your personal experience a brand you believe did well with each. It could be three different brands or one brand for all three. Support your answer with specific information and links to the social media pages illustrating your discussion.

9-28. Figure 9.6 identifies strategies brands can use with social media. Find an example of each strategy in social media not described in the textbook. Provide the link, explain why it is an example of the strategy, and your evaluation of whether the strategy was good or bad, and why.

9-29. Using a blog search engine, locate an example of an interactive blog. Evaluate the blog. Is it effective? Why or why not?

9-30. Use a search engine to locate an example of viral marketing. Evaluate the viral marketing. Was it effective? Why or why not?

Blog Exercises

Access the authors' blog for this textbook at the URLs provided to complete these exercises. Answer the questions that are posed on the blog.

9-31. Hooters: **http://blogclowbaack.net/2014/05/12/hooters-chapter-9/**

9-32. Covergirl: **http://blogclowbaack.net/2014/05/12/covergirl-chapter-9/**

9-33. Social Media: **http://blogclowbaack.net/2014/05/12/social-media-chapter-9/**

Student Project

CREATIVE CORNER

Carlos just opened his own hot dog and pastry stand in downtown St. Louis. He believes social media could be used to build awareness of his stand and to build a customer base. Carlos believes having the unique combination of hot dogs and pastries provides him with a combination meal (hot dog, pastry, and drink) that counters what a fast-food restaurant would offer. Develop a social media marketing campaign for Carlos that includes the following elements:

- Objectives (or reasons) for the social media marketing campaign
- Social networking sites he should utilize
- Social media strategies
- Metrics he can use to measure success of the social media campaign
- Banner ad that Carlos can place on Facebook (design this for him)

In developing the campaign, be sure to provide a rationale to Carlos for your suggestions.

CASE 1 POST-IT: MAKING THE ORDINARY EXTRAORDINARY

Sooner or later, every business person comes into contact with a Post-it note. These sticky, functional tools have become part of everyday life in homes, offices, and other places. The product remains a steady, profitable staple of the 3-M portfolio. Jesse Singh, vice president for the stationery and office supplies division of 3M in Minnesota, notes "If you think about the product, it's iconic; it's been in the market over 30 years," and, until recently, the strategy to sell it was by "taking a functional view of the brand."[43]

In 2013, a new $10 million marketing campaign was launched, with a fresh intent. The new approach utilized messages in television commercials, online ads, the company's website, and through social media. The idea was to suggest Post-it notes could be so much more. The campaign emphasized "customization," or the tendency exhibited by younger consumers to want personalized messages from mass media and individualized uses for goods.

With the theme "Go ahead" driving the campaign, customers were encouraged to find new ways to use this longstanding product. Soon "Post-it" wars emerged between local offices, as employees used Post-its to create images and other designs on external windows. Further, the product's flexibility led Singh to know that "They're using it to communicate, using it to collaborate, using it to organize themselves." In a somewhat surprising turn of events, 3-M's research revealed that many customers felt a strong emotional connection to Post-its.

Post-it hosts an "Idea Headquarters" website that helps people find unique uses for the tool, including becoming more productive and reducing the tendency to procrastinate. Social media posts seek out additional methods for taking advantage of the item's distinctive characteristics.

Television commercials supported all other efforts, with messages targeting moms to show different ways they use Post-its to organize their days; millennials to be creative in posting the notes to remind themselves about events and to communicate with others (sort of a paper "tweet," according to one observer) as well as to help them remain optimistic; and to a married man who uses a Post-it note to remind himself to "keep the honeymoon going."

Post-it's marketing team faces two trends as the future unfolds. The first involves making the product itself more appealing and amenable to these novel applications. One response has been to increase the number of colors beyond the traditional yellow and more common colors. The second may become a more daunting issue over time. The "generic" problem occurs when a brand becomes so well-accepted that the brand name is used to describe the item, no matter which company sells it. Examples include Band-aids, Xerox copies, and Scotch tape. Don't be surprised if you hear the product more regularly referred to as "Post-it brand" in advertisements for the product in the future. Doing so has been the most common response to the generic problem.

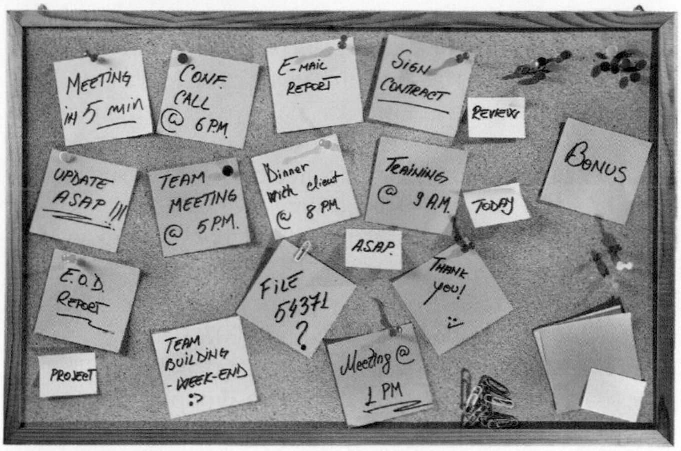

Photorack/Fotolia

▲ Post-it notes have been in the market for over 30 years.

In the meantime, the 2013 campaign was "the first time we're including all these forms of (media) creativity under one banner," said Jeff Odiorne, executive creative director at Grey New York advertising agency. He continued, "Consumers have taken it upon themselves to figure out how to use the brand in unconventional ways. It's a brand that consumers love so much, they've made it what it is today," he adds. "The real things that real people do or have done, we want to put those on stage."[44]

9-34. Which social media sites are best suited to this type of promotional campaign? Why?

9-35. How could consumers, fans, and the company take advantage of new video-posting technologies to promote the Post-it brand?

9-36. What were the marketing objectives of the "Go ahead" campaign?

9-37. Would social listening be of value to Post-it's marketing team? If so, how? If not, why not?

9-38. Which social media marketing strategies should Post-it's team use? Provide justification for your response.

CASE 2 VIVE HOY

The market for carbonated soft drinks represents one of the largest and most lucrative targets in the United States and around the world. Coca-Cola and Pepsi have dominated the industry for many years. As the competition continues to evolve, each seeks out groups to attract and retain. Recently, PepsiCo reinvigorated its own efforts to capture the Hispanic share in the United States.

Advertising Age reported that in 2004 PepsiCo ranked number 6 on the magazine's list of the Top 50 Advertisers in Hispanic Media, spending $68.5 million. Then, the company had dropped to number 27, spending $41 million in 2007. The next year, the company dropped off the list and remained in that position for four years. At the same time, Coca-Cola dropped its spending dramatically to the same group, although the organization still spent $29.8 million in 2011, with a ranking of number 48 on the Top 50 list.

Javier Farfan, senior director for cultural branding at PepsiCo, noted that, "One of the key reasons I came here is to figure out how to dive deeper into the Hispanic space." Suggesting that the company had somewhat "lost its way," Farfan said, "In the carbonated category, exponentially, growth is going to come from Latinos. There's the population growth, but we're also more prone to drink soda. So it became really important and strategic for Pepsi to get into that space."

One of the outcomes was the "Vive Hoy" or "Live for Now" campaign and tagline associated with a new wave of television commercials. Farfan noted, "There's a new mainstream evolving. It's a different state of mind. Latinos don't want to be separate; they want to be included. "We want to nod and wink to them in places where they actually engage with media. Latinos watch MTV as much as Univision."[45]

To more fully attract Hispanic patrons, Pepsi launched two new products, Paradise Mango and Cherry Vanilla. Both were designed to attract Hispanic customers.

In addition to mainstream advertising and new products, *Marketing Daily* notes another fertile ground. Hispanic consumers are "Social Media Catalysts," according to the magazine. A recent study conducted for Unilever revealed that Hispanic consumers are "twice as likely to either share content or click on shared content than Americans in general." The report's data indicates that, "Hispanic consumers are also more influential on social media: content they share garners more "click-backs" (the act of clicking shared links to view the shared content) than content shared by non-Hispanic consumers."

Although Hispanic consumers read more on mobile devices than other groups, they are less inclined to share from those devices. At the same time, the youngest Hispanic consumers do not have reservations about sharing from mobile devices, which indicates the potential to reach them in ways that would lead to a larger community of advocates for Pepsi.[46]

JB325/Fotolia

▲ Pepsi launched the "Vive Hoy" campaign to attract Hispanic consumers.

The next generation of marketing efforts will likely integrate messages for Hispanic and non-Hispanic consumers as society becomes more blended. The net result will likely be an expanding marketplace for companies that are able to attract individual groups while at the same time reaching the mainstream audience.

9-39. The *Marketing Daily* article noted that Hispanics, "are less likely to use Pinterest or Twitter and twice as likely to use email and nearly 50 perccent more likely to use blogging channels such as Tumblr and Blogger." How should PepsiCo's marketing team respond to these statistics?

9-40. What social media marketing goals should PepsiCo seek to achieve with Hispanics? Why?

9-41. Which social media marketing tactics do you believe will be most effective for PepsiCo when seeking to reach the Hispanic audience? Which would be least likely to succeed? Defend your responses.

9-42. How might social listening be of value to PepsiCo with regard to the Hispanic market? Justify your answer.

9-43. What metrics would you use to measure the success of a social media marketing campaign directed to Hispanics? Justify your answer.

MyMarketingLab

Go to **mymktlab.com** for the following Assisted-graded writing questions:

9-44. Discuss the current trends of consumer video-sharing. Examine reasons brands have become involved in social media marketing. For each of the trends you identify, elaborate on ways brands can use social media marketing to reach video-sharing consumers. Be sure to justify your choices of social media marketing.

9-45. Brands are excited when something the company posts on the internet goes viral and spreads like wildfire among consumers. What factors contribute to a brand's posting going viral? Discuss how the social media strategies of content seeding, real-time marketing, interactive blogs, and consumer-generated reviews lead to a successful viral marketing attempt or unsuccessful viral marketing.

Chapter 10 Alternative Marketing

Chapter Objectives

After reading this chapter, you should be able to answer the following questions:

10.1 How can buzz marketing, guerrilla marketing, lifestyle marketing, and experiential marketing enhance a marketing communications program?

10.2 What methods can be used to effectively employ product placements and branded entertainment?

10.3 Why has the use of alternative media venues, especially video game advertising, grown in marketing communications programs?

10.4 How have in-store marketing and point-of-purchase displays evolved into effective communication and sales tools?

10.5 How can brand communities enhance brand loyalty and devotion?

10.6 What methods are used to adapt alternative marketing programs to international marketing efforts?

Overview

Traditional mass media advertising faces many challenges. Although advertisers are not ready to abandon radio, television, magazines, newspapers, and out-of-home programs, they know that many new and valuable media outlets have emerged. As a result, alternative marketing programs and alternative media are on the rise. Marketers spend increasing numbers of dollars finding ways to reach potential customers in new and innovative formats. Successful advertising and promotional programs often take advantage of these new alternative approaches, including those targeted to individual segments domestically and consumers in other countries for international firms.

HEBREW NATIONAL

Gourmet Hot Dogs

Hebrew National makes gourmet Kosher hot dogs. Kosher literally means "fit to eat." According to the company's website, "For more than 100 years, Hebrew National® has followed strict dietary law, using only specific cuts of beef that meet the highest standards for quality, cleanliness, and safety—so artificial flavors, colors, fillers, and by-products simply don't make the cut." The company began as a mom-and-pop operation located on the Lower East Side of New York City that has grown into the largest, most recognized Kosher brand in America.[1]

The Bratskeir Company, a full-service advertising and marketing communications agency, described the problem faced by Hebrew National this way: the brand's "higher price was a barrier to trial and purchase of its better-tasting, higher-quality franks." The insight drawn by the company was, "Moms who try Hebrew National hot dogs love the taste and quality and understand why they cost more. They are influenced by, and readily influence, other moms. They like to do good for others as do well for their families."[2]

The company's agency searched 12 cities for 250 PTA presidents, Hispanic community leaders, and Jewish mothers to serve on "mom squads." The moms' sport-utility vehicles were emblazoned with the Hebrew National logo. The "mom squads" hosted backyard hot dog barbecues and distributed discount coupons at community events. Bratskeir noted that, "They took their show on the road, holding sampling events at Little League games, soccer tournaments, and other neighborhood events, all summer long" and "Moms distributed coupons everywhere they went. For every coupon redeemed, we donated a package of hot dogs to ConAgra's Kid's Cafés, which feeds thousands of children from poor families."

Mark Kleinman, vice president of sales and marketing, used to think only outrageous products were worthy of alternative marketing strategies. He stated, "But even a loved American food like the hot dog can generate a lot of discussion." The net result was an impressive growth in sales and visibility for this company and its products.[3]

Tyler Olson/Fotolia

▲ "Mom squads" were recruited to host backyard hot-dog barbecues and pass out coupons for Hebrew National Kosher hot dogs.

This chapter presents four topics. First, it identifies major alternative marketing programs: buzz marketing, guerrilla marketing, product placements and branded entertainment, and lifestyle marketing. Next, it describes a series of marketing tactics associated with alternative media. Third, in-store marketing will be examined. Finally, brand communities are discussed. The international implications of these new forms of alternative media are also presented.

Alternative Marketing Programs

objective 10.1

How can buzz marketing, guerrilla marketing, lifestyle marketing, and experiential marketing enhance a marketing communications program?

Developing alternative marketing programs requires creativity and imagination. Marketers identify new places where a consumer's path intersects with a brand's presence or creates a new intersection point. They then prepare attention-getting marketing messages for those points of contact, which provides the opportunity to supplement or replace mass media advertising with more targeted methods.

In essence, the goal remains the same as for traditional media. Marketing professionals continue to look for innovative ways to reach a target audience. Alternative marketing programs and alternative media venues provide widely accepted options.

Scott Cooner, Inc

▲ Traditional media advertising is an important component of any alternative marketing program.

Figure 10.1 lists common alternative marketing choices. These programs seldom operate independently. A guerrilla marketing campaign might also include buzz and lifestyle marketing components. The same campaign may contain digital components and traditional media.

Alternative marketing relies on buzz, word-of-mouth, and lifestyle messages at times when consumers are relaxing and enjoying hobbies and events. Integrating these venues into a coherent integrated marketing program that speaks with a clear voice and message should be the goal.

Buzz Marketing

Buzz marketing has become one of the fastest-growing areas in alternative marketing. Estimated expenditures for these programs total more than $1 billion annually. **Buzz marketing**, or *word-of-mouth marketing*, emphasizes consumers passing along information about a product. A recommendation by a friend, family member, or acquaintance carries higher levels of credibility than an advertisement. Buzz can be more powerful than the words of a paid spokesperson or endorser. As shown in Figure 10.2, word-of-mouth endorsements can be supplied by consumers who like a brand and tell others, consumers who like a brand and are sponsored by a company to speak to others, or by company or agency employees who talk about the brand.

Consumers Who Like a Brand

A consumer who truly likes a brand and tells others about it creates the ideal marketing situation. Enthusiasts deliver these messages in person or via the internet in various ways. Many musical groups have achieved fame through this type of word-of-mouth support by those who have seen the bands in bars or as part of a small concert or tour. The ad for Five Star Fitness Center on the next page features Rheagan, who is passionate about exercise and a fan of Five Star Fitness. She shares this enthusiasm with anyone who will listen.

Sponsored Consumers

Many companies sponsor individuals as agents or advocates to introduce new products. It works best when these individuals, or ambassadors, also like the brand. A program can involve individuals talking one-on-one to others, or they can host house or block parties to present the product to a group of friends and family.

- Buzz marketing
- Guerrilla marketing
- Lifestyle marketing
- Experiential marketing
- Product placement and branded entertainment

▲ **FIGURE 10.1**
Forms of Alternative Marketing

- Individuals who truly like a brand
- Individuals who are sponsored by a brand
- Company or agency employees

▲ **FIGURE 10.2**
Types of Buzz Marketing Approaches

Brand Ambassadors Customer evangelists, or brand ambassadors, are typically individuals who already like the brand that they sponsor. The company offers incentives and rewards in exchange for advocacy. Marketers select an ambassador based on his devotion to the brand and the size of his social circle. Once recruited, an ambassador delivers messages to her family, friends, reference groups, and work associates. Some are asked to develop grassroots, no- or low-cost marketing events and to promote the brand on the internet through blogs or on social networks such as Facebook. Brand advocates are advised to be upfront and honest about their connections with the brand.

On move-in day at the University of North Carolina, students wearing American Eagle Outfitter shirts volunteered to help new students move into their dorms. They cheerfully unloaded cars and lugged belongings to dorm rooms. They passed out American Eagle coupons, water canisters, and Eagle pens as they helped the students. The helpers were student brand ambassadors. An estimated 10,000 college students work as ambassadors for a variety of companies, including American Eagle, Red Bull, NASCAR, Microsoft, and Hewlett-Packard. In exchange for promoting a particular brand, they receive discounts and/or merchandise.[4]

Photographer Steven Palowsky Photography LLC, Instagram@stevenpalowsky

▲ Rheagan generates buzz for Five Star Fitness Center because she is passionate about exercise and the facility.

Procter & Gamble took advantage of a similar approach for a series of products through the efforts of Justin Breton, a student at Boston University. He spent about 15 hours per week talking about PUR, a water filtration system from Procter & Gamble. Justin was one of 100 college ambassadors hired by P&G to pitch items ranging from PUR to Herbal Essences hair products. The students prepared their own marketing plans and earned up to $2,500 per semester. They were required to submit regular reports and were monitored by P&G and RepNation.[5] The approach helped Procter & Gamble place products in the hands of consumers and provided students with opportunities to create unique marketing ideas.

▼ Many companies employ college students to pitch products ranging from air filtration systems to cell phones to computer software.

© Andres Rodriguez/Fotolia

House or Block Parties Many brand ambassadors host house or block parties. Nestlé Purina spent $50,000 on 1,000 house parties to market a new line of dog food, Chef Michael's Canine Creations. Purina identified childless individuals with household incomes greater than $60,000 who love to pamper their pets. House Party, a firm that matches brands with party hosts, located the homes for Purina. Dianna Burroughs hosted a party in her Manhattan West Village condo. Fourteen guests and their dogs arrived to sample the filet-mignon-and-potato-flavored kibbles from Chef Michael's Canine Creations. House Party's other clients include Avon, Procter & Gamble, Kraft, Mattel, Hershey's, and Ford.[6]

Vgstudio/Fotolia

▲ BzzAgent recruits individuals who are influencers among their friends and associates to serve as brand ambassadors.

BzzAgent offers parties and the ambassador approach for its clients. Suzanne Ermel, a 30-year-old unemployed lawyer, serves as a BzzAgent ambassador for a boxed wine, Black Box. At the grocery store, when she sees a shopper put a box of wine in her shopping cart, Suzanne stops the shopper, declaring "Don't do it! This [Black Box wine] is just a couple of dollars more and you're going to like it a lot more." She adds, "I've pointed Black Box out to random people shopping for wine." She invites friends to her house for a blind tasting party and serves Black Box wine without mentioning the brand name. She then solicits comments from her guests and reveals the name of the wine. The Black Box buzz marketing campaign sought to "increase trial, advocacy, and impact sales."[7] The key to these events was that the host was an influencer among his or her friends and associates.

Company Employees

A final group of advocates includes company or agency employees. The company or agency decides whether they should pose as customers or identify themselves as being affiliated with the company. The Word of Mouth Marketing Association (WOMMA) argues that individuals should be upfront and clearly identify themselves as being with the company.

A few years ago, Wal-Mart featured a blog about two ordinary people, Laura and Jim, trekking across the Unites States in an RV and staying in Wal-Mart parking lots. The blog appeared to be written by a couple who were avid customers of Wal-Mart. The blog received considerable attention after *BusinessWeek* exposed Jim as a professional photojournalist employed by Edelman, Wal-Mart's public relations firm. Both Wal-Mart and Edelman received considerable criticism regarding the program because of the lack of transparency.[8]

The Word of Mouth Marketing Association provides guidelines for companies seeking to generate word-of-mouth communications through employees, agency employees, or even sponsors or agents. It encourages:

- Honesty of relationship—be honest about the relationship between consumers, advocates, and marketers.
- Honesty of opinion—be honest in presenting opinions about the brand, both good and bad.
- Honesty of identity—identify honestly who you are.[9]

Buzz Marketing Stages

As shown in Figure 10.3, some compare buzz marketing to how a virus replicates. The process consists of three stages: inoculation, incubation, and infection.[10] The inoculation stage corresponds to the product being introduced. During incubation, a few innovators or trendsetters try the product. In the infection stage, widespread use of the product occurs.

- Inoculation—the product is introduced
- Incubation—the product is used by a few innovators or trendsetters
- Infection—widespread use of the product occurs

▶ **FIGURE 10.3**
The Stages of Buzz Marketing

Wholly Guacamole/ Fresherized Foods

▲ Wholly Guacamole's marketers used social media to create buzz about its alliance with the TV show *The Biggest Loser*.

Only a few companies have been successful deploying buzz marketing during the inoculation stage, or product introduction. In most cases, buzz marketing does not work well at this stage unless the company employs brand agents or brand ambassadors. Otherwise, generating word-of-mouth communication can be virtually impossible. Previous research suggests that true customer-generated buzz occurs only after awareness of the product has emerged. That awareness typically requires advertising through traditional channels.[11] Now, however, social media can provide an alternative method for developing awareness of a new product or brand. Through blogs and social networking, brand managers can generate awareness and buzz, especially if they can locate some early adopters who are passionate about the brand and are willing to share that enthusiasm within their spheres of influence.

Buzz Marketing Preconditions

Advertising and buzz communication programs from actual customers typically cannot create a successful buzz by themselves unless the preconditions listed in Figure 10.4 are met. The brand must be unique, new, or perform better than current brands. It should stand out and have distinct advantages over competitors. Although not essential, memorable advertising helps to produce buzz. Intriguing, different, and unique advertising captures attention and can inspire talk among people. Getting consumers involved can enhance word-of-mouth communications.

Stride Sugarless Gum developed a website to complement the company's traditional advertising. The campaign featured the tagline, "Stride gum lasts a ridiculously long time." The company invited consumers to share what they would like to do for a ridiculously long time and post photographs of these activities on the Stride microsite developed for Sugarless Gum.[12]

Buzz marketing works for two primary reasons. First, as noted, people trust someone else's opinion more than paid advertising. Second, consumers like to render their opinions and share their thoughts. Many exhibit an innate desire for social interaction and are concerned about the welfare of others. Sharing an opinion can build a person's ego and sense of self-worth, especially when the opinion leads to happiness or satisfaction with a particular product.

Stealth Marketing

A special form of buzz marketing, **stealth marketing**, applies surreptitious practices to introduce a product to individuals while not disclosing or revealing the presenter's true relationship with the brand. Someone posing as a tourist might ask people to take a photo with a new camera and then talk to them about the camera. An attractive model ordering a beer or soft drink can tell everyone about how great it tastes. In both instances, the company pays someone to extol the product's benefits.

One stealth marketing ploy that received national attention was a 6-minute video entitled "Bride Has Massive Hair Wig Out" featuring a young bride-to-be who was unhappy with her haircut. In the video, she starts hacking off her hair just prior to the wedding ceremony. Her friends try in vain to stop her. It turns out she was acting. It was a cleverly produced video ad for Unilever's Sunsilk Haircare brand produced

- Product must be unique, new, or superior
- Brand must stand out
- Advertising should be
  - Memorable
  - Intriguing
  - Different
  - Unique
- Consumer involvement with the brand

▲ **FIGURE 10.4**
Preconditions of Buzz Marketing

AntonioDiaz/Fotolia

▲ After asking someone to take her picture, this individual can then talk about the camera.

by its advertising agency. Thinking it was a real bride and real situation, the "Wig Out" video attracted millions of online viewers, was tweeted to thousands, appeared on blogs, received a feature story on CNN, and became the subject of talk shows before Unilever revealed the truth about the stealth marketing campaign.[13]

Stealth marketing thrives in the online world, most notably on social media, due to the ease of creating videos and offering brand endorsements. Most people are not likely to pass along traditional advertisements and clips. The result has been a rise in stealth approaches as an alternative.

Some argue that stealth marketing represents a shrewd way to reach consumers and generate buzz. At the same time, the Word of Mouth Marketing Association emphasizes the importance of honesty of relationship and honesty of identity. The Federal Trade Commission (FTC) has issued an opinion letter supporting the Word of Mouth Marketing Association regarding the full disclosure of any paid individuals in ads. The enticement to create stealth marketing campaigns that generate buzz remains, and the debate over its ethical implications will likely continue.

Guerrilla Marketing

Guerrilla marketing programs obtain instant results using limited resources. The concept was developed by Jay Conrad Levinson. Historically, guerrilla marketing offers one of the most successful alternative media marketing programs. Its tactics rely on creativity, quality relationships, and the willingness to try unusual approaches. These programs were originally aimed at small businesses; however, now a wide array of firms takes advantage of guerrilla marketing tactics. Guerrilla marketing emphasizes a combination of media, advertising, public relations, and surprises to reach consumers.

Guerrilla marketing utilizes alternative tactics and venues to focus on finding unique ways of doing things. To be successful, the marketing department must change its thinking process in the marketing department. Discovering "touchpoints" with customers constitutes the first step. Touchpoints include the places where the customers eat, drink, shop, hang out, and sleep. Next, the marketing team identifies unique and memorable ways to reach consumers at one or more of those touchpoints. To do so requires imagination and unorthodox thinking.

Social media and guerrilla marketing tactics were part of the re-launch of Twinkies after Hostess went bankrupt and the brand disappeared from store shelves. Brand loyalists passed along the tagline "sweetest comeback in the history of ever" throughout social media. Guerrilla teams, Twinkie the Kid mascot, and food trucks were sent to major markets. The campaign cost $3 million and generated so much demand that the company could barely keep up. Customers purchased 85 million Twinkie cupcakes, with another 100 million ordered by retailers.[14]

Figure 10.5 compares guerrilla marketing to traditional marketing. Guerrilla marketing tends to focus on specific regions or areas. Rather than a national or international campaign, the approach concentrates on personal communication. The objective should be to create excitement that spreads to others by word-of-mouth. Guerrilla marketing involves interacting with consumers, not just sending out a message. Building relationships with customers should be the outcome. By enticing individuals to react or to do something, the program enhances the chance that a message will hit home. Advertisements reach consumers where they live, play, and work in ways that are noticed. The eventual

FIGURE 10.5
Traditional vs. Guerrilla Marketing

Traditional Marketing	Guerrilla Marketing
• Requires money	• Requires energy and imagination
• Geared to large businesses with big budgets	• Geared to small businesses and big dreams
• Results measured by sales	• Results measured by profits
• Based on experience and guesswork	• Based on psychology and human behavior
• Increases production and diversity	• Grows through existing customers and referrals
• Grows by adding customers	• Cooperates with other businesses
• Obliterates the competition	• Aims messages at individuals and small groups
• Aims messages at large groups	• Uses marketing to gain customer consent
• Uses marketing to generate sales	• "You Marketing" that looks at how can we help "You"
• "Me Marketing" that looks at "My" company	

relationships that evolve help create brand loyalty and positive recommendations to other consumers. Consequently, guerrilla marketing requires an aggressive, grassroots approach to marketing. It should produce buzz. When carried out properly, guerrilla marketing becomes a powerful marketing weapon. Figure 10.6 identifies six reasons why companies should use guerrilla marketing tactics.

Pink Jacket Creative generated buzz about Engobi, a caffeine-enhanced snack chip, during the inoculation stage of the buzz process, which can be extremely difficult. As shown in the photo in this section, "Engobi Girls" were employed to distribute free samples of the chips and to generate interest in prospective customers as part of an ingenious guerrilla marketing campaign.

FIGURE 10.6
Reasons for Using Guerrilla Marketing

- To find a new way to communicate with consumers
- To interact with consumers
- To make advertising accessible to consumers
- To impact a spot market
- To create buzz
- To build relationships with consumers

Pink Jacket Creative

"Engobi Girls" were a central component of the guerrilla marketing campaign created by Pink Jacket Creative for a new type of snack chips.

Karns foods

▲ Karns Foods can use lifestyle marketing to acquaint consumers with its quality meat department.

Lifestyle Marketing

Another program that assists companies making contacts with consumers in more offbeat and relaxed settings, **lifestyle marketing**, involves identifying marketing methods associated with the hobbies and entertainment venues of the target audience. Lifestyle marketing includes contacting consumers at places such as farmer's markets, bluegrass festivals, citywide garage sales, flea markets, craft shows, stock car races, and other places where large concentrations of potential customers convene. A local grocer such as Karns Foods can use these types of venues to acquaint consumers with its quality meat department.

A wide range of consumer lifestyles creates potential target groups, from relatively standard habits to more edgy and extreme behaviors. The energy drink Red Bull and the producers of the energy snack PowerBar gave free samples to people attending sports events, including football and baseball games. The concept was that people who watch sports would be more inclined to try the product. Covergirl offered cosmetics to women attending a fashion show with the idea that females in attendance would be more concerned about personal appearance. Finding a venue where consumers go for relaxation, excitement, socialization, or enjoyment and then matching it with the brand's target market constitutes the key to lifestyle marketing.

Experiential Marketing

Another alternative marketing form, **experiential marketing**, combines direct marketing, personal selling, and sales promotions into a single consumer experience. It typically involves direct marketing through interactive means such as special events and free samples. Experiential marketing seeks to engage consumers with the brand, rather than merely providing free samples. Bruce Burnett, chief executive of i2i Marketing suggests that experiential marketing, "gives consumers the opportunity to question as well as gain hands-on experience with a brand, allowing them to be more intimate with it, leading to a higher conversion rate."[15]

▼ Tracy is passing out samples of a new drink as part of an experiential marketing program.

JackF/Fotolia

Cadillac developed a three-part experiential program aimed toward current and perspective buyers. All three events were by invitation only. The first element featured a series of 14 golf clinics that paired golf instruction by the David Leadbetter Gold Academy with test drives of the Cadillac. The second element included a culinary tour in 13 different markets paired with the Cadillac SRX model. The third element, a five-track based event, displayed a souped-up V-Series Cadillac sedan in a half-day of high-performance driving and education session led by the Skip Barber Racing School. Invitees participated in three modules: slalom breaking, lane change, and lap driving. GM's head of North American marketing Chris Perry stated that the experiential programs fit the Cadillac brand well because "the Cadillac customer is one who is more entrepreneurial spirited, perhaps more interested in the latest technology, always looking for the new ideas and thinking, more outer directed."[16]

Jack Morton Worldwide created an experiential marketing campaign for Cotton, Inc. aimed at 18- to 34-year-old women. The traveling mall exhibit presented the songs "The Fabric of Our Lives" and "Dixie" sung by contemporary artists Zooey Deschanel (indie rock), Miranda Lambert (country), and Jazmine Sullivan (R&B). Mall shoppers were able to look into the singers' closets, which were filled with cotton clothes. Shoppers could also record a personal version of "The Fabric of Our Lives." The campaign's budget was $500,000 to $1 million. The exhibit provided mall shoppers with hands-on contact with cotton fabrics.[17]

To increase the probability that a positive experience will occur from an experiential marketing event, companies should follow these steps:

Step 1 Choose a clear, concise market segment to target.

Step 2 Identify the right time and place to involve consumers with the brand. Choose opportunities that fit with consumers' lives and when they can engage with the brand emotionally and logically.

Step 3 Make sure the experience reveals clearly the brand's promise and represents the brand well to consumers.

Allowing consumers to enjoy the benefit of a good or service before actually making a purchase gives the program the greatest chance for success.[18]

Product Placements and Branded Entertainment

objective 10.2
What methods can be used to effectively employ product placements and branded entertainment?

Most marketers believe getting a product noticed has become increasingly difficult. In response, many firms increased product placement and branded entertainment expenditures. Each couples the popularity of an entertainment venue with a product or company.

Product Placements

The planned insertion of a brand or product into a movie, television show, or program, a **product placement** serves the purpose of influencing viewers. Product placements have been a part of motion pictures since the beginning of the industry in the 1890s. Lever Brothers placed the company's soap brand in some of the early films. In the 1930s, Buick created a ten picture deal with Warner Brothers for placements. Several tobacco companies paid actors to endorse and use the brands. Early television programs, such as the *Colgate Comedy Hour*, were sponsored by brands.

The biggest surge in product placement occurred in 1982 after Reese's Pieces were used to lure E.T. out of hiding as part of the plot of the movie. The placement of the Reese's Pieces spurred a 65 percent increase in sales following the movie's release.[19] With that surge, product placements continued to grow for both brands and TV shows. During a recent month, *American Idol* led all television shows with 208 paid product placements. The top brand in terms of product placement was Coca-Cola.[20] Figure 10.7 displays the top six brands and top six television shows for product placements.

Top Brands (Total occurrences/month)

- Coca-Cola 99
- AT&T 76
- Chevrolet 45
- Ford 39
- Apple 32
- Everlast 32
- Nike 32

Top Shows (Total occurrences/month)

- *American Idol* 208
- *Celebrity Apprentice* 127
- *America's Next Top Model* 88
- *Biggest Loser* 88
- *Amazing Race* 69
- *Shedding the Wedding* 40
- *Dancing with the Stars* 38

FIGURE 10.7
Top Television Production Placements

Advertisers believe product placements lead to increased awareness and more positive attitudes toward the brand. In a few isolated cases, sales of a brand have increased. In most instances, however, no immediate impact on sales occurs. Research by Nielsen reveals the following about product placements:

- Brands placed within "emotionally engaging" television programs were recognized by 43 percent more viewers.
- Brand recognition increased 29 percent for brands placed in highly enjoyed programs.
- Positive brand feelings increased by 85 percent for brands placed in popular programs.[21]

Brand placement presents the advantage of a low cost per viewer, especially for movies. After a movie has finished at the cinema, it will usually be converted to a DVD format for movie rentals. From there, the movie may be adapted for television viewing on syndicated outlets or one of the premium movie channels. It might also be made available on TV through video-on-demand. This expands a movie's reach beyond the cinema screen to other venues where it may be seen multiple times by individuals.

Harley-Davidson hired Davie Brown Entertainment to locate appropriate product placement opportunities in movies, television, music, and video games. For the first time in Harley-Davidson's history, the company relied on product placements as its core marketing strategy. According to Dino Bernacchi, director of advertising and promotions for Harley-Davidson, "We want to use [product placement] to socialize Harley-Davidson motorcycling.... Entertainment can sensationalize the excitement and thrill of riding to the point of moving people to check it out." Only three percent of American consumers own a motorcycle, but another 15 to 20 million have the desire to buy one. Harley-Davidson's marketing team believed strategic product placements would encourage those on the edge to go ahead and make purchases.[22]

M.Camerin/Fotolia

▲ Harley Davidson emphasized product placement in television shows, movies, music, and video games in a recent marketing campaign.

Recently, MillerCoors signed an exclusive product placement deal with Turner Broadcasting. Only MillerCoors products would be shown on TNT- and TBS-created shows. Product placement included cans of beer, barware, taphandlers, and trucks. While MillerCoors did not have control of the scripts for the various television shows, the brewery's marketing team provided input on each of its brands and how they could be used. For instance, Blue Moon appeals to women and was therefore featured in *Rizzoli & Isles*. Miller Lite was featured in *Dallas* because the city of Dallas contains a large group of Miller Lite customers.[23]

Branded Entertainment

The integration of entertainment and advertising by embedding brands into the storyline of a movie, television show, or other entertainment medium is **branded entertainment**.[24] In an episode of the CTV drama, *The Eleventh Hour*, for example, Nicorette was integrated into a story about a character trying to quit smoking. The movie *Up in the Air* starring George Clooney prominently displayed American Airlines and Hilton Hotels. The movie's plot involves Clooney's character logging ten million miles on American so he can have his name emblazoned on the plane and ride along with American Airlines' chief pilot. Actual American Airlines planes were used in the film. Many of the hotel scenes were filmed at

Hilton locations. Integrating the brands into the story made them much more noticeable to the viewing audience.[25]

The use of branded entertainment has increased with the rise of reality television shows that simulate "real-world" situations. The success of branded entertainment in reality shows has led to its use in scripted television shows. Branded entertainment may also be found in novels, plays, songs, and movies.

- Media
- Supporting promotional activities
- Consumer attitudes toward placements
- Placement characteristics
- Regulations

▲ **FIGURE 10.8**
Key Factors Influencing the Effectiveness of Product Placement and Branded Entertainment

Achieving Success

Figure 10.8 identifies the major factors that influence the success of brand placements and branded entertainment. The specific medium or media involved has an impact on effectiveness. Placement clutter has caused some television programs to lose clout. For instance, 4,349 product placements were used during Fox's *American Idol* show from January to May in one season.[26] Only the prominent brands were noticeable, such as the red plastic cups of Coca-Cola in front of the judges. Most were lost in the mass of brands appearing on the show.

Product placements and branded entertainment work because no "call to action" appears. Instead, increasing brand awareness and generating positive feelings toward the brand are the goals. When a consumer's favorite actor enjoys a particular brand or her favorite show contains a particular brand, it becomes more likely that the individual will transfer those positive feelings to the brand. People between the ages of 15 and 34 are more likely to notice brands placed in a movie or show. Also, individuals in North America and the Asia-Pacific area are more receptive than viewers in Europe. When a consumer sees a brand placement of a product that he has purchased, it may reinforce the idea that a wise decision was made, further validating the original purchase decision.[27]

Company Tactics The manner in which marketers place the brand into a movie or show will be important. Brand insertions work best when they seem logical. In other words, the most effective placements are those woven into the program in ways that appear to be natural parts of the story. Brands shown in the background that seem to be artificially inserted will be less effective.

For some companies, product placements in movies deliver the advantage of bypassing legislation and guidance intended to control advertising to children and young adults. A study of the top 25 box office movies revealed that 32 percent were rated for viewing by adolescents and contained prominent brand placements for tobacco products. If these companies would have tried to advertise directly to teens, they would have encountered numerous regulations and possibly severe penalties.[28]

Budgets for product placements and branded entertainment have been increasing for several reasons. First, a brand's appeal may be stronger when it appears in a non-advertising context. Second, the perception of what others think of a brand is important to consumers. For many, it can be more important than how the consumer views the brand. Seeing the brand used in a television show, a movie, or a book makes the brand appear to be acceptable and even desirable. Third, seeing others use the brand provides reassurance for individuals who have already purchased the item.

Fourth, for individuals who place little value in brand names and branded products, having a brand placed in a program provides evidence of the brand's advantages. The evidence may be strong enough for them to consider purchasing the item. In these cases, the brand does not have to directly persuade the consumer of its merits. It does so through the acceptance and use of the product by the actor or the story in the program.

▼ Seeing brands used in television shows and movies can make the brand look more acceptable and desirable.

Gstockstudio/Fotolia

The Media's Perspective For moviemakers and television producers, money represents the primary motivation behind product placements and branded entertainment. In the past, brand mentions were incidental or used by movie producers to create realism in a film. They now generate additional income. Martha Stewart charges $10,000 for a 30-second placement on her show. For a one-time mention in the show with a product close-up, the price goes up to $100,000. For a 2-minute branded entertainment segment with two or three talking points, the price rises to more than $250,000.[29]

In summary, brand placements present an excellent method to increase share of mind and build brand awareness. Although some believe that certain programs have become saturated with product placements, they continue to be utilized. If clutter becomes too severe, usage will likely decline, but only if the impact on consumer responses and attitudes also declines.

Alternative Media Venues

objective 10.3
Why has the use of alternative media venues, especially video game advertising, grown in marketing communications programs?

In upper New York, before crossing one of the five bridges operated by the New York State Bridge Authority, a driver must pay a toll or present an EZ-pass. Advertisements now appear on the mechanical arms that come down at the toll booth for a popular tourist attraction called Headless Horseman Hayrides and Haunted Houses. Owner Nancy Jubie reported, "This is so in-your-face advertising, we couldn't pass it up." The cost to put the name of her business on a toll booth arm for 3 months was $18,000.[30] Many companies look for unusual and unlikely places to attract attention. Figure 10.9 identifies some of the alternative forms of media.

- Video games
- Cinema
- Subways
- Street and mall kiosks
- Stairs
- Escalators
- Parking lots
- Airlines
- Shopping bags
- Clothes

▲ **FIGURE 10.9**
Examples of Alternative Media

Video Game Advertising

Product placements in video games have become common. Products can be part of a stand-alone game purchased at a retail store and played on the computer, or they can be placed in an internet video game. In-game brand placement enjoys all of the advantages of brand placements and branded entertainment. Video game advertising reaches young people who have become more difficult to contact through traditional media. In addition, it has the added feature of interactivity. Advertisers spend approximately $7 billion per year on in-game advertising because it presents an attractive market for the following reasons:

- 75 percent of all U.S. internet users spend at least one hour a month playing online games.
- 27 percent average 30 hours a month playing games.
- The primary game-playing market segment is 16- to 34-year-old males.
- The fastest-growing video game market segment is females.[31]

Video game advertising takes several forms (see Figure 10.10). The original and most widespread form of video game advertising involves locating a brand placement in the game. It can take the form of a billboard in a racing game, a Coke vending machine, or a McDonald's restaurant that is permanently integrated into the game. With the cost of producing a game now in the $20 to $30 million range and $1 to $5 million more to launch a game, game producers welcome product placement advertising as a source of revenue.

- In-game advertisements
- Rotating in-game advertising
- Interactive ads
- Game-related Websites
- Advergames
- Sponsored downloads
- Mobile game apps

▲ **FIGURE 10.10**
Video Game Advertising

The number of game-related websites has exploded in recent years. Rather than placing ads in the game itself, advertisers place ads on these gaming sites. Although the exact number of gaming websites has not been identified, estimates suggest that more than 6,000 exist. Some receive as many as seven million visits per year.[32]

Numerous companies offer video games to be played on branded websites. These branded video games are called **advergames**. Axe, Maxwell House, Holiday Inn, Arby's, Baskin-Robbins, and Suave are companies offering advergames. Instead of creating a special microsite for these games, the advergames are usually placed on free gaming portals such as Kewlbox (www.kewlbox.com). Ninety percent of the games on the site are advergames and are offered for free. They are played 500,000 to 700,000 times per day.[33] Blockdot.com research indicates that consumers have positive feelings about brands that sponsor advergames. More specifically, 83 percent of consumers think positively about companies that underwrite advergames, and 70 percent are more likely to buy products from companies that sponsor the games.[34]

In addition to game-related websites, advertisers are attracted to the social gaming market. According to Nielsen, gaming has passed email as the second most popular online activity just behind social networking. Of the 800 million individuals on Facebook, 53 percent have played games on the site, and 20 percent play them regularly.[35]

Another popular new approach involves mobile gaming that drives traffic into retail outlets. Buffalo Wild Wings, for instance, features a fantasy football game app that requires consumers to play it in the store to be eligible for prizes. Cosi, a newly established sandwich restaurant, requires gamers to visit a store to determine if they are winners. In both instances, the mobile game apps drive customer traffic to retail outlets where they are more likely to purchase food items.[36]

AlexandreNunes/Fotolia

▲ The primary game-playing market segment is 16- to 34-year-old males.

Benefits IGA Worldwide research revealed that the majority of gamers hold positive attitudes about seeing ads in video games, if the ads are well done and fit the scene. The study noted that 82 percent of gamers find the games to be just as enjoyable when ads were present. A 44 percent increase in recall of brands resulted from ads presented in games when compared to awareness prior to exposure in the video game. Positive brand attribute associations also increased.[37]

Online video games present advertisers with the luxury of generating quality web metrics. Advertisers can track the length of ad exposure in an online game. In most cases, the marketers are able to tie in demographic information to find out who views the in-game ad, how long they play, and how often. These metrics then make it possible to target ads specifically to the consumer, demographic group, location profile, or type of player.[38]

▼ Approximately 40% of gamers are now female, many starting to play games at a young age.

Eleonore H/Fotolia

New Video Game Technology Product placements within a game face the disadvantage of soon becoming static. Consequently, the player no longer notices it. To combat this problem, Massive, a new media company, has pioneered a technology that rotates or changes ads in online video games in real time. Advertisers insert new ads and products into the online game each time the person plays it. By changing the ads, the marketing team delivers time-sensitive promotions, and the advertising remains current. Massive can make the advertisement interactive, allowing the player to click on it for additional information. Additional technology can measure how much of a billboard or product placement a player sees during the game depending on their in-game actions. Technology can then fine tune the player's surroundings so that the missed ad will reappear later in the game.[39]

Females and Video Games In the past, most marketers believed that mostly teens and young adult males enjoyed video games. Today, IDC Research estimates that females constitute 40 percent of all gamers. One recent estimate suggests that more than 130 million females play video games.

The introduction of new games, such as *Littlest Pet Shop* and *Charm Girls* for girls plus *Your Shape, Just Dance, Wii Fit Plus*, and *Sports Active* for women, has built demand. Ubisoft's *Imagine* video game series, which sold 14 million copies in 3 years, features games

Wavebreakmedia Micro/Fotolia

▲ More women are needed to design and produce games for the female market.

in which girls can play the role of a ballerina or explore female-dominated professions. WomenGamers.com connects with women who enjoy video games. The site offers reviews of games and posts various types of commentary articles.

Many believe more can be done to entice women into the market. Courtney Simmons, public relations director for Sony Online Entertainment (SOE), recently spoke to an invitation-only crowd at the Game Developers Conference in San Francisco. Simmons enjoys playing video games with her three children. She argues that women are being "gamed down to," because "there is a lack of understanding about how women play." Simmons wants "more women making games," she says, "making more games that women want to play."

EA conducted extensive market research about what female users want in a game. The company's marketing team discovered that girls like it better when the pets make eye contact with the player. Studies and sales data indicate that women are more likely to play handheld casual games, such as the Nintendo DS, along with more socially-oriented games.

From a marketing communications perspective, gaming offers considerable potential. As more females purchase gaming devices and play games tailored to them, sales will increase. Further, the ability to reach girls, young women, and mature women with products placed in the games or advertising messages embedded in them presents a potentially powerful new method to develop brand awareness and brand loyalty in an alternative medium.[40]

Cinema Advertising

▼ A street kiosk advertisement for Unleashed Dog Parks created by the Pink Jacket Creative advertising agency.

Pink Jacket Creative

Prior to a movie showing, most theaters present advertisements during pre-feature programming. Some products may have direct relationships with the movie; others are totally unrelated. Although clutter exists in the sense that the commercials often run consecutively and will be mingled with new movie previews, they are delivered to what is essentially a "captive" audience waiting for the feature to start.

Cinema advertising rarely appears at the center of an integrated ad campaign, but that was the case with HP's launch of the Photosmart Premium printer with TouchSmart Web. According to Tariq Hassan, HP's vice president of marketing, "We had to create more awareness; we had to touch the consumer. The theater was a natural fit." The cinema campaign included a 30-second spot in the pre-feature programming at 17,300 theaters and 2,600 plasma screens in theater lobbies. It also executed an interactive "lobby domination" strategy in 15 theaters in New York, Chicago, San Francisco, San Diego, Miami, and Houston. Theater lobbies were turned into branded events with banners, signage, holographic 3-D kiosks, and large manned booths where the printer was demonstrated. The campaign delivered 50,000 product demonstrations averaging 6 minutes in length and a total of 700,000 lobby impressions.[41]

Other Alternative Media

A number of additional media alternatives are available. Ads now appear on subways and other public facilities as local and state governments struggle to balance budgets. Parking lots, stairs, and escalators all feature advertising displays. Airlines increase revenues by presenting advertisements on flight-ticket jackets and using in-plane signage. Shopping bags, clothes, and restaurant menus provide additional advertising venues.

Alternative media provided an important component of the advertising campaign for Unleashed Dog Parks created by the Pink Jacket

◀ A bus wrap advertisement for Unleashed Dog Parks created by the Pink Jacket Creative advertising agency.

Pink Jacket Creative

Creative advertising agency. As shown in the two photos in this section, Pink Jacket added a street kiosk ad and a bus wrap ad to reinforce the billboards that were running. The objective was to reach people during routine moments in their daily lives.

The out-of-home component of a recent Kraft Lunchables with Fruit campaign was unique in its use of alternative venues. The company descended on the three largest U.S. markets—Chicago, New York, and Los Angeles—with news about fruit offered on numerous street corners. In partnership with Feeding America, interactive storefronts were developed. Consumers could engage with the storefront materials to contribute to Feeding America. In addition to the interactive storefronts, Lunchables took over bus shelters with dynamic lenticular printing, dominated billboards, sides of buildings, and Times Square.

A new innovative form of alternative media utilizes facial recognition technology. A digital display in a shopping mall with this technology can recognize a female in her 20s standing in front of it. Ads touting makeup, shoes, fashions, and ice cream then pop up. If a man in his 50s moves in front of the display, a different set of ads appears.

The popularity of using nontraditional formats to deliver advertising messages continues to increase. Each time an innovative marketing professional identifies a new venue, a segment of the advertising community jumps on board. These methods make it possible to send messages that either cut through or go around clutter to reach people in moments when they may be more receptive to an advertisement's content.

In-Store Marketing

objective 10.4
How have in-store marketing and point-of-purchase displays evolved into effective communication and sales tools?

Consumers make approximately 60 percent of all purchase decisions while in a retail store.[42] Except for point-of-purchase (POP) displays, many marketing departments do not pay much attention to in-store marketing. Funds devoted to it represent a small percentage of advertising and marketing budgets. This may mean that some companies are missing opportunities.

To understand the potential of in-store advertising, consider what affects consumers as they purchase clothing. In a survey of about 600 consumers, 52 percent said that in-store signage, displays, or point-of-purchase displays influenced their decisions, far outdistancing print advertising and word-of-mouth communications.[43] Figure 10.11 displays a complete list of these influences.

▶ **FIGURE 10.11**
Types of Advertising that Most Influenced Clothing Purchases

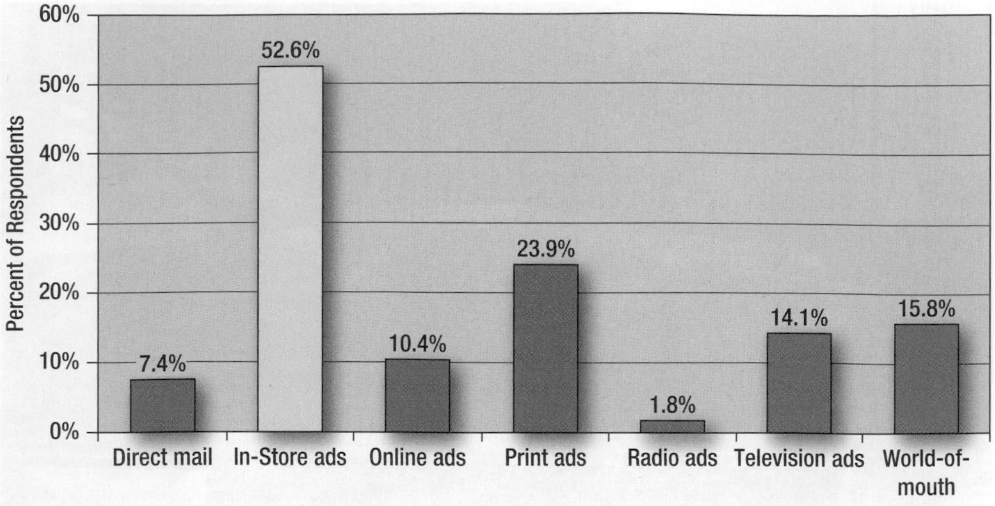

▲ Approximately 60 percent of all purchase decisions are made in the retail store.

In-Store Marketing Tactics

The in-store shopping experience has a major impact on purchase decisions. In a survey of shoppers, 69 percent called the in-store time the "make or break" experience. "Understanding high potential shopper strike zones has become increasingly critical, given the intensified battle for consumer loyalty and share of mind in-store," commented D'Anna Hawthorne, strategic director at Miller Zell, a retail consulting firm. Companies now try to engage consumers, not just merchandise items on a shelf. According to consumers, end-aisle displays and merchandise displays are the most engaging. Ceiling banners and overhead mobiles are the least engaging.[44]

The use of color, light, and sound has long been a part of in-store marketing. Retailers may also add *motion*. Placing and using video screens and television monitors to present messages represents the newest and most expensive in-store marketing tactic. Many static signs have been replaced with high-technology mediums. Also, shopping carts with static signs that are broken or unreadable are being replaced with video screens. Digital media within the store offers retailers the opportunity to customize messages to fit the store and the aisle where the display is located.[45]

Airplay America produces The Salon Channel, a retail television channel and digital signage network for beauty salons. Programming consists of human interest and lifestyle stories. Beauty shop patrons spend an average of 30 to 45 minutes per salon visit. The Salon Channel provides entertainment, including features about nationally recognized stylists and the latest hairstyles, along with advertisements for products and services, many of which are related to beauty and fashion.[46]

Wal-Mart follows the same path. In the past, Wal-Mart's ads appeared on all in-store televisions at the same time. With new technologies, the marketing department distributes ads geared to each department within a store and for specific aisles. Rather than hanging television monitors from the ceiling, flat-screen panel monitors are placed at eye level in the aisles, which leads to greater ad recall. Marketers placed digital monitors at end-caps and near other displays. These television monitors contain advertising pertinent to the end-cap or the merchandise being displayed. To fully appreciate the potential impact of this form of in-store advertising, consider each week 68 million viewers watch the combined national television newscasts on ABC, CBS, and NBC. The number of shoppers at Wal-Mart each week tops 127 million. The potential audience for a commercial on the

Wal-Mart television system will be nearly twice as large as an advertisement on the three national newscasts.[47] In addition, the Wal-Mart ad reaches consumers as they shop and while they consider purchasing options.

Social Media and In-Store Tactics

The rise of social media usage has led to attempts to use it to drive store traffic. Social media can be integrated with other in-store tactics. Marketers place QR codes on the product's package or label and on store shelves that offer instant coupons. Mobile coupons may be accessed via social media that can then be redeemed at the retail store.

Banana Republic recently offered a unique alliance with Match.com. The clothing store sponsored an in-store Valentine's Day meet-and-greet mixer in key markets of Chicago, San Francisco, Los Angeles, and New York. Individuals from Match.com met each other after hours at the selected store to become acquainted. Fashion and lifestyle blogger Joy D. Cho was enlisted to share her personal love story on her blog *Oh Joy*. Cho and her husband re-created their first date in a Banana Republic outlet. Photos of the date were posted on Facebook, Twitter, Instagram, and Pinterest. Individuals were also encouraged to share their favorite photos taken inside the store on social media for a chance to be included in the Valentine's Day album posted by Banana Republic on Facebook.[48]

Boyers Foods

▲ In-store signage at Boyer's offering a faster, better shopping experience.

Point-of-Purchase Marketing

Traditionally, one of the most important components of in-store marketing has been **point-of-purchase (POP) displays**, which include any form of special exhibit that advertises merchandise. Retailers locate point-of-purchase displays near cash registers, at the end of an aisle, in a store's entryway, or anywhere they might be noticed. Point-of-purchase advertising includes displays, signs, and devices used to identify, advertise, or merchandise an outlet, service, or product. POP displays can serve as an important aid to retail selling.

Point-of-purchase displays remain highly effective tools for increasing sales. Coca-Cola reports that only 50 percent of soft drink sales are made from the regular store shelf. The other 50 percent results from product displays in other parts of the store. American Express discovered that 30 percent of purchases charged on the American Express card came from impulse decisions by customers seeing the "American Express Cards Welcome" sign.

Research indicates that an average increase in sales of about nine percent occurs when one POP display is used. Only about half of POP displays actually impact sales; however, those that increase purchases do so by an average of nearly 20 percent. Consequently, point-of-purchase advertising remains attractive to manufacturers.[49]

Currently, manufacturers spend more than $17 billion each year on point-of-purchase advertising materials. Manufacturers place the greatest percentage of POP materials in

▼ Point-of-Purchase displays are often located near cash registers to encourage impulse buys.

Tyler Olson/Fotolia

restaurants, food services, apparel stores, and footwear retailers. The fastest-growing categories include fresh, frozen, or refrigerated foods and professional services.[50]

Manufacturers view point-of-purchase displays as an attractive way to display a brand more prominently in front of customers. Many retailers hold a different perspective, believing that POP materials should either boost sales for the store or draw customers into the store. Retailers are not interested in the sales of one particular brand, but instead want to improve overall sales and store profits. Retailers prefer displays that educate consumers and provide information. As a result, retailers are more inclined to set up displays to match the retailer's marketing objectives.

Designing Effective Point-of-Purchase Displays

Effective POP displays clearly communicate the product's attributes. A quality display incorporates the price and other promotional information. It encourages the customer to stop and look, pick up the product, and examine it. A customer who stops to examine a product on display becomes more likely to buy the item.

▼ Using POP displays that are integrated with Kraft's advertisements for Kraft Parmesan Cheese increases the chances of being noticed by shoppers.

Kraft Foods, Inc.

A successful display makes a succinct offer that the customer immediately understands. In most cases, a display has a limited time to capture the customer's attention. If it fails, the customer simply moves on to other merchandise. Colors, designs, merchandise arrangements, and tie-ins with other marketing messages are critical elements of effective POP displays.

The best point-of-purchase displays are integrated with other marketing messages. Logos and message themes used in advertisements appear on the display. A study by the Saatchi & Saatchi advertising agency revealed that consumers make purchase decisions in just four seconds. On average, a consumer only looks at a display or signage for three to seven seconds.[51] Tying a POP display into current advertising and marketing messages increases the chances it will be noticed. Effective displays present any form of special sales promotion that a company offers. Customers quickly recognize tie-ins with current advertising and promotional themes as they view displays. Figure 10.12 lists some additional pointers for point-of-purchase advertising.

Measuring Point-of-Purchase Effectiveness

Manufacturers and retailers both seek to measure the effectiveness of POP displays. Linking the POP display into a point-of-sale (POS) cash register

- Integrate the brand's image into the display.
- Integrate the display with current advertising and promotions.
- Make the display dramatic to get attention.
- Keep the color of the display down so the product and signage stand out.
- Make the display versatile so it can be easily adapted by retailers.
- Make the display reusable and easy to assemble.
- Make the display easy to stock.
- Customize the display to fit the retailer's store.

▶ **FIGURE 10.12**
Effective Point-of-Purchase (POP) Displays

makes it easier to gather results. Items on the display are coded so that the POS system picks them up. Then, individual stores measure sales before and during a point-of-purchase display program by using cash register data. The data also helps the retailer's management team decide when it is time to withdraw or change a display as sales begin to decline. The technology enables retailers to identify the displays that generate the largest impact on sales. A retailer might deploy this method to test different types of POP displays in various stores. The most effective displays can then be expanded to a larger number of stores.

From the manufacturer's viewpoint, point-of-sale data helps to improve POP displays. The data may also be used to strengthen partnerships with retailers. These bonds help the manufacturer weather poor POP showings. Retailers are more willing to stay with a manufacturer that tries to develop displays that benefit both parties.

Brand Communities

objective 10.5
How can brand communities enhance brand loyalty and devotion?

The ultimate demonstration of brand loyalty and brand devotion takes the form of **brand communities**. In most cases, a symbolic meaning behind the brand links individuals to the brand community and other owners of the brand. Interactions between the customers and the product lead to a sense of identity and inclusion. A set of shared values and experiences that integrate with feelings about the brand becomes the result.

Brand communities do not form for every product or company. They cannot be created by the product itself; however, a marketing department can facilitate and enhance a community experience. A company with a strong brand community maintains a positive image, has a rich and long tradition, occupies a unique position in the marketplace, and enjoys a group of loyal, dedicated followers.[52] Figure 10.13 highlights some of the reasons that brand communities exist. Most brand communities require some type of face-to-face interactions, although the internet does provide a venue for members to contact each other and to blog about the product.

- Affirmation of the buying decision
- Social identity and bonding
- Swap stories
- Swap advice and provide help to others
- Feedback and new ideas

▲ **FIGURE 10.13**
Reasons Brand Communities Form

Jeep, Harley-Davidson, and Apple all enjoy loyal brand communities. In each case, the brand owners come from diverse populations. The highly successful Jeep Jamboree and Camp Jeep events give owners opportunities to share driving experiences, tell stories, and share ideas. Most of the interactions among customers occur during the company-sponsored barbecue. They also take place during roundtable discussions hosted by a Jeep engineer or other Jeep employee.

Many, if not most, of the attendees at a Camp Jeep event have no experience driving a Jeep off-road. Among those who have, some use a "tread lightly" ethos, whereas others have mud-covered vehicles from heavy off-road adventures. First-timers at the camp

Skyjaker Suspension

◀ The popularity of the reality TV show *Duck Dynasty* has increased enthusiasm for the brand community around the Skyjacker brand.

FIGURE 10.14
Ways to Enhance Brand Community Spirit

- Create member benefits to encourage new customers to join a group.
- Provide materials to the group that are not available anywhere else.
- Involve firm representatives in the groups.
- Sponsor special events and regular meetings.
- Promote communications among members of the group.
- Build a strong brand reputation.

are often timid and afraid they might not fit in, but soon find they do as repeaters fully welcome anyone and everyone to the Jeep community. The vehicle provides the common bond that brings individuals together, regardless of demographic and psychographic differences.

Harley-Davidson features a highly successful brand community program. Several years ago, the company's leadership team helped create a unique brand community spirit. An organization called HOG formed around the Harley brand. In return, Harley-Davidson offered benefits, such as information about community gatherings along with special marketing offers for accessories, to HOG members. The benefits are only available to the HOG group, which encourages new Harley-Davidson owners to join the HOG brand community.

Marketers seek to facilitate and enhance the community in which owners can interact. Figure 10.14 provides information on ways a marketing team can assist in creating a brand community.

Building a brand community begins with sponsoring events that bring product owners together. As noted, Jeep sponsors the jamborees and a camp. Harley-Davidson sponsors rides, rallies, and local events. These events help create a brand community spirit that leads to bonding between owners. Eventually, this produces a sense of social identity.

Company representatives should become involved in club events. Jeep engineers attend events and mingle with customers. They provide advice and encouragement to any new owner about to take his or her vehicle off-road for the first time. Harley managers, including the CEO, ride Harleys to rallies to talk with owners.

In addition to company-sponsored events, other venues for interaction can be encouraged. The internet offers another place for owners to talk. They can visit through blogs, chat rooms, or social network microsites. A company can become involved in these exchange venues. Employees should openly identify themselves. Brand communities enjoy company involvement and want an honest exchange of comments.

While providing venues and means for enhancing a brand community spirit, the company continues other advertising and marketing programs. Brand communities normally emerge for brands with strong images. Such images must be maintained. Marketers feature the pride of owning the brand in advertisements, making its uniqueness and position in the marketplace clear.

International Implications

objective 10.6
What methods are used to adapt alternative marketing programs to international marketing efforts?

Alternative marketing can be used to reach minority groups within the United States. An example of buzz marketing occurred when the Clamato company sought to increase brand awareness among U.S. Latinos. The firm gave 2,000 agents a 32-ounce bottle of Clamato and 10 coupons. The agents reached 34,000 potential customers, and positive opinions of the drink rose from 32 to 78 percent.[53]

Alternative marketing methods are also being tried in other countries. Starbucks and Pepsi combined efforts to produce a movie series called *A Sunny Day*. The film follows a girl from the Chinese countryside to the big city, where she discovers love, blogging, Starbucks, and Pepsi. The series was tailored for Shanghai's subway and the 2.2 million who ride it each day. The story was made into a soap opera-style script featuring short daily segments. A website featured story snippets each day for those who missed seeing it on the subway and wanted to know what happened. The Shanghai subway has a network of 4,000 flat-screen monitors that provide train information, clips of soccer highlights, entertainment news, and advertising. Marketers pay to run ads, just like they would on television. *A Sunny Day* was the system's first venture into a short miniseries, with episodes each day for 40 weeks.[54]

Brand communities have emerged in other countries. Jeep employed the brand community concept to build a brand presence in China. The first Jeep was introduced in China in 1983 by American Motors through a joint venture in Beijing; however, recent sales of Jeep have slowed. In response, the first three-day Camp Jeep in China was created. It attracted 700 Jeep owners and 3,000 participants. The event included off-road courses, bungee jumping, a hiking course, wall climbing, a soccer field, and an off-road ATV course. Musical entertainment and time slots for karaoke enthusiasts were provided.[55] The event's purpose was to renew Jeep's strong brand name and to create a strong sense of community among current Jeep owners in China. Through these individuals, Jeep's marketing team hoped to generate word-of-mouth, or buzz, for the Jeep brand, driving new customers to the Jeep brand.

The clutter problems that plague U.S. advertisers are present around the world. The tactics used to overcome it domestically may be adapted to international operations. Firms from other nations can adapt alternative media tactics. International conglomerates will likely respond with new and creative alternative marketing programs.

INTEGRATED campaigns in action

Interstate Batteries

Interstate Batteries employed its internal marketing department to launch a geo-targeted online media plan for all company battery centers located in cities throughout the United States. The objectives of the campaign were to:

- Increase awareness of all Interstate Battery Centers
- Drive traffic to all Interstate Battery Centers
- Create awareness of key brand messages

Interstate Batteries featured an online display advertising to create awareness and provide information about the location of its stores. The campaign was geo-targeted by each store's market ZIP codes. Consumers who clicked on the ads were taken to a geo-specific landing page that provided information about the closest All Battery Center. The campaign targeted the 25 to 54 age group with the selected ZIP codes surrounding each of the battery stores.

Online metrics to measure the success of the campaign were determined prior to the launch. Metrics included click-through rates, coupon redemptions, changes in sales, and the number of transactions at the retail stores. Additional online metrics included the number of individuals who enlarged the map, submitted information by email, and printed the coupon.

The Interstate Battery Center digital campaign is located at the Pearson Instructor's Resource Center (www.pearsonhighered.com). The campaign includes a PowerPoint presentation outlining the details of the campaigns and examples of the collaterals. Video by the Interstate Batteries marketing team explaining the campaign is available.

Interstate Batteries

Summary

Alternative media enjoys many success stories. Well-known brands, such as Ben & Jerry's and Starbucks, have emerged using very little traditional advertising. Each found new methods to establish a brand presence, including alternative media and alternative marketing methods. Starbucks built a community of coffee lovers through local involvement and word-of-mouth.

The four forms of alternative marketing programs are buzz marketing, stealth marketing, guerrilla marketing, and product placement. Buzz marketing, or word-of-mouth marketing, places the emphasis on consumers passing along information about a brand. The consumers can be those who like a brand, sponsored consumers, or company insiders. Some consider using company insiders to be unethical, which means care should be given before starting such programs.

Stealth marketing uses surreptitious practices to introduce a product to individuals or fails to disclose or reveal the true relationship with the brand. It has also drawn ethical criticism.

Guerrilla marketing programs are designed to obtain instant results with limited resources through creativity, high-quality relationships, and a willingness to try unusual approaches. Lifestyle marketing involves the use of marketing methods associated with the hobbies and entertainment venues of the target audience. Experiential marketing combines direct marketing, field marketing, and sales promotions into a single consumer experience.

Product placements are planned insertions of a brand or product into a movie, television program, or some other media program. Branded entertainment facilitates the integration of entertainment and advertising by embedding brands into the storyline of a movie, television show, or other entertainment medium.

Numerous alternative media venues exist. They include mobile phone advertising, video game advertising and advergames, cinema advertising, airline in-flight advertising, and others. Use of these media has been on the increase.

In-store marketing programs take two forms. New tactics include the use of high-tech video screens and television monitors in new and more visible places. This includes tailoring messages to individual parts of the store. Traditional point-of-purchase advertising continues to be widely utilized. Recently, POP advertising incorporated newer technologies to increase its effectiveness.

Brand communities evolve when consumers feel a great deal of brand loyalty and devotion. They form around events, programs, and exchanges of information. A company with a strong brand and a devoted marketing team can assist in the formation and continuance of brand communities.

Alternative media choices are utilized to reach minority groups in the United States in unique new ways. They are also expanding into international markets. As advertising clutter increases, the use of these media is likely to grow and will likely become cluttered as well.

Key Terms

alternative marketing The use of buzz, word-of-mouth, and lifestyle messages at times when consumers are relaxing and enjoying hobbies and events

buzz marketing An emphasis on consumers passing along information about a product to others; also known as *word-of-mouth marketing*

stealth marketing The use of surreptitious practices to introduce a product to individuals without disclosing or revealing the true relationship with the brand

guerrilla marketing Programs designed to obtain instant results through the use of limited resources by relying on creativity, high-quality relationships, and the willingness to try new approaches

lifestyle marketing Marketing methods associated with the hobbies and entertainment venues of the target audience

experiential marketing A program that combines direct marketing, field marketing, and sales promotions into a single consumer experience

product placement The planned insertion of a brand or product into a movie, television show, or some other media program

branded entertainment The integration of entertainment and advertising by embedding brands into the storyline of a movie, television show, or other entertainment medium

advergames Branded video games

point-of-purchase (POP) displays Any form of special display that advertises merchandise

brand communities A link that forms due to an association between the brand, a consumer, and others who own or purchase the brand

MyMarketingLab

Go to **mymktlab.com** to complete the problems marked with this icon ✪.

Review Questions

10-1. What is needed to create alternative marketing programs by marketers?

10-2. What is a sponsored consumer?

10-3. What does a brand ambassador do and what are the controls?

10-4. The Word of Mouth Marketing Association provides guidelines for companies. What are they?

10-5. What is a sponsored consumer?

10-6. What is guerrilla marketing? How does it differ from traditional marketing?

10-7. What are the fundamental requirements of guerrilla marketing in order for it to work?

10-8. How do consumer lifestyles create potential target groups?

10-9. What are product placements and branded entertainment? What do they have in common?

10-10. Identify the alternative media venues described in this chapter.

10-11. Describe the forms of video game advertising, including advergames.

10-12. What is in-store marketing? Why is it important?

10-13. What new in-store marketing tactics are being utilized?

10-14. What is point-of-purchase advertising? Why is it important?

10-15. How have new technologies changed some forms of point-of-purchase advertising?

10-16. What is a brand community?

10-17. What should a company's marketing team do to assist in the development and growth of brand communities?

10-18. Is the use of alternative media growing or declining in international markets? Explain why.

Critical Thinking Exercises

DISCUSSION QUESTIONS

10-19. Think about a product category where you have a high knowledge of the various brands. Pick one of the major brands. Discuss the characteristics the brand would want for a brand advocate, ambassador, or evangelist. What type of offers would it take from the company to create a strong brand ambassador? Discuss each of the stages of buzz marketing as it relates to the brand you identified. Which stage is the brand in now? Justify your answer. Discuss each of the preconditions of buzz marketing as it relates to your chosen brand.

10-20. Many consumer websites feature reviews with a number of stars. These are peer reviews by previous customers. Are you influenced by these types of reviews? Do you think they are genuine?

10-21. Can you think of a lifestyle marketing program or an experiential marketing campaign that you encountered? What was your reaction? Was the approach effective? Why or why not? What about with other consumers? If you have not experienced lifestyle or experiential marketing, think of a situation and brand where you think it would be effective. Explain why.

10-22. Imagine being approached by the owner of a small clothing boutique. She has heard about guerrilla marketing and wants to try it. Why should she use guerrilla marketing? What are the pros and cons? What guerrilla marketing techniques would you suggest?

10-23. Find a movie or television show that you have already watched and enjoyed. Watch it again, but this time, make a list of all of the product placements in the file. Identify if each was a prominent placement, if the actor used the brand, or if it was just in the background. When you finish, discuss the product placements that were the most effective and those that were the least effective. What made the placement effective? What made it ineffective?

10-24. Do you play video games? If so, approximately how many hours a month do you play games (including online games)? What advertising have you noticed in the games? How effective was the advertising?

10-25. A prominent position in a store has a price tag attached to it. It is common practice for a manufacturer to pay to have their products featured on an "end gondola" in retail stores. Visit three or four stores and see which products have paid for these positions. Are they the same brands in each one? Share your findings.

10-26. Go to a nearby retail store and talk to the manager or one of the employees. Ask them about the store signage, including point-of-purchase displays. Ask the employee to discuss what signage is effective and why. As a customer, did you agree with the manager's or employee's viewpoint? Why or why not?

Integrated Learning Exercises

10-27. Access **http://women.igda.org**. What is your overall opinion of this website? How can it be beneficial to a marketing manager? How can it be beneficial to females who want to pursue video game design? Go to the parent website **www.igda.org**. What types of information are available at this site?

10-28. Access the Word of Mouth Marketing Association website at **www.womma.org**. What features did you find on the site? What resources are available? What benefits does the site provide to a business? Is there any value for a consumer?

10-29. Type "buzz marketing" into an online search engine. Find two advertising agencies or marketing agencies that offer buzz marketing expertise. What types of buzz marketing services does each provide? Which company do you think offers the best buzz marketing program? Why?

10-30. Type "guerrilla marketing" into an online search engine. Find two agencies that offer guerrilla marketing services. Describe what type of services each offers. Go to an article database and type in "guerrilla marketing." Find two articles about guerrilla marketing that interest you. Summarize the articles.

10-31. Every country or region will have a creative advertising agency that tries to break the mould. They are the marketing and advertising innovators pushing the boundaries all the time. Do they push the boundaries of legality? Identify an example and comment on their work and their types of client.

10-32. Point-of-purchase displays should be an important component of a firm's IMC program. Research indicates that effective displays have a positive impact on sales. Access the following firms that produce point-of-purchase displays. Which firm's site is the most attractive? Which firm would be the best from the standpoint of developing displays for a manufacturer? Explain.

a. Displays2Go (**http://www.displays2go.com**)
b. Vulcan Industries (**www.vulcanind.com**)
c. Display Design & Sales (**www.displays4pop.com**)

Blog Exercises

Access the authors' blog for this textbook at the URLs provided to complete these exercises. Answer the questions that are posed on the blog.

10-33. Coca-Cola: **http://blogclowbaack.net/2014/05/12/coca-cola-chapter-10/**

10.34. Harley Davidson: **http://blogclowbaack.net/2014/05/12/harley-davidson-chapter-10/**

10.35. Buzz marketing: **http://blogclowbaack.net/2014/05/12/buzz-marketing-chapter-10/**

Student Project

CREATIVE CORNER

Ugg is the brand name for an Australian company that sells big, bulky sheepskin boots. The company's marketing team wondered if it would be possible to get fashion-conscious consumers to even consider the boots. Instead of advertising to the fashion-conscious consumer, Ugg's marketing team targeted high-profile fashion influencers. They successfully contacted and convinced Kate Hudson and Sarah Jessica Parker to wear the items. Then Oprah Winfrey praised Uggs on one of her shows. At that point, the boots became fashionable, and retailers couldn't keep them in stock.[56]

Ugg became successful using unique alternative marketing methods. Access Ugg's website at **www.uggaustralia.com** to learn about the company's products and the company itself. Suppose Ugg wanted to initiate a buzz marketing campaign at your university and that the company leaders contacted you for marketing advice. First, they would like to recruit some brand ambassadors as advocates for their brand. Your first task, therefore, is to design a flyer to post around campus announcing that Ugg wants to hire brand ambassadors. Before you can design the flyer, you must decide on the relationship the ambassador will have with Ugg and the type of reward or payment she will receive. After you design the flyer, your second task is to design a buzz marketing program that you believe Ugg and the new brand ambassador should use on your campus.

CASE 1 TIGER BALM: REINVIGORATING A LIFESTYLE

Companies know that there are huge financial benefits in the business of effective pain relief. Analgesics, a category of pain medication, continues to evolve as the ageing population and changing lifestyles have increased the likelihood of aches. According to Euromonitor International, retail sales of topical analgesics reached an estimated value of $4 billion in 2009. Consumers are also increasingly turning to herbal remedies, which are believed to offer a more natural approach to healing. Figures from Euromonitor International show that sales of herbal products grew by 35 percent from 2004 to 2009, accounting for about 16 percent of spending on consumer health products.

The century-old topical ointment Tiger Balm is a traditional brand that millions rely on for the quick relief of aches and pains. Tiger Balm has evolved from its humble origins to become a household name in 100 countries around the world.

Packaged in hexagonal jars that bear the label of a leaping tiger in their logos, the ointment is offered primarily within the Chinese market. Tiger Balm's founder, Aw Chu Kin, a Chinese herbalist in Burma, passed on the product's secret formula to his sons and made them promise to donate some of the sales proceeds of the ointment to charity. Due to the success of Tiger Balm, the company Haw Par was created. It soon grew to become a conglomerate, with interests in several industries and in 1926 the headquarters were moved to Singapore. As business flourished, so did the company's philanthropy. Tiger Balm has contributed much to local communities, especially for education and welfare concerns.

Tiger Balm's heritage is a great brand story. However, although Tiger Balm had strong brand awareness among consumers, it had become associated with older adults. Tiger Balm needed to reinvigorate itself to appeal to younger consumers.

The 1990s was an exciting time for Tiger Balm. It started to leverage its brand equity and expand its product range to suit changing consumer needs. It also implemented a lifestyle approach in its marketing. Tiger Balm began to package the balm in various forms and sizes to meet a more international market and to appeal to those who were involved in sports. Repositioning the brand as a personal care product rather than an ancient home remedy made the brand more appealing to a younger generation. Tiger Balm products are now classified into three lines: Tiger Balm with You at Home, Tiger Balm with You at Work, and Tiger Balm with You at Play.

Although Tiger Balm has seen sales grow in many parts of the world, it is inevitable that the brand will face challenges in the various markets that it competes in. To improve its market share, Tiger Balm has to adopt innovative marketing ideas and stay relevant. Tiger Balm now uses online advertising platforms, such as YouTube and Google. On its website (www.mytigerbalm.com), consumers can ask questions, obtain assistance in analyzing symptoms, and buy recommended products. By providing a total brand experience, the brand is able to stay relevant and connected with consumers. As part of its strategy to increase its brand recall in the minds of Indian consumers, Tiger Balm became the associate sponsor of the cricket team Chennai Super Kings for Indian Premier League Season 3. To create excitement for cricket enthusiasts and to relate to its consumers, Tiger Balm ran a contest in major Indian cities. Winners were provided exclusive opportunities to dine with the Chennai Super Kings team or win VIP match tickets. As a designated official "health and fitness partner" of the Chennai Super Kings, Tiger Balm won the hearts of the large Indian cricket community.

Leungchopan/Shutterstock

▲ To reach a new and younger audience, Tiger Balm used the internet to customize relationships with its customers.

In line with its brand philosophy, Tiger Balm is still very much into doing good deeds and supports and sponsors many charities. Such a commitment to philanthropy is Tiger Balm's way of creating an emotional connection with its customers and the community at large and to set the brand apart from the competition.

Even with substantial changes in the business and marketing landscape, Tiger Balm has remained focused on delivering its brand promise and the core value of its products while seeking and engaging alternative marketing strategies to stay relevant. The journey will continue for Tiger Balm, as it innovates alongside people's changing lifestyles—at home, at work, and at play.[57]

10-36. Propose an integrated lifestyle marketing program for Tiger Balm products based on a tie-in with a chosen sporting activity. Include both traditional and nontraditional promotional tools.

10-37. Describe a possible guerrilla marketing campaign for Tiger Balm.

10-38. Identify any opportunities for product placements for Tiger Balm products.

10-39. Is there a potential overlap between the brand community for Tiger Balm and the cricket community? Describe the ways that Tiger Balm's marketing department could build and enhance the relationship between the two communities.

CASE 2 HOTCOW: SEE AND REMEMBER, EXPERIENCE AND UNDERSTAND

In an increasingly competitive market, agencies need to come up with new ways of marketing products in a cost-effective manner that delivers precisely what they promise to their clients. Hotcow is a central London marketing agency that specializes in alternative marketing methods. Its repertoire includes guerrilla marketing, buzz marketing, sampling, hit squads, PR stunts, experiential events, road shows, and word-of-mouth marketing. Its goal is to make the best use of mobile marketing, viral marketing, and social media to get maximum exposure and deliver brand value for its clients. The agency won the Institute of Promotional Marketing's award for planning and executing brand experience campaigns at point of purchase in 2010. Hotcow has also won several other awards for its work for Thomson Fly, Honey Monster Foods, and Charlotte's Web. The agency also includes Neurofen, Aer Lingus, The Body Shop, and Endemol among its clients.

Rehan Qureshi/Shutterstock

▲ Hotcow stages elaborate brand events in order to cut through the noise in crowded markets.

Hotcow has a reputation for implementing effective alternative marketing techniques, principally word-of-mouth, or buzz, marketing that aims to attract early adopters to spread the word for the brand. Social networking sites, such as Facebook and MySpace, and YouTube can be powerful and effective marketing tools. The trick is to create something that gets people excited enough to get them blogging, texting, and tweeting, effectively making the brand part of the conversation they are having with their peers. That way other people will listen and get swept up in the conversation.

Hotcow calls its approach experiential marketing. It is essentially a logical extension of customer relationship marketing in that it focuses on establishing a connection with the consumer. It is vital to have a good understanding of the consumers' mindset and create an experience for them that they will not forget. The goal is for consumers to relate to the brand and for the marketing to leave a lasting impression on them that will encourage purchases into the future.

Experiential marketing works well as a live event. In March 2010, Honey Monster Foods gave the agency the task of refreshing consumers' fondness for its Honey Monster cereal character. The agency had a customized monster truck tour the UK; at each tour stop they put on special events that showcased the Honey Monster product. The main target was families, who stopped by during their shopping trips to have their photographs taken with the Honey Monster. The agency also staged live events using brand performers, with the purpose of creating a memorable experience by encouraging interaction.

The nonalcoholic beverage sector is a highly competitive, fast-growing, global market. Lifestyle marketing can be used to create a buzz about a product by paying careful attention to a target market's profile and characteristics. One of Hotcow's clients, Innocent Drinks, stages an annual weekend festival in Regents Park that targets health-conscious consumers. The net result is that Innocent Drinks is the second-fastest rising brand in the UK in terms of recognition.

Another hot brand that Hotcow has designed promotions for is Red Bull. One of Red Bull's promotions is Flugtag, which was first held in Vienna, Austria, in 1991. Red Bull, an energy drink, uses its slogan "Red Bull Gives You Wings" quite literally by holding events where teams are asked to design their own flying machines and compete with one another. Over 10,000 entrants have been involved in 20 cities around the world. The events are fun experiences for the participants and the crowds. They are a great example of using experiential marketing to target a specific type of consumer.

Red Bull continues to engage in traditional advertising, but it is increasingly using alternative forms of marketing, such as the Flugtag events. More than 11 million people are registered as "liking" Red Bull on Facebook, and it has some 90,000 followers on Twitter. Red Bull also sponsors extreme competitive events, such as the Red Bull X Fighters, a form of freestyle motor-cross, which attracts huge live audiences and extensive television and media coverage. The term *guerrilla* marketing was coined by Jay Conrad Levinson. The idea is to come up with a promotional idea that cannot be ignored. It requires imagination and creativity. Agencies like Hotcow use a blend of publicity stunts, street teams and theater, street stencilling, and lamppost advertising to reach target markets.

The term *guerrilla marketing* does suggest a degree of illegality, but this is often not the case, because in most cases all the legal permissions to run the event or the stunt are obtained in advance.[58]

10-40. Is a buzz marketing program a good idea for every type of product? Why or why not?

10-41. What are the key elements of guerrilla marketing?

10-42. Are there any ethical concerns to consider when using guerrilla marketing?

10-43. How might experiential marketing work on a larger scale? Can you think of any examples of this from your own country?

10-44. Brand-sponsored live events are a widely used marketing strategy. What are the potential benefits to a brand with this form of promotion?

MyMarketingLab

Go to **mymktlab.com** for the following Assisted-graded writing questions:

10-45. Think about a product category where you have a high knowledge of the various brands. Pick one of the major brands. Discuss the characteristics the brand would want for a brand advocate, ambassador, or evangelist. What type of offers would it take from the company to create a strong brand ambassador? Discuss each of the stages of buzz marketing as it relates to the brand you identified. Which stage is the brand in now? Justify your answer. Discuss each of the preconditions of buzz marketing as it relates to your chosen brand.

10-46. Access Ugg's website at **www.uggaustralia.com**. Evaluate the website in terms of its effectiveness, freshness, and the use of alternative marketing methods. What traditional marketing methods did you see? Do you think Ugg has effectively merged traditional and nontraditional advertising methods? Why or why not?

Part 4

IMC PROMOTIONAL TOOLS

Chapter 11 Database and Direct Response Marketing and Personal Selling

Chapter Objectives

After reading this chapter, you should be able to answer the following questions:

11.1 What role does database marketing, including the data warehouse, data coding and analysis, and data mining, play in creating and enhancing relationships with customers?

11.2 How can database-driven marketing communication programs help personalize interactions with customers?

11.3 How do database-driven marketing programs create sales and build bonds with customers?

11.4 When should direct response marketing programs be used to supplement other methods of delivering messages and products to consumers?

11.5 What are the tasks involved in developing successful personal selling programs for consumers and businesses?

11.6 How should database marketing and personal selling programs be adapted to international settings?

Overview

The fourth section of this textbook examines the promotional tools that help acquire and retain customers, as displayed in Figure 11.1. This chapter examines database programs, direct response marketing, and personal selling. Database marketing provides a new communication link with customers. This, in turn, helps to produce higher levels of customer acquisition, customer retention, and customer loyalty. Database marketing has become increasingly crucial. New technologies associated with the internet and computer software make it easier to build and develop strong database programs. Sales promotions, both consumer and trade promotions, are presented in Chapter 12, followed by public relations and sponsorship programs in Chapter 13.

Successful businesses continually acquire new customers and work to retain them. Repeat customers purchase more frequently and spend more money. Maintaining repeat business is far less expensive than constantly replacing those who turn to other companies. Personal selling, such as that carried out by Paula Ramirez, plays a key role in many organizational marketing outcomes.

SELLING PHARMACEUTICALS

Paula Ramirez

Courtesy of Paula Ramirez

Of the many forms of selling that take place, one of the more complex tasks involves convincing physicians about the merits of new drugs. Doctors are extremely busy and do not have time to listen to a sales pitch or read lengthy articles or literature about drugs. For a salesperson to see a physician requires patience, because getting past secretaries, receptionists, and nurses (gatekeepers) can be challenging.

Paula Ramirez is a sales representative for Strativa Pharmaceuticals. She has been successful because she understands the classic steps of selling to business clients, whether she calls on a CEO of a large corporation or a physician at a local medical clinic. Her approach includes collecting information, making sales calls, leaving samples, developing relationships, closing, and following up.

When collecting information about physicians, Paula stated, "Right now we're using an online system that allows me to take the physician's name and upload his or her information from a database. Further details regarding the physician's practice then becomes available. I try to learn about the staff, including their names, like and dislikes of each person–as much information as I can." Paula maintains personal information about each employee, such as "Kids in Little League" or "from Wyoming" in the client's file in order to make a personal connection. She says, "The more I know about each individual, the easier it is to interact with them and develop a personal relationship. I have found that friendship is an important key to personal selling."

Through her selling experience now and in the past with other companies, Paula has learned the importance of handling objections and closing sales. She recognizes that objections mean the person is interested. "Your task at that point is to answer the objection in terms of your product," she says. Once objections have been answered sufficiently, it is time to close, to ask for the sale. "You have to ask. You can't be afraid of a no answer because a "no" does not always mean "no," it means not right now. Don't give up. Go back, because there is another objection that you have not sufficiently answered."

The first part of this chapter examines database marketing, including data warehouses, data coding, and data mining as well as data-driven communications and marketing programs. Three data-driven marketing programs are permission marketing, frequency programs, and customer relationship management systems. Databases are used for direct response marketing techniques, including direct mail, email, television programs, telemarketing, and traditional and alternative media. Databases are a key component of personal selling. Finally, international differences in these programs are considered.

objective 11.1
What role does database marketing, including the data warehouse, data coding and analysis, and data mining, play in creating and enhancing relationships with customers?

Database Marketing

Database marketing involves collecting and utilizing customer data for the purposes of enhancing interactions with customers and developing customer loyalty. Successful database marketing emphasizes identifying customers and building relationships with them.

▶ **FIGURE 11.1**
Overview of Integrated Marketing Communications

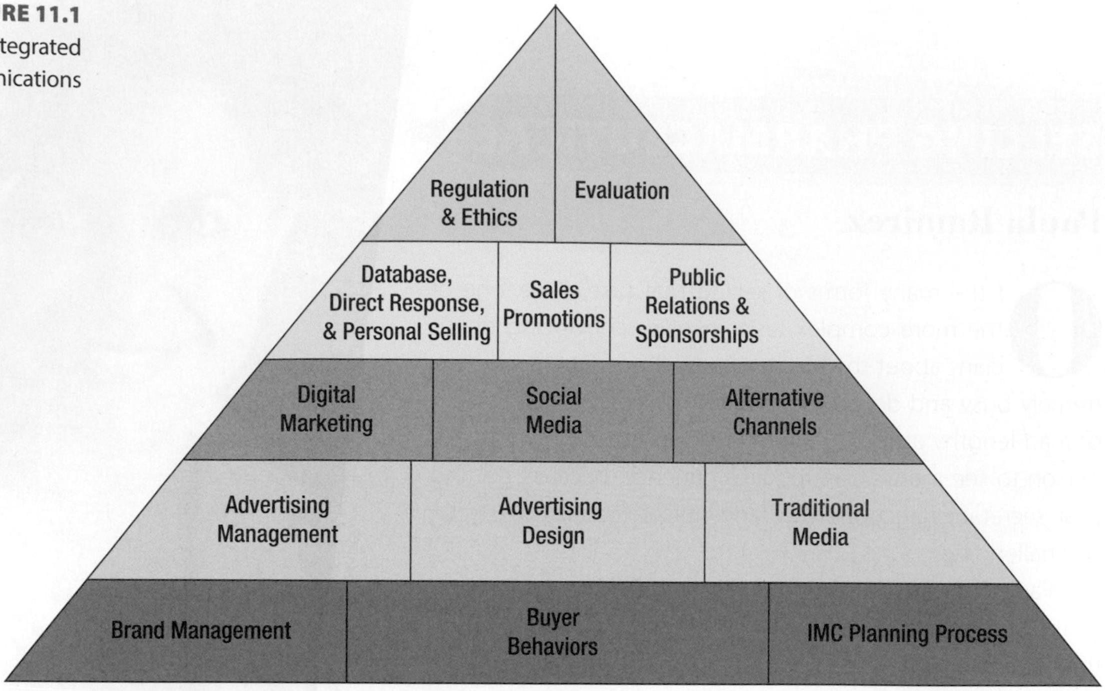

© AntonioDiaz/Fotolia

▲ The primary focus of database marketing is customer retention and developing positive relationships.

This includes understanding the lifetime values of various customers and the development of customer retention efforts. Enhancing customer loyalty constitutes the primary benefit of database marketing. Although database marketing can be used for selling products, retention and relationships remain the primary focus.

A number of retail boutiques have captured the power of database marketing. When shoppers visit the store, the sales staff can access data regarding their preferences, sizes, previous purchases, and other information. Purchases are followed up with thank-you notes. Customers receive notices when new shipments of clothes arrive and are sent invitations to special events. Loyalty to these boutiques remains high. Some customers who have moved away return to buy merchandise. One vital ingredient stands out: Data are used to make customers feel special and develop relationships with them. Although selling occurred, it does not drive the database program. Figure 11.2 displays the tasks associated with database marketing. Of these, building the data warehouse and data coding are the two key activities described next.

▶ **FIGURE 11.2**
Tasks in Database Marketing

- Building a data warehouse
- Database coding and analysis
- Data mining
- Data-driven marketing communications
- Data-driven marketing programs

Building a Data Warehouse

Successful database marketing requires a quality **data warehouse**, which holds all customer data. The IT department and marketing team distinguish between an operational database and the marketing database when building a data warehouse. An *operational database* holds the individual's transactions with the firm and follows accounting principles. The marketing department manages the *marketing database*, which contains information about current customers, former customers, and prospects. Examples of data and analyses found in a standard marketing data warehouse include:

- Customer names and addresses
- Email addresses and digital records of visits to the company's website
- History of every purchase transaction
- History of customer interactions such as inquiries, complaints, and returns
- Results of any customer surveys
- Preferences and profiles supplied by the customer
- Marketing promotions and response history from marketing campaigns
- Appended demographic and psychographic data from sources such as Knowledge Base Marketing or Claritas
- Database coding such as lifetime value and customer segment clusters

Collecting customer names and addresses is the easiest part of developing the database. Gathering the other information that turns the data warehouse into a powerful marketing and communication tool can be more challenging.

The marketing team typically employs a system for updating addresses, because approximately 20 percent of Americans move each year. When individuals fill out a change of address form with the U.S. Postal Service, the information is sent to all of the service bureaus authorized to sell the information to businesses. A company that sends database names to one of these bureaus receives address updates for only a few cents per hit, or per individual that moves. Updating mailing addresses occurs at least once each year, depending on how often the company uses the database and the frequencies of contacts.

▼ Contact information is an important component of building a data warehouse for a business-to-business company such as Scott Powerline & Utility Equipment.

Bobbie Williams/Scott Equipment

Email and Internet Data

Email addresses continue to be essential elements of a quality database. The internet and email provide cost-effective channels of communication to be used in building relationships with customers. Most database programs take advantage of digital tracking to register and store website visits and browsing patterns. This information allows for personalization of the firm's website for each customer. When someone logs on to the site, a greeting such as "Welcome back, Stacy," can appear on the screen. The tracking technology makes it possible for the system to recognize that Stacy, or at least someone using her computer, is accessing the website. If Stacy has purchased products or browsed the catalog, then the content of the pages can be tailored to contain the products she has an interest in buying.

Purchase and Communication Histories

Effective database programs maintain detailed customer purchase histories. The database records every interaction between the company and customer. When a customer sends an email to tech support, the information will be placed in the database. Any person who returns a product or calls customer service to complain has the information documented. Purchases and interaction histories determine future communications with customers and assist the marketing team in evaluating each customer's lifetime value and other customer value metrics.

Personal Preference Profiles

Purchase and visit histories do not provide complete information. Quality database marketing programs include profiles with specific information about each customer's personal preferences. These profiles and personal preference files may be constructed in various ways, including customer surveys and through information provided on an application for a loyalty card.

Every time the company initiates a contact with a customer, the information should be placed in the database, along with the customer's response. This information provides a rich history of what works and what does not. It further allows for customization of communication methods for each customer, which leads to the highest probability of success.

Customer Information Companies

Oftentimes, demographic and psychographical information are not available through internal company records. In these cases, the information can be obtained by working with a marketing research firm that specializes in collecting customer data. Knowledge Base Marketing, Donnelly, Dialog, and Claritas are four companies that market this type of information.

Data from website visits can be combined with offline information provided by firms such as Acxiom and Datran Media. Once merged, companies can store the information in cookies to allow for future customization and personalization of websites and communications with customers. For instance, based on income level and past purchasing habits, two women in adjoining offices can access the same cosmetics website; one might see a $300 bottle of Missoni perfume and the other might see the $25 house brand.[1]

Geocoding

The process of adding geographic codes to each customer's record so that customer addresses can be plotted on a map, or **geocoding**, helps decision makers finalize placements of retail outlets and directs marketing materials to specific geographic areas. Geocoding combines demographic information with lifestyle data. This assists the marketing team in selecting the best media for advertisements.

One version of geocoding software, CACI Coder/Plus, identifies a cluster in which an address belongs. A group such as Enterprising Young Singles in the CACI system contains certain characteristics such as enjoying dining, spending money on DVDs and personal computers, and reading certain magazines. A retailer might then target this group with mailings and special offers.[2]

▼ Geocoding allows a boutique, such as Chic Shaque, to target customers in specific geographic areas around its retail stores.

Joplin Globe

Database Coding and Analysis

Database coding and analysis provide information for the development of personalized communications. They assist in creating marketing promotional campaigns. Common forms of database coding include lifetime value analysis, customer clusters, and location-data tracking.

Lifetime Value Analysis

The **lifetime value** figure for a customer or market segment estimates the present value of future profits the individual or segment will generate over a lifetime relationship with a brand or firm.[3] Many marketing experts believe a market segment value provides more accurate information, because it sums costs across a market segment. Individual lifetime value calculations normally only contain costs for single customers.

The figures needed to calculate the lifetime value of a consumer or set of consumers are revenues, costs, and retention rates. Revenue and costs are normally easy to obtain, because many companies record these numbers for accounting purposes. Retention rates require an accurate marketing database system.

The cost of acquiring a new customer constitutes a key figure. It can be calculated by dividing the total marketing and advertising expenditures in dollars by the number of new customers obtained. As an example, when a company spends $200,000 dollars and acquires 1,000 new customers as a result, the acquisition cost becomes $200 per customer ($200,000 divided by 1,000).

The cost of maintaining the relationship represents another important amount. It measures all costs associated with marketing, communicating, and maintaining the database records. Obtaining these records may be more problematic, because such costs are usually for a campaign, which makes allocating costs to a single customer difficult. Computer and database technology can average or allocate a portion of these costs to individual customer records or to a lifetime value segment.

The lifetime value figure will be the end product for either individual customers or a customer segment. A lifetime value figure for a customer segment of $1,375 represents the amount of revenue, on average, that each customer will generate over his or her lifetime. By communicating with and marketing to the customer segment, the company may be able to increase the lifetime value. A lifetime value analysis informs the company's customer contact and service personnel regarding a customer's potential worth to the company.

▼ Progressive Bank can take advantage of customer clustering to identify the best prospects for its trust and wealth management services.

French Creative

Customer Clusters

Marketers use coding systems to group customers into clusters based on a wide variety of criteria. A bank may group customers based on the number of accounts, types of accounts, and other relationships a customer may have with the organization. For example, customers with home mortgages above $100,000 with balances of 30 to 60 percent remaining may be targeted for a home equity loan. A clothing retailer might group customers by the type of clothing each group purchases and then develop marketing programs for the various groups. Teenagers who purchase Western wear would be in a different cluster than teenagers who prefer hip, trendy fashions.

Unified Western Grocers, a wholesale cooperative association serving more than 3,000 grocery stores, used a customer cluster analysis to reduce 19 different advertising campaigns and programs for the various stores it served down to four, based on customer commonalities. The four clusters that emerged from the analysis were affluent urban and suburban households; mid-downscale rural seniors; large, low-income urban households; and non-acculturated

Hispanics. The marketing team designed advertisements and created shelf allocations of brands for each of the four customer clusters. The approach reduced advertising design costs and led to more effective advertising.[4]

Location-Data Tracking

The newest form of data analytics is based on information provided by mobile GPS technology. Cell phone companies such as Verizon can track customer locations and combine it with profile information. This type of information may be valuable to sports properties as well as restaurants and retailers. For instance, the Phoenix Suns basketball team's marketers took advantage of the technology to better understand fans who attended games. This information helped target specific businesses as potential sponsors.

A company such as Verizon can obtain location data to track the movement of individuals inside a sports arena as well as their activities outside the facility. These data are aggregated and then *hashed*—the process of anonymizing the data so that specific individuals cannot be identified. The data provides information regarding the restaurants or businesses patrons visited prior to attending a game as well as after a game. The marketing team then adds profile data from companies such as Experian in order to segment consumers by demographics. The ability to target specific market segments based on their actual patronage behavior at the game and the businesses around the facility becomes the result.[5]

Data Mining

Data mining involves using computer data analysis software to study data to find meaningful information and help build relationships. Data mining includes two activities: building profiles of customer segments and/or preparing models that predict future purchase behaviors based on past purchases.

▼ Data mining can be used by Weaver to build profiles of its customers that would be good targets for the company's various services.

Katie Mcgee

Data mining assists the marketing team in building profiles of the firm's best customers. These profiles, in turn, help identify prospective new customers. They can be used to examine "good" customers to see if they are candidates for sales calls that would move them from "good" to a higher value. Companies offering different types of goods and services develop multiple profiles. The profiles assist in targeting sales calls and help identify cross-selling possibilities.

The marketing team at First Horizon National Bank employed data mining tactics to expand the company's wealth management business by studying consumer groups. Data regarding existing customers from the mortgage side of the firm's business made it possible to locate the best prospects for investment services. Linking the data mining program with cross-selling resulted in an increase in company revenues from $26.3 million to $33.8 million in just one year.[6]

Marketers for the retailer American Eagle developed a data mining method to analyze consumer responses to price markdowns. The information helped the team determine when to cut prices and by how much in order to optimize sales. Markdown programs were geared to individual stores, because consumers responded differently in each outlet.[7]

The second data mining method involves developing models that predict future sales based on past purchasing activities. Marketing professionals at

Staples, Inc. prepared a modeling program to examine the buying habits of the company's catalog customers. The program identified the names of frequent buyers who were then sent customized mailings.

The specific type of information needed determines the dating mining method. Once the information contained in the data has been analyzed, the team can design targeted marketing programs. Profiles and models assist in creating effective marketing campaigns. A direct-mail program to current customers differs from one designed to attract new customers. The data provide clues regarding the best approach for each customer segment.

Data coding and data mining serve three purposes (see Figure 11.3). First, they assist in developing marketing communications. Marketing employees utilize the information to choose types of promotions, advertising media, and the message to be presented to each group of customers. Second, they help in developing marketing programs. Third, companies that employ salespeople can use the information to qualify prospects and make personal sales calls on those individuals or businesses that offer the greatest potential. Specific sales activities are described in the following sections.

- Develop marketing communications
- Develop marketing programs
- For personal sales
  - Qualify prospects
  - Information for sales calls

▲ **FIGURE 11.3**
Purposes of Data Coding and Data Mining

Database-Driven Marketing Communications

objective 11.2
How can database-driven marketing communication programs help personalize interactions with customers?

Building a database, coding the information, and performing data mining make it possible to utilize the output for the purpose of establishing one-on-one communications with customers. Personalized communications build relationships and lead to repeat business and customer loyalty. They may help move the company and its products from brand parity to brand equity. A database marketing program contains tools to personalize messages and keep records of the types of effective and ineffective communications. The internet offers the key technology for database-driven communications. Figure 11.4 highlights the importance of the internet in customer interactions.

Identification Codes

A database-driven marketing program starts with assigning individual customers IDs and passwords that allow them to access components of the website that are not available to those who simply visit the site without logging on. IT professionals tie IDs and passwords to cookies on each customer's computer in order to customize pages and individual offers. When the system works properly, the customer does not have to log in each time. Instead, the cookie automatically does it for the person. For example, each time a user accesses Barnes & Noble, he receives a personalized greeting, such as "Welcome, Jim." Next, when Jim places an order, he does not have to type in his address or credit card information. The database contains this information and it comes up automatically, which saves Jim time and effort and increases the probability he will buy something.

Companies send specialized communications after the sale. A series of messages follows the purchase. First, the buyer receives an email confirming the order and thanking her. The email contains a tracking code that she can access to locate her order at any time. The message includes an estimated shipping date. Some companies include

- It is the cheapest form of communication.
- It is available 24/7.
- Metric analysis reveals that the customer read the message, the time it was read, and how much time was spent reading it.
- Customers are able to access additional information whenever they want.
- It can build a bond with customers.

◀ **FIGURE 11.4**
The Importance of the Internet in Customer Communications

WavebreakMediaMicro/Fotolia

▲ Sending birthday wishes to customers can enhance brand attitude, brand patronage, and brand loyalty.

an email in the interim stating that the order has reached the warehouse. Then, another email can be sent when the order is pulled and shipped.

Personalized Communications

An effective database-driven communication program relies on customer profiles and any other information about customer preferences to help individualize messages. Clothing retailers often send emails about new fashions that have arrived. These emails do not go to every person in the database. Only to those who have indicated a desire to have access to the information or who have indicated they have an interest in fashion news receive the messages. These customers often believe they are receiving special "inside" information.

Marketing employees build lists of loyal patrons who will be sent birthday greetings based on customer profile data. Recently, a steak and seafood restaurant sent a card and offered a $10 birthday discount to 215,600 persons who provided their birthdates. The cost of mailing the birthday card and discount was $90,000. Patrons redeemed approximately 40 percent of the cards. Each birthday customer brought an average of two other people, and those individuals paid full price for their meals. The result was $2.9 million in revenues derived from the program.[8]

A survey by Fulcrum revealed that 74 percent of individuals who received a birthday message from a business thought more positively about the company, and 88 percent of the positive reactions translated into increased brand loyalty. Greetings from brands in the food and beverage industry generated the most positive responses. Birthday wishes with discounts were more effective than birthday greetings sent without incentives. Clearly personalized communications offer an effective means of increasing brand loyalty.[9]

Customized Content

In addition to personalized communications, data can be analyzed in order to customize content. Netflix tracks what movie buffs watch, search for, and rate. The company tracks the time of day, date, the device used (smartphone, tablet, or PC), where individuals browsed, and where they scrolled on a page. The information aids the company in suggesting movies to the person and helps stream the suggestions to the individual's most-often checked device at the best time. For instance, if the browsing history indicates that an individual searches for and watches romantic comedies on Friday nights, then a suggestion would be sent to the person's mobile phone or tablet that morning or the day prior. Netflix estimates that 75 percent of viewer selections result from these data-driven recommendations.[10]

In-Bound Telemarketing

Contacts made by telephone work the same way as internet contacts. The service-call operator immediately sees the identity of the person calling. Customer data appears on the screen in front of the in-bound telemarketer. The operator treats the caller in a personalized manner. When the company calculates a lifetime value code, the operator knows the customer's value and status. The operator asks about a recent purchase or talks about information provided on the customer's list of preferences or a customer profile. The operator greets and treats each customer as an individual, not as a random person making an in-bound call.

Newcomer, Morris and Young Inc.

◀ A bank such as Ouachita Independent Bank can incorporate trawling to identify individuals who have just moved into the community and may be looking for a banking institution.

Trawling

Database marketing includes a procedure called **trawling**, or the process of searching the database for a specific piece of information for marketing purposes. Home Depot's trawling program locates individuals who have recently moved. The company's marketing team knows that when people buy new homes, they often need home improvement merchandise. Most of the time, these items include merchandise sold at Home Depot.

Other marketers trawl a database to find anniversary dates of a special purchase, such as a new car. Car dealerships send a correspondence on each year's anniversary of a car purchase to inquire about customer satisfaction and interest in trading for a newer vehicle. A retailer can trawl for individuals who have not made a purchase within the last three months or who purchased a lawnmower last year. Trawling presents a wide variety of ways to communicate with specific individuals who meet a particular criterion.

Database-Driven Marketing Programs

objective 11.3
How do database-driven marketing programs create sales and build bonds with customers?

Database-driven marketing programs take many forms. They may be undertaken in conjunction with other marketing activities. Some of the more common programs include permission marketing, frequency programs, and customer relationship management efforts.

Permission Marketing

A strong backlash by consumers against spam and junk mail continues to grow. Consequently, many marketing departments have turned to **permission marketing**, a program in which companies send promotional information to only those consumers who give the authorization to do so. Permission marketing programs can be offered on the internet, by telephone, or through direct mail. Response rates are often higher in permission programs, because customers only receive requested marketing materials or those for which consent was given. Results are enhanced when permission marketing programs utilize database technology to segment customers, although not every person who signs up for permission marketing becomes a valuable customer.

Figure 11.5 lists the steps of a permission marketing program. Permission can be obtained by providing incentives for volunteering, such as information, entertainment, a gift, cash, or entries in a sweepstakes. Any information provided should be primarily educational and focus on the company's product or service features.

Reinforcing the relationship requires an additional new incentive beyond the original gift. Relationships can be enhanced when marketers acquire more in-depth information

FIGURE 11.5
Steps in Building a Permission Marketing Program

1. Obtain permission from the customer.
2. Offer the consumer an ongoing curriculum that is meaningful.
3. Reinforce the incentive to continue the relationship.
4. Increase the level of permission.
5. Leverage the permission to benefit both parties.

about a consumer such as hobbies, interests, attitudes, and opinions. The information may be tailored to entice additional purchases by offering special deals.

Keys to Success in Permission Marketing For a permission marketing program to succeed, the marketing team ensures that the recipients have agreed to participate. Unfortunately, some consumers have been tricked into joining permission marketing programs. One common tactic involves automatically enrolling customers in permission marketing programs as they complete online surveys or purchase items online. Opting out of the program requires the individual to un-check a box on the site. Although this approach increases the number of individuals enrolled, the technique often creates bad feelings.

The marketing materials should be relevant to the consumers receiving them. Far too many people who have joined permission marketing programs encounter situations in which they provide no input and are bombarded with extraneous marketing messages. This does not create loyalty and runs counter to the purpose of a permission program.

One recent survey revealed that 80 percent of consumers stopped reading permission emails from companies because they were shoddy or irrelevant. Another 68 percent said the emails came too frequently, and 51 percent reported they lost interest in the goods, services, or topics of the emails. On the whole, consumers delete an average of 43 percent of permission emails without ever reading them.[11]

To overcome these challenges, the marketing team monitors responses and customizes the permission program to meet individual customer needs. Database technology allows for customization by tracking responses and browsing behavior. When a customer regularly accesses a website through a link in an email sent by the company to read the latest fashion news, the behavior can trigger email offers and incentives on fashions related to the news stories and links the customer followed. An individual who does not access the website and does not appear to be interested in fashion news receives a different type of email offer. By capitalizing on the power of database technology, a firm can enhance the permission marketing program and make it beneficial to the company and the customer.

▼ Permission marketing can target individuals interested in fashion news.

.Shock/Fotolia

Permission Marketing Enticements Figure 11.6 notes the top reasons for opting into email programs. Winning a sweepstakes tops the list. Also, individuals who are already customers of the company may be more inclined to examine the company's products.[12] Enticing them into the permission marketing program will be easier than trying to attract new patrons.

Figure 11.7 provides a list of motives that help retain customers in a permission marketing relationship. As shown, consumers remain with such programs for many reasons.[13]

Permission marketing programs have the potential to build strong, ongoing relationships with customers when they offer something of

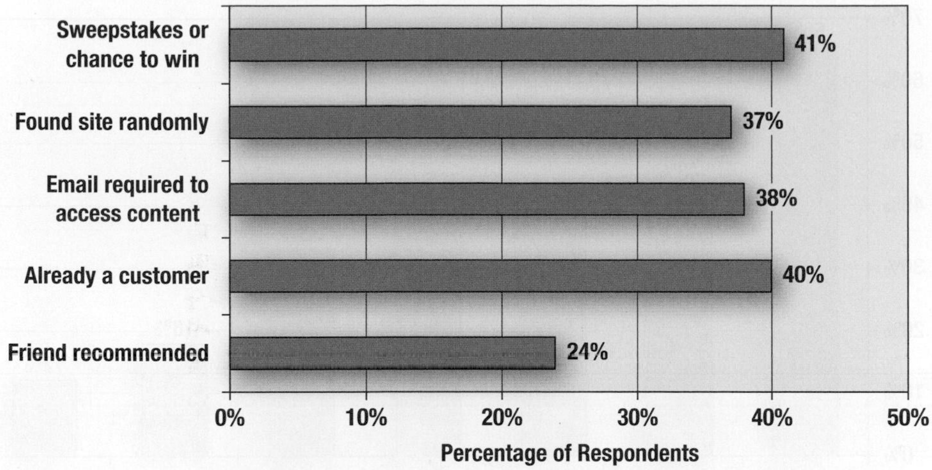

FIGURE 11.6
Reasons Consumers Opt into Email Permission Programs

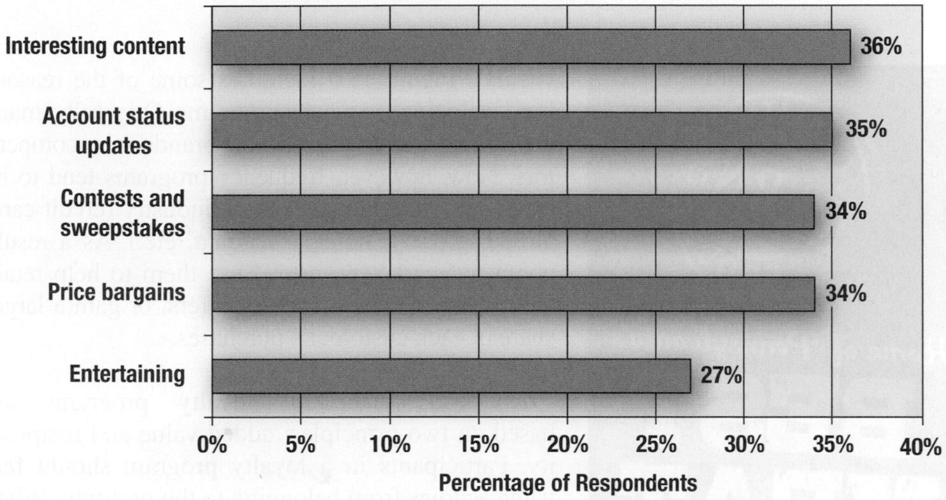

FIGURE 11.7
Reasons Consumers Remain in a Permission Marketing Program

value. To optimize permission marketing, firms feature empowerment and reciprocity. **Empowerment** means consumers believe they have power throughout the relationship and not just at the beginning when they agreed to join the program. They can make decisions and have choices about what to receive.

To maintain positive attitudes, consumers should be given rewards along the way, not just at the beginning. This creates feelings of **reciprocity**, or a sense of obligation toward the company. Only rewarding customers for joining the program will be a mistake. Empowerment and reciprocity lead the customer to believe the company values the relationship, which increases the chances the consumer will continue to be an active participant.

Frequency Programs

A company offers free or discounted merchandise or services for a series of purchases in a **frequency program** or **loyalty program**. These enticements encourage customers to make repeat purchases. In the airline industry, frequent-flyer programs offer free flights after a traveler accumulates a certain number of miles. Grocery stores grant special discounts when purchase totals reach a certain amount within a specified time period.

Chief Marketing Officer (CMO) Council research indicates that two-thirds of consumers belong to loyalty programs. On average, households are enrolled in 14 programs, but only actively participate in about six. Figure 11.8 provides a list of benefits of such programs mentioned by customers and the percentage that cites each benefit.[14]

▶ **FIGURE 11.8**
Benefits of Loyalty Programs Cited by Consumers

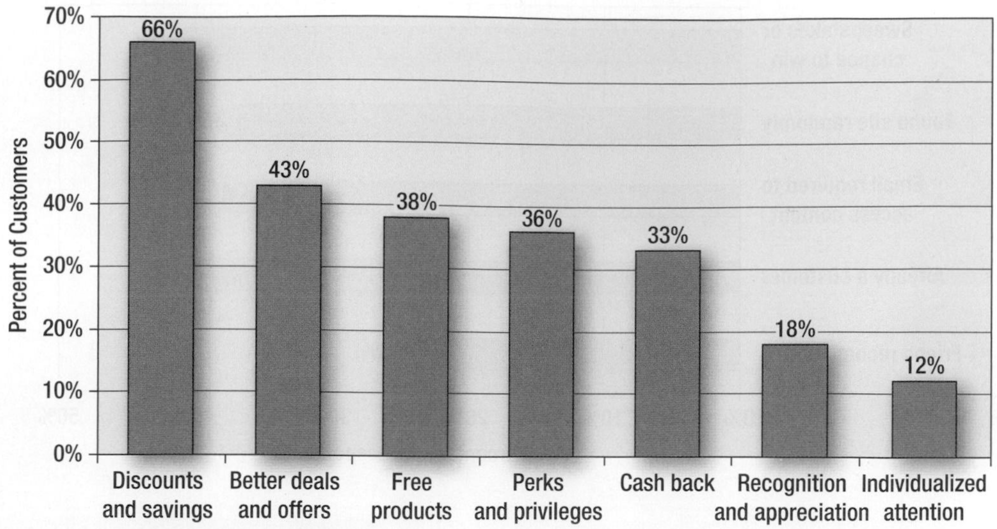

Karns foods

▲ An advertisement for Karns Quality Foods encouraging consumers to sign up for the store's loyalty program.

Goals Figure 11.9 identifies some of the reasons for developing frequency programs. Originally, many were developed to differentiate brands from competitors. Now, however, frequency programs tend to be offered by all companies in an industry (credit card, airline, grocery, hotel, restaurant, etc.). As a result, company marketers instead use them to help retain customers, match competitor offers, or gain a larger share of each customer's purchases.

Principles Successful loyalty programs are based on two principles: added value and reciprocity. Participants in a loyalty program should feel value accrues from belonging to the program. When the customer in turn rewards the perceived value by making additional purchases, it creates a sense of reciprocity. When the customer and the company both benefit from the relationship, it continues.

Recent research suggests that the more effort a customer expends to participate in a frequency program, the greater the value of the reward becomes. Many consumers are willing to put forth greater effort to obtain luxury rewards as opposed to necessity rewards. Shoppers at a grocery store are more likely to give higher levels of effort in order to receive a free overnight stay at a nearby local resort or a free meal at a nice restaurant than they would for a $20 gift certificate for food.

Data-Driven Customization Collecting data assists the marketing team in customizing loyalty programs to meet each individual's needs. Mass offers may not be as effective, because customers feel they are being "sold" rather than "rewarded." CVS Pharmacy's marketer understood this principle when they launched the ExtraCare loyalty program. Individuals who belonged to ExtraCare received a tailored version of the weekly print circulars. The data collected from the member's purchases leads to suggestions of sale items along with individualized discounts and coupons. These promotional offers were not for competing brands or products that do not interest card members. Instead, they were for brands and products card members regularly purchased. In the

- Maintain or increase sales, margins, or profits
- Increase loyalty of existing customers
- Preempt or match a competitor's offer
- Encourage cross-selling
- Differentiate the brand
- Discourage entry of a new brand

◀ **FIGURE 11.9**
Goals of Frequency or Loyalty Programs

words of one customer who likes to drink Coke products rather than Pepsi, "For me to be able to get a coupon to buy more Coke is a lot more relevant. I value more getting coupons for products I like, not for products I don't care for, which is wasting my time."

▲ Restaurants often use loyalty cards to encourage customers to return more often.

Monkey Business/Fotolia

Maximize Motivation Effective loyalty programs maximize a customer's motivation to make another purchase. Many times, marketers target moderate users with frequency programs. Light users seldom make purchases and cost more to maintain in the program than they spend. High users already make frequent purchases and are unlikely to increase their purchasing levels. Consequently, moderate users represent the most valuable target group.

Research indicates that a *variable ratio reward schedule* is superior to regularly scheduled rewards in motivating additional purchases. A variable ratio means that customers receive intermittent reinforcements. They do not know exactly when a reward will be given or the size of the incentive. The random reward schedule should be frequent enough to encourage them to make ongoing purchases.[15]

Although many consumers have frequency cards, they may not always use them. The marketing manager of a locally-owned restaurant noticed he had a large number of customers who had not recently used their Frequent Diner Club cards. Trawling identified 4,000 Frequent Diner Club members who had not earned any points during the previous three months. To motivate these past customers, the restaurant sent a letter to each of the 4,000 offering a $5 discount on dinner. The offer was good for 35 days. The cost of the mailing was $1,800. Results were:

- The average number of member visits per day increased from 25 to 42 during the promotion and to 29 per day after the promotion ended.
- Average visits by individual members holding cards increased both during and after the promotion.
- Incremental sales increased by $17,100 during the promotion and by $4,700 after the 35-day promotion.

By spending $1,800, the promotion led to reactivations by about 600 people who had not dined at the restaurant in 3 months. Of the nearly 600 who were motivated to come back during the promotion, 147 dined at the restaurant after the promotion was over.[16]

Customer Relationship Management

Customer relationship management (CRM) programs provide a method to employ databases that customize products and communications with customers, with the goals of higher sales and profits. Successful CRM programs build long-term loyalty and bonds with customers through a personal touch, facilitated by technology. Effective customer relationship management programs go beyond the development of a database and traditional selling tactics to the mass customization of both communications and products.

Two primary CRM metrics are the lifetime value of the customer and share of customer. The lifetime value concept has already been described in an earlier chapter. As noted, it measures the potential level of purchases to be made by an individual or market segment.

The second metric, share of customer, is based on the concept that some customers are more valuable than others and that, over time, the amount of money a customer spends

Advertisement for Centric Federal Credit Union furnished by Emogen Marketing

▲ Centric Federal Credit Union can use a CRM program to enhance relationships with its current customers.

with a firm can be increased. **Share of customer** refers to the percentage of expenditures a customer makes with one particular firm compared to total expenditures in that product's category. Share of customer measures a customer's potential value. The question becomes, "If more is invested by the company in developing a relationship, what will the yield be over time?" When a customer makes only one-fourth of his purchases of a particular product category with a specific brand, increasing the share of the customer would mean increasing that percentage from 25 percent to a higher level, thus generating additional sales revenues. The ultimate goal would be leading the customer to make 100 percent of his purchases with one brand.[17]

Kellogg's CRM database holds information from 18 million consumers. Among these, 3.5 million individuals have become part of Kellogg's Family Rewards Program. Each Kellogg product package provides a unique, 16-digit code. Members submit these codes online in exchange for points that can be redeemed for discounts or free prizes, such as toys or sports equipment. The code tells Kellogg the type of product, the package size, and the store where the product was purchased. The information creates a history of every Kellogg purchase the individual made, when it was made, and where it was made. These data allow the company's marketing group to prepare specific offers designed to match the person's past purchasing behaviors. In addition, the data assist in developing marketing communications that are better aligned with consumer preferences and that facilitate the cross-selling of Kellogg products.[18]

In general, CRM marketing programs should enhance customer loyalty. When a hotel's check-in person knows in advance that a business traveler prefers a nonsmoking room, a queen-size bed, and reads *USA Today*, these items can be made available as the guest arrives. Training hotel clerks and other employees to rely on the database helps them to provide better service, thereby increasing loyalty from regular customers. Any organization's marketing department can adapt these techniques to fit the needs of its customers and clients.

In addition to permission marketing, frequency programs, and CRM systems, other marketing programs can result from database analysis. Internet programs, trade promotions, consumer promotions, and other marketing tactics may be facilitated by using the database.

objective 11.4
When should direct response marketing programs be used to supplement other methods of delivering messages and products to consumers?

Direct Response Marketing

One program closely tied to database marketing, **direct response marketing** (or **direct marketing**), involves targeting products to customers without the use of other channel members. Figure 11.10 identifies the most typical forms of direct response marketing

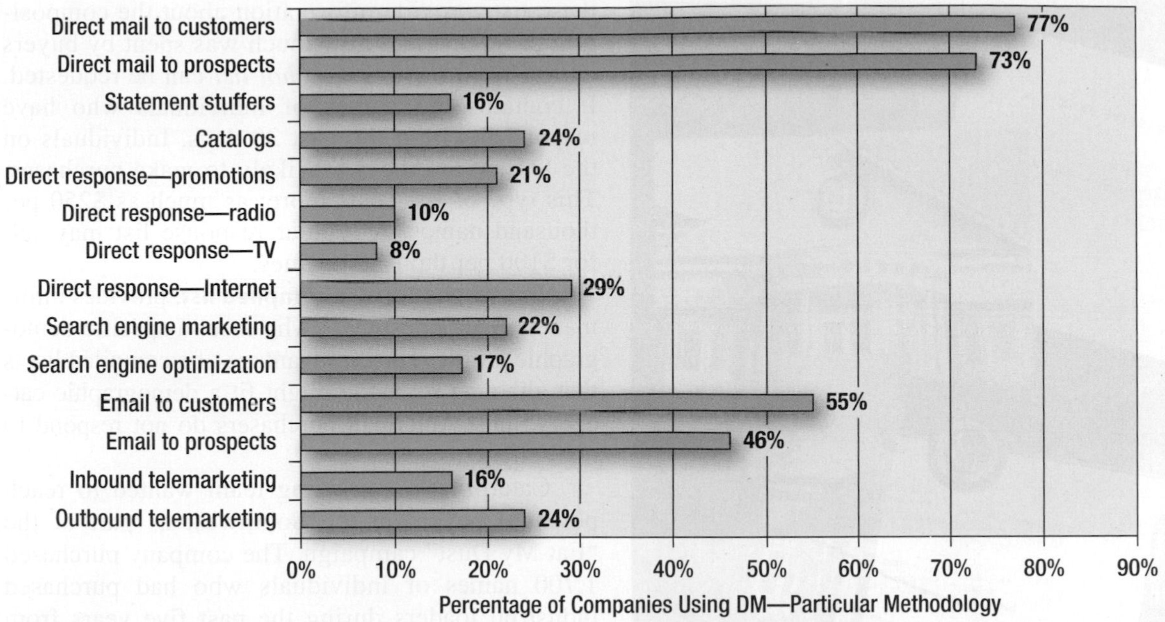

▲ **FIGURE 11.10**
Methods of Direct Response Marketing

and the percentages of companies using them. Notice that direct marketing can be aimed at customers as well as prospects. According to the Direct Marketing Association, about 60 percent of a typical direct marketing budget targets prospecting for new customers; the other 40 percent is spent retaining current customers.[19]

Many pharmaceutical companies employ direct response advertising, especially on television and in magazines. A recent study revealed that this direct response approach works. Ads for prescription medications by pharmaceuticals prompted almost one-third of Americans to ask their doctors about a particular brand of medicine and 82 percent of those who asked doctors received some type of prescription. The prescription was for the advertised brand 44 percent of the time; for another drug, 56 percent of the time. Sometimes, doctors prescribed the advertised brand as well as another brand.[20]

Individuals and companies respond to direct response marketing in a number of ways, such as by telephone, email, visiting a retail location, or using a PURL (personalized URL). PURLs offer the advantage of preloading all of the individual's personal data to a website, which can then customize the information and any offer. They also assist in tracking the individual's onsite activities and in making real-time changes to offers.[21]

Direct Mail

As shown in Figure 11.10, direct mail remains the most common form of direct response marketing. Direct mail targets both consumers and business-to-business customers. The quality of the mailing list normally determines the success of a direct mail program. Companies utilize two sources when compiling a mailing list: the firm's internal database and/or a commercial list.

The company's marketing department parses an internal list and separates active members from inactive members. Prospective new customers receive different direct mail pieces with messages designed to entice repeat purchases. Mailing direct offers to individuals (or businesses) who have not purchased recently but who have purchased in the past often yields a better response rate than cold-call mailing lists from brokers.

Types of Commercial Lists A company can purchase a commercial list as either a response list or a compiled list. A **response list** consists of customers who have made purchases or who have responded to direct mail offers in the past. Brokers selling

Courtesy of French Creative

▲ Progressive Bank can take advantage of direct mail to target specific financial service customers.

these lists provide information about the composition of the list and how much was spent by buyers on the list. In addition, a *hot list* can be requested. It contains the names of individuals who have responded within the past 30 days. Individuals on the hot list are the most likely to make purchases. This type of list costs more: as much as $250 per thousand names. A regular response list may sell for $100 per thousand names.

The second form, a **compiled list**, provides information about consumers who meet a specific demographic profile. The disadvantage of a compiled list is that although someone might fit a demographic category, most American purchasers do not respond to mail offers.

Caterpillar's marketing team wanted to reach potential buyers in the Southwest as part of the "Eat My Dust" campaign. The company purchased 1,700 names of individuals who had purchased industrial loaders during the past five years from Equipment Data Associates, a Charlotte, North Carolina, firm that compiles detailed purchasing histories of more than 870,000 U.S. contractors. Rea & Kaiser's Nichols agency designed a sweepstakes to win a new Cat 414E. An eye-catching direct mail piece urged contractors to sign up either online, by mail, or at a local Caterpillar dealer. Standard response rates are less than one percent; the response rate for the "Eat My Dust" direct mailer was 18 percent.[22] The highly targeted list made the difference.

Skyjaker Suspension

▲ Catalogs are an important component of Skyjacker's Integrated Marketing Communications Program.

Catalogs

Many consumers enjoy catalogs and view them at their leisure. Catalogs have a longer-term impact because they are kept and shared. Catalogs feature a low-pressure direct response marketing tactic that gives consumers time to consider goods and prices. Many marketers believe that online shopping has replaced catalogs; however, some research suggests that this is not the case. More than half of online shoppers browse a catalog prior to making the online purchase and more than 30 percent have a catalog in hand when placing the online order. More than 85 percent of survey respondents said they had purchased an item online after seeing it in a catalog first.[23]

Successful cataloging requires an enhanced database. Many catalog companies, such as L.L.Bean and JCPenney, create specialty catalogs geared to specific market segments. The specialty catalogs have a lower cost and a higher yield, because they reach individual market segments.

Catalogs are essential selling tools for many business-to-business marketing programs. They provide more complete product information to members of the buying center as well as prices for the purchasing agent. When combined with an internet presence, a catalog program can facilitate a strong connection with individual customers.

Mass Media

Television, radio, magazines, and newspapers provide additional tools for direct response advertising. Direct response TV commercials are slightly longer (60 seconds), which allows a potential buyer time to find a pen to write down a toll-free number, an address, or a website. Catchy, easy-to-remember contact information is often used, such as "1-800-Go-Green" or "www.gogreen.com." Repeating the response format helps customers remember how to respond. Often a "call-now" prompt concludes the commercial.

Television also features infomercials for various types of products, such as exercise equipment and cooking tools. Cable and satellite systems have led to the creation of numerous direct response channels. The Home Shopping Network remains one of the most successful. Essentially, the channel runs 24-hour infomercial programs. Other channels feature jewelry, food, and shoes.

Direct response techniques are also presented on radio stations and in magazines and newspapers. Radio does not have the reach of television, but it can be designed to match the type of station format. Radio ads repeat the response number or website frequently so that consumers can make contacts.

Print media can be sent to various market segments. Newspaper advertisements may feature website information and other quick-response formats. The same holds true for magazines. Both contain website information and toll-free numbers.[24] The more ways provided to respond to an ad, the higher the response rate.

Internet and Email

The internet offers a valuable form of direct marketing. Consumers can respond directly to ads placed on a website, and direct response advertisements can be placed on search engines and used in emails.

As shown in Figure 11.10, email continues to be a frequently used form of direct response marketing. Email provides a cost-effective method of reaching prospects. It helps build relationships with current customers through personalization of communications and by presenting marketing offers tailored to each consumer's needs, wants, and desires. For business-to-business marketers, email works better than postal mail and other direct marketing forms when the recipient is familiar with the company.[25]

By placing ads on search engines and using search engine optimization, firms make direct response offers directly to individuals and businesses in the market for particular products. A direct response ad for fruit trees that appears when a person types in "apple trees" will be more effective than one that appears when a person searches on "iPad" or "office furniture."

Direct Sales

In the consumer sector, companies such as Amway, Mary Kay, and Avon rely on direct sales. The salesperson contacts friends, relatives, coworkers, and others and provides them with small catalogs or marketing brochures. Alternatively, individuals host parties and invite friends and relatives to see products.

Mark is the Avon flanker brand designed for teenagers and women under 30. In launching a new line of cosmetics, Mark's marketing group brought direct selling into the digital and social media age by hiring 40,000 "Mark Girls" to work in the United States. Mark Girls are primarily women between

▼ More than 40,000 "Mark Girls" work in the United States for Avon.

the ages of 18 and 24 who use grassroots methods to sell Mark cosmetics and fashion accessories in dorms, through sororities, and via Facebook. The brand offers personalized e-boutiques, iPhone apps, and a Facebook e-shop. Kristiauna Mangum is a marketing major at Ohio State University. She is also a sales manager for Mark and manages 155 other Mark girls, earning commissions that range from 20 to 50 percent of the product's price.[26]

Telemarketing

Telemarketing takes place in two ways: inbound or outbound. *Inbound telemarketing* occurs when an individual initiates a call to a company. When a customer places an order, cross-selling can occur by offering other products or services. At times, customers make inbound calls to register complaints or talk about problems. Direct response marketing can provide information about how to solve the problem. For example, when a customer calls a mortgage company because of a late fee, the person can be encouraged to sign up for a direct pay program, which means the customer does not have to worry about possible mail delays.

The least popular method for direct marketing is *outbound telemarketing*. New legislation now requires prior consent before outbound sales calling or texting to a cell phone. This law has greatly reduced the attractiveness of outbound telemarketing. Successful outbound programs are tied into databases that identify the customers or prospects who have had prior relationships with the company. Only those individuals are contacted. An outbound telemarketing program that contacts customers who have not purchased in a year can help bring those customers back. A company that purchased a copy machine can be called to inquire about interest in paper and toner.

Personal Selling

objective 11.5
What are the tasks involved in developing successful personal selling programs for consumers and businesses?

Personal selling offers a face-to-face opportunity to build relationships with consumers. It takes place in both consumer and business-to-business transactions. Personal selling may result in the acquisition of new customers in addition to influencing current customers to increase levels of purchases. It can also be used to service and maintain existing relationships. The goal of personal selling should not be limited to making sales. Developing longer-term relationships with customers represents a second key objective. **Relationship selling** seeks to create a customer for life, not for a single transaction.

Figure 11.11 identifies the standard steps in the selling process. A quality data warehouse accompanied by effective database technologies provides key tools that assist in personal selling.

Generating Leads

Producing quality leads constitutes the first personal selling task, especially for business-to-business programs. Figure 11.12 identifies some of the most common methods. Personal sales calls are costly, which makes generating quality leads crucial.

Referrals generate the most ideal leads, because most recommendations are made by satisfied individuals. Referrals give the salesperson a head start. Making contact with purchasing agents or buyers in business organizations can be difficult. Dropping the name of the person who gave the referral helps the salesperson get past a gatekeeper.

- Generating leads
- Qualifying prospect
- Knowledge acquisition
- Sales presentation
- Handling objections
- Sales closing
- Follow-up

FIGURE 11.11
Steps in the Selling Process

Also, if someone has given a referral, then the potential lead becomes more receptive to the sales call and has a more positive attitude toward the salesperson. The best referrals come from current customers. Those made by other channel members, vendors, and acquaintances can also be useful because they allow the salesperson to get a foot in the door with a potential prospect.

- Refferals
- Database-generated leads
- Networking
- Directories
- Cold calls

▲ **FIGURE 11.12**
Methods of Generating Sales Leads

For generating leads, databases provide quality information, especially internal databases. Most of these leads originate from some type of advertising or inquiry. Direct response ads in various media can generate leads. Online ads on various websites or search engines also produce leads. Individuals may send an email inquiry or request additional information through the company's website. Databases provide quality leads through trawling and analytical techniques, such as data mining. These methods identify leads with higher sales potential.

Other less desirable means of generating sales leads are networking, directories, and cold calls. Although these approaches may produce some leads, they are time consuming and less productive. Networking in civic and professional organizations allows salespeople to make personal contacts. Directories may be obtained from the federal government, professional organizations, or research firms that provide the names of companies that purchase specific products or those in a given industry. The challenge becomes locating quality leads from the list. Cold calls are the worst method of generating leads. The salesperson has no idea whether the company or individual has any interest in the product.

Qualifying Prospects

Every name or prospect may not be viable. Also, all prospects do not offer equal value. With this in mind, qualifying prospects means evaluating leads on two dimensions: (1) the potential income the lead can generate and (2) the probability of acquiring the prospect as a customer. Based on the outcomes of these evaluations, determinations can be made regarding the best methods of contact and what happens with the lead. The high cost of making personal sales calls means that only the best leads warrant personal visits. Some prospects receive telephone calls or emails from an inside salesperson. Others may be mailed or emailed marketing materials but are not contacted directly by a salesperson.

Once the leads are analyzed using the two categories—sales potential and probability of acquisition—they are then placed into categories, or buckets, with the leads high on both dimensions as the best, or "A" leads. These leads normally receive a call from the sales staff. The second best group, or "B" leads, often will be contacted by a telemarketer or through email. "C" leads receive marketing materials and are encouraged to make inquiries if interested. Leads that score low on both dimensions may be kept in a database and monitored for future action in case the lead's situation changes.

Knowledge Acquisition

During the knowledge acquisition phase, the company's salespeople or other members of the sales department gather materials about the prospect. Figure 11.13 identifies typical information. The more a salesperson knows about a prospect before making the sales call, the higher the probability of making a sale or gaining permission to demonstrate the company's prospect.

▼ Leads can be generated through business personnel clicking on this digital banner ad for LUBA Workers' Comp.

LUBA Workers' Comp

FIGURE 11.13
Knowledge Acquisition Information

- Understand the prospect's business.
- Know and understand the prospect's customers.
- Identify the prospect's needs.
- Evaluate the risk factors and costs in switching vendors.
- Identify the decision makers and influencers.

The Sales Presentation

The initial sales call can be designed to gather information, discuss bid specifications, answer questions, or to close the deal with a final pitch or offer.[27] The exact nature of the first sales call depends on the information gathered prior to the call. Also, the stage of the buying process affects the presentation. The types of sales presentations used typically fall into one of these categories: stimulus-response, need-satisfaction, problem-solution, and mission-sharing.[28]

A **stimulus-response** sales approach, or a "canned" sales pitch, involves specific statements (stimuli) designed to elicit specific responses from customers. The salesperson normally memorizes the stimulus statement (the pitch). Telemarketers, retail sales clerks, and new field sales reps often rely on this method.

The **need-satisfaction** sales approach strives to discover a customer's needs during the first part of the sales presentation and then to provide solutions. The salesperson should skillfully ask the right questions. She should understand the customer's business and customers. Once a need has been identified, the rep then shows how the company's products meet that need.

The **problem-solution** sales approach requires employees from the selling organization to analyze the buyer's business. It usually involves a team of individuals such as engineers, salespeople, and other experts. The team investigates a potential customer's operations and problems, and then offers feasible solutions.

In the last approach, **mission-sharing**, two organizations develop a common mission. They then share resources to accomplish that mission. This partnership resembles a joint venture as much as a selling relationship.

.shock/Fotolia

▲ Understanding customer needs provides the basis for the need-satisfaction sales approach.

Handling Objections

Companies and individuals seldom make purchases after a sales presentation without raising some objections or concerns. Salespeople anticipate objections and carefully answer them. Figure 11.14 lists the most common methods of handling objections.

With the *head-on approach*, the salesperson answers the objection directly. Doing so, however, suggests that the customer or prospect is wrong. Consequently, the salesperson should use tact. No one likes being told he is in error. The salesperson takes care to not offend the customer.

To avoid a confrontation, some salespeople employ an *indirect approach*. This method allows the salesperson to never really tell the customer he is wrong. Instead, the salesperson sympathizes with the customer's viewpoint and then provides the correct information.

When the customer's objection is partially true, the salesperson may utilize the *compensation method*. With this approach, the salesperson replies "yes, but..." and then explains the product's benefits or features that answer the customer's objection.

Some customers do not have specific objections but are anxious or worried about the consequences of switching to a new vendor. For this situation, a sales rep can apply the *feel, felt, found* method. The salesperson permits the customer to talk about her fears or worries. In response, the salesperson can relate personal experiences or experiences of other customers who had the same fears and worries and how the product resulted in a positive experience.

- Head-on approach
- Indirect approach
- Compensation method
- "Feel, felt, found"

▲ **FIGURE 11.14**
Methods of Handling Objections

Closing the Sale

Often, the most important element of the sales call is the closing; however, it may also be the most difficult part. Salespeople often experience feelings of rejection or failure when prospects or customers say "no." Successful salespeople are masters at making the close. Figure 11.15 identifies some of the most common sales-closing methods. The one to be used depends on the personality of the salesperson, the personality of the prospect, and the situation surrounding the sales call.

With the *direct close*, the salesperson asks for the order outright. The approach may be used when objections have been answered and the salesperson believes the prospect is ready to buy.

When the salesperson cannot be sure if the prospect is ready, he can try the *trial*. With this approach, the salesperson solicits feedback that provides information regarding the customer's reaction, without asking directly for the sale. A positive reaction leads the salesperson to ask for the order. If not, then he returns to the sales presentation. The salesperson may also *summarize* the product's benefits and how it meets the customer's needs prior to asking for the order.

- Direct close
- Trial close
- Summarization close
- Continuous "yes" close
- Assumptive close

▲ **FIGURE 11.15**
Methods of Closing Sales

Sometimes a salesperson asks a serious of questions along the way, ensuring the customer will *continuously* respond "yes." By answering "yes" to smaller questions about the benefits of a product, when it comes time to ask for the order the customer may be more likely to respond with a "yes."

A salesperson can also *assume* the customer will say "yes." She might ask, "How many cases do you want?" or "How would you like this to be shipped?"

▼ With the summarization close, the salesperson shows how the product meets the customer's needs.

Creativa/Fotolia

Follow Up

Keeping customers happy after a purchase can result in repeat business, customer loyalty, and positive referrals. Quality follow-up programs are cost-effective ways to retain customers, which is much cheaper than continually finding new ones. Unfortunately, following up may be neglected by the sales staff, especially if the salesperson receives commission on new sales but not on follow-up activities. In this situation, the company must designate other employees to follow up to ensure that customers are satisfied with their purchases.

International Implications

objective 11.6
How should database marketing and personal selling programs be adapted to international settings?

Database marketing faces the same challenges as other aspects of an IMC program when a firm moves into the international arena. These include differences in technology, which make data collection and analysis more difficult due to issues such as language and internet availability. Further, local laws may limit the methods by which information can be collected as well as the types of information a company seeks and/or shares with other companies.

In many parts of the world, customers may only live a few miles apart yet reside in different countries. For example, the European Union consists of many nations in close proximity. Therefore, decisions must be made as to whether data will be country specific.

Programs such as permission marketing, frequency, and customer relationship management are subject to legal restrictions as well as cultural differences. In some instances, they may be highly accepted. Such is the case for permission marketing in Japan. In many Asian cultures, the giving of gifts takes on added meaning. This may indicate that stronger bonds between customers and companies are important in personal selling.

Direct marketing programs should be adapted to local conditions. Mail delivery systems may be easier to access in some countries than others. The same holds true for telephone systems, internet access, and other technologies. Infomercials may not be possible in countries with state-run television systems. A company's marketing team considers all local legal, social, cultural, technological, and competitive conditions before embarking on an international database-driven marketing program or direct marketing program.

Some international companies have moved to the forefront of data-based marketing programs. For example, Land, a Russian high-end supermarket chain, has implemented interactive kiosks that create recommendation-styled grocery lists for customers who use the brand's loyalty cards.[29]

Marketers also adapt personal selling tactics to specific countries. Local culture and customs must be carefully observed prior to making a sales call. A cultural assimilator will often be assigned help the sales team understand the nuances of a specific region or nation such as methods of greeting people, the manner in which gender differences are treated, dining customs, time awareness, personal space in communication, and other factors that affect interpersonal interactions.

Summary

Database marketing has become a vital element of a complete IMC program. The two key activities involved at the most general level—identifying customers and building relationships with them—have an impact on numerous other IMC tasks. It is more cost-effective to retain customers than to seek out new ones. Further, the actual message may change when communicating with long-time, loyal customers.

Building a data warehouse begins with collecting data to be used by the marketing department. Beyond basic information, such as a customer's name, address, and email address, other key data include the customer's purchase history and preferences. Geocoding involves adding geographic codes to customer records, which assists in selecting media and creating messages targeted to specific groups.

Database coding and analysis leads to either lifetime value analysis of customers or the clustering of customer groups based on customer spending patterns. Data mining programs involve building profiles of customer segments and/or preparing models that predict future purchase behaviors based on past purchases. The information gathered from data coding and data mining leads to the development of data-driven marketing communications and marketing programs.

Database-driven marketing communication programs are facilitated by effective identification codes that allow for personalization of messages and interactions. An effective database-driven communication program relies on customer profiles combined with other information available regarding specific customers. In-bound telemarketing programs, trawling, advertising, and lifetime value segment programs can be fine-tuned for individual customers.

Database-driven marketing programs include permission marketing, frequency programs, and customer relationship management systems. Permission marketing is a selling approach in which the customer agrees to receive promotional materials in exchange for various incentives. Frequency programs are incentives customers receive for repeat business. Both are designed to create customer loyalty over time. CRM is designed to build long-term loyalty and bonds with customers through the use of a personal touch facilitated by technology.

Direct response or direct marketing efforts may be made by mail, catalog, phone, mass media, the internet, or email. Direct mail programs remain popular as outbound telemarketing programs continue to diminish.

The goal of many personal selling programs—relationship selling—should be to create a customer for life rather than for a single transaction. The steps involved in personal selling include generating leads, qualifying prospects, knowledge acquisition, designing effective sales presentations, handling objections, closing the sale, and following up. Each of these activities can be made more effective through the use of quality database management programs.

Key Terms

data warehouse The place where customer data are held

geocoding Adding geographic codes to customer records to make it possible to plot customer addresses on a map

lifetime value The present value of future profits a customer generates over his or her life in a relationship with a brand or firm.

data mining The process of using computer data analysis software to mine data for meaningful information and relationships

trawling The process of searching the database for a specific piece of information for marketing purposes

permission marketing A form of database marketing in which the company sends promotional materials to customers who give the company permission to do so

empowerment Consumers believe they have power throughout the seller–consumer relationship, not just at the beginning when they agreed to join a frequency program

reciprocity A sense of obligation toward a company that results from receiving special deals or incentives such as gifts

frequency (or loyalty) program A marketing program designed to promote loyalty or frequent purchases of the same brand (or company)

customer relationship management (CRM) Programs designed to build long-term loyalty and bonds with customers through the use of a personal touch facilitated by technology

share of customer The percentage of expenditures a customer makes with one particular firm compared to total expenditures in that product's category

direct response (or direct) marketing Vending products to customers without the use of other channel members

response list A list of customers who have made purchases or who have responded to direct mail offers in the past

compiled list A list consisting of information about consumers who meet a specific demographic profile

relationship selling Developing long-term relationships with customers rather than focusing on a single transaction

stimulus-response A sales approach, often called a "canned" sales pitch, that uses specific statements (stimuli) to elicit specific responses from customers

need-satisfaction A sales approach in which the salesperson strives to discover a customer's needs during the first part of the sales presentation and then provides solutions to those needs

problem-solution A sales approach that requires employees from the selling organization to analyze the buyer's operations and offer ways to solve their problems

mission-sharing A sales approach in which two organizations develop a common mission and then share resources to accomplish that mission

Review Questions

11-1. What is the primary benefit of database marketing?

11-2. Give examples of data and analyses that can be found in a standard marketing data warehouse.

11-3. Why are customer email addresses so useful?

11-4. What is the purpose of customer preference profiles?

11-5. How do you calculate the cost of acquiring a new customer?

11-6. How might a financial institution cluster their customers?

11-7. In location data tracking, what is meant by the term "hashed"?

11-8. Explain how consumer profile information is used when sending communications to customers.

11-9. What is trawling?

11-10. Describe a permission marketing program. What are the key benefits of this approach?

11-11. What are the keys to an effective permission marketing program?

11-12. Describe a frequency program.

11-13. What is customer relationship management?

11-14. What is meant by the term share of customer?

11-15. What is direct response marketing?

11-16. Explain how response lists and compiled lists are used in direct mail programs.

11-17. Explain the two ways infomercials are presented as parts of a direct response program.

11-18. What is relationship marketing?

11-19. What steps are involved in the personal selling process?

11-20. Identify the four types of sales presentations typically used by sales reps.

11-21. What types of closing methods are available to salespeople?

Critical Thinking Exercises

DISCUSSION QUESTIONS

✪ **11-22.** Assume you are the account executive at a database marketing agency. A local music retailer with four stores has asked you to develop a database for the company. How would you build a data warehouse? What information should be in the databases? Where and how would you obtain the data?

✪ **11-23.** Hickory Outdoor is a retail store that sells fishing, hunting, camping, and other outdoor equipment and supplies, including various items for a number of outdoor sports. The company has built a database of its customers over the last five years. The marketing team can use data mining to improve their marketing efforts. Suggest ways data mining can be used. What type of marketing programs would you suggest based on data mining? What other types of marketing programs can be developed from the database?

11-24. Karen's Formal Dress is a retailer specializing in formal and wedding wear. She has a database with more than 3,000 names of individuals who have purchased or rented formal wear. She would like to develop a permission marketing program. How can the marketing team encourage individuals to give permission to receive marketing materials? Once the company has the customer's permission, how can the relationship be continued to make it beneficial to both the consumer and to Karen's Formal Dress? Describe the methodology Karen should use in her permission marketing program, including the types of materials, methods of distribution, and incentives.

✪ **11-25.** A primary reason for developing a frequency program is to encourage customers to be loyal to a business or brand. For each of the following products, discuss the merits of a frequency program. What types of incentives would individuals need to join the frequency club and then to continue participation in the program?

a. Local restaurant
b. Auto repair service
c. Printing service
d. Clothing retailer

11-26. Examine the forms of direct response marketing shown in the graph in Figure 11.10. Which ones have you responded to in the past? Which ones are most likely to influence your purchase decisions? Which ones are the least likely? Explain for each method your personal responses over the last year.

11-27. The marketing team for Hickory Outdoor (see question 23) is seeking to use direct response advertising to accomplish two goals: (1) to sell specific merchandise and (2) to encourage individuals to visit the store or its website. Which types of direct response advertising would be the most effective? Why? What type of direct response offers should Hickory Outdoor make?

11-28. Examine the direct marketing methods highlighted in Figure 11.10. Evaluate each method for the following types of businesses. Which ones would be the best? Which ones would not work as well? Justify your answers.

a. Shoe store
b. Sporting goods retailer
c. Internet calendar and game retailer (sells only via the internet)
d. Manufacturer of tin cans for food-processing companies

11-29. Interview five individuals. Ask each person whether they have ever received any sales calls on either their landline or their mobile phone. If they have had such calls, have they ever bought anything as a result of the call? Was the call from a business they were already buying from or had bought from in the past? What are their views about telemarketing? Do they feel that it is sufficiently regulated in your own country? Share your own findings with the rest of the class.

11-30. Formal and staged sales presentations at hotels and other venues are fairly common across the world. How are the potential customers identified and persuaded to attend? What kinds of incentives are offered? Are they common in your own country? Do you know any one that has attended one? Were they persuaded by the slick sales presentation?

Integrated Learning Exercises

11-31. Pick a company that sells clothing. Go to the company's website. What evidence do you see of database marketing and of personalization of the website? Describe a database marketing program the company could use to reach consumers such as yourself.

11-32. Go to website for Scotts Miracle Gro at **www.scotts.com**. What evidence do you see of database marketing and of personalization? Review the concepts presented in the section "Database-Driven Marketing Communications." What steps could Scotts take to develop data-driven communications with visitors to the website as well as individuals who make purchases?

11-33. A number of companies specialize in database marketing. You are the manager of a small chain of eight Chinese food restaurants. Review the websites of each of the following companies. Outline what each company offers. Which one would be the best for your company? Why?

a. Database Marketing Group (**www.dbmgroup.com**)
b. Advanced Marketing Consultants (**www.marketingprinciples.com**)
c. Dovetail (**www.dovetaildatabase.com**)

11-34. *DMNews* is a trade journal for database marketing and CRM programs. Access the website at **www.dmnews.com**. What types of information are available on the site? How could this help companies with database marketing and CRM programs? Access and read one of the articles from the journal. Write a paragraph about what you learned.

11-35. CentricData is a database marketing firm that specializes in mid-size to large retailers. Access the website at **www.centricdata.com**. What types of services does CentricData offer? How could this company help a retail store develop a database marketing program?

11-36. The Direct Marketing Association (DMA) is a global trade association of business and nonprofit organizations that use direct marketing tools and techniques. Access the trade organization's website at **www.the-dma.org**. What services does the DMA provide its members? What value would this be to a business in developing a direct marketing program?

11-37. A primary key in successful direct marketing is the quality of the list used. One company that specializes in compiling lists is U.S. Data Corporation. Access the company's website at **www.usdatacorporation.com**. What types of lists does the company offer? Access one of the lists and discuss how a company could use U.S. Data Corporation for a direct response marketing campaign. What services does U.S. Data Corporation offer?

11-38. You are the marketing manager of a small jewelry retail chain in your own country. You feel that a direct response marketing campaign would boost both short- and long-term sales. Find a business that offers DR marketing lists appropriate to your market. How would you choose from their lists? What other services does the business offer you and would it be valuable for the campaign? Could they handle the entire campaign under your instruction?

11-39. Use the internet to find three websites of companies and organizations that offer advice to salespeople. Write a report about the methods the sites suggest and how those tactics compare to the materials presented in this chapter.

Student Project

CREATIVE CORNER

Lilly Fashions sells fashionable, trendy clothes. The company's primary target customer is 20- to 30-year-old females with an average income of $40,000 and some college. Lilly's marketing team wants to capitalize on the concepts of database marketing and direct response marketing. Design a newspaper advertisement that encourages females in the company's target market to visit the retail store and join Lilly's loyalty program. In addition, design a direct mail piece that would go to individuals who are currently in the database but who have not made a purchase within the last three months. Prepare another email that can be sent to members in the database on the person's birthday offering them a free meal at a local restaurant, if they come to the store to pick up the meal voucher. This promotion is a joint promotion with the restaurant, which shares in the cost, which means the restaurant must also be part of the email.

Blog Exercises

Access the authors' blog for this textbook at the URLs provided to complete these exercises. Answer the questions that are posed on the blog.

11-40. Database marketing: **http://blogclowbaack.net/2014/05/12/database-marketing-chapter-11/**

11-41. Direct response marketing: **http://blogclowbaack.net/2014/05/12/direct-response-marketing-chapter-11/**

11-42. Personal selling: **http://blogclowbaack.net/2014/05/12/selling-chapter-11/0**

CASE 1 SALON SENSATIONAL

The world of beauty enhancement continually changes. Jennifer Swann, owner and manager of Salon Sensational, recognizes that she must constantly adapt to new trends in order to keep her company on top. Jennifer owns four salons, located in Medford and Portland, Oregon. The salons serve both male and female clients. Her current operation offers hair care of all types, manicures, pedicures, and includes space rentals to two popular local massage therapists. The company also sells a line of top quality hair care products including shampoo, conditioner, and coloring rinses.

Salon Sensational has been involved in local community events. Most notably, each year the salon provides low-cost pink hair accents to sponsor Breast Cancer Awareness efforts. Also, twice each year stylists provide free services to low income members of the community as part of a city-wide program for the disadvantaged, held at the local city auditorium.

Jennifer has created a program designed to keep her stylists on the cutting edge. Each receives financial incentives in order to attend training sessions for creating the newest hair styles. She also maintains an incentive system designed to encourage stylists to sell and cross-sell the hair care products that the salon offers.

Five years ago, Jennifer purchased a sophisticated computer software system that allows her to track all customer interactions with the salon, including records of past appointments, purchases of products, methods of payment (cash versus charge), along with notes about past complaints as well as past compliments. The system maintains appointment schedules and also identifies customers who have routinely canceled or not kept their appointments.

Repeat business represents the staple of the salon industry. When customers routinely return, stylists stay busy and the total company benefits. Customer referrals also help to build volume in terms of appointments.

Currently, Jennifer is looking for ways to increase purchase frequencies and facility utilization. She recognizes that care must be given to avoid alienating clientele members by appearing to "hard sell" them hair care products or additional visits. At the same time, she knows that part of the frequency displayed by customers is the result of building strong bonds and relationships between individuals and their stylists as well as Jennifer herself.

One approach to building revenues would be to add new services, such as cosmetology. In that way, a person getting ready for a major event, such as a prom or wedding would be able to have her hair styled, nails polished, and make-up set up, all in the same location. The question is whether sufficient demand for such a new service exists. She would have to invest in a minor amount of remodeling in order to be able to provide the service.

JackF/Fotolia

▲ Jennifer styling the hair of one of her customers.

At the same time, Salon Sensation enjoys a positive reputation in both cities. Many customers report high levels of loyalty. The goal is to build on those aspects in order to continue to succeed.

11-43. Identify the types of data Jennifer should collect from her customers and how she could obtain it.

11-44. Suppose Jennifer wants to start a loyalty card program to build her database. Design a flyer that could be handed to customers of the salons encouraging them to join the loyalty program. What benefits would customers receive? In exchange, what information would Jennifer request from each customer?

11-45. Once the database is built, what database-driven marketing communications should Salon Sensational send out to individuals in its database?

11-46. Which direct response marketing programs would be helpful to Jennifer? How would they be of value? Explain how Jennifer could use each to increase purchase frequencies and visits to her salons.

11-47. What types of personal selling tactics should stylists use? Which should not be used? Why?

11-48. What methods for overcoming objections would best serve Salon Sensational when selling hair care products?

CASE 2 THE TRAVEL AGENCY DILEMMA

Leisure time travel remains a common pursuit across a variety of markets. Numerous forces influence consumers as they seek out restful, adventuresome, romantic, and family-oriented vacations. Factors such as gasoline and airline ticket prices, economic conditions, political unrest, and the changing world of technology factor into personal and family decisions regarding places to go, things to do, people to see, and events to enjoy.

Travel agencies experience the influence of these forces as directly as any other group. When gas prices rise, consumers take shorter trips. When airline tickets are at a premium, travelers look for bargains or seek other alternatives. Unemployment, political turmoil in places such as Mexico and Europe, and other considerations cause people to either stay at home or change travel plans.

The most direct influence on the travel agency business has been the internet and its popular travel sites. Travelocity, Priceline.com, and other airline booking sites allow consumers to shop online for the best air fares and travel times. Hotels.com plus numerous hotel chain-run booking sites, which also offer frequency programs, make it possible to find the most ideal hotel arrangement without the use of a travel agency. Many internet-savvy consumers no longer feel the need to call or drive to a local travel agency. These individuals have become convinced that they are able to match any price or travel arrangement that an agency can find.

To compete in this intense environment, agency managers seek ways to deliver value-added services that entice consumers to continue to utilize their companies. Among the potential methods to maintain customer loyalty are offers of convenience, skill at finding better prices than consumers can obtain online, and the ability to package travel into one-price programs. Many travel agencies create agreements with hotels, cruise lines, and airlines to offer better prices than consumers will receive from other vendors.

Travel agencies can also offer suggestions regarding combinations of activities such as fine dining with an elaborate hotel. Many agency employees visit numerous destinations, seeking to obtain better quality information about local attractions that would go unnoticed by travelers to a specific area.

In the future, the question remains as to whether travel agencies will be able to continue to compete. Only with carefully constructed service programs and quality marketing efforts will it be possible to maintain a set of clientele as the world of internet shopping continues to increase.

1000words/Fotolia

▲ With access to the internet, many tourists see little value in the services provided by travel agencies.

11-49. How might database marketing, including the data warehouse, data coding and analysis, and data mining, help a travel agency create and enhance relationships with customers and potential customers?

11-50. How could data-driven marketing programs, including permission marketing, frequency programs, and customer relationship management systems, be useful to travel agencies?

11-51. Discuss each of the direct response marketing techniques in relation to marketing travel agencies.

11-52. What personal selling tactics are most important to travel agency employees as they work with customers and potential customers?

11-53. Discuss the pros and cons of each of the methods of handling objections in personal selling in relation to a couple who are hesitant to purchase a vacation to one of the Caribbean islands.

11-54. Discuss the pros and cons of each of the closing methods in personal selling in relation to a couple who are hesitant to purchase a vacation to one of the Caribbean islands.

MyMarketingLab

Go to **mymktlab.com** for the following Assisted-graded writing questions:

11-55. Karen's Formal Dress is a retailer specializing in formal and wedding wear. She has a database with more than 3,000 names of individuals who have purchased or rented formal wear. She would like to develop a permission marketing program. How can the marketing team encourage individuals to give permission to receive marketing materials? Once the company has the customer's permission, how can the relationship be continued to make it beneficial to both the consumer and to Karen's Formal Dress? Describe the methodology Karen should use in her permission marketing program, including the types of materials, methods of distribution, and incentives.

11-56. Pick a company that sells clothing and go to its website. What evidence do you see of database marketing and personalization of the website? Describe a database marketing program the company could use.

Chapter 12 Sales Promotions

Chapter Objectives

After reading this chapter, you should be able to answer the following questions:

12.1 What differences exist between consumer promotions and trade promotions?

12.2 How can the various forms of consumer promotions help to pull consumers into stores and push products onto the shelves?

12.3 How do different types of customers respond to consumer promotions?

12.4 What types of trade promotions can help push products onto retailers' shelves and eventually to end users?

12.5 What concerns exist for manufacturers considering trade promotions programs?

12.6 What issues complicate international sales promotions programs?

Overview

It may be tempting to think that a high-quality advertising program completes the task of promotion. It does not. A fully integrated marketing communications program includes additional key activities. This chapter describes sales promotions programs. **Sales promotions** consist of all of the incentives offered to customers and channel members to encourage product purchases.

Sales promotions take two forms: consumer promotions and trade promotions. Companies offer **consumer promotions** directly to customers and potential customers. Consumer promotions are aimed at those who actually use the product, or end users. They may be individuals or households. Another end user may be a business that consumes the product, when the item is not resold to another business. In other words, companies offer consumer promotions in both consumer markets and business-to-business markets.

Trade promotions are only allotted in the distribution channel. **Trade promotions** consist of the expenditures or incentives used by manufacturers and other members of the marketing channel to purchase goods for eventual resale. Trade promotions provided to other firms help push products through to retailers.

DUBAI SHOPPING FESTIVAL

The Dubai Shopping Festival (DSF), also known as "Layali Dubai" in Arabic, is one of the most famous shopping fiestas in the world. It is the region's largest and longest running shopping and entertainment extravaganza. The DSF has had around 35 million visitors since 1996, who have spent close to $20 billion in shopping malls, airlines, hotels, and entertainment outlets. The one-month-long festival, with the slogan "One Family, One World, One Festival," offers visitors some of the major and best brands in the world at low prices. Dubai has low import duties and no taxation, and therefore offers amazing value to the bargain hunter. Even the major brands which are widely available are less expensive in Dubai than in their country of origin.

Ilona Ignatova/Shutterstock

Sponsorships and sales promotion tie-ins were widely used. The Lexus Mega Raffle entitles coupon buyers the dream opportunity to take home a Lexus LX570 car as well as $28,000 in cash. The Nissan Grand Raffle gives shoppers at the DSF the chance to drive home a Nissan SUV every day. The Dubai Gold and Jewellery Group participate in the DSF with a gold promotion effort which gives away prizes worth millions during the festival.

As well as concerts featuring popular stars, there are a number of events to entertain visitors to the DSF, including a dolphin show and a sound and light show. There is also a desert camp in which families and visitors have the option of renting tents for days or choosing from the endless number of activities designed for adventure enthusiasts.

The DSF was segregated into many major attractions with the purpose of entertaining the city's many visitors who come from around the world, and who all have different needs. It also aimed to make the expatriate population more loyal to the country as they can enjoy their own culture in Dubai every year.

The Dubai Shopping Festival is an excellent example of how various sales promotion techniques can be used to promote not only products and services but also countries, helping to boost tourism and bring development into Dubai by attracting investments and spending. Its continued success is proven by the large number of tourists from not only the Gulf Cooperative Council (GCC) but also the rest of the world.[1]

objective 12.1
What differences exist between consumer promotions and trade promotions?

In the past, some marketing experts believed that any type of sales promotion, whether consumer or trade, eroded brand equity by shifting the focus to price. Now, however, many company leaders recognize that properly managed promotions differentiate a brand from the competition, helping to build brand awareness and improving a brand's image.[2]

The marketing team designs promotional programs to help the company achieve its IMC objectives and to support a brand's position. In the early stages of a product's life cycle, promotions match advertising and other efforts focused on brand awareness, creating opportunities for trial purchases and stimulating additional purchases. Later, the goal shifts to strengthening a brand, increasing consumption, fending off competition, or finding new markets. As noted above, the Huggies brand has taken advantage of sales promotions programs.

This chapter examines consumer promotions first, followed by trade promotions. Although the presentations are separate, the marketing team designs both at the same time. The adjustments made to sales promotions programs in international markets are also described.

Consumer Promotions

objective 12.2
How can the various forms of consumer promotions help to pull consumers into stores and push products onto the shelves?

Enticing a consumer to take the final step and make the purchase constitutes a primary goal for a consumer promotions program. Advertising creates the interest and excitement that brings the consumer to the store. Marketers then use other tactics. In addition to leading to the final decision to buy an item, consumer promotions programs help generate store traffic and enhance brand loyalty.

During recent Super Bowls, Denny's offered free breakfast to anyone who came into the restaurant from 6:00 a.m. to 2:00 p.m. on the Tuesday following the game. Each year, roughly two million Americans took advantage of the offer. Some waited in line for hours for a breakfast. The promotion's goal, according to CEO Nelson Marchioli, was to "re-acquaint America with Denny's." He added, "We've never been thanked this much—and folks are saying they'll come back." The cost of the entire promotion, including food, labor, and the Super Bowl commercial, was about $5 million. In exchange, Denny's earned something money alone cannot buy; a powerful positive public relations blitz. The promotion garnered as much as $50 million in free, positive media news coverage. The company received 40 million hits on its website in the week following the Super Bowl, suggesting a highly successful consumer promotions program.[3] Figure 12.1 identifies the most common consumer promotions.

- Coupons
- Premiums
- Contests and sweepstakes
- Refunds and rebates
- Sampling
- Bonus packs
- Price-offs

▲ **FIGURE 12.1**
Types of Consumer Promotions

Coupons

A coupon offers a price reduction to the consumer. It may be a percentage off the retail price, such as 25 or 40 percent, or an absolute amount, such as 50 cents or $1. Companies print almost 300 billion coupons per year, and on average consumers redeem about 2.5 billion. The 0.85 percent redemption rate represents approximately $3.87 billion in savings for consumers, or around $1.55 per coupon.[4] Nearly 80 percent of all U.S. households redeem coupons, and almost two-thirds are willing to switch brands with coupons.[5]

▼ Coupons for Wholly Guacamole and Jennie-O Turkey products are part of this advertisement.

Wholly Guacamole/Fresherized Foods

Coupon Distribution

Manufacturers issue approximately 80 percent of all coupons. Most coupons are sent through print media, with the vast majority distributed through **freestanding inserts (FSI)**, or sheets of coupons distributed in newspapers, primarily on Sunday. FSI represent almost 90 percent of all coupons distributed, although the percentage has declined as consumers switch to digitally-delivered coupons.[6] Figure 12.2 identifies the various forms of coupon distribution.

FSI and print media remain popular for several reasons. First, the consumer makes a conscious effort to clip or save the coupon. Second, coupons create brand awareness. The consumer sees the brand name on the coupon even when it is not redeemed. Third, FSI encourage consumers to purchase brands on the next trip to the store. Consumers are more likely to purchase a couponed brand and remember the name when they redeem a coupon, which helps move the brand to a consumer's long-term memory.

Digital coupons continue to grow in popularity. About 15 percent of the U.S. population, or 45 million consumers, redeem digital coupons. Digital coupon users tend to be more affluent and better educated. The average household income for a digital coupon user is $97,000. One-third has earned a college degree. Websites make it easy for consumers to find and print coupons, download them onto mobile devices, or transfer them to a loyalty card. Retail stores, including JCPenney, Kroger, and Safeway, feature technologies that permit consumers to redeem coupons from cell phones. CVS Pharmacy customers can scan a loyalty card at a kiosk inside the store entrance to receive instant coupon offers and in-store specials based on their purchase histories. Ease of use spurs the growth of digital coupons.[7]

- Print media
  - Freestanding inserts (FSIs)
- Direct mail
- In- or on-package
- In-store
  - Scanner delivered
- Digital
- Employee delivered

▲ **FIGURE 12.2**
Methods of Distributing Coupons

Types of Coupons

Coupons are distributed in retail stores, offered digitally from the internet or in a store, such as CVS, and may be placed on or near packages. In each instance, the consumer can immediately redeem the coupon at the store through an *instant redemption coupon* program. The coupons often lead to trial purchases and purchases of additional packages of a product. Many grocery stores sponsor a company to cook a food product and offer free samples along with coupon giveaways, which represents another form of instant redemption couponing.

Coupons can be placed inside packages so that customers cannot redeem them quite as quickly. This encourages repeat purchases. These coupons are called *bounce-back coupons*.

Some retailers issue coupons at the cash register. An item being scanned at a cash register triggers a *scanner-delivered coupon*. The coupon is often for a competing brand, thereby encouraging brand switching the next time a consumer makes a purchase.

To encourage purchases of additional products, manufactures provide *cross-ruffing coupons*, which means placing a coupon on one product for another product. For example, a coupon for French onion dip may be placed on a package of potato chips. Cross-ruff coupons should be for products that logically fit together and that are often purchased and consumed simultaneously. Occasionally, a manufacturer uses cross-ruffing to encourage consumers to purchase another of its products. Kellogg's may place a coupon on a Rice Krispies box for another cereal, such as Frosted Flakes or

Boyers Foods

▲ Coupons for brands sold at Boyer's grocery store.

an oatmeal product. This couponing tactic encourages consumers to purchase within the same brand or family of products.

Disadvantage of Coupons

Customers who have a brand preference redeem approximately 80 percent of all coupons.[8] Some believe that offering price discounts through coupons to customers who are willing to pay full price does not make sense. Manufacturers, however, argue that these consumers may be willing to stock up on the item, which means they do not buy from the competition. It might also result in the consumer using more of the product. In essence, manufacturers recognize that these brand-preference customer redemptions are a "necessary evil" in mass distribution programs. To avoid sending coupons to current customers, firms may send direct mail coupons to non-loyal customers, thereby targeting nonusers and the competitor's customers.

Premiums

Premiums are prizes, gifts, or other special offers consumers receive when purchasing products. The consumer pays full price for the original good or service with a premium and receives something free. Others offer additional items at a reduced price, such as buy one and get the second at half price.

Types of Premiums

- Free-in-the-mail
- In- or on-package
- Store or manufacturer
- Self-liquidating

▲ **FIGURE 12.3**
Types of Premiums

Figure 12.3 identifies four major types of premiums. *Free-in-the-mail premiums* are gifts individuals receive for purchasing products. To receive the gift, the customer mails in a proof of purchase to the manufacturer who then sends the gift to the buyer. More than one purchase may be required to receive some gifts, such as three proofs of purchase.

Credit card companies employ premiums to entice individuals to sign up for various products. Instead of providing a proof of purchase, the consumer activates the card to receive an incentive, which ranges from cash back on a purchase to merchandise and frequent-flier miles.

In- or *on-package premiums* are usually small gifts, such as toys in cereal boxes. The gift may be disguised or packaged so the consumer must buy the product to see the premium, as is the case with Cracker Jack. At other times, the gift will be attached to the package, such as a package of blades with the purchase of a razor.

▼ A premium offer of "free small tots" by Sonic and Wholly Guacamole.

Wholly Guacamole/Fresherized Foods

Store or *manufacturer premiums* are gifts given by either the retail store or the manufacturer when the customer purchases a product. Fast-food restaurants lure children through a toy that accompanies the purchase of a child's meal. Hyundai recently offered a unique premium. With the purchase of a new Hyundai Equus, with the suggested retail price of $50,000, customers received a free Apple iPad loaded with the 300-page owner's interactive manual. The iPad included a leather slipcase with the car's service appointments preloaded and scheduled.[9]

The fourth type, a *self-liquidating premium*, requires the consumer to pay a small amount of money for the gift or item. The premium may be offered for only $4.99 plus shipping and handling and two proofs of purchase from boxes of Cheerios. The premium is called self-liquidating because $4.99 covers the premium's cost. The manufacturer may also receive money for shipping and handling so that consumers pay for most or all of the expense of the item.

Karns foods

◀ An advertisement for Karns Foods featuring both premiums and coupons.

Keys to Successful Premium Programs

Successful premium programs include several common elements (Figure 12.4). First, the premium should match the target market. A target market consisting of older, high-income individuals can be reached with a premium such as china or fine crystal. If the market is children, a cartoon figure or a character from Disney or Sesame Street becomes more attractive.

The best premiums reinforce the firm's image. They should not be low-cost trinkets. Giving cheap merchandise insults customers and damages the firm's image. Premium

- Match the premium to the target market
- Carefully select the premiums (avoid fads, try for exclusivity)
- Pick a premium that reinforces the firm's product and image
- Integrate the premium with other IMC tools (especially advertising and POP displays)
- Don't expect premiums to increase short-term profits

◀ **FIGURE 12.4**
Keys to Successful Premium Programs

Courtesy of Alliance One Advertising

▲ A newspaper ad for The Toggery offering a premium "Buy 1 get the 2nd at 50% off."

programs succeed when they tie in with the firm's products to enhance the image of the product and the brand.[10]

Premiums should be integrated with the other components of the IMC program. General Mills recently offered collectable Star War premiums tied in with the recent Star Wars movie. The premium effort was supported by in-store pallet displays, FSIs, and digital efforts on sites such as MyBlogSpark.com, StarWars.com, and Lucasfilm's Twitter. In addition, to drive awareness of the promotion, General Mills added a 10-second tag to television spots for the cereal brands with the premiums inside the box.[11]

Some marketing experts believe overusing coupons damages a brand's image. Conversely, premiums might actually enhance an image. Picking the right type of premium becomes the key. Premiums can be used to boost sales; however, they usually are not as successful as coupon sales. Nevertheless, premiums remain a valuable consumer promotional tool.

In the United States, companies spend approximately $24 billion on premiums each year.[12] Although premiums add value and enhance the brand, they are less effective at increasing profits. Therefore, a clear relationship between the premium's intention and IMC goals should be established. Logically, the goal relates to image rather than profit.

Contests and Sweepstakes

Each year, companies spend approximately $1.9 billion on the various games, contests, and sweepstakes that appear in both consumer and business markets.[13] The prize list largely determines the success or failure of these appeals. Members of the target market for the contest or sweepstakes must desire the prizes in order to entice them to participate.

Contests

The words *contest* and *sweepstakes* tend to be used interchangeably, yet some differences exist, primarily legal. *Contests* normally require the participant to perform an activity. The winner will be selected from the group that performs best or provides the most correct answers. Often, contests require a participant to make a purchase to enter. In some states, however, forcing consumers to make a purchase to enter a contest is illegal. In developing contests, the marketing team first investigates the state and federal laws that apply.

Contests range from the bikini contests at local nightclubs to popular television shows such as *Jeopardy* or *American Idol* in which contestants must answer questions or win competitions to earn prizes. Although some contests are mostly chance, others require skill. For example, Dr. Pepper encouraged visitors to the website deviantART.com to submit designs for a Dr. Pepper-themed outdoor mural. The winner, Rey Jawahir of Hillsborough County, Florida, was selected from among 2,105 entries. He won a trip to Brooklyn to see the mural, a $3,000 iPad, and various deviantART.com perks. The contest generated 314,000 page views besides mentions on Facebook, Twitter, and other social media sites.[14]

Sweepstakes

No purchase is required to enter a sweepstakes. Consumers enter as many times as they wish, although companies can restrict customers to one entry per visit to the store or location. Probability dictates the chances of winning a sweepstakes. The odds of winning must clearly be stated on all point-of-purchase (POP) displays and advertising materials. In a sweepstakes, the probability of winning each prize must also be published in advance.

Wholly Guacamole/Fresherized Foods

▲ An advertisement for Wholly Guacamole promoting a contest with high perceived value, a free trip.

Perceived Value

People enter contests and sweepstakes that they find interesting or challenging. Consumers do not enter every contest or sweepstakes they encounter. Instead, they selectively choose. The decision will be based on the perceived value of the contest or sweepstakes prize combined with the odds of winning. The greater the perceived odds of winning, the more likely a person will participate.

The perceived value of a contest or sweepstakes consists of two components: extrinsic value and intrinsic value. The *extrinsic value* represents the actual attractiveness of the prize (a car versus a free sandwich). The greater the perceived extrinsic value, the more likely people will become involved. *Intrinsic values* are those associated with participating. A contest requiring the demonstration of a skill, such as the one with recipes or an essay contest, entices entry by individuals who enjoy demonstrating that skill. Extrinsic rewards become secondary. Instead, participants enjoy competing and demonstrating their abilities. This, in part, explains the popularity of fantasy football and baseball leagues and "pick the winner" sports contests such as the NCAA basketball tournament each spring.

Sears recently launched a national "More Green Across America" contest that encouraged individuals to nominate baseball fields, playgrounds, and other community green spaces. The contestants sent photos and wrote short essays about why the area deserved a makeover. Baseball Hall-of-Famer Mike Schmidt appeared as the campaign's spokesperson. Sears narrowed the list down to ten worthy projects and then asked the public to vote for the winner. The grand prize winner received a new yard tractor, mower, line trimmer, edger, and blower as well as a visit from the Sears Blue Lawn & Garden Crew to help complete the beautification project.[15]

To encourage consumers to continue participating in a contest, the extrinsic values of prizes can be increased by allowing small, incremental rewards. A consumer who wins a soft drink or a sandwich in a sweepstakes at Subway may be more likely to continue participating. Scratch-and-win cards tend to be effective because the reward is instant.

▼ This advertisement for fantasy fishing by Bassmaster appeals to outdoorsmen.

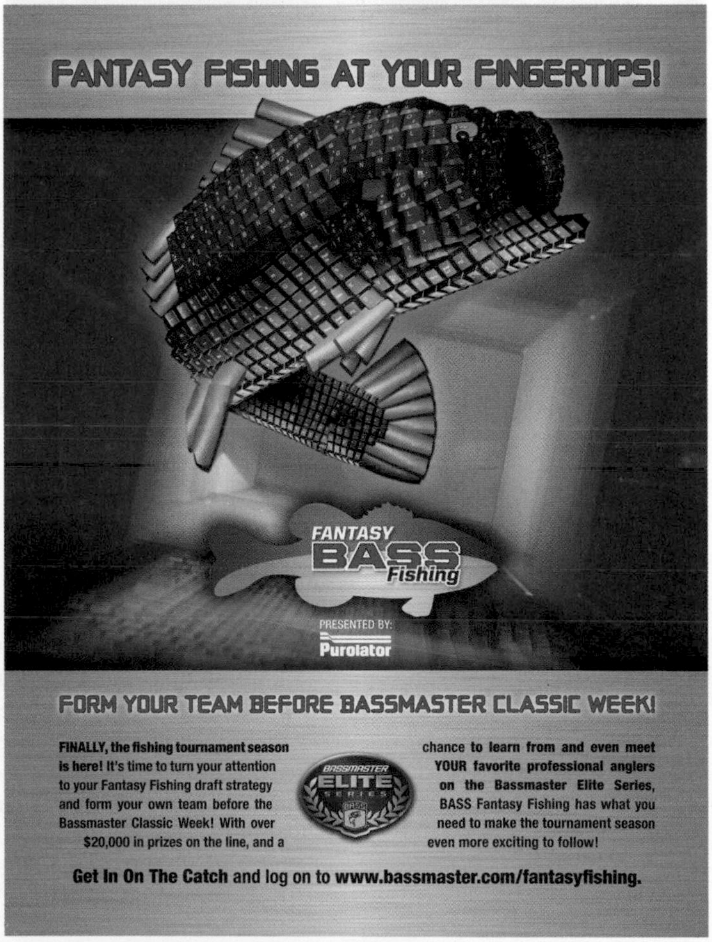

Courtesy of Newcomer, Morris & Young, Inc.

The Internet and Social Media

The internet offers a popular location for contests and sweepstakes. It provides opportunities for individuals to see a prize's intrinsic value by creating interactive games to challenge a contestant's ability. The internet also features data-capturing capabilities. Internet contests cost less to set up and run than other types of promotions.

The newest trends in contests and sweepstakes include social media. Microsoft, Sephora, NASCAR, Comcast, Chik-fil-A, Wholly Guacamole, and McDonald's have created Twitter sweepstakes or have used Twitter and social media sites to enlist participants for a contest or sweepstakes. Marketers use the sweepstakes or contest to ignite a viral buzz about the brand.[16]

Skyjaker Suspension

▲ This advertisement for Skyjacker offers a $35 cash back rebate on purchases of Hydro or Nitro shocks.

Goals of Contests and Sweepstakes

Although contests and sweepstakes routinely increase customer traffic, the question remains as to whether they actually boost sales. Some do, others do not. Marketers recognize that intrinsic rewards tend to draw consumers back. This means online games are exciting prospects, because they can be structured to create intrinsic value.

Refunds and Rebates

Refunds and rebates are cash returns given to consumers or businesses following the purchase of a product. Consumers pay full price for the product but can mail in some type of proof of purchase. The manufacturer then refunds a portion of the purchase price. A *refund* is a cash return on what are called "soft goods," such as food or clothing. *Rebates* are cash returns on "hard goods," which are major ticket items such as automobiles and appliances.

Customers claim only about 30 percent of all rebates. For rebates valued at $50 or more, the percentage rises to about 65 percent. The inconvenience associated with obtaining the rebate represents the primary reason for low response rates. Too many steps or the long waiting times associated with "snail mail" are common complaints about rebates. Many consumers wait two to three months to receive a rebate check.[17]

Rebate programs often suffer from diminished effectiveness, because consumers have come to expect them. Car dealers often find that customers will wait until rebates are offered. As a result, no new purchase activity takes place without a rebate program, which delays the purchase process. Further, increasing the amount of a rebate no longer seems to spur additional sales, yet discontinuing or reducing rebate levels tends to have an immediate negative impact.

Refunds and rebates achieve the greatest successes when they are perceived as new or original. When they become an entrenched part of doing business, they are expected discounts. To be effective, rebates and refunds should change the buyer's behavior, either by leading to a more immediate purchase or by causing the customer to change brands.

Sampling

Sampling is the actual delivery of a product to consumers for their use or consumption. In business-to-business markets, samples of products may be given to potential clients. Sampling also can be featured in the service sector. For example, a tanning salon may offer an initial visit free to encourage new customers to try its facilities. Dentists and lawyers use sampling when they provide an initial consultation free of charge.

In a survey of 1,800 consumers, more than one-third of those who tried a sample purchased the product during the same shopping trip. Fifty-eight percent indicated they would buy the product again. Nearly one-fourth said they bought the product being sampled instead of the brand they intended to purchase.[18] This means sampling constitutes an effective method of getting consumers to try and purchase a particular brand.

Sample Distribution

Figure 12.5 lists various methods of samples distribution. The most common consumer method, *in-store distribution*, delivers the sample in the store such as when an employee cooks a food product and gives it to customers on site. *Direct sampling* means items are mailed or delivered door-to-door to consumers. In the business-to-business sector, salespeople often deliver direct samples to prospects or to current customers to encourage them to try the company's brand or a newly introduced product.

Response samples are made available to individuals or businesses responding to a media offer on television, on the internet, from a magazine, through social media, or by some other source. *Cross-ruffing* sampling plans provide samples of one product on another. A laundry detergent with a free dryer sheet attached to the package is a cross-ruffing sample.

- In-store distribution
- Direct sampling
- Response sampling
- Cross-ruffing sampling
- Media sampling
- Professional sampling
- Selective sampling

▲ **FIGURE 12.5**
Methods of Distributing Samples

Media sampling means the sample is included in the media outlet. Recently, samples for Dr. Scholl's Her Open Shoes insoles were affixed to heavy-stock paper in magazines including *In Style, All You, Shape*, and *Glamour*. Women could remove the insole and test it on one foot and compare it to the other foot that did not have an insole. Approximately 3 million were distributed. One month after the run, 11 percent of subscribers had purchased insoles and nearly 60 percent said they planned to make purchases. Approximately 57 percent had peeled the sample insole out of the magazine and 37 percent said they actually tested it.[19]

Salespeople give *professional samples* to professionals, such as doctors, who then provide patients with the free drug samples. *Selective samples* are distributed at a site such as a state fair, parade, hospital, restaurant, or sporting event. For instance, Procter & Gamble distributed 40,000 samples across 25 of its brands in Manhattan. The company opened "pop-up boxes" in five different street locations to distribute the sample. Stylists were on hand to deliver beauty tips and some celebrities stopped by the temporary box stands.[20]

In recent years, marketers have increased usage of freestanding inserts to distribute samples. A variety of products have been distributed in newspapers, including breakfast bars, coffee, shampoo, snacks, tea, and automotive cleansers. In Hollywood, 70,000 "all natural, gluten free" dog biscuits were distributed in *The Hollywood Reporter*. Companies that use the FSI method in newspapers do so because the approach breaks through the clutter and captures attention. The newspaper is an "invited medium." Consequently, consumers may be more receptive when samples are included in the paper.[21]

▼ Sampling can be used by Maxwell House Coffee to encourage consumers to try various versions of the product.

mcgarrybowen

Benefits of Sampling

Product sampling presents an effective way to introduce a new item, generate interest in it, and collect information about consumers. Internet-based response sampling programs have become popular with both consumers and manufacturers. Bristol-Myers/Squibb was one of the first companies to utilize the internet for product sampling. The company gave a free sample of Excedrin to individuals who requested one. Potential customers had to be willing to provide their names, addresses, and email information. In addition to the 12-pack sample of Excedrin, consumers received coupons for additional purchases, along with the quarterly *Excedrin Headache Relief Update Newsletter*. This form of response has the advantage of sampling only the consumers who requested the product. Companies normally can gather additional information to be added to a database. Seventy percent of those who requested a sample online were willing to complete a survey to receive the item.[22]

Successful Sampling Programs

As with the other consumer promotions, sampling will be related to and based on the IMC plan. Sampling encourages a trial use by a consumer or a business. The approach becomes most effective when it introduces a new product or a new version of a product to a market. Samples also help to promote a current product to a new target market or to new prospects.

Successful sampling involves targeting the right audience at the right venue at the right time. Mass sampling will not be nearly as cost-effective as targeted sampling. For example, Chanel recently sent a sample of its No. 5 fragrance in a package mailer to the 1.2 million subscribers of *Vogue* magazine. With a median income of $63,000, the readership of *Vogue* fits the target audience of the affluent Chanel brand. The sample was included in the December issue, just in time for making a Christmas gift suggestion. The sample coupled with several ads in the December issue of *Vogue* created an effective targeted sampling campaign.[23]

Bonus Packs

When an additional or extra number of items are placed in a special product package, it is a bonus pack. Examples include offering four bars of soap for the price of three or three free AA batteries in a bonus pack containing nine batteries. Typical bonuses range from 20 to 100 percent of the normal number of units in a package. A 30 percent bonus is the most common.

Types of Bonus Packs

Figure 12.6 identifies the major objectives of bonus packs. Increasing the size or quantity of the package can lead to greater product use. When a package that contains eight small candy bars increases by four more bars, consumers are likely to eat more, because they are readily available. This will not be true for products with constant consumption rates. If Colgate offers a bonus pack with an additional tube of toothpaste, consumers do not use more of the product. In effect, this delays the next purchase. Manufacturers offer these types of bonus packs because they preempt the competition. A consumer with a large quantity of the merchandise on hand becomes less likely to switch brands.

Keys to Successful Bonus Packs

Bonus packs reward customer loyalty by presenting, in effect, free merchandise. Bonus packs can lead to brand switching if the consumer has used the brand previously. Facing purchase decisions, consumers may opt for brands that offer more product at the regular or special price. The packages present an advantage that competitive brands are not offering.

Bonus packs tend to be popular with manufacturers, retailers, and customers. A retailer can build a positive relationship with a manufacturer that features a bonus pack to increase brand switching and stockpiling. Retailers gain an advantage because the bonus pack

- Increase usage of the product
- Match or preempt competitive actions
- Stockpile the product
- Develop customer loyalty
- Attract new users
- Encourage brand switching

FIGURE 12.6
Bonus Pack Objectives

offers a "bargain" or "value" through the retail outlet. Customers enjoy bonus packs because it feels like they are getting free merchandise. For products with high levels of competition, the bonus pack approach helps maintain brand loyalty and reduces brand switching at a minimal cost.

Bonus packs rarely attract new customers, because they have not previously purchased the brand. Obtaining an extra quantity increases purchase risk rather than reducing it. Most customers do not like to waste a product by throwing it away when they are dissatisfied. Marketing research indicates that when the bonus is small (20 to 40 percent), consumers often believe the price per unit has not truly changed. Unfortunately, a large bonus, such as doubling the amount, may lead consumers to believe that the price was first increased to compensate for the additional quantity. In that instance, increasing the size of a bonus captured the consumer's attention but did not convey the desired message.[24]

Kraft Foods, Inc.

▲ This advertisement for Karns Quality Foods includes a bonus pack offer.

Price-Offs

A price-off is a temporary reduction in the price of a product to the consumer. A price-off can be physically marked on the product, such as when a bottle of aspirin shows the regular retail price marked out and replaced by a special retail price (e.g., $8.99 marked out and replaced by $6.99). Producing a label with the price reduction pre-marked forces the retailer to sell the item at the reduced price. This ensures the price-off incentive will be passed on to consumers. At other times, the price-off will not be printed on the actual item but instead on a point-of-purchase display, sign, or shelf.

Benefits of Price-Offs

Price-offs help stimulate sales of existing products. They entice customers to try new products, because the lower price reduces the financial risk of making the purchase. They encourage customers to switch in brand parity situations or when no strong brand loyalty exists. In cases where consumers do have a preference, a price-off on a favorite brand encourages stockpiling of the product and possibly increased consumption of the item.[25] A consumer who purchases additional breakfast bars due to a price-off tends to consume more breakfast bars. Again, this will not be true for products such as deodorant or toothpaste. Stockpiling those types of products only delays the next purchase and does not increase consumption. Similar effects occur in the business-to-business arena when price-offs are offered.

Price-offs have proven to be successful consumer promotions for two reasons. First, the price-offs have the appeal of a monetary savings. Second, they grant immediate rewards. Unlike rebates, refunds, contests,

▼ A Boyer's advertisement offering price-offs on various seafood items.

Boyers Foods

FIGURE 12.7
Advantages and Disadvantages of Price-Offs

Advantages	Disadvantages
• Stimulate sales	• Negatively impact profits
• Encourage product trial	• Encourage price-sensitivity
• Encourage brand switching	• Negative impact on brand image
• Stockpiling and increased consumption	

Courtesy of Platinum Motorcars

▲ A price-off promotion by Platinum Motorcars offering 20 percent off on a 2-day rental if the consumer mentions seeing this advertisement.

sweepstakes, and other promotional incentives, consumers do not have to wait to receive the incentive.

Problems with Price-Offs

Although price-offs are easy to implement and can have a sudden impact on sales, at times they cause problems. Sales may increase, but the program might cause a negative impact on a company's profit margin. It normally takes at least a 30 to 60 percent increase in sales to offset each five percent price reduction.

Price-off programs encourage consumers to become more price-sensitive. In the same way that customers respond to rebates, they can either wait for a price-off promotion or choose another brand that happens to be on sale. In addition, when used too often, price-offs may lead to a negative impact on a brand's image. David Hale, CEO of Good Eats, noted, "Deep discounting doesn't build loyalty or consistency—it's cheapening your brand."[26] Again, price-off programs should be incorporated into the firm's overall IMC program. Figure 12.7 summarizes the benefits and problems with price-off promotions.

Overlays and Tie-Ins

At times, companies combine two or more consumer promotions activities into a single campaign, called an *overlay*. To attract Chinese consumers in Canada, Tropicana combined sampling with coupons. Free samples (50,000 cups of orange juice) were given out along with 30,000 coupons at a Chinese New Year's celebration in Vancouver. Asians who live in the United States and Canada are not typically large users of coupons; however, Tropicana Canada's research indicated that the Chinese consider oranges to be harbingers of good luck. A few weeks after the promotion, 40 percent of the coupons were redeemed, and sales of Tropicana orange juice among the Chinese community in Canada increased considerably.[27]

Developing a consumer promotion with another product or company is another common strategy, called a *tie-in*. *Intracompany tie-ins* are the promotion of two different products within one company using one consumer promotion. An alternative method involves partnering with another company, which is an *intercompany tie-in*. Fast-food restaurants often use tie-ins with movies and toys to create attractive children's promotions. Stand-alone, overlay, and tie-in programs deserve careful planning to maximize these effects.

Planning for Consumer Promotions

In planning the consumer promotions component of the IMC, the program should support the brand image and the brand positioning strategy. To ensure this occurs, marketers consider the target audience. Researchers identify the core values present in the target audience as well as opinions regarding the firm's products, especially as they relate to the competition. After gathering the information, the marketing team finalizes the consumer promotions plan. In terms of promotions, consumers can be divided into the four categories shown in Figure 12.8.

Promotion-prone consumers regularly respond to various consumer promotions and like to purchase products that are on-deal. They tend to clip coupons on a regular basis, enter contests and sweepstakes, purchase bonus packs, and respond to other promotional offers. In contrast, for **price-sensitive consumers**, price remains the primary, if not only, criterion used in making a purchase decision. Brand names are not important, and these individuals will not pay more for them. They take advantage of any type of promotion that reduces the price.

Courtesy of Alliance One Advertising

▲ A price-off and coupon offer for Eskamoe's Frozen Custard & More.

Brand-loyal consumers purchase only one particular brand and do not substitute, regardless of any deal being offered. They make the necessary effort to purchase their chosen brand. More common are **brand-preference consumers** who consider a small set of brands for which they have a strong attachment. When promotions are offered for one of their chosen brands, it becomes the one to be purchased. These consumers ignore a promotion for brands not in the brand preferred set, regardless of the size or type of promotion.

Consumers do not fit into one of the four categories for all purchases. They may tend to be one of the four types, but promotion or brand preferences change across product and service categories. A beer drinker may be extremely promotion prone; a wine drinker may be quite brand loyal. The same beer drinker may be extremely loyal to a pizza brand, and the same wine drinker may be price sensitive when it comes to buying potato chips.

In planning promotions, the marketing team understands that promotion-prone consumers look for on-deal brands. Price-sensitive consumers purchase the cheaper brand, regardless of whether it is on-deal or off-deal. Therefore, these two types of consumers are not highly attractive to pursue with consumer promotions unless the promotional goal is to increase sales, market share, or customer traffic. There will be little or no future allegiance to the brand.

Brand-loyal consumers only redeem promotions for their favored brands. Offering a promotion to this group makes little sense, because they will buy the brand anyway. Brand-preferred consumers represent the ideal group to target market, especially when the promotion features a brand in their preference sets. This can enhance loyalty toward the brand and prevents them from purchasing a competing brand. It may also move the consumer closer to brand loyalty.

objective 12.3
How do different types of customers respond to consumer promotions?

- Promotion-prone
- Brand-loyal
- Brand-preferred
- Price-sensitive

◀ **FIGURE 12.8**
Types of Consumers in Relation to Consumer Promotions

© michaeljung /Fotolia

▲ Brand-preferred consumers are the ideal group to target.

Manufacturers should incorporate retailer objectives into promotions programs. It does little good to create a promotion that will be popular with consumers if retailers are not willing to work with the manufacturer to enhance the promotional offer. Retailers prefer promotions that benefit them. The primary reasons retailers support manufacturer consumer promotions programs are to:

- Increase store traffic
- Increase store sales
- Attract new customers
- Increase the basket size[28]

The promotions program revolves around the theme of the IMC program while keeping in mind where the promotions will be seen by the consumer. Specific goals associated with the product, the target market, and the retail outlets are first formulated. Building-brand constitutes a long-term goal; generating sales is more short range. Price-based offers normally are designed to attract new customers or to build sales. Marketers use other consumer promotions, such as high-value premiums to enhance a firm's image over time.

objective 12.4

What types of trade promotions can help push products onto retailers' shelves and eventually to end users?

Trade Promotions

Trade promotions are incentives designed by members of the trade channel to entice another member to purchase goods for eventual resale. Trade promotions are aimed at retailers, distributors, wholesalers, brokers, or agents. A manufacturer offers trade promotions to convince another member of the trade channel to carry its goods. Wholesalers, distributors, brokers, and agents offer trade promotions to persuade retailers to purchase products for eventual resale.

Twenty years ago, trade promotions represented only about 25 percent of a manufacturer's marketing budget; today, it reaches nearly 70 percent. Trade promotions often constitute the second largest expense for a manufacturer after the cost-of-goods sold. Trade promotions account for approximately 17 percent of gross sales revenues for manufacturers.[29]

Trade promotions contribute to many successful IMC programs. Unfortunately, in other companies, the individual responsible for trade promotions may not be involved in the IMC planning process. Leaders in these firms often view trade promotions as merely a means for placing products onto retail shelves or satisfying a channel member's request. As a result, little consideration may be given to matching the IMC program when developing trade promotions programs.

A variety of trade promotions tools exist. Individual companies select trade promotions techniques based on several factors. These factors include the nature of the business (manufacturer versus distributor), the type of customer to be

▼ When developing promotions, Chic Shaque's marketing team first seeks to understand the type of consumers that shop at its retail store.

Joplin Globe

FIGURE 12.9
Types of Trade Promotions

- **Off-invoice allowance:** A per-case rebate paid to retailers for an order.
- **Slotting fees:** Money paid to retailers to stock a new product.
- **Exit fees:** Money paid to retailers to remove an item from their SKU inventory.

FIGURE 12.10
Types of Trade Allowances

influenced (e.g., retailer versus wholesaler), company preferences, and the objectives of the IMC plan. Figure 12.9 lists the primary types of trade promotions.

Trade Allowances

Trade allowances provide financial incentives to other channel members to motivate them to make purchases. Trade allowances take a variety of forms, including the ones in Figure 12.10. Each makes it possible for the channel member to offer discounts or other price-reduction deals to its channel customers.

Off-Invoice Allowances Off-invoice allowances are financial discounts given for each item, case, or pallet ordered. They encourage channel members to place orders. Approximately 35 percent of all trade dollars go to off-invoice allowances, making them the largest expenditure among trade promotions tools.[30] As with refunds, rebates, and price-offs in the consumer sector, many retailers are reluctant to purchase merchandise without some type of trade allowance. In addition, tremendous competitive pressure to offer trade allowances exist as companies selling the same type of products compete for limited shelf space.

Slotting Fees The most controversial form of trade allowance, **slotting fees**, are funds charged by retailers to stock new products. As shown in Figure 12.11, retailers justify slotting fees in various ways.[31] First, retailers spend money to add new products to inventories and to stock merchandise. An unsuccessful product means the retailer's investment in inventory represents a loss, especially when the retailer has stocked the product in a large number of stores. Slotting fees recover some of the loss.

Second, adding a new product in the retail store means providing shelf space. Shelves are already filled. Adding a new product means either deleting brands or products or reducing the amount of shelf space allocated to them. In both cases, the retailer spends both time and money creating space for a new product.

Third, slotting fees make it easier for retailers to make decisions about new products. A typical supermarket carries 35,000 SKUs (stock-keeping units). The supermarket's managers evaluate 10,000 to 15,000 new products per year. Most will fail. Consequently, retailers believe charging slotting fees forces manufacturers to weed out high-risk product introductions. The average total cost in slotting fees for a nationally introduced product ranges from \$1.5 to \$2 million.[32] Consequently, retailers contend that slotting fees force manufacturers to conduct careful test marketing on products before introducing them. Such testing limits the number of new products offered each year. This, in turn, drastically reduces the number of new product failures.

Finally, slotting fees add to the bottom line. Many products have low margins or markups. Slotting fees generate additional monies to support retail operations. Estimates suggest that between 14 and 27 percent of trade promotion monies given to retailers go directly to the retailer's profits.[33]

- Cost of adding new products to inventory
- Re-allocating shelf space
- Aids decision on choosing new products to stock
- Add to the profit margin

FIGURE 12.11
Retailers' Justifications of Slotting Fees

Art Allianz/Fotolia

▲ Retailers charge slotting fees to place new products on store shelves.

The other side of the argument comes from manufacturers, who claim slotting fees are practically a form of extortion. Many manufacturers believe slotting fees cost too much and are unfair in the first place. These fees compel manufacturers to pay millions of dollars to retailers that could be dedicated to advertising, sales promotions, or additional marketing efforts.

Slotting fees can prevent small manufacturers from getting products into stores because they cannot afford them. Some large retail operations have small-vendor policies; however, placing merchandise remains extremely challenging.

Exit Fees Instead of paying a slotting allowance, some retailers ask for **exit fees**, which are monies paid to remove an item from a retailer's inventory. This approach may be useful when a manufacturer introduces a new size of a product or a new version, such as a 3-liter bottle of Pepsi or Pepsi Diet Vanilla. PepsiCo already has products on the retailer's shelves. Adding a new-sized container or new variety of the product involves lower risk and is not the same as adding a new product. Rather than charging an upfront fee, such as a slotting allowance, retailers request exit fees if the new version of the product fails or if one of the current versions must be removed from the inventory. Four percent of retailers charge exit fees, compared to the 82 percent using slotting fees.[34]

Trade Allowance Complications In offering trade allowances to retailers, manufacturers assume that a portion of the price reduction will be passed on to consumers. This occurs only about half of the time. When consumers receive a portion of the price allowance, retailers often schedule competing brands, so they can have at least one special offer going at all times. Thus, one week Pepsi offers a reduced price and the next week Coke offers a discount. The two products are rarely promoted on-deal at the same time. By offering only one on-deal at a time, the retailer always has a reduced priced brand for the price-sensitive consumer. The retailer also can charge the brand-loyal consumer full price 50 percent of the time. While accomplishing these goals, the retailer receives special trade allowances from both Pepsi and Coke.

▼ Trade promotions offered to retailers are often passed on to customers in terms of lower prices or discounts.

Karns Foods

In an effort to increase profit margins, retailers engage in two activities: forward buying and diversion. *Forward buying* occurs when a retailer purchases extra amounts of a product while it is on-deal. The retailer then sells the on-deal merchandise after the deal period ends, saving the cost of purchasing the product at the manufacturer's full price. *Diversion* takes place when a retailer purchases a product on-deal in one location and ships it to another location where it is off-deal. For example, a manufacturer may offer an off-invoice allowance of $5 per case for the product in France. Diversion tactics mean the retailer purchases an excess quantity in France and has it shipped to stores in other European countries. To do so, retailers first examine the potential profits to be earned, less the cost of shipping the product to other locations. Shipping costs tend to be relatively high compared to trade allowances offered. Consequently, retailers do not use diversion nearly as much as forward buying.

Trade Contests

To achieve sales targets and other objectives, channel members sometimes provide trade contests. Winners receive prizes or cash, or **spiff money**. Contests are held at every level within the channel. They can be between brokers or agents, wholesalers, or retail stores. To prevent undue influence of contests on buyers, a number of large organizations prohibit employees from participating in vendor contests. Although influencing salespeople represents exactly what a contest seeks to accomplish, many large retail organizations do not want buyers participating, because these buyers make purchase decisions for as many as 500 to 2,500 stores and participating in a contest may result in poor decisions.

© bst2012/Fotolia

▲ Trade contests were held among travel agents to increase cruise ship bookings.

In recent years, the demand for cruise ship vacations has steadily decreased. As a result, cruise lines have used a combination of advertising, consumer promotions, and trade promotions to attract patrons. Royal Caribbean International offered travel agents cooperative advertising programs featuring TV commercials, newspaper ads, as well as an email template to contact potential travelers.

Norwegian Cruise Lines enrolled 5,500 agents in a "Sale of All Sails" promotional contest. Prizes were based on bookings. Each agent that set up a Holland America cruise was enrolled in the trade contest. The prizes offered included a free cruise with five veranda staterooms. The Princess Cruise line offered booking agents the chance to win a West Coast sailing cruise with a mini-suite. One cruise was awarded each week during a 90-day period. Offering travel agents the chance to win prizes and cruises for themselves caused many of them to be motivated to book cruises for the lines holding the contests.[35]

Trade Incentives

Trade incentives are similar to trade allowances. The difference is that **trade incentives** involve the retailer or channel member performing a function in order to receive the funds. The purpose, however, remains the same as for trade allowances: to encourage the channel member either to push the manufacturer's brand or to increase purchases of that brand. Figure 12.12 identifies three major types of trade incentives.

Cooperative Merchandising Agreements The most comprehensive trade incentive, a cooperative merchandising agreement (CMA), is a formal agreement between the retailer and manufacturer to undertake a two-way marketing effort. The CMA can be

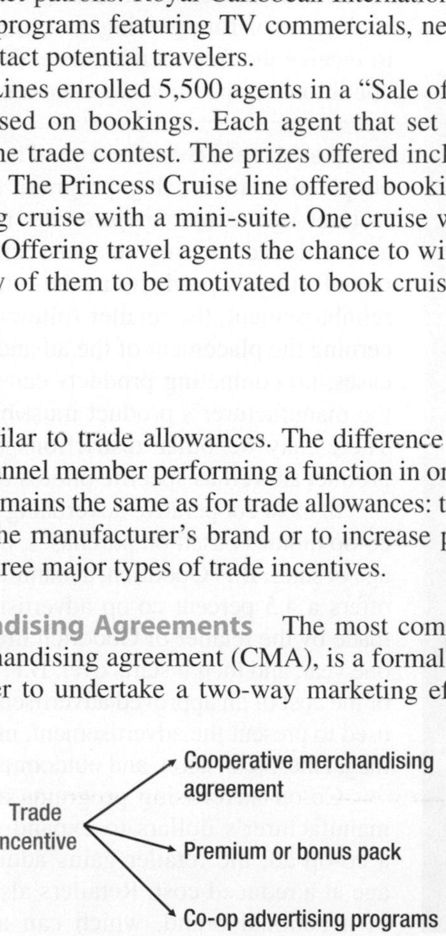

◀ **FIGURE 12.12**
Types of Trade Incentives

for a wide variety of marketing tasks. A CMA may feature the manufacturer's brand as a price leader in an advertisement. A cooperative agreement may be created in which a retailer will emphasize the manufacturer's brand as part of an in-house offer made by the store or feature the manufacturer's brand on a special shelf display.

Cooperative merchandising agreements remain popular with manufacturers because the retailer performs a function in order to receive the allowance or incentive. The manufacturer retains control of the functions performed. Also, if price allowances are made as part of the CMA, the manufacturer knows that the retailer passes a certain percentage or the entire price discount on to the consumer. CMAs allow manufacturers to create annual contracts with retailers. These longer-term commitments reduce the need for last-minute trade incentives or trade allowances.

CMAs also benefit retailers. The primary advantage, from the retailer's perspective, is that the program allows them to develop *calendar promotions*, which are promotional campaigns the retailer plans for customers through manufacturer trade incentives. Signing an agreement allows a retailer to schedule the weeks a particular brand will be on sale and offset the other weeks with other brands. Calendar promotions make it possible to always have one brand on sale while the others are off-deal and to rotate the brands on sale. By arranging sales through trade incentives, the margins for the retailer stay approximately the same for all brands, both on-deal and off-deal, because they rotate. As a result, the retailer effectively moves the price reductions given to customers to manufacturers rather than absorbing them. A store may feature Budweiser on-deal one week and Heineken the next. Loyal beer drinkers stay with their preferred brand, while price-sensitive consumers can choose the on-deal brand and the store retains a reasonable markup on all beers sold.

Premiums and Bonus Packs Instead of providing the retailer with a price discount, a manufacturer might give free merchandise in the form of a premium or bonus pack. For example, a manufacturer would offer a bonus pack of one carton for each 20 purchased within the next 60 days. The bonus packs are free to the retailer and are awarded either for placing the order by a certain date or for agreeing to a minimum-size order. Often, to receive the free merchandise, the retailer must meet both conditions: a specified date and a minimum order size.

▼ A co-op advertisement for Bob's Furniture Gallery featuring both the Flexsteel and Thomasville brands.

Joplin Globe

Cooperative Advertising The final trade incentive, a cooperative advertising program, occurs when the manufacturer agrees to reimburse the retailer a certain percentage of the advertising costs associated with advertising the manufacturer's products in the retailer's ad. To receive the reimbursement, the retailer follows specific guidelines concerning the placement of the ad and its content. In almost all cases, no competing products can be advertised. Normally, the manufacturer's product must be displayed prominently. There may be other restrictions on how to advertise the product as well as specific photos or copy that must be used.

In most cooperative advertising programs, retailers accrue co-op monies based on purchases, normally a certain percentage of sales. B.F. Goodrich, a manufacturer of automobile tires, offers a 4.5 percent co-op advertising fund on all purchases made by the retailer of Goodrich tires. The money accrues for one year, and then it starts over. B.F. Goodrich pays 70 percent of the cost of an approved advertisement. Any medium may be used to present the advertisement, including radio, newspaper, magazines, television, and outdoor advertising.[36]

Co-op advertising programs allow retailers to use the manufacturer's dollars to expand advertising programs. In a co-op ad, the retailer gains additional advertising coverage at a reduced cost. Retailers also benefit from the image of a national brand, which can attract new or additional customers to the store. Wal-Mart recently expanded co-op advertising efforts with major manufacturers, who contributed more than $400 million toward Wal-Mart's annual advertising budget. In Wal-Mart's system, manufacturers have considerably more creative input into the ads and are prominently displayed in the ad instead of taking minor roles.[37]

Manufacturers also benefit from co-op ads. By sharing advertising expenditures with retailers, the manufacturer gains additional exposure at a lower cost. More important, almost all co-op advertising programs are tied to sales. The retailer accrues co-op advertising dollars based on a certain percentage of sales. Thus, to obtain the co-op money, the retailer must promote the brand prominently and purchase the product for resale. Consequently, a wide variety of cooperative advertisements appear regularly in every medium for both consumer and business-to-business products.

Trade Shows

Many business-to-business marketing programs include appearances at trade shows. They benefit both manufacturers and retailers. From a manufacturer's standpoint, a trade show provides the opportunity to discover potential customers and sell new products. Relationships with current customers can be strengthened at the show. A trade show often grants the opportunity to investigate the competition. Many times, trade shows establish a situation in which the manufacturer's sales team meets directly with decision makers and buyers from business-to-business clients. A trade show can strengthen the brand name of a product as well as the company's image.

From the retailer's perspective, a trade show helps buyers to compare merchandise and to make contacts with several prospective vendors in a short period of time. In some cases, the retailers negotiate special deals. Trade shows represent an ideal place for buyers and sellers to meet in an informal, low-pressure setting to discuss how to work together effectively.

Some national and international trade shows are attended by thousands of buyers. A trade show will succeed if manufacturers seek out key buyers and try to avoid spending too much time with nonbuyers. Figure 12.13 identifies five categories of buyers who attend trade shows. Many marketers try to weed out the education seekers who are not interested in buying. Manufacturer's agents concentrate efforts on three groups: solution seekers, buying teams, and power buyers. Asking the right questions identifies solution seekers and buying teams. The power buyers are more difficult to find because they do not want to be identified. They often do not wear badges at trade shows, which means vendors are never sure who they are.

In the United States, few deals are finalized during trade shows. Buyers and sellers meet, discuss, and maybe even negotiate, but seldom complete the sale. Instead, manufacturers collect business cards as leads to be followed up later. This procedure varies for international customers. International attendees tend to be senior executives with the authority to make purchases. They fit into the power-buyer category listed in Figure 12.13. U.S. manufacturers know that the international attendee often wishes to conduct business during the show, not afterward. The international attendees spend more time at each manufacturer's booth. They stay longer in order to gather and study information in greater detail. The international guest, who pays more for travel expenses, wants more in-depth information than an American counterpart requires.

- **Education seekers** Buyers who want to browse, look, and learn but are not in the buying mode
- **Reinforcement seekers** Buyers who want reassurance they made the right decision in past purchases
- **Solution seekers** Buyers seeking solutions to specific problems and are in the buying mode
- **Buying teams** A team of buyers seeking vendors for their business; usually are in the buying mode
- **Power buyers** Members of upper management or key purchasing agents with the authority to buy

FIGURE 12.13
Five Categories of Buyers Attending Trade Shows

Imtmphoto/Fotolia

▲ International attendees at trade shows often wish to conduct business during the show, not afterward.

The number of international trade show visitors has increased as competition continues to expand globally. The increase in international participants has caused trade show centers to set up more meeting spaces, conference centers, and even places to eat where buyers and sellers meet and transact business.

Trade shows have changed in other ways. Niche and regional shows are replacing large national and international shows. For example, in the 1990s, many megasports trade shows were attended by everybody in the sporting goods business. The National Sporting Goods Association World Sports Expo in Chicago attracted in excess of 90,000 attendees. That number has dwindled to fewer than 40,000 today. Now, manufacturers and retailers attend specialty trade shows featuring only one sport or regional shows that focus on one section of the country. Smaller shows are less expensive to set up. Many company leaders believe they provide higher-quality prospects and better opportunities to bond with customers and offer more quality one-to-one time with customers and potential customers. In contrast, it is relatively easy to get lost in the crowd at a bigger show.[38]

Concerns with Trade Promotions

objective 12.5

What concerns exist for manufacturers considering trade promotions programs?

Effective marketing teams incorporate trade promotions into the overall IMC effort. In many companies, this does not occur, primarily due to employee pay structures. Sales and brand managers face quotas; and when sales fall behind, one quick way to boost them is to offer retailers a trade deal. Further, company leaders often evaluate brand managers based on the sales growth of a brand. Trade deals become the easiest way for a brand manager to ensure continuing growth. The pattern of using trade deals to reach short-term quotas rather than long-term image and theme-building will not change until top management adopts a new approach. The IMC process succeeds when it emphasizes the long-term horizon and the company's compensation structure changes to match.

▼ Strong brands, such as Philadelphia Cream Cheese, do not rely as heavily on trade promotions.

Kraft Foods, Inc

A strong brand image causes retailers to stock the product even when fewer trade deals are offered, because a strong brand by itself can help pull customers into retail stores. A customer who considers Sony to be a strong brand in the stereo marketplace asks for that brand in an electronics retail store. This makes stocking Sony an advantage, even with limited trade promotions offers.

The cost of trade promotions continues to pose another concern. Manufacturers spend billions of dollars each year on them. These costs are often passed on to consumers in the form of higher prices. Estimates suggest that 11 cents out of every dollar spent for a consumer product goes directly for the cost of trade promotions.[39] The goal should be to keep the cost at a reasonable level. Money should be spent wisely, rather than simply getting into "bidding wars" with competitors. Trade promotions dollars have the greatest long-term impact when they help build relationships and help achieve other key IMC goals.

An unfortunate situation occurs when merchandise does not move until a trade promotion incentive has been offered. In the grocery industry, the majority of all purchases made by retailers are on-deal with some type of trade incentive. The constant use of deals has trimmed manufacturer margins on products and created competitive pressures to conform.

If a manufacturer tries to halt or cut back on trade promotions, retailers replace the manufacturer's products with other brands or reduce shelf space to give more room to manufacturers offering better deals.

One way to correct these problems would be to spend more on advertising focused on building or rebuilding a brand's image. Also, the marketing team should be certain promotions fit the brand's image. "If it doesn't fit," writes Brian Sullivan in *Marketing News*, "don't use it."[40] Unfortunately, to spend more on advertising means cutting trade promotions incentives. The risk becomes that other competitors will move in by giving better trade promotion deals to retailers and gain shelf space as a result. Then, the cycle begins again.

Managing trade promotions programs constitutes a challenging part of the marketing planning process because such a large percentage of the marketing budget goes to trade promotions. Effective IMC programs achieve a balance between all elements of the promotions mix and identify clear goals and targets for trade promotions programs. Only then will the company be able to compete on all levels and not just through a cycle of trade promotions bidding wars.

International Implications

objective 12.6
What issues complicate international sales promotions programs?

Consumer promotions are adapted to the countries in which they are offered. Two complications occur: legal and cultural. Any coupon, premium, contest, sweepstakes, or price change must fit with local legal regulations. The marketing team investigates any potential legal problems before launching an international consumer promotions program.

Culturally, citizens in some countries may take a dim view of some promotions. For instance, in some cultures, those who redeem coupons may be viewed as being of lower socioeconomic status, which may dissuade some from using them. Participation in contests or sweepstakes may violate religious norms in other nations.

The same holds true for trade promotions. Laws vary regarding discounts, spiff money, slotting fees, and exit fees. These issues may also be reflected in cultural values. And, as previously noted, the ways in which managers in companies around the world participate in trade shows varies.

Finally, the emphasis placed on sales promotions will be different, depending on the company involved and the country in which that company operates. Both small companies seeking to do business in foreign countries and large international conglomerates will need to adjust to local conditions when employing these marketing tactics. At the same time, the goal remains to be certain that the efforts match the company's image and overall approach to marketing communications.

Summary

An IMC program incorporates all four elements of the promotions mix. Advertising may be considered to be the main "voice" of the IMC message. At the same time, the sales promotion part of the mix, including trade and consumer promotions, plays a crucial role in the success or failure of the overall marketing program.

Attracting customers by using consumer promotions includes the use of coupons, premiums, contests and sweepstakes, refunds, rebates, samples, bonus packs, and price-off deals. These items should be combined with specific promotional goals to have the desired impact on customers. Consumer promotions are often used to boost sales and can be an excellent short-term method to increase sales or a firm's market share. They also provide a means of introducing new products. Often, a consumer promotion prompts consumers to at least try the product, where selling it at the regular price will not. Coupons and contests have been successful tactics for gaining new customers. Consumer promotions can boost sales of a particular brand, and evidence suggests that they increase sales of the overall product category rather than just take sales away from competitors.

Trade promotions complement consumer promotions. The use of trade allowances, trade contests, trade incentives, and participation in trade shows helps the manufacturer or member of the marketing channel maintain positive contact with other organizations and moves products toward the retailer. Trade promotions work best when they are integrated into other IMC efforts rather than being viewed as a necessary evil or simply as a short-term tool to increase sales.

Internationally, sales promotions can be used when they are chosen based on the characteristics, attitudes, laws, regulations, and cultural nuances of a given geographic region. The primary objective of any promotions program must always be to enhance the message sent forth in other aspects of the IMC program in a manner that helps the company reach its long-term marketing objectives in a cost-effective and positive fashion.

Key Terms

sales promotions All of the incentives offered to customers and channel members to encourage product purchases

consumer promotions Incentives directly offered to a firm's customers or potential customers

trade promotions Expenditures or incentives used by manufacturers and other members of the marketing channel to purchase goods for eventual sale

freestanding inserts (FSIs) Sheets of coupons distributed in newspapers, primarily on Sunday

promotion-prone consumers Consumers who are not brand loyal and regularly respond to promotions such as coupons, price-off plans, or premiums, only purchasing items that are on-deal

price-sensitive consumers Consumers for whom price is the primary, if not only, criterion used in making a purchase decision

brand-loyal consumers Consumers who purchase only one particular brand and do not substitute, regardless of any deal being offered

brand-preference consumers Consumers who prefer a small set of brands

trade allowances Financial incentives provided to other channel members to motivate them to make purchases

slotting fees A form of trade allowance in which funds are charged by retailers to stock new products

exit fees Monies paid to remove an item from a retailer's inventory

spiff money Rewards given as contest prizes to brokers, retail salespeople, stores, wholesalers, and agents

trade incentives Funds given that require the retailer to perform a function in order to receive the dollars

MyMarketingLab

Go to **mymktlab.com** to complete the problems marked with this icon ✪.

Review Questions

12-1. Define sales promotion. What are the two main categories of sales promotions?

12-2. What are the sales promotion objectives for new products or services?

12-3. What is meant by the term "freestanding insert"?

12-4. What is a premium? What types of premium programs can companies use?

12-5. What is the purpose of an instant redemption coupon?

12-6. What is an in- or on-pack premium?

12-7. What are the circumstances or requirements for a premium program to work?

12-8. What are the two usual factors that influence whether someone enters a competition?

12-9. How is a refund different from a rebate?

12-10. What are the primary types of samples?

12-11. What benefits and problems are associated with sampling?

12-12. What are the benefits of offering bonus packs?

12-13. What benefits and problems are associated with price-off tactics?

12-14. What is an overlay? A tie-in?

12-15. What four categories of consumers can be associated with consumer promotions?

12-16. What are the major types of trade allowances?

12-17. What is a slotting fee? An exit fee?

12-18. Who are the targets of consumer promotions in most cases?

12-19. What complications are associated with trade allowances?

12-20. How does the spiff money relate to trade contests?

12-21. What are the main types of trade incentives?

12-22. Describe a cooperative merchandising agreement.

12-23. How are premiums or bonus packs used as trade incentives?

12-24. How can a cooperative advertising program benefit both a manufacturer and a retailer?

12-25. Describe how to effectively utilize trade promotions.

12-26. What problems must be overcome when developing international sales promotions programs?

Critical Thinking Exercises

DISCUSSION QUESTIONS

12-27. In many developed countries the age group market with the greatest disposal income is the grey one. It is difficult to target and very diverse in its tastes and needs. Choose a product that would appeal to the grey market. What sales promotions would you choose? Where would you feature these promotions? How would you get to the grey market? How significant is the grey market in your own country? Can you learn lessons from the way products and services are marketed to them?

12-28. Refer to the list of consumer promotions in Figure 12.1. Discuss each one in terms of your personal usage. Which ones do you use? How often? Why?

12-29. Design a magazine advertisement with a detachable coupon or premium for one of the following products. Be sure to put an expiration date and other restrictions on the use of the coupon or premium. You may want to do an internet search to see some sample coupons or premiums before you design yours.

- **a.** SunBright Tanning Salon
- **b.** Dixie Printing
- **c.** Hamburger Haven
- **d.** BriarPatch Ice Cream

12-30. The Rawlings Sports Equipment Company plans to increase sales of baseball gloves this season. The company intends to use a coupon program. Discuss the pros and cons of each method of coupon distribution listed in the chapter for Rawlings. Which method or methods should Rawlings use? Why?

12-31. To maintain a strong brand image, Revlon's marketing team decides to use a premium for each of its lipstick products. What type of premium would you suggest for Revlon for each of the target markets listed here? Which premium would you use? Justify your answers.

- **a.** Females, ages 60 +
- **b.** Teenagers, ages 14 to 19
- **c.** College students, ages 18 to 25
- **d.** Professional females, ages 30 to 50

12-32. How often do you enter contests or sweepstakes? What was the last contest you entered? Why did you enter? Discuss the importance of extrinsic and intrinsic rewards in entering contests and sweepstakes. If you seldom or never enter contests and sweepstakes, why? What type of intrinsic and extrinsic rewards would it take for you to enter?

12-33. Video games generate major revenues for many companies. One manufacturer decided to use sampling as a method to reach the primary target market—males between the ages of 15 and 30. The sampling could have been distributed in one of two ways. First, the actual game could be loaded on a computer for targeted individuals. Second, potential customers could be sent an abbreviated version of the game. Which sampling method would be best? Using the list of sampling methods provided in the chapter, discuss the pros and cons of each sampling method in terms of this new video game. Which type and method of sampling would you recommend? Why?

12-34. Consumers can be divided into four broad categories in terms of how they respond to consumer promotions: promotion prone, brand loyal, price sensitive, and brand preference. Identify two services or goods that would fit into each category for you personally. For example, you may be promotion prone when you buy soft drinks (your favorite brand is "What's on Sale"), but be very brand loyal when you buy shoes (Nike, Reebok). What determines which type of category you fit into for the various products you discussed?

12-35. Sales promotions that are allowed in your own country may not necessarily be allowed in all of the countries in your region. The situation may also be reversed. Compare and contrast the range in two other countries with your own.

12-36. As with the other consumer promotions, international expansion requires understanding the laws and customs of each country and culture. In Saudi Arabia and other Muslim countries, Clinique had to modify its sampling techniques. In the United States and Western cultures, Clinique provides cosmetics samples in retail outlets for customers to try. In the United States, women normally sell retail cosmetics; in Saudi Arabia, men do. At the same time, Muslim custom prohibits a man from touching a woman if she is not a relative. Female customers must either apply the cosmetics themselves or bring their husbands to the store with them.

Asking a female customer "What color are your eyes?" constitutes a grave offense in Saudi Arabia because the eyes are believed to be the gateway to the soul. Asking her about skin tone does not make sense because women keep their faces covered. Sampling is important for Clinique in Saudi Arabia.[41]

How would you organize a sampling program in light of these cultural factors? What other consumer promotions could be used? If you have someone in your class from a Muslim country, ask your classmate to discuss the use of consumer promotions in her home country.

Integrated Learning Exercises

12-37. Coupons remain a popular form of consumer promotions. Access the following websites. What are the advantages and disadvantages of each to a consumer? How do the websites impact manufacturers? How do they impact retailers?

a. Coupon Country (**www.couponcountry.com**)
b. CoolSavings (**www.coolsavings.com**)
c. SmartSource (**www.smartsource.com**)
d. Coupons.com (**www.coupons.com**)

12-38. Sweepstakes and contests provide excellent methods for building customer traffic to a retail outlet and interest in a brand. Certain firms assist in the development of sweepstakes and contests. This is important due to a variety of legal restrictions imposed by different states. Access the following websites. What types of services does each offer? How do the companies assist in developing a contest or sweepstakes? Which firm would you choose if you were responsible for developing a contest or a sweepstakes program for a new brand of cosmetics?

a. Promotion Activators, Inc. (**www.promotionactivators.com**)
b. Compliance Sweepstakes Services (**www.compliancesweeps.com**)
c. Ventura Marketing & Promotion (**www.sweepspros.com**)

12-39. Examine the following websites. What types of promotions are available? What are the objectives of the various consumer promotions? Do the promotions on the websites mesh with the company's advertising and consumer promotions at retail outlets? Explain.

a. Taco Bell (**www.tacobell.com**)
b. Hershey's (**www.hersheys.com**)
c. Huggies (**www.huggies.com**)
d. Papa John's (**www.papajohns.com**)

12-40. One widely read journal featuring promotional marketing is *Promo*. Access the website at **http://chiefmarketer.com/promotional-marketing**. Examine the table of contents and access the various areas. After exploring the site, write a short report about what is available at the website and how it can be used to assist companies wanting to develop various promotions.

12-41. Use a search engine to find your country or region-specific version of the websites for Apple, Samsung, and Toshiba. What promotions are they running at the moment? Are these promotions in association with, or independent of, local retailers? Are they trying to convince you to order direct?

Student Project

CREATIVE CORNER

Access the official website of the Corpus Christi Hooks minor league baseball team. From the following list of special days, pick two and then design two different ads. Make sure each advertisement features a consumer promotion that is either mentioned on the website (under "Promotions" or "Promotions Calendar") or that you come up with on your own.

Opening Day	*Cinco de Mayo*
Mother's Day	Father's Day
Fourth of July	Labor Day
Play-off Games	Championship Celebration

Blog Exercises

Access the authors' blog for this textbook at the URLs provided to complete these exercises. Answer the questions that are posed on the blog.

12-42. Papa John's: **http://blogclowbaack.net/2014/05/12/papa-johns-chapter-12/**

12-43. Brookshire's: **http://blogclowbaack.net/2014/05/12/brookshires-chapter-12/**

12-44. Consumer promotions: **http://blogclowbaack.net/2014/05/12/consumer-promotions-chapter-12/**

CASE 1 DULUX PAINT: SALES PROMOTIONS IN CONSUMER AND TRADE MARKETS

Owned by AkzoNobel (formerly ICI), Dulux is a brand of paint that is available across the world. The Dulux brand name has been in existence for over 80 years and the paint is sold to consumers for home decorating via DIY stores. It is also sold under the brand name Dulux Trade to professional decorators and contractors, who buy through DIY stores and trade distributors. The paint market is highly competitive and Dulux competes with a number of paint brands including store own brands.

In the UK, Dulux is the market leader and offers a range of paint and coating products for interior and exterior decoration. They also offer an in-store mixing service to help customers to coordinate color schemes, together with information on decorating and advice on planning and designing decorating projects. Dulux has a strong track record in innovation and new product development and is also involved in sustainability initiatives such as recycling and sponsoring community activities such as painting local community facilities.

An old English sheepdog has become the advertising mascot for Dulux and has featured in their advertising in the UK since 1961. The association between the dog and the brand has become so strong that the breed is often referred to as "the Dulux dog." Dulux uses a variety of media and promotional tools to market the brand to consumer and trade markets using advertising in TV and press and a range of sales promotions. Their consumer and trade website have links to social networking sites such as Facebook, Twitter, and Pinterest and there are product demonstration videos available on the trade website designed to present specialist guidance and advice to the trade professional.

Advertising raises awareness of new Dulux products and can visually present creative examples of color schemes and room design through TV and online advertising. To further encourage purchases, sales promotions offer added value and incentives in both consumer and trade markets in a highly competitive market and play an important role in the marketing communications strategy for Dulux.

There are a number of methods that Dulux uses to promote to the consumer market. Instant redemption, date-specific, money off coupons are used to encourage consumers to purchase from the Dulux range; these vouchers are made available in print or can be digitally downloaded. Sampling is also used; consumers can also order color testers online or buy in-store. These testers are samples of the product that provide a small amount of the chosen paint plus a brush and give the consumer the opportunity to try out the color at home before selecting and buying the final product. Consumers are also offered the opportunity to enter online competitions to win prizes such as a cuddly toy version of the famous Dulux dog.

In order to attract the trade professional market, Dulux uses promotions such as providing details of trade distributor and store locations on their website and offering marketing

Luanateutzi/Shutterstock

▲ Many different areas of a company must be involved in planning and execution in order to produce a successful IMC.

support to retailers and trade, who in turn carry price offers and Dulux sales promotions. Date-specific digital and press coupons are used in trade outlets to offer money off on the Dulux Trade product range. Money off promotions are supported by advertising in specialist painting and decorating trade magazines together with in-store point-of-sale materials such as leaflets and posters. Dulux also provides free color guides as brochures or downloads, as well as color swatches for trade professionals to show to their customers, together with design and application advice to support commercial projects. Dulux Trade also supports their trade customers by attending specialist trade shows such as the UK's National Painting and Decorating Show, where the Dulux sales team can demonstrate products and provide advice and information on the latest products, technological developments, and application techniques.[42]

12-45. What are the benefits of offering a paint sampling service?

12-46. What are the potential disadvantages of offering money off coupons for the Dulux brand?

12-47. What is the role of specialist trade fairs in the Dulux marketing communications strategy?

12-48. How can sales promotion help to grow sales of Dulux paint through DIY trade outlets?

12-49. How can sales promotion help to differentiate the Dulux brand from store own brands?

12-50. What role can online competitions play in the Dulux marketing communications strategy?

12-51. Visit the Dulux trade website at http://dulux.tradedecorating.co.uk/index.jsp. What benefits does the website offer to the trade professional?

12-52. How can the effectiveness of sales promotion be measured?

CASE 2 MARKETING SPORTS EQUIPMENT

The term "sports" has many meanings, depending on the context and those involved in a conversation. Some may be inclined to think of college and professional athletes playing games at the highest level in front of large crowds. Others view sports as being related to physical fitness. Other groups think in terms of "leisure time" or "children's recreation."

Regardless of the type of sports one considers, Academy Sports + Outdoors offers the equipment, clothing, and support services consumers need to engage in activities as varied as camping, fishing, boating, barbeques, as well as participating in mainstream sports such as baseball, basketball, soccer, and football, as fans or as participants. Large, brightly lit retail outlets feature a wide variety of merchandise for the majority of sporting and outdoor activities in 130 stores placed in 11 different states in the United States.

Academy Sports + Outdoor competes with numerous vendors, including Dick's Sporting Goods, Modell's, Bass Pro Shop, and big box retailers Wal-Mart, Kmart, and Target. Sports participants can also visit specialty shops, such as golf pro shops and smaller fishing stores and outlets.

Consumer groups range from casual backyard athletes to serious hunters, fishermen (and women), Little League sponsors and teams, and families looking for equipment to take on a camping expedition. As a result, discovering which target markets are the most lucrative remains an important challenge for each retail chain in this marketplace.

Academy Sports + Outdoor's management team has chosen to offer guns and other types of hunting equipment. Retailers offering firearms often encounter controversy, both from those opposed to guns and members of major gun lobbies.

Recently, an additional challenge faced major sports retailers. A declining economy forced many consumers to consider which purchases were absolutely necessary and which product purchases could be put on hold. At the same time, some families chose simpler, less expensive vacations and recreational activities, such as camping and home entertainment through games such as badminton and table tennis.

Academy Sports + Outdoor defines itself as "the destination for active-minded families." The company's mission defines the goals of providing an "unparalleled shopping experience," creating a trusting relationship with customers, and promoting a high-quality working environment for company associates that includes the opportunity to advance within the company.

It is not surprising that the company receives "an overwhelming volume of requests" for sponsorship activities. Company leaders have established well-defined criteria for examining inquiries. Any organization seeking a sponsorship tie-in must make the request three months in advance and can expect to wait as long as five weeks for a response. A similar backlog exists for its donations and charitable activities.

Elenathewise/Fotolia

▲ Families are an important target market for Academy Sports + Outdoors.

In the future, Academy Sports + Outdoor will continue to expand. Company policies regarding relationships with suppliers remain an important priority. In any case, as long as people continue to enjoy a wide variety of recreational activities, the potential for further growth remains possible.

12-53. What are the primary target markets for Academy Sports + Outdoor?

12-54. For each of the target markets identified in the preceding question, what types of consumer promotions should Academy Sports + Outdoor offer? Justify your response.

12-55. Suppose you are the vice president of marketing at Academy Sports + Outdoor. Examine the list of consumer promotions shown in Figure 12.1. Discuss the pros and cons of each promotion if the target market is active-minded families with children under 18 and incomes between $30,000 and $70,000.

12-56. From your answer to the preceding question, pick one of the promotions you feel is the best to reach the designated target market. Design a newspaper ad using that promotion. Be sure to include restrictions such as usage and expiration date.

MyMarketingLab

Go to **mymktlab.com** for the following Assisted-graded writing questions:

12-57. According to Kim James, sales promotion manager for Eckerd Drug, "The teen and preteen segments are important because they (teens) are developing buying habits and loyalties during these ages and are our future loyal consumers." In addition to established brands such as Cover Girl and Maybelline, Eckerd Drug now stocks brands such as Bonne Bell, Jane, and Naturistics. Which consumer promotions would be the best to attract teens and preteens to the cosmetics department of Eckerd Drug? Why? What tie-ins or overlays would you recommend? Why?

12-58. The Rawlings Sports Equipment Company plans to increase sales of baseball gloves this season. The company intends to use a coupon program. Discuss the pros and cons of each method of coupon distribution listed in the chapter for Rawlings. Which method or methods should Rawlings use? Why?

Chapter 13 Public Relations and Sponsorship Programs

Chapter Objectives

After reading this chapter, you should be able to answer the following questions:

13.1 What relationships exist between public relations and the marketing activities performed by a company?

13.2 How can the public relations functions help to build better relationships with all internal and external stakeholders?

13.3 What types of positive, image-building programs can companies feature as parts of a public relations program?

13.4 What steps can companies take to prevent or reduce image damage when negative events occur?

13.5 How can marketers tie sponsorships to public relations efforts to strengthen a customer base?

13.6 What roles can event marketing play in creating customer excitement and brand loyalty?

13.7 How can companies adapt public relations programs, sponsorships, and event marketing to international settings?

Overview

The traditional promotions mix consists of advertising, sales promotions, personal selling, and public relations efforts. The first three elements in the mix have been presented. This chapter covers the fourth element: public relations. The sponsorship and event programs that tie into public relations efforts are also examined.

Public relations efforts, sponsorships, and event programs contribute to the overall IMC approach. The same unified message appears in every marketing endeavor, from the appearance of the company's letterhead and stationery to advertisements, promotional items, information in press releases, and in any sponsorship program. Making sure each component of a firm's IMC plan speaks with one voice remains the goal. Extending this objective to public relations and sponsorships constitutes an important task for the marketing team.

THINK BLUE, THINK VOLKSWAGEN

Monty Rakusen/Cultura/photolibrary.com

Since production started in the German town of Wolfsburg in 1945, the Volkswagen Group (VW) has built ninety-four production facilities worldwide, from the north of Sweden to South Africa and from Mexico to China. Every working day, more than 500,000 employees are involved in the manufacturing of nearly 35,000 cars. Not surprisingly, the corporation ranks among the leading car manufacturers in the world. The Volkswagen website, however, states the company does more than producing and selling cars. In its public communication, the company stresses its goal again and again: to make a sustainable contribution to global mobility by offering attractive, safe, and environmentally sound vehicles.

Volkswagen has paid a lot of attention to innovations, activities, and campaigns in the field of ecological sustainability. In 2005 the company introduced the Polo BlueMotion, an eco-friendly car, which was followed by a range of energy-saving BlueMotion technologies. In 2010 the global "Think Blue" campaign was launched to encourage people to drive more responsibly and adopt a greener lifestyle. In this respect, Volkswagen Sweden pioneered with "The Fun Theory": safe driving, recycling, and health initiatives were promoted by means of viral videos featuring funny ideas. Within the Volkswagen group the idea to contribute to a more sustainable future is also promoted: there is a "Think Blue Factory" concept to promote more efficient production. Volkswagen is certainly investing in such green strategies to sell more cars and raise profits, but they are also meant to create goodwill that, in turn, might lead to a more positive image and better relationships with the firm's stakeholders.

Volkswagen tries hard to practice what it preaches. Over the years, the car manufacturer has supported sustainable and safe driving projects, initiatives, and events all over the world. In Brazil, the company has invested in hydroelectric power plants to generate renewable energy, while local VW employees have been trained in how to reduce their environmental impact. In China, Volkswagen has sponsored road safety programs on television and environmental education courses at school.

The company has also supported many societal initiatives in the field of science, employment, health, art, and sports. In South Africa and Mexico, for instance, Volkswagen has set up projects in impoverished communities, such as the "A Day for the Future" project, in which the workers of an adjacent VW plant are donating one day's salary to help disadvantaged children. Volkswagen sponsors artwork and exhibitions in the Museum of Modern Art in New York and is also involved in other art support projects in the United States. Volkswagen became a Tier One partner for the 2014 Olympic and Paralympic Winter Games in the Russian city of Sochi.

Wolfsburg, Volkswagen's home base, has always been a company town: most of the 50,000 workers live near the local factory or in the surrounding region. Naturally, many buildings, associations, and events in Wolfsburg are supported by VW. The best example of this is the sponsorship of the local soccer club, Vfl Wolfsburg, playing in the Volkswagen Arena. For Volkswagen, the team—it won the German championship in 2009—is a strong brand ambassador. As the town's main employer, VW has been active in local and regional development projects for many years. For instance, when Volkswagen and Wolfsburg were facing economic problems in the 1990s, the company established the Wolfsburg AG, a public-private company aimed at the promotion of regional growth initiatives. This resulted in the development of the entertainment complex "Autostadt," which boosted the local economy. Volkswagen also acts as a sponsor of nature conservation projects aimed at the protection of local plants, birds, and insects in the countryside near Wolfsburg.

However, not all stakeholders are impressed by Volkswagen's efforts. At the Frankfurt Car Exhibition in 2011, activists from Greenpeace hung a banner near the Volkswagen stand, claiming "Climate destruction made in Germany." This was accompanied by an internet campaign which blamed Volkswagen for falsely presenting activities as environmentally friendly. In the same year, the corporation was also accused of misleading advertising on fuel saving of its passenger cars. German regulations in this field make use of an eight-point scale, while VW mistakenly employed its own nine-point scale. However, for Volkswagen the overall publicity balance has been quite favorable. In 2011 the company won several awards for the credibility of its social responsibility, among them being the International German PR Award.[1]

This chapter begins with a discussion of the nature of a public relations function within an integrated marketing plan. Second, sponsorship programs and event marketing tactics are outlined to show how the company can make quality contacts with existing customers, new prospects, vendors, and others. Successful positive public relations and sponsorship programs enhance the firm's image, and its brands become better known because they are perceived more favorably in the marketplace. The chapter concludes with an examination of international issues associated with public relations efforts.

Public Relations

objective 13.1
What relationships exist between public relations and the marketing activities performed by a company?

In Hollywood, one well-worn phrase is "There's no such thing as bad publicity." This may be true for a bad-boy actor trying to get his name out to the public; however, in the world of marketing and communications, bad publicity can be worse than no publicity. Many business organizations spend countless hours fending off negative comments while trying to develop positive and noticeable messages and themes.

The **public relations (PR) department** manages publicity and other communications with every group in contact with the company. Some of the functions performed by the public relations department are similar to those provided by the marketing department. Others are quite different. The two may cooperate with and consult each other, yet each has a unique role. To illustrate, consider the two-pronged approach used by the Mexico Tourism Board to increase tourism. The first component of the campaign featured a branding effort carrying the tagline "The Place You Thought You Knew." Second, public relations employees designed efforts aimed at countering Mexico's drug-and-violence image that has been often portrayed by U.S. media. The two programs sought to change Americans' perceptions of Mexico.[2]

Some marketing experts argue that public relations should be part of the marketing department, just as advertising, trade promotions, and consumer promotions are under the jurisdiction of the marketing manager. Others suggest that public relations activities are different and cannot operate effectively within a marketing department. Instead, a member of the public relations department should serve as a consultant to the marketing department. Still others contend that a new division, called the "department of communications," should be created to oversee both marketing and public relations activities.

▼ Company leaders decide who should handle the public relations activities.

Internal versus External Public Relations

Deciding who will handle various public relations activities will be the first major decision company leaders make. They can be managed by an internal public relations officer or department. Other companies hire public relations firms to complete special projects or all public relations functions. When a company retains a public relations agency, normally an internal company employee takes charge of internal public relations, because most public relations firms deal only with external publics.

The decision criteria used in selecting advertising agencies can be applied to selecting a public relations firm. Developing a trusting relationship with the public relations agency and clearly spelling out what the firm expects from the agency become high priorities.

JD Bank

▲ The marketing department at JD Bank concentrates on building a strong brand that can be reinforced through positive public relations efforts.

Public Relations Tools

Public relations employees utilize a number of tools, including company newsletters, internal messages, public relations releases, correspondences with stockholders, annual reports, and various special events. Even the bulletin board in the company's break room conveys messages to internal stakeholders.

Capturing **hits**, or mentions of a company's name in news stories, constitutes one common goal of a public relations firm. Hits can be positive, negative, or neutral in terms of their impact. Each improves the chance that consumers will see the name of a company in a news-related context, which can increase brand or company awareness; however, the agency also considers the type of image portrayed. It may be a more prudent strategy to seek fewer hits while making sure that mentions of the company are in a positive light that reinforces the firm's IMC theme.

When employing a public relations firm, the agency's personnel should be familiar with the client's IMC approach. Then, members of the public relations firm work on ideas that reinforce the theme. The firm develops special events, activities, and news releases designed to strengthen the company's voice.

Public Relations Functions

objective 13.2
How can the public relations functions help to build better relationships with all internal and external stakeholders?

Public relations activities are not standard marketing functions. The marketing department concentrates on customers and the channel members en route to those customers, such as wholesalers and retail outlets. In contrast, the public relations department focuses on a variety of internal and external stakeholders, including employees, stockholders, public interest groups, the government, and society as a whole.

Figure 13.1 displays five key public relations functions. These tasks are completed by public relations personnel, whether they are internal employees or members of a public relations company hired to perform those functions.

- Identify internal and external stakeholders
- Assess the corporate reputation
- Audit corporate social responsibility
- Create positive image-building activities
- Prevent or reduce image damage

◀ **FIGURE 13.1**
Public Relations Functions

Identifying Stakeholders

Each recipient of company communications is important. Any constituent who makes contact with a company should receive a clear, unified response. A **stakeholder** is a person or group who has a vested interest in the organization's activities. Vested interests may include:

- Profits paid as common stock dividends
- Loan repayments a lending institution seeks to receive
- Sales to the company or purchases made from the company
- Wages paid to employees
- Community well-being
- A special-interest topic

In essence, a wide variety of items can cause people or other companies to believe they hold a stake in the firm's activities. Public relations employees observe stakeholders and, when appropriate, target them with communications. Figure 13.2 identifies the primary internal and external stakeholders that the public relations department monitors.

Communications with each of these stakeholder groups are crucial. To ensure consistency, company leaders develop a communication strategy that fits with the IMC plan and corporate image. The overall message to each stakeholder stays the same. Then, each message can be tailored to meet the different expectations of the various audiences. By customizing the content, style, and channel of communication, each stakeholder group receives a message that best resonates with it, yet it remains consistent with other messages.

In addition to sending communications to individual stakeholders, the public relations department closely studies the actions and opinions of each group. When changes in attitudes, new views, or serious concerns develop, the public relations department remains ready to respond. The department will be responsible for making certain all communications to each of these publics consistently present the firm's message and image.

Internal Stakeholders

Effective managers know the value of quality internal communications. Employees provide a powerful channel of communication to people outside the organization. They can either enhance or damage a firm's reputation. What employees say to others has a much higher level of credibility than what a company says about itself. Word-of-mouth communications, including informal statements by employees, impact purchasing, and investing decisions.[3]

Employees receive a constant stream of information from the company. The same holds true for other internal stakeholders, such as corporate shareholders and labor unions. Many of these individuals are not in the marketing and public relations departments. They should still be aware of what the company seeks to achieve with the IMC program, even if it means presenting only basic information. Those closest to the marketing department, such as employees serving customers, will be more acutely aware of the nature of the IMC plan, including how the company's message theme should be transmitted to constituents.

To communicate effectively with employees, the public relations department works closely with the human resource (HR) department. Publications and communications aimed at employees should be consistent with the image and message the firm espouses to customers and others. When a firm advertises that its employees are always ready to assist customers,

- Employees
- Unions
- Shareholders
- Channel members
- Customers
- Media
- Local community
- Financial community
- Government
- Special-interest groups

FIGURE 13.2
Stakeholders

the public relations team makes sure employees are aware of the message. Employee behaviors should reflect the advertising theme being conveyed to customers. The HR department looks for and hires workers who are attracted to that approach. Performance appraisals and rewards can be structured to favor those who buy into the company's IMC approach. This emphasis on providing quality information about company activities extends to every public relations event and sponsorship program.

Community Trust Bank

▲ An advertisement for Community Trust Bank offering a new mobile app.

The Community Trust Bank advertisement shown in this section highlights a new mobile app that allows individuals to bank anytime and anywhere. Employees who are aware of this ad can communicate the same message when dealing with prospective customers who contact the bank.

External Stakeholders

Overseeing external communications continues to be a daunting task, because the company has little or no influence over how external publics perceive organizational activities. External stakeholders include groups such as the media, the local community, the financial community, the government, and special-interest groups. The company has no control over what these groups say or how they interpret information about the company. The public relations agency continually disseminates positive information and quickly reacts to any negative publicity or complaints.

A totally integrated communications program accounts for all types of messages an organization delivers to internal and external stakeholders. Every contact point provides the opportunity for a quality message to be sent. The marketing department creates contact points with customers and potential customers. To complement this effort, the public relations department deals with the myriad of contact points that are not created or planned, yet may be just as critical. An unplanned contact point, such as a news story or an individual talking to an employee of the firm at a social gathering allows the firm to build a positive image or minimize the impact of any negative messages that are circulating. Dealing with unplanned contact points will be challenging. Continuing investigations of what goes on around the firm will be one key to keeping constituents satisfied while trying to insulate the firm from negative publicity.

▼ A strong brand name, such as Kraft, is a valuable asset that must be protected.

Kraft Foods, Inc.

Assessing Corporate Reputation

A corporation's reputation is fragile and valuable. Well-received corporate and brand names enhance businesses during the good times and protect them when a crisis or problem occurs. A company's reputation influences consumer decisions regarding which brands to purchase. Investors elect where to place money based on corporate reputations. These assessments also affect potential employees as they decide whether to apply for work in any given organization.

Corporate scandals, accounting fraud, and economic and financial downturns have reduced consumer confidence in the business community. The Edelman's Trust Barometer reported that 56 percent of individuals surveyed

▶ FIGURE 13.3
Activities that Affect a Company's Image

Image-Destroying Activities
- Discrimination
- Harassment
- Pollution
- Misleading communications
- Deceptive communications
- Offensive communications

Image-Building Activities
- Empowerment of employees
- Charitable contributions
- Sponsoring local events
- Selling enviromentally safe products
- Outplacement programs
- Supporting community events

said they do not trust businesses to do the right thing.[4] Company actions as well as actions of individuals within an organization impact a firm's reputation. Figure 13.3 identifies activities that can harm an organization's reputation and activities that can enhance a firm's reputation.

Assessing and managing a company's reputation will be as important as promoting its products. Yet, with all that is at stake, fewer than half of the companies in the United States have someone assigned to monitor corporate reputation. As a result, many company leaders have little idea what consumers, investors, employees, and the public think or say about the firm. A company cannot effectively pursue a public relations program when company leaders do not know what people believe about the organization.

Assessment begins when public relations employees conduct surveys and interviews in order to reveal perceptions of the organization. Monitoring online chatter, tweets, and social media produces additional information. These efforts can be completed internally or are performed by an outside company such as a public relations firm. Examining both external and internal views of the corporation's reputation produces a complete view of the organization.

▼ This advertisement for the Medical Center of Southeast Texas emphasizes water safety.

Courtesy of Alliance One Advertising

Corporate Social Responsibility

Corporate social responsibility is an organization's obligation to be ethical, accountable, and reactive to the needs of society. It means companies align values for the greater good of society and take actions that have positive effects. Globalization and increased pressures from the public for corporate transparency have led to an increasing emphasis on social responsibility. Bradley K. Googins, director of the Boston College Center for Corporate Citizenship, stated that, "Quality used to be the difference between brands, then it was technology. Now, it really comes back to reputation. It's really the question of who you want to do business with and the relationship between the consumer and the product."[5]

Business experts agree that socially responsible firms are more likely to thrive and survive in the long term. Companies engaged in positive activities generate quality publicity and engender customer loyalty. Firms that work to eliminate unfair practices, pollution, harassment, and other negative activities are more likely to stay out of court, and the company suffers fewer negative word-of-mouth comments by unhappy employees or consumers. Managing these activities properly can lead to a positive corporate image.

A new trend in corporate social responsibility, **purpose marketing**, or **pro-social marketing**, involves advertising that focuses on the values, behavior, and beliefs of the company. The messages show how the company or brand operates in a socially responsible fashion. Outwear and sports-equipment brand Patagonia, for instance, focuses on social initiatives rather than investing in traditional brand advertising. According to Joy Howard, vice president of marketing at Patagonia, "We have a mission to solve problems in the world." Recently, the company encouraged consumers to embrace sustainability by mending their clothing rather than buying new items. Another Patagonia initiative focused on removing dams across the United States to promote river restoration. Patagonia executives believe it is important to use "business to help solve environmental problems."[6]

The public relations department works with the marketing department to make sure internal publics are made aware of a corporation's social responsibility efforts. The department then informs the general public about these activities while seeking to enhance the firm's image.

Creating Positive Image-Building Activities

objective 13.3
What types of positive, image-building programs can companies feature as parts of a public relations program?

In an effort to positively influence the views that consumers and other stakeholders have about a company, many firms engage in cause-related marketing and green marketing. These planned events draw positive attention to the organization as a solid corporate citizen, one committed to social responsibility. The public relations department sends out messages in the form of press releases and holds press conferences to highlight these positive, image-building activities.

Cause-Related Marketing

A **cause-related marketing** program ties marketing activities with a charity in order to generate goodwill. U.S. businesses pay more than $1.5 billion each year for the right to use a nonprofit organization's name or logo in company advertising and marketing programs.[7] This type of partnership agreement between a nonprofit cause and a for-profit business assumes that consumers prefer to purchase from companies that support good causes. Marketers engage in cause-related marketing to develop stronger ties and to move consumers, as well as businesses, toward brand loyalty. A Cone Communications and Roper Starch Worldwide survey revealed that:

- 78 percent of consumers are more likely to purchase a brand associated with a cause they care about.
- 54 percent would be willing to pay more for a brand associated with a cause they care about.

French Creative

▲ An advertisement for Progressive Bank highlighting its involvement in the community.

These benefits lead companies to get involved. Relationships that do not yield positive benefits to the business sponsor do not last long. In choosing a cause, the marketing and public relations teams concentrate on issues that relate to the company's business. Supporting these efforts makes the activity more credible to consumers.

When a fit exists, positive reactions emerge. Dick's Sporting Goods created a unique cause-related effort featuring students struggling in some way, such as a boy with the death of his grandfather and a girl dismissed by peers at a fast-food restaurant. The program, called "Sports Matters," was designed to show the emotional struggles of student athletes while raising $2 million to fund sports programs disbanded at financially strapped schools.[8]

In addition to social media-based cause-related marketing programs, companies also use games. Social gaming company Zynga produces games including Farmville, CityVille, and Mafia Wars that reach more than 230 million players a month. After the earthquake and tsunami hit Japan, Mark Pincus, CEO of Zynga, incorporated cause-related marketing into ten of the company's games by creating a virtual fan to blow virtual air. Players could purchase the virtual fan for $5, with all of the proceeds going to relief efforts in Japan. The campaign lasted one week and raised $600,000.[9]

Benefits to Nonprofit Organizations Cause-related marketing also assists nonprofit organizations. Competition has increased in both the business world and the nonprofit world. An increasing number of nonprofit organizations compete for contributions and gifts. Strategic relationships with businesses can boost contributions to a nonprofit organization. A General Mills Yoplait campaign recently raised more than $10 million for the Susan G. Komen Breast Cancer Foundation. Featuring the slogan, "Save Lids to Save Lives," General Mills donated ten cents for each Yoplait lid that was returned by consumers.[10] The relationship resulted in direct increases in revenues for Yoplait and positive publicity for the foundation.

Most of the time, corporate leaders select the nonprofits they wish to support. Occasionally, the reverse occurs. Alice Berkner, founder of the International Bird Rescue Research Center, obtained a small grant to test major dish soaps for cleaning birds harmed by oil spills. Procter & Gamble's Dawn detergent worked the best. When first approached by Berkner about supporting the cause, P&G turned her down. Then, during the 1989 Exxon Valdez oil spill, volunteers used Dawn on the oil-covered birds to remove the black crude. Media coverage was extensive. Now Dawn donates around $100,000 annually to the research center. A television commercial created by Kaplan Thaler Group shows a baby duck, penguin, and seal being washed with Dawn detergent. There is no voiceover, just the song "Wash Away" sung by Joe Purdy. The copy on the screen states that Dawn has helped save thousands of animals caught in oil spills.[11]

A complex linkage exists between public relations and cause-related marketing. To benefit from cause-related marketing, company leaders want publicity. Yet, if the company publicizes too much, people think the cause is only being used for commercial gain. Further, when the company supports an unrelated cause, consumers may conclude that the business merely seeks to benefit from the nonprofit's reputation, which may lead some to stop buying the company's products or to believe the company wishes to cover up unethical behaviors.

▼ A large percentage of Americans believe in recycling waste materials.

Daisy Daisy/Fotolia

Many consumers have become skeptical about the motives behind giving to various charities. In a survey of British consumers, the vast majority said a company should spend funds on communications about cause-related efforts. The same survey indicated that two-thirds also said the amount spent should not be significant. The majority of those surveyed said their purchase decisions are influenced by the causes a company supports. This makes informing people about a company's cause-related activities necessary; however, doing so involves walking a thin line between publicizing and what might be viewed as corporate self-aggrandizement.[12] Even though most people understand that a business must benefit from the relationship, they still tend to develop negative views when they believe that the business exploits a relationship with a nonprofit.

Green Marketing and Pro-Environmental Activities

Green marketing is the development and promotion of products that are environmentally safe. Most consumers favor green marketing. One recent survey indicated that 58 percent of Americans try to save electricity, 46 percent recycle newspapers, 45 percent return bottles or cans, and 23 percent buy products made from or packaged in recycled materials.[13]

Although consumers say they support green marketing and environmentally safe products, actual purchases of such products only occur when all things are considered equal. Most consumers often will not sacrifice price, quality, convenience, availability, or performance for the sake of the environment. According to David Donnan, a partner with consulting firm A.T. Kearny,

"Every consumer says I want to help the environment. I'm looking for eco-friendly products. But, if it's one or two pennies higher in price, they're not going to buy it. There is a discrepancy between what people say and what they do.[14]

To benefit from green marketing, the company's marketing team identifies the segments that are most attracted to environmentally friendly products. In the United States, consumers can be divided into five groups based on their propensity to purchase green products and their attitudes about environmental issues. Only nine percent of American consumers are classified as "True Blue Greens," and another six percent are classified as "Greenback Greens." The True Blue Greens are active environmentalists who support environmentally safe products and shop for green brands. The Greenback Greens purchase environmentally safe products but are not politically active. The other three groups, Sprouts, Grousers, and Basic Browns, are less committed or not committed to environmental protections.[15]

In making a choice about the degree of emphasis to place on green marketing, managers ask three questions. First, what percentage of the company's customer base fits into the green marketing segments? Second, can the brand or company be differentiated from the competition along green lines in such a way that it can become a competitive advantage? Third, will the company's current target market be alienated by adopting a green marketing approach?

Promoting Green Activities Almost all firms say they are pro-environment and provide information on company websites about environmental activities. The amount of effort given to publicize these activities varies widely.[16] Coca-Cola tries to protect the environment, but most people are unaware of the company's efforts. Coca-Cola has invested in various recycling programs and recyclable package designs but does not publicize the activities due to concerns that the information might reduce the product's appeal to some of the company's audience.

Promoting the direct, tangible benefits of a product first, with the environmental benefits presented as secondary factors, can be an alternate approach. The Toyota Prius was launched with an emphasis on fuel efficiency. Consumers were told they would spend less on gas. The fact that the Prius was an environmentally advanced, fuel-efficient hybrid vehicle was mentioned but not stressed. The idea was that strong environmentalists would believe buying a hybrid car is important. For those who were not strong environmentalists, it did not matter, because the car delivered fuel efficiency.

A new approach involves creating green products within brand lines. Levi Strauss sells designer jeans made from recycled plastic bottles. Nike's "FlyKnit" shoes are produced with yarn instead of leather uppers. The shoes are designed for a better fit as well as reduction in waste. In both instances, reaching green-oriented customers is the goal.[17]

Some companies integrate environmental activities into an overall business design and marketing approach. This approach works best when the primary customer base consists of True Blue Greens and the Greenback Greens. The Body Shop, Patagonia, Honest Tea, and Seventh Generation feature this approach. Honest Tea embeds social responsibility into every company activity, from the manufacturing process to the marketing of products. The company features biodegradable tea bags, organic ingredients, and community partnerships. Honest Tea's marketing program emphasizes concern for and support of environmental and social issues.

▼ Companies such as Honest Tea and Seventh Generation have demonstrated concern for the environment.

Fotofreundin/Fotolia

Seventh Generation has produced natural-ingredient cleaning products for 21 years. Although well-known to environmentally conscious shoppers, few people had ever heard about the Seventh Generation brand. To increase awareness, the company's leaders hired Minneapolis-based Carmichael Lynch to develop a series of print and television commercials about the brand's safety and green ingredients. The campaign's goal was to educate consumers about the products and the importance of protecting the environment.[18]

Greenwashing Most business leaders believe their companies should be involved in protecting the environment and creating green products; however, the marketing emphasis varies. Companies that claim to make green products have been exposed by bloggers who point out that they are not. Faking green, or **greenwashing**, damages a company's reputation when such information appears on blogs and other social media. Honesty and transparency constitute two important ingredients in an environmentally friendly IMC program.

objective 13.4
What steps can companies take to prevent or reduce image damage when negative events occur?

Preventing or Reducing Image Damage

Another important public relations function, **damage control**, involves reacting to negative events caused by a company error, consumer grievances, or unjustified or exaggerated negative press. Bad publicity and negative events quickly damage a corporate brand image. A strong company image that took years to build can be rapidly destroyed. British Petroleum (BP) continues to suffer from the negative publicity surrounding the company's oil spill in the Gulf of Mexico. Sales at Target stores plummeted after customer credit card data was breached.

Bad news travels fast, and it is not always the media that generates negative publicity. Sometimes negative word-of-mouth communications come from customers, employees, or other individuals connected with the company. The internet makes it possible for individuals to report bad experiences and post negative comments for thousands to see in a very short time.

Damage control applies to two situations. The first occurs when the firm has made an error or has caused legitimate consumer or public grievances. The second takes place when unjustified or exaggerated negative press appears. Defending an organization's image and handling damage control takes two forms: proactive prevention strategies and reactive damage-control strategies (see Figure 13.4).

- Proactive Strategies
  - Entitlings
  - Enhancements
- Reactive Strategies
  - Internet Interventions
  - Crisis management programs
  - Apology strategy
  - Impression management techniques

▲ **FIGURE 13.4**
Damage-control Strategies

Proactive Prevention Strategies

Proactive prevention means that rather than waiting for harmful publicity to appear and then reacting, many firms charge certain employees with minimizing the effects of any future bad press in advance. These approaches help prevent negative publicity from emerging in the first place. Two proactive prevention techniques include entitlings and enhancements.[19] **Entitlings** are attempts to claim responsibility for positive outcomes of events. **Enhancements** are attempts to increase the impact of the desirable outcome of an event in the eyes of the public.

Berc/Fotolia

▼ Entitling takes place when a firm associates with an athlete who wins at the Olympics or in other types of competition.

Entitling takes place when a firm associates its name with a positive event. For example, being the official sponsor of a U.S. Olympic team that wins a gold medal ties the company's name to the athletic achievements of people who do not work for the firm, yet the firm claims responsibility for some aspect of their successes.[20] An advertising campaign by TD Ameritrade featured the stories of seven athletes showing their lifelong journey to make the Olympics and the fortitude required of long-term investors. The theme of the ads was that Ameritrade can help investors reach long-term goals, one small step at a time, just as these athletes reached the Olympics, one step at a time.[21]

Enhancements occur when the marketing or public relations department suggests that something relatively small is a bigger deal. Any "buy American" program promoted as being patriotic as well as good for the economy (and local workers) seeks to enhance the image of the company that markets the items. Press releases pointing out the "buy American" feature help underscore these advantages to consumers.

- Internet interventions
- Crisis management programs
- Apology strategies
- Impression management

▲ **FIGURE 13.5**
Reactive Damage-control Strategies

Reactive Damage-Control Strategies

Company leaders often must react to unforeseen events. In these instances, managers work diligently to blunt the effects of unwanted bad publicity by every means possible. Reactive damage-control strategies companies use to reduce negative publicity include internet interventions, crisis management programs, apology strategies, and impression management techniques (see Figure 13.5)

Internet Interventions Firms combat negative online word-of-mouth with **internet interventions**. Social media and blogs help consumers share negative word-of-mouth and talk about bad experiences. Consumers around the world tell horror stories about companies or products. Individuals can say anything online, even when it unfairly portrays various industries, companies, or brands.

Internet outlets allow people to vent emotions, which can injure a company's reputation. Companies including Ford, Pepsi, Toyota, and Southwest Airlines use software and assign employees to monitor internet postings, social media comments, and tweets. Even with these technological tools, however, monitoring everything said about a company remains a daunting task. It can involve hundreds of posts per day. Employees must quickly decide which to investigate further. Marcus Schmidt, a senior marketing manager for Microsoft suggests, "If you start seeing a lot of people retweeting it, then you know to pay attention."

Recently, Coke's software identified a Twitter post by a frustrated consumer who was not able to redeem a prize from the MyCoke rewards program. The consumer's profile indicated that he had more than 10,000 followers. Adam Brown, Coke's head of social media, posted an apology on the individual's Twitter profile and offered to help. The consumer received the prize. He later changed his Twitter avatar to a photo of himself holding a bottle of Coke. Brown noted, "We're getting to a point if you're not responding, you're not being seen as an authentic type of brand."[22]

Not every activity warrants a formal reaction. Still, social listening keeps the company's leadership informed about what people are saying and thinking.

▼ Social listening allows a company to know what its customers are saying and thinking.

Monkey Business/Fotolia

Crisis Management A company either accepts the blame for an event, offers an apology, or refutes the charges in a forceful manner in a **crisis management** program. A crisis may be viewed as a problem or an opportunity. Often, a crisis contains the potential to improve the firm's position and image.

When PepsiCo encountered claims that hypodermic needles were found in its products, the management team quickly responded with photographs and videos demonstrating that such an occurrence was impossible, because the bottles and cans are turned upside down before being filled with any soft drink. Next, footage of a con artist slipping a needle into a bottle was shown. This fast and powerful answer eliminated the negative publicity, and Pepsi was able to make a strong statement about the safety of its bottling methods.

FIGURE 13.6
Elements of an Apology Strategy

1. An expression of guilt, embarrassment, or regret
2. A statement recognizing the inappropriate behavior and acceptance of sanctions for wrong behavior
3. A rejection of the inappropriate behavior
4. Approval of the appropriate behavior and a promise not to engage in inappropriate behavior
5. An offer of compensation or penance to correct the wrong

Unfortunately, some company leaders only make matters worse, as was the initial reaction of Toyota to quality problems with its vehicles. Continual denials were not well-received, especially when the problems kept occurring. Many consumers became angry when it was revealed that Toyota's management team had been aware of the issues for a long time without seeking to correct them. Eventually, the president of Toyota Motors, Akio Toyoda, was summoned to Washington to testify before the House Committee on Oversight and Government Reform.

Realizing its image was quickly eroding and the outcry against the company was building, Toyota launched a full-scale public relations campaign with print, television, and social media networks. Full-page newspaper ads and several television spots were prepared in which Toyota announced a temporary halt in production followed by an apologetic, but reassuring, message that Toyota would pull through the crisis. At the same time, the company created a social media response room staffed with individuals who monitored online conversations and responded to consumer concerns.[23]

Apology Strategies Another reactive damage-control strategy, an **apology strategy**, occurs when an investigation reveals that the firm was at fault. Any sincere apology should be offered quickly. The apology should include the five elements listed in Figure 13.6.[24]

Companies offer apologies in situations for minor violations or at times in which the firm or person cannot deny responsibility. It can become an effective strategy for creating an emotional bond with the public. Consumers are less likely to remain angry with a company that admits a mistake. When customers believe the apology was sincere and heartfelt, they normally forgive the company and at times feel more positively toward the organization afterward.

Apology strategies are used in situations in which the violation is minor or cannot be denied.

Gino Santa Maria/Fotolia

Mountain Dew offered an apology when the brand faced intense criticism for an advertisement entitled "Felicia the Goat" that was viewed as racist and misogynist. The company bought Twitter ads to apologize to consumers and then ran a series of mainstream ads asking the public for its forgiveness. According to Sabrina Horn, CEO of a public relations firm, "Mountain Dew clearly wants to make sure its audiences know they are sorry. The best thing anyone in a situation like this should do is to admit fault immediately. The instances where companies hesitate to respond or don't admit fault are the ones we remember forever."[25]

Impression Management Trying to project a certain type of image, or **impression management**, includes "the conscious or unconscious attempt to control images that are projected in real or imagined social interactions."[26] In order to maintain or enhance an image, individuals and corporations attempt to influence the identities they display to others. Each can be projected in a manner that maximizes positive characteristics while minimizing any negative elements.

Any event that threatens a person's image or a company's desired identity creates a predicament. When faced with one, public relations officials make concerted efforts to reduce or minimize the negative consequences. When the predicament cannot be avoided or concealed, then an individual or company engages in any remedial activity that reduces the potentially harmful consequences, including expressions of innocence, excuses, justifications, and other explanations.

An *expression of innocence* means company leaders provide information designed to convince others (clients, the media, and the government) that the company was not associated with the event that caused the predicament. In other words, they say, "We did not cause this to happen. Someone (or something) else did."

Excuses are explanations designed to convince the public that the firm and its leaders are not responsible for the predicament or that it could not have been foreseen. Thus, they should not be held accountable for the event that created the predicament. They might say, "It was an act of God. It was totally unavoidable. It was the random act of an individual."

Justifications involve using logic designed to reduce the degree of negativity associated with the predicament. Making the event seem minor or trivial is one method. Suggesting that the firm had to proceed in the way it did ("We outsource some of the production process because if we don't we'll be out of business, and our other employees will lose their jobs") is another form of justification.

Other explanations may be created to persuade individuals that the cause of the predicament does not truly represent what the firm or individual is really like. In other words, the case was the exception rather than the rule, and customers should not judge the firm too harshly. You will hear comments such as "This was a singular incident, and not indicative of the way we do business."[27] This strategy was used by Carnival Cruise Lines after its cruise ship, the Triumph, caught fire and stranded 3,200 passengers and crew members for five days. In addition to declaring it was an isolated incident, the company also invited ten active participants on Instagram to take a cruise and then post comments and pictures about their experiences.[28]

Each company's management team, marketing department, and public relations specialists should be acutely aware of the speed with which events can cause great damage to a firm's image. Managers may pursue proactive and reactive measures to make sure the firm survives negative publicity with less long-term damage.

Sponsorships and Event Marketing

objective 13.5
How can marketers tie sponsorships to public relations efforts to strengthen a customer base?

To build brand loyalty and other positive feelings toward a company, many marketing leaders utilize sponsorships and event marketing. These programs create situations in which prospects, customers, vendors, and others in unique situations gather together. People who attend sponsored activities or special events already have favorable feelings about the activity taking place. These positive attitudes are easily transferred to a company that provides funding.[29]

Forms of Sponsorships

Sponsorship marketing means that the company pays money to sponsor someone, some group, or something that is part of an activity. A firm can sponsor a long list of groups, individuals, activities, and events. Various businesses sponsor everything from local Little League baseball and soccer teams to national musical tours, NASCAR drivers, and sports stadiums.

In North America, companies spend approximately \$16.3 billion each year on sponsorships and events.[30] Figure 13.7 provides a breakdown of the spending. Sports account for about 70 percent of all sponsorships. Sporting events are popular and often attract large crowds. In addition to the audience attending the game or competition, many more watch on television. Popular athletes can be effective spokespersons. If possible, the firm

▼ Companies often sponsor youth baseball to enhance its image among consumers.

Tammykayphoto/Fotolia

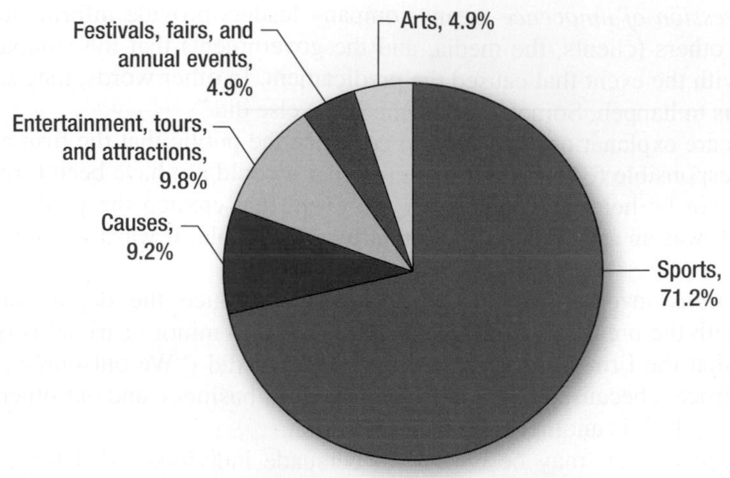

FIGURE 13.7 Marketing Expenditures on Sponsorships

should be the exclusive sponsor of the person or team, which makes it easier to remember than when there are multiple sponsors.

Sponsorships became a major part of Ford's integrated advertising and marketing push for the Ford F-Series Super Duty pickup trucks. Although the integrated campaign included television ads, print ads, and online chats, the central component of the campaign was the sponsorship of Toby Keith's concert tour, "America's Toughest Tour." The Ford F-Series trucks were highly visible at the concerts, with truck-themed set pieces on stage and at least one F-Series truck actually on the stage. In addition to the concert tour, Ford also sponsored a Monster Jam truck show and individual professional bull riders. The company sponsors the Future Farmers of America, the American Quarter Horse Association, and the Dallas Cowboys.[31]

Instead of the major sports, many brand managers invest in endurance competitions such as Tough Mudder, Spartan Race, and CrossFit Games. Under Armour, Wheaties, and Advil Tough sponsor the 10–12 mile Tough Mudder obstacle course race. The more rigorous Spartan Race includes a time factor. CrossFit Games holds a series of exceedingly difficult workouts from eponymous and cult conditioning programs. Reebok serves as the title sponsor of both the Spartan Race and CrossFit Games. These unique sports venues were chosen because the participants and attendees both tend to be more social-media savvy than the general population and are more likely to share their involvements through various social media networks.[32]

Some organizations have moved away from sports sponsorships toward cultural events such as classical music groups and jazz bands, visual art exhibits by noted painters, dance troupes, and actors for various theater performances. Cultural sponsorships may not be the best match for every firm. They are most effective for products sold to affluent consumers. Consequently, financial institutions often become the primary sponsors of these types of performers and performances. In the past, some institutions provided funds without receiving recognition. Now firms leverage philanthropic efforts by having the name of the company strongly associated with the cultural activity. This includes printing the name of the firm on programs and regularly mentioning the brand or corporate name as the entity responsible for arranging for the artist to be present at the event. Also, sponsors usually receive choice seats at performances that can be given to key clients.

Television offers another option for sponsorships, which can be tied to product placement efforts. For example, Coca-Cola, Ford, and AT&T sponsored the popular television show *American Idol*. Each company paid $35 million for the right

▼ Interstate is a successful sponsor of NASCAR.

Jane Koenecke/Interstate Batteries

to be part of one of the most watched TV shows, to post online content, and to run off-air, co-branded marketing programs. Ford featured its vehicles in music videos sung by the final 12 contestants. Ford also gave away a Ford Escape Hybrid to the top two finalists. In terms of product placement, Coca-Cola had branded cups placed in the center on the judges' table and Coke graphics were visible behind the contestants as they were interviewed. AT&T benefited greatly from the sponsorship by being responsible for the text-message voting tabulations each week. AT&T also featured *Idol* downloads, ring tones, and videos of bad auditions and poor performances.[33]

French Creative

▲ A non-profit, such as Med Camps, often pursues corporate sponsors to help fund the organization's activities for children.

Social Media and Blogs A new format involves sponsoring bloggers. Colleen Padilla, a 33-year-old mother of two and author of the popular website Classy Mommy (classymommy.com), has reviewed nearly 1,500 products, including microwave dinners, Nintendo Wii, and baby clothes. Her site attracts 60,000 unique visitors every month. Companies eagerly send her products to test and, if she likes them, to post positive comments on the site. When she does not like an item, nothing will be posted. Padilla tells her readers if the brand was sent to her. She also includes videos featuring brands, including Healthy Choice, labeled as "sponsored posts."

For some bloggers, such as Drew Bennett, product sponsorships have become a lucrative business. Bennett began with a photo-a-day blog that mushroomed into sponsored products at his site BenSpark.com. He has written more than 600 posts for firms such as X-Shot, a telescope camera extender. Bennett typically earns between $5.35 and $10 per post. Most product sponsors pay Bennett between 11 and 68 cents each time a reader moves from his site to the brand's site.

Kmart used a similar approach to generate positive buzz. Through 800 blog posts and 3,200 Twitter messages, Kmart reached 2.5 million people. The campaign began with six popular bloggers receiving a $500 gift card to shop at Kmart and then writing about their experiences.[34]

Sponsorship Objectives

Measuring the direct impact of a sponsorship program may be difficult. Sponsorships can be designed to accomplish a variety of objectives. They can seek to:

- Enhance a company's image
- Increase a firm's visibility
- Differentiate a company from its competitors
- Showcase specific goods and services
- Help a firm develop closer relationships with current and prospective customers
- Sell excess inventory

The Green Turtle restaurant built visibility and a positive image through a sponsorship program. The company sponsored Amelia's Ace of Hearts Ride to raise money for breast cancer. Approximately 200 of the 400 bike riders registered at the restaurant, and 300 people celebrated at an after-party in the restaurant. The event raised $28,000 for the charity. Leho Poldmae, an employee of The Green Turtle reported, "These events and sponsorships put the human aspect into marketing. They are much more powerful than ads in touching and reaching customers."[35]

Event Marketing

objective 13.6
What roles can event marketing play in creating customer excitement and brand loyalty?

Event marketing and sponsorship marketing are similar. The primary difference is that sponsorship marketing involves a person, group, or team. **Event marketing** takes place when a company supports a specific event. Also, event marketing and lifestyle marketing are closely related. Both often include setting up a booth or display and maintaining a physical presence at an event. For instance, in the advertisement for the Wild Flower shown in this section, the company is identified as a sponsor of the "Taste of Home Joplin Show."

Sponsoring the right event provides a company with brand-name recognition and helps develop closer ties with vendors and customers. Events boost morale for the employees who participate in or attend them. Sponsoring local events such as the Special Olympics often generates free publicity. These events can also be used to enhance the company's image in the local community.

As is the case with sponsorships, many event marketing programs feature sports. Other events are related to lifestyles. A rodeo sponsored by Lee Jeans, a music concert held by a local business, or a health fair conducted by a local hospital are all examples of event marketing.

Event marketing has proven to be especially successful with Hispanic consumers. It can be an excellent method of building brand awareness and building brand loyalty. Renata Franco of Cox Communications notes that, "Hispanics are much more community-centered. Events do really well." When Cox Communications sponsors a Hispanic event, the company employs bilingual brand ambassadors who can personally speak to attendees.[36]

▼ The Wild Flower is a sponsor of the "Taste of Home Joplin Show."

Joplin Globe

Selecting Sponsorships and Events

Several key steps are involved in selecting a sponsorship or an event. To ensure the maximum benefit, companies follow the steps highlighted in Figure 13.8.

Determining Objectives

Company leaders outline communication objectives before becoming involved in a sponsorship or an event. For an objective of rewarding customers, marketers look for sponsorships or events that major customers would enjoy. Some objectives are more internally oriented, especially those designed to increase employee involvement or to boost morale. These can be achieved by finding opportunities internal members will like.

- Determine objectives
- Match the audience to company's target market
- Promote the sponsorship or event
- Advertise at the event
- Track results

◀ **FIGURE 13.8**
Steps in Selecting a Sponsorship or Event

Externally-oriented objectives include maintaining market share, building a stronger brand presence, enhancing the product or firm's image, and increasing sales.

Matching the Audience to the Company's Target Market

In choosing a sponsorship or an event, the marketing team matches the audience profile with the company's target market. A firm sponsoring a singer at a music show attended mainly by women works best when the company's primary customers are female. Marketing executives also consider how the individual participant or group image relates to the firm's image. A contestant in an upscale event, such as a piano competition, may be sponsored by a tuxedo or formal gown company. The sponsors of the Women's Bassmaster Tour shown in the advertisement in this section are a good match with the participants who attend Tour events.

Promoting the Event

Advertising and public relations releases promote sponsorships and events. Company officials give extra effort to contacting interest groups that would benefit from the event. An event such as a local Special Olympics requires commercials, contacts with the press, and finding ways to reach parents and relatives of those who might participate. Sponsorship of NASCAR by Interstate Batteries involves highlighting the partnership in advertising and public relations efforts.

▼ Matching the audience profile with the company's target market is important when selecting sponsorships.

Courtesy of Newcomer, Morris & Young, Inc.

Advertising at the Event

Sponsors insist on placement of the company's name and logo and other product information in every advertisement and brochure for the event. Many attendees of games and events keep programs as souvenirs. Placing the sponsor's name and message on the program generates an advertisement with a longer lifespan. The sponsoring business maximizes brand-name exposure by connecting the firm's name with the event's marketing program. The marketing team works closely with the event management team to make sure the company's name receives prominent attention in all materials associated with the occasion.

Tracking Results

Some events and sponsorships turn out better than others for the sponsor. To determine the best opportunities, the marketing team tracks results. In addition to sales, employees can monitor how many pieces of literature were given to attendees, the number of samples

Tyler Olson/Fotolia

▲ Sponsoring an event, such as a rodeo, allows companies to reach consumers in a less-cluttered environment.

distributed, or the number of visitors to the sponsor's display booth. Further, marketing research measures brand awareness or brand image before and after the event to discover whether any new level of awareness or higher image emerged.

Tracking results helps the business evaluate its investment. Company leaders and marketing managers then decide whether the sponsorship or particular event was beneficial and if the organization should sponsor the event or similar events in the future.

When Victoria's Secret launched the brand Pink, it was coupled with a unique event marketing promotion during spring break. The goal was to reach 18- to 24-year-old females. The event began with a three-story pink box set up on a beach in Miami. Advertisements, internet postings, street teams of employees giving out fliers, aerial signs, posters in nearby hotels, and public relations press releases built excitement during the five-day countdown. Many spring breakers showed up at the pink box. They were treated to a fashion show and a live concert by No Mercy. After the concert, Victoria's Secret Pink gift cards were distributed, and the company hosted nightclub parties. The unique marketing event spurred sales of the new Pink brand and the Victoria's Secret brand. The Victoria's Secret marketing team completed the evaluation stage and discovered a significant increase in Pink brand sales in the Miami area and a dramatic rise in other Victoria's Secret brand sales.[37]

An Advertising Research Foundation study revealed that intentions to purchase a branded product increased from 11 to 52 percent among consumers who attended a brand-sponsored event. Further research suggests that purchase intentions translate into sales about half the time. The Advertising Research Foundation study investigated events sponsored by Frito-Lay, State Farm, and Coca-Cola. Sports-related sponsorships and events tended to have the best results.[38]

Cross-Promotions

A cross-promotion with an event sponsor or other companies involved helps boost the impact of the sponsorship. A **cross-promotion** is a marketing event that ties together companies and activities around a specific theme. Recently, eBay partnered with Sony and Baskin-Robbins to create a unique event called "Camp eBay." During the summer months, consumers typically go outdoors to enjoy the warm weather and are not logged onto the internet. Consequently, eBay's marketing team decided to go to consumers. Camp eBay was eBay's first attempt at event marketing. The management team sought to create awareness of eBay and educate people who do not use the site. The program also encouraged existing buyers and sellers to be more active in the summertime.

The Camp eBay program began with the purchase of a refurbished school bus. It went on a mobile marketing tour of six high-traffic areas: the Indy 500, CMA Fan Fest, eBay Live, Taste of Chicago, the Ohio State Fair, and the Minnesota State Fair. The school bus classroom drew 52,000 people who attended 30-minute sessions about how to use eBay. Participants earned badges redeemable for prizes that were furnished by Sony and Baskin-Robbins. The prizes were worth a total of $85,000. In addition, eBay pitched tents at 20 Clear Channel Entertainment venues that hosted nearly 400 concerts. The impact of this event marketing program was that 45 percent of existing users increased purchases, leading to an overall increase in sales of two percent during the promotion and nine percent after the event.[39]

Sponsorship programs and event marketing have increased in popularity during the past decade due to the potential to interact with consumers on a one-to-one basis. In the future, sponsorships and event marketing tie-ins with other media, especially the internet (and specifically social media), will rise. Rock concerts, boat shows, music fairs, and a wide variety of other, more specialized programs are likely to be featured by various companies. Many marketing experts believe that making contacts with customers in personalized ways that do not directly involve sales calls are valuable activities. Event marketing and sponsorship programs create that type of contact.

International Implications

objective 13.7
How can companies adapt public relations programs, sponsorships, and event marketing to international settings?

The public relations function has become increasingly valuable in the international arena for several reasons. First, the growing number of international firms creates the need to make sure the company will be viewed in a positive light in every country in which it does business.

Second, the impact of terrorism and war over the past decade has heightened sensitivities between many nations. Any company conducting business in a foreign land will have a public relations officer in charge of monitoring news stories and other events so that the firm can react to negative press.

Third, at times companies suffer from negative publicity when false information is being transmitted. KFC endured rumors and reports that the company was selling chickens vaccinated with unapproved antibiotics and growth hormones and that the ice used in soft drinks sold by the company contained more bacteria than toilet water. Company officials worked diligently to restore the firm's image in the minds of Chinese consumers. Volkswagen and GlaxoSmithKline create similar responses when the companies were criticized by official Chinese media sources.

Corporate social responsibility also has no national boundaries. Many heated debates have taken place regarding outsourcing. Critics argue that nations other than the United States have enjoyed the advantages of unfair wage rates and the ability to pollute freely, thereby cutting costs and attracting businesses to them. Any multinational corporation or company conducting business in foreign lands should be aware of these criticisms and find effective ways to respond.

Many sponsorships now include international events. Some of the more visible ones are found in sports, most notably automobile racing and soccer. Sportswear brand Adidas signed an agreement with the NBA to be the league's official supplier in Europe and worldwide. The sponsorship represents a major effort by Adidas because NBA merchandise is sold in more than 100,000 stores in 100 countries on six continents.[40]

The principles that guide the development of sponsorships domestically apply equally well to any international involvements. To fully prepare an effective sponsorship program in an international setting, the marketing team employs a cultural assimilator to ensure correct usage of a foreign language, the legality of the sponsorship, and that it does not violate any local cultural norms. As the world continues to become smaller, with increasing interactions between countries, companies, and individuals, the growth of multinational sponsorships should continue.

▼ Basketball has become a popular sponsorship for international brands.

Cristovao31/Fotolia

INTEGRATED campaigns in action

Wayport Austintatious

The Wayport company is the world's largest internet hotspot provider. Pink Jacket Creative advertising agency executive Bill Breedlove said, "If you're in a Marriott hotel, or a McDonald's, they even have Starbuck's now, you're logging onto their site. They specialize in verticals that are health care, such as regional hospitals and major hospital chains as well hospitality, and QSRs [quick-service restaurants]."

Pink Jacket Creative was able to provide a combination of buzz marketing and trade show expertise in one event. According to Breedlove, "There was a trade show in Austin, Texas. It was for the hospitality industry. They came to us with a challenge. Like any trade show challenge, they wanted to get the top executives from the top hotel chains away from the floor of the trade show and in their own environment, so that their salespeople can work on them, and everybody wants that. "Then we took the folks to this bar that we had redecorated and had a little shindig, and their salespeople got to mingle, and it was quite successful. They were making appointments right and left with their marketing people and technology folks. So it was fun and highly successful."[41]

The Austintatious trade show campaign is located at the Pearson Instructor's Resource Center (www.pearsonhighered.com). The campaign includes a PowerPoint presentation outlining the details of the campaigns and examples of the collaterals as well as some photos of the event. Also available is video commentary by Bill Breedlove and Elena Baca.

Courtesy of Pink Jacket Studio

▲ A Willie Nelson impersonator was one of the entertainers at the Austintatious nightclub takeover.

Courtesy of the authors

▲ This Austintatious billboard was seen by trade show attendees at the Austin airport.

Summary

The public relations department plays a major role in an integrated marketing communications program, whether the department is separate from marketing or combined as part of a communications division. Public relations efforts are oriented to making sure that every possible contact point delivers a positive and unified message on behalf of the company.

Any person or group with a vested interest in the organization's activities is a stakeholder. Internal stakeholders include employees, unions, and stockholders. External publics include members of the marketing channel, customers, the media, the local community, financial institutions, the government, and special interest groups.

To reach all intended audiences, the public relations department has a series of tools available. These include company newsletters, internal messages, public relations releases, correspondence with stockholders, annual reports, and various special events. A bulletin board in the company's break room can be used to convey messages to internal stakeholders.

In the attempt to build a favorable image of the company, the public relations department develops special events, such as altruistic activities, and cause-related marketing programs. Care must be taken to make certain these acts are not perceived with cynicism and skepticism. This means being certain that any good deed matches with the company's products and other marketing efforts. A natural fit between an altruistic event and the company's brand is more readily accepted by various members of the public.

The public relations team tends to damage control when negative publicity arises. Proactive and reactive tactics help maintain a positive image for the company. Damage-control tactics include internet interventions, crisis management programs, and impression management techniques.

Sponsorship programs enhance and build the company's image and brand loyalty. A sponsorship of an individual or group involved in an activity—whether a sporting event, a contest, or a performance by an artistic group—can be used to link the company's name with the popularity of the player involved. Sponsorships should match with the firm's products and brands.

Event marketing occurs when a firm sponsors an event. A strong physical presence at the event is one of the keys to successfully linking an organization's name with a program. To do so, the firm determines the major objective of the sponsorship, matches it with company customers and publics, and ensures that the firm's name is prominently displayed on all event literature.

Managing public relations, sponsorships, and event marketing programs requires company leaders to assess the goals and the outcomes of individual activities. A cost–benefit approach may not always be feasible, but the marketing team should be able to track some form of change, whether it is increased inquiries, the number of samples passed out at an event, or a shift in the tenor of news articles about the organization. The public relations department serves as the organization's watchdog, making sure those who come in contact with the company believe the firm is working to do things right and to do the right things.

Key Terms

public relations (PR) department A unit in a firm that manages publicity and other communications with all of the groups that make contact with the company

hit The mention of a company's name in a news story

stakeholder A person or group with a vested interest in a firm's activities and well-being

corporate social responsibility An organization's obligation to be ethical, accountable, and reactive to the needs of society

purpose marketing (pro-social marketing) Promoting a brand or company by focusing on values, behavior, and beliefs of the company to sell the company's products

cause-related marketing Matching marketing efforts with some type of charity work or program

green marketing The development and promotion of products that are environmentally safe

greenwashing Activities presented as being green or environmentally friendly that are not

damage control Reacting to negative events caused by a company error, consumer grievances, or unjustified or exaggerated negative press

entitlings Attempts to claim responsibility for positive outcomes of events

enhancements Attempts to increase the impact of a desirable outcome of an event in the eyes of the public

internet interventions Confronting negative publicity on the internet, either in website news releases or by entering chat rooms, blogs, or social networks

crisis management Either accepting the blame for an event and offering an apology or refuting those making the charges in a forceful manner

apology strategy Presenting a full apology when the firm has made an error

impression management The conscious or unconscious attempt to control images projected in real or imagined social situations

sponsorship marketing When the company pays money to sponsor someone or some group that is participating in an activity

event marketing When a company pays money to sponsor an event or program

cross-promotion A marketing event that ties together companies and activities around a specific theme

MyMarketingLab

Go to **mymktlab.com** to complete the problems marked with this icon ✪.

Review Questions

13-1. Should public relations be an integral part of the overall marketing effort? Provide some reasons why this should not be the case. Give an alternative solution to the question.

13-2. How is PR work split when an agency is used?

13-3. In PR terms, what are hits? How are they assessed and handled by PR people?

13-4. Once public relations have identified likely stakeholders, what happens next?

13-5. In the area of social responsibility, what is purpose marketing or pro-social marketing?

13-6. Why would a business pay to have the logo of a charity on their letterhead or website?

13-7. What are the dangers if a business overplays its charity work?

13-8. What is greenwashing?

13-9. What reactive damage-control techniques are available to the public relations team?

13-10. Describe entitlings and enhancements.

13-11. What five elements are parts of an apology strategy?

13-12. What four forms of impression management are used to combat negative events?

13-13. What is sponsorship marketing?

13-14. Describe an event marketing program. What must accompany the event in order to make it a success?

13-15. What are cross-promotions? How are they related to event marketing programs?

13-16. How are public relations programs and sponsorships adapted to international companies?

Critical Thinking Exercises

DISCUSSION QUESTIONS

13-17. "There's no such thing as bad publicity." Maybe, but bad publicity has caused corporations to collapse and millions have been taken off the value of other corporations. Find a good example of bad publicity for an organization in your country. What happened? Did the organization survive the bad publicity? What action did they take? Was the bad publicity actually justified?

13-18. How should a business respond to persistent criticisms from consumers and others on social media? Should they take this kind of criticism as seriously as they might take a piece in the professional media or ignore it?

13-19. One of the vice presidents of a small but highly respected bank in a local community was charged with sexual harassment by a female employee. What types of communications should be prepared for each of the internal and external stakeholders listed in the chapter? Which stakeholders would be the most important to contact? Why?

✪ **13-20.** Is the local community important to a manufacturing firm that sells 99 percent of its products outside the area? Does it really matter what the local people say or believe about the manufacturer as long as the firm's customers are happy? Explain your answer.

✪ **13-21.** What causes do you support or are special to you? Do you know which corporations sponsor or support the causes? If not, see if you can find literature or websites that contain that information. Why do you think corporations choose a particular cause to support? What benefits do corporations receive from sponsorships?

13-22. When Starbucks opened its first coffee shop inside a public library, ten percent of all proceeds from coffee sold there went to support the operation of the library. Describe the benefits to Starbucks of this type of sponsorship. What benefits accrue to the library? Some consumers feel this type of sponsorship is inappropriate because it involves a for-profit company selling products in a government entity. Examine the various methods of damage control. Which method or methods should a library use to reduce the criticism and to prevent any negative fallout? Justify your choice.

13-23. Managers often are the most difficult group for the public relations department to reach. To entice employees to reach departmental goals, managers often communicate using memos or verbal messages. These messages may conflict with the IMC theme. For example, in an effort to trim costs, a manager may send a memo to all employees telling them to use only standard production procedures. Through verbal communications, employees learn that anyone caught violating or even bending the policy to satisfy a customer will be immediately reprimanded. The manager's action suggests that even though he wants employees to provide customer service, in actuality they had better not do anything that is not authorized. Employees soon get the message that management cares only about costs, not the customer. Employees will perceive any advertising message about customer service as a big joke. Write a memo to employees that supports the IMC goal of quality customer service, yet alerts them to the need to follow standard operating procedures. Is there anything else you would do to ensure that employees do not receive conflicting messages?

13-24. Sponsorships are now a major component of professional sports. Football, basketball, baseball, and golf all have sponsors. Many stadiums are now named for companies. What would be the benefit of a clothing brand, such as Kate Spade, investing a large budget into sport sponsorships? What are the disadvantages? Examine the various sponsorship objectives. Which objective or objectives should Kate Spade pursue? Why? Outline the steps Kate Spade would utilize in choosing a sponsor for its brand.

13-25. The shortage of state funds for universities and colleges has led many university leaders to consider using sponsorships to generate revenues. What would you think about your university having the stadiums and different sports having corporate names? Discuss the pros and cons of your school using corporate sponsors to fund athletics.

Integrated Learning Exercises

13-26. Although some firms handle public relations activities internally, many firms retain public relations firms to work on special projects and to handle unique situations. The Public Relations Society of America (PRSA) is one of the major associations for PR practitioners. In Canada, the primary association is the Canadian Public Relations Society (CPRS). Access the websites of these two organizations at **www.prsa.org** and **www.cprs.ca**. What types of information does each provide? What types of services are offered? How would these organizations be beneficial to various companies?

13-27. Access the online version of *PRWeek* at **www.prweek.com**. What type of information is available? How would this site be valuable to a PR practitioner? How could it be used by a firm seeking a public relations agency? How could it be used by a marketing manager?

13-28. The American Institute of Philanthropy ranks many charities. Access the website at **www.charitywatch.org**. How does the Institute rate the charities? How can this information be used by a company to determine which charities to support?

13-29. A number of companies offer services to help firms plan and develop sponsorships. One company is IEG. Access the website at **www.sponsorship.com**. Review the site. Identify the various services offered by IEG. If you were the marketing manager for a company that wanted to develop a sponsorship program, how could IEG help? Be specific.

13-30. Many companies participate in event marketing to accomplish various objectives. Access the following companies that assist firms with event marketing. What type of services does each offer? What is your evaluation of each of the companies? If you were hosting an event, which company would you hire? Why?

a. Advantage International, LLC (**www.advantage-intl.com**)
b. Fuse Youth Marketing Agency (**www.fusemarketing.com**)
c. RPMC Event and Promotion Agency (**www.rpmc.com**)

13-31. Sponsorship of charities, sports events, and worthy institutions is big business. It brings in countless millions to the charities or other organizations and gives the sponsor a massive boost in their exposure. Identify who sponsors three of the following and the benefits to them:

a. UEFA Champions League (**www.uefa.com**)
b. Médecins Sans Frontières (**www.msf.org**)
c. Stichting INGKA Foundation (**www.ikeafoundation.org**)
d. Qatar World Cup (**www.fifa.com/worldcup/qatar2022**)
e. Wellcome Trust (**www.wellcome.ac.uk**)
f. Mohammed bin Rashid Al Maktoum Foundation (**www.sheikhmohammed.com**)
g. Red Crescent (**www.redcrescent.org**)

Blog Exercises

Access the authors' blog for this textbook at the URLs provided to complete these exercises. Answer the questions that are posed on the blog.

13-32. Interstate Batteries — **http://blogclowbaack.net/2014/05/05/interstate-batteries-chapter-13/**

13-33. Adidas — **http://blogclowbaack.net/2014/05/05/adidas-chapter-13/**

13-34. Crisis Management — **http://blogclowbaack.net/2014/05/05/crisis-management-chapter-13/**

Student Project

CREATIVE CORNER

Circle K Ranch has been selling, training, and boarding horses for almost 20 years. With the recent downturn in the economy, however, Circle K experienced a decline in all facets of its business. In talking with some marketing students at the local university, the owner of Circle K Ranch, Kathy Kroncke, wondered about using cause-related marketing, sponsorships, and even event marketing to boost the awareness and image of her business. She recently added horseback riding to her list of services and developed a 10-mile ride that goes through a local state park. So far, business has not been what she expected, despite research that indicated a high level of interest in riding, especially by 15- to 40-year-old females. Design a cause-related marketing program, a sponsorship program, and an event marketing program for Circle K Ranch. After you have designed each of the programs, choose the one you think would be the best for Circle K Ranch. Design a newspaper ad featuring the program. What other methods would you use, both traditional and nontraditional, to publicize the program you chose?

CASE 1 NEW DRUG FACES PUBLIC RELATIONS AND MARKETING CHALLENGES

It is unusual for a new product to create a vehement public response from both supporters and detractors. One such product, which was approved by the FDA in 2006 and made widely available in 2007, is Gardasil. The drug was developed by Merck and Company.

Gardasil is provided in the form of a vaccine. It was developed to prevent cervical cancer by blocking infection from human papillomavirus (HPV), which is spread through sexual contact. The Food and Drug Administration permits Gardasil to be used by females ages nine through twenty-six, with the goal of inoculating girls before they become sexually active. Although the vaccine does not prevent every form of papillomavirus, it does treat four of the most common, including 100 percent prevention of the most common type and 70 percent of the four most common types combined.

Nearly half a million women are diagnosed with cervical cancer each year. According to some experts, Gardasil might make it possible to eliminate cervical cancer within a generation. It is also a victory for Merck, the fourth-biggest U.S. drug maker, which has focused increasingly on vaccines and may generate \$3 billion in annual sales from Gardasil alone. "It's important from a public health perspective because you're eliminating a cancer," said Les Funtleyder, an analyst in New York for Miller Tabak & Co. "The subtle point is these guys are creating new drugs for important health problems, which is what a pharma is supposed to do."

Gardasil requires three doses to be given over six months. In 2007, each dose costs around \$120. Consequently, affordability may determine how effective the drug is in quelling cervical cancer. About 80 percent of cases are in poorer countries. "Critical to success will be ensuring that women in the world's poorest countries—where cervical cancer hits hardest—have rapid and affordable access to this lifesaving new tool," said Gabriel N. Hortobagyi, a physician at the University of Texas M.D. Anderson Cancer Center in Houston and president of the American Society of Clinical Oncology. HPV is one of the most common sexually transmitted viruses in the world, and it causes genital warts as well as cancer. About 20 million people in the United States are infected, according to the U.S. Centers for Disease Control and Prevention (CDC).

Why the controversy? Many social conservatives fear that providing the vaccine may provide subtle approval for young women to engage in sex, much in the same way as providing birth control information and condoms are sometimes condemned. Some of the response was in regard to the recommendations from a panel of experts assembled by the CDC. The panel issues widely followed guidelines, including recommendations for childhood vaccines that become the basis for vaccination requirements set by public schools. The panel recommended that the vaccine be required.

Merck company officials and others noted that research indicates the best age to vaccinate would be just before puberty to make sure children are protected before they become sexually active. The vaccine would probably be targeted primarily at girls but could also be used on boys to limit the spread of the virus. "If you really want to have cervical cancer rates fall as much as possible as quickly as possible, then you want as many people to get vaccinated as possible," said Mark Feinberg, Merck's vice president of medical affairs and policy, noting that, "school mandates have been one of the most effective ways to increase immunization rates." That is the view being pushed by cervical cancer experts and women's health advocates.

© Deklofenak/Fotolia

▲ Many young girls could benefit from the HPV virus vaccine Gardasil.

Not surprisingly, a major clash emerged, mostly notably when the state of Texas made it a requirement to have the vaccine in order to be admitted to school. The battle lines were primarily drawn over girls being forced to take a medicine, with or without parental consent, along with the concerns expressed about sexual activity.

Company officials from Merck worked carefully with both governmental agencies and other groups to reduce concerns. In 2008, the company began advertising Gardasil in television commercials entitled "One Less" and "Guard Yourself." A powerful point is made: By taking the medicine, one less person will become infected.

13-35. Describe the stakeholders and the positions of each group involved in this controversy.

13-36. Outline the positive public relations opportunities available to promote Gardasil.

13-37. Describe how Merck should respond to negative publicity and complaints about the product.

13-38. Could Merck use cause-related marketing effectively, or would it be construed as a means of marketing the drug?

CASE 2 STANDARD CHARTERED SINGAPORE MARATHON: PUBLIC RELATIONS AND MARKETING OPPORTUNITIES

The Standard Chartered Singapore Marathon is an annual international marathon held on the first Sunday of December each year, organized by Singapore Sports Council, a government-funded body tasked to built a holistic sports environment in Singapore. Standard Chartered Bank is the title sponsor of the event. The Standard Chartered Singapore Marathon has recorded increasing levels of participation from both local and international runners and in 2010 attracted a record 60,000 participants—a 10-fold increase from the race's debut in 2002.

Standard Chartered Bank is a global banking group that operates in more than 70 countries. It is a trusted brand that is known internationally for its high standards in business and social responsibility. Standard Chartered Bank opened its first branch in Singapore in 1859. It was given the license to operate as a Qualifying Full Bank by the Monetary Authority of Singapore in 1999, allowing it to serve both consumer and wholesale banking customers. It is an important employer for the Singapore economy, with a staff of about 5,700 working in branch banking, global consumer and wholesale business, technology, and operations functions.

Standard Chartered Bank Singapore has been the title sponsor of the Standard Chartered Singapore Marathon since 2002. Its long-standing relationship with the Singapore Sports Council reflects the bank's strong belief in its commitment to the community and its willingness to go the extra mile for its stakeholders, the essence of which is captured in its brand statement "Here for Good."

The Standard Chartered Singapore Marathon 2010 featured a number of cash incentives to increase the level of competition among elite runners and new routes to accommodate more runners and to enhance the race day experience. Among the new incentives for runners in the Elite and Open categories were the "Champion Fund" for winning athletes who plan to return for the 2011 marathon and the "Time Bonus" for those runners who met certain target times. The total prize money amounted to $355,707, making the Standard Chartered Singapore Marathon 2010 an attractive race for elite runners and branding it as Asia's premier marathon.

The Standard Chartered Singapore Marathon 2010 also featured a variety of programs to engage the larger community. For example, Run for Good was an initiative by Standard Chartered Bank to use the race to raise funds for Club Rainbow (Singapore). Club Rainbow works with hospitals to provide a full range of support for children and youths up to the age of 20 who suffer from major illnesses. Individuals were able to donate directly to the fund or to sign up as a Run for Good participant. Run for Good participants solicited funds through their own networks and were able to set up personalized online profiles on the Club Rainbow (Singapore) website to promote the cause.

xc/Shutterstock

▲ By sponsoring the Singapore Marathon, Standard Chartered Bank reinforces the message that it is "Here for Good."

The Standard Chartered Kids Dash was a 750 m race for children 13 years and younger. The race was a bonding event for families with young children to enjoy the carnival atmosphere and experience one of Asia's best road races.

The Standard Chartered Singapore Marathon 2010 also featured a hospitality package to encourage companies to promote healthy living and build teamwork and morale among their staff. Companies put together teams of runners who raised funds for charity. The hospitality package included a complimentary massage for runners at the end of the race.

Ray Ferguson, the regional CEO of Standard Chartered Bank, Singapore and Southeast Asia, believes that the Standard Chartered Singapore Marathon can be an iconic event in

Singapore's sporting calendar, because it has the ability to engage staff, customers, and the community at large.[42]

13-39. Discuss the positive public relations opportunities for Standard Chartered Bank Singapore as the titled sponsor of the Standard Chartered Singapore Marathon since 2002.

13-40. Explain the advantages and disadvantages of using cause-related marketing (Club Rainbow Singapore) with event marketing.

13-41. Discuss any other programs that Standard Chartered Bank Singapore can initiate to leverage its sponsorship of the Standard Chartered Singapore Marathon.

MyMarketingLab

Go to **mymktlab.com** for the following Assisted-graded writing questions:

13-42. When Starbucks opened its first coffee shop inside a public library, ten percent of all proceeds from coffee sold there went to support the operation of the library. Describe the benefits to Starbucks of this type of sponsorship. What benefits accrue to the library? Some consumers feel this type of sponsorship is inappropriate because it involves a for-profit company selling products in a government entity. Examine the various methods of damage control. Which method or methods should a library use to reduce the criticism and to prevent any negative fallout? Justify your choice.

13-43. Sponsorships are now a major component of professional sports. Football, basketball, baseball, and golf all have sponsors. Many stadiums are now named for companies. What would be the benefit of a clothing brand, such as Kate Spade, investing a large budget into sport sponsorships? What are the disadvantages? Examine the various sponsorship objectives. Which objective or objectives should Kate Spade pursue? Why? Outline the steps Kate Spade would utilize in choosing a sponsor for its brand.

Part 5

IMC ETHICS, REGULATION, AND EVALUATION

Chapter 14 Regulations and Ethical Concerns

Chapter Objectives

After reading this chapter, you should be able to answer the following questions:

14.1 Which agencies and laws regulate marketing communications?

14.2 What are the relationships between puffery, deception, and substantiation?

14.3 What legal remedies can agencies use to correct deceptive communications practices?

14.4 How do the three major industry regulatory agencies help keep advertising and business practices from injuring customers or other businesses?

14.5 What ethical criticisms have been registered against advertising and marketing practices?

14.6 Which marketing tactics raise ethical concerns?

14.7 How can marketers apply the various ethical frameworks and ethics programs to their activities and actions?

14.8 What international issues influence the discussion of legal and ethical marketing activities?

Overview

The final level of an IMC program includes making certain the communications program meets ethical and legal requirements and is properly evaluated. This part of the text examines these topics. Figure 14.1 displays the completion of an IMC program.

The fields of marketing and marketing communications have long been the subject of scrutiny from the general public, special interest groups, and the government. This may not be surprising. In marketing and sales, money is involved as people make purchases. Many individuals and organizations express concern about the public trust and the well-being of the community. When companies sell goods and services that can injure people or cause harm in some other way, criticisms and legal actions likely will follow.

REEBOK PAYS $25 MILLION SETTLEMENT

Piotr Marcinski/Fotolia

The running shoe and sport shoe industry has dealt with criticism and concern for years. Complaints have been registered regarding the high prices of shoes, the foreign labor used to produce them, and the strong amount of social pressure parents and children face to purchase the most fashionable and cutting-edge models, at the expense of other, more practical and necessary merchandise.

Recently, Reebok encountered a new controversy. The company's Easy Tone and Run Tone product lines in the toning shoes market are produced with a rounded or otherwise unstable sole. Companies including Reebok, New Balance, and Skechers make such shoes and claim they force wearers to use more muscle to maintain balance while working out. The different shoe styles for running, walking, and training sell for about $100. Reebok sold more than five million pairs in the United States and 10 million abroad. Toning shoes became a $1.1 billion market in a short period of time.

In ads for the Easy Tone and Run Tone lines, Reebok made specific claims. One commercial featured a super fit women who assures viewers that Easy Tone sneakers strengthen hamstrings and calves by up to 11 percent and tone one's butt (gluteus maximus muscles) "up to 28 percent more than regular sneakers, just by walking." And, as Ellie Krupnick from the Huffington Post noted, "How was Reebok planning on backing that up, exactly?"

The Federal Trade Commission (FTC) stepped in. The agency ordered Reebok to pay a $25 million settlement, because the products failed to fulfill the body-shaping promises claimed in the ads. The FTC ruled that Reebok made unsupported advertising claims. David Vladeck, director of the FTC's Bureau of Consumer Protection, said, "The FTC wants national advertisers to understand that they must exercise some responsibility and ensure that their claims for fitness gear are supported by sound science."

Reebok maintained its stance regarding the shoes, stating that, "We stand behind our Easy Tone technology—the first shoe in the toning category that was inspired by balance-ball training. Settling does not mean we agree with the FTC's allegations; we do not. We have received overwhelmingly enthusiastic feedback from thousands of Easy Tone customers, and we remain committed to the further development of our Easy Tone line of products. Our customers are our number one priority, and we will continue to deliver products that they trust and love."

Reebok was not the only company admonished by the FTC. Skechers agreed to pay $41 million regarding advertising and marketing of a similar product. In both situations, the Federal Trade Commission concluded that the claims made by the companies were misleading.[1]

This chapter examines two interrelated topics. The first part features a description of the legal environment surrounding marketing and marketing communications. The second part presents views of ethics, morals, and social responsibility as they relate to marketing, advertising, and promotions. In essence, those involved in marketing programs should consider both the letter of the law—regulations and other legal limitations—as well as the spirit of the law. Guided by both personal principles and organizational guidelines, marketing professionals work to ensure that their actions are both legal and ethical.

▶ **FIGURE 14.1**
Integrated Marketing Communications

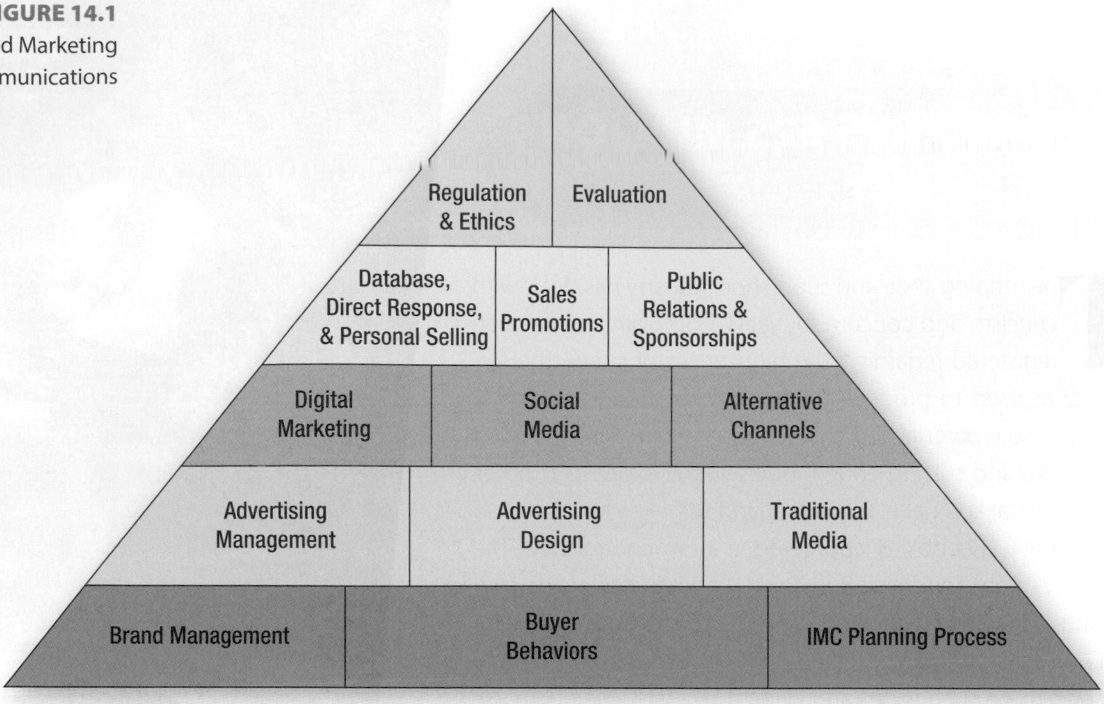

Marketing Communications Regulations

objective 14.1
Which agencies and laws regulate marketing communications?

The U.S. federal government has enacted considerable legislation designed to keep companies from taking unfair advantage of consumers and other businesses. Various states regulate for-profit companies and other organizations. Many of these federal and state laws are enforced by regulatory agencies. This section reviews governmental actions in the areas of legislation and regulation of company marketing practices (see Figure 14.2).

Governmental Regulatory Agencies

Governmental agencies serve as watchdogs to monitor for potential violations of the law, some of which are only partially related to marketing. For example, the Food and Drug Administration (FDA) regulates and oversees the packaging and labeling of products. The FDA also monitors advertising on food packages and advertisements for drugs, yet its primary responsibilities are ensuring food quality and drug safety.

▼ The FCC monitors advertising directed toward children.

Petro Feketa/Fotolia

The Federal Communications Commission (FCC) regulates television, radio, and the telephone industry. The FCC grants (and revokes) operating licenses for radio and television stations. The FCC also holds jurisdiction over telephone companies. The FCC does not have jurisdiction over the content of advertisements transmitted by mass media. The FCC does not control which products may be advertised; however, the organization does monitor advertising directed toward children. FCC rules limit television stations to 12 minutes per hour of children's advertisements

- Food and Drug Administration (FDA)
- Federal Communications Commission (FCC)
- U.S. Postal Service (USPS)
- Bureau of Alcohol, Tobacco and Firearms (ATF)
- Federal Trade Commission (FTC)

FIGURE 14.2
Government Regulatory Agencies

during weekdays and 10 minutes per hour on weekends. Recently, Viacom agreed to pay $1 million for programming on Nickelodeon that violated the time limitation 600 times in the span of one year.[2]

The U.S. Postal Service (USPS) holds jurisdiction over all mailed marketing materials. The USPS investigates mail fraud schemes and other fraudulent marketing practices. The Bureau of Alcohol, Tobacco and Firearms (ATF) rules when the sale, distribution, and advertising of alcohol and tobacco are at issue. Ordinarily, the governmental agency that examines incidents involving deceptive or misleading marketing tactics is the Federal Trade Commission (FTC).

The Federal Trade Commission

The **Federal Trade Commission**, or **FTC**, which was created in 1914 by the passage of the Federal Trade Commission Act, presides over marketing communications. The act's original intent was to create a federal agency to enforce antitrust laws and to protect businesses from one another. It had little authority over advertising and marketing communications except when an advertisement was considered to be unfair to the competition, thereby restricting free trade.

Unfair and Deceptive Marketing Practices

In 1938, Congress passed the Wheeler–Lea Amendment to Section 5 of the Federal Trade Commission Act to increase and expand the authority of the FTC and to prohibit false and misleading advertising. The agency was granted the authority to stop unfair or deceptive advertising practices and to levy fines when necessary. The law provided the FTC access to the courts to enforce the law and ensure that violators abide by FTC rulings.

A firm can violate the act even when the company did not expressly intend to deceive. An advertisement or communication is deemed to be deceptive or misleading when:

1. A substantial number of people or the "typical person" is left with a false impression or misrepresentation that relates to the product.
2. The misrepresentation induces people or the "typical person" to make a purchase.

Consumers may be misled by advertisements, mailings, corporate literature, labels, packaging, website materials, and oral and written statements made by salespeople. This gives the government a great deal of latitude in dealing with deceptive practices.

Deception versus Puffery

objective 14.2
What are the relationships between puffery, deception, and substantiation?

Puffery can be legally used in advertisements and marketing messages. **Puffery** exists when a firm makes an exaggerated statement about its goods or services. The key difference, in terms of the FTC and the courts, between puffery and a claim is that puffery does not constitute a *factual statement*. In contrast, a *claim* makes a factual statement that can be proven true or false. Firms may make puffery statements without proving them; claims must be substantiated or proven in some manner.

Terms normally associated with puffery include words such as *friendliest, best, greatest*, and *finest*. A firm can advertise "our brand is the best" or "our signature dishes use only the finest ingredients." Courts and the regulatory agencies view these statements as puffery and believe that consumers expect firms to use them routinely in their advertisements. An advertisement for Karns Foods stating "Home of Pennsylvania's Best Meat Department"

▶ This Interstate Batteries billboard advertisement provides an example of using puffery by stating its products are "outraegously dependable."

Interstate Battery Systems International, Inc.

constitutes one form of puffery. The statement cannot be proven true or false but rather is a matter of opinion.

The word *best* will normally be accepted as puffery. The word *better* has been construed to imply a comparison. The term has recently been tested through the FTC, the National Advertising Division of the Better Business Bureau, and the courts. Papa John's use of the phrase "Better Ingredients, Better Pizza" was found to be puffery, as was the phrase "Only the best tomatoes grow up to be Hunt's."

In another situation, Progresso made the statement "Discover the Better Taste of Progresso" in company advertisements. The slogan was challenged by Campbell's Soup Company, which argued that Progresso's "better taste" phrase was puffery. Representatives for Campbell's contended that taste tests can be used to determine if one food product tastes better than other brands. The courts agreed and ordered Progresso to either modify the phrase or prove that Progresso soups do taste better.[3]

Quick service restaurants and other food providers have begun using words such as "wholesome, fresh, natural, and local" to avoid scrutiny by the FTC that was created by ads making health-related claims. Such vague words have no specific marketing-related meaning. In addition, consumers accept them. Darren Tristano, vice president at Technomic, commented, "More traditional health claims on the menu tend to get adverse reactions by the customer because they associate healthy claims with less taste. The newer descriptors are designed around the idea that the food is better for you."[4]

▼ This advertisement for Karns Foods uses puffery by stating it is the "Best Meat Department."

Karns Food

Substantiation of Marketing Claims

The concept of substantiation applies to claims that are not puffery. **Substantiation** means that an advertising claim or promise

Courtesy of Alliance One Advertising

◀ Southwest General Hospital features puffery in this advertisement by stating its heart care is first, and "second to none."

must be proven with data, facts, or through competent and reliable evidence. Failure to do so can result in a lawsuit or governmental action.

An advertisement featuring an endorser must contain truthful statements representing the person's experiences or opinions. When a commercial uses an expert endorsement, the statements must be based on legitimate tests performed by professionals in the field. In the advertisement for Skyjacker shown in this section, reality TV star of Duck Dynasty Willie Robertson states, "I've spent my life in the swamps of Louisiana. Skyjacker helps me look at ruts in my rearview mirror."

All marketing claims must reflect the typical experience a customer would expect to encounter from the use of a good or service, unless the advertisement clearly and prominently states otherwise. A few years ago, a Kleenex Cottonelle advertisement made the claim that the product was softer. Kleenex provided actual touch tests by consumers as evidence. The company then used engineering and lab tests to show that Kleenex tissue consists of 24 percent more cottony, soft fiber. Thus, Kleenex was able to substantiate the claim. Substantiation may not always be easy. To increase the probability the substantiation will be accepted by the FTC and courts, company leaders use the following principles:[5]

▼ A Skyjacker advertisement featuring with Willie Robertson of *Duck Dynasty* as an endorser.

lee mcguire/Skyjacker Suspensions

1. The federal government assumes consumers read ads broadly and do not pay much attention to fine print and qualifying language. Thus, hiding a qualifier at the bottom of the ad or using words such as *usually, normally*, or *under typical situations* somewhere in the ad is not normally accepted as substantiation.
2. The evidence has to be for the exact product being tested, not for a similar product, regardless of the similarity.
3. Evidence should come from or be accepted by experts in the relevant area of the product and would be considered valid and reliable by the experts. Studies conducted by the company or something found on the internet is not acceptable.
4. The FTC and courts consider the totality of the evidence. If the company has one study that supports the claim but there are four studies by other independent organizations that indicate something different, then the evidence will not be accepted as valid substantiation.

Regardless of the type of communication, the FTC prohibits unfair or deceptive marketing communications. Marketers must substantiate claims through competent and reliable evidence. Unfortunately, a great deal of gray area

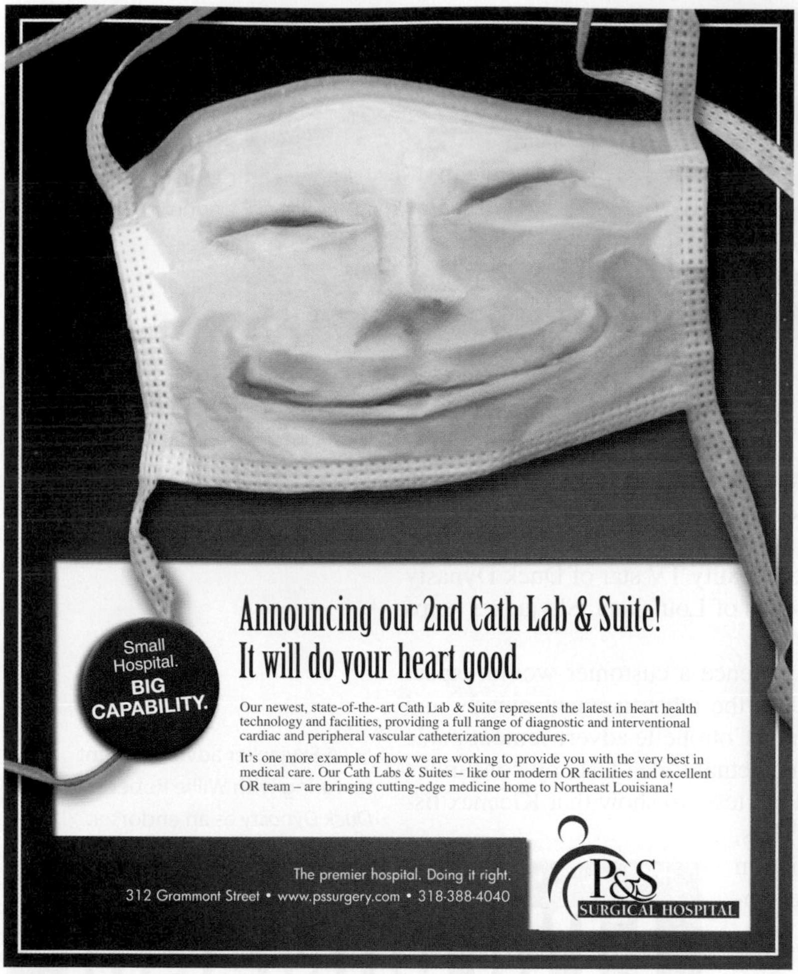

French Creative

▲ The claim in this advertisement that P & S Surgical Hospital is "the premier hospital" was substantiated through two different inpatient surveys.

exists between puffery and a claim that must be substantiated. Consequently, lawsuits are filed and governmental agencies are required to address complaints and suspected violations of the law. These agencies and their rulings strongly affect individual marketing practices as well as company actions.

How Investigations Begin

An investigation into misleading or deceptive advertising can be triggered in a number of ways. Sources of complaints can be registered by:

- Consumers
- Businesses
- Congress
- The media

Each can raise questions about what appears to be an unfair or deceptive practice. Investigations by the FTC remain confidential at first, which protects the agency and the company under investigation.

Consent Orders

When the FTC believes a law has been violated, it issues a **consent order**. Company leaders who sign consent orders agree to stop a disputed practice without admitting guilt.

ADT signed consent agreements with the FTC concerning three spokespersons for the company's security system. These spokespersons were conveyed as independent experts and appeared on NBC's *Today Show*, other TV shows, radio news programs, and blogs promoting ADT's Pulse security systems. Although the spokespersons were portrayed as independent experts, all were paid by ADT's public relations department. One was paid more than $300,000, another more than $200,000, and all were given security systems with monitoring free of charge. Under the consent agreement, ADT agreed to make it clear these experts were paid by ADT. They also had to remove reviews and endorsements from the brand's website and blog that were misrepresented as independent reviews and disclose any reviews or endorsements when there was any type of material connection with ADT.[6]

objective 14.3
What legal remedies can agencies use to correct deceptive communications practices?

FTC Settlements

Occasionally, rather than agreeing to a consent order, company leaders accept a settlement with the FTC. This occurred when a number of auto dealerships were charged by the FTC with deceptive and misleading advertising and marketing practices. One dealer, Fowlerville Ford in Michigan, sent 30,000 mailers to consumers telling them they had won a prize that they could collect at the dealership. Not one of 30,000 recipients actually won or collected a prize. Another dealership, Norm Reeves Honda Superstore, advertised that consumers would pay zero down on a lease when in fact the copy did not mention the substantial fees and other charges that consumers were required to pay upon signing a contract. A dealer in Texas, Southwest Kia, advertised that consumers could purchase a vehicle for a very low monthly payment when in fact they would owe a large, final balloon payment at the end of more than $10,000. In each of these cases, the dealership signed a settlement with the FTC.[7]

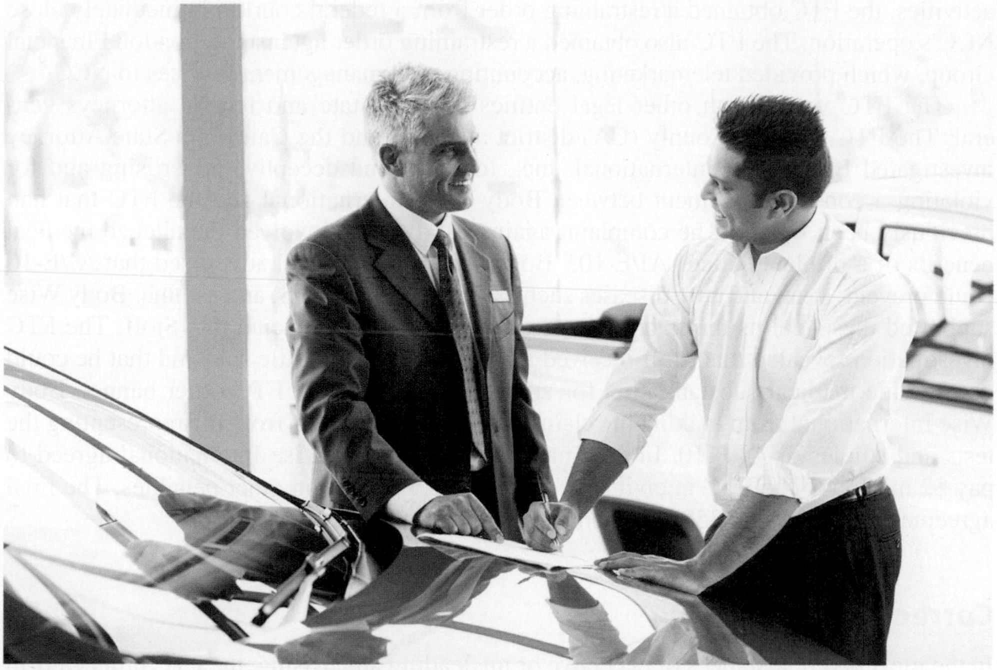

Michael jung/Fotolia

◀ The FTC investigated a number of auto dealerships for allegations of deceptive and misleading advertising.

Administrative Complaints

Most FTC investigations end with the signing of a consent order or settlement. When one cannot be reached, the FTC issues an **administrative complaint**. At that point, a formal proceeding similar to a court trial will be held before an administrative law judge. Both sides submit evidence and render testimony. At the end of the administrative hearing, the judge makes a ruling. When the judge concludes a violation of the law has occurred, a *cease and desist order* is issued. The order requires the company to stop the disputed practice immediately and refrain from similar practices in the future. A company that is not satisfied with the decision of the administrative law judge can appeal the case to the full FTC commission.

The *full commission* holds hearings similar to those before administrative law judges. Rulings follow presentations of evidence and testimony. Any company that is dissatisfied with the ruling of the full FTC commission can appeal the case to the U.S. Court of Appeals and further, to the highest level, the U.S. Supreme Court. The danger to a company that appeals a case is that consumer redress can be sought at that point. This means any company found guilty of violating laws can be ordered to pay civil penalties.

Courts and Legal Channels

Occasionally, the FTC uses the court system to stop unfair and deceptive advertising and marketing communications practices. This takes place when a company violates previous FTC cease and desist orders or when the negative effects of a company's activities are so severe that they require immediate action. The latter occurred in a case involving the National Consumer Council (NCC), a debt reduction and negotiation firm based in Santa Ana, California. The FTC investigation found that the National Consumer Council encouraged consumers to stop paying their debts once they signed up with NCC for debt reduction. At the same time, NCC did not normally start negotiation with debtors for six months. By then, the customer's debtors were irate and not willing to negotiate. In the meantime, the NCC customer had been making payments into a fund at NCC. Charges and monthly fees were being withdrawn for payment to NCC. Many customers did not know NCC was making the charges. Eventually, the customers discovered that not only did NCC ruin their credit ratings, but they were also deeper in debt than when they signed on. Almost all of them were forced to declare bankruptcy. Due to the severity of NCC's activities, the FTC obtained a restraining order from a federal court to immediately close NCC's operation. The FTC also obtained a restraining order against the London Financial Group, which provided telemarketing, accounting, and management services to NCC.[8]

The FTC works with other legal entities such as state and federal attorneys general. The FTC, Orange County (CA) district attorney, and the California State Attorney investigated Body Wise International, Inc., for false and deceptive advertising and for violating a consent agreement between Body Wise International and the FTC that had previously been signed. The complaint against Body Wise involved the alleged medical benefits of a product called "AI/E-10." Body Wise International advertised that AI/E-10 could prevent, treat, and cure diseases such as cancer, HIV/AIDS, and asthma. Body Wise supported these claims through the expert testimony of a physician, Dr. Stoff. The FTC investigation revealed that Stoff received royalties for every bottle sold and that he could not provide medical substantiation for any of the claims. The FTC order banned Body Wise International from making the claims and prohibited Stoff from misrepresenting the tests and studies of AI/E-10. In the final settlement, Body Wise International agreed to pay $2 million to the FTC in civil penalties and $1.5 million in other penalties. The final agreement contained a $358,000 monetary judgment against Dr. Stoff.[9]

Corrective Advertising

In the most severe instances of deceptive or misleading advertising, the FTC orders a firm to prepare **corrective advertisements**. These rare situations occur when the members of the FTC believe that discontinuing a false advertisement will not be sufficient. When the FTC concludes that consumers believed the false advertisement, it can require the firm to produce corrective ads to bring consumers back to a neutral state. Consumers should return to the beliefs they held prior to the false or misleading advertising.

The FTC ordered corrective advertising for the Novartis Corporation. The judgment was based on false and deceptive advertisements of a product called Doan's analgesic. During the investigation, members of the FTC concluded that Doan's claim of greater efficiency than competing products was not substantiated. The FTC ordered Novartis to immediately cease comparative advertising and to make this statement in corrective ads: "Although Doan's is an effective pain reliever, there is no evidence that Doan's is more effective than other pain relievers for back pain." Novartis was ordered to spend $8 million advertising the statement and include it for one year in all advertisements, except for 15-second broadcast ads. Unhappy with the order, leaders at Novartis filed a lawsuit in federal court against the FTC; however, the federal court upheld the FTC order.[10]

▼ The FTC issued a trade regulation ruling that bloggers must reveal if they are being compensated in any way by a company when endorsing a brand.

Tagstock2/Fotolia

Trade Regulation Rulings

The final type of action the FTC takes, a **trade regulation ruling**, applies to an entire industry. Normally, the commission holds a public hearing and accepts both oral and written arguments. The commission then makes a ruling that applies to every firm within an industry. As with other FTC rulings, decisions can be challenged in the U.S. Court of Appeals.

The recent rise in personal blogs led to an explosion of product reviews by bloggers. Often, bloggers are paid or receive free merchandise to post positive comments. Blogger Jessica Smith was given a Ford Flex to use for one month plus a free gas card in exchange for a positive review. Microsoft sent bloggers a free laptop loaded with the newest Microsoft operating system. After investigating these practices, the FTC issued a ruling that bloggers who review products must disclose any connection with the advertiser or product, whether the product provided was free or if they were compensated in any way. The ruling also applies to celebrities who promote products on talk shows or on Twitter.[11]

A similar industry trade ruling occurred with gift cards issued by retailers. Many retailers were charging dormancy fees for cards that were not used immediately and many had expiration dates. Consumers did not receive this information at the time of purchase. The FTC issued a ruling that any merchant issuing a gift card must "boldly" display any fees or expiration dates on the card.[12]

Industry Oversight of Marketing Practices

objective 14.4
How do the three major industry regulatory agencies help keep advertising and business practices from injuring customers or other businesses?

Federal regulatory agencies cannot handle all industry activity. Although industry regulatory agencies have no legal power, they reduce the load on the FTC and the legal system. The three most common and well-known industry regulatory agencies are all a part of the Council of Better Business Bureaus: the National Advertising Division, the National Advertising Review Board, and the Children's Advertising Review Unit (Figure 14.3).

Council of Better Business Bureaus

The Council of Better Business Bureaus provides resources to both consumers and businesses. Consumers and firms may file complaints with the bureau about unethical business practices or unfair treatment. The bureau compiles a summary of all charges leveled against individual firms. Customers seeking information about the legitimacy of a company or its operations can contact the bureau. The bureau provides a carefully worded report containing any complaints against the company and reveals the general nature of customer concerns. The Better Business Bureau helps individuals and businesses make sure they are dealing with a firm with a low record of problems.

- National Advertising Division (NAD)
- National Advertising Review Board (NARB)
- Children's Advertising Review Unit (CARU)

▲ **FIGURE 14.3**
Industry Self-Regulatory Agencies

National Advertising Division Complaints about advertising or some aspect of marketing communications are referred to the National Advertising Division (NAD) of the Council of Better Business Bureaus for review. The NAD reviews the specific claims, and NAD lawyers collect information and evaluate data concerning the complaint to determine whether an advertiser can substantiate a claim. If not, the NAD negotiates with the advertiser to modify or discontinue the advertisement. When the firm's marketing claim can be substantiated, the NAD dismisses the complaint.

Individuals and companies may file complaints about unfair ads. Most complaints are from competing brands and deal with comparative ads. A few do not deal directly with a competitor but are the result of misleading advertising. Such was the case with a print ad for Maybelline Mascara featuring model Freja Beha Erichsen. In the ad, Erichsen's eyelashes looked impressively voluminous and, according to the copy, it was because of Maybelline's "patented supersonic jumbo brush that loads on big, sleek, volume instantly" which produces lashes eight times bigger. Fine print at the bottom of the ad indicated Erichsen's eyebrows were also enhanced with lash inserts.

▼ The NAD investigated a print ad for Maybelline Mascara.

Antonioguillem/Fotolia

After reviewing the advertisement, the NAD ruled the ad was "literally false" because the image of Erichsen was "not an accurate depiction of the volume that can be achieved by applying the mascara alone without the use of lash inserts" and therefore should be discontinued. L'Oreal, owner of the Maybelline brand, argued that at the bottom of the ad, it was disclosed the model's eyebrows were styled with lash inserts. In response, the

NAD said it is "axiomatic that disclosures that contradict or substantially change the main message in an advertisement are inadequate to prevent inaccurate consumer takeaways."[13]

The Maybelline decision illustrates the power of the NAD and is typical of NAD recommendations. In 95 percent of the cases when the NAD recommends an ad be discontinued or modified, the company voluntarily complies with the decision. The NAD is not a legal entity, which means companies do not have to abide by a decision.

National Advertising Review Board When a complaint cannot be resolved by the NAD or the advertiser appeals the NAD's decision, it will be referred to the National Advertising Review Board (NARB), which is composed of advertising professionals and prominent civic individuals. When the NARB rules that the firm's advertisements cannot be substantiated, it orders the firm to discontinue the advertisements in a manner similar to a consent order by the FTC. The NARB is a private board. When the business or firm being accused refuses to accept the NARB ruling, the matter will be turned over to the FTC or the most appropriate federal regulatory agency.

The NARB recently investigated a dispute between Minute Maid and Tropicana. Minute Maid was ordered to modify ads because the copy claimed that consumers preferred Minute Maid orange juice to Tropicana by a 2:1 margin. Tropicana lodged a complaint and won when it was heard by the NAD. Minute Maid disagreed with the NAD ruling and appealed to the NARB. Minute Maid complained that the decision by the NAD placed an unnecessary and unfair burden on comparative advertising, because all claims relative to a competitor must be substantiated. The National Advertising Review Board supported the NAD and issued an order for Minute Maid to comply with the ruling.[14]

Few cases are appealed to the NARB. Over a two-year period, only 19 decisions out of 339 made by the NAD were appealed to the National Advertising Review Board. None were overturned by NARB. Sixteen were upheld and in three cases part of the decision was upheld and other aspects were overturned.[15]

If a company is dissatisfied with the decision of the NARB or refuses to abide by the decision, the next step in the appeal process will be taken by the Federal Trade Commission. The NARB seldom refers a case to the FTC. Such an action has been taken only four times in the past 25 years. The last was a case dealing with Winn-Dixie, which made direct price comparisons with competitors. The NARB found that Winn-Dixie was using prices that were up to 90 days old. The NARB ruled that any price comparisons made in an advertisement by Winn-Dixie must use prices that are no more than seven days old. The decision to forward the case to the FTC was made when Winn-Dixie refused to modify the ads and accept the NARB ruling.[16]

Children's Advertising Review Unit The Children's Advertising Review Unit (CARU) investigates and monitors all forms of advertising in all media directed toward children younger than 12 years old. It also monitors online privacy practices of websites targeted at children younger than age 13. The CARU operates in a manner similar to the NAD.

▼ The Children's Advertising Review Unit (CARU) monitors all forms of advertising directed toward children.

Karelnoppe/Fotolia

In addition to handling complaints about advertising to children, CARU began prescreening ads directed to children. CARU now examines more than 300 ads per year. The prescreening allows CARU to highlight any potential problems with an advertisement before it goes into production. CARU has also issued a series of guidelines to help advertisers prepare ads for children. Figure 14.4 highlights these guidelines.[17]

Children younger than age 12 do not have the same reasoning abilities as adults. Consequently, the CARU stresses the importance of advertisers acting responsibly. Advertisements must show a toy as if a child were playing with it. It must

- Ads for toys should not create unreasonable expectations. Toys shown in acts should look and act as they would if a child were playing with it.
- Ads should not blur the line between fantasy and reality.
- Ads should have clear and visible disclosures about what items come with a toy and what items do not.
- Items that require adult supervision must be shown with adults supervising the child.
- Products and ad content should be appropriate for children.

FIGURE 14.4
CARU Guidelines for Advertising to Children

- Lower cost
- Faster resolution
- Heard by attomeys and business professionlas with experience in advertising

FIGURE 14.5
Advantages of Using the CBBB to Regulate Advertising

convey the difference between any fantasy used in a commercial and the reality when the child plays with the toy. When accessories are shown, the commercial must clearly state that the accessories do not come with the original toy so the child will not be disappointed. If an item such as a trampoline is advertised, then adult supervision must also be shown in the advertisement.

Advantages to Using Self-Regulation Industry-based actions are designed to control the marketing communications environment and limit legal actions that will be required by the courts or a governmental agency. As highlighted in Figure 14.5, industry regulatory agencies offer several benefits over FTC and legal remedies. Agencies normally hear cases sooner and at a lower cost to the companies involved. Further, attorneys and business professionals with experience in advertising hear the complaints. Although FTC judges may some have familiarity with the advertising industry, they often have less extensive knowledge than the individuals involved in the CBBB's agencies.

Effective management, however, will be proactive rather than reactive. Company leaders can work to create an image of a socially responsible firm. This creates a far better approach than reacting to the constant scrutiny of angry consumers and regulatory agencies.

IMC and Ethics

objective 14.5
What ethical criticisms have been registered against advertising and marketing practices?

In many instances, an advertising or marketing practice may be legal but be ethically suspect. This section considers various marketing and advertising tactics. Then ethical frameworks and responses involving them are described.

Ethics and morals constitute the key principles used to guide a person's activities in the world of commerce. **Morals** are beliefs or principles that individuals hold concerning what is right and what is wrong. **Ethics** are moral principles that serve as guidelines for both individuals and organizations. Many ethical and moral concerns affect the fields of marketing, advertising, and marketing communication. At the most general level, several major concerns and criticisms have arisen, including the items provided in Figure 14.6.

1. Advertisements cause people to buy more than they can afford.
2. Advertising overemphasizes materialism.
3. Advertising increases the costs of goods and services.
4. Advertising perpetuates stereotyping of males, females, and minority groups.
5. Advertisements often make unsafe products, such as alcohol and tobacco, seem attractive.
6. Advertisements often are offensive.
7. Advertising to children is unethical.

FIGURE 14.6
Ethical Concerns Regarding Advertising

Olesiabilkei/Fotolia

▲ One criticism of advertising is that it causes consumers to buy more than they can afford.

Ethics and Advertising

Some critics complain that advertisements cause people to *buy more than they can afford*. It is closely connected to the comment that advertising *overemphasizes materialism*. A case can be made that many commercials do indeed stress luxury, social standing, and the prestige of being first to purchase an item. At the same time, the messages are still just commercials. Those who defend advertising point out those consumers should be responsible for spending money wisely.

Advertising has been alleged to *increase the costs of goods and services*. This argument has been made for many years. Advertising professionals note that without consumer awareness, products would not be purchased, because consumers would not know of their existence. Further, advertising widens the base of potential customers and may increase repeat business. Additional sales lead to economies of scale and lower prices rather than increasing them.

▼ Elderly people are sometimes stereotyped in advertising.

iofoto/Fotolia

Perpetuating Stereotypes

Many social commentators suggest that advertising and other forms of media perpetuate stereotyping of men, women, and minority groups. This leads to several questions. For instance, is segmentation the same as stereotyping? In an era in which the term *political correctness* routinely appears, debate defining "acceptable" continues. In marketing, some of the categories in which market segments are identified include age, race, gender, social status, and income. When marketing to or portraying different individuals from these categories, do advertisers use clichés that are no longer appropriate?

Advertisements may portray a market segment as one-dimensional figures rather than reflecting the complexities of specific gender, racial, or age segments. Teens may be depicted as rebellious, carefree, and sexually starved. Asian Americans may be shown in advertising as technological experts—knowledgeable, savvy, and even mathematically adept or intellectually gifted. They are usually shown in ads for business-oriented or technical products. From a marketing perspective, it is much easier to group people into smaller subgroups with common interests. Is it unethical, bad business, or simply a practical matter to represent or misrepresent consumers in these ways?

Advertising Unsafe Products

Marketing has been associated with unsafe products such as alcohol, cigarettes, and other potentially harmful items. By the age of 18, the average American teen has viewed more than 100,000 beer commercials. The use of sexuality and social acceptance combined with humor makes the products in commercials appear desirable. Critics of the brewing industry and marketing agree that many beer commercials encourage underage drinking and build brand loyalty or brand switching in a population that should not even use the product. Occasional underage drinking can lead to an addiction in a few months, because underage drinkers are less developed mentally, physically, and emotionally. The question becomes: Do a few public relations advertisements represent a real attempt to reduce underage drinking, or are they designed to placate the government and critics?

The same holds true for tobacco products. Numerous charges have been made arguing that tobacco companies focus on reaching young people through characters such as Joe Camel. Any marketing professional entering the field should consider his or her comfort level with such approaches.

After tobacco advertising on television was banned by the government, marketers created a series of tactics to make certain company products are mentioned on the air. Sponsorships of the Virginia Slims Tennis and Marlboro Cup Racing came under scrutiny, because sportscasters state the names of the products while reporting scores and results.

Ivan Montero/Fotolia

▲ Sex in advertising has the potential to be offensive to individuals domestically as well as those in other countries.

Offensive Advertisements

Many adult products require tasteful advertising and marketing programs, even when they are free to be shown through any medium. Feminine hygiene products, condoms, and other personal adult products may be featured in practically any venue. Marketing professionals should select media that are appropriate as well as create ads that will not offend.

In the international arena, the responsibility becomes even greater. In many Islamic countries, advertisements for personal hygiene or sexually-related products are offensive. Company leaders should explore cultural differences before undertaking any kind of marketing campaign.

Another ethical issue that has arisen concerns the use of nudity and sexuality in advertising. Marketing professionals must carefully consider what the limits should be. Suggesting that sex sells is simply not enough, nor is making a defensive claim about freedom of speech or freedom of expression. Ethics, morals, and a clear conscience should serve as additional guides when a company pushes the limits of sexuality in advertising.

Advertising to Children

A continuing controversy in the field of marketing is the ethical acceptability of advertising to children. Children represent a tremendous level of spending and buying power, more than $20 billion annually. Critics question the tactics used to reach them.

Mary Pipher, clinical psychologist and author of *The Shelter of Each Other*, suggests that, "No one ad is bad, but the combination of 400 ads per day creates in children a combination of narcissism, entitlement, and dissatisfaction."[18] Ads targeted to children employ multiple tactics, including building brand awareness through images and logos, featuring toys and collectibles, and developing tie-ins with television programs and movies, including the *Hannah Montana* phenomenon. Characters such as Barney, Ronald McDonald, and Harry Potter vend everything from food to toys to clothes.

▼ From a social perspective, advertising to children remains a controversial issue.

Anatoliy Samara/Fotolia

With so many potential venues to sell directly to children and to put pressure on their parents, many company leaders believe it is best to "get them while they're young." From a societal perspective, however, the question remains as to whether such impressionable young minds should be subjected to so many messages.

▶ **FIGURE 14.7**
Ethical Issues in Marketing

- Brand infringement
- Professional services marketing
- Gifts and bribery
- Spam and cookies
- Ambush marketing
- Stealth marketing

Marketing and Ethics

objective 14.6
Which marketing tactics raise ethical concerns?

Ethical dilemmas arise in places other than advertisements. Many times, however, a connection exists between a marketing program and what takes place in the marketing communications arena. Figure 14.7 reviews some of these issues.

Brand Infringement

Numerous ethical challenges have been associated with brand management. One continuing problem, **brand infringement**, occurs when a company creates a brand name that closely resembles a popular or successful brand, such as when the Korrs beer company was formed. In that case, the courts deemed the brand an intentional infringement, and the name was abandoned. Another brand-infringing company ordered by the courts to give up the name was Victor's Secret.

The brand infringement issue becomes more complex when a brand becomes so well-established that it may be considered a generic term, such as a Kleenex tissue or a Xerox copy. Band-Aid encountered the problem in the 1970s, forcing the marketing team to make sure the product was identified as "Band-Aid Brand Strips" rather than simply "band aids," to keep the competition from using the name. The most vulnerable new brand name may be Google, as in "I Googled myself" or "I Googled it."

A newer form of unethical behavior, internet *domain squatting* or *cyber squatting*, is the questionable practice of buying domain names (barnesandnoble.com, kohls.com, lebronjames.com, etc.) that are valuable to specific people or businesses in the hopes of making a profit by reselling the name. At the extreme, whitehouse.com was a pornographic website. Any new company trying to build a presence in the marketplace may find itself stifled by domain squatters. Names matter, and cyber squatters are willing to take advantage of these activities to make profits at some else's expense.[19]

Marketing of Professional Services

Is it ethical to advertise a physician's services or new drugs? For many years, attorneys, dentists, and physicians did not advertise for fear of being viewed as "ambulance chasers." Recently, the trend has gone in the opposite direction. For example, a dermatologist will advertise a "skin rejuvenation" practice with only a bare mention that it is part of a medical practice. Critics argue that this takes medicine into the area of merchandising and suggest that doing so is deceptive.

▼ Attorneys and physicians who advertise have been criticized as "ambulance chasers."

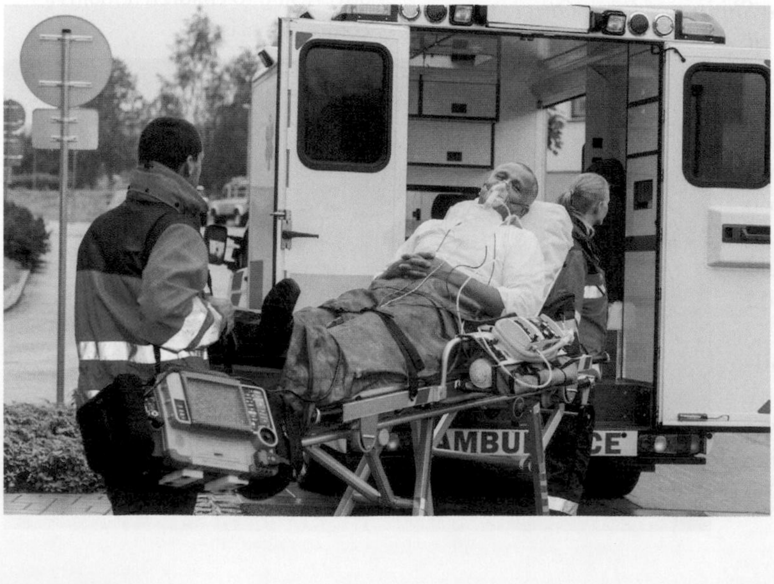

People injured by accidents, poor medical care, or bad medications are encouraged to call a toll-free number for information on how they can obtain compensation. Other ads encourage people to get rid of bad debts by filing bankruptcies. Critics of medical advertising have suggested attorneys are now chasing the same ambulances, hoping for large settlements of which they receive a substantial portion.

Pharmaceutical companies spend millions of dollars advertising new drugs. A great deal of discussion has taken place with regard to sexual dysfunction products. Unfortunately, many young men are buying and using the drugs for recreational purposes. Marketing critics complain that advertising and promotional tactics encourage this type of misuse.

The marketing of herbs, supplements, and other untested products has also created concern. Claims are made regarding their contributions to energy level, sexual stamina, and mental acuity. Other products are marketed using unsubstantiated reports about weight loss.

Physicians, pharmaceutical companies, and attorneys have the right to market their services. The ethical questions deal with how these services are presented to the public.

Gifts and Bribery in Business-to-Business Marketing Programs

When marketing to other businesses, close personal contacts are often common, both in personal sales calls and in other venues, such as trade shows. Gifts and bribery represent two of the more serious ethical concerns.

To influence sales, purchasing agents and other members of the buying company are often the recipients of gifts, meals, entertainment, and free trips. From a personal ethics standpoint, many concerned leaders question accepting personal gifts designed to influence business decisions. The International Olympics Committee wrestles with this issue when selecting sites for games. Exorbitant gifts, meals, and entertainment have been used by various cities in an effort to sway the selection process.

Closely tied with the issue of receiving gifts is offering or accepting bribes. These can be related to gaining governmental contracts or making business contacts. Without them, permits may not be granted or can be very difficult to obtain. In Germany and France, the government actually allows companies to write off bribes as tax deductions.

Spam and Cookies

Technology creates a double-edged sword for marketers. On the one hand, it leads to ingenious new ways to quickly reach a set of consumers with a key message and to keep in continuous contact with those customers. On the other hand, it can be invasive and intrusive and presents ethical dilemmas for those working on the web.

Numerous complaints about spamming have been raised. Even with anti-spam legislation, individuals continue to receive unwanted emails. One university in the Midwest receives about 100,000 emails a day, of which approximately 95,000 are spam. Should this be considered an ethical issue or simply a practical matter? Either way, spamming remains a controversial practice.

Cookie technology allows a company's website to track a browser's activities and other websites a consumer has visited. The technology allows a firm to customize and personalize web content to match a consumer's interest. A Harris Interactive survey revealed that 95 percent of consumers believe it is at least somewhat important that companies know "who I am, my buying history, past problems or complaints, preferences, and billing record."[20] At the same time, many consumers express concerns about privacy issues and what firms do with the information collected. Primary questions raised are:

- Should an internet company be allowed to gather this information?
- Should the company be allowed to sell the information to other companies?

Answers fall into two categories: legal and moral. Although it may be legal to collect and transfer consumer information in this manner, the ethical issue remains. Marketing professionals continue to experience the need for quality information. They try to balance this need with the ethical ramifications of invading privacy rights. Failure to do so may result in long-term implications for both the company and those who use the internet to shop for products.

Ambush Marketing

The rise of dollars spent on sports sponsorships and the use of athletes as endorsers has been accompanied by a rise in **ambush marketing**, which is "a brand's attempt to associate itself with a team or event without buying the rights to do so."[21] Official sponsorships

▸ FIGURE 14.8
Recall of Olympic Sponsors

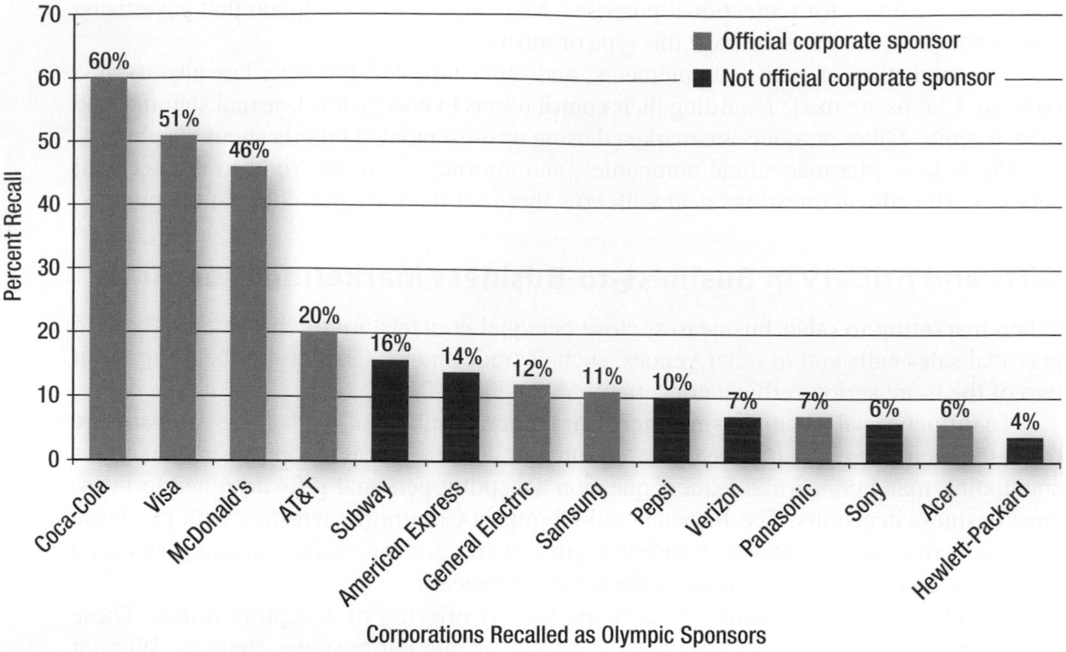

Mdestil/Fotolia

▲ Ambush marketing occurs when a brand is associated with a team or sporting event and is not an official sponsor.

often cost millions. Consequently, some firms have looked at alternative methods of capitalizing on a major sporting event without paying for the rights to be an official sponsor.

To understand the potential impact of ambush marketing, consider Figure 14.8. Chadwick Martin Bailey of Boston surveyed individuals asking them to recall the official sponsors of the Winter Olympics. In Figure 14.8, the bars in blue represent the $40 million companies paid to become official sponsors. The companies indicated by red were not official sponsors, although consumers thought they were. Some of this confusion was deliberately created. Figure 14.9 identifies the primary categories of ambush marketing.

Direct ambush marketing occurs when a firm intentionally designs an advertising or marketing campaign to capitalize on a major sporting event. The firm seeks to appear to be an official sponsor without stating whether it is or is not a sponsor. VISA was the official credit card sponsor of the Olympics. American Express was not; however, during and after the Olympics, American Express ran television commercials with scenes of Barcelona, Spain (the site of the Summer Olympics) and a message that said, "You don't need a visa" to visit Spain.

Verizon was also not an official sponsor of the Olympics, but the company ran ads stating that it was a sponsor of the U.S. speed skating team. The result of the campaign was that seven percent of viewers of the Olympics thought Verizon was a sponsor, more than some of the companies that paid the $40 million sponsorship price tag.[22]

Indirect ambush marketing occurs when a firm suggests or hints it is associated with a sporting event when it is not. With **allusion ambushing**, an organization creates an impression that it is a sponsor when it is not. During a recent Summer Olympics, Nike ran a series of ads

▸ FIGURE 14.9
Types of Ambush Marketing

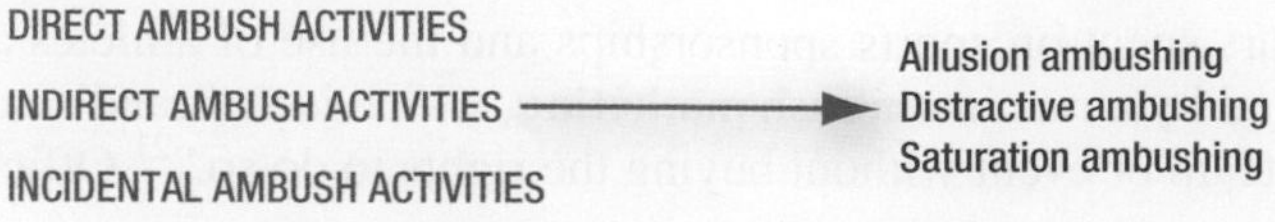

centered on the number 8, which is a symbol of good luck in China, where the games were held. Nothing was said about the Olympics or even the athletes competing in the events. **Distractive ambushing** involves a company designing a promotion or event near a major sporting event. At a recent Winter Olympics, MasterCard, which was not an official sponsor, sent two catering trucks to busy intersections in Vancouver every day to distribute cups of coffee and cocoa. As a result, MasterCard's logo was seen all over downtown Vancouver on cups and napkins. **Saturation ambushing** happens when a firm increases advertising and marketing during a major event such as the NCAA basketball tournament. No mention is made of the event, but the brand will be seen numerous times by viewers of the event, not only during but also before and after the event. This method works best when an event lasts several days such as the NCAA basketball tournament or the Olympics.[23]

Incidental ambushing takes place when consumers associate a brand with an event without any intentional or indirect effort on the part of the company. At recent collegiate swimming events as well as the Olympics, announcers have mentioned Speedo's LZR Racer swimsuit worn by swimmers. Speedo gained considerable brand exposure, but it was incidental and not planned by Speedo's marketing team.

None of these ambushing tactics are illegal; however, some question whether such approaches are ethical. Clearly, direct and indirect ambush marketing approaches capitalize on the popularity of the event without paying the price to be an official sponsor.

micromonkey/Fotolia

▲ Stealth marketing involves pitching the benefits of a brand without revealing you are paid to do so.

Stealth Marketing

Some companies have used the buzz method of **stealth marketing**. The approach entices consumers to look at a product through a personal contact without them realizing the person making the pitch is actually paid or compensated in some way.

Jonathan Margolis, CEO of the Michael Alan Group and co-author of the book *Guerilla Marketing for Dummies*, believes the risks of stealth marketing outweigh the benefits. He says, "It might work if the product is good enough, but ultimately the consumer is being duped. It's risky to stage something that people think is a natural occurrence. There is a potential for backlash. Consumers don't like being deceived, and brands don't want to look bad."[24]

A recent event illustrates why Margolis believes stealth marketing borders on being unethical. An attractive 26-year-old woman was paid by BlackBerry to go to nightclubs and bars and flirt with well-dressed men. She enticed the men to pay attention to her, handed them her BlackBerry, and asked them to put their phone numbers in the phone, with the promise she would call. She had no intention of calling; rather, she sought to show them the phone, get them to hold it, and use it while she talked about how much she loved it. Many view that level of deception as unethical.

Not all marketers agree. Jason Van Trentlyon, president of Street Guerilla Marketing, argued, "Stealth marketing has a greater potential to make a more sincere impact on the public as opposed to a TV or billboard ad. People are inundated with so many blatant advertisements on TV and in magazines that they don't pay attention anymore. This is a way of creating buzz, and any buzz is good buzz."[25]

Responding to Ethical Challenges

objective 14.7
How can marketers apply the various ethical frameworks and ethics programs to their activities and actions?

The foundation and frameworks for ethical guidelines are derived from several sources. These include philosophy, law, religion, and common sense.

One *philosophy of life* involves maximizing pleasure and minimizing pain. This idea represents **hedonism**. Critics note that life is often more than the simple pursuit of pleasure and avoidance of pain. **Homeostasis** is the natural craving for balance. People balance a variety of urges throughout life.

The **law** offers guidelines regarding right and wrong as well as what is acceptable and what is not within a geographic area. Legal systems are designed to tell people what they can and cannot do. Remember, however, that not all legal systems are the same.

Many **religions**, or belief systems, profess a version of the philosophy summarized by the *Golden Rule*: Do unto others as you would have them do unto you. Acting in a morally acceptable manner starts with treating others well. Still, specific religious ideologies vary widely. Many disagreements about what is right or wrong exist. Respect, tolerance, discussion, compromise, and accommodation should become ethical guidelines when the religious views of others contradict your own.

In general, one overriding constant may be that ethical actions, moral correctness, and social responsibility all boil down to *common sense*. Two processes can be used to analyze an ethical concept. The first is logic and reasoning, which leads to common sense conclusions. One's conscience may become muted over time if it is continually ignored; however, most people know when they are doing something right or wrong. The second element of common sense is gut instinct. Deep down inside, most people know when something is appropriate or inappropriate. A person's inner thoughts and gut reaction should never be ignored in an ethical reasoning process.

Ethics Programs

Various individuals and groups have responded to the need for a more ethical environment by creating ethics training programs, codes of ethics, and ethics consulting systems. These attempts are designed to assist individual employees, managers or supervisors, and others within a company facing ethical challenges or dilemmas.

Ethics Training Programs

Ethics training can take place at several points. Early moral training occurs in many families as part of growing up, both in secular settings and in religious organizations. Those attending college receive further instruction. The Association to Advance Collegiate Schools of Business (AACSB), a major accrediting body for schools of business, places a strong emphasis on ethics instruction for over a decade.

Many corporations now add ethics topics into new-employee training programs as well as manager training systems. Some are self-created; others are developed in conjunction with professional organizations and nearby colleges and universities.

Codes of Ethics

Codes of ethics are created in two ways. The first appears within professional organizations. In marketing, two key organizations are the American Marketing Association (AMA) and the American Academy of Advertising (AAA). The AMA code of ethics may be found on the organization's website (www.marketingpower.com).

The second way ethical codes are developed is within business organizations. Many firms have written and revised ethical codes. Figure 14.10 displays some common components of codes of ethics.

Ethics Consulting Systems

Numerous individuals and organizations are willing to provide counsel regarding ethical dilemmas. Some employ "ethics hotlines" through which a concerned employee can make contact to discuss an ethics problem. The services offered by such organizations

- The purpose of the code, including (1) regulation of behavior and (2) inspiration to employees.
- A statement of aspirations often included in a preamble that outlines the ideals a company aspires to for its employees. The statement should include the values and principles of the organization.
- A list of principles.
- A list of rules, if needed.
- A statement regarding how the code was created.
- How the code will be implemented.
- How the code will be publicized internally to employees.
- How the code will be publicized externally to constituents and publics.
- How the code will be embraced.
- A statement regarding how and when the code will be revised.
- Most of the time, values, principles, and rules are listed in order of importance.

FIGURE 14.10
Components of Codes of Ethics

vary. Some provide additional instruction, whereas others offer ethical consultations designed to build in-house ethics advisors as well as formulate codes of ethics.

Ethics and social responsibility concerns all boil down to the actions and decisions made by individuals and groups. Any person entering the fields of marketing and advertising should carefully consider what he or she considers to be acceptable and unacceptable acts prior to taking a position as well as while working within any role. The term *whistle-blower* describes an individual who is willing to go public with charges about an organization doing something that is illegal or unethical. Making the choice to be a whistle-blower is difficult; it can cause a career setback and make the individual vulnerable to lawsuits and other retaliatory actions. Failure to take action is also a choice. One's conscience and belief system provide the ultimate guides as to when and how to respond to moral issues.

International Implications

objective 14.8
What international issues influence the discussion of legal and ethical marketing activities?

Each individual country has its own set of laws regarding what is legal and what is not in the areas of marketing, promotions, and advertising. The marketing department should make sure these laws and regulations are clearly understood and companies try to comply with them. For instance, in China it is important to remember the Communist Party is always in charge. Censorship rules are vague but enforced by the Communist Party. Rules governing the internet are also vague but again can be censored and enforced by the party. Finally, trademarks belong to the first entity that registers it, not the first person or company that uses it. While pro-business, China creates ethical and legal challenges for U.S. companies.

Legal systems vary. In the United States and many Western countries, *common law* is based on local customs, traditions, and precedents. Legal history, previous cases, and national customs serve as guides, and judges typically have more discretion in making legal decisions.

Civil law, which is present in many European countries, is based on a broad set of legal principles, and decisions are made based on legal codes that have been written over time. This gives judges less flexibility.

Theocratic law is based on religious teachings. The foundation of the most common form of theocratic law, Islamic law, is the *Koran* and *Sunna*. Many Islamic countries regulate transactions in different ways. For instance, merchants cannot charge interest in an Islamic system.

Moral reasoning follows a similar pattern in international marketing. One cannot assume that a given system of ethics and morals is completely acceptable in another country. For example, views of the roles of men and women in society vary widely. Any marketing program with an international outreach should employ a cultural assimilator to help individuals understand ethical principles present in other nations.

Summary

To enforce fair standards in the areas of advertising and marketing communications, a number of governmental agencies take action when needed. These include the Federal Trade Commission, the Food and Drug Administration, the Federal Communications Commission, and others. Each tries to keep unfair marketing activities from taking place.

The primary agency regulating marketing communications, the FTC, makes special efforts to stop instances of unfair or deceptive practices. In conjunction with the courts, the FTC and other governmental agencies regulate the majority of companies and industries in the United States. The FTC regulates cases of fraudulent practices targeted at individual consumers as well as conflicts between businesses. Through the use of consent orders, administrative complaints, cease and desist orders, and full commission hearings, the FTC makes its findings and rulings known to the parties concerned. Court actions and corrective advertising programs are utilized in more severe cases. Trade regulation rulings apply when an entire industry has been found guilty of an infraction.

Ethics and morals constitute key principles that can be used to guide a person's activities in the world of commerce. Morals are beliefs or principles that individuals hold concerning what is right and what is wrong. Ethics are moral principles that serve as guidelines for both individuals and organizations.

Marketing and marketing communications activities are affected by ethical and moral concerns. Some of the more common complaints about advertising include issues of materialism and overconsumption. Also, there are criticisms that advertising perpetuates stereotypes, features unsafe products, sends out offensive messages, is deceptive, and unfairly targets children. Each of these issues requires consideration by anyone entering the profession.

Marketing programs are also subject to ethical concerns. Brand infringement, questionable medical marketing and advertising programs, business-to-business tactics, and internet marketing programs have come under scrutiny. Responses to these criticisms are the responsibility of top management, the marketing department, and those associated with public relations.

A number of ethical frameworks and guidelines are available. Those in the field of marketing may be guided by concepts regarding social responsibility. Also, ethics programs consisting of ethics training, codes of ethics, and ethics consulting systems are available to those facing dilemmas or wishing to pose questions.

The issues of legality and morality are present in the international arena as well. Each is complicated by different bodies of law and views of ethics in various nations. Companies seeking to expand internationally should be aware of these differences in order to find ways to respond to them.

Key Terms

Federal Trade Commission (FTC) A federal agency that presides over marketing communications

puffery What takes place when a firm makes an exaggerated claim about its products or services without making an overt attempt to deceive or mislead

substantiation Firms must be able to prove or back up any claims made in their marketing communications

consent order A directive issued when the FTC believes a violation has occurred

administrative complaint A formal proceeding similar to a court trial held before an administrative law judge regarding a charge filed by the FTC

corrective advertisements Ads that bring consumers back to a neutral state, so consumers once again hold beliefs they had prior to being exposed to a false or misleading advertisement

trade regulation ruling Findings that implicate an entire industry in a case of unfair or deceptive practices

morals Beliefs or principles that individuals hold concerning what is right and what is wrong

ethics Moral principles that serve as guidelines for both individuals and organizations

brand infringement Occurs when a company creates a brand name that closely resembles a popular or successful brand

ambush marketing A brand's attempt to associate itself with a team or event without buying the rights to do so

direct ambush marketing When a firm intentionally designs advertising or marketing to capitalize on a major sporting event without becoming a sponsor

indirect ambush marketing When a firm suggests or hints that it is associated with a sporting event when it is not

allusion ambushing When a firm creates an impression that it is a sponsor when it is not

distractive ambushing When a firm designs a promotion or event near a major sporting event without sponsoring the event

saturation ambushing When a firm increases advertising and marketing during a major event without mentioning or sponsoring the event

incidental ambushing A brand is associated with an event without any intentional or indirect effort on the part of the company

stealth marketing A tactic in which consumers are enticed to look at a product through a personal contact without them realizing that the person making the pitch is paid or compensated

hedonism Maximizing pleasure and minimizing pain

homeostasis The natural craving for balance

law Governmental guidelines for what is right and wrong as well as what is acceptable and what is not within a geographic area

religions Belief systems

MyMarketingLab

Go to **mymktlab.com** to complete the problems marked with this icon ✪.

Review Questions

14-1. In the United States, which organization has jurisdiction over mailed marketing materials?

14-2. How are consumers referred to in terms of rules regarding misrepresentation?

14-3. Why might the word "best" be acceptable when "better" is not?

14-4. Give an example of qualifying language in an advertisement.

14-5. If the FTC believes that a violation has been committed it will issue a consent order. What happens next?

14-6. What is a consent order and what does it mean for both parties?

14-7. If a judge issues a "cease and desist" order in the United States, what are the implications for the business?

14-8. What is a consent order?

14-9. What is an administrative complaint?

14-10. What is the purpose of a corrective advertisement?

14-11. What is a trade regulation ruling? How does it differ from other Federal Trade Commission rulings?

14-12. What is the relationship between the Council of Better Business Bureaus and the National Advertising Division?

14-13. What is the primary function of the National Advertising Review Board?

14-14. How does the Children's Advertising Review Unit operate?

14-15. Define ethics and morals.

14-16. Identify the types of ethical complaints regarding advertising.

14-17. What is brand infringement?

14-18. What types of ethical issues have been raised regarding medical marketing and advertising?

14-19. Describe the ethical issues associated with internet marketing.

14-20. Describe all of the forms of ambush marketing.

14-21. What is stealth marketing? How does it create an ethics debate?

14-22. Name the three types of ethics programs that can be used to help marketing professionals cope with moral challenges.

Critical Thinking Exercises

DISCUSSION QUESTIONS

14-23. Manufacturers of processed foods need to pay particular attention to ensuring that full ingredients are listed on the packaging. These need to be accurate and to list the ingredients in order of their weight or contribution to the overall volume of the product. Some products need to be marked as suitable for or unsuitable for particular people for religious reasons. Equally, there is a requirement to show whether the product is suitable for vegetarians, vegans, or those with allergies or intolerances. How is this managed by manufacturers in your own country? What guidelines and legal requirements are in force?

14-24. Should grossly misleading advertisements be stopped before they are ever broadcast or printed? What are the checks and balances in place in your own country to perform this task? Is it a fool-proof system?

14-25. One of the industries closely watched by the FTC is the weight-loss industry. Find three advertisements from magazines, newspapers, or television that deal with weight loss. What claims were made? Do you believe the claims are truthful and legitimate? How do you, as a consumer, distinguish between what is truthful and what is deceptive?

✪ **14-26.** Advertising directed toward children remains a hot topic among parents and educators. Many feel that advertising unfairly targets children and creates materialistic desires. By the time a child is three years old, she already knows many brands of products, such as McDonald's. What is your opinion of advertising to children? Is the current regulation enough, or should it be more stringent?

14-27. One of the criticisms of advertising is that it causes people to buy more than they can afford. Each year, a large number of people in United States declare bankruptcy, often because they have overspent. Do you agree that advertising causes people to buy more than they can afford, or is advertising just responding to the materialistic desire of individuals? Defend your response.

✪ **14-28.** Advertising does increase the cost of goods and services, but a common defense is that advertising provides people with knowledge about availability of products, which allows consumers to make more intelligent decisions. Do you think this is a valid defense of advertising? Why support the importance of advertising? What other defense could you offer to support the importance of advertising?

14-29. Think about advertisements you have seen or heard recently and identify one that you believe is offensive. Why was it offensive? Why do you think the advertiser ran the ad if it is offensive? Do you think offensive ads can be effective? Why or why not?

14-30. What is your opinion of alcohol and tobacco advertising? Should alcohol and tobacco companies have the same freedom to advertise as other product manufacturers? Do you think it is a danger for children to see alcohol or tobacco ads? Does it influence their desire to use these products?

14-31. Using sex to sell products is another area that many consumers find offensive. Locate two print ads or ads on television that are highly sexual in nature, one that you consider offensive and one that you consider is appropriate. What makes the difference? Are there too many ads that use sexual themes?

14-32. You have seen advertisements by attorneys and medical professionals. Discuss your opinion about these advertisements? Do you think ads by attorneys just increase the number of lawsuits and bankruptcies? Why do medical professionals such as doctors and dentists advertise? Does it affect your opinion of their professionalism? Why or why not?

14-33. Do you believe that ethics can be learned, or is it something an individual has internally? Why or why not? Suppose a company has hired you to teach ethics to its employees. Discuss the concepts of hedonism, homeostasis, law, religion, and common sense as it would relate to teaching a seminar to new employees on ethics. How would ethics training, code of ethics, and an ethics consulting system be used as part of the training class?

Integrated Learning Exercises

14-34. In most countries there is a statutory body or a self-managing organization charged with the responsibility of policing marketing and advertising. Find the website of the one in your country and study the scope of its work and the sanctions it can impose.

14-35. The FTC's Bureau of Consumer Protection works for the consumer to prevent fraud, deception, and unfair business practices in the marketplace. Access the FTC's website at **www.ftc.gov** and go to the Consumer Protection section of the site. What information is available? Find an article or recent event from the website and write a short report. How does the FTC's Bureau of Consumer Protection safeguard consumers?

14-36. Access the FTC's website at **www.ftc.gov**. Access each of the following components of the website. What type of information does each section contain? Why is it important?

a. Competition
b. Economics
c. Policy

14-37. One of the primary functions of the FTC is to investigate possible false and deceptive advertising and marketing practices. Access the FTC website at **www.ftc.gov**. Go to the "Actions" section of the site. Read through the list of recent actions. Find two that are interesting. Review the cases and write a brief report on each case. What were the results of the FTC investigation?

14-38. Access the FTC website at **www.ftc.gov**. Go to the "News" section of the website. Read through the list of recent actions. Find two that are interesting. Review the cases and write a brief report on each case. What were the results of the FTC investigation?

14-39. The Council of Better Business Bureaus is an important industry organization for businesses as well as consumers. Access the website at **www.bbb.org**. What information is available on the site? Go to the "Consumer" section of the website. How can the BBB assist consumers? What types of information is available to consumers?

14-40. Access the website of the Council of Better Business Bureaus at **www.bbb.org**. Go to the "Business" section of the website. What information is available? Briefly describe each component of the "Business" section of the website and how it may benefit a business.

14-41. The National Advertising Division (NAD) of the Council of Better Business Bureaus can be found at **www.nadreview.org**. Access the site. Look through the recent cases the NAD has investigated. Find two of interest to you. Write a report about each case, discussing the issues and the findings of the NAD.

14-42. The Children's Advertising Review Unit (CARU) of the Better Business Bureau can be found at **www.caru.org**. Access the site. Look through the recent cases the CARU has investigated. Find two of interest to you. Write a report about each case discussing the issues and the findings of the CARU.

14-43. Protecting the privacy of children is an important function of the Children's Advertising Review Unit (CARU). Access the CARU website at **www.caru.org**. Go to the "Privacy Program" component of the site. Discuss the information that is available on the site. How does this protect children? How is it beneficial to parents?

Blog Exercises

Access the authors' blog for this textbook at the URLs provided to complete these exercises. Answer the questions that are posed on the blog.

14-44. Reebok – **http://blogclowbaack.net/2014/04/24/reebok-chapter-14-2/**

14-45. Federal Trade Commission – **http://blogclowbaack.net/2014/04/24/federal-trade-commission-chapter-14/**

14-46. Better Business Bureau - **http://blogclowbaack.net/2014/04/28/bbb-chapter-14/**

Student Project

CREATIVE CORNER

Solidax ADX was developed in the United States in 2005 and was recently rated by the Weight Loss Institute to be the best weight-loss product on the market. Solidax ADX is based on synephrine, chromium picolinate, and pyrovate and is designed to suppress appetite and increase metabolism and calorie expenditure. Unlike other diet pills, it does not have negative central nervous effects. The ingredients found in Solidax have been proven to be effective in controlled, laboratory-based human weight-loss studies.[26]

Concerned about recent FTC investigations of false and deceptive advertising of competing brands, the makers of Solidax ADX want a print ad that will be effective but not subject to FTC investigation. Based on the information provided, design a print advertisement for Solidax ADX.

CASE 1 THE TRUTH ABOUT YOGURT

You don't have to look far to discover that many health professionals believe in the health benefits of yogurt. Elaine Magee, writing for WebMD, notes that, "our body needs to have a healthy amount of 'good' bacteria in the digestive tract, and many yogurts are made using active, good bacteria." Yogurt contains probiotics, or the good bacteria that promotes healthy digestion. Yogurt also contains protein, which helps prevent osteoporosis, and Vitamin D, which provides additional skeletal benefits.[27]

So how does a company get in trouble promoting the health benefits of yogurt? By overstating its advantages over the competition. Dannon, which produces Activia and DanActive, recently paid $45 million in a class action lawsuit to settle complaints regarding its advertising. The company's commercials suggested that the products were "clinically" and "scientifically" proven to regulate digestion and boost immune systems in campaigns featuring actress Jamie Lee Curtis, who called the yogurt "tasty." ABC News noted that, "Both yogurts sell at a 30 percent premium over other brands because they claim special bacterial ingredients that the company advertised as clinically proven to help strengthen immune systems and regulate digestion."

Art Allianz/Fotolia

▲ A female consumer examining various brands of yogurt.

"This was a disingenuous advertising campaign that promised something that hasn't been proven," Dr. Roshini Rajapaksa, a gastroenterologist, told ABC News. John Climaco, one of the two attorneys who brought the suit, reported, "The judge agreed that the company was making claims it simply hadn't proven."[28]

Dannon's executive team disputed the court's findings, stating that the company settled to avoid the cost and distraction of litigation. Further, "The lawsuit claims the advertising was not true. Dannon stands by its advertising and denies it did anything wrong."

Still, the terms of the settlement required Dannon to remove the words "clinically" and "scientifically proven" from product labels and advertisements. Instead, the words "clinical studies show," or something similar, could be substituted. The court also required the company to say that Activia and DanActive yogurts are food rather than treatments or cures for medical disorders or diseases. The company was forced to remove the word "immunity" from DanActive labels and ads. Also, the firm was told to include a qualifier to the advertising claim the yogurt "helps strengthen your body's defenses" or "helps support the immune system." Such a statement only pertains, "when (the products are) eaten regularly as part of a balanced diet and healthy lifestyle," according to the judge's order. "This is victory for just about anyone who benefits from accuracy in food labeling," attorney Climaco concluded.[29]

14-47. How do the concepts of deception, puffery, and substantiation apply to this case?

14-48. Could Dannon's executive team have avoided such an expensive outcome? If so, how?

14-49. Do you agree that the term "clinical studies show" is significantly different than, "scientifically proven" or "clinically proven"? Should the judge have been more specific about what wording could or could not be used?

14-50. What ethical or moral guidelines, if any, did Dannon violate?

14-51. What role should advertising and marketing communications play in explaining the health benefits of basic products such as yogurt?

CASE 2 ASSESSING SMART CHOICES

One continuing trend in the United States is an interest in the content of food products. Many consumers want to buy foods that promote good health and nutrition. One recent effort that generated a substantial amount of controversy was the Smart Choices Program, which was created by the nonprofit American Society of Nutrition. Ten large food manufacturers enrolled in the program, including Kellogg's and Kraft.

Monkey Business/Fotolia

▲ The Smart Choice endorsement suggests a nutritional healthy product.

Under the system, a food product had to meet a specific set of guidelines to qualify for the Smart Choices endorsement. The system was based on the federal Dietary Guidelines for Americans developed by a conglomerate of food industry leaders, academics, nutritionists, and public interest organizations. Accepted products received permission to print a front-of-package or front-of-box label, in the form of a large green checkmark, with the phrase "Smart Choices Program and Guiding Food Choices" underneath. The logo clearly suggested an endorsement of a nutritional program, and many critics believed consumers would interpret the label as carrying a governmental stamp of approval.

Any company wishing to place the Smart Choices label and logo was required to pay up to $100,000 per year for the right to do so. Quickly, manufacturers of a series of foods, including sugary cereals, snacks, and sandwich spreads, paid the money. Among the products that featured the endorsement were Fruit Loops, Kid Cuisine Cheeseburgers, Teddy Grahams, and Kraft Macaroni and Cheese. And as one industry observed noted, the more products receiving the label, the greater the amount of money the American Society of Nutrition was able to collect from a food producer.

It did not take long for the reactions to grow strong. Following a *CBS Evening News* report and other exposures in various media, companies began to withdraw support for the Smart Choices Program logo. Charges were raised that conflicts of interest could not be avoided using the system as it had been implemented. The Food and Drug Administration (FDA) issued a Guidance for Industry letter in October, 2010. The agency announced that it would analyze food labels with the intent of identifying any that might be misleading. The FDA also announced it would develop a universal front-of-packaging labeling system that all food manufacturers must follow. The FDA did not name the Smart Choices Program specifically in the letter, but the program subsequently decided to suspend the use of the logo.

The Friedman Sprout, which is the official student newspaper for the Friedman School for Nutrition Science and Policy, published an article wondering if the school's reputation had been damaged by the involvement of the school's dean with The American Society of Nutrition.

The American Society of Nutrition continues operations. Its chief officer remains with the organization. The organization has announced intentions to follow new FDA guidelines for labels on packages and to become re-involved with the food manufacturers that had originally participated in the program.[30,31]

14-52. Why would the FDA become involved in this situation? What legal standard might have been violated?

14-53. What actions could the FDA have taken beyond writing a Guidance for Industry letter?

14-54. Do you believe the American Society of Nutrition violated any ethical standards? If so, which ones?

14-55. Do you believe the food manufacturers that sold sugary cereals and junk food carrying the Smart Choices Program label violated any ethical standards? If so, which ones? Explain.

14-56. Should the food manufacturers continue associating with the American Society of Nutrition? Why or why not?

14-57. Do you believe the dean of the School for Nutrition Science and Policy violated any ethical standards? If so, which ones? Explain.

MyMarketingLab

Go to **mymktlab.com** for the following Assisted-graded writing questions:

14-58. Do you believe that ethics can be learned, or is it something an individual has internally? Why or why not? Suppose a company has hired you to teach ethics to its employees. Discuss the concepts of hedonism, homeostasis, law, religion, and common sense as it would relate to teaching a seminar to new employees on ethics. How would ethics training, code of ethics, and an ethics consulting system be used as part of the training class?

14-59. Protecting the privacy of children is an important function of the Children's Advertising Review Unit (CARU). Access the CARU website at **www.caru.org**. Go to the "Privacy Program" component of the site. Discuss the information available on the site. How does this protect children? How is it beneficial to parents?

Chapter 15 Evaluating an Integrated Marketing Program

Chapter Objectives

After reading this chapter, you should be able to answer the following questions:

15.1 What are the three broad categories of evaluation tools used to evaluate IMC systems?

15.2 How do marketing teams match evaluation methods with IMC objectives?

15.3 What forms of message evaluations can be conducted to assess IMC programs?

15.4 Which evaluation criteria are suggested by the positioning advertising copytesting (PACT) system?

15.5 How do online evaluation systems assist advertising managers in assessing the quality of a firm's internet activities?

15.6 What types of behavioral evaluations can be employed to assess IMC programs?

15.7 What criteria should be used to assess the overall IMC program?

15.8 How are evaluation programs adjusted to match international operations?

Overview

John Wanamaker, a well-known nineteenth-century department store owner, was among the first to use advertising to attract customers to his store. He once remarked, "I know half the money I spend on advertising is wasted, but I can never find out which half." Evaluating the effectiveness of advertising has become increasingly difficult. In today's environment, company executives demand measurable results because of the high costs of advertising campaigns. The challenge for advertising account executives and others who prepare ads continues to be offering evidence that those campaigns are successful.

To meet the growing insistence for accountability, research and media experts spend time and energy seeking to develop new and accurate measures of success. These measures, known as **metrics**, attempt to accurately portray the effectiveness of a marketing communications plan, which may not be easy.

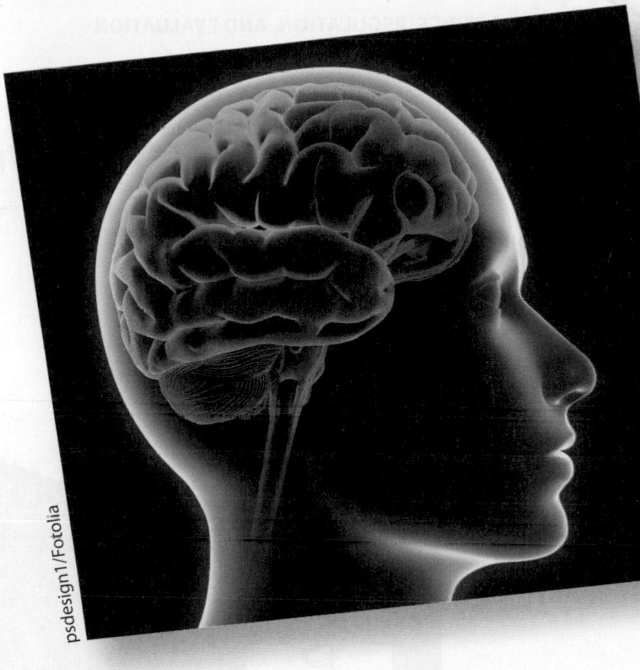
psdesign1/Fotolia

SANDS RESEARCH, INC.

Neuromarketing on the Cutting Edge

If any one theme emerges from the interviews with members of the various advertising agencies featured in this textbook, it would be that company executives demand clear and convincing evidence that marketing and advertising actually work. Tangible measures such as increases in store traffic, website hits, coupon redemptions, and sales provide behavioral evidence. Many times other factors influence these outcomes, and a lag occurs between the time the advertisement was run until any corresponding behavior resulted.

Advertising agencies continue to look for methods to refine the development and delivery of marketing messages. Several techniques exist, including recall tests and studies of brand perceptions and loyalty. Finding real-time data suggesting that an advertisement has captured and kept a viewer's attention is what remains.

Sands Research, Inc., led by its chairman and chief science officer, Dr. Steve Sands, is a leading neuromarketing firm. The company pioneered developments in applications that draw on cognitive neuroscience technology to provide unique insights into consumer responses to television and print advertisements, product packaging, and digital media. By combining its technology with before-and-after-questionnaires, Sands Research provides a comprehensive, objective analysis of the viewer's engagement in the marketing material presented by an advertiser.

Recently, Dr. Sands announced a breakthrough in the rapidly growing area of applying neuroscience to market research. Sands Research uses high-density arrays of EEG (electroencephalograph) sensors to capture brainwave activity across the full brain at 10,000 times a second, per sensor. In essence, this means the firm has the ability to study the impact a message has on capturing a person's attention and track times of peak interest as the person stays engaged with that message.

Traditional methods designed to analyze the impact of an advertisement with rating statements and open-ended questions tend to be verbally biased. They may also fail to completely measure the impact of the nonverbal components of commercials, including music and visuals. Creative people have long suspected that traditional research approaches, such as recall testing, unfairly reward overly rational advertising and penalize emotional executions.

Research suggests that when commercials quickly capture attention, they tend to generate more "peak" moments during the run. Peak moments of attention increase positive feelings toward commercials and potentially influence recall. Peaks are likely to occur when:

- Important news is provided; for example, the announcement of a strong price promotion.
- Inciting incidents appear, typically those involving a moment strongly charged with negative emotion to set up a joke or storyline.
- Surprising moments or turning points in stories take place.
- The delivery of climatic moments or punch lines occurs.

The value of these new techniques may be enhanced through the understanding that three different memory systems may be involved in developing a person's view of a brand: knowledge memories, emotion or episodic memories, and action or procedural memories of bodily experiences and physical sensations. Evidence from these studies suggests that these memories might be stored in different parts of the brain. Consequently, a rational and verbal memory might be reported, but emotional or episodic memories may not. This would explain the underreporting of the impact of musical and visual cues in advertisements.

The full impact of these new technologies has yet to be realized. At the least, Sands Research suggests the company can help an advertiser create an advertisement with the greatest potential for capturing attention from storyboard to the run of the commercial. And, an exciting new era in marketing measurement may be well underway.[1]

▶ This advertisement for Scott Equipment could be evaluated using message evaluation techniques, such as ad recall or attitudes toward the message

Courtesy French Creative

This chapter considers the methods available for evaluating components of an IMC program. Three broad categories of evaluation tools can be used to evaluate IMC systems: message evaluations, online evaluations, and respondent behavior evaluations.

Evaluation Metrics

objective 15.1

What are the three broad categories of evaluation tools used to evaluate IMC systems?

Three primary metrics may be used to evaluate marketing communications (see Figure 15.1). **Message evaluation techniques** examine the message and the physical design of the advertisement, coupon, or direct marketing piece. Message evaluation procedures include the study of actors in advertisements as well as the individuals who speak in radio ads. A message evaluation program reviews the cognitive components associated with an ad, such as recall and recognition, as well as emotional, attitudinal, and behavioral intention responses.

Online evaluation metrics examine online advertising and marketing campaigns. The internet provides a unique set of metrics and techniques that are not available for traditional media. In addition to click-throughs, marketers can track such metrics as dwell rate and dwell time. The internet provides highly accurate, real-time measures of consumer reactions.

Respondent behavior evaluations address visible customer actions, including store visits, inquiries, or actual purchases. This category contains evaluation technique measures that feature numbers such as the amount of coupons redeemed, hits on a website, and changes in sales.

- Message evaluation techniques
- Online evaluation metrics
- Respondent behavior evaluations

▲ **FIGURE 15.1**
Primary Metrics Used to Evaluate Marketing Communications

The emphasis on providing compelling proof that advertising actually works has led to a greater emphasis on respondent behaviors. Higher sales, increases in store traffic, a greater number of daily hits on a website, and other numbers-based outcomes appeal to many managers. At the same time, message evaluations, online metrics, and behavioral responses help the marketing manager and advertising team build short-term results and achieve long-term success.

Matching Methods with IMC Objectives

objective 15.2

How do marketing teams match evaluation methods with IMC objectives?

Marketers choose methods of evaluation that match the objectives to be measured.[2] An advertising campaign with the objective of increasing customer interest in and recall of a brand will be assessed using the level of customer awareness as the metric. Normally, this means the marketing team measures awareness before, during, and after the ads have run. At other times, objectives focus on customer actions. Redemption rates can measure the success of a campaign featuring coupons.

Several levels are used to analyze an advertising or IMC program. They include:

- Short-term outcomes (sales, redemption rates)
- Long-term results (brand awareness, brand loyalty, or brand equity)
- Product- and brand-specific awareness
- Awareness of the overall company
- Affective responses (liking the company and a positive brand image)

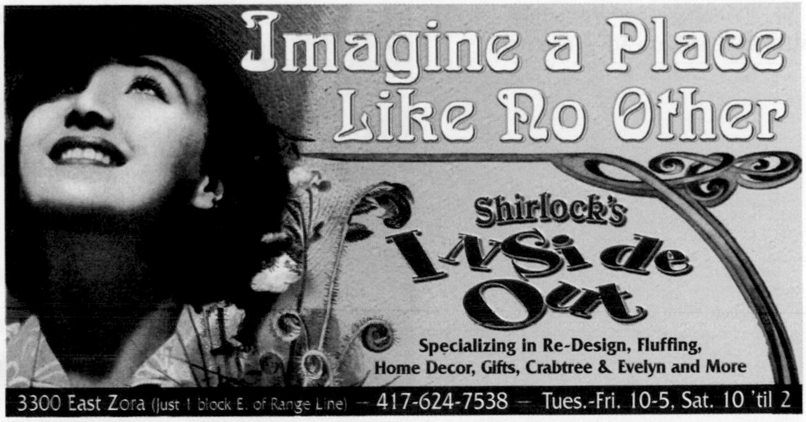

Joplin Globe

▲ A number of extraneous events might affect the impact of this ad for Shirlock's Inside Out advertisement.

The temptation sometimes arises to overemphasize the first factor, short-term outcomes, without considering the long-term impact of a campaign or marketing program. The company's marketing team endeavors to maintain a voice that carries across campaigns over time.

In light of the overall marketing and advertising goals, the marketing manager then considers the various options for evaluating advertising. Selection of evaluation procedures takes place prior to launching a campaign. An advertisement placed in a trade journal can contain a code number, a special telephone number, or a special internet microsite to track responses. For coupons, premiums, and other sales promotions, code numbers are printed on each item to identify the source.

In general, careful planning prior to initiating an IMC program allows the evaluation of the campaign to be easier and more accurate. At the same time, the evaluation of a specific advertisement or marketing piece may be difficult, because many factors can affect the outcome being measured. For instance, a retailer may run a series of newspaper and radio ads to boost store traffic. In order to measure the impact of the ads, the retailer keeps records of store traffic before, during, and after the campaign. Unfortunately, the traffic count might be affected by various factors, even something as simple as the weather. If it rains for two days, the traffic count will be lower. Further, the store's chief competitor may run a special sale during the same time period, which also affects traffic. A TV program, such as the season finale of a major series, or even a special program at the local high school (commencement, school play), could have an impact. In other words, many extraneous factors could affect results. When reviewing an advertising program, marketing professionals consider these factors.

Performing one analysis normally does not adequately assess the influence of the impact of marketing communications on a company's image. Even though store traffic was low, the ad may have been stored in the buyer's long-term memory, which may make a difference later. Conversely, the same ad may have been awkward or offensive in some way. The store owner might believe the weather affected the outcome instead of a poor advertising design. Consequently, company leaders consider short- and long-term implications when assessing an IMC program.

Message Evaluations

objective 15.3
What forms of message evaluations can be conducted to assess IMC programs?

Evaluation or testing of advertising communications occurs at every stage of the development process. This includes the concept stage before an advertisement is produced. Testing at that stage often involves soliciting the opinions of a series of experts or from "regular" people. Ads can be tested after completion of the design stage but prior to development. Advertising creatives often design television commercials using a storyboard such as the one shown on the next page for Interstate Batteries. Print ads can be analyzed using artist sketches.

▶ A storyboard for an Interstate Batteries television advertisement.

Jane Koenecke/Interstate Batteries

Although ads and marketing pieces can be tested prior to production, most advertising agencies perform a small amount of pretesting, primarily due to the lack of reliable test results. Elena Petukhova from The Richards Group advertising agency notes that, "We really don't trust the results of pretests using boards because the format makes a difference. Consumers are used to seeing the finished product, so when you show them a mockup or sketch, they tend not to see it very positively. It is difficult for them to make the transition to what the ad will look like after production, and in their minds they compare it to finished ads, which produce low evaluation scores. Whenever possible, we wait until after production to test ads."[3]

As shown in Figure 15.2, individual companies and advertising agencies employ three primary methods to evaluate advertising campaign messages: advertising tracking research, copytesting, and emotional reaction tests. Each fits differing circumstances, advertising methods, and IMC objectives. For the future, a promising method of advertising evaluation involves cognitive neuroscience.

Advertising Tracking Research

One common method of evaluation involves tracking an advertisement by one of the major advertising research firms, such as Nielsen IAG or Millward Brown. Tracking research examines ads that have launched. This in-market research method monitors a brand's performance and advertising effectiveness. Tests are performed at specific times or intervals or continuously. Ad tracking provides a general measure of the effect of the

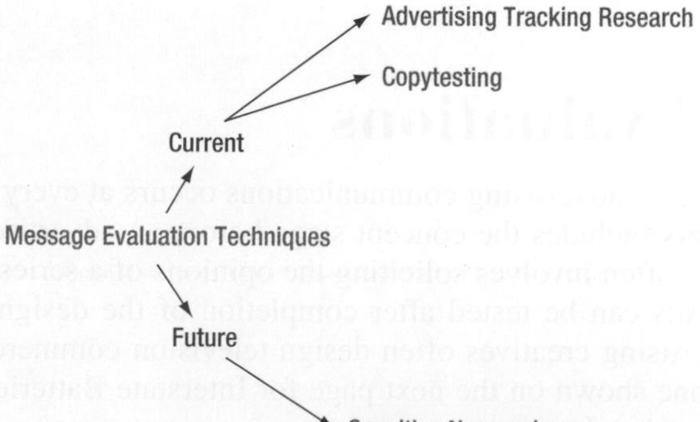

▶ **FIGURE 15.2**
Evaluating Advertising Messages

media weight (i.e., spending level), the effectiveness of the media buys, and the quality of the ad's message and execution. Ad tracking examines the relative impact of a message compared to the competition and over time.

Nielsen IAG provides ad tracking. The company offers a syndicated database of real-time brand and ad performance tracking based on more than 210,000 television program episodes and 250,000 commercials. In addition to television ads, the service applies to the evaluation of internet ads and in-cinema campaigns. Nielsen conducts thousands of surveys daily measuring viewer engagement with TV programs and the effectiveness of each advertisement on network and cable television channels.[4]

mcgarrybowen

▲ Marketers for Maxwell House coffee might take advantage of ad tracking research to measure the success of the "Stay Grounded" ad campaign.

Ad Tracking Methodology With ad tracking, research respondents are usually shown a brief portion of an advertisement or a few stills from a TV ad with the brand name removed or not visible. Researchers ask respondents if they recognize the company, which measures brand and ad recognition. Subjects are then asked to identify the brand being advertised, which measures unaided brand awareness. Those that cannot correctly identify the sponsor are given a list of brands and asked to identify the correct brand, which measures aided brand awareness. In addition to recognition and unaided and aided brand awareness, tracking research also measures:

- Memorability
- Likeability
- Unaided and aided message recall
- Unaided and aided campaign recall

Similar techniques are available for magazines. Mediamark Research & Intelligence's AdMeasure tracks recall and response to advertisements in every issue of 200 magazine titles. Affinity offers a competing service, the American Magazine Study Print Ad Ratings, which contains ad measurements across 125 magazine titles.[5]

When the mcgarrybowen agency created a campaign for Burger King, employees engaged in ad tracking to measure the brand's impression score. Both Burger King and its primary rival were measured with YouGov Brandindex's impression score which asks respondents, "Do you have a general positive feeling about the brand?" Prior to the campaign launch, Burger King's impression score was 24.4 compared to McDonald's score of 48.9. During the campaign, Burger King's score rose to a high of 45.1 then dropped at the end to 38.4. At the same time, McDonald's impression score fell to 34.8. By assessing these results before, during, and after the campaign, marketers from Burger King and mcgarrybowen were able to obtain more accurate measures of the campaign's effectiveness in creating a more positive impression of the restaurant chain.[6]

Report Cards and Benchmarks Dave Snell of The Richards Group reported the information provided by Nielsen IAG offers a continuous "report card" as well as a "benchmark." During the second or third week of a new campaign, ad tracking research provides two types of information about a new advertisement's performance. First, it shows how the new ad performs in comparison to the brand's competitors. Second, it indicates how well the advertisement performed in relation to those from previous campaigns.

Nielsen IAG also builds a benchmark for a company as it measures ad performance over months and years. These benchmark data are especially valuable when a new campaign

Kirtan Patel/Philadelphia Cream Cheese

▲ Ad tracking can help marketers for Philadelphia Cream Cheese detect when wear out begins to occur.

launches. Advertisers compare new messages to previous ones along various dimensions to ensure the commercials performed as expected. The benchmark from previous ads provides a better indicator of performance than comparisons with competitors or ads for similar products.

Tracking services also "help us to know when wear-out is beginning to set in," says Dave Snell. Measuring the advertisement's effectiveness on a biweekly basis and graphing those measures indicate when an advertisement starts to lose its impact. At that point, the agency and client can switch to a new campaign, bring back a previous ad, or modify the current commercial.

The Richards Group's Elena Petukhova notes that ad tracking includes the disadvantage of failing to provide any diagnostics. The data indicate how the ad performs in relation to the competition, against previous ads, and over time. They do not yield information regarding the reasons an advertisement did not perform well. Other types of research explore the reasons why an advertisement failed. In essence, ad tracking research indicates when an advertisement has worn out or is not performing, but it does not tell the agency what to do.

Copytesting

The second form of message evaluation, **copytests**, assesses the finished marketing piece or one in the final stages of development. Copytesting elicits responses to the main message of the advertisement as well as the presentation format. Television and print ads have long been evaluated using copytesting procedures. Online print and video ads were seldom copytested, but that trend is changing. According to Jeff Cox, CEO of ARS Group which performs copytesting, about 75 percent of the firm's clients now test at least some of their digital ads during development.[7]

Common copytesting techniques include portfolio tests, theater tests, and online tests. A **portfolio test** displays a set of print ads containing the one being evaluated. A **theater test** displays a set of television ads, including the one being studied. The individuals who participate do not know which piece is under scrutiny. Both techniques mimic reality in the sense that consumers normally are exposed to multiple messages, such as when a radio or television station plays a series of commercials in a row or when a set of newspaper ads appears on a single page. The tests also allow researchers to compare the target piece with other marketing messages. For these approaches to produce the optimal findings, all of the marketing pieces shown must be in the same stage of development, such as preproduction ads or finished ads.

Internet copytesting can replace both the portfolio and theater tests. Online copytesting costs less and provides more immediate results. The Millward Brown advertising firm features online testing procedures, including copytesting. Typically, an agency client performs copytests five to eight times per year. The tests deliver information regarding the in-depth potential of an ad under ideal circumstances. When they are conducted online, consumers pay more attention to the ad than they would for a television show, radio program, or while reading a magazine. Therefore, copytesting results offer a measure of the advertisement's potential when it receives the viewer's complete attention.

Copytesting follows finished ads that have already been launched. Millward Brown typically studies the ad using 150 respondents. Quantitative questions address issues such as:

- Breakthrough ability
- The brand message and image

- The level of the ad and brand memory
- Levels of enjoyment
- What the ad communicates
- How well the intended message was communicated
- Potential responses (i.e., likelihood of making a purchase)
- Persuasive power of the advertisement
- Engagement of the viewer with the ad and brand

Testing Emotional Reactions In addition to these measures, Millward Brown prepares a second-by-second emotional reaction chart that indicates how viewers feel about an advertisement to be shown on television. As they watch the commercial on a computer screen, respondents move the computer mouse to indicate their feelings—one direction for positive feelings and the other direction for negative feelings. By superimposing these 150 emotional reaction tests onto one graph, the client sees how the feelings and emotions of the respondents change throughout the commercial. This information has value because it indicates points at which emotions turn. Although the test does not measure the level of emotion but rather changes in emotion, these data provide sufficient evidence for the agency to develop hypotheses or best practice ideas to assist in making future advertisements.

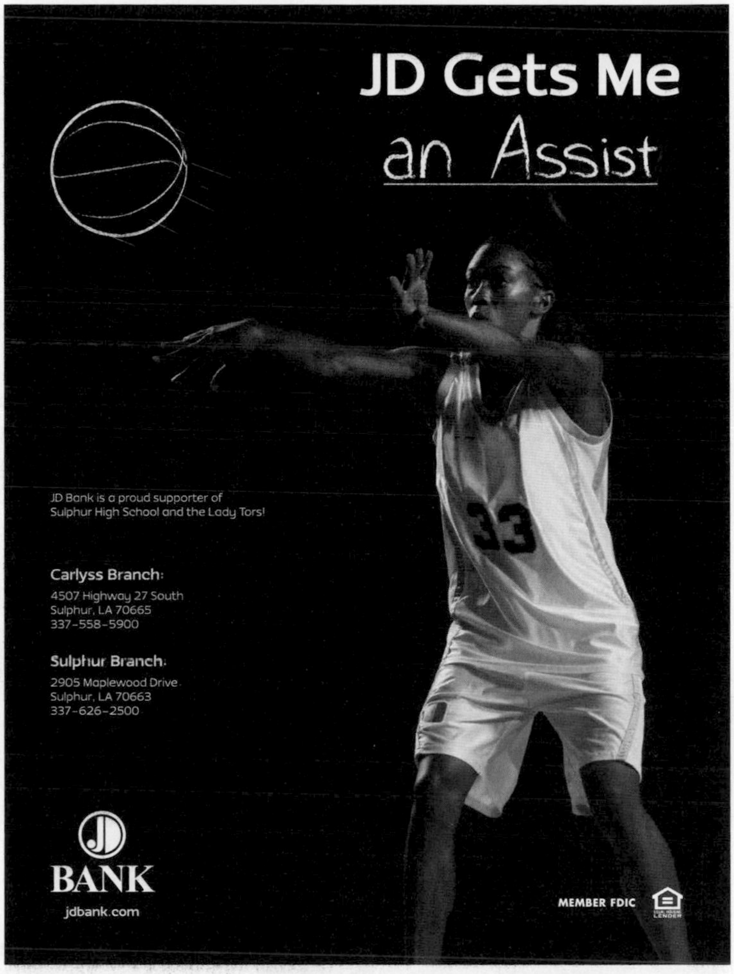

JD Bank

▲ Emotional reaction tests provide valuable information to advertising agencies and brand managers.

Verbatim Comments The final pieces of information provided to clients by Millward Brown and other agencies are the verbatim comments of the respondents. Each respondent presents, in his or her own words, thoughts about the advertisement. According to Dave Snell from The Richards Group, "These verbatim comments are extremely valuable to us because they provide a written commentary on what people think about the ad and what thoughts are foremost from watching the ad."[8] Millward Brown asks a number of open-ended questions to engage respondents and gain a deeper understanding of their thought processes. The research team also requests respondents to tell the story of the ad, which provides additional valuable insights. The Richards Group's Elena Petukhova commented that, "It can tell you a lot about the ad, both positive and negative. It tells you what the customer sees and thinks and how the ad story came across to them."[9]

As noted previously, ad tracking does not generate information regarding the reasons an ad did not perform well or what to do to correct it. Copytesting procedures can generate some of this information. Advertising creatives can then determine what to do next. By using continuous ad tracking and copytesting, an agency builds a benchmark for a particular client on an advertisement's performance. The agency also gains insights into what works and what does not work for consumers for that particular product category and brand.

Copytesting Controversies Controversies regarding copytesting remain. A number of advertisers and marketers strongly believe the method favors rational approaches over affective and conative (action-inspiring) methods. To correct this potential deficiency, some research firms add emotional tests to copytesting procedures.

Further, some marketers believe copytesting prior to production stifles the creativity needed to produce ads that will stand out in the clutter. Recently, creatives working for brands—including Nike, Volkswagen, Budweiser, and Target—have been allowed to skip the copytesting phase of advertising design and move straight into production. When the agency Wieden + Kennedy created "the man your man could smell like" campaign for Old Spice cologne, the brand's parent firm Procter & Gamble allowed Wieden to skip the concept testing stage completely. Also, the approval process for the Old Spice campaign was streamlined to just one P&G executive.[10]

Unless the client insists on preproduction copytests, agencies now move directly into production and perform the tests after the ad launches. Many advertisers believe copytests are likely to lead creatives to design ad messages about the product benefits that are believable and understandable to members of a focus group or panel. Many consumers in focus groups know little, if anything, about how to create an effective advertisement. Most creatives believe it does not make sense to have them serve as final judges of an advertisement's quality.

Although a number of marketing professionals do not favor using copytests at all, the majority believe they are necessary, primarily due to accountability issues. Jeff Cox, CEO of copytesting agency ARS Group, argues that, "Copytesting can squelch creative, but the marketplace and the world's largest advertisers see value in doing this."[11] When the time comes to support a decision for a high-dollar advertising campaign, advertising agency and company executives want evidence that supports the investment. Also, advertising agencies can use the results of copytesting to perfect future ads and campaigns by understanding what works and what does not work in a given marketplace.

▼ Emotional reaction tests provide valuable information to advertisers, such as Progressive Bank.

French Creative

Emotional Reaction Tests

Many advertisements seek to elicit emotional responses from consumers. Emotional ads are based on the concept that messages eliciting positive feelings are more likely to be remembered. Also, consumers who have positive attitudes toward ads develop more favorable attitudes regarding the product. This, in turn, should result in increased purchases.[12]

Measuring the emotional impact of an advertisement can be difficult. The simplest method involves asking about an individual's feelings and emotions after viewing a marketing communication piece. An alternative method, a **warmth monitor**, relies on the notion that feelings of warmth are positive when they are directed toward an ad or a product. To measure warmth, subjects are asked to manipulate a joystick or the mouse on a computer while watching a commercial, moving one direction for warmer and another for cooler.[13]

Members of the faculty at the University of Hawaii developed the first warmth meter. Individuals viewed advertisements in a theater-type lab featuring a big-screen television. Those who felt negatively about what they were watching pulled a joystick downward. Those who felt more positively pushed the joystick in the opposite direction. As they watched a commercial, the subjects constantly moved the joystick, thereby conveying their feelings during every moment of the ad. The results of the 20 participants were tallied into one graph and then placed over the commercial. This technology allowed the advertiser to see the parts of the message that elicited positive emotions and which parts elicited negative emotions.[14]

Reactions and Opinions designed a similar technology for use on the internet. The company can easily poll 1,000 or more people who view an advertisement online. As individuals watch the ad on streaming video, the participants use a mouse to move a tab on a sliding scale from 1 to 10. When they like what they see, they slide the tab toward the 10. Those who do not like what they see slide the tab toward the 1. After the data have been collected, a graph will be superimposed over the advertisement to indicate the likable and dislikable parts of the message. The internet offers the advantage of allowing subjects to provide ratings at their convenience. If the agency needs a focus group to discuss the ad, subjects can be selected from the participants. The focus group session can also be held online.[15]

Another approach to measuring emotional reactions, **biometric research**, involves measuring physiological reactions to advertisements and marketing messages. The Innerscope company specializes in biometric research. Carl Marci, CEO and chief science officer stated that, "Innerscope strongly believes that unconscious emotional responses direct attention, enhance learning, and memory, and ultimately drive behaviors that our clients care about." Innerscope puts test subjects in a living room setting. A device on the television tracks eye movement to track the subject's attention to stimuli. At the same time, a special belt worn by the subject collects data regarding the person's heartbeat, perspiration levels, respiration, and body movements. By integrating all of these biological measures, Innerscope measures the level of emotional engagement of viewers during every second of the ad via their emotional, unconscious responses to what they see.[16]

Time Warner built a 9,600-square-foot media lab in Manhattan for its own operation but also leases to clients for biometric research. The cost ranges from $50,000 for basic focus groups to $120,000 for research featuring biometrics. The company makes biometric belts available to measure physiological reactions to ads. Cameras measure eye movements and two-way mirrors allow for client observation.[17] Rather than rely on consumers telling researchers how they are reacting via some type of warmth meters, biometrics measure actual emotional reactions. Individuals can lie about how they feel with a warmth meter, but bodily reactions to ads are more difficult to fake.

Cognitive Neuroscience

In recent years, significant advances have occurred in **cognitive neuroscience**, a brain-image measurement process that tracks brain activity. As noted in the opening vignette for this chapter, it tracks the flow and movement of electrical currents in the brain. One study using cognitive neuroscience (psychophysiology) demonstrated that the currents in a subject's brain indicated a preference for Coke or Pepsi that are the same as for the product a person chooses in a blind taste test. According to neuroscientist Justin Meaux, "Preference has measurable correlates in the brain; you can see it." Richard Siberstein, an Australian neuroscientist, took physiological measurements of the brain to show that successful ads tend to generate higher levels of emotional engagement and long-term memory coding.[18]

Consider a sexually provocative advertisement under development. Individual members of a focus group may enjoy the ad but cover up these feelings by saying it was sexist and inappropriate. Their responses may be due to the desire for social acceptance. In a copytest for the same ad, a respondent may also offer socially acceptable answers even though he is not face-to-face with the researcher. The individual may not move the computer mouse to report his true feelings in a study using an emotional monitor. The negative stigma attached to sex in advertising often affects self-reported reactions. A physiological arousal test, such as cognitive neuroscience, might provide a better indicator of a person's true response. Many advertising researchers believe physiological arousal tests provide more accurate information than emotional reaction tests, because physiological arousal is more genuine.[19]

Cognitive neuroscience is likely to produce a more accurate assessment of this billboard than a copytest.

The most recent research in this area has been undertaken by companies such as EmSense, Neuro-Focus, Sands Research, and OTX Research. These companies experiment with portable devices that measure both brain waves and biologic data. Coca-Cola employed this methodology to select ads to run on the Super Bowl. Coke produced a dozen ads that were evaluated by the EmSense device. The EmSense device measures brain waves and monitors breathing, heart rates, blinking, and skin temperatures as consumers watch ads. Through these physiological measurements, Coca-Cola researchers determined which ads to use. Some Super Bowl commercials were modified to produce higher levels of emotions.[20]

Frito-Lay engaged in neuroscience to test product packaging. Company marketers discovered that matte beige bags of potato chips picturing potatoes and other healthier ingredients did not trigger anterior cingulated cortex activity (the area of the brain associated with guilt) as much as shiny potato chip bags.

Frito-Lay's chief marketing officer, Ann Mukherjee, said, "Brain-imaging tests can be more accurate than focus groups." After a focus group rejected a Cheetos advertisement, Frito-Lay tested the commercial using neuroscience methods. The ad featured a woman taking revenge on someone in a Laundromat by putting orange snack food in a dryer that was full of white clothes. The focus group participants felt the prank made Frito-Lay look mean-spirited. The neuroscience test indicated that women loved the commercial.[21]

Cognitive neuroscience reveals physiological reactions to a message. It shows where brain activity occurs and, to some extent, the level of activity. It can identify times when a test subject becomes enthralled with a message. It also indicates when the person merely focuses on the logo or an attractive woman in the commercial. The methodology identifies positive and negative emotions and the intensity of the emotions by the amount of neurons firing. This methodology enables scientists (and marketers) to understand the information being processed, where it is being processed, and how the individual reacted to the ad or marketing piece. Although still in its infancy, cognitive neuroscience offers great potential for evaluating advertising and marketing.

Evaluation Criteria

objective 15.4
Which evaluation criteria are suggested by the positioning advertising copytesting (PACT) system?

Each of the evaluation programs mentioned thus far require quality evaluation criteria. One helpful program, **positioning advertising copytesting (PACT)**, was created by 21 leading U.S. advertising agencies to help evaluate television ads.[22] Even though PACT examines the issues involved in copytesting television ads, the principles apply to any type of message evaluation system and all types of media. Figure 15.3 lists the nine main principles to follow when testing a written or verbal marketing communication piece.

Any advertising procedure should be *relevant to the advertising objective being tested*. For a coupon promotion designed to stimulate trial purchases, marketers should evaluate the coupon's copy in order to determine its ability to stimulate those purchases. An evaluation of attitudes toward a brand requires a different instrument.

- Testing procedure should be relevant to the advertising objectives.
- In advance of each test, researchers should agree on how the results will be used.
- Multiple measures should be used.
- The test should be based on some theory or model of human response to communication.
- Tha testing procedure should allow for more than one exposure to the advertisement, if necessary.
- In selecting alternate advertisements to include in the test, each should be at the same stage in the process as the test ad.
- The test should provide controls to avoid biases.
- The sample used for the test should be representative of the target sample.
- The testing procedure should demonstrate reliability and valldity.

FIGURE 15.3
Copytesting Principles of PACT

Researchers should agree about how the results are going to be used when selecting test instruments. They should also agree on the design of the test in order to obtain the desired results. This becomes especially important during the preparation stage of an advertisement's development because many tests are used to determine whether the advertisement eventually will be created.

The research team should select a *cutoff score* to be used following the test. This prevents biases from affecting findings about the ad's potential effectiveness. Many advertising agencies use test markets for new advertisements before they are launched in a larger area. A recall method used to determine if people in the target market remember seeing the ad should contain a prearranged cutoff score. In other words, the acceptable percentage may be established so that 25 percent of the sample should remember the ad in order to move forward with the campaign. An advertisement that does not achieve the percentage has failed the test.

Using multiple measures allows for more precise evaluations of ads and campaigns. A well-designed ad may fail one particular testing procedure yet score higher on others. Consumers and business buyers who are the targets of marketing communications are complex human beings. Various people perceive individual ads differently. As a result, advertisers usually try to develop more than one measure to be certain greater agreement can be reached about whether the ad or campaign will succeed and reach its desired goals.

The test to be used should be *based on some theory or model of human response to communication*, which makes it more likely that the test will accurately predict the human response. Enhancing the odds that the communication will produce the desired results (going to the website, visiting the store, or making a purchase) when an ad launches becomes the objective.

Tracey Altman/Fresherized Foods

▲ This advertisement for Wholly Guacamole includes a coupon and offer for free potato tots, which means the message evaluation could focus on its ability to stimulate purchases.

Many testing procedures are based on a single exposure. Although in many cases this may be sufficient for research purposes, sometimes *multiple exposures* are necessary to obtain reliable test results. For complex ads, more than one exposure may be needed. The human mind comprehends only so much information in one viewing. The marketing team should make sure a person can and will comprehend the message to determine whether it achieve the desired effects.

Often ads are tested in combination with other ads to disguise the one being examined. Placing the test marketing piece in with others means the test subjects do not know which one is being evaluated. This prevents personal biases from affecting judgments. To ensure valid results, *the alternative ads should be in the same stage of process development*. When ad copy is being tested prior to ad development, the alternative ads should also be in the ad copy development stage.

Next, adequate controls are put in place to *prevent biases and external factors from affecting results*. To help control external factors, researchers often utilize experimental designs. When conducting experiments, researchers hold as many things as constant as possible and manipulate one variable at a time. With a theater test, the temperature, time of day, room lighting, television program, and ads shown should all be the same. Then, the researcher may display the program and ads to an all-male audience followed by an all-female audience. Changing a single variable (gender) makes it possible to see if the ad, in a controlled environment, was perceived differently by men as opposed to women.

Field tests can also be effective. Testing marketing communications in real-world situations offers value, because they approximate reality. When conducting field tests, such as mall intercepts, those performing the testing seek to control as many variables as possible. Thus, the same mall, same questions, and same ads are shown. Then, researchers manipulate age, gender, or other variables one at a time.

Courtesy of Joplin Globe.

▲ Using PACT principles helps ensure a better evaluation of this advertisement for Chic Shaque.

As with any research procedure, sampling procedures are important. The *sample being used should be representative of the target population*. A print ad designed for Spanish-speaking Hispanic Americans should be tested using a Spanish questionnaire or interview format.

Finally, researchers continually try to make tests *reliable and valid*. Reliable means "repeatable." In other words, if the same test were given five times to the same person, the individual should respond in the same way each time. If a respondent is "emotional" on one iteration of a warmth test and "neutral" when the ad is shown a second time, the research team will wonder if the test is reliable.

Valid means "generalizable." Valid research findings can be generalized to other groups. For instance, when a focus group of women finds an ad to be funny, and then a group of men reacts in the same way, the finding that the humor was effective becomes more valid. This would be an increasingly valuable outcome if the results were generalizable to people of various ages and races. Many times an ad may be reliable, or repeatable in the same group, but not valid or generalizable to other groups of consumers or business buyers.

The PACT principles have value when agencies design tests of short-term advertising effectiveness. They also help when marketers seek to understand larger and more long-term issues such as brand loyalty and identification with the company. Generating data documenting that what a company is doing works should be the objective. When this occurs, the company and its advertising team have access to valuable information.

Online Evaluation Metrics

objective 15.5
How do online evaluation systems assist advertising managers in assessing the quality of a firm's internet activities?

To evaluate digital marketing communications from the internet, a number of metrics are available that provide hard and soft data. Figure 15.4 identifies methods of measuring digital marketing and the percentage of companies using each method.

Click-throughs remain the primary method used to measure the impact of online advertising. The number of click-throughs provides an idea of how many people see an

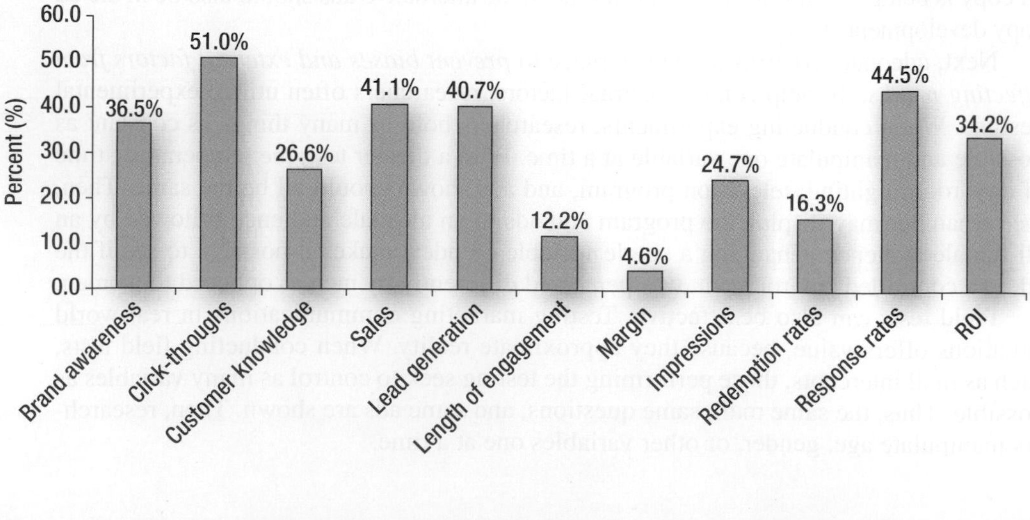

▶ **FIGURE 15.4**
Measuring Effectiveness of Digital Marketing

online ad, click it, and go to the website. Once there, additional metrics, such as length of engagement, dwell rate, dwell time, redemption rates, response rates, and sales, become available. Redemption rates and response rates occur when visitors to the site take an action. Sales occur when the individual makes the purchase online. *Dwell rate* measures the proportion of ad impressions that resulted in a user engaging with the ad, such as clicking it or just mousing over it. *Dwell time* measures the amount of time users spend engaged with a particular advertisement. *Length of engagement*, a newer metric, measures how long the person stays at a website. It offers a surrogate of a person's interest in the product and the site being visited.

Tracey Altman/Fresherized Foods

▲ Click-throughs offer a common metric used to measure the impact of banner ads, such as this one for Sonic and Wholly Guacamole.

AdKnowledge introduced an online management tool called MarketingMatch Planner to evaluate internet advertising campaigns. MarketingMatch Planner software includes two components: Campaign Manager and Administrator. Campaign Manager records traffic to a site and performs postpurchase analysis. Administrator integrates web ad-buy data and performance analysis with the firm's accounting and billing systems. In addition, MarketingMatch Planner can integrate third-party data, including audience demographics, from the following sources:

- MediaMetrix for basic demographics
- NetRatings for gross rating points (GRP) and other ratings instruments
- Psychographic data from SRI Consulting
- Website ratings and descriptions from NetGuide
- Web traffic audit data from BPA Interactive[23]

Marketers view digital data results in light of the company's IMC objectives. An IMC objective of building brand awareness requires something other than online sales data to be assessed. An internet ad might bring awareness to a brand but not lead to an online purchase. This may occur when a consumer or business uses the internet to gather information but then makes the actual purchase at a retail store or by telephone. In that situation, the analysis of an internet advertising campaign may not reflect all of the brand awareness or sales that the campaign generated.

One of the newest forms of online evaluations is measuring and monitoring *web chat*. A company called WiseWindow developed software (Mass Opinion Business Intelligence, MOBI) that can swiftly analyze large numbers of opinions on the web, blogs, Twitter, and social networking sites such as Facebook. MOBI provides continuous, real-time information concerning consumer sentiment about a brand, business, or advertising campaign from millions of sites virtually instantaneously. Companies including Kia, Best Buy, Viacom, Cisco Systems, and Intuit utilize the software to analyze how customers, employees, and investors feel.

Gaylord Hotels applied sentiment analysis software called Clarabridge to determine how customers feel about the company's network of upscale resorts. From the sentiment analysis, Gaylord concluded that the first 20 minutes of a guest's visit were the most

▼ A number of different metrics can be used to evaluate websites, such as this one for DuPage Medical Group.

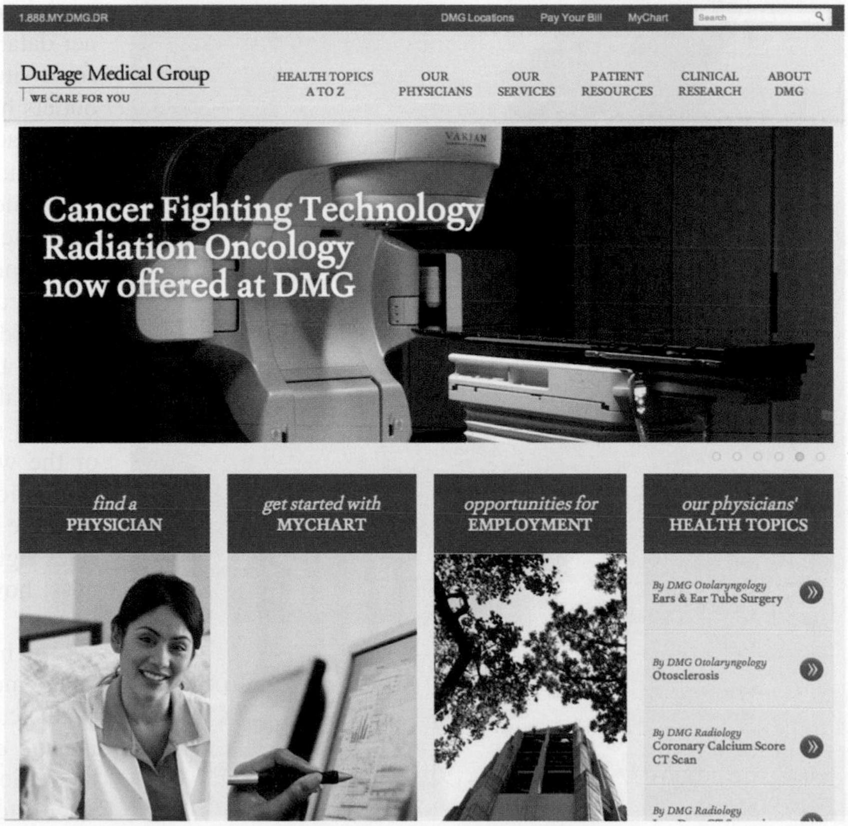

DuPage Medical Group

critical and there were five ways the company could increase the likelihood that guests would recommend the hotel to others. For instance, the web chat analysis revealed it was important to take a new guest to a location rather than just point out where it was or show them on a map. Before this sentiment analysis, Gaylord believed the company had to do 80 things. David C. Kloeppel, chief operating officer for Gaylord Hotels, stated, "We learned that the first 20 minutes of the hotel experience was of vital importance to our guests. Our hypothesis became, if we could perfect the first 20 minutes of the experience, we could drive positive overall guest satisfaction."[24]

objective 15.6
What types of behavioral evaluations can be employed to assess IMC programs?

Behavioral Evaluations

The first part of this chapter regarding message evaluations focuses on insights into what people think and feel. Some marketers contend that sales represent the only valid evaluation criterion. An advertisement may be fun and enjoyable, but if sales do not increase, it was ineffective. The same reasoning applies to other marketing communication tools, such as consumer promotions, trade promotions, and direct marketing tactics.

While it may be true that tangible results should be the bottom line of any marketing program, not all communication objectives can be measured using sales figures. Leaders of companies with low brand awareness may be most interested in the visibility and memorability aspects of a communication plan, even though a marketing program designed to boost brand awareness does not result in immediate sales.

Measuring the results of a consumer promotion campaign featuring coupons using sales figures is easier than measuring the results of a television advertising campaign. Consequently, effective promotions evaluations involve the study of both message and behavioral elements. This section describes behavioral measures shown in Figure 15.5.

- Sales
- Response rates
- Redemption rates
- Test markets
- Purchase simulation tests

▲ **FIGURE 15.5**
Behavioral Measures

▼ This Scott Equipment advertising campaign resulted in an increase in sales.

Bobbie Williams/Scott Equipment

Sales and Response Rates

Measuring changes in sales following a marketing campaign is relatively simple. Retailers collect information from universal product codes (UPCs) and scanner data. These data are available on a weekly and, in some situations, daily basis for each store. Many retail outlets have access to real-time sales information that can be accessed at any point during the day.

Scanner data make it possible for company leaders to monitor sales and help both the retailer and the manufacturer discover the impact of a particular marketing program. At the same time, extraneous factors can affect sales. In a multimedia advertising program, it would be difficult to know which advertisement moved the customer to action. A company featuring a fall line of jackets may be affected by a cold snap. If so, what caused the customer to buy—the ad or the weather? Firms utilizing trade and consumer promotion programs must account for the impact of both the promotion and the advertising when studying sales figures. Sales provide one indicator of effectiveness; however, they may be influenced by additional factors.

As highlighted in Figure 15.6, advertisements may be the most difficult component of the IMC program to evaluate, for several reasons. As just noted, distinguishing *the effects of advertising from other factors* may be difficult. Advertisements create short- and long-term effects, and consumers and businesses see them in many different contexts. The direct impact of one advertisement or one campaign on sales will be difficult to decipher.

Advertising often has a delayed impact. Many times, consumers encounter ads and are persuaded to purchase the product but will not actually make the purchase until later when they actually need the item. A woman may be convinced that she wants to buy a new pair of jeans in response to a sexy and effective advertisement by Calvin Klein. Still, rather than buying them herself, she leaves several well-placed hints for her husband before her next birthday, which could be several months later. The problem could be that her husband purchased another brand or a different gift. So, she either waits for another special occasion for her husband to buy the jeans or she makes the purchase herself at a later time.

Consumers often decide to make purchases based on an advertisement but *change their minds when they arrive at the retail store.* A competing brand may be on sale, the store could be out of the desired brand, or the salesperson could persuade the customer that another brand is better. In each case, the ad was successful on one level but another factor interfered before the purchase was made.

Further, *the brand being advertised may not be part of the consumer's evoked set.* Upon hearing or seeing the ad, however, the brand moves into the evoked set. Thus, even when an individual does not consider the brand at first, it will be in the future when the need arises or when the consumer becomes dissatisfied with a current option.

Advertising helps generate brand awareness and brand equity. Although sales may not be the result immediately, *the ad may build brand equity*, which, in turn, influences future purchases.

A wide variety of responses to marketing communications programs are available besides sales. Figure 15.7 lists some of the responses that can be tracked.

- Influence of other factors
- Delayed impact of the ads
- Consumers changing their minds while in the store
- Whether the brand is in the consumer's evoked set
- Level of brand equity

▲ FIGURE 15.6
Factors that Make Advertising Difficult to Evaluate

- Changes in sales
- Telephone inquiries
- Response cards
- Internet responses
- Direct-marketing responses
- Redemption rate of sales promotion offers—coupons, premiums, contests, sweepstakes

▲ FIGURE 15.7
Tracking Marketing Responses

Promotions Measuring the effects of trade and consumer promotions, direct marketing programs, and personal selling on actual sales is relatively easy. Manufacturers study the impact of trade promotions by observing changes in sales to the retailers at the time the company offers promotions. The same holds true for consumer promotions, such as coupons, contests, and point-of-purchase displays. Many manufacturers' representatives push hard to get retailers to prominently place the company's point-of-purchase displays. At the same time, the retailer might be more interested in the effects of the display on sales. Using scanner data, both the retailer and the manufacturer can measure the impact of a display. Retailers normally prefer point-of-purchase displays that have demonstrated the ability to boost sales.

Toll-Free Numbers One method of measuring the impact of an advertisement, direct mail piece, TV direct offer, or price-off discount to a business customer involves assigning a toll-free number to each marketing piece. A great deal of information can be collected during an inbound call. Sales data can be recorded and demographic information gathered. Psychographic information may then be added by contacting various commercial services.

In business-to-business situations, a toll-free number provides contact names to help the vendor discover who performs the various functions in the buying center. As a result, a toll-free number provides sales data to determine which marketing program would be best and generate valuable information that can be tied to the sales data. Knowing who responds to an offer helps marketers better understand customers and develop the right approach for each target group.

QR Codes and Facebook Likes Two new methods of evaluation are QR code responses and Facebook likes. Many ads include QR codes consumers can access with their mobile phones. Some link to a company's website, while others offer special deals or information. The advertisement for Kraft Parmesan Cheese on the next page includes a QR code. The marketing department counts how many individuals access the code. They also gather information about individuals who accessed the QR code.

With the increased popularity of Facebook, a new measure of a brand's popularity is the number of individuals who "like" a brand. Employees count the number of likes

Courtesy of Alliance One Advertising

▶ One Measure of effectiveness of this O'Nealgas advertisement is the increase in the number of phone calls made for pricing and scheduling.

and correlate the likes to special offers that are made on the brand's Facebook. Many marketers consider fans "liking" a brand or something a brand does as a surrogate for word-of-mouth endorsement.

Kraft Foods, Inc.

▼ Kraft Foods' marketing team can measure how many individuals accessed the QR code contained in the ad for for Parmesan cheese.

Response Cards Response cards collect customer information as the forms are filled out at the time of an inquiry. Response cards carry the disadvantage of providing less data. Consequently, commercial sources are needed to obtain additional demographic and psychographic information, because response cards solicited from current customers contain information the firm may already have in its database.

Internet Responses Internet responses provide quality behavioral measures. By using cookies, a marketing team obtains considerable information about the person or business making the inquiry. In addition, many times the person or business responding voluntarily provides a great deal of helpful information. Responses to direct advertising through internet views may also be tracked.

The Canadian Tourism Commission tested direct-response ads placed on television, radio, direct mail, and online. Each ad used a different URL for viewers to access for additional information. To the tourist, there was no perceivable difference, because each URL took the person to the designated Canadian Tourism site. The Tourism Commission could track which ad the person viewed and which URL the person used. This made it possible to count the number of visitors from each of the direct-response advertisements.[25]

Tracey Altman/Fresherized Foods

◀ Wholly Guacamole's marketers can evaluate this brand alliance campaign with Disney using the redemption rate for the mail-in rebate.

Redemption Rates Marketers study various kinds of redemption rates to measure behavioral effectiveness. Employees code coupons, premiums, rebates, contests, sweepstakes, and direct-mail pieces and record redemption rates. Comparing a current campaign with previous campaigns makes it possible to examine changes made in the design or advertisement's execution. The marketing team reviews the results in light of positive or negative changes in redemption rates.

Immediate changes in sales and redemptions offer another form of behavioral evaluation. An advertiser or company may use them but fail to see "the forest for the trees." One campaign, advertisement, or promotions program should be viewed in the context of all other marketing efforts. Behavioral measures work best when the team sees them as part of the bigger picture.

Test Markets

Test markets allow company leaders to examine the effects of a marketing effort on a small scale before launching a national or international campaign. The marketing team is able to examine several elements of a marketing communication program in one setting. If the test market achieves success, then the likelihood that the national campaign will be effective improves. Test markets measure the effects of a campaign in a new country before launching a full-scale international effort. Test market programs are used to assess:

- Advertisements
- Consumer and trade promotions
- Pricing tactics
- New products

Test markets provide cost-effective methods to analyze and then make changes in marketing efforts before millions of dollars are spent on something that might not accomplish its objectives. Advertisements can be modified, promotions revised, and pricing policies revisited before undertaking a more widespread program. For example, McDonald's tested new ads that touted cleaner restaurants and friendlier service. The goal of the commercials was to test a campaign emphasizing McDonald's effort to improve in-store and drive-through service. Two television spots and one radio spot were produced and aired in Tampa and Seattle. Reactions from the test markets provided McDonald's marketing team and the advertising agency with information about the impact of the ad campaign, the parts of the message that should be modified, and whether the campaign should be launched nationally.[26]

Test markets hold the advantage of resembling an actual purchasing situation more than any of the other tests. Making sure the site selected for the test market strongly resembles the target population becomes the key. A product targeted toward senior citizens should be studied in an area with a high concentration of seniors.

Katie Mcgee

▲ A test market can be used to evaluate various aspects of an advertising campaign for Weaver before it is launched in the seven cities where offices are located.

A test market campaign should resemble the national or full marketing plan, if possible. A lengthy time lapse may cause a company to experience differing results. Marketers try to make sure the test market provides a mirror image of the actual marketing program.

A test market might be as short as a few days or as long as two to three years. A test that is too short may yield less reliable results. If the test market is too long, the national market situation may change and the test market may no longer be a representative sample. The greater drawback is that the competition can study what is going on, which gives them time to react to the proposed marketing campaign.

Competitive Responses Competing companies often respond to test market programs in one of two ways. First, some introduce a special promotion in the test market area in order to confound the results. This may reduce sales for the tested product, making the campaign appear to be less attractive than it actually was. The second approach involves not intervening in the test market, but instead using the time to prepare a countermarketing campaign. Firms that use this tactic are ready when the national launch occurs, and the impact may be that the test market results are not as predictive of what will happen.

Scanner Data Scanner data make it possible for results from test market campaigns to be made quickly available. The figures help determine the acceptability of test market results. A firm can design several versions of a marketing campaign in different test markets. Scanner data assist marketers in comparing the sales from each test market to determine which version works best. For example, in one test market the firm may present an advertising campaign only. In the second test market, coupons may be added to the ad program. In the third test market, a premium will be combined with advertising. The results from each area help the marketing team understand which type of marketing campaign fared best.

Test markets provide the opportunity to test communication ideas in more true-to-life settings. Test markets examine trade and consumer promotions, direct marketing, and other marketing communication tools. They are not quite as accurate when assessing advertising, because changes in sales take longer and the test market program may not be long enough to measure the full impact. In any case, test markets offer valuable instruments to examine specific marketing features and more general communications campaigns.

▼ Rather than field test markets, researchers can use simulated shopping exercises.

Yuri Arcurs/Fotolia

Purchase Simulation Tests

Instead of test markets, marketing researchers employ purchase simulation tests. *Simulated purchase tests* present a cost-effective approach to examine purchase behaviors. Research Systems Corporation (RSC) specializes in purchase simulation studies. RSC tests the impact of commercials by studying consumer behaviors in a controlled laboratory environment.

Consumers are asked if they would be willing to buy products in a variety of ways, using various methods. They might be asked about purchase intentions at the end of a laboratory experiment. In this situation, however, intentions are self-reported and may be a less accurate predictor of future purchase behaviors. RSC does not request consumer opinions, ask them to describe their attitudes, or even ask if they plan to purchase the product. Instead, RSC creates a simulated shopping experience. Subjects choose from a variety of products they would see on a store shelf. After completing a simulated shopping exercise, the subjects are seated and watch a television preview containing various commercials. The participants are asked to view the TV program as they would watch any TV show at home. The test ad is placed in with other ads, and the subjects do not know which ad is being tested.

After completing the preview, the subjects participate in a second shopping exercise. Researchers then compare the products chosen in the first shopping trip to those selected in the second. Shifts in brand choices are at least partly due to the effectiveness of the advertisement, because it was the only variable that changed.

This methodology provides the advantage of using test procedures that do not rely on opinions and attitudes. Among other things, this means that RSC's procedure would work in international markets as well as domestic markets.[27] In some cultures, subjects tend to seek to please the interviewer who asks questions about opinions and attitudes. As a result, the answers are polite and socially acceptable. The same subjects may also seek to provide answers they think the interviewer wants to hear. By studying purchases instead of soliciting opinions, subjects are free to respond in a more forthright fashion.

Any methodology designed to tap into behaviors rather than emotions and feelings features a built-in advantage. Opinions and attitudes change and may be quickly affected by other variables. Observing behaviors and changes in behaviors gets more quickly to the point of the experiment, which is whether the buyer can tangibly be influenced by a marketing communications tool.

In summary, the systems available to examine respondent behaviors are response rates, online metrics, test markets, and purchase simulation tests. Marketers employ programs in conjunction with one another and also with the message evaluation techniques described earlier. None of these approaches is used in a vacuum. Instead, the data generated and findings revealed are tested across several instruments and with numerous groups of subjects. In that manner, the marketing department manager and the advertising agency can try to heighten the odds that both short- and long-term goals can be reached through the ads, premiums, coupons, and other marketing communications devices used. Even then, the job of evaluation is not complete.

Evaluating the Overall IMC Program

objective 15.7
What criteria should be used to assess the overall IMC program?

As has been noted throughout this textbook, the expenditures companies make for marketing communications has led CEOs and other executives to push for greater accountability. These individuals, as well as stockholders and boards of directors, want to know what type of return results when a firm spends a large sum of money on an advertising campaign or other marketing activity. They seek to discover the *return on investment (ROI)* of an advertising and promotions program.

Little agreement exists regarding what "ROI" means when applied to a marketing program. No consensus takes place regarding how to measure marketing ROI. In one study, more than 70 percent of marketers said it would be difficult to measure the impact of advertising and marketing on sales. The same number predicted that it would be extremely difficult for the marketing industry to reach any agreement on what constitutes ROI for marketing. The most common are behavioral responses, such as incremental sales, total sales, and market share.[28]

This confusion will likely continue, even as company executives try to justify advertising and marketing expenditures. Consequently, those in the marketing profession keep trying to identify ways to measure the impact of marketing communications, ultimately in dollars and cents.

- Market share
- Innovation
- Productivity
- Physical and financial resources
- Profitability
- Manager performance and development
- Employee performance and attitudes
- Social responsibility

▲ **FIGURE 15.8**
Overall Health of a Company

Many years ago, Peter Drucker outlined a series of goal areas that indicate organizational health. These goals (listed in Figure 15.8) match well with the objectives of an IMC program.[29] As marketers struggle to find a way to measure the ROI of marketing communication expenditures, understanding the various measures of overall health of an organization can provide valuable insight on how marketing communications contributes.

Market share has long been linked to profitability. It demonstrates consumer acceptance, brand loyalty, and a strong competitive position. The IMC planning process should help the marketing team understand both market share and the relative strengths and weaknesses of the competition. IMC programs are designed to hold and build market share.

Innovation includes finding new and different ways to achieve objectives. This applies to many marketing activities, including new and unusual trade and consumer promotions, public relations events and sponsorships, e-commerce and social media programs, and the firm's advertising efforts.

Productivity reflects the industry's increasing emphasis on results. IMC experts are being asked to demonstrate tangible results from IMC campaigns. Both short- and long-term measures of the effects of advertisements and promotions demonstrate the "productivity" of the organization in terms of gaining new customers, building recognition in the marketplace, determining sales per customer, and through other measures.

Physical and financial resources are important to an IMC program. Physical resources include the most up-to-date computer and internet capabilities. The firm must provide sufficient financial resources to reach this goal. Communication devices that keep the firm in contact with consumers constitute vital elements in the long-term success of an IMC plan.

Profitability remains vitally important to the marketing department and the overall organization. Many IMC managers know that more than sales are at issue when assessing success. Sales must generate profits in order for the company to survive and thrive.

Manager performance and development may be an overlooked part of an IMC program. Effective marketing departments and advertising agencies should develop pipelines of new, talented creatives, media buyers, promotions managers, webmasters, and others in order to succeed in the long term. Also, new people should be trained and prepared for promotion for more important roles.

Employee performance and attitudes reflect not only morale within the marketing department, but also relations with other departments and groups. An effective IMC plan consists of building bridges with internal departments so that everyone is aware of the thrust and theme of the marketing program. Satisfied and positive employees help the firm promote its image.

Social responsibility can be linked to the long-term well-being of an organization. Brand equity and loyalty are hurt when the firm is known for illegal or unethical actions. Therefore, marketing leaders should encourage all of the members of an organization to act in ethically and socially responsible ways.

When these goals are reached, the firm's IMC program works well. Beyond these targets, IMC plans should continually emphasize the evolving nature of relationships with customers. Retail consumers and business-to-business buyers should be constantly contacted to find out how the company can best serve their needs.

Simply stated, every chapter in this book implies a series of key performance targets for IMC programs that can guide the actions of the marketing department and the advertising agency both in the short term and for the long term. Firms that are able to maintain one clear voice in a cluttered marketplace stand the best chance of gaining customer interest and attention as well as developing long-term bonds with all key publics and stakeholders. An effective IMC program helps set the standards and measure performance and, in the end, becomes the model for marketing success for the entire organization.

objective 15.8
How are evaluation programs adjusted to match international operations?

International Implications

Many of the techniques described in this chapter are available worldwide. IMC programs should be assessed in several ways, including domestic results, results in other countries, and as an overall organization.

Individual advertisements and promotional programs are examined within the countries in which they appear. Due to differing standards regarding advertising content, they must be evaluated in light of local cultures and purchasing habits.

Many times, advertising and promotional programs are assessed across national boundaries. For example, a campaign launched in Europe leads to evaluations in individual countries including France, Spain, and Italy, but also as a collective, such as the European Union. Measures of attitudes are difficult to collect. Sales are easier to assess due to the use of the Euro in all of these nations; however, inflation rates and other statistics are affected by local conditions.

It is advisable to contract with local advertising agencies to discover which techniques are most viable in other countries. In some nations, using coupons may be viewed as a sign of poverty, and users are either secretive or embarrassed about redeeming them. In those situations, it helps to study results in light of cultural norms.

Numerous multinational conglomerates assess advertising and promotional efforts through regional offices. Pacific Rim information will be combined with information from Europe, Africa, and other places. The goal is to make sure an overall image and theme is projected worldwide.

Summary

Assessing an IMC program often involves examining the effects of individual advertisements. These efforts are conducted in three major ways: message evaluations, online evaluation metrics, and evaluating respondent behaviors. Numerous techniques are available. Most of the time, marketing managers and advertisement agencies apply several different methods in order to get the best picture of an ad's potential for success. Advertisements are studied before they are developed, while they are being developed, and after they have been released or launched.

The guiding principles for any marketing tool include agreement on how test results will be used, pre-establishing a cutoff score for a test's results, employing multiple measures, basing studies on models of human behaviors, creating multiple exposures, testing marketing instruments that are in the same stage of development, and preventing as many biases as possible while conducting the test. Many times, certain members of the marketing team may not be objective, especially when they had the idea for the ad or campaign. In these instances, companies retain an outside research agency to study the project.

Message evaluations take place at every stage of the development process. Methods that may be employed include advertising tracking research, copytesting, emotional reaction tests, and cognitive neuroscience.

Positioning advertising copytesting (PACT) is primarily used to evaluate television advertisements. Nine key principles are involved. The principles may be applied to any type of message evaluation system and all types of media.

Online evaluation metrics include the use of click-throughs, dwell rates, dwell time, and length of engagement. Interactive data are carefully evaluated in light of the company's IMC objectives. The newest form of evaluation is measuring and monitoring web chat.

Behavioral evaluations consist of sales and response rates, toll-free number responses, response cards, internet responses, and redemption rates. Test markets assess advertisements, consumer and trade promotions, pricing tactics, and acceptance of new products. Purchase simulation tests offer cost-effective methods to analyze the impact of advertising and promotion on immediate consumer purchase responses.

IMC plans guide the entire company. Therefore, more general and long-term criteria should be included in any evaluation of an IMC program. When the IMC theme and voice are clear, the company is achieving its long-range objectives, the principles stated in this book are applied efficiently and effectively, and the company is in the best position to succeed at all levels, including in all international operations.

Key Terms

metrics Measures designed to accurately portray the effectiveness of a marketing communications plan

message evaluation techniques Methods used to examine the creative message and the physical design of an advertisement, coupon, or direct marketing piece

online evaluation metrics Methods used to examine online advertising and marketing campaigns

respondent behavior evaluations Methods used to examine visible customer actions, including making store visits, inquiries, or actual purchases

copytests Tests used to evaluate a marketing piece that is finished or in its final stages prior to production

portfolio test A test of an advertisement using a set of print ads, one of which is the ad being evaluated

theater test A test of an advertisement using a set of television ads, including the one being evaluated

warmth monitor A method to measure emotional responses to advertisements

biometric research A method to measure physiological reactions to advertisements and marketing messages

cognitive neuroscience A brain-image measurement process that tracks brain activity

positioning advertising copytesting (PACT) Principles to use when assessing the effectiveness of various messages

MyMarketingLab

Go to **mymktlab.com** to complete the problems marked with this icon ✪.

Review Questions

15-1. How do message evaluation techniques work and what do they reveal about the message to the researcher?

15-2. What do respondent behavior evaluations look at and why are they important?

15-3. How does planning help IMC evaluation?

15-4. Outline the levels that are used to analyze an advertising or IMC program.

15-5. In addition to recognition and unaided and aided brand awareness, what does tracking research measure?

15-6. What is the purpose of copy-testing an advertising or marketing piece?

15-7. What kind of copy-testing can replace both portfolio and theater testing? What are the advantages?

15-8. What are the positioning advertising copytesting principles that help advertisers prepare quality ads and campaigns?

15-9. Define the terms click-throughs, dwell rate, dwell time, and length of engagement. How are these measures used to evaluate marketing communications?

15-10. What are the primary forms of behavioral evaluations that can be used to test advertisements and other marketing pieces?

15-11. How are behavioral responses to marketing messages measured?

15-12. What items can be evaluated using test markets?

15-13. Describe a purchase simulation test.

15-14. Name and describe the criteria that can be used to assess the impact of the overall IMC program, as noted in this chapter.

15-15. What differences occur when international marketing programs are assessed?

Critical Thinking Exercises

DISCUSSION QUESTIONS

15-16. Create an advertising approach for one of the following products. Describe your idea in three or four sentences. Organize a small focus group of four other students in class. Ask the group to evaluate your advertising concept. What did you learn from the exercise?

a. Retail pet store
b. Baseball caps
c. Computers
d. Sweaters
e. Watches

15-17. Organize a small focus group of four or five other students in your class or individuals you know. Pick a daily newspaper and identify a group of competing print ads. Are there common features? Which ads are more effective and why? Write a summary of the evaluation of the ads and criteria used.

15-18. Form a group of five other students or individuals. Ask each to identify at least two advertisements each from different media. These should include television, radio, print, and the internet. Get them to write down what appeals to them and why the advertisements stand out. Are there any advertisements that stand out for negative reasons? What are these reasons? Ask each student to read his or her list comparing ads that were liked or stood out for negative reasons. What were the differences?

15-19. Are sales figures important when evaluating integrated marketing communications? How should hard data such as redemption rates and store traffic be used in the evaluation of marketing communications? In terms of accountability, how important are behavioral measures of IMC effectiveness?

15-20. From the viewpoint of a marketing manager of a large sporting goods manufacturer, what types of measures of effectiveness would you want from the $5 million you pay to an advertising agency for an advertising campaign? Knowing that evaluations cost money, how much of the $5 million would you be willing to spend to measure effectiveness? What type of report would you prepare for your supervisor?

15-21. A clothing manufacturer spends $6 million on trade promotions and $3 million on consumer promotions. How would you measure the impact of these expenditures? If an agency was hired to manage these expenditures, what type of measures would you insist the company utilize?

15-22. Examine a current magazine. Make a record of how many advertisements include methods for measuring responses. That is, how many list a code number, a toll-free number, or a website? Listing a toll-free number or a website does not ensure that the agency or firm will know where the customer obtained that information. How can the advertising agency or firm track the responses from a specific advertisement in the magazine you examined?

15-23. In some Asian countries, it is improper to talk about oneself. Therefore, people often are too embarrassed to answer questions about feelings and emotions. Those who do answer the questions would tend to provide superficial answers. Explain the advantages of a simulated purchasing test methodology in this situation. What other methods of evaluating feelings and emotions could an agency use in Asian countries?

Integrated Learning Exercises

15-24. Pick three print advertisements that include website URLs. Visit each site. Was the website a natural extension of the advertisement? What connection or similarities did you see between the website and the advertisement? Do you think your response was tracked? How can you tell?

15-25. Decision Analysts, Inc. is a leading provider of advertising and marketing research. Access the company's website at **www.decisionanalyst.com** and investigate the various services the company offers. Examine the advertising research services available. Write a short report about how advertising research services provided by Decision Analysts could be used.

15-26. Before committing to an expensive marketing and advertising campaign, it is always important to test ideas, concepts, and delivery first. Find organizations that offer this testing in your country. What services do they offer? Is this time and money worthwhile?

15-27. AdKnowledge is a firm that excels at measuring internet traffic and internet advertising. Access the website at **www.adknowledge.com**. What services does the company offer? Describe a research project you feel this company could do successfully to assist in advertising or internet research.

15-28. ComScore is a firm that measures internet traffic and internet advertising. Access the website at **www.comscore.com**. What services does the company offer? Describe a research project you feel this company could do successfully to assist in advertising or internet research.

15-29. Millward Brown provides marketing and advertising evaluations. Access the company's website at **www.millwardbrown.com**. Describe the various services offered by the company. Suppose you want to evaluate an advertising campaign for Forever 21 clothes. Identify and discuss the Millward Brown tools you would use.

Student Project

CREATIVE CORNER

After leaders at PepsiCo and Starbucks became concerned about the diminishing supply of fresh, clean water, the companies teamed together to sell Ethos Water. The product's distribution has expanded, and it is now sold in major grocery stores, convenience stores, and drug stores. The goal of Ethos Water is to ensure that children throughout the world have clean water.

Access the Ethos Water website at **www.ethoswater.com**. After reviewing the site, design a print ad for a magazine aimed at college students in your area. When you have finished designing the ad, trade your ad with another student or ask him or her to show it to 10 students not enrolled in this class. Explain to the student how to conduct a copytest to gather attitudes and opinions about the ad. Before conducting the copytest, make a list of questions you want to ask. Some suggestions are:

15-30. Have you ever heard of Ethos Water?

15-31. What do you think is the primary message of this advertisement?

15-32. Does the copy make sense? Is it understandable?

15-33. Does the visual attract your attention?

15-34. What types of feelings does the ad elicit?

15-35. How likely would you be to access the Ethos Water website for more information?

15-36. What is your overall evaluation of the advertisement?

It is important that someone else conduct the copytest for you to gain honest answers. Respondents are less likely to be honest, especially about any negative feedback, if you show them the advertisement and they know you designed it.

CASE 1 DORITOS ACADEMY TURKEY: THE SUCCESS STORY OF SOCIAL MEDIA COMMUNICATION

PepsiCo's Frito-Lay brand, the world's largest snack company with operations in more than 40 countries, entered the Turkish market through the acquisition of Uzay Gıda in 1993. Frito-Lay has always been successful in communicating with young consumers who are keen on trying new brands.

In 2011, to increase its market share and to strengthen its brand image the company launched a new product, Doritos Fritos. To increase awareness, traditional sales and marketing channels were used simultaneously with the internet, including the use of social media. After the company identified young people aged 18–24 as the target group, research about their lifestyles, interests, tastes, and social media usage was carried out. The information collected was used to create a "virtual academy" with unusual fun and ambiance with the slogan "adding spice to life."

The company's communication team established a guideline comprising three criteria: taking risk (being brave), integration (integrated use of all communication channels), and measurement and listening to the voice of the consumer. At the heart of the campaign is the Web page (http://www.doritosakademi.com), which was designed to be a platform for entertainment. Virtual campus life was created and the social networks such as Facebook, Twitter, and YouTube were integrated onto the platform. In the virtual academy, information about the academy and the instructors are supplied besides the class notes and entertaining videos. In the commercials the famous Turkish star Huysuz Virjini appeared as the Rector and Megan Fox introduced the "Doritos Fritos Shots."

Profiles were created on Facebook and Twitter for the virtual characters (professors and the academy staff), social media activities were planned, and gifts were offered to increase the number of participants (academy enrollment). For example, the company distributed free Doritos Fritos for registration, and members of the virtual academy were able to buy priority tickets to see Madonna in concert. By Fall 2011 the company allocated 20 percent of the total communication budget to social media campaigns and with this comprehensive work, the

Nancy R. Cohen/Photodisc

▲ Following a strong social media campaign, Doritos is seeing a real growth in market share.

Doritos Academy gained 15,000 followers and obtained almost 600,000 likes on Facebook. According to SocialBakers, monthly increase in the number of fans reached 84,000 and the number of people talking about "Doritos Academy" reached 40,000. By November 2012, "Doritos Akademi" was the 34th fastest growing page on Facebook in Turkey. Messages sent 24/7 by the instructors of the Academy maintained the liveliness of the Web page. Involving the consumers in the co-creation process increased the success of the company and the loyalty of the consumers. By November 2012, this loyalty provided the highest market share for the brand in Turkey.[30]

15-37. What IMC objectives are important to Doritos?

15-38. What long-term IMC criteria should be used to assess the Doritos brand?

15-39. What are the relations between segmentation, targeting, and the IMC?

15-40. What examples can you give about the IMC for other companies?

15-41. What could be the differences between B2B and B2C from the aspect of IMC?

CASE 2 SPYCH MARKET ANALYTICS

A new age of marketing communication evaluation may be under way. Spych Marketing Analytics, which was founded in 2008, provides innovative solutions for companies seeking a better understanding of the future market environments, including the Gen Y and Millennial consumer segments, the advancement of technology, and the quickly evolving world of customer experience. The company tries to delve into the insights and emotions of these groups, providing an innovative portal into the psyches of these markets through its program called Empathic Youth Research and other mixed methodological approaches to consumer insights. CEO Benjamin Smithee argues that, "You have to look at the foundations and fundamentals of the advertising industry, and right now we are seeing a dramatic paradigm shift in the ways marketing communications are delivered and consumed." The media include traditional advertising venues, public relations, but also social media and mobile technologies, utilized by an evolving set of consumers.

Company employees work to enhance every aspect of the market research process. On its website, the organization proclaims, "… we create natural environments for our respondents, evoking rich insights and opinions that surface only through truly natural and empathic interactions." Further, "The Spych Experience maximizes the return your team obtains from each project overcoming fallacies often associated with traditional youth research."

To achieve these ideals, the company employs innovative concepts regarding marketing metrics and consumer understanding. The concepts are based on the importance of going beyond simply engaging customers to include "re-advertising." CEO Benjamin Smithee notes a new model in which "sharing" becomes a second important outcome from a marketing effort as shown in Figure 15.9.

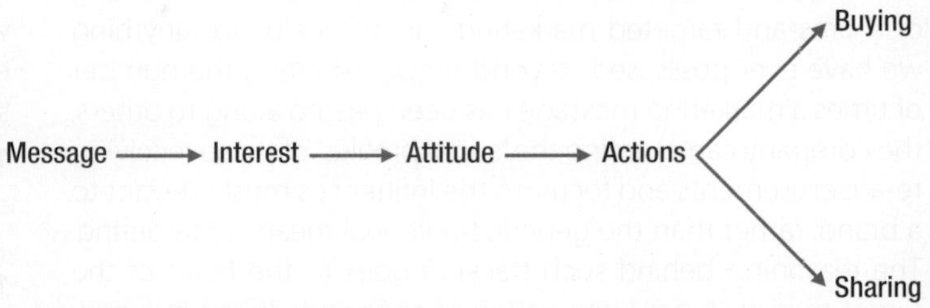

▲ **FIGURE 15.9**
Moving from Message to Buying/Sharing

Spych seeks to identify levels of engagement in terms of "intensity," in which a message is shared with friends and others. The concepts of "share-ability" and "virality" take on particular importance in Spych parlance. As Spych Marketing Analytics brand strategist Landon Ledford notes, "We ask the question, does this pass the traditional advertising test and then lead to sharing?" He notes that in previous times, an ad might be shared with one or two other people, such as when a person would tear an advertisement out of a newspaper or magazine and give it to a friend. Now, a message can quickly be re-posted to 200-plus Facebook friends.

In essence, Spych bases its conclusions regarding a message's success with "engagement" with an advertisement being

◀ Spych Brand Strategist Landon Ledford and CEO Ben Smithee.

Courtesy of the authors.

measured first by "click commitment," which is the willingness of a person to click on an ad on a medium such as Twitter, making that decision in three seconds or less, and second by "socialization," or passing the advertisement on to others.

Taking the next step, new technologies allow for tracking of shares and targeted marketing capabilities unlike anything we have ever possessed. Beyond simply counting the number of times a marketing message has been passed along to others, the company can examine the "social profiles" of those receiving re-advertisements and focus on the influences most relevant to a brand, rather than the generic traditional means of targeting. The reasoning behind such tracking goes to the heart of the target market. A new generation of consumer shops in a new manner, communicates through channels that have not been previously available, and responds to companies and marketing messages in ways we have never seen.

The ultimate goals of these measures and concepts remain the same as in any traditional marketing effort. Return visits to various vendors, repeat purchases, word-of-mouth endorsements, and feeling a connection (brand loyalty) with a company, all of which lead to increased sales over time suggest that a marketing program has achieved success. Re-advertising and sharing with others enhance the prospects of reaching the right audience, sending the right message, and creating long term relationships with the company. As CEO Smithee summarized, "The more layers you can seamlessly integrate, the better chance of getting something sticky."

15-42. Would the concepts used to measure marketing success match with the message evaluation methods presented in this chapter? Why or why not?

15-43. Compare the concepts used by Spych with the terms "behavioral response" and "attitudinal response."

15-44. What roles do "emotions" and "logic" play in the Spych approach to marketing communications?

15-45. What roles do social media and hand-held technologies such as smartphones play in today's marketing environment? How will they evolve in the future?

MyMarketingLab

Go to mymktlab.com for the following Assisted-graded writing questions:

15-46. Are sales figures important when evaluating integrated marketing communications? How should hard data such as redemption rates and store traffic be used in the evaluation of marketing communications? In terms of accountability, how important are behavioral measures of IMC effectiveness?

15-47. ComScore is a firm that measures internet traffic and internet advertising. Access the website at www.comscore.com. What services does the company offer? Describe a research project you feel this company could do successfully to assist in advertising or internet research.

Endnotes

Chapter 1

1. "Virgin Atlantic: Still Red Hot campaign," *ThinkBox*, http://www.thinkbox.tv/server/show/ConCaseStudy.1631, accessed December 7, 2012; Virgin Atlantic, website, http://www.virginatlantic.com/gb/en.html, accessed December 7, 2012; Virgin Atlantic (2012), Student Information Pack, http://www.virginatlantic.com/en/gb/allaboutus/ourstory/forstudents.jsp, accessed December 7, 2012.
2. Donald Baack, "Communication Processes," *Organizational Behavior* (Houston: Dame Publications, Inc., 1998), pp. 313–37.
3. Brian Morrissey, "Chick-fil-A's Strategy: Give Your Fans Something to Do," *Brandweek* 50, no. 35 (October 5, 2009), p. 40.
4. James G. Hutton, "Integrated Marketing Communications and the Evolution of Marketing Thought," *Journal of Business Research* 37 (November 1996), pp. 155–62.
5. Diane Brady, "Making Marketing Measure Up," *BusinessWeek* (December 13, 2004), pp. 112–13; "Top 10: Issues Facing Senior Marketers in 2007," *Advertising Age* 78, no. 17 (April 23, 2007), p. 23.
6. "Unilever Cuts Agency, Production Spending Even as Ad Costs Rise," *Advertising Age*, February 2, 2012, http://adage.com/print/232485.
7. Andrew McMains, "Ad Spending Trends Reveal No Surprises," *Adweek* 48, no. 44 (December 3, 2007), p. 9.G14
8. Alison Circle, "Marketing Trends to Watch," *Library Journal* 134, no. 16 (October 1, 2009), pp. 26–29.
9. Katherine Rosman, "In Digital Era, What Does Watching TV Even Mean?" October 8, 2013, *http://online.wsj.com/news/articles/SB10001424052702303442004 5*.
10. Mark Walsh, "Microsoft Highlights Usage Across Device Pathways," *Online Media Daily*, March 14, 2013, *www.mediapost.com/publications/article/195786*.
11. Lauren Keller Johnson, "Harnessing the Power of the Customer," *Harvard Management Update* 9 (March 2004), pp. 3–5; Patricia Seybold, *The Customer Revolution* (London: Random House Business Books, 2006).
12. Lauren Indvik, "U.S. Online Retail Sales to Reach $327 Billion by 2016, http://mashable.com/2012/02/27/ecommerce-327-billion-2016-study, accessed March 9, 2012.
13. Katy Keim, "Don't Be Fooled: Social-Media Consumers Aren't in a Relationship with You," *Advertising Age*, May 29, 2013, *http://adage.com/print241722*.
14. Ibid.
15. "Doritos Launches First Global Campaign," *Advertising Age*, March 6, 2013, *http://adage.com/print/240173*.
16. M. N. Tripathi, "Customer Engagement—Key to Successful Brand Building," *The XIMB Journal of Management* 6, no. 1 (March 2009), pp. 131–40.
17. Jean-Noel Kapferer, "The Roots of Brand Loyalty Decline: An International Comparison," *Ivey Business Journal* 69, no. 4 (March–April 2005), pp. 1–6.
18. Debbie Howell, "Today's Consumers More Open to Try New Brands," *DSN Retailing Today* 43, no. 20 (October 25, 2004), pp. 29–32.
19. Jana Lay-Hwa Bowden, "The Process of Customer Engagement: A Conceptual Framework," *Journal of Marketing Theory & Practice* 17, no. 1 (Winter 2009), pp. 63–74.
20. "Study: Subway's Advertising Most Effective in Restaurant Space," *Advertising Age*, October 16, 2013, *http://adage.com/print/244761*; Colleen Rothman and Gina Gapp, "Perceptions of Restaurant Advertising," *Technomic* white paper, Issue 3, September 2013.
21. Stephen J. Gould, Dawn B. Lerman, and Andreas F. Grein, "Agency Perceptions and Practices on Global IMC," *Journal of Advertising Research* (January–February 1999), pp. 7–26.
22. Ibid.
23. Jane L. Levere, "A Campaign from Jaguar to Show its Wild Side," *The New York Times*, February 26, 2012, http://www.nytimes.com/2012/02/27/business/media/jaguar-ad-campaign.
24. Karlene Lukovitz, "Eight O'Clock Coffee Ups Marketing for Brand Refresh," *Marketing Daily*, August 16, 2013, http://www.mediapost.com/publications/article/206930/eight-oclock-coffee-ups-marketing-for-brand-refre.html. Eight O'Clock Coffee, 2013, http://www.eightoclock.com/. Daily Coffee News, "Eight O'Clock Coffee Unveils Brand Redesign, Marketing Plans," August 14, 2013, http://dailycoffeenews.com/2013/08/14/eight-oclock-coffee-unveils-brand-redesign-marketing-plans/.
25. Emirates website, www.emirates.com/english/, accessed November 15, 2010.

Chapter 2

1. V. Mabrey and S. Rosenberg (2008). Can Julia Stewart Save Applebee's? ABC Nightline, April 2, http://abcnews.go com/Business/CEOProfiles/story?id=4573076&page=1, retrieved July 25, 2011; Jeff Bailey, "Reinventing Applebee's," *Forbes Women: Power Women*, December 2, 2009, http://www.forbes.com/2009/12/02/restaurant-business-applebees-ihop-julia-stewart.html, accessed March 5, 2012; Applebee's, IHOP Parent Say Sales Are Up, *U.S. Equities, Forbes.com*, September 23, 2010, http://www.forbes.com/2010/09/23/applebees-ihop-parent-says-sales-are-up-marketnewsvideo.html, accessed March 5, 2012; Applebee's Girl's Night Out: http://technorati.com/social-media/article/applebees-using-social-media-to-bring/#ixzz1oMGa6Jp7
2. Arun Sudhaman, "Brand Quality Still Key to Corporate Reputation: Edelman," *Media Asia* (November 19, 2004), p. 8.
3. Shelly Banjo, "Wal-Mart Ads Tout American Success Story, *The Wall Street Journal*, May 3, 2013, http://online.waj.com/article/SB10001424127887324582004578460 9.
4. Based on "2013 Ranking of Top 100 Brands," *Interbrand*, www.interbrand.com/en/best-globa-brands/2013/top-100-list, accessed September 30, 2013.
5. "Nokia Rethinks Global Marketing as a Challenger Brand," *Advertising Age*, http://adage.com/print/242956, July 3, 2013.
6. Brad Dorfman, "Exclusive: Kraft's New Marching Orders: Make Today Delicious," *Reuters* (http://uk.reuters.com/articlePrint?articleID=UKN15243520090217), February 17, 2009.

7. Interview with Jami Salter, Scott Equipment, November 25, 2013.
8. Katya Andressen, "4 Ways to Reinvent Your Brand," www.ragan.com/Main?Articles/46743.aspx, May 22, 2013; "Comeback Kids: Haggar, Keds Stage Brand Revival," *Advertising Age*, October 30, 2011, http://adage.com/print/230721.
9. Stuart Elliott, "L'eggs Returns to TV Advertising," *The New York Times Media Decoder*, April 7, 2011, http://mediadecocer.blogs.nytimes.com/2011/04/07.
10. "How PMH Gave Target Its Signature Look," *Advertising Age*, March 18, 2012, http://adage.com/print/233378.
11. Paul McNamara, "The Name Game," *Network World* (April 20, 1998), pp. 77–78.
12. Max Du Bois, "Making Your Company One in a Million," *Brand Strategy,* no. 153 (November 2001), pp. 10–11.
13. Michael J. De La Merced, "Kraft, Mondelez and the Art of Corporate Rebranding," *The New York Times*, March 21, 2012, http://dealbook.nytimes.com/2012/03/21.
14. Pamela W. Henderson and Joseph A. Cote, "Guidelines for Selecting or Modifying Logos," *Journal of Marketing* (April 1998), pp. 14–30.
15. Daniel Andreani, "Go Ahead, Change the Ugly Logo," http://smartblogs.com/leadership/2013/06/12/go-ahead=change-that-ugly-logo, June 12, 2013.
16. Robert Klara, "New American Airlines Logo Triggers Ire and a Sense of Déjà vu," *Adweek*, www.adweek.com/news/advertising-branding/new-american-airlines-logo-triggers-ire-and-a-sense-of-deja-vu," January 18, 2013
17. Natalie Zmuda, "What Went into the Updated Pepsi Logo," *Advertising Age* (http://adage.com/print?article_id=132016), October 27, 2008.
18. Karl Greenberg, "Stanley Brand Update Ready for Action," *Marketing Daily*, www.mediapost.com/publications/article/202016, June 9, 2013.
19. Andrew Adam Newman, "Nestle Adds Premium Brand in Still Water Arena," *The New York Times*, www.nytimes.com/2013/06/10/business/media/nestle-adds-premium-brand-in-still-water-arena, June 9, 2013.
20. Interview with Tracy Altman, Wholly Guacamole, November 7, 2013.
21. Natalie Zmuda, "What Went Into the Updated Pepsi Logo?"
22. "Branding Isn't Just for Large Companies with Deep Pockets Anymore," *Smart Business* 4, no. 2 (May 2009), pp. 20–21.
23. Andrew Ehrenberg, Neil Barnard, and John Scriven, "Differentiation or Salience," *Journal of Advertising Research* (November–December 1997), pp. 7–14.
24. Stuart Elliott, "A Campaign Linking Clean Clothes with Stylish Living," *The New York Times* (www.nytimes.com/2010/01/08/business/media/08adco.html), January 8, 2010.
25. "How PMH Gave Target Its Signature Look," *Advertising Age*, March 18, 2012, http://adage.com/print/233378.
26. "Brand Keys 2013 Customer Loyalty Index Finds Seismic Shift I How Consumers Emotionally Engage with Products, Services," Press Release, http://brandkeys.com/wp-content/uploads/2013/02/2013-CLEI-Press-Release-FINAL-Overall.pdf.
27. "Brandz Top 100 Most Valuable Global Brands 2010," Millward Brown Optimor, www.millwardbrown.com, accessed March 16, 2012.
28. Kusum L. Ailawaldi, Scott A. Neslin, and Donald R. Lehman, "Revenue Premium as an Outcome Measure of Brand Equity," *Journal of Marketing* 67, no. 4 (October 2003), pp. 1–18; Don E. Schultz, "Understanding and Measuring Brand Equity," *Marketing Management*, Spring 200, Vol. 9, No. 1, pp. 8–9; Tanya Irwin, "Apple, Hershey's, Sprite Top Youth Brands," *MediaPost News*, October 26, 2011, www.mediapost.com/publications/article/161108.
29. Christopher Heine, "Check Out the Top 100 Beloved Brands," *Adweek*, www.adweek.com/news/advertising-branding/check-out-the-top-100-beloved-brands, October 10, 2013.
30. John N. Frank, "Walking the Private Label–National Brands Tightrope," *Buyer*, Vol. 25, No. 5 May 2011, pp. 16–21.
31. Stephanie Hilderbrandt, "What's in Store for Private Label," *Beverage Industry*, Vol. 102, No. 9, September 2011, pp. 18–22.
32. Terri Goldstein, "Battling Brand Malpractice," *BrandWeek.* (www.brandweek.com/bw/content_display/news-and-features/direct/e3i422dde68f61e91f2f602f6a04ac4d207), November 2, 2009; Ellen Byron, "At the Supermarket Checkout, Frugality Trumps Brand Loyalty," *The Wall Street Journal* (http://online.wsj.com/article/SB122592835021203025.html), November 6, 2008.
33. Jack Neff, "Study: Cutting Spending Hurts Brand Long Term," *Advertising Age* (http://adage.com/print?article_id=135790), April 6, 2009.
34. Dongdae Lee, "Image Congruence and Attitude Toward Private Brands," *Advances in Consumer Research* 31 (2004), pp. 435–41.
35. Rusty Williamson, "Penney's Launching New Line," *Women's Wear Daily (WWD)* 191, no. 83 (April 19, 2006), p. 2.
36. Kelly Nolan, "Apparel & Accessories: A Label for Every Style at JCP," *Retailing Today* 45, no. 14 (August 7, 2006), pp. 27, 36.
37. John Kalkowski, "Private Labels Are Booming."
38. Vanessa L. Facenda, "A Swift Kick to the Privates," *Brandweek* 48, No. 31 (September 3, 2007), pp. 24–28.
39. Kris Perry, "Do You Help Your Customers Sell or Market?" *Paperboard Packaging* 89, no. 11 (November 2004), p. 8.
40. "Packaging Affects Brand Loyalty," *Supermarket News* 53, no. 45 (November 7, 2005), p. 36.
41. Andrea Zoe Aster, "Good Drinks Come in Smart Packaging," *Marketing Magazine* 109, no. 32 (October 4–11, 2004), pp. 13–15.
42. Serena Ng, "P&G Changes Tide Pods Packaging to Look Less Like Candy," http://online.wsj.com/article/SB10001424127887324694904578600260338869552.html, accessed November 19, 2013.
43. Stuart Elliott, "A Redesigned Brand Hopes to Avoid Tropicana Storm," *The New York Times, Media Decoder*, August 31, 2011, http://www.mediacoder.blogs.nytimes.com/2011/08/31.
44. Heidi Tolliver-Walker, "The Top Five Most Effective Ways to Use QR Codes on Packaging," *Seybold Report: Analyzing Publishing Technologies*, Vol. 12, No. 1, January 9, 2012, pp. 2–6.
45. "Banana Republic CMO Talks New Mad Men Collection, Unifying the Brand," *Advertising Age*, http://adage.com/print/240484, March 25, 2013.
46. Andrew McMains, "To Compete Locally, Global Brands Must Adapt," *Adweek.com* (http://adweek.com/pt//cpt&title=To+compete+locally.html), September 25, 2008.
47. Johnny K. Johansson and Ilkka A. Ronkainen, "Consider Implications of Local Brands in a Global Arena."
48. Nina Hidayat, "The Gardenia Bread Wars," *VenusBuzz*, January 3, 2012, http://www.venusbuzz.com/archives/4041/thegardenia-bread-wars/; "Gardenia: Malaysia's Strongest Brands," *Superbrands Volume VI*, http://www.superbrands.com/my/pdfs/CSB_MY_FA_GARDENIA.pdf, accessed December 2012.
49. Arçelik A.Ş., website, http://www.arcelikas.com/, accessed December 2012; Euromonitor International website, http://www.euromonitor.com, accessed December 2012; "Arçelik

A.Ş. 2011 Annual Report," http://www.arcelikas.com/UserFiles/file/ArcelikFRENG2011.pdf, accessed December 2012; Firlar Belma and Pelin Dündar, "Effect of the Use of Mascots at Advertisements to Brand Awareness," *The Journal of International Social Research*, 4, no. 19 (Fall 2011); Social Bakers website, http://www.socialbakers.com, accessed December 2012; "En Etkili 20 Kampanya," Capital, http://www.capital.com.tr/en-etkili-20-kampanya-haberler/19811.aspx, accessed December 2012.

Chapter 3

1. Rachel Kam, "The Secret of Secret Recipe," *The Star*, March 21, 2009, http://biz.thestar.com.my/news/story.asp?file=/2009/3/21/business/3471796&sec=business, accessed November 15, 2010; Secret Recipe website, www.secretrecipe.com.my, accessed November 15, 2010.
2. Jeffrey B. Schmidt and Richard A. Spreng, "A Proposed Model of External Consumer Information Search," *Journal of Academy of Marketing Science* 24, no. 3 (Summer 1996), pp. 246–56.
3. Merrie Brucks, "The Effect of Product Class Knowledge on Information Search Behavior," *Journal of Consumer Research* 12 (June 1985), pp. 1–15; Schmidt and Spreng, "A Proposed Model of External Consumer Information Search."
4. Laura M. Buchholz and Robert E. Smith, "The Role of Consumer Involvement in Determining Cognitive Responses to Broadcast Advertising," *Journal of Advertising* 20, no. 1 (1991), pp. 4–17; Schmidt and Spreng, "A Proposed Model of External Consumer Information Search"; Jeffrey J. Inman, Leigh McAllister, and Wayne D. Hoyer, "Promotion Signal: Proxy for a Price Cut," *Journal of Consumer Research* 17 (June 1990), pp. 74–81; Barry J. Babin, William R. Darden, and Mitch Griffin, "Work and/or Fun: Measuring Hedonic and Utilitarian Shopping Value," *Journal of Consumer Research* 20 (March 1994), pp. 644–56.
5. Schmidt and Spreng, "A Proposed Model of External Consumer Information Search."
6. M. Fishbein and Icek Ajzen, *Belief, Attitude, Intention, and Behavior: An Introduction to Theory and Research* (Reading, MA: Addison-Wesley, 1975).
7. Richard P. Bagozzi, Alice M. Tybout, C. Samuel Craig, and Brian Sternathal, "The Construct Validity of the Tripartite Classification of Attitudes," *Journal of Marketing* 16, no. 1 (February 1979), pp. 88–95.
8. "Jeep Leads List of 25 Most Patriotic Brands," *USA Today*, www.usatoday.com/story/driveon/2013/07001/most-patriotic-brands-jeep/2481337, July 1, 2013.
9. Discussion of cognitive mapping based on Anne R. Kearny and Stephan Kaplan, "Toward a Methodology for the Measurement of Knowledge Structures of Ordinary People: The Conceptual Content Cognitive Map (3CM)," *Environment and Behavior* 29, no. 5 (September 1997), pp. 579–617; Stephan Kaplan and R. Kaplan, *Cognition and Environment, Functioning in an Uncertain World* (Ann Arbor, MI: Ulrich's, 1982, 1989).
10. Laura Green, "Esurance Builds it Brand Power to Attract New Customers," *Smart Business*, www.sbnonline.com/index.php?option=com_k2&view=item&id, May 31, 2013.
11. Discussion of heuristics and multiattribute model based on William L. Wilkie and Edgar A. Pessemier, "Issues in Marketing's Use of Multiattribute Models," *Journal of Marketing Research* 10 (November 1983), pp. 428–41; Peter L. Wright, "Consumer Choice Strategies: Simplifying vs. Optimizing," *Journal of Marketing Research* 11 (February 1975), pp. 60–67; James B. Bettman, *An Information Processing Theory of Consumer Choice* (Reading, MA: Addison-Wesley, 1979).
12. "Truvia Takes Aim at Rival Sugar Substitutes With Wellness Push," *Advertising Age*, http://adage.com/print/244587, October 8, 2013.
13. Mark Sneider, "Create Emotional Ties with Brand for Sales," *Marketing News* 38 (May 15, 2004), pp. 44–45.
14. Peter Leimbach, "Role Reversal: Mr. Mom Goes Shopping," Adweek.com (www.adweek.com/aw/content_display/news/agency/33i1a1890f91e4cda9a5b3c3348b4c85509), July 1, 2009.
15. Lucia Moses, "Millennial Guys Are Turning to Makeup," *Adweek*, www.adweek.com/news/advertising-branding/millennial-guys-are-turning-makeup-150313, June 19, 2013.
16. "The Domestication of Man: More Men Taking on Cleaning Chores," *Quirk's Marketing Research Review*, August 2011, Article 20110826-3.
17. Mark Dolliver, "Alas, Free Time Comes at a Price," *Adweek* 45, no. 34 (September 13, 2004), p. 42; Mark Dolliver, "More Money or More Time?" *Adweek* 42, no. 11 (March 12, 2001), p. 44.
18. Discussion of second-chancers based on Richard Halverson, "The Customer Connection: Second-Chancers," *Discount Store News* 37, no. 20 (October 26, 1998), pp. 91–95.
19. "LGBT Consumers Warm to Ads Targeted to Gays," *eMarketer Digital Intelligence*, September 1, 2011, www.emarketer.com/articles/print.aspx?1008571.
20. Stuart Elliott, "Luxury Hotels Market the Memories They Can Make," *The New York Times*, September 13, 2011, www.nytimes.com/2011/09/14.
21. "Boomers Bend the Trends," *Private Label Buyer* 21, no. 4 (April 2007), p. 14.
22. Karl Greenberg, "Reebok: Huge New Campaign Touts Healthy Lifestyle," *Marketing Daily*, www.mediapost.com/publications/article/193657, February 15, 2013.
23. Discussion based on Frederick E. Webster, Jr., and Yoram Wind, "A General Model for Understanding Organizational Buyer Behavior,"*Marketing Management* 4, no. 4 (Winter–Spring 1996), pp. 52–57; Patricia M. Doney and Gary M. Armstrong, "Effects of Accountability on Symbolic Information Search and Information Analysis by Organizational Buyers," *Journal of the Academy of Marketing Science* 24, no. 1 (Winter 1996), pp. 57–66; Rob Smith, "For Best Results, Treat Business Decision Makers as Individuals," *Advertising Age's Business Marketing* 84, no. 3 (1998), p. 39.
24. Patricia M. Doney and Gary M. Armstrong, "Effects of Accountability on Symbolic Information Search and Information Analysis by Organizational Buyers," *Journal of the Academy of Marketing Science* 24, no. 1 (Winter 1996), pp. 57–66.
25. Herbert Simon, *The New Science of Management Decisions,* rev. ed. (Upper Saddle River, NJ: Prentice Hall, 1977).
26. Webster and Wind, "A General Model for Understanding Organizational Buyer Behavior"; Doney and Armstrong, "Effects of Accountability on Symbolic Information Search and Information Analysis by Organizational Buyers"; James A. Eckert and Thomas J. Goldsby, "Using the Elaboration Likelihood Model to Guide Customer Service-Based Segmentation," *International Journal of Physical Distribution & Logistics Management* 27, no. 9–10 (1997), pp. 600–15.
27. Patrick J. Robinson, Charles W. Faris, and Yoram Wind, "Industrial Buying and Creative Marketing," *Marketing Science Institute Series* (Boston: Allyn & Bacon, 1967).
28. Adapted from Webster and Wind, "A General Model for Understanding Organizational Buyer Behavior."
29. Eugene F. Brigham and James L. Pappas, *Managerial Economics,* 2d ed. (Hinsdale, IL: Dryden Press, 1976).

30. Charles A. Weber, John R. Current, and Desai Anand, "Vendor: A Structured Approach to Vendor Selection and Negotiation," *Journal of Business Logistics* 21, no. 1 (2000), pp. 134–69.
31. Discussion of dual channel marketing is based on Wim G. Biemans, "Marketing in the Twilight Zone," *Business Horizons* 41, no. 6 (November–December 1998), pp. 69–76.
32. Ibid.
33. Ibid.
34. Robert Duboff, "True Brand Strategies Do Much More Than Name," *Marketing News* 35, no. 11 (May 21, 2001), p. 16.
35. D. Ballantyne and R. J. Varey, "Creating Value-In-Use Through Marketing Interaction: The Exchange Logic of Relating, Communicating and Knowing," *Marketing Theory* 6, no. 3 (2006), pp. 335–48; G. D. Pires, J. Stanton, and R. Paulo, "The Internet, Consumer Empowerment and Marketing Strategies," *European Journal of Marketing* 40, no. 9/10 (2006), pp. 936–49; T. Park, *et al.*, "Effective Advertising on Mobile Phones: A Literature Review and Presentation of Results from 53 Case Studies," *Behaviour & Information Technology* 27, no. 5 (September–October 2008); S. L. Vargo and R. F. Lusch, "Service-Dominant Logic: Continuing the Evolution," *Journal of the Academy of Marketing Science*, 36 (2008), pp. 1–10; "Yemeksepeti.com," *Twitter*, https://jp.twitter.com/yemeksepeti; http://www.yemeksepeti.com/TR/Sehir-Secim/a.ys?redirectUrl=Default.aspx, accessed December 12, 2012; "Yemeksepeti Case Study," *StrongMail*, http://www.strongmail.com/pdf/sm_casestudy_yemeksepeti.pdf, accessed 12 December, 2012; "Yemeksepeti.com," YouTube, http://www.youtube.com/watch?v=R9j4AgX76UE, accessed December 12, 2012; "Yemeksepeti," *AceFlex*, http://aceflex.knowbase.org/usa/yemeksepeti.asp, accessed December 12, 2012.

Chapter 4

1. Interview with Stan Richards, The Richards Group, February 5, 2010.
2. Stuart Elliott, "Playing Up a Scotsman's Lawn Expertise," *The New York Times*, March 12, 2012, http://www.nytimes.com/2012/03/13/business/media/playing-up-the-lawn-ken-of-a-scotsman.html?adxnnl=1&adxnnlx=1413558370-4/ADusALTgFnCmH7dtUPLw.
3. Andrew Adam Newman, "Two Sides to a Deodorant Campaign," *The New York Times*, www.nytimes.com/2013/03/11/business/media/degree-deodorant, March 10, 2013.
4. Nancy Pekala, "Marketing to Today's Women: Focus on Life Stages, Not Ages," *Marketing Matters Newsletter*, American Marketing Association, November 10, 2009.
5. Ibid.
6. Cecilia King, "Marketers Target Moms Armed with Smartphones," *The Washington Post*, June 24, 2011, www.washingtonpost.com/business/economy/marketers-target-moms-armed-with-smartphones/2011/06/24.
7. Simon Goodall, "How to Connect with the Heart and Mind of the Male Shopper," *Advertising Age*, March 29, 2011, http://adage.com/print/149623.
8. Brian Braiker, "The Next Great American Consumer," *Adweek*, September 26, 2011, www.adweek.com/print/135207.
9. Lucia Moses, "Tweens Have a Big Say in Household Spending," *Adweek*, www.adweek.com/news/advertising-branding/tweens-have-big-say-household-spending-150570, June 26, 2013.
10. "Status, Fashion, and the Search for Value Driving Teen Spending," *Quirk's Marketing Research Media*, http://quirksblog.com/blog/2013/05/29/status-fashion-and-the-search-for-value-driving-teen-spending, May 29, 2013.
11. Gary Evans, "This Consumer Has Cash, But She's Tired," *Furniture Today* 31, no. 50 (August 27, 2007), pp. 1, 42.
12. Gavin O'Malley, "Marketers Advised to Target Ethnic Preferences," *Online Media Daily*, November 29, 2011, www.mediapost.com/publications/article/153175.
13. Tanya Irwin, "Ram Truck Hispanic Effort Most Comprehensive," *Media Post News Marketing Daily*, September 28, 2011, www.mediapost.com/publications.
14. Karlene Lukovitz, "Kraft Mac & Cheese Launches New Hispanic Creative," *Marketing Daily*, www.mediapost.com/publications/article/199450, May 2, 2013; "Brand of Opportunity: Domino's Hispanic Campaign Features Franchisee," *Advertising Age*, http://adage.com/print/242873, June 27, 2013.
15. Rebecca Piirto Heath, "Psychographics," *Marketing Tools* (November–December 1995), pp. 74–81.
16. SRI Consulting Business Intelligence (www.sric-bi.com, accessed January 3, 2008); Dana-Nicoleta Lascu and Kenneth E. Clow, *Marketing Principles*, Textbook Media, 2012.
17. Jane L. Levere, "We Have Dinner, Drinks, Swimming … Oh, and Gambling, Too," *The New York Times*, April 2, 2012, www.nytimes.com/2012/04/02/business/media.
18. "How To Get Millennials to Love and Share Your Product," *Advertising Age*, http://adage.com/print/243624, August 14, 2013.
19. David Feldman, "Segmentation Building Blocks," *Marketing Research* (Summer 2006), pp. 23–29.
20. PRIZM, "My Best Segments" (www.claritas.com/MyBestSegments/Default.jsp, accessed January 3, 2008).
21. Ronald L. Zallocco, "Benefit Segmentation of the Fitness Market," *Journal of Health Care Marketing* 12, no. 4 (December 1992), p. 80.
22. Susan Pechman, "Custom Clusters: Finding Your True Customer Segments," *Bank Marketing* 26, no. 7 (July 1994), pp. 33–35.
23. "Dairy Queen Effort Thinks Beyond the Blizzard to Burgers and Fries," *Advertising Age*, http://adage.com/print/241602, May 21, 2013.
24. Andrew Adam Newman, "Carnival Cruise Campaign Focuses on the First-Timers," *The New York Times*, December 20, 2011, www.nytimes.com/2011/12/21/business/media.
25. Gene Koprowski, "Bovine Inspiration," *Marketing Tools* (October 1996), pp. 10–11.
26. "How Swanson Broth is Adopting to the Foodie Age," *Advertising Age*, http://adage.com/print/244371, September 25, 2013.
27. Andrew Adam Newman, "Yes, the Diner's Open. How About a Seat at the Counter?" *The New York Times*, February 1, 2011, www.nytimes.com/2011/02/02/business/media/02adco.html.
28. Lionell A. Mitchell, "An Examination of Methods of Setting Advertising Budgets: Practice and Literature," *European Journal of Marketing* 27, no. 5 (1993), pp. 5–22.
29. Gregory Bresiger, "It's Ad Infinitum," *New York Post*, May 1, 2011, www.nypost.com/f/print/news/business/it_ad_infinitum_3ThF9rxodhlKnSkcIjdTPK.
30. James E. Lynch and Graham J. Hooley, "Increased Sophistication in Advertising Budget Setting," *Journal of Advertising Research* 30, no. 1 (February–March 1990), pp. 67–76.
31. James O. Peckham, "Can We Relate Advertising Dollars to Market Share Objectives?" *How Much to Spend for Advertising*, M. A. McNiver (ed.) (New York: Association of National Advertisers, 1969), p. 30.
32. "Higher Gear," *Promo Industry Trends Report* (www.promomagazine.com, accessed January 2, 2008).

33. "2004 Advertising to Sales Ratios for 200 Largest Ad Spending Industries," *Adage* (www.adage.com, accessed February 26, 2005).
34. Ingrid Lunden, "Nielsen: Old School TV Reigns Supreme at 58% of Ad Spend, Internet Display up 27% in Q2," http://techcrunch.com/2013/10/22/nielsen-internet-display-ad-spend-up-27-in-q2-but-old-school-tv-reigns-supreme-at-58-of-all-spend, October 22, 2013.
35. Shannon Dortch, "Going to the Movies," *American Demographics* 18, no. 12 (December 1996), pp. 4–8.
36. About Benihana, http://www.benihana.com/about/corporate-information/, accessed December 20, 2013.
37. Why is Facebook Blue? The Science Behind Colors in Marketing," fastcompany.com, http://www.fastcompany.com/3009317/why-is-facebook-blue-the-science-behind-colors-in-marketing, retrieved December 20, 2013.
38. Interview with Benny Black, February 18, 2010, by Donald Baack and Kenneth E. Clow.

Chapter 5

1. Jerry Olson and Thomas J. Reynolds, "Understanding Consumers' Cognitive Structures: Implications for Advertising Strategy," *Advertising Consumer Psychology,* L. Percy and A. Woodside, eds. (Lexington, MA: Lexington Books, 1983), pp. 77–90; Thomas J. Reynolds and Alyce Craddock, "The Application of the MECCAS Model to Development and Assessment of Advertising Strategy," *Journal of Advertising Research* 28, no. 2 (1988), pp. 43–54.
2. Laurie A. Babin and Alvin C. Burns, "Effects of Print Ad Pictures and Copy Containing Instructions to Imagine on Mental Imagery That Mediates Attitudes," *Journal of Advertising* 26, no. 3 (Fall 1997), pp. 33–44.
3. Marc Bourgery and George Guimaraes, "Global Ads: Say It with Pictures," *Journal of European Business* 4, no. 5 (May–June 1993), pp. 22–26.
4. Gerard J. Tellis, "Study: Advertising Half as Effective as Previously Believed," *Advertising Age*, June 26, 2011, http://adage.com/print/228409.
5. Margaret Henderson Blair, "An Empirical Investigation of Advertising Wearin and Wearout," *Journal of Advertising Research* 40, no. 6 (November–December 2000), pp. 95–100.
6. Ibid.
7. Gerard J. Tellis, "Study: Advertising Half as Effective as Previously Believed," *Advertising Age*, June 26, 2011, http://adage.com/print/228409.
8. "Leaner Ad Budgets Mean More Marketers Rely on In-House Agencies," *Advertising Age*, http://adage.com/print/243976, September 5, 2013.
9. G+G Advertising (**www.gng.net**, accessed January 16, 2010); "G&G Advertising," *Agency Compile* (**www.agencycompile.com/factsheet/factsheet.aspx?agency_id=7823**, accessed January 16, 2010).
10. Bruce Horovitz, "Amateur Doritos Ad Maker Could Win $1M… and a Job," *USA Today, Money*, accessed November 27, 2011, www.usatoday.com/money/media/story/2011-09-26.
11. Prashant Malaviya, "Consumer-Generated Ads: Good for Retention, Bad for Growth," *Forbes*, www.forbes.com/sites/onmarketing/2013/07/02/consumer-generated-ads-good-for-retention-bad-for-growth, July 2, 2013.
12. E.J. Schultz and Rupal Parekh, "Behind Kraft's Seismic Shift: Why It's Shaking Up Its Shops," *Advertising Age*, November 15, 2010, http://adage.com/print?article_id=147105.
13. Suzanne Vranica and Daniel Fitzpatrick, "BofA Reviews Ad Strategy," *Wall Street Journal*, January 12, 2012, http://online.wsj.com/article/SB10001424052970204257504577155 0.
14. Heather Jacobs, "How to Make Sure Your Pitch Is Heard," *B&T Weekly* 57, no. 2597 (February 8, 2007), pp. 14–16.
15. Interview with Jane Hilk, Senior Vice President of Marketing, Oscar Mayer, January 28, 2010.
16. Emily Bryson York, "Behind Kraft's Marketing Makeover: From New Ad Agencies to New Attitude," *Advertising Age* (http://adage.com/article?article_id=141943), February 8, 2010.
17. Jacobs, "How to Make Sure Your Pitch Is Heard."
18. Steve Miller, "VW Is Going Outdoors, Literally," *Brandweek.com* (http://brandweek.com/VW+IS+Going+Outdoor), June 23, 2008.
19. Jack Neff, "The Newest Ad Agencies: Major Media Companies," *Advertising Age* (http://adage.com/print?article_id=140712), November 3, 2008.
20. "Media Agencies Make Mark as Content Creators," *Advertising Age*, April 24, 2011, http://adage.com/print/227163.
21. Interview with Jane Hilk, Sr. Vice President of Marketing, Oscar Mayer, January 28, 2010.
22. H. Rao Unnava and Deepak Sirdeshmukh, "Reducing Competitive Ad Interference," *Journal of Marketing Research* 31, no. 3 (August 1994), pp. 403–411.
23. Naveen Donthu, "A Cross-Country Investigation of Recall of and Attitudes Toward Comparative Advertising," *Journal of Advertising* 27, no. 2 (Summer 1998), pp. 111–21.
24. "Survey: Clients Must Improve Quality of Briefs to Agencies if They Want Better Work," *Advertising Age*, http://adage.com/print/241065, April 24, 2013.
25. Henry A. Laskey and Richard J. Fox, "The Relationship Between Advertising Message Strategy and Television Commercial Effectiveness,"*Journal of Advertising Research* 35, no. 2 (March–April 1995), pp. 31–39.
26. Herbert E. Krugman, "Memory Without Recall, Exposure Without Perception," *Journal of Advertising Research* 40, no. 6 (November–December 2000), pp. 49–55; David Kay, "Left Brain Versus Right Brain," *Marketing Magazine* 108, no. 36 (October 27, 2003), p. 37.
27. "Picking Up the Pace," *Marketing News* 36, no. 7 (April 1, 2002), p. 3.
28. Laurel Wentz and Bradley Johnson, "Top 100 Global Advertisers Heap Their Spending Abroad," *Advertising Age* (http://adage.com/print?article_id=140723), November 30, 2009.

Chapter 6

1. Mark Dolliver, "Assessing the Power of Ads," *Adweek.com* (http://adweek.com/aw/content_display/news/agency/e3i34e2ede5adb7e1e8aa21d1f4fa3b2d0b), June 22, 2009.
2. Henry A. Laskey, Ellen Day, and Melvin R. Crask, "Typology of Main Message Strategies for Television Commercials," *Journal of Advertising* 18, no. 1 (1989), pp. 36–41.
3. David Aaker and Donald Norris, "Characteristics of TV Commercials Perceived as Informative," *Journal of Advertising Research* 22, no. 2 (1982), pp. 61–70.
4. **www.campbellsoupcompany.com/atw_usa.asp** (accessed January 12, 2008).
5. Wolfgang Gruener, "Nintendo Wii Surrenders Market Share in Weak Game Console Market," *TG Daily* (**www.tgdaily.com/trendwatch-features/43289**), July 17, 2009.
6. Tony Smith, "Intel Extends Market Share Gains," *Register Hardware* (**www.reghardware.co.uk/2007/04/20/intel_vs_amd_q1_07/print.html**), April 20, 2007.

7. Shailendra Pratap Jain and Steven S. Posavac, "Valenced Comparisons," *Journal of Marketing Research* 41, no. 1 (February 2004), pp. 46–56.
8. Dhruv Grewal and Sukumar Kavanoor, "Comparative Versus Noncomparative Advertising: A Meta-Analysis," *Journal of Marketing* 61, no. 4 (October 1997), pp. 1–15; Shailendra Pratap Jain and Steven S. Posavac, "Valenced Comparisons," *Journal of Marketing Research* 41, no. 9. (February 2004), pp. 46–56.
9. "Microsoft's Google-Bashing Try Campaign Is Actually Working," *Advertising Age*, http://adage.com/print/244691, October 15, 2013.
10. Aaron Baar, "Subaru Taps Nostalgia for the First Car," *Marketing Daily*, February 26, 2012, www.mediapost.com/publications/article/168531.
11. Stuart Elliott, "In New Ads, Stirring Memories of Commercials Past," *The New York Times*, January 12, 2012, www.nytimes.com/2012/01/13/business/media/stirring-memories-of-commercials-past.
12. Joanne Lynch and Leslie de Chernatony, "The Power of Emotion: Brand Communication in Business-to-Business Markets," *Journal of Brand Management* 11, no. 5 (May 2004), pp. 403–420.
13. Based on Rosemary M. Murtaugh, "Designing Effective Health Promotion Messages Using Components of Protection Motivation Theory," *Proceedings of the Atlantic Marketing Association* (1999), pp. 553–57; R. W. Rogers and S. Prentice-Dunn, "Protection Motivation Theory," *Handbook of Health Behavior Research I: Personal and Social Determinants,* D. Gochman, ed. (New York: Plenum Press, 1997), pp. 130–32.
14. Ibid.
15. Michael S. Latour and Robin L. Snipes, "Don't Be Afraid to Use Fear Appeals: An Experimental Study," *Journal of Advertising Research* 36, no. 2 (March–April 1996), pp. 59–68.
16. Martin Eisend, "A Meta-Analysis of Humor Effects in Advertising," *Advances in Consumer Research–North American Conference Proceedings* 34 (2007), pp. 320–23.
17. James J. Kellaris and Thomas W. Cline, "Humor and Ad Memorability," *Psychology & Marketing* 24, no. 6 (June 2007), pp. 497–509.
18. Theresa Howard, "Windex Birds Make Clean Sweep as Most-Liked Ads," *USA Today* (December 18, 2006), p. 7B (Money).
19. Matthew Creamer, "Marketing's Era of Outrage," *Advertising Age* 78, no. 7 (February 12, 2007), pp. 1, 26.
20. "Sex Doesn't Sell," *The Economist* 373, no. 8399 (October 30, 2004), pp. 62–63.
21. Andrew Adam Newman, "Selling a Household Cleaning Product on Its…Sex Appeal?" *The New York Times* (**www.nytimes.com/2009/11/13/business/media/13adco.html**), November 13, 2009.
22. Sandra O'Loughlin, "Hanes Shows Some 'Love' in Battle for Intimates," *Brandweek* 48, no. 9 (February 26, 2007), p. 11.
23. Bob Garfield, "Dentyne Spot Makes It Seem That Naysayers Have a Point," *Advertising Age* 76, no. 5 (January 31, 2005), p. 41.
24. Based on G. Smith and R. Engel, "Influence of a Female Model on Perceived Characteristics of an Automobile," *Proceedings of the 76th Annual Convention of the American Psychological Association* 15, no. 3 (1968), pp. 46–54; Leonard Reid and Lawrence C. Soley, "Decorative Models and the Readership of Magazine Ads,"*Journal of Advertising Research* 23 (April–May 1983), pp. 27–32; R. Chestnut, C. LaChance, and A. Lubitz, "The Decorative Female Model: Sexual Stimuli and the Recognition of Advertisements," *Journal of Advertising* 6 (Fall 1977), pp. 11–14.
25. Jessica Severn, George E. Belch, and Michael A. Belch, "The Effects of Sexual and Non-Sexual Advertising Appeals and Information Level on Cognitive Processing and Communication Effectiveness," *Journal of Advertising* 19, no. 1 (1990), pp. 14–22.
26. Tom Reichart, "Sex in Advertising Research: A Review of Content, Effects, and Functions of Sexual Information in Consumer Advertising," *Annual Review of Sex Research* 13 (2002), pp. 242–74; D. C. Bello, R. E. Pitts, and M. J. Etzel, "The Communication Effects of Controversial Sexual Content in Television Programs and Commercials," *Journal of Advertising* 3, no. 12 (1983), pp. 32–42.
27. "Note to Chrysler: Gutter Humor Has No Place in Ads," *Automotive News* 78, no. 6064 (October 27, 2003), p. 12.
28. Tom Reichart, "Sex in Advertising Research: A Review of Content, Effects, and Functions of Sexual Information in Consumer Advertising," *Annual Review of Sex Research* 13 (2002), pp. 242–74; Andrew A. Mitchell, "The Effect of Verbal and Visual Components of Advertisements on Brand Attitude and Attitude Toward the Advertisement," *Journal of Consumer Research* 13 (June 1986), pp. 12–24.
29. Bruce Horovitz, "Risqué May Be Too Risky for Ads," *USA Today* (April 16, 2004), p. 1B.
30. Julie Naughton and Amy Wicks, "Eva's Seduction: Calvin Klein Stirs Controversy with Mendes Ads," *Women's Wear Daily* 196, no. 25 (August 4, 2008), p. 1.
31. Kate Lunau, "Study Finds Real Women Don't Sell," *Maclean's* 121, no. 33 (August 25, 2008), p. 34.
32. Howard Levine, Donna Sweeney, and Stephen H. Wagner, "Depicting Women as Sex Objects in Television Advertising," *Personality and Social Psychology Bulletin* 25, no. 8 (August 1999), pp. 1049–58.
33. Steve Oakes, "Evaluating Empirical Research into Music in Advertising: A Congruity Perspective," *Journal of Advertising Research* 47, no. 1 (March 2007), pp. 38–50.
34. Andrew Hampp, "A Reprise for Jingles in Madison Avenue," *Advertising Age*, September 6, 2010, http://adage.com/pring?article_id=145744.
35. Felicity Shea, "Reaching Youth with Music," *B&T Weekly* 54, no. 2491 (October 1, 2004), pp. 16–17.
36. Brian Steinberg, "The Times Are a-Changin' for Musicians and Marketers," *Advertising Age* 78, no. 43 (October 29, 2005) p. 43.
37. Nicole Rivard, "Maximizing Music," *SHOOT* 48, no. 4 (February 23, 2007), pp. 17–21.
38. Douglas Quenqua, "What's That Catchy Tune? A Song for Car Insurance Makes the Charts," *The New York Times* (**www.nytimes.com/2007/12/31/business/media/31allstate.html**), December 31, 2007.
39. Stuart Elliott, "Godiva Rides in a New Direction," *The New York Times* (**www.nytimes.com/2009/11/16/business/media/16adnewsletter1.html**), November 16, 2009.
40. Joanne Lynch and Leslie de Chernatony, "The Power of Emotion: Brand Communication in Business-to-Business Markets," *Journal of Brand Management* 11, no. 5 (May 2004), pp. 403–20; Karalynn Ott, "B-to-B Marketers Display Their Creative Side," *Advertising Age's Business Marketing* 84, no. 1 (January 1999), pp. 3–4.
41. Stephanie Thompson, "Big Deal," *Mediaweek* 7, no. 44 (November 24, 1997), p. 36; Judann Pollack, "Big G Has Special Cheerios for Big '00," *Advertising Age* (June 14, 1999), pp. 1–2.

42. Jim Hanas, "Rotoscope Redux," *Creativity* 10, no. 1 (February 2002), pp. 40–41.
43. Interview with Stan Richards by Donald Baack and Kenneth E. Clow, January 20, 2010.
44. Aaron Baar, "For Stein Mart, It's Love at First Find," *Marketing Daily*, September 10, 2011, www.mediapost.com/publications.
45. Matthew Warren, "Do Celebrity Endorsements Still Work?" *Campaign (UK)* 44 (November 2, 2007) p. 13.
46. "Angelina Joli to be $10m face of Louis Vuitton," *Marketing*, www.marketingmagazine.co.uk/news/1067170, accessed May 3, 2011.
47. "Highest Paid Athletes," *Buzzle.com*, www.buzzle.com/articles/highest-paid-athletes.htmil, accessed April 16, 2012.
48. Jonathan Wexler, "Who Is the Athlete With the Most Endorsements?" Playing Field Promotions (**www.playingfieldpromotions.com/blog/438/who-is-the-athlete-with-the-most-endorsements**), June 9, 2009.
49. Interview with Stan Richards by Donald Baack and Kenneth E. Clow, January 20, 2010.
50. Laura Petrecca, "Small Companies Seek Publicity from Celebrities," *USA Today*, www.usatoday.com/cleanprint/?1296061644796, accessed January 26, 2011.
51. Claire Murphy, "Stars Brought Down to Earth in TV Ads Research," *Marketing* (January 22, 1998), p. 1.
52. Kamile Junokaite, Sonata Alijosiene, and Rasa Gudonaviciene, "The Solutions of Celebrity Endorsers Selection for Advertising Products," *Economics & Management* 12, no. 3 (2007), pp. 384–90.
53. Stuart Elliott, "La-Z-Boy, Meet Brooke Shields," *The New York Times*, November 29, 2010, www.nytimes.com/2010/11/29/business/media/29adnewsletter1.html.
54. "Betty White Voted America's Most Trusted Celebrity: Poll," *Reuters*, August 18, 2011, www.reuters.com/assets/print?aid=USTRE77H2WE20110818.
55. Roobina Ohanian, "Construction and Validation of a Scale to Measure Celebrity Endorsers' Perceived Expertise," *Journal of Advertising* 19, no. 3 (1990), pp. 39–52.
56. Kenneth Hein, "Danica Patrick Talks GoDaddy, Pepsi," *Brandweek* (**www.brandweek.com/bw/content_display/news-and-features/direct/e3i7a35e791d5c**), November 30, 2009.
57. Dipayan Biswas, Abhijit Biswas, and Neel Das, "The Differential Effects of Celebrity and Expert Endorsements on Consumer Risk Perceptions," *Journal of Advertising* 35, no. 2 (Summer 2006), pp. 17–31.
58. David J. Moore and John C. Mowen, "Multiple Sources in Advertising Appeals: When Product Endorsers Are Paid by the Advertising Sponsor," *Journal of Academy of Marketing Science* 22, no. 3 (Summer 1994), pp. 234–43.
59. Raymond R. Burke and Thomas K. Srull, "Competitive Interference and Consumer Memory for Advertising," *Journal of Consumer Research* 15 (June 1988), pp. 55–68.
60. Karen Robinson-Jacobs, "With Employees in Ads, Pizza Hut Goes for Slices of Life," *The Dallas Morning News*, November 17, 2010, www.dallasnews.com/sharedcontent/dws/bus/stories.
61. Safe Food Centre website, www.safoodcentre.com.au, accessed November 16, 2010; Charlie's Group website, www.charliesgroup.co.nz, accessed November 16, 2010.
62. Mavi US website, http://us.mavi.com/, accessed December 2012; Mavi Turkey website, http://tr.mavi.com/, accessed December 2012; Perlin Turgut, "Making the Perfect Fit," *Time Magazine*, February 23, 2003, http://www.time.com/time/magazine/article/0,9171,425833,00.html.

Chapter 7

1. UEFA Champions League website, www.uefa.com/uefachampionsleague, accessed November 11, 2010; SportsPro Media website, www.sportspromedia.com, accessed November 11, 2010.
2. Creative Blog: Top 35 TV Commercials, Oreos, http://www.creativebloq.com/3d/top-tv-commercials-12121024, retrieved January 14, 2014.
3. Mickey Marks, "Millennial Satiation," *Advertising Age* 14 (February 2000), p. S16; J. Thomas Russell and W. Ronald Lane, *Kleppner's Advertising Procedure*, 15th ed. (Upper Saddle River, NJ: Prentice Hall), 2002, pp. 174–75.
4. Larry Percy, John R. Rossiter, and Richard Elliott, "Media Strategy," *Strategic Advertising Management* (2001), pp. 151–63.
5. Kate Maddox, "Media Planners in High Demand," *BtoB* 89, no. 13 (November 8, 2004), p. 24.
6. Arthur A. Andersen, "Clout Only a Part of Media Buyer's Value," *Advertising Age* 70, no. 15 (April 5, 1999), p. 26.
7. Ibid.
8. Herbert E. Krugman, "Why Three Exposures May Be Enough," *Journal of Advertising Research* 12, no. 6 (1972), pp. 11–14.
9. Erwin Ephron and Colin McDonald, "Media Scheduling and Carry-over Effects: Is Adstock a Useful Planning Tool," *Journal of Advertising Research* 42, no. 4 (July–August 2002), pp. 66–70; Laurie Freeman, "Added Theories Drive Need for Client Solutions," *Advertising Age* 68, no. 31, p. 18.
10. Larry Percy, John R. Rossiter, and Richard Elliott, "Media Strategy," *Strategic Advertising Management* (2001), pp. 151–63.
11. Ibid.
12. Jack Loechner, "TV Advertising Most Influential," *Media Post Research Brief*, March 23, 2011, www.mediapost.com/publications/?fa=articles.printfriendly&art_aid=147033.
13. Diane Holloway, "What's On? Ads, Ads, and Maybe a TV Show," *Austin American Statesman* (**www.austin360.com/tv/content/movies**/television/2005/10/11tvcolumn.html, accessed January 17, 2008), October 11, 2005.
14. Jack Neff, "Future of Advertising? Print, TV, Online Ads," *Advertising Age* (**www.adage.com/print?article_id=136993**), June 1, 2009; Gregory Solman, "Forward Thought: Ads A-Ok on DVRs," *Hollywood Reporter* (http://hollywoodreporter.com), December 27, 2007.
15. Steve McClellan, "Audit Finds Nielsen's C3 Ratings Hurt Advertisers," *Media Daily News*, September 19, 2011, www.mediapost.com/publications/article/158818.
16. Brian Steinberg, "Simon Who? Idol Spots Still Priciest in Prime Time," *Advertising Age*, October 18, 2010, http://adage.com/pring/146495.
17. Adapted from Brian Steinberg, "Sunday Night Football Remains Costliest TV Show," *Advertising Age* (http://adage.com/article?article_id=139923), October 26, 2009; "List of Top 20 Prime-time Programs in the Nielsen Ratings for Sept. 28–Oct. 4," *Entertainment Daily* (http://blog.taragana.com/e/2009/10/06/list-of-top-20-prime-time-programs-in-the-nielsen-ratings-for-sept28-oct4), October 6, 2009.
18. Karlene Lukovitz, "Regional Gain Uses TV to Take On Big Pizza Brands," *Marketing Daily*, November 15, 2011, www.mediapost.com/publications/article/162392.
19. Andy Fixmer, Ian King, and Cliff Edwards, "DirecTV Upends Ad Model with Toyota Spots of Auto Geeks," *Bloomberg Businessweek* www.businessweek.com/printer/articles/596492, September 23, 2013.

20. Gavin O'Mally, "Social Media Chatter Ups Live TV Stats," *MediaPost News*, March 22, 2012, www.mediapost.com/publications/articl/170743; Jack Loechner, "TV Advertising Most Influential," *Media Post Research Brief*, March 23, 2011, www.mediapost.com/publications/?fa=articles.printfriendly&art_aid=147033.
21. Anthony Crupi, "Commercial Breaks Aren't Twitter Breaks," *Adweek*, www.adweek.com/news/advertising-branding/commercial-breaks-arent-twitter-breaks, September 18, 2013.
22. Ki Mae Heussner, "Social Data Uncovers Brand, TV-Show Affinity," *Adweek*, December 22, 2011, www.adweek.com/print/137243.
23. Susan Kuchinsakas, "Brands Increase Recall with TV/Digital Mix, Google Says," *ClickZ*, December 6, 2011, www.clickz.com/print_article/clikz/stats/2130484.
24. Gabriel Beltrone, "Ads Trump Football in Super Bowl Survey," *Adweek*, www.adweek.com/news/advertising-branding/ads-trump-football-in-super-bowl-survey, January 24, 2013; Stuart Elliott, "Mainstays Will Reappear in the Big Game Again," *The New York Times*, January 27, 2012, www.nytimes.com/2012/01/27/business/media/mainstays-will-reappear-in-the-big-game-once-again.
25. Stuart Elliott, "Before the Toss, Super Bowl Ads," *The New York Times*, February 2, 2012, www.nytimes.com/2012/02/03/business/media/before-the-toss-super-bowl-ads; Stuart Elliott, "Before Sunday, A Taste of the Bowl," *The New York Times*, February 3, 2012, www.nytimes.com/2011/02/04/business/media/04adco.html. G28
26. Interview with Stan Richards, The Richards Group, February 4, 2010; Rupal Parekh, "Behind the Scenes of Bridgestone's Super Bowl Spots," *Advertising Age*, February 8, 2010, pp. 4–5.
27. Doug McPherson, "Into Thin Air," *Response* 18, no. 5 (February 2010), pp. 40–45.
28. Interview with Mary Price by Donald Baack and Kenneth E. Clow, January 20, 2010.
29. Doug McPherson, "Into Thin Air," *Response* 18, no. 5 (February 2010), pp. 40–45.
30. Sarah Mahoney, "Taco Tweets Fuel Texas C-Store's Advertising," *Media Post News, Marketing Daily*, February 9, 2011, www.mediapost.com/publications/?fa=Articles.print_aid=144522.
31. Morianna Morello, "Why Print Media—and Why Now?" *Response* 17, no. 8 (May 2009), p. 77.
32. Edward C. Baig, "DirecTV Takes the Dive with SI's Swimsuit Issue," *USA Today Money*, February 1, 2012, www.usatoday.com/money/media/story/2012-02-01/directv-takes-the-dive-with-sis-swimsuit-issue.
33. Nat Ives, "If You're Rich, You Still Have Time to Read," *Advertising Age* (**www.adage.com/print?article_id=130685**), September 2, 2008.
34. Erik Sass, "Newspaper Ads Still Guide Shopping," *Media Daily News*, April 13, 2011, www.mediapost.com/publications/?fa=Articles=148632.
35. Bill Gloede, "Best Use of Newspapers," *Adweek* 48, no. 25 (June 18, 2007), pp. SR22–23.
36. Erik Sass, "Newspaper's Digital Audience Skews Younger, More Affluent," *Media Daily News*, December 13, 2011, www.mediapost.como/publications/article/164161.
37. *Marketer Trees 2009* (http://adage.com/marketertres09), December 28, 2009.
38. Lindsay Morris, "Studies Give 'Thumbs Up' to Mags for Ad Awareness," *Advertising Age* 70, no. 32 (August 2, 1999), pp. 16–17; Rachel X. Weissman, "Broadcasters Mine the Gold," *American Demographics* 21, no. 6 (June 1999), pp. 35–37.
39. Stacey Pratt, "Planning Casebook," *Mediaweek*, no. 1230 (October 20, 2009), p. 17.
40. "ABM Releases Harris Study Data: B2B Advertising Highly Effective," *Min's B2B* 9, no. 26 (June 26, 2006), p. 8.
41. Kate Maddox, "Top 100 B-to-B Advertisers Increased Spending 3% in '06," *BtoB* 92, no. 11 (September 10, 2007), pp. 25–30.
42. Ibid.
43. Eric Pfanner, "TV Still Has a Hold on Teenagers," *The New York Times* (**www.nytimes.com/2009/12/14/business/media/14iht-cache14.html**), December 14, 2009.
44. Joe Mandese, "Power Shift," *Broadcasting & Cable* 135, no. 53 (December 12, 2005), p. 12.
45. Martin Croft, "Media Indies Take on Networks with Consortium," *Marketing Week* 29, no. 28 (July 13, 2006), p. 13.
46. Interview with Bill Breedlove by Donald Baack and Kenneth E. Clow, January 21, 2010.
47. Jack Neff, "Media Buying & Planning." *Advertising Age* 70, no. 32 (August 2, 1999), pp. 1–2.
48. Alison Smith, Duracell Releases Ad Featuring Deaf Seahawks Fullback Derrick Coleman: Urges People to Use Your Power, NFL.com http://nesn.com/2014/01/duracell-releases-ad-featuring-deaf-seahawks-running-back-derrick-coleman-urges-to-trust-your-power-video/, retrieved January 14, 2014.
49. Yahoo! Sports. Want Goosebumps? Watch this commercial featuring deaf Seahawks fullback Derrick Coleman, January 14, 2014, http://sports.yahoo.com/blogs/nfl-shutdown-corner/want-goosebumps-watch-commercial-featuring-deaf-seahawks-fullback-173222906—nfl.html, retrieved January 14, 2014.
50. Tim Nudd, Deaf NFL Player Derrick Coleman Tells His Story in a Terrific Duracell Ad, *Adweek*, January 13, 2014, http://www.adweek.com/adfreak/deaf-nfl-player-derrick-coleman-tells-his-story-terrific-duracell-ad-154952, retrieved January 14, 2014.

Chapter 8

1. Toucan Limited website, www.toucan.ae, accessed November 16, 2010; Tobago Online Booking Engine, www.visittobago.gov.tt, accessed November 16, 2010; Tobago House Assembly website, www.tha.gov.tt, accessed November 16, 2010.
2. Brian Morrissey, "Real Time: The Web's New Prime Time," *Adweek* (**www.adweek.com/aw/content_display/news/digital/e3i15f4e2b3b4a487b3b5cd5347ebd07cbf**), May 25, 2009.
3. Cate T. Corcoran, "Delivering the Goods: E-tailing Sales to Rise But Gains Seen Slowing," *Women's Wear Daily* 197, no. 94 (May 5, 2009), p. 94.
4. Michael Stich, Jim Leonard, and Jennifer Rooney, "Ring Up E-Commerce Gains with True Multichannel Strategy," *Advertising Age* 79, no. 10 (March 10, 2008), p. 15.
5. "Consumers Embrace Internet as Regular Shopping Tool," *Australian Giftguide* (October–December 2009), p. 10.
6. Amy Cravens, "How New Devices, Networks, and Consumer Habits Will Change the Web Experience," *Giga Omni Media White Paper*, January 22, 2013 (www.pro.gigaom.com).
7. David Sparrow, "Get 'em to Bite," *Catalog Age* 20, no. 4 (April 2003), pp. 35–36.
8. Amanda Gaines, "Leading the Charge," *Retail Merchandiser* 49, no. 6 (November–December 2009), pp. 16–19.
9. Mike Fletcher, "How to Create the Perfect E-Commerce Website," *Revolution* (March 2009), pp. 60–63.
10. Joab Jackson, "E-Consumers Get Smart," *CIO* 23, no. 7 (February 1, 2010), p. 18.

11. Gwen Moran, "Check Out Your Checkout," *Entrepreneur* 38, no. 1 (January 2010), p. 38.
12. Lisa Cervini, "Free Shipping Offers Fueling Online Sales," *This Week in Consumer Electronics* 20, no. 24 (November 21, 2005), p. 16.
13. "Data-Insecurity Fears Said to Hamper Online Shopping," *CardLine* 9, no. 13 (March 27, 2009), p. 34.
14. Suzanne Beame, "Consumer Confidence in Online Shopping Sites Is on the Rise," *New Media Age* (November 15, 2007), p. 15.
15. "Online Consumers Happy to Be Tracked," *The Wall Street Journal*, December 5, 2011, http://blogs/wsj.com/tech-europe/2011/12/05/online-consumers-happy-to-be-tracked.
16. "Multiscreen Campaign Importance Rises with Smart Device Use," *eMarketer*, November 25, 2013, www.emarketer.com/articles/print.aspx?R=1010413.
17. Roger Matus, "Mobile Action Codes in Magazine Advertising," white paper from Nellymoser, Inc. (www.nellymoser.com), p. 4.
18. Shama Hyder Kabani, "Online Marketing Plan," The Marketing Zen Group (**www.marketingzen.com**), pp. 9–13.
19. March Cohen, "A Revolutionary Marketing Strategy: Answer Customers' Questions," *The New York Times*, www.nytimes.com/2013/02/28/business/smallbusiness, February 27, 2013.
20. William Launder, "Marketers Seek Extra Edge to Go Viral," *Wall Street Journal*, http://online.wsj.com/article/SB10001424127887323980604579031391201753578, August 25, 2013.
21. Lauren Johnson, "McDonald's Puts Location at Core of iTunes Radio Launch Campaign," *Mobile Marketer*, www.mobilemarketer.com/cms/news/advertising/16531, November 5, 2013.
22. Rimma Kats, "Applebee's Drives Foot Traffic via Targeted Location-Based Mobile Campaign," www.mobilecommercedaily.com/applebees-drive-foot-traffic-via-targeted-location-based-mobile-campaign, May 15, 2013.
23. "Timberland, Kenneth Cole Track Shoppers Who Opt-In for Deals," *Advertising Age*, http://adage.com/print/243811, August 26, 2013.
24. Mark Walsch, "Location-Based Mobile Ads Deliver Best Engagement, Performance," *Online Media Daily*, www.mediapost.com/publications/article/192780, February 6, 2013.
25. Lucia Moses, "Online Video Ads Have Higher Impact Than TV Ads," *Adweek*, www.adweek.com/news/advertising-branding/online-video-ads-have-higher-impact-than-tv-ads-148982, May 1, 2013.
26. Zach James, "Forget Amazon. YouTube is Where Shoppers Do Research," *Adweek*, www.adweek.com/videowatch/forget-amazon-youtube-is-where-shoppers-do-research-152068, August 28, 2013.
27. Mike Shields, "Social Sites Not as Video Ad Friendly as Content, E-mail," *Mediaweek* (**www.mediaweek.com/mw/content_display/news/digital-downloads/metrics**), November 18, 2009.
28. Beth Snyder Bulik, "Does Your Company Need a Chief Blogger?" *Advertising Age* 79, no. 15 (April 14, 2008), p. 24.
29. Sarah Halzack, "Marketing Moves to the Blogosphere," *Washingtonpost.com* (**www.washingtonpost.com/wp-dyn/content/article/2008/08/24/AR20080824051517**), August 25, 2008.
30. Ibid.
31. Basil Katz, "Email Newsletters Aim for Inbox and Wallet," *Reuters* (**www.reuters.com/articlePrint?articleId=USTRE5894XI20090910**), September 10, 2009.
32. Karen J. Bannan, "The Mandate to Integrate," *BtoB* 94, no. 12 (September 28, 2009), p. 23.
33. "Re-Marketing Helps Boost Online Shoppers' Baskets," *Data Strategy* 3, no. 7 (May 2007), p. 9.
34. Ingrid Lunden, "Nielsen: Internet Display Advertising Grew 32% in 2013," http://techcrunch.com/2014/01/27/nielsen-internet-display-advertising-grew-32-in-2103, January 27, 2014.
35. "Online Ad Spending Consolidates Among Search, Banners, Video," *eMarkter Digital Intelligence*, February 3, 2012, www.smarketer.com/articles/print.aspx?R=1008815.
36. Brian Morrissey, "Beefing Up Banner Ads," *Adweek* (**www.adweek.com/aw/content_display/news/digital/e3if04360897e1103df4b92464543af6649**), February 15, 2010.
37. Josh Quittner, Jessi Hempel, and Lindsay Blakely, "The Battle for Your Social Circle," *Fortune* 156, no. 10 (November 26, 2007), pp. 11–13.
38. "Is Online Advertising Getting Too Complex?" *Advertising Age*, http://adage.com/print/245070, November 1, 2013.
39. Suzanne Vranica, "Web Display Ads Often Not Visible," *Wall Street Journal*, http://online.wsj.com/article/SB10001424127887324904004578537131312357490, November 10, 2013.
40. Michael Fielding, "We Can All Get Along," *Marketing News*, May 15, 2007, p. 4.
41. Paula Andruss, "Personalized URLS," *Marketing News*, September 1, 2008, p. 10.
42. "Problem Solved," *BtoB* 92, no. 15 (November 12, 2007), p. 21; "Online Ad Spending Consolidates Among Search, Banners, Video," *eMarketer Digital Intelligence*, February 3, 2012, www.smarketer.com/articles/print.aspx?R=1008815.
43. "Problem Solved," *BtoB* 92, no. 15 (November 12, 2007), p. 21.
44. Jack Neff, "Why CPG Brands Better Buy Paid Search," *Advertising Age* (http://adage.com/print?article_id=130353), August 18, 2008.
45. Josh Quittner, Jessi Hempel, and Lindsay Blakely, "The Battle for Your Social Circle," *Fortune* 156, no. 10 (November 26, 2007), pp. 11–13.
46. "Google Searches for Success in Local Ads," *Advertising Age*, March 1, 2011, http://adage.com/print/149140.
47. Lynda Radosevich, "Going Global Overnight," *InfoWorld* 21, no. 16 (April 19, 1999), pp. 1–3.
48. "Visa and comGateway Bring Black Friday Savings to Hong Kong's Online Shoppers," November 20, 2012, www.visa-asia.com; Jennifer Booton, "America's Black Friday Frenzy Goes Global," *Fox Business*, December 4, 2012, www.foxbusiness.com/industries/2012/12/04/globalizing-america-retail-culture; "China's Singles Day Beats the U.S. Black Friday on e-sales," *Advertising at China Smack*, December 3, 2012, www.advertising.chinasmack.com/2012/chinas-singles-day-beats-the-us-black-friday-on-e-sales.html.
49. "Arab Media Outlook 2011–2015," Arab Media Forum, http://www.arabmediaforum.ae/en/amo.aspx, accessed December 9, 2012; "LivingSocial Shuts up Shop in Middle East," *The National*, http://www.thenational.ae/business/retail/livingsocialshutsup-shop-in-middle-east#ixzz2EZyaP7kC, accessed December 9, 2012; "Group Buying Websites Battle for Middle East Shoppers with Online Bargains," Wamda.com, http://www.wamda.com/2012/02/group-buying-websites-battle-for-middleeastshoppers-with-online-bargains, accessed December 9, 2012; "Group Buying; Good or Bad for Business?," *Web, News & Features*, ITP.net, http://www.itp.net/585502-groupbuying-goodor-bad-for-business, accessed December 9, 2012.

Chapter 9

1. http://eatwholly.com/our-story.html.
2. Christopher Heine, "Study: Women Love Social Media More Than Men," *Adweek*, www.adweek.com/news/technology/study-women-love-social-media-more-than-men, December 30, 2103.
3. Maeve Duggan and Joanna Brenner, "The Demographics of Social Media Users–2012," *Pew Research Center*, www.pewresearch.org, February 14, 2013.
4. Daniel Frankel, "Report: Facebook, Google Overtake Yahoo in Display Ad Market Share," *PaidContent.org*, February 22, 2012, http://cnt.to/pUc.
5. Brian Womack, "Facebook Boosts Targeting Options for Advertisers," *Bloomberg*, www.bloomberg.com/news/print/2-13-10-15/facebook-boosts-targeting-options-for-advertisers, October 15, 2013.
6. Reed Albergotti, "Few Facebook Users Share Daily, Survey Says," *Wall Street Journal*, http://online.wsj.com/news/articles/SB1000142405270230448511045, February 3, 2014; Scott Martin, "Facebook's Teens Plummet as Elders Surge," *USA Today*, www.usatoday.com/story/tech/2014/01/16/facebooks-teens-plummet-as-elders-surge, January 16, 2014.
7. John Koetsier, "Twitter and Social Commerce: Facebook Generates 10X Shares, 20X Traffic, 30X Customers," http://venturebeat.com/2013/10/25/twitter-facebook-and-social-commerce-facebook-generates-10x-shares-20x-traffic-30x-customers," October 25, 2013.
8. Brian Morrissey, "Brands Seek Fans on Facebook," *Adweek.com* (http://adweek.com/aw/content_display/news/digital/e3id3d058ba458918f0fc8ec45), October 12, 2009.
9. Mark Walsh, "Study: Social Media Pays," *Media Post News, Online Media Daily*, (**www.mediapost.com/publications/?fa=Articles_aid=110120**), July 20, 2009.
10. Yoree Koh, "Twitter Users' Diversity Becomes an Ad Selling Point," *Wall Street Journal*, http://online.wsj.com/news/articles/SB100014240527023044191045, January 20, 2014.
11. Todd Wasserman, "Starbucks 'Tweet-a-Coffee' Campaign Prompted $180,000 in Purchases," http://mashable.com/2013/12/05/starbucks-tweet-a-coffee-180000, December 5, 2013.
12. Claire Cain Miller, "Marketing Small Businesses with Twitter," *The New York Times* (**www.nytimes.com/2009/07/23/business/smallbusiness/23twitter.html**), July 23, 2009.
13. Zach James, "Fans Crush Brands When It Comes to YouTube Branded Content Pales in Comparison to User-produced Fare," *Adweek*, www.adweek.com/videowatch/fans-crush-brands-when-it-comes-youtbue-150262, June 13, 2013.
14. Tim Nudd, "Meet Devin Graham, Advertising's Daredevil," *Adweek*, www.adweek.com/news/advertising-branding/meet-devin-graham" February 11, 2014.
15. Vindu Goel, "Is Instagram Another Path to Riches for Facebook?" http://bits.blogs.nytimes.com/2014/02/18/is-instagram-another-path-to-riches-for-facebook, February 18, 2014.
16. Joe McCarthy," Bloomingdale's Balances Selfies with Beauty Tips in Instagram," www.luxurydaily.com/bloomingdales-balances-selfies-with-beauty-tips-in-instagram, October 31, 2013; Steve Smith, "Lipton Rides Instagram's Positive Mood," www.mediapost.com/publications/article/192807, February 6, 2013.
17. Christina Binley, "More Brands Want You to Model Their Clothes," *The Wall Street Journal*, http://online.wsj.com/article/SB100014241278873242160045784830, May 15, 2013.
18. Chris Heine, "Amazon is Among Pinterest's Best Retailers for the Holidays," *Adweek*, www.adweek/com/news/technology/amazon-is-among-pinterests-best-retailers-for-the-holidays, December 12, 2103; Karlene Lukovitz, "Land 'O Lakes Pinterest Promo Helps Fight Hunger," *Marketing Daily*, www.mediapost.com/publications/article/195218, March 7, 2013.
19. "Social Strategies for 2014," *Wildfire by Google Whitepaper, Ad Age Content Strategy Studio*, October 2013; Michael A. Stelzner, "2013 Social Media Marketing Industry Report," *Social Media Examiner*, www.socialmediaexaminer.com, 2013.
20. Karlene Lukovitz, "Hooters Dives into Social Media," *Marketing Daily*, www.mediapost.com/publications/article/206785/hooters-dives-into-social-media, August 14, 2013.
21. Galen Callen, *Wholly Guacamole & Disney Report*, October 2011.
22. Aaron Baar, "Social Interactions Affect Brand Perceptions," *Marketing Daily*, www.mediapost.com/publications/article/193609, February 19, 2013.
23. Bruce Horovitz, "Hate Talk Won't Derail Mixed-Race Cheerios Ad," *USA Today*, www.usatoday.com/story/money/business/2013/06/02/cheerios-general-mills-commerical-mixed-race-ad/2384587, June 3, 2013.
24. "How Social Data Influenced Hyatt to Pull Part of Campaign Days Before Launch," *Advertising Age*, http://adage.com/print/243539, August 8, 2013.
25. Doug Pruden and Terry Vavra, "How to Find and Activate Your Best Potential Advocates," http://smartblogs.com/social-media/2014/01/27//how-to-fin-and-activate-your-best-potential-advocaates, January 27, 2014.
26. Jack Neff, "Buzzkill: Coca-Cola Finds No Sales Lift from Online Chatter," *Advertising Age*, www.adage.com/article/cmo-strategy/240409, March 18, 2013.
27. "McKinsey Finds Social Buzz Can Affect Sales–Negatively Anyway," *Advertising Age*, http//adage.com/print/242039, June 11, 2013.
28. Lara Vogel, "L'Oreal on Social Media: 3 Ideas Worth Stealing." *Hoosh Meaningful Numbers*, September 3, 2013, http://blog.hoosh.com/loreal-on-social-media-3-ideas-worth-stealing/, retrieved March 10, 2014.
29. Amit Bapna and Ravi Balakrishnan, "Brand Using Social Media to Learn About Consumer Preferences, *The Economic Times*, December 4, 2013, http://articles.economictimes.indiatimes.com/2013-12-04/news/44757376_1_facebook-app-facebook-india-social-media, retrieved March 10, 2014.
30. *Wholly Biggest Loser Final Report*, June 2011.
31. "5 Ways to Encourage Customers to Share Your Content," *Marketo White Paper*, www.marketo.com, 2013.
32. "Esurance Hands Out That $1.5 Million, Releases Mind-Boggling Stats," *Adweek*, www.adweek.com/adfreak/esurance-hands-out-that-15-million," accessed February 10, 2104.
33. Adam McKibbin, "These Brands Scored Big on Sunday Without Expensive TV Spots," *Adweek*, www.adweek.com/brandshare/these-brands-scored-big-on-sunday-without-expensive-tv-spots-155290, February 3, 2014.
34. "5 Ways to Encourage Customers to Share Your Content," *Marketo White Paper*, www.marketo.com, 2013.
35. Paul Farhi, "Oreo's Tweeted Ad Was Super Bowl Blackout's Big Winner," *Style*, http://articles.washingtonpost.com/2013/-02-4/lifestyles/36741262, February 4, 2013.
36. "Adobe Readies Its Super Bowl Real-Time War Room," *Advertising Age*, http;//adage.com/print/291400, January 30, 2014.
37. Christopher Heine, "Starbucks Pushes Snow Day on Facebook, Twitter," *Adweek*, www.adweek.com/news/technology/starbucks-pushes-snow-day-on-facebook-twitter," February 8, 2013.

38. Rick Wion, "McDonald's Finds Quick Social Response Requires Nimble Planning," *eMarketer*, www.emarketer.com/articles/print/1009716, March 8, 2013.
39. David Ensing, "Consumers Take Online Reviews with a Grain of Salt," www.quirks.com/articles/2013/20131026, October 2013.
40. Andrew Adam Newman, "A Campaign for Clothes by a Guy Not Wearing Any," *The New York Times* (**www.nytimes.com/2009/10/29/business/media/29zappos.html**), October 29, 2009.
41. Todd Wasserman, "So Your Ad Went Viral–Big Deal," http://mashable.com/2013/12/12/so-your-ad-went-viral-big-deal, December 12, 2013.
42. Lenna Garibian, "Digital Influence: Blogs Beat Social Networks for Driving Purchases," *MarketingProfs*, www.marketingprofs.com/charts/print/2013/10336, March 18, 2013.
43. Stuart Elliot, "3-M says, 'Go Ahead, Make Something of It," The New York Times, January 28, 2013, http://www.nytimes.com/2013/01/28/business/mutfund/3m-says-go-ahead-make-something-of-it.html?pagewanted=all&_r=1&, retrieved March 5, 2014.
44. Ibid.
45. Natalie Zmuda, "Pepsi Refocuses on Hispanics," *Advertising Age,* July 24, 2013, http://adage.com/article/hispanic-marketing/pepsi-refocuses-hispanics-flavors-tagline/236269/, retrieved March 6, 2014.
46. Karl Greenberg, "Hispanic Consumers Are Social Media Catalysts," *Marketing Daily,* February 20, 2014, http://www.mediapost.com/publications/article/219954/hispanic-consumers-are-social-media-catalysts.html, retrieved March 6, 2014.

Chapter 10

1. Hebrew National, http://www.hebrewnational.com/kosher-products, retrieved March 16, 2014.
2. Bratskeir Company, "Woman Bites Dog: Trumping Price with Taste, http://www.bratskeir.com/hebrewnatl.html, retrieved March 16, 2014.
3. Bloomberg Business Week Magazine, July 29,2001, "Buzz Marketing," http://www.businessweek.com/stories/2001-07-29/buzz-marketing, retrieved March 16, 2014.
4. Natasha Singer, "On Campus, It's One Big Commerical," *The New York Times*, September 11, 2011, www.nytimes.com/2001/09/11/business-at-colleges-the-marketers-are-everywhere.
5. Laurie Burkitt, "Procter & Gamble Taps Co-Eds to Sell Products," *Forbes.com* (**www.forbes.com/2009/09/09/procter-gamble-repnation-cmo-network-readyu_print.html**), September 9, 2009.
6. Laurie Burkitt, "Marketers Break Into Homes By Sponsoring Parties," *Forbes.com* (**www.forbes.com/2009/08/19/purina-house-party-cmo-network-houseparty_print.html**), August 19, 2009.
7. Andrew Adam Newman, "Putting Boxed Wine to the Taste Test," *The New York Times*, October 11, 2011, www.nytimes.com/2011/10/12/business/media-boxed-wine-firms-claim-theyll-pass-the-taste-test.
8. Angelo Fernando, "Transparency Under Attack," *Communication World* 24, no. 2 (March–April 2007), pp. 9–11.
9. Ibid.
10. Jim Matorin, "Infectious 'Buzz Marketing' Is a Smart Way to Build Customer Loyalty at Your Operation," *Nation's Restaurant News* 41, no. 18 (April 30, 2007), pp. 18–20.
11. Kate Niederhoffer, Rob Mooth, David Wiesenfeld, and Jonathon Gordon, "The Origin and Impact of CPG New-Product Buzz: Emerging Trends and Implications," *Journal of Advertising Research* 47, no. 4 (December 2007), pp. 420–26.
12. Ibid.
13. Chris Powell, "The Perils of Posing," *Profit* 26, no. 2 (May 2007), pp. 95–96.
14. T. L. Stanley, "Twinkies Relaunch as Dude Food," *Adweek*, www.adweek.com/news/advertsing-brand/hostess-twinkie-relaunch-brands-treat-dude-food-151734, August 7, 2013.
15. Becky Wilkerson, "Bringing Brands to Life," *Marketing* (**www.marketingmagzine.co.uk**), February 18, 2009, pp. 35–38.
16. "Karl Greenberg, "Cadillac in the Performance Swim Lane With V-Centric Events," *MediaPost News, Marketing Daily*, April 20, 2011, www.mediapost.com/publications/?fa=articles.printfriendly&art_aid=149076.
17. Stuart Elliott, "King Cotton Goes on Tour," *The New York Times* (**www.nytimes.com/2009/08/24/business/media/24adnewsletter1.html**), August 24, 2009.
18. Derek Drake, "Prove the Promise of Your Brand," *Adweek* 50, no. 35 (October 5, 2009), pp. S11–S12.
19. Simon Hudson and David Hudson, "Branded Entertainment: A New Advertising Technique or Product Placement in Disguise?" *Journal of Marketing Management* 22, no. 5/6 (July 2006), pp. 489–504.
20. "Product Placement Hits High Gear on American Idol, Broadcast's Top Series for Brand Mentions," *Advertising Age*, April 18, 2011, http://adage.com/pring/227041.
21. Linda Moss, "Nielsen: Product Placements Succeed in 'Emotionally Engaging' Shows," *Multichannel News* (**www.multichannel.com/index.asp**), December 10, 2007.
22. Stacy Straczynski, "Harley-Davidson Revs Product Placement," *Adweek* (**www.advweek.com/aw/content_display/news/agency/e3i84436228620cd549875945**), November 12, 2009.
23. "The Only Beer in TNT and TBS Shows Now Comes from MillerCoors," *Advertising Age*, http://adage.com/print/240451, March 20, 2013.
24. Simon Hudson and David Hudson, "Branded Entertainment: A New Advertising Technique or Product Placement in Disguise?" *Journal of Marketing Management* 22, no. 5/6 (July 2006), pp. 489–504.
25. Andrew Hampp, "How American Airlines Got a Free Ride in 'Up in the Air,'" *Advertising Age* (http://adage.com/print?article_id=141059), December 14, 2009.
26. Cecily Hall, "Subliminal Messages," *Women's Wear Daily* 195, no. 2 (January 3, 2008), p.12.
27. Marc Graser, "More Ads Set for Videogames," *Variety*, September 13, 2011, www.variety.com/article/VR1118042795; Simon Hudson and David Hudson, "Branded Entertainment: A New Advertising Technique or Product Placement in Disguise?" *Journal of Marketing Management* 22, no. 5/6 (July 2006), pp. 489–504.
28. Raj Persaud, "The Art of Product Placement," *Brand Strategy,* no. 216 (October 2007), pp. 30–31.
29. Burt Helm, "Marketing: Queen of the Product Pitch," *BusinessWeek* (April 30, 2007), pp. 40–41.
30. "Hey, Advertisers: New York Has a Bridge to Sell You," *Advertising Age*, October 26, 2011, http://adage.com/print/230643.
31. Jessica E. Lessin, "Expenses Mount for App Launches," *The Wall Street Journal*, http://online.wsj.com/article/SB100014241278873243458045784252, April 17,2013; Theresa Howard, "As More People Play, Advertisers Devise Game Plans," *USA Today* (July 11, 2006), p. Money, 3b.

32. Ibid.
33. Ibid.
34. Rita Chang, "Advergames: A Smart Move, If Done Well," *Advertising Age* (http://adage.com/print?article_id=131786), October 16, 2008.
35. Heather Chaplin, "Players Lend a Helping Hand or Thumb," *Adweek*, April 20, 2012, www.adweek.com/print/139461; "Brands Friending Social Gaming Amid New Web Craze," *The Wall Street Journal*, August 8, 2010, http://online.wsj.com/article/SB1000142405274870465750457541180412583242 6.html.
36. Rebecca Borison, "Fall Into Cosi Sweepstakes," www.mobilecommercedaily.com/cosi-drives-in-store-traff-with-game, accessed October 10, 2013.
37. Mike Shields, "IGA: Most Gamers Cool with In-Game Ads," *Mediaweek.com* (http://mediaweek.com/mw/content_display/news/digital-downloads/gaming/e3i8d91a7147083886bfb91a8ee5978c1a7), June 17, 2008.
38. Susan Catto, "Are You Game?" *Marketing Magazine* (November 26, 2007, Supplement), pp. 18–19.
39. Ibid.
40. WomenGamers.com (**www.womengamers.com/news/2010/03/11/breaking-down-female-demographic**), May 3, 2010; Yukari Iwatani Kane, "Videogame Firms Make a Play for Women," *The Wall Street Journal* (http://online.wsj.com/article/SB1000142405274870488240457446365277788 5432.html), October 13, 2009; CNN.com (www.cnn.com/2008/TECH/ptech/02/28/women.gamers/index.html), May 3, 2010.
41. Katy Bachman, "HP Employs Cinema Experience to Push Printer," *Mediaweek* (**www.mediaweek.com/mw/content_display/news/out-there/place-based/e3i4cb8ab6**), November 29, 2009.
42. Kenneth Hein, "Study: In-Store Marketing Beats Traditional Ads," *Sales & Marketing Management* 161, no. 6 (November 2009), p. 57.
43. Amy Johannes, "Snap Decisions," *Promo* 18, no. 11 (October 2005), p. 16.
44. Kenneth Hein, "Study: In-Store Marketing Beats Traditional Ads," *Sales & Marketing Management* 161, no. 6 (November 2009), p. 57.
45. Tim Dreyer, "In-Store Technology Trends," *Display & Design Ideas* 19, no. 9 (September 2007), p. 92.
46. Ibid.
47. Michael Bellas, "Shopper Marketing's Instant Impact," *Beverage World* 126, no. 11 (November 15, 2007), p. 18.
48. Sarah Mahoney, "Banana Republic, Match.com Spread V-Day Love," *Marketing Daily*, www.mediapost.com/publications/article/192845, February 6, 2013.
49. "POP Sharpness in Focus," *Brandweek* 44, no. 24 (June 6, 2003), pp. 31–36; David Tossman, "The Final Push—POP Boom," *New Zealand Marketing Magazine* 18, no. 8 (September 1999), pp. 45–51.
50. Betsy Spethmann, "Retail Details," *Promo SourceBook 2005* 17 (2005), pp. 27–28.
51. RoxAnna Sway, "Four Critical Seconds," *Display & Design Ideas* 17, no. 11 (November 2005), p. 3.
52. Catja Prykop and Mark Heitmann, "Designing Mobile Brand Communities: Concept and Empirical Illustration," *Journal of Organizational Computing & Electronic Commerce* 16, no. 3/4 (2006), pp. 301–23.
53. Sinclair Stewart, "More Marketers Using Word of Mouth to Whip Up Sales," *Seattle PI* **www.seattlepi.com/business/344656_wordofmouth24.html**, December 23, 2007.
54. James T. Areddy, "Starbucks, PepsiCo Bring 'Subopera' to Shanghai," *The Wall Street Journal Online* (http://online.wsj.com/public/article_print/SB119387410336878365.html), November 1, 2007, p. B1.
55. Thomas Clouse, "Camp Jeep Comes to China," *Automotive News* 82, no. 6281 (November 12, 2007), p. 48.
56. Jeff Weiss, "Building Brands Without Ads," *Marketing Magazine* 109, no. 32 (October 4–11, 2004), p. 22.
57. Tiger Balm website, www.tigerbalm.com, accessed November 9, 2010; My Tiger Balm website, www.mytigerbalm.com, accessed November 9, 2010; "Waging War on Pain," Euromonitor International, www.euromonitor.com, accessed November 9, 2010; Robin D. Rusch, "Tiger Balm Fit for an Emperor," *Brand Channel*, April 16, 2001, www.brandchannel.com; "Made in Singapore," *Marketing Magazine*, August 2007, www.marketing-interactive.com; "Tiger Balm Associates with Chennai Super Kings for IPL-3," India Infoline News Service, April 1, 2010, www.factiva.com.
58. Hotcow website, www.hotcow.co.uk, accessed November 6, 2010; Red Bull website, www.redbull.co.uk, accessed November 6, 2010.

Chapter 11

1. Stephanie Clifford, "Ads Follow Web Users, and Get More Personal," *The New York Times* (**www.nytimes.com/2009/07/31/business/media/31privacy.html**), July 31, 2009.
2. Leo Rabinovitch, "America's 'First' Department Stores Mines Customer Data," *Direct Marketing* 62, no. 8 (December 1999), pp. 42–45.
3. Jason Q. Zhang, Ashutosh Dixit, and Roberto Friedman, "Customer Loyalty and Lifetime Value: An Empirical Investigation of Consumer Packaged Goods," *Journal of Marketing Theory & Practice* 18, no. 2 (February 2010), pp. 127–139.
4. Elliot Zwiebach, "Wholesalers Segment Shoppers Using Lifestyle Clusters," *Supermarket News* 55, no. 7 (February 12, 2007), p. 23.
5. "Verizon Uses Phone Data to Connect Consumer Dots for NBA Teams," *Advertising Age*, http://adage.com/print/245178, November 8, 2013.
6. Howard J. Stock, "Connecting the Dots," *Bank Investment Consultant* 13, no. 3 (March 2005), pp. 28–31.
7. Jordan K. Speer, "Digging Deep: Extreme Data Mining," *Apparel Magazine* 45, no. 12 (August 2004), p. 1.
8. Arthur M. Hughes, "The Importance of Customer Communications," *Database Marketing Institute* (**www.dbmarketing.com/articles/ART233.html**), August 23, 2007.
9. "Consumers Appreciate Birthday Wishes from Brands," *Quirk's* http://quirksblog.com/blog/2013/12/04/consumers-appreciate-birthday-wish-from-brands, December 4, 2013.
10. "Data Mining Boosts Netflix Subscriber Base," *Advertising Age*, http://adage.com/print/243759, September 2, 2013.
11. Joseph Gatti, "Poor E-Mail Practices Provoking Considerable Customer Defection," *Direct Marketing* (December 2003), pp. 1–2.
12. Joseph Gatti, "Most Consumers Have Reached Permission E-Mail Threshold," *Direct Marketing* (December 2003), pp. 1–2.
13. Ibid.
14. Mark Dolliver, "Gauging Customer Loyalty," *Adweek* (**www.adweek.com/aw/content_display/news/agency/e3i4a73f5d7451749a37c7fca20**), February 16, 2010.
15. Mark A. Santillo, "Active Engagement," *Greater Games Industry Catalog* 12 (Spring 2010), p. 14.

16. Arthur M. Hughes, "The Importance of Customer Communications," *Database Marketing Institute* (**www.dbmarketing.com/articles/ART233.html**), August 23, 2007.
17. "CRM Metrics," *Harvard Management Update* 5, no. 3 (March 2000), pp. 3–4.
18. "Kellogg Cracks the Code on Loyalty," *Advertising Age*, http://adage.com/print/243342, July 29, 2013.
19. Richard H. Levey, "Prospects Look Good," *Direct* 16, no. 6 (December 1, 2004), pp. 1–5.
20. Julie Appleby, "As Drug Ads Surge, More Rx's Filled," *USA Today* (**www.usatoday.com/news/health/2008–02–29-drugs-main_N.html**), February 29, 2008.
21. Paula Andruss, "Personalized URLs," *Marketing News*, September 1, 2008, p. 10.
22. Jeff Borden, "Eat My Dust," *Marketing News* 42, no. 2, February 1, 2008, pp. 20–22.
23. Kyle Stock, "Why the Analog Catalog Still Drives Digital Sales," *Bloomberg Businessweek*, www.businessweek.com/printer/articles/165812, November 7, 2013.
24. Based on Jay Kiltsch, "Making Your Message Hit Home: Some Basics to Consider When…," *Direct Marketing* 61, no. 2 (June 1998), pp. 32–34.
25. Daniel B. Honigman, "Sweet Science," *Marketing News* 41, no. 16 (October 2, 2007), pp. 16–17.
26. Camille Sweeney, "Avon's Little Sister Is Calling," *The New York Times* (**www.nytimes.com/2010/01/14/fashion/14SKIN.html**), January 14, 2010.
27. Ken Le Meunier-FitsHugh and Nigel F. Piercy, "Does Collaboration Between Sales and Marketing Affect Business Performance," *Journal of Personal Selling & Sales Management* 27, no. 3 (Summer 2007), pp. 207–220.
28. Patricia R. Lysak, "Changing Times Demand Front-End Model," *Marketing News* 28, no. 9 (April 25, 1994), p. 9.
29. Christopher Heine, "Grocery Chain will Pitch Store Patrons with Amazon-Like Recommendations," *Adweek*, December 9, 2013, http://www.adweek.com/news/technology/grocery-chain-will-pitch-store-patrons-amazon-recommendations-154379, retrieved March 21, 2014.

Chapter 12

1. Gulf News website, http://gulfnews.com/, accessed December 2012; Dubai Events website, http://www.dubaievents.ae, accessed December 2012; Guide to Dubai website, http://www.guide2dubai.com, accessed December 2012.
2. Mariola Palazon-Vidal and Elena Delgado-Ballester, "Sales Promotions Effect on Consumer-Based Brand Equity," *International Journal of Market Research* 47, no. 2 (2005), pp. 179–205.
3. Bruce Horovitz, "2 Million Enjoy Free Breakfast at Denny's," *USA Today* (**www.usatoday.com/money/industries/foo.2009/02/03-denny's_N.html**), February 10, 2009.
4. Patricia Odell, "Now in Vogue," *PROMO* (http://promomagazine.com/incentives/marketing_vogue/index.html), December 1, 2009.
5. Joe Mandese, "Marketers Hold the Promo Line in 2011, Coupon Volume Drops for First Time in Years," *Media Daily News*, January 4, 2012, www.mediapost.com/publications/article/165125
6. Erik Sass, "Is Digital Coupons' Rise Print Insert's Demise?" *MediaPost News* (**www.mediapost.com/publications/?fa=Articles.showArticle&art_aid=122690**), February 18, 2010; Patricia Odell, "Now in Vogue." *PROMO* (http://promomagazine.com/incentives/marketing_vogue/index.html), December 1, 2009.
7. Erik Sass, "Is Digital Coupons' Rise Print Insert's Demise?" *MediaPost News* (**www.mediapost.com/publications/?fa=Articles.showArticle&art_aid=122690**), February 18, 2010; Allen Adamson, "CMOs: Your Brand Is on Digital Time," *Forbes* (**www.forbes.com/2010/02/02/digital-branding-apple-ipad-cmo-network-allen-adamson**), February 2, 2010.
8. Elizabeth Gardener and Minakshi Trivedi, "A Communication Framework to Evaluate Sales Promotion Strategies," *Journal of Advertising Research* 38, no. 3 (May–June 1998), pp. 67–71.
9. "Hyundai Adds Luxury Glitz with iPad-based Owner's Manual," *PROMO* (http://promomagazine.com/incentives/news/0407-hyundai-adds-ipad-manual/index.html), April 7, 2010.
10. Don Jagoda, "The Seven Habits of Highly Successful Promotions," *Incentive* 173, no. 8 (August 1999), pp. 104–05.
11. Karlene Lukovitz, "General Mills Ties Into 3D Star Wars Release," *Marketing Daily*, January 23, 2012, www.mediapost.com/publications/article/166262.
12. "Prizewinning Growth," *PROMO* (http://promomagazine.com/contests/marketing_prizewinning_growth/index.html), July 1, 1998.
13. Patricia Odell, "Spending Up by a Nose," *PROMO* (http://promomagazine.com/contests/marketing_spending_nose/index.html), December 1, 2009.
14. Christopher Heine, "Dr. Pepper's Outdoor Mural Contest Thrives Online," September 15, 2001, www.clickz.com/news/2109658/dr-peppers-outdoor-mural-contest-thrives-online.
15. Sarah Mahoney, "Sears Launches Yard Guru Campaign," *Marketing Daily* (**www.mediapost.com/publications/?fa=Articles.printFriendly&art_aid=125255**), March 31, 2010.
16. Brian Morrissey, "Brand Sweepstakes Get Twitterized," *Adweek* (**www.adweek.com/aw/cn\content_display/news/digital/e3ied5661580e6e68a1834a7e3**), November 22, 2009.
17. Sandra Block, "Rattled About Rebate Hassles? Regulators Starting to Step In," *USA Today* (March 22, 2005), p. 3b.
18. Kenneth Hein, "Study: Sampling Works," *Brandweek.com* (**www.brandweek.com/bw/content_display/news-and-features/shopper-marketing/e3i32e9c3e84ea86c79e3ae157688c1ad0a**), September 29, 2008.
19. Andrew Adam Newman, "Dr. Scholl's Widens Its Insole Campaign," *The New York Times* (**www.nytimes.com/2010/04/01/business/media/01adco.html**), March 31, 2010.
20. Kyle Stock, "The Logic Behind P & G's Old-School Manhattan Giveaway," *Bloomberg Businessweek*, www.businessweek.com/print/articles/126706, June 19, 2013.
21. Pete Wetmore, "Inserts Branch Out Beyond Print Fliers," *Advertising Age* 75, no. 16 (April 19, 2004), p. N-6.
22. Betsy Spethman, "Introductory Offer," *PROMO* 16 (2004), p. 27; Jennifer Kulpa, "Bristol-Myers Squibb Breaks Ground with Direct Response Product Sampling Website," *Drug Store News* 19, no. 7 (April 7, 1997), p. 19.
23. Rachel Lamb, "Chanel Taps Vogue Supplement to Spark Holiday Gift-Giving," *Luxury Daily*, November 23, 2011, www.luxurydaily.com/chanel-taps-vogue-supplment-to-spark-holiday-gift-giving.
24. Beng Soo Ong and Foo Nin Ho, "Consumer Perceptions of Bonus Packs: An Exploratory Analysis," *Journal of Consumer Marketing* 14, no. 2–3 (1997), pp. 102–12.
25. David R. Bell, Ganesh Iyer, and V. Padmanaghan, "Price Competition Under Stockpiling and Flexible Consumption,"

Journal of Marketing Research 39, no. 3 (August 2002), pp. 292–304.
26. "Papa John's Tries to Hold the Price of Its Pies," *Advertising Age*, March 4, 2012, http://adage.com/print/233109.
27. Showwei Chu, "Welcome to Canada, Please Buy Something," *Canadian Business* 71, no. 9 (May 29, 1998), pp. 72–73.
28. Walter Heller, "Promotion Pullback," *Progressive Grocer* 81, no. 4 (March 1, 2002), p. 19.
29. Miguel Gomez, Vithala Rao, and Edward McLaughlin, "Empirical Analysis of Budget and Allocation of Trade Promotions in the U.S. Supermarket Industry," *Journal of Marketing Research* 44, no. 3 (August 2007), pp. 410–24.
30. Ibid.
31. K. Sudhir and Vithala Rao, "Do Slotting Allowances Enhance Efficiency or Hinder Competition?" *Journal of Marketing Research* 43, no. 2 (May 2006), pp. 137–55.
32. Paula Bone, Karen France, and Richard Riley, "A Multifirm Analysis of Slotting Fees," *Journal of Public Policy & Marketing* 25, no. 2 (Fall 2006), pp. 224–37.
33. "Study: Trade Dollars Up," *Frozen Food Age* 50, no. 2 (September 2001), p. 14.
34. Walter Heller, "Promotion Pullback," *Progressive Grocer* 81, no. 4 (March 1, 2002), p. 19.
35. "Cruise Selling Season Kicks Off with Agent Promotions and Optimism," *Travel Agent* 319 (January 3, 2005), p. 9.
36. Roger A. Slavens, "Getting a Grip on Co-Op," *Modern Tire Dealer* 75, no. 3 (March 1994), pp. 34–37.
37. Jack Neff, "Wal-Mart Ups the Ante with Brand Co-op Ads—in More Ways than One," *Advertising Age* (http://adage.com/article?article_id=140743), November 30, 2009.
38. Jennifer Gilbert, "The Show Must Go On," *Sales & Marketing Management* 155, no. 5 May 2003), p. 14.
39. Walter Heller, "Promotion Pullback," *Progressive Grocer* 81, no. 4 (March 1, 2002), p. 19.
40. Brian Sullivan, "Make Sure Promotional Items Fit Brand Perfectly," *Marketing News* 35, no. 19 (September 10, 2001), p. 15.
41. Donald Baack, *International Business* (New York: Glencoe McGraw-Hill, 2008), pp. 28–49.
42. "Dulux Trade Launches Voucher Promotion," Professional Builders Merchant, http://www.professionalbuildersmerchant.co.uk/news/article/dulux_trade_launches_voucher_promotion/, accessed December 6, 2012; Dulux website, http://www.dulux.co.uk/index.jsp, accessed December 6, 2012; Dulux Trade website, http://dulux.trade-decorating.co.uk/index.jsp, accessed December 6, 2012; "Dulux, Let's Colour," *Superbrands*, http://www.superbrands.uk.com/dulux, accessed December 6, 2012; The National Painting and Decorating Show 2012 website, http://www.paintshow.co.uk/index.php, accessed December 6, 2012.

Chapter 13

1. "Volkswagen: *Facts and Figures Navigator 2012*," Volkswagen Group, http://www.volkswagenag.com/content/vwcorp/info_center/en/publications/2012/03/navigator-2012—facts-andfigures.bin.html/binarystorageitem/file/Navigator_21_09_2012_en_WEB.pdf, accessed December 7, 2012; "Volkswagen Group, Sustainability Report 2011," Volkswagen Group, http://www.volkswagenag.com/content/vwcorp/info_center/en/publications/2012/04/SR_2011.bin.html/binarystorageitem/file/VWAG_NHB_2011_e_web_neu.pdf, accessed December 7, 2012.
2. "Mexico Leans on PR to Lure Back Tourists," *Advertising Age*, June 26, 2011, http://adage.com/pring/228385.
3. Jenny Dawkins, "Corporate Responsibility: The Communication Challenge," *Journal of Communication Management* 9, no. 2 (November 2004), pp. 106–17.
4. Heather Chaplin, "Players Lend a Helping Hand – or, Thumb," *Adweek*, April 10, 2012, www.adweek.com/print/139461.
5. Michael Fielding, "Companies that Behave Responsibly Earn Good Rep, Consumers' Attention," *Marketing News* 41, no. 8 (May 1, 2007), pp. 17–18.
6. "Why Advertising is Dead Last Priority at Outerwear Marketer Patagonia," *Advertising Age*, http://adage.com/print/245712, December 17, 2013.
7. Suzanne Vranica, "NBC Universal Tees Up Cause-Related Shows," *The Wall Street Journal* (http://online.wsj.com/article/SB10001424052748704112904574477872926288910.html), October 19, 2009.
8. "Dick's Taps Amateurs to Make Case That Sports Matter," *Advertising Age*, http://adage.com/print/292025, March 7, 2014.
9. Heather Chaplin, "Players Lend a Helping Hand – or, Thumb," *Adweek*, April 10, 2012, www.adweek.com/print/139461.
10. Nan Xiaoli and Heo Kwangiun, "Consumer Responses to Corporate Social Responsibility (CSR) Initiatives," *Journal of Advertising* 36, no. 2 (Summer 2007), pp. 63–74.
11. Andrew Adam Newman, "Tough on Crude Oil, Soft on Ducklings," *The New York Times* (**www.nytimes.com/2009/09/25/business/media/25adco.html**), September 25, 2009.
12. Dawkins, "Corporate Responsibility: The Communication Challenge."
13. Jill Meredith Ginsberg and Paul N. Bloom, "Choosing the Right Green Marketing Strategy," *MIT Sloan Management Review* 46, no. 1 (Fall 2004), pp. 79–84.
14. Stephanie Clifford and Andrew Martin, "As Consumers Cut Spending, Green Products Lose Allure," *The New York Times*, April 21, 2011, www.nytimes.,com/2011/04/22/business/energy-environment/22green.html.
15. Jill Meredith Ginsberg and Paul N. Bloom, "Choosing the Right Green Marketing Strategy, *MIT Sloan Management Review* 40, no. 1 (Fall 2004) pp. 79–84.
16. Examples based on Ginsberg and Bloom, "Choosing the Right Green Marketing Strategy."
17. Joan Voight, "Green is the New Black," *Adweek*, www.adweek.com/news/advertising-branding/green-is-the-new-black, October 23, 2013.
18. Tanya Irwin, "Seventh Generation Debuts First National Campaign," *Marketing Daily, MediaPost News* (**www.mediapost.com/publications/?fa=Articles.printFriendly&art_aid=120626**), January 14, 2010.
19. Marvin E. Shaw and Philip R. Costanzo, *Theories of Social Psychology,* 2nd ed. (New York: McGraw-Hill, 1982), p. 334.
20. Rich Thomaselli, "New Orleans is a Super Bowl Winner," *Advertising Age* (adage.com/superbowl10/article?article_id=141988), February 8, 2010.
21. Andrew Adam Newman, "TD Ameritrade Commercials Link Olympics and Investing," *The New York Times*, www.nytimes.com/2013/12/09/business/media/td-ameritrade-commericals-link-olympics-and-investing, December 6, 2013.
22. Sarah E. Needleman, "For Companies, A Tweet in Time Can Avert PR Mess," *The Wall Street Journal* (online.wsj.com/article/SB1249258302403003.html), August 3, 2009.
23. Michael Bush, "The Cult of Toyota," *Advertising Age* (http://adage.com/print?article_id=142335), March 1, 2010; Rich Thomaselli, "Toyota Sends in Jimi Lentz for Cross-Media Saatchi-Led PR Control," *Advertising Age* (http://adage.com/print?article_id=141856), February 1, 2010; Laurie Burkitt,

"From Trusted to Busted: Brands Have a Credibility Crisis," *Forbes* (**www.forbes.com/1010/02/25/toyota-tiger-consumer-faith-cmo-network-trusted-to-be-busted**), February 25, 2010.

24. Shaw and Costanzo, *Theories of Social Psychology,* 2nd ed., p. 334.
25. Christopher Heine, "Mountain Dew Uses Twitter Ads to Promote Apology," *Adweek*, www.adweek.com/news/technology/mountain-dew-uses-twitter-ads-to-promote-apology, May 2, 2013.
26. Shaw and Costanzo, *Theories of Social Psychology,* 2nd ed., p. 329.
27. Ibid, p. 333.
28. Jane L. Levere, "Spot Shares Moments of Better Cruise Memories," *The New York Times*, www.nytimes.com/2013/09/19/business/media/spot-shares-moments-of-better-cruise-memories, September 18, 2013.
29. Nigel Pope, Kevin E. Voges, and Mark Brown, "Winning Ways," *Journal of Advertising* 38, no. 2 (Summer 2009), pp. 5–20.
30. "Events & Sponsorships," *2008 Marketing Fact Book, Marketing News* 42, no. 12 (July 15, 2008), p. 26.
31. Karl Greenberg, "Ford Intros Integrated Push for F-Series," *Marketing Daily, MediaPost News* (**www.mediapost.com/publications/?fa=Articles.printFriendly&art_aid=125753**), April 8, 2010.
32. "Brands Stake Out a Place on Courses of Jaw-Dropping Endurance Competitions," *Advertising Age*, http://adage.com/print/291097, January 17, 2014.
33. Gail Schiller, "Idol Sponsors Coke, Ford, AT&T Paying More," *Brandweek.com* (http://login.vnuemedia.com/bw/esearch/article_display.jsp?vnu_content_id=1003696656), January 15, 2008.
34. Pradnya Joshi, "Approval by a Blogger May Please a Sponsor," *The New York Times* (**www.nytimes.com/2009/07/13/technology/internet/13blog.html**), July 13, 2009.
35. Patricia Cobe, "Working the Neighborhood," *Restaurant Business* 108, no. 11 (November 2009), pp. 20–26.
36. David Tanklefsky, "Events-based Campaigns, Experiential Marketing Prove Successful Among Hispanic Consumers," B&C (**www.broadcastingcable.com/article/print/355270-Hispanic_TV_Summit_Promotion**), September 24, 2009.
37. Betsy Spethmann, "A Winning Season," *PROMO* 18, no. 1 (December 2004), pp. 32–41.
38. Kenneth Hein, "Study: Purchase Intent Grows with Each Event," *Brandweek* 49, no. 4 (January 28, 2008), p. 4.
39. Diane Anderson, "eBay's Campy Road Tour: One on One, No Mosquitoes," *Brandweek* 46, no. 10 (March 7, 2005), p. R6.
40. Jonathan Clegg, "NBA, Adidas Shoot for Europe," *The Wall Street Journal* (http://online.wsj.com/article/SB10001424052748704896104575140032574551 3978.html), March 23, 2010.
41. Personal interview with Bill Breedlove by Kenneth E. Clow and Donald Baack, January, 2010.
42. Standard Chartered Marathon Singapore website, www.marathonsingapore.com/Home.aspx, accessed November 8, 2010; Singapore Sports Council website, www.ssc.gov.sg/publish/Corporate/en.html, accessed November 8, 2010; Standard Chartered website, www.standardchartered.com/home/en/index.html#, accessed November 8, 2010.

Chapter 14

1. Sarah Skidmore, "Reebok to Pay $25 Million over Toning Shoe Claims," Business Week, September 28, 2011, http://www.businessweek.com/ap/financialnews/D9Q1P9PG0.htm, accessed March 16, 2012.
2. Ellie Krupnick, "Reebok Reaches $25 Million Settlement Over Toning Sneakers," The Huffington Post, November 28, 2011, http://www.huffingtonpost.com/2011/09/28/reebok-settlement-toning-sneakers_n_985141.html, accessed March 16, 2012.
3. "Broadcasters Breach Kids Rules," *Marketing Magazine* 109, no. 35 (November 1, 2004), p. 4.
4. Bart Lazar, "This Column Is the Best One You'll Ever Read," *Marketing News* 38, no. 13 (August 15, 2004), p. 8.
5. "Fast Feeders Serve Up Fresh Buzzwords," *Advertising Age*, March 7, 2011, http://adage.com/print/149264.
6. Katy Bachman, "FCT Busts ADT for Failing to Disclose Paid Endorsers," *Adweek*, www.adweek.com/news/advertising-branding/ftc-busts-adt-for-failing-to-disclose-paid-endorsers, March 6, 2014.
7. Jamie LaReau, "Dealerships Settle Deceptive Advertising Charges in FTC Sweep," *Automotive News*, www.autonews.com/article/20140109/RETAIL07/140109857, January 9, 2014.
8. Robert Hof, "What Facebook's FTC Privacy Settlement Means to Marketers," *Forbes*, November 29, 2011, www.forbes.com/sites/orberthof/2011/11/29/what-facebook-ftc-privacy-settlement-means-to-marketers.
9. "FTC Takes Aim at Another Credit Counseling Firm," *Mortgage Servicing News* 8, no. 7 (August 2004), p. 21.
10. "Body Wise International to Pay $3.5 Million to Settle Federal and State Deceptive Advertising Charges," Federal Trade Commission (**www.ftc.gov**, accessed September 20, 2005).
11. Debbi Mack, "FTC Use of Corrective Advertising Upheld," *Corporate Legal Times* 10, no. 108 (November 2000), p. 80.
12. Tim Arango, "Soon, Bloggers Must Give Full Disclosure," *The New York Times* (**www.nytimes.com/2009/10/06/business/media/06adco.html**), October 6, 2009; Douglas MacMillan, "Blogola: The FTC Takes on Paid Posts," *BusinessWeek* (**www.businessweek.com/print/technology/content/may2009/tc20090518_532031.html**), May 19, 2009.
13. Andrew Adam Newman, "Mascara Ads: Thick Lashes, Fine Print," *The New York Times*, www.nytimes.com/fashion/mascara-ads-thisck-lashes-fine-print, November 12, 2013.
14. Seth Stevenson, "How New Is New? How Improved Is Improved?" *Slate* (**www.slate.com/toolbar.aspx?action=print&id=2221968**), July 13, 2009.
15. Andrew Adam Newman, "In Criticizing Rival Products, a Dove Campaign is Called Unfair," *The New York Times*, www.nytimes.com/2013/06/25/business/media/in-criticizing-rival-products, June 24, 2013.
16. "Minute Maid Complains, but NARB Forces Change," *Advertising Age* 68, no. 15 (April 14, 1997), p. 51.
17. "NARB Sends Winn-Dixie Complaint to FTC," *Advertising Age* 67, no. 52 (December 23, 1996), p. 2.
18. Wayne Keeley, "Toys and the Truth," *Playthings* 106, no. 2 (February 2008), p. 8.
19. Mary Pipher, *The Shelter of Each Other* (New York: Ballentine Books, 1996).
20. Internet Marketing Register (**www.marketing-register.com**, accessed February 28, 2005).
21. Beth Snyder Bulik, "Consumers to Providers: Do You Know Who I Am?" *Advertising Age* 79, no. 10 (March 10, 2008), p. 8.
22. Simon Chadwick and Nicholas Burton, "Ambush!" *The Wall Street Journal* (http://online.wsj.com/article/SB10001424052970204731804574391102699362862.html), January 25, 2010.
23. Ibid; Aaron Baar, "Olympics Sponsors Benefit, As Do Competitors," *Marketing Daily* (**www.mediapost.com/publications/?fa=Articles.printFriendly&art_aid=122665**), February 17, 2010.
24. Chadwick and Burton, "Ambush!" Anne Kingston, "The Outlaws," *Maclean's* 123, no. 8 (March 8, 2010), pp. 48–49.

25. Jacob E. Osterhout, "Stealth Marketing: When You're Being Pitched and You Don't Even Know It," *NY Daily-News* (**www.nydailynews.com/lifestyle/2010/04/19_stealth_marketing**), April 19, 2010.
26. Ibid.
27. Elaine McGee, "The Benefits of Yogurt," WebMD, http://www.webmd.com/diet/features/benefits-of-yogurt, retrieved April 19, 2014.
28. Troy McMullen, "Dannon to Pay $45 Million to Settle Yogurt Lawsuit," ABC News, http://abcnews.go.com/Business/dannon-settles-lawsuit/story?id=9950269, retrieved April 19, 2014.
29. Ibid.
30. **www.nutrition.about.com, www.conagrafoods.com, www.mcdonalds.com, www.foodproductdesign.com, www.fritolay.com**, and **www.nlm.nih.gov**, all accessed March 13, 2008.
31. Kelly Dumke and Rachel Zavala, "The Controversy Surrounding Smart Choices," *The Friedman Sprout* (http://friedmansprout.wordpress.com/2009/12/02/the-controversy-surrounding-smart-choices/), December 2, 2009; Randall Pinkston, "Experts Say Industry Food Labels Deceptive," *CBS Evening News* (www.cbsnews.com/stories/2009/09/06/eveningnews/main5291352.shtml), September 6, 2009; "Smart Choices?" *CBSNewsOnline* (www.youtube.com/watch?v=dWMVcURE-eE, accessed May 18, 2010); Rebecca Ruiz, "Eight Puzzling Food Labels," *Forbes* (www.forbes.com/2009/09/23/food-labels-healthy-lifestyle-health-smart-choices-nutrition.html), September 23, 2009.

Chapter 15

1. http://www.sandsresearch.com/, accessed September 14, 2010.
2. Gordon A. Wyner, "Narrowing the Gap," *Marketing Research* 16, no. 1 (Spring 2004), pp. 6–7.
3. Interview with Elena Petukhova, The Richards Group, May 17, 2010, by Kenneth E. Clow.
4. "Nielsen IAG" (http://en-us.nielsen.com/tab/product_families/iag, accessed May 19, 2010).
5. Lucia Moses, "Publishers Offer TV-Like Metrics, But Will Buyers Bite?" *Mediaweek*, (**www.mediaweek.com/mw/content_display/news/magazines-newspapers/e3ieea0d35**), January 17, 2010.
6. "Has Burger King's First Mcgarrybowen Ad Helped the Brand?" *Advertising Age*, September 19, 2011, http://adage.com/print229832.
7. "Copy Testing Coming to Digital Marketing," *Advertising Age*, February 27, 2011, http://adage.com/print/149100.
8. Interview of David Snell by Kenneth E. Clow, May 17, 2010.
9. Interview with Elena Petukhova, The Richards Group, May 17, 2010, by Kenneth E. Clow.
10. Andrew McMains, "P&G Does Dan Wieden's Bidding," *Adweek*, June 27, 2011, www.adweek.com/print/132903.
11. "Copy Testing Coming to Digital Marketing," *Advertising Age*, February 27, 2011, http://adage.com/print/149100.
12. Steven P. Brown and Douglas M. Stayman, "Antecedents and Consequences of Attitude Toward the Ad: A Meta-Analysis," *Journal of Consumer Research* 19 (June 1992), pp. 34–51.
13. Douglas M. Stayman and David A. Aaker, "Continuous Measurement of Self-Report or Emotional Response," *Psychology and Marketing* 10 (May–June 1993), pp. 199–214.
14. Freddie Campos, "UH Facility Test Ads for $500," *Pacific Business News* 35, no. 23 (August 18, 1997), pp. A1–A2.
15. Patricia Riedman, "Discover Why Tests TV Commercials Online," *Advertising Age* 71, no. 13 (March 27, 2000), pp. 46–47.
16. Jon Lafayette, "Biometric Study: Broadcast Ads Make Web Work Better," May 9, 2011, www.broadcastingcable.com/article/print/467935.
17. Amy Chozick, "These Lab Specimens Watch 3-D Television," *The New York Times*, January 24, 2012, www.nytimes.com/2012/01/25/business/media/a-media-lab-will-test-consumers-reactions.
18. Bruce F. Hall, "On Measuring the Power of Communications," *Journal of Advertising Research* 44, no. 2 (June 2004), pp. 181–88.
19. Hall, "On Measuring the Power of Communications."
20. John Capone, "Microsoft and Initiative Strive for Better Advertising Through Neuroscience," *Online Media Daily* (**www.mediapost.com/publications/?fa=Articles.printFriendly&art_aid=118835**), December 9, 2009; Steve McClellan, "Mind Over Matter: New Tools Put Brands in Touch with Feelings," *Adweek* (http://www.adweek.com/aw/content_display/news/media/e3i975331243e08d74c5b66f857ff12cfd5), February 18, 2008.
21. Laurie Burkitt, "Battle for the Brain," *Forbes* 184, no. 9 (November 16, 2009), pp. 76–78.
22. Based on PACT document published in *Journal of Marketing* 11, no. 4 (1982), pp. 4–29.
23. http://www.adknowledge.com/usa/index.php, accessed September 14, 2010.
24. Rachel King, "Sentiment Analysis Gives Companies Insights into Consumer Opinion," *Bloomberg Business*, March 1, 2011, www.businessweek.com/print/technology/content/feb2011/tc20110228_366762.htm.
25. Chris Dillabough, "Web Lets Canadian Tourism Test Media Effectiveness," *New Media Age* (October 31, 2002), p. 12.
26. Kate MacArthur, "McDonald's Tests Ads That Focus on Service," *Advertising Age* 74, no. 1 (January 6, 2003), p. 3.
27. Tim Triplett, "Researchers Probe Ad Effectiveness Globally," *Marketing News* 28, no. 18 (August 29, 1994), pp. 6–7.
28. Paul J. Cough, "Study: Marketers Struggle to Measure Effectiveness," *Shoot* 45, no. 29 (August 20, 2004), pp. 7–8.
29. Peter Drucker, *Management: Tasks, Responsibilities, Practices* (New York: Harper & Row, 1974).
30. sosyalmedya.co website, http://sosyalmedya.co/doritosakademi/; http://www.doritosakademi.com/html/, accessed November 8, 2012; Frito-Lay Turkey website, http://www.fritolay.com.tr/sirket/tarihce.aspx, accessed November 8, 2012; Frito-Lay website, http://www.fritolay.com/about-us/history.html, accessed November 8, 2012; Social Bakers website, http://www.socialbakers.com, accessed November 8, 2012; Hurriyet Daily News website, http://www.hurriyetdailynews.com, accessed November 8, 2012; Euromonitor International website, http://www.euromonitor.com, accessed November 8, 2012; Digital Age website, http://www.digitalage.com.tr/News.aspx?NewsId=828; http://acikhava.wordpress.com/2011/10/17/frito-lay-fritos-doritosakademiacikhava-kampanyasi/, accessed November 8, 2012.

Name Index

S

Subject Index

A

B

C

D

E